EXTERNAL ECONOMIC POLICY SINCE THE WAR

VOLUME I

EXTERNAL ECONOMIC POLICY SINCE THE WAR

Volume I

THE POST-WAR FINANCIAL SETTLEMENT

BY

L. S. PRESSNELL

LONDON

HER MAJESTY'S STATIONERY OFFICE

Printed for Her Majesty's Stationery Office by Commercial Colour Press, London E7.
Dd.738216, C7, 6/87, PS.5250527.

CONTENTS

CHAPTER 5: THE WASHINGTON TALKS SEPTEMBER – OCTOBER 1943

CHAPTER 6: 1944: DEADLOCK IN COMMERCIAL POLICY, PROGRESS IN MONETARY POLICY

CHAPTER 7: THE FORMATION OF INTERNATIONAL MONETARY POLICY 1944 – 45: BRETTON WOODS AND AFTER

CHAPTER 8: SLOW PROGRESS ON TRADE POLICY 1944 – 45

CHAPTER 9: THE SHAPING OF POST-WAR FINANCIAL POLICY

CHAPTER 10: NEGOTIATING THE AMERICAN LOAN OF 1945

CHAPTER 11: THE NEGOTIATIONS FOR THE CANADIAN LOAN 1946

CHAPTER 12: CONCLUSION: AN INCOMPLETE FINANCIAL SETTLEMENT

APPENDICES

LIST OF TABLES IN APPENDIX 27

PREFACE

The official history of external economic policy since the second world war could not have been written as though its starting point were the defeat of Japan in August 1945. The stance of economic policy, both ahead of the coming of peace and after its sudden arrival, was shaped by the adverse economic impact of the war and by wartime discussions and international undertakings.

The deterioration of the balance of payments was the most striking economic effect of the war. On current account the volume of exports in 1945, though above the worst wartime levels, was less than half—forty-six percent—of that in 1938, the last full peacetime year. On capital account, disposals of part of Britain's overseas assets, together with accumulation of external debt roughly three times as great as those disposals, were roughly equivalent to the loss of four-fifths of pre-war overseas assets.

From March 1941, however, the US provision of extensive Lend-Lease aid had held this grave position largely in suspense, so far as British action to correct it was concerned. Meanwhile, as the 'Consideration' for Lend-Lease, Britain undertook, by Article VII of the Mutual Aid Agreement of 1942, to work towards the liberalisation of international trade and payments after the war. Following from this commitment, the US expected that Britain would participate in the new monetary institutions to be formed under the Bretton Woods agreements of July 1944, and, in respect of commercial policy, in a parallel, proposed 'International Trade Organisation'. With the end of the war, and the end of Lend-Lease, the balance of payments burst out of its virtual suspense: the reckoning had now to be faced.

Such were the influences felt in the Anglo-American financial negotiations of September – December 1945. Under the resulting financial agreement the USA granted Britain a line of credit of $3.75 billion; the terms of settlement of US Lend-Lease and of Britain's reciprocal aid were agreed. The credit had the twofold aim of assisting the recovery of the British economy and of its external equilibrium, and of allowing Britain 'to assume the obligations of multilateral trade' (agreement section 3). The agreement provided, therefore, both the culmination of wartime developments and the setting of the stage for e..ternal

xi

policy in peacetime. This, the first of two volumes, is concerned broadly with events up to the conclusion of the agreement and its immediate consequences. The second volume will continue the narrative to 1960.

The Official Civil Histories of the second World War could not be concerned in detail with problems of the peace. Although they have nevertheless provided invaluable illumination of some landmarks in the preparations for the peace, it has been necessary to construct a map of events, as it were, from the original records. British official sources have been the mainstay throughout. Since the overriding purpose has been to follow the evolution of British official policy, anything more than limited resort to records of policies and decisions elsewhere, of which British officials and ministers were unaware, would have distorted the presentation of the evolution of British policy as experienced within government. The principal records used have been those of HM Treasury and the Cabinet Office, with reference where appropriate to those of other areas of government. These records are at once a blessing in terms of their scope and detail, and a handicap in respect of their immense volume. Short cuts may occasionally be possible with such material, but there is no real escape from detailed, sometimes tedious, work on day to day working files if there is to be any prospect of sensing how policy was shaped. On a single matter of apparently minor, though inescapable, importance, a 'file' may run into numerous sub-files and then yet more files beyond those, while each file or sub-file may contain a hundred or more papers, and a paper may be relevant to several distinct topics.

In respect of published sources (other than official histories) explicit references have been restricted to those which have become standard sources, or which fill gaps in official records, or which offer interpretations significantly different from those indicated by the official records.

Indispensable help has come from many who were involved in the events discussed here; from other students of them; from archivists and librarians; and, far from least, from officials in Government departments, especially those in departmental record sections, in the Public Record Office, and in the Cabinet Office Historical Section. To all of them my gratitude is immeasurable. In some cases, personal recollection has unlocked puzzles, as have diaries and other personal papers; such sources have also been particularly helpful in re-creating the atmosphere in which policy evolved, and by giving leads to further inquiry. A number of those consulted have given generously of their time in commenting on drafts of some or all of the chapters. The best form of thanks is to stress that I should not wish the book to have been published without their assistance. A special debt is owed to my wife, who has been of inestimable help throughout, and has prepared the index.

Acknowledgements

Thanks are especially due to the following:

Mr Paul Bareau, Sir George Bolton, Lord Boothby, Mr Roy Bridge, Vice-Admiral Sir Richard Brockman, Sir Alec Cairncross, Sir Richard ('Otto') Clarke, Lord Cobbold, Sir Edgar Cohen, Lord Coleraine, Sir Edmund Compton, Mr Douglas Jay, Mr A Van Dormael, Sir Edward and Lady Ford, Mr A T K Grant, The Earl of Halifax, Sir Frederic Harmer, Dr J K Horsefield, Lt-Gen Sir Ian Jacob, Lord Kahn, Sir John Lang, Lady Kathleen Lee, Sir Percivale Liesching, Mr L P T Thompson-McCausland, Mr D F McCurrach, Sir John Martin, Professor J E Meade, Professor D E Moggridge, Sir Edward Playfair, Lord Plowden, Sir Jeremy Raisman, Sir Denis Rickett, Lord Robbins, Lord Roberthall, Professor R S Sayers, Lord Sherfield, Sir Arthur Snelling, Sir Roger Stevens, Dr Nita Watts.

The Bank of England, the British Library of Political and Economic Science, Churchill College Archives.

List of Abbreviations and Guide to References

BPP British Parliamentary Papers (HMSO London), followed by date of Session and volume number.

FRUS *Foreign Relations of the United States* (Government Printing Office, Washington DC), followed by number or title of volume.

JMK The Collected Writings of John Maynard Keynes (London), followed by volume and page numbers:

XXI *Activities* 1931 – 9: World Crises and Policies in Britain and America (1982).

XXIII *Activities* 1940 – 3: External War Finance (1979).

XXIV *Activities* 1944 – 6: The Transition to Peace (1979).

XXV *Activities* 1940 – 4: Shaping the Post-War World: The Clearing Union (1980).

XXVI *Activities* 1941 – 6: Shaping the Post-War World: Bretton Woods and Reparations (1980).

XXVII *Activities* 1940 – 6: Shaping the Post-War World: Employment and Commodities (1980).

Documentary references are to British official records, unless otherwise described, with Class and reference numbers in the Public Record Office (AVIA, BT, CAB, DO, FO, PREM, T), or with those of the original departmental files.

The dates of telegrams are of their times of origin wherever possible. Occasionally telegrams were despatched a day or more later than their times of origin; in consequence the numerical order of a series of telegrams may not reflect their precise chronological order.

CHAPTER 1

The Nature of the Problem

(1) THE POST-WAR SETTLEMENT

The conclusion of the Anglo-American Financial Agreement in December 1945, and the simultaneous publication of agreement on the broad approach to international discussions of commercial policy, represented an attempt to settle both Britain's wartime financial problems and the direction of her external economic policy in the peace. The settlement partially collapsed in August 1947, barely more than one year after the United States had ratified it in July 1946, and less than six weeks after the requirement of convertibility for currently earned sterling, an essential feature of the agreement, had been fulfilled. In an exposition of external economic policy, a policy which had made such an uncertain start between 1945 and 1947, a major preliminary task is therefore to explore the origins of the settlement of 1945. This introductory chapter sketches the broad trends which came together at the end of 1945; subsequent chapters examine in more detail some major influences in the evolution of post-war economic policies.

(2) THE FOUR EXTERNAL PROBLEMS

When in August 1945, much earlier than most had expected, hostilities in the second world war ended, the British Government faced four 'external' economic problems that were closely related. First, and of considerable urgency, the almost immediate termination of financial assistance under 'Mutual Aid' from the United States and Canada necessitated the securing of finance for essential supplies.

Second, there was the settlement of wartime financial obligations, in particular to the USA and Canada. Under Mutual Aid, originating on the American side as Lend-Lease some months before America's entry into the war in December 1941, and on the Canadian as a variety of financial assistance, Britain had received from and provided to the two countries supplies and services on the basis that settlement would be postponed until the end of the war. Further, Britain had accumulated massive net liabilities to numerous overseas countries. At the end of June 1945, shortly before the end of the war, these had already reached £3,355 million. They were largely in sterling: 'the sterling balances' which were to overshadow the post-war economy. Just over

I

£3 billion were 'quick' liabilities, which in principle the creditors could spend at short notice; before the war, apart from the exceptional fluctuations of 1938 – 9, something over £500 million was probably a 'normal' level[1] (for fuller details, *see below,* Appendix 21, p 413). A very rough indication of the potential burden of the greatly increased balances is given by a comparison with the value of pre-war merchandise exports, which in 1938 was £471 million. Post-war export prices were expected to be roughly double those of pre-war.[2] Allowing for a comparable rise in working balances to £1,000 million, the remaining balances would then be equivalent to about two and a half years of exports at their 1938 volume. It was, however, hoped to raise the volume of exports (which at the end of the war were only forty-two per cent of that in 1938) towards a level at least fifty per cent higher.[3] The increased balances, net of working balances, would then be equivalent, *ceteris paribus*, to one and two-thirds' years of that enhanced amount.

In the view of Lord Keynes,* at the opening of the Anglo-American financial negotiations in Washington in September 1945, rather less than one-sixth of the overall total was not particularly intractable. Some liabilities were governed or were expected to be governed by special arrangements, such as the monetary and payments agreements negotiated with numerous countries during the war to regulate the expenditure of sterling; certain obligations, mainly to Portugal, would have to be met in gold; and liquidation of British assets in Latin American countries was expected to go some way to meet liabilities there.[4] By far the largest creditors, however, for approximately £2.7 billion, were the sterling area countries: the Empire, the Commonwealth (except Canada), and a few other countries, notably in the Middle East, where there was substantial British expenditure during the war. These countries traditionally conducted substantial trade with Britain and with each other; they financed their overseas trade as a whole in sterling, and held their international reserves largely—during the war almost entirely—in sterling. Thus, the growth of the sterling area's balances reflected not only Britain's heavy expenditure on goods and services from trading partners and the scarcity of British exports and shipping, but also the greater pooling of gold and foreign exchange accruals in exchange for sterling; exchange controls in individual sterling countries restricted expenditure outside the sterling area in order to minimise drawings on the central 'dollar pool'. In

---

* KEYNES, John Maynard, 1st Baron 1942 (1883 – 1946); Member of the Chancellor of the Exchequer's Consultative Council 1940 – 46; Director of the Bank of England 1941 – 46; Chairman of United Kingdom Delegation, UN Monetary and Financial Conference, Bretton Woods, 1944; various missions to the USA 1941 – 46, including negotiations for US Loan to Britain 1945; appointed a Governor of the International Bank for Reconstruction and Development, February 1946.

short, Britain's gold and dollar reserves were those of the sterling area as a whole. Moreover, despite recovery from very low levels during the war, the reserves bore a far less favourable ratio to sterling balances at the end than at the beginning: roughly one to seven, compared with one and a quarter to one. So great a deterioration illuminated the major post-war problems of the future of the balances and the limited scope for drawing on the reserves to meet Britain's post-war balance of payments difficulties.

A third economic problem was the apparent indispensability of long-term finance from abroad, mainly from the USA but also from Canada, in order to balance Britain's external accounts during the transition to a peacetime economy, a process expected to take several years. 'Commercial exports', though above their worst wartime levels, were running at not much more than two-fifths of their 1938 volume in the first nine months of 1945. Imports were down to barely three-fifths of their 1938 volume. In *value* terms, the trade deficit, which had averaged £388 million annually in the last three full pre-war years (1936 – 8) was thought likely to reach £500 – 700 million in 1946;[5] although its narrowing subsequently was to be expected, worsened terms of trade were expected to be a constraint. Net invisible earnings, which had not quite covered the trade gap before the war (some disinvestment had occurred) had shrunk drastically; moreover high government expenditure overseas, far above its modest pre-war level, was expected to swamp, or at best to offset, net invisible earnings in the early post-war years. Recovery of that part of net invisible earnings represented by shipping, one-third of the pre-war total, could be anticipated, but not that of the remaining two-thirds, which had come largely from interest, profits, and dividends. Those receipts had fallen as a result of wartime dislocation, particularly in south-east Asia, but more lasting deterioration was implicit in massive external disinvestment. Disposal of overseas assets accounted for about one-quarter of this. The remainder consisted largely of two items. One was the reduction in gold and dollar reserves. The other and far larger comprised the greatly increased sterling balances which, in default of a drastic settlement, would involve heavy servicing costs. The total amount of disinvestment was equivalent to rather more than eighty per cent of the estimated total of net overseas assets before the war.[6]

The stark prospects for trade and for the balance of payments as a whole embodied a particularly critical problem in the prospective shortage of US and Canadian dollars. The United Kingdom's dependence on imports from North America had increased during the war; it was likely to remain high, at least during the reconstruction period. There would be heavy demands on Britain's own resources, not only for her own reconstruction needs but also from those of war-devastated countries in Europe and elsewhere. The USA was the only other major source of supply, but dollars were almost universally scarce. Hence there would be severe constraints on Britain's ability to export to North America in the early post-war years. Further, the traditional relief provided by the dollar earnings of overseas sterling countries was likely to be attenuated: those countries imported relatively more from the USA than before the war, and Britain would be making 'unrequited exports' to them if they used excess sterling balances to acquire British goods and services. The scope for Britain to offset its dollar deficits, by surpluses with the rest of the sterling area and the latter's surpluses with the USA, had therefore diminished.

Estimates of the prospective cumulative deficit, and hence of the amount of overseas aid that might have to be sought, before the achievement of sustainable equilibrium in the balance of payments, were necessarily rough and bold. During 1944–5, the Economic Section of the War Cabinet Offices, in co-operation with the Treasury, the Board of Trade, and the Bank of England attempted such forecasting (largely in extension of estimates made even earlier, in 1941–2). They assumed that the war against Japan would last two years after Germany's defeat, and that recovery would continue for a further three years. The cumulative deficit was put within a range of £1,300 million to £2,000 million (see Appendix 27). Keynes adapted these estimates. He made various assumptions about the reduction of major potential burdens on the balance of payments: notably about the containment of expenditure of excess sterling balances, and the reduction of government expenditure overseas. By summer 1945 his calculations had led to the conclusion that it would be necessary to seek aid of $5,500 million (£1,375 million): $5,000 million (£1,250 million) from the USA, and $500 million (£125 million) from Canada.

Fourth, by no means least, indeed probably the major inspiration of the settlement, Britain was broadly committed to the evolution with the United States of proposals for world trading arrangements that would be far less restrictive than those of the inter-war years.

The link between these four problems was Article VII of the Mutual Aid Agreement of February 1942 between Britain and the USA; the spirit of this was embodied in comparable agreements between the USA and other countries to which it extended Lend-Lease. Article VII formally associated wartime with future peacetime arrangements by its provision that 'in return for aid' under the Lend-Lease Act of March 1941 Britain should render appropriate benefits to the USA. The American Lend-Lease legislation had not specified those benefits, beyond stating simply that they were to be in any form 'which the President deems satisfactory'.[7] With the unhappy experience of war debts after the first world war in the drafters' minds, Article VII stated that 'the terms and conditions [should not] burden commerce between the two countries [but should] include provision for agreed action . . .' to expand economic activity. The action would be directed towards 'the elimination of all forms of discriminatory treatment in international commerce, and to the reduction of tariffs and other trade barriers . . .' There should be early discussions about the attainment of these objectives.[8] These obligations became known, using a routine term encountered elsewhere to denote compensation for American trading concessions, as 'The Consideration'. The manner of its possible implementation was to colour Anglo-American relations and the preparations for peace during the rest of the war; it was to dominate the settlement devised during the negotiations of September–December 1945 which, though commonly described as financial negotiations are equally to be regarded as 'Article VII negotiations'.

(3) ARTICLE VII

The Administration's need to seek regular Appropriations from Congress and to provide it with reports at least every ninety days ensured ample scope for public scrutiny of Lend-Lease and of the 'benefits' therefrom to the USA. The particular stress of Article VII on 'The Consideration' in terms of commercial policy found its rationale in the concern of both countries to avoid after the war the mistakes of the past in international trade. On the American side the Administration had displayed since 1934, in the Reciprocal Trade Agreements Act, a determination to lower the trade barriers its predecessors had erected, but to do so only in exchange for reciprocal concessions by other countries. It was determined to end discriminatory practices, particularly those from which it claimed to suffer under the system of preference that had been developed following the Imperial Economic Conference held at Ottawa in 1932. American endeavours to contain and eventually to reduce or eliminate Imperial Preference had begun before the war in trade agreements with Canada in 1935, and above all in 1938 with both Canada and Britain respectively. Britain's wartime restrictions upon trade put question marks, however, over the worth of the Anglo-American Trade Agreement, indeed over its eventual survival after the war, for it had a nominal duration of only three years (it was, however, to be prolonged until formally terminated in 1962[9]). Further, the development of exchange control and notably of the dollar-pooling, dollar-economising of the sterling area added to Imperial Preference a twin source of American unease over alleged discrimination. Britain's wartime search to earn more dollars gave the State Department, under the quasi-missionary leadership of its Secretary, Mr Cordell Hull,* an opportunity to press its 'trade expansion' programme even before the emergence of Lend-Lease. With the advent of that massive aid, the supply of dollars was

* HULL, Cordell (1871–1955); Secretary of State of the United States of America, 1933–44.

not overtly to depend upon Anglo-American accord over trade policy, but the terms of the eventual settlement of Lend-Lease would. This was an important, real, but potentially delicate distinction, for disaccord over post-war plans could obviously influence the general atmosphere in which the repeated frictions over Lend-Lease/Mutual Aid were produced.

The British reaction to American aspirations to freer trade was less to dissent than to doubt their applicability in the context of Britain's economic and political problems. Even before the war the balance of payments had been weak at the same time as unemployment was high. The realisation of certain overseas assets to finance the war was further weakening it by the loss of invisible earnings. Moreover, by ensuring indispensable finance, Lend-Lease permitted the drastic reduction of British exports, as recognised in the 'Export White Paper' of September 1941, and thereby deepened the trough from which overseas earnings would have to be hauled after the war. The post-war external problem had become clear enough during 1940 – 41. It was to be analysed by the Economic Section of the War Cabinet Offices during the discussions on post-war plans associated with the evolution of 'The Consideration' in 1941 – 42 in what may be regarded as a foundation memorandum for many governmental discussions and many subsequent memoranda during the rest of the war.[10] The elaboration of this produced a formidable programme. Exports would have to be greatly increased and imports restrained. Overseas debts would have to be held at bay if they could not be reduced. Five years at least would be required for the economy to recover to a sustainable equilibrium, overseas aid being somehow secured meanwhile (see Appendix 27).

So much was understood within the British Government, but this was agreement upon the nature of the problem, whereas there was disagreement upon the policy implications of both wartime and pre-war economic tribulations. To the extent that the differences were primarily of political philosophy they appeared clear enough, though scarcely easy to resolve in a wartime coalition. Some major differences cut across parties, however; nor were the Government's economic advisers united in their recommendations. Although much was done to prepare domestic policies for the transition and for the better Britain it was hoped to construct, the temptation was strong to defer rather than to decide upon external commitments at the height of the war. The scent of peace brought a different but no less powerful drag upon decision in the weakening of the wartime cement of coalition between, and indeed within, parties, diminishing the last chances of consensus on post-war policy. Perhaps even more conducive to procrastination was the genuine, eventually desperate, hope that some major decisions might become unnecessary or less burdensome by the removal of the

6

worst threats to the post-war balance of payments. Hence there was ministerial discouragement of official discussion of long-term plans towards the end of the war: might there not be some 'Grand Assize' at which the two allies would herald the peace with the spirit of mutual aid, by balancing the accounts and then cancelling them?[11] As for the specific financial problems of Britain in the peace, hopes of a new 'brainwave' comparable with Lend-Lease for the war were not confined to the British side of the Atlantic, although there they were inevitably stronger, surviving into the early days of negotiations in autumn 1945. How far such hopes were warranted must remain substantially conjectural, given the removal from power before the end of the war, by the death of President Roosevelt* in April 1945 and by Mr Churchill's[†] electoral defeat in the summer, of the two statesmen who had handled with remarkable success the delicate problems of Mutual Aid; upon them the hopes for comparable achievement in dealing with the problems of peace had ultimately rested. Conjectural also must be the impact of the early end of the war against Japan. To use the jargon then current, the completion of the war against Germany, Stage I ('Phase I' to the Americans), was separated from the commencement of Stage III, the transition to a peacetime economy, by only three months instead of the eighteen months that had been officially forecast as necessary for Stage II, the concentration of the war against Japan alone. Stage III arrived, therefore, before preparations had been made for it and when, indeed, there had been struggle enough to try to secure satisfactory Anglo-American arrangements for Stage II.

(4) DIFFICULTIES OVER LEND-LEASE

Three closely related anxieties affected Britain's passage towards a peacetime economy during the closing months of the war, from late 1944 to August 1945. These concerned the operation of Lend-Lease (the name and the American procedures continued after the formal transformation into Mutual Aid); uncertainty over the relaxation of constraints upon Britain's export trade; and the level of the gold and dollar reserves.

That there were continuous frictions in Lend-Lease arrangements is scarcely surprising. The transfer of resources between countries was bound to involve problems about the recipient country's own supply capacity. In the case of non-military items, were they supporting a

---

* ROOSEVELT, Franklin Delano (1882–1945); President of United States, 1933–45; Democratic Party.
† CHURCHILL, Winston Leonard Spencer, KG 1953 (1874–1965); Prime Minister, First Lord of the Treasury, and Minister of Defence, 1940–45; Leader of the Opposition, 1945–51; Minister of Defence, 1951–52; Prime Minister and First Lord of the Treasury, 1951–55.

civilian sector too large for wartime? Did they contribute to an unfair sustenance of one partner's export competitiveness after the war? As the junior partner Britain was sensitive to such queries, to which American constitutional and political habits gave an abrasive character. As early as November 1943 certain capital goods had been excluded from Lend-Lease.[12] The flood of supplies and hence of finance associated with the invasion of Europe in June 1944 strengthened American surveillance, particularly of proposed non-military supplies, not only for the conclusion of the German war but also for the coming concentration on Japan. Matters were settled in principle at the 'OCTAGON' meeting at Quebec between President Roosevelt and Mr Churchill in September 1944, and subsequently in some detail by a 'Combined Committee' in Washington during October-December 1944. Britain now expected to maintain during Stage II roughly the same military effort in relation to the USA as in Stage I, but the expectation that both countries would begin the shift to a peacetime economy implied a decline in the absolute amount of military aid. Britain argued, however, and secured agreement, that *non*-military needs would scarcely change since civilians would need as much food, etc, as before, and for these requirements Lend-Lease was expected to be broadly sustained.[13] Unfortunately, these arrangements stopped short of decisions about the manner of ending Lend-Lease and about a replacement of it to help Britain in the reconstruction period; yet Lend-Lease had been widely regarded in the United States, as had Mutual Aid in Canada, as essentially a wartime expedient, and all parties including the United Kingdom had long recognised that it would end with the war.

Lend-Lease supplies flowed less satisfactorily than expected after the Quebec and Washington discussions of autumn 1944, and more sluggishly than before. A rough indication of the slowdown is provided by deliveries of army supplies to Britain from the US. As a proportion of expected deliveries, they had reached 85 per cent in 1943 and 75 per cent in 1944; in the first four months of 1945 the proportion was two-thirds on the tighter basis for Stage II or as little as one-half on the ampler basis of Stage I. By April 1945, indeed, as Germany's defeat approached, a widely diffused deceleration was apparent.[14] By then, too, alarming uncertainties were gathering over Lend-Lease and Stage III. When renewing the Lend-Lease Act in April 1945, the American Congress had attached an amendment prohibiting the use of Lend-Lease funds for post-war relief and reconstruction; only the vote of the Senate Chairman, Vice-President Truman,* defeated a further amendment to forbid the use in exports of any Lend-Lease materials regardless of previous undertakings. President Roosevelt's death in

* TRUMAN, Harry S. (1884-1972); Vice-President of the USA, 1945; President 1945-53; Democratic Party.

April 1945 made Mr Truman the President who signed the amended Bill.[15] Three weeks later, the surrender of Germany led to his being advised to sign an order which was intended to reduce Lend-Lease forthwith, but which US officials treated as requiring the stoppage of all Lend-Lease supplies.[16] The rationale may have been a desire to warn the Soviet Union, whose actions in former German-occupied territories in Eastern and South-eastern Europe the American Administration felt to be contrary to understandings reached at the Yalta Conference in February 1945.[17] The day before the President signed his order, the Chancellor of the Exchequer had sent a reminder to the US Foreign Economic Administration of the arrangements for Stage II agreed the previous autumn, and announced subsequently to Parliament. For Britain the new President's action would have been devastating; but it was immediately retracted.[18] Even so, it was a danger signal. On three counts difficulties were already increasing. It now seemed likely that dollars might be needed for food and equipment supplied to British forces not engaged in the war against Japan; that meant in particular the occupation forces in Germany. Second, the reduction of their own war production made the American military authorities reluctant to supply material which Britain could apparently supply herself; but this implied an obvious check to Britain's reduction of her own war production and to the reconversion agreed at Quebec and Washington. Third, drastically accelerating declines in American supplies hampered British preparations for participation in the conclusion of the war against Japan.[19] The fluctuating uncertainties and hopes of mid-1945 persisted against a background of two months' delay between the British Prime Minister's request to the President for clarification, on 28 May, and the latter's formal reply on 29 July. If this now set out the facts, they were grim: warlike supplies were to be limited to those directly required for the war against Japan.[20] During this waiting period there had, it is true, been tolerably reassuring news in that the usual Appropriations Bill to implement the renewed Lend-Lease Act, though providing much smaller funds for Britain than hoped, at least seemed to secure for the year June 1945 to June 1946 non-munitions supplies, eg, food, on the basis agreed in late 1944. There was, however, a double caveat: the American Administration reiterated to Congress that Lend-Lease would not be used for post-war reconstruction, and also stated that it would cease entirely within perhaps a month of Japan's defeat.[21]

In his reply of 29 July, the American President had accepted the British suggestion that discussions on Stage III, ie, on the transition from a war to a peace economy, should be held later that summer in Washington, but within days Japan had surrendered under nuclear bombardment, so that Stage III was about to open before discussions on it could be commenced. Quite predictably, in strict accord with the

9

American law and with the reports and expectations of British officials, but none the less to the horror of the British Government and to that of the British public, Lend-Lease was abruptly terminated, subject to some limited exceptions.[22] Thereafter a different basis had to be sought for the finance of American supplies to Britain.

(5) THE REVIVAL OF EXPORTS

A second major anxiety in the move to a peace economy arose from the drastic rundown of Britain's exports during the war. This had been partly a deliberate policy to concentrate resources upon war production, immediate survival being more important than the future of the balance of payments. It became particularly drastic when Lend-Lease assured essential imports, but also introduced new complications, for British exports might now embody Lend-Lease materials, or materials for which such supplies were substitutes. More generally the maintenance, let alone the apparent strengthening anywhere of British exports during the war, tended to foster unease and resentment amongst erstwhile American exporters, who felt their own trading prospects to be handicapped by war constraints, whereas British exporters might be using Lend-Lease aid, the product of such constraints, to gain unfair advantage. No matter whether those feelings were justified or were a cover for less worthy motives, the feelings existed, as also did the irritant for Britain of American oversight of the use of Lend-Lease supplies. It was to diminish the scope for such friction that exports had been allowed to shrink drastically.

In September 1941, the Foreign Secretary was to address a formal memorandum on British export policy to the American Ambassador in London. The 'Export White Paper' as this became known declared that Britain would use for export neither Lend-Lease supplies nor their substitutes nor, so far as possible, scarce materials of any kind.[23]

This commitment certainly allowed the 'export problem to go underground in the long middle stretch of the war' in the sense that Lend-Lease had displaced exports as the dominant source of external finance.[24] Difficulties over the use and therefore the supply of Lend-Lease materials none the less persisted, so that there were early and repeated British endeavours to moderate the asperities of export policy. It did not prove possible, however, to develop specific proposals for the withdrawal of the Export White Paper and for securing export freedom until the end of 1944. During 1944, exports, which in 1941 had been fifty-six per cent of their volume in 1938, had fallen to thirty-one per cent of that last full pre-war year. It was the British aim to raise this to about sixty-seven per cent during the first year of Stage II, say from early 1945 to early 1946; a more ambitious, though necessary aim was to raise it to 150 per cent (or even to 175 per cent) within a few years[25] (see Appendix 27).

At Quebec in September 1944 the American President and the British Prime Minister agreed, somewhat obscurely, that Lend-Lease supplies should not be used in the revival, for which Mr Roosevelt was anxious, of Britain's exports, but that there would be no conditions attaching to Lend-Lease that would obstruct that recovery. This imprecision doubtless reflected not only American political caution ahead of the November Presidential election for Mr Roosevelt's fourth term, but also the intention, as yet unformulated, of the President and of his Secretary of the Treasury, Mr Morgenthau,* that aid of some kind must be provided to assist Britain's recovery. Thus, a rundown of Lend-Lease would be of less consequence to Britain whilst at the same time it would also satisfy Congress that no change was being made in Lend-Lease policy.[26] Conceivably some on both the American and British sides foresaw compensation for Britain in the enhanced opportunity for her exports that might result from the deliberate destruction of major German industries after the war, but such influence as they exercised proved fleeting. The 'Morgenthau Plan' for the 'pastoralisation' of Germany had preoccupied the Secretary of State at Quebec. It encountered, however, such overwhelming opposition that, notwithstanding the signature by the President and a sceptical Prime Minister of a document giving it some support, it failed to become part of official Anglo-American policy.[27]

For the subsequent Washington negotiations in October and November the detailed British case for help in Stage II, including export freedom, was embodied in a very carefully prepared and substantial 'book' dubbed 'the PhD thesis'.[28] British representatives sought to regain export freedom by the withdrawal of the Export White Paper on 1 December 1944. During strenuous negotiations the American representatives, concerned to avoid any appearance of disturbance to the established principles of Lend-Lease administration, preferred to await VE day, the end of the German war, and thus formally the commencement of Stage II, but even so with disturbing qualifications. The British team proposed the exclusion from Lend-Lease of various supplies; to assuage American fears, Lord Keynes gave an assurance that everything would be done to avoid a restrictive, discriminatory operation of the sterling area's pool of scarce dollars. After further strenuous discussions and further plunges into American hesitations about anything that appeared to modify Lend-Lease before the end of the war, Lord Keynes was able to report his understanding that there was 'the certainty of complete export freedom after VE day and, by administrative action, the substance of it from 1 January next'.[29] Thus, a real beginning could be made to restore exports. There remained, however, clouds of complete un-

---

* MORGENTHAU, Henry, Jr. (1891–1967); Secretary of the Treasury, USA, 1934–45.

certainty about the extent and direction of recovery until there could be discussions about the provision of external finance and about commercial policy in Stage III.

(6) THE GOLD AND DOLLAR RESERVES

The third problem to influence Britain's move towards a peacetime economy (the other two being Lend-Lease and a degree of export freedom) was the question of the adequacy of her gold and dollar reserves, which were shared with the rest of the sterling area. In the context of the massive accumulation of sterling debt, the need for postwar imports for reconstruction, and the pressure to abjure quantitative and discriminatory controls on trade, Britain's—the Sterling Area's—exiguous reserves towards the end of the war might have been seen as focusing her grave financial position, but the Americans maintained a crucially blurred view of them. A constant irritant during the war, this foreshadowed difficulties in securing finance for the peace. Britain's reserves, accompanied by significant parts of her longer-term investment in the USA, had virtually disappeared before the enactment of Lend-Lease; indeed, American political considerations had been held by the Administration to require this. Thereafter, although reserves recovered from near-zero they suffered strict American policing lest it be supposed that they were increasing at the American public's expense.[30] Meanwhile the accumulation of sterling debt and the further loss of assets (eg, by the Dominions' and India's use of excess sterling to repatriate British-held debt), magnified the contrast between financial burdens and the ability to sustain them.[31]

At the Washington discussions in late 1944 the British concern to stem an expected decline in reserves met not just a welcome American relaxation of pressure, but also help, albeit less than both countries hoped, to strengthen them. Even so, it would have been premature to assume that there was a shared view on the nature of Britain's financial problem. American thinking, which British comment scarcely tried to discourage, assumed the elimination or the neutralisation of excessive sterling liabilities after the war. Moreover, in July 1945 at the Potsdam Conference President Truman reproduced for the Prime Minister the standard American misconceptions that increases in Britain's reserves warranted less Lend-Lease assistance. The Chancellor of the Exchequer swiftly cabled clarification and correction for Mr Churchill to give to the President.[32] He stressed not only that the reserves, at a level to which the Americans had not taken exception in autumn 1944, had risen from temporary causes, but also and above all that the grave disparity between reserves and liabilities had in fact increased. With only a month, as it was to prove, to the end of the war the incident was a warning that the US Administration appeared to be still unable or unwilling to share Britain's sombre view of her external financial position.

CHAPTER 1, SOURCE REFERENCES

1. US–UK Economic Negotiations in Washington, Tables laid before the US–UK Top Committee, 14 September 1945: GEN 89/3, in CAB 78/37 and PREM 8/35. See also *Statistical Material presented during the Washington Negotiations*, Cmd 6707, December 1945, *British Parliamentary Papers (hereafter BPP)*, 1945–6, XXI, Table 6. The estimate of something over £500 million ('a little over $2 billion' with an exchange rate of $ 4.03 to the £) was cited by Lord Keynes in his exposition to the Top Committee: GEN 80/21 in CAB 130/6; *The Collected Writings of John Maynard Keynes* (hereafter *JMK*), XXIV, p 476. That estimate, later statistics were to indicate, understated the pre-war level. From the end of 1931, a few months after their temporary depletion during the 1931 crisis, the half-yearly level of balances rose from £411 million to as much as £808 million at the end of 1937 before beginning their protracted decline associated with increasing international tension during 1938 and 1939; they fell to £542 million at the end of June 1939 and to £517 million at the end of December, thereafter beginning their inexorable wartime growth: *Reserves and Liabilities 1931 to 1945*, Cmd 8354, September 1951, *BPP* 1950–1, XXI.

2. Keynes to US–UK Top Committee, 13 September 1945, GEN 80/20, CAB 130/6; *JMK* XXIV, p 470.

3. Cmd 6707, Section III.

4. Mr J M Keynes (from June 1942 Lord Keynes) had been appointed a member, unsalaried, of the Chancellor of the Exchequer's new Consultative Council in June 1940: R S Sayers, History of the Second World War, *Financial Policy 1939–45* (London 1956), p 45. Effectively he was a wide-ranging adviser, dominating the Treasury, with exceptional access to officials and Ministers.

5. The valuation of imports in 1936–8, which was on a cif (cost, insurance, freight) basis is that given in Cmd 6707, Appendix VII Table 10. The range of £500–700 million for the estimated trade deficit in 1946 reflects revisions and the contrast between the use for imports of the cif basis and that of fob (free on board), the latter being lower than the former. Shortly before the Washington negotiations Keynes had estimated the trade deficit for 1946 at £700 million, with imports valued cif, but subsequently reduced this to £650 million, which Mr R W B Clarke of the Treasury equated on an fob basis to £500 million. See Appendix 27, 'Forecasting the Post-War Balance of Payments', Tables 3(a) and 3(b).

6. Cmd 6707, Appendix VI & Table 9; C H Feinstein, *National Income, Expenditure and Output of the United Kingdom* 1855–1965 (Cambridge 1972), p 205 and p T110, Table 50.

7. H D Hall, History of the Second World War, *North American Supply* (London 1955), Appendix III, 'The Lend-Lease Act' of 1941, Section 3(b) on p 506.

8. Ibid, Appendix V, 'The Master Lend-Lease Agreement' of 1942, pp 512–13. The agreement was published as a White Paper, *United States No 1 (1942), Agreement between the Governments of the United Kingdom and the United States of America on the Principles applying to Mutual Aid in the Prosecution of the War against Aggression*, Cmd 6341, *BPP* 1941–2, IX.

9. The treaty was formally terminated in 1962 by an Exchange of Notes, which recorded that its 'substantial provisions...were rendered inoperative by the Supplementary Agreement of...1947': Cmnd 1897, December 1962, *Treaty Series No 78 (1962), Third Supplementary List of Ratifications, Accessions, Withdrawals, &c, for* 1962, *BPP* 1962–3, XXXVII, p 1014.

10. 'The United Kingdom's Post-War Balance of Payments', memorandum of 31 January 1942, with related papers, in T230/4 and T236/302.

11. J Keith Horsefield, *The International Monetary Fund 1945–65. Twenty Years of International Monetary Co-operation* (3 vols, Washington DC 1969), I, p 53, citing E F Penrose, *Economic Planning for the Peace* (Princeton, N J, and London 1953), p 55.

12. Hall, op cit, pp 280, 438.

13. Ibid, pp 443–4.

14. Ibid, pp 451–3.

15. G C Herring, 'The United States and British Bankruptcy 1944–45: Responsibilities Deferred', *Political Science Quarterly* LXXXVI (1971), pp 271–3; Harry S Truman, *Year of Decisions 1945* (London 1955), pp 47, 101–2. Mr Truman's account does not refer to the further, defeated, amendment, and mistakenly records the defeat of the amendment which was in fact passed, prohibiting the use of Lend-Lease appropriations for relief, etc.

16. The background to the new President's original order is given in Truman, op cit, pp 145–6.

17. Jim Bishop, *FDR's Last Year April 1944–April 1945* (London 1975), p 528.

18. Hall, op cit p 455; Truman, op cit, p 145.

19. Hall, op cit, pp 457–8.

20. Ibid, pp 458–9; Truman, op cit, pp 409–10.

21. Hall, op cit, p 457.

22. Ibid, p 461.

23. *United States No 2 (1941). Correspondence respecting the policy of His Majesty's Government in connexion with the use of materials received under the Lend-Lease Act,* Cmd 6311, September 1941, *BPP* 1940–41, VIII. See also Hall, op cit, pp 295–6, Sayers, op cit, pp 398–405, and W K Hancock & M M Gowing, History of the Second World War, *British War Economy* (London 1949), pp 244–5.

24. Hancock & Gowing, op cit, p 245.

25. For attempts to have the Export White Paper modified or withdrawn, 1943–4, see PREM 4/17/13; E L Hargreaves and M M Gowing, History of the Second World War. *Civil Industry and Trade* (London 1952), pp 161–3. On wartime and post-war exports, Hancock & Gowing, op cit, pp 520–1; History of the Second World War. *Statistical Digest of the War,* prepared in the Central Statistical Office (London 1951), Table 142.

26. Hall, op cit, p 444.

27. For the Prime Minister's attitude, see papers in PREM 4/18/6, especially telegrams GUNFIRE 166 and 169 of 15 September 1944 to the Deputy Prime Minister and War Cabinet (whose reply in telegram CORDITE 300 of 16 September congratulated him); *Foreign Relations of the United States,* (hereafter *FRUS*), *The Conference at Quebec 1944* (Washington DC 1972), pp 324–8, 342–4, 359–63, 466–7; Winston S Churchill, *History of the Second World War. VI Triumph and Tragedy* (London 1954), pp 138–9. See also *FRUS,* op cit, pp 101–5, 128–43, 390–1; *FRUS, The Conferences at Malta and Yalta 1945* (Washington DC 1955), pp 134–5; Sir John Colville, *Footprints in Time* (London 1976), pp 166–7 and *The Churchillians* (London 1981), pp 33–34; The Earl of Avon, *The Eden Memoirs. The Reckoning* (London 1961), pp 475–6; Sayers, op cit, p 469; D Rees, *Harry Dexter White* (New York 1973), pp 254–75; *JMK* XXIV, p 128, n 1. For an extended account of the Morgenthau Plan, see Warren F Kimball, *Swords or Ploughshares? The Morgenthau Plan for Defeated Nazi Germany 1943–46* (Philadelphia, New York, San José and Toronto 1976).

28. By Mr E A G (later Sir Austin) Robinson: A S J Baster, *Reconstruction,* CAB 102/619.
29. Hancock & Gowing, op cit, p 532; Sayers, op cit, p 473; Hall, op cit, pp 445–6.
30. Sayers, op cit, pp 437–44.
31. Ibid, pp 438–40.
32. Hall, op cit, p 459. President Truman's note to Mr Churchill, 17 July 1945, Mr Churchill's telegram TARGET 65 to Chancellor, 18 July, and Chancellor's telegram ONWARD 61 of 18 July to Mr Churchill: PREM 4/17/15.

CHAPTER 2

Trade, Dollars, and Trade Policy 1941 – 42

(1) PRE-WAR TRADE POLICY

By 1939, the British economy had for several years been moving decisively away from the relative lack of official controls which had characterised it before 1914, and to a considerable degree up to September 1931. Recent though this development was, perhaps indeed because it was so recent, it had already been challenged. During the war, it was to be challenged further, by some British as well as by the American participants in preparations for the peace; the settlement of 1945 was to seek to modify the trade and monetary policies which had evolved during the inter-war years.

Britain's nineteenth century policies of free trade and of an open monetary system had been modified in two stages in the quarter of a century before 1939. The first comprised the war of 1914 – 18 and the 1920s. The McKenna duties of 1915 to protect certain industries were a major relaxation of free trade principles. Even more significant was the crumbling in 1917 of Britain's long resistance to Imperial Preference, although the Conservatives' electoral defeat in 1923 delayed its implementation. The second stage came with the world slump from 1929, in which the 1931 financial crisis came to overshadow subsequent economic policies. Protective tariffs were virtually generalised except for food in 1932; agriculture, however, was given increasing shelter from overseas competition by quantitative restrictions.

The monetary system had changed no less dramatically. Following the difficult years of the restored gold standard of 1925 – 31, and after its collapse in September 1931, it no longer rested on rigid exchange rates. The pound had become nominally a floating currency. The formal establishment of the Exchange Equalisation Account in 1932 sought to shield the exchange rate and the domestic economy against undue disturbance from abrupt international transfers of short-term capital ('hot money'). There was in consequence a loosening of the links between international and domestic monetary developments. Further, the restriction of capital export, which had been intermittent since 1915, became almost continuous from 1931, with exceptions for Empire and foreign sterling-using countries. Not least, long-standing international trading and monetary relations crystallised during and after 1931 into the sterling system of countries which held their reserves in sterling and which, in a world of violent exchange fluctuations and of exchange control, kept their currencies freely exchangeable and virtually stable in terms of sterling.

Reasons and justifications could be enumerated, though not here, for these arrangements. To those outside them, especially to the United States, the element of discrimination was particularly resented, and challenges to those new trade and monetary policies were quickly made. Even without the rest of the Empire, Britain was the world's largest trader; moreover, Imperial Preference favoured the competitors of the badly depressed American producers of food and raw materials. Equipped with the Reciprocal Trade Agreements Act of 1934, the United States Administration sought to diminish Imperial Preference, particularly by the Anglo-American Trade Agreement of 1938.

The modification of British monetary policy was less formal and less extensive. Within 18 months of Britain's resort to a floating exchange rate, the new American Administration under President Roosevelt had begun in March 1933 to out-float, as it were, the pound sterling. Although the rise in the sterling and then in the dollar price of gold between 1931 and 1934 eased the problem of international liquidity, the floating and depreciation of the American dollar in 1933–4 was to put sterling back into, indeed above, its old pre-1931 over-valuation in terms of the dollar. The retention by a few countries ('the Gold Bloc'), notably by France, of their gold parities allowed Britain to continue a degree of floating. This came to an end in September 1936 with the devaluation of the French franc, with which was associated an understanding between Britain, the USA, and France (subsequently joined by several other countries). This was the Tripartite Declaration, by which the three countries agreed to seek stable exchange rates, and to notify each other of impending changes in them[1]. This understanding embodied both a partial rejection of the immediate American past of monetary isolationism, and a forward look towards the world-wide system of stable but adjustable exchange rates of the International Monetary Fund that was to emerge from the Bretton Woods Conference of 1944.

Thus, even before their close association during the war years induced keener scrutiny of their respective external economic policies, Britain and the USA had begun to modify them in the light both of self-interest and of their somewhat differing visions of international arrangements that would be more orderly and less destructive than those of the inter-war years. The war itself led British thinking along three sorts of paths. One pointed to the development of imperial trade. This would have involved tight restrictions on non-empire trade and an extension of Imperial Preference. American policy before the war, and, as will be seen, during the war, virtually eliminated this possibility.

17

A second path merits particular attention. This envisaged the controlled development of trade through barter deals and bilateral payments agreements, allied with such restrictions upon trade and payments that the war seemed to have justified. In extreme form this was 'Schachtian', following the policies of Dr Hjalmar Schacht* (President of the Reichsbank until 1939) and of other Nazi economic experts. Britain's inclination to such policies was understandable and ran through much wartime discussion of economic policy. 'After the last war', Keynes declared[2] at the end of 1940

> 'laissez-faire in foreign exchange led to chaos. Tariffs offer no escape from this. But in Germany Schacht and Funk[†] were led by force of necessity to evolve something better. In practice they have used their new system to the detriment of their neighbours. But the underlying idea is sound and good. In the last six months the Treasury and the Bank of England have been building up a system which has borrowed from the German experience all that was good in it. If we are to meet our obligations and avoid chaos in international trade after the war, we shall have to retain this system...'

There would be no alternative to Schachtian policies, he was to write some months later[3], unless some ideal international system could be established—'Utopia' as his plans for a Clearing Union were to be dubbed—though he was soon to modify, but not to abandon wholly his Schachtian advocacy. Moreover, the Bank of England, as technicians responsible for operating foreign exchange policy, were to maintain a steadfast view that monetary and trade controls of a Schachtian character, though it did not so describe them, could scarcely be avoided in the post-war years.

The occasion for this presentation of Keynes's Schachtian views was a series of anxious reports from Switzerland in autumn 1940 about the alleged fear of businessmen in countries not occupied by the Nazis that a British victory would see London indifferent to its economic leadership of Europe; rather than face post-war economic disorder, they might seek accommodation with the Nazis' 'New Economic Order' and thereby strengthen instead the chances of a German victory. Britain was therefore urged to publicise counter-proposals to what was regarded largely as German propaganda. This task was remitted to Keynes, from whose prologue to a memorandum on 'Proposals to counter the German "New Order"' the extract in the preceding paragraph is taken. The memorandum itself was in much

* SCHACHT, Dr Hjalmar Horace Greely (1877–1970); President of the Reichsbank 1924–30 and 1933–39; Reichsminister of Economics 1934–37.
† FUNK, Walther, (1890–1960); Reichsminister of Economics 1937; President of the Reichsbank 1939.

more general terms with no good word for German economic methods. The nearest reference to Schachtianism was its statement that 'The arrangements we are now slowly perfecting, by which international exchange returns to what it always should have been, namely a means for trading goods against goods, will outlast the war.' It offered a pledge to establish an international exchange system that would make markets and materials open to all, with the help after liberation of a European Reconstruction Fund to provide credit[4]. This memorandum was intended for a major ministerial pronouncement, and was so used in a speech by the Foreign Secretary, Mr A Eden*, in May 1941[5]. Before then, however, it had been widely circulated, possibly without the revealing prologue; it was read and pondered by the Prime Minister, Mr Churchill, and his close advisers; it was also shown to Mr Harry Hopkins†, President Roosevelt's confidant[6]. An influential trend in British thinking had therefore been expounded in advance of joint Anglo-American preparations for the post-war world.

The third path came into view with Lend-Lease in March 1941. This path pointed towards the extension of the policies of the American Reciprocal Trade Agreements Act and of the Tripartite Agreement. It was symbolised by Article VII of the Mutual Aid Agreement of February 1942, with its vision of world trade free from discrimination and from most species of restriction, and with its commitment to discuss measures to realise that vision. Chapter 3 is concerned with Article VII.

(2) WAR NEEDS AND POST-WAR POLICY

For Britain the choice of path depended partly upon the likely state of her economy at the end of the war. This looked sombre at an early stage. Britain in 1939 could scarcely face the cost of a major war, save with the most skilful financing and with overseas aid: from the Empire, from the sterling area, and from the USA. The first would provide men, materials, and gifts. The second, largely overlapping in composition with the Empire, would provide 'short-term' loans—the sterling balances—representing banking claims on Britain due to, but not fully utilised by, countries which kept their international reserves wholly or largely in sterling. The third, the USA, would eventually provide financial aid in Lend-Lease. All three would yield further resources by their purchases of British assets overseas, such as secur-

---

* EDEN, Robert Anthony, KG 1954, 1st Earl of Avon 1961 (1897–1977); Secretary of State for Dominion Affairs, 1939–40; Secretary of State for War, 1940; Secretary of State for Foreign Affairs, 1940–45; Leader of House of Commons, 1942–45; Secretary of State for Foreign Affairs and Deputy Prime Minister, 1951–55; Prime Minister and First Lord of the Treasury, 1955–57.

† HOPKINS, Harry L (1890–1946); Secretary of Commerce, USA, 1938–40; until 1945, Special Adviser and Assistant to President of USA.

ities and factories, and all three involved the accumulation of heavy indebtedness by Britain.

The gearing of the home economy to war and the procurement of additional overseas resources were bound to take time. Moreover, there was initially a cautious husbanding of external resources to regulate their use over the three years' horizon of full economic mobilisation for war; but they were in any case scanty in relation to Britain's needs. Further the unreality of 'the Phoney War', from September 1939 to April 1940, discouraged the sense of urgency in developing a war economy that emerged only with the disasters of April – June 1940. Even so, it had become clear shortly before that overseas resources were unlikely to last on existing projections of expenditure beyond 1941. Then, in June 1940, it was decided to commit forthwith virtually all the country's external resources to the war effort. Further, with the fall of France, Britain took over French war contracts in the USA, adding thereby an extra burden then estimated at some £125 million (it proved to be some 15 per cent higher). These decisions of mid-1940 brought into view the early exhaustion of Britain's overseas resources.[7]

To increase overseas reserves, Britain had already been exploring two main possibilities, both of which led to delicate Anglo-American discussions about post-war commercial policy. One was to increase exports. These were required, it should be stressed, not just to secure foreign exchange to pay for obviously essential war materials, but also to provide countries supplying food and raw materials with essential goods, including spare parts for British manufactured equipment, which they could not readily obtain elsewhere. There was also an insurance element involved, in the British fear of permanently losing overseas markets, for instance in South America. The other major source of possible overseas funds was financial aid from North America, especially from the USA, but also in substantial amounts from Canada. Initially, in autumn 1940, these two approaches of exports and finance were not co-ordinated. Subsequently they overlapped to form a backcloth to discussions about post-war economic policies that were to continue intermittently from mid-1941 to their climax in September-December 1945.

(3) THE EXPORT DRIVE AND US TRADE POLICY

The export drive had been symbolised by the establishment in February 1940 of an 'Export Council'.[8] The American President himself was to approve this policy, urging Britain even in July 1940 'to force out' exports.[9] A direct increase of exports to the USA seemed essential; the possibility of the indirect earning of dollars by exports to, for instance, Latin American countries was dimmed by their own unfavourable balance with the USA as well as by their existing difficulties in meeting their obligations to Britain. In November 1940, therefore, the Washington representatives of the Export Council, with other Board of Trade officials, opened negotiations with the State Department. These were bound to be difficult. Only recently had there been a significant abatement in mutual suspicions over commercial policy by the conclusion of the Anglo-American Trade Agreement of 1938. Even before, however, its formal ratification in November 1939, the outbreak of war had brought import controls and exchange controls. Britain was now restricting imports, including those from the USA, while continuing to admit Empire supplies freely. The British desire to increase exports to the USA therefore faced, not surprisingly, certain obstacles. Technically, it required a further modification of American tariffs; it also raised questions about the future of the trade agreement, and inevitably also about post-war commercial policy.

Prolonged discussion developed about what the American participants described[10] as a suitable 'Consideration', a word that was soon to haunt Anglo-American economic relations until the end of 1945. Britain's increased war purchases would not suffice; trading concessions would have to be matched by trading concessions. The Americans sought specifically an abatement of Imperial Preference, and proposed that the resultant mutual concessions should be embodied in a supplementary trade agreement to be 'terminable shortly after the war'. Imperial Preference quickly became the sticking point it was to remain thereafter. The Dominions would have to be consulted, which would cause delay and reveal their resentment, argued the British. Eventually, bilateral negotiations between the USA and the individual Dominions, which opened in summer 1941, seemed to offer a way out on preferences, though not an answer to the American fear that the 1938 agreement might lapse.

The Board of Trade's negotiations soon proved embarrassing to the Treasury, which, shortly after they commenced, became involved in a succession of discussions with the United States Administration eventually centring on trade policy. First, a Treasury mission reached Washington early in December 1940, following the re-election of President Roosevelt.[11] This resumed the search, which electoral considerations had suspended in July, for financial assistance. The mission was associated with the formulation of the Lend-Lease proposals,[12] and after their passage into law in March 1941 wrestled with the implications of the American requirement of a 'Consideration', which was to emerge as a commitment about post-war commercial policy. In August 1941, the Atlantic Charter, the product of the meeting at sea of President Roosevelt and Mr Churchill, added further emphasis to discussions of post-war economic policy. Finally, in September 1941, Britain sought by 'the Export White Paper' to allay American concern about the use of Lend-Lease supplies; in effect, Britain affirmed her policy of reducing exports to the barest minimum.

It was in late December 1940, with its own representatives engaged in Lend-Lease financial discussions, that the Treasury 'suddenly discovered' that the Board of Trade was exploring the possibilities of a supplementary trade agreement, which involved assumptions about post-war economic policy contrary to those of the Treasury. A month later the threat of disarray in policy seemed likely to disappear, for the Board of Trade hoped that the negotiations could fade away. Agreement, the Board recognised, would be elusive should the Dominions prove difficult to persuade, and would in any case involve dishonesty if in fact Britain really envisaged the management of trade after the war along the lines canvassed in Keynes's recent paper against a 'New Order'.[13] The enactment of Lend-Lease during March 1941 might seem to have transformed the export question, even to have made it irrelevant, but such proved to be far from the case. On the one hand, Britain still needed dollar earnings, to meet old commitments and to pay for items not covered by Lend-Lease. On the other hand, in contrast to much of the United States Administration, the State Department did not lose interest in trading arrangements with Britain; in particular, it continued to press for a trade agreement. It feared lest restrictive post-war policies by Britain should stimulate pressure on the United States Government to end the 1938 Trade Agreement, encouraging those who favoured 'hemisphere solidarity' in inter-American trade, and bringing the risk of a trade war with Britain.[14] Thus, the trade talks continued, entangling with the Treasury's discussions, but retaining awhile their separate character, until in mid-1941, they suddenly faced collapse. Tension emerged between the Board of Trade and the Treasury, and Anglo-American relations trembled a little. What had happened?

(4) SCHACHTIANISM

A shock for Britain over post-war commercial policy was by mid-1941 already in the making from the American side, and it was probably fortuitous that in fact it developed from the British side. During the spring of 1941, the Board of Trade had seemed to be moving towards the broad American position. It pointed out in May that the 1938 agreement was subject to six months' notice of termination from the end of the year; a supplementary trade agreement, accompanied by bilateral agreements between the USA and the principal Empire countries would therefore provide a desirable safeguard against a post-war tariff war. Above all, the Board of Trade seemed to contemplate constraints upon Britain's use of quantitative restrictions on imports and of exchange control after the war.[15] This approach had already evoked apprehension in the Treasury and in the Bank of England, when in late June Keynes, who had been in Washington for a month (see below p 30), declared to the State Department's principal expert on commercial policy, Mr Harry Hawkins*, that bilateral trading arrangements might be inevitable for Britain in the post-war transition. With Sir Frederick Phillips,† the chief Treasury representative in Washington, Keynes elaborated this thesis to Mr J A Stirling,‡ the Board of Trade's representative. Sketching out the harsh prospect for Britain's post-war balance of payments which the Economic Section had prepared, they stressed that 'Any return to pre-war conditions, particularly as regards trade between the United States and the United Kingdom, is impossible'. Shipping losses, Lend-Lease obligations, the fall in overseas earnings, and the needs of reconstruction, not to mention the possible diversion of South African gold from the British market, all combined to require an increase of exports over the pre-war level of at least 50 per cent. This could be accomplished only by the bilateral method of relating imports from countries to the exports they took.[16]

Both the Treasury in London and the State Department in Washington were momentarily stunned by this intervention which, reported the chief Board of Trade representative in the trade talks, 'had practically caused a deadlock'.[17] Yet if identified, and reprobated by some as a characteristic Keynesian *faux pas* in its forthrightness, the incident involved no more than the expression of views that were broadly those of the British Government, and which had been discussed in transatlantic cables. For Keynes himself, they were the expression of 'Schachtian' views he had already presented to the British Government in December 1940. Above all, the incident doubtless had the merit of clarification: much larger than the relatively limited question of earning extra dollars for war finance which had spawned it, the true issue was that of the principles of Britain's external economic policy after the war. The furore of mid-1941 helped to shift this to where the United States Administration was in any case shortly to place it, in the heart of the discussions about the Lend-Lease 'Consideration'. At first, however, Mr Hawkins was so disturbed by the political implications of Keynes's comments, and so certain that Mr Cordell Hull would find them unacceptable, that he hesitated to report them to the Secretary of State.[18] 'A situation of some delicacy' had arisen, the Board of Trade representative cabled to London, thereby feeding the simmering annoyance of the Treasury (and of the Bank of England) with the Board of Trade for having 'committed the Government to these Anglo-American trade agreement discussions

---

* HAWKINS, Harry C (b. 1894), US Department of State.
† PHILLIPS, Frederick KCMG 1933; GCMG 1942 (1884–1943); Joint Second Secretary HM Treasury; represented HM Treasury in USA, 1940–43.
‡ STIRLING, John Ashwell (1891–1965); Assistant Secretary, Board of Trade, 1935–51.

without letting us know'. The words, those of Sir Richard Hopkins*
of the Treasury, reached the eyes of the Chancellor, who marked
them with his red pencil.[19] In an endeavour to extricate the
Government the Chancellor, the President of the Board of Trade,
and the Foreign Secretary jointly told the Ambassador that while
they accepted the exposition by Keynes and Phillips of the post-war
need for bilateralism, and recognised that such arrangements would
transgress the principle of the most-favoured-nation clause in
international commercial treaties, there was not necessarily an
impasse. The 1938 agreement allowed import restrictions in wartime:
as it would be unreasonable for those to be withdrawn immediately
war ended, there was arguably no threat, in their continuance
during the transition, to the validity of the agreement, although that
might be fortified by specially negotiated arrangements. Thus,
argued London, the trade negotiations could be continued: the
United States might, however, prefer to lift the particular problem
of post-war import policy out of the trade talks for further
discussions.[20]

These developments had jumped the American gun on post-war
policy. Indeed, President Roosevelt had given Keynes in late May
1941 the impression of reluctance to discuss post-war plans, especially
if they came from Britain and anticipated possible American
proposals.[21] In fact, during May the President had given instructions to the State Department, transferring to it a task originally
assigned to the US Treasury (below p 29), to prepare a draft
Anglo-American agreement about Lend-Lease;[22] this was being
completed when the 'situation of some delicacy' arose. The State
Department could therefore be more accommodating than Mr
Hawkins's original shocked reaction suggested. It doubted London's interpretation of the 1938 agreement, and Mr Hawkins
warned that the possibility of British bilateralism would 'sour' every
friend of Britain in the State Department. Moreover, American
traders would resent paying taxes to provide Lend-Lease for
countries which discriminated against their exports. Hawkins urged
the desirability of grasping the present opportunity for agreement;
he stressed the need for Britain to demonstrate the absence of purely
selfish motives in the choice of policies; and he resisted the British
inclination to leave crucial issues 'to solve themselves after the war'.
He nevertheless suggested, doubtless more aware than his British
counterpart of imminent American action to that end, that general
principles might be settled outside the trade discussions. In short,
the State Department virtually echoed the British Ministers' view

---

* HOPKINS, Richard Valentine Nind, KCB 1920 (1880–1955); Second Secretary,
HM Treasury 1932–42; Permanent Secretary, HM Treasury, 1942–45.

about separating the two issues, the specific and the general, and Mr Hawkins envisaged further trade discussions for August.[23]

During August and September 1941 missions from New Zealand, Australia, and South Africa arrived in or were on the way to Washington to open bilateral trade discussions with the United States Administration, which also had talks with representatives of the Indian Government.[24] The British discussions, however, were suddenly torpedoed early in September. Claiming that the Export White Paper was overwhelming it with fresh work, the Board of Trade recalled its chief negotiator (who had been 11 months in Washington) to help. No doubt, too, the White Paper had also appeared to diminish the immediate relevance of the trade talks. This latest upheaval produced consternation in the Treasury and in the Bank; whatever their earlier disgruntlement, they appreciated the value of having an expert observer in Washington to persuade the Dominions' representatives to weigh the possible effect on post-war sterling trade, and on the system of Imperial Preference as a whole, of any new trading arrangements they might contemplate.[25] By now, however, intense domestic and transatlantic debates about 'the Consideration' for Lend-Lease were overshadowing the relatively subordinate matter of a trading agreement, the talks about which faded away, as did those between the Dominions and the USA, to be suspended in summer 1943.[26] The subsequent, intermittent, discussions of commercial policy during the rest of the war were to continue on the more general level. The principal and embarrassing achievement of Britain's trade mission in 1940–41 was to bring out very clearly, before Lend-Lease did so even more sharply, the American divergence from leading elements in British thinking about post-war economic policy.

CHAPTER 2, SOURCE REFERENCES

1. R S Sayers, *The Bank of England* 1891 – 1944 (3 vols, Cambridge 1976), II, pp 475 – 81 and III, pp 280 – 1.

2. Proposals to counter the German 'New Order', 1 December 1940, T 247/85; *JMK* XXV, pp 7 – 10.

3. See below, p 70.

4. T 247/85.

5. Ibid, tels 2377 of 26 May 1941 and 2405 of 28 May, British Ambassador in Washington (Lord Halifax) to Mr Eden; Eden to Halifax, tel 2923 of 30 May; Keynes to Mr Nigel Ronald of Foreign Office, 2 June.

6. Mr Eden to Prime Minister, 30 January 1941, and Prime Minister to Mr Eden 24 May, PREM 4/100/5.

7. Sayers, *Financial Policy,* pp 366 – 7.

8. E L Hargreaves & M M Gowing, History of the Second World War. *Civil Industry and Trade* (London 1952), p 51.

9. Mr J A Stirling from Washington to Mr R J Shackle, Board of Trade, tel 168 SHACK 11 January 1941, and Sir Ronald Campbell from Washington to Mr Eden, Foreign Secretary, No 421 (4/81), 24 April 1941, T 160/1200.

10. Mr D'Arcy Cooper from Washington to Shackle, Board of Trade, tel 641(R), 12 December 1940, ibid.

11. The visit was originally expected in November 1940 and that date is given on the relevant file, and in Sayers, *Financial Policy,* pp 369,567. In fact it took place in early December 1940: see eg, tel 2900,3 Dec 1940, Marquess of Lothian from Washington to London, T 160/1051.

12. Warren F Kimball, *The Most Unsordid Act* (Baltimore 1969), pp 133 – 7 *passim.*

13. Mr S D Waley of the Treasury to Lord Catto and Sir Richard Hopkins, 27 December 1940, and also Hopkins to Sir Horace Wilson, 2 July 1941; Sir Arnold Overton of the Board of Trade to Mr S D Waley, 20 January 1941: T 160/1200.

14. J J Wills of Board of Trade to Waley, 30 April 1941, ibid.

15. Board of Trade to Stirling in Washington, tel 2222, 25 April 1941, and Sir Frederick Phillips from Washington to Treasury, tel 2334, 24 May 1941, ibid.

16. J A Stirling from Washington to Board of Trade, tels 3101 and 3102 of 4 July 1941, ibid; Phillips to Treasury, tel 2334, 24 May, CAB 117/52; R F Harrod. *The Life of John Maynard Keynes* (London 1952), p 513.

17. Memo by Sir Arnold Overton, 28 June 1941, reporting telephone call from Washington by Stirling, T 160/1200.

18. Stirling from Washington to Board of Trade, tel 3101, 4 July 1941, ibid.

19. Stirling to Board of Trade, tel 3102, 4 July 1941, ibid, and handwritten note by Hopkins, 12 July 1941, with initials K W (Kingsley Wood), 13 July 1941, ibid.

20. Tel 4074, London to Washington, 16 July 1941, ibid.

21. Keynes from Washington to Treasury, tel 2439, 29 May 1941, CAB 117/52, also in T 160/1105.

22. Warren F Kimball, 'Lend-Lease and the Open Door: The Temptation of British Opulence, 1937 – 1942', *Political Science Quarterly* LXXXVI (1971), pp 243 – 9; Dean Acheson, *Present at the Creation* (London 1970), p 28.

23. Stirling's report of 23 July on his talk with Mr H Hawkins, ibid.

24. Tel 2064, Washington to London, 9 May 1941 (New Zealand); tel 3865, Washington to London, 24 August 1941 (Australia); tel 1087, United Kingdom High Com-

missioner in S. Africa to Dominions Office, 12 September 1941, ibid.

25. E W Playfair to Waley, 13 September 1941; Hopkins to Playfair, 15 September 1941; Mr C F Cobbold of Bank of England to Waley, 16 September 1941, ibid.

26. *FRUS* 1943 III (Washington 1963), pp 107–10.

CHAPTER 3

The Price of Lend-Lease: 'The Consideration'

(1) THE CONCEPT OF A 'CONSIDERATION'

Scarcely less surely than the search for dollars by exporting, the search for direct financial aid from the USA led to discussions of post-war commercial policy. This followed the Lend-Lease Act of March 1941, by which, in the interests of its own defence, the United States would provide extensive aid to foreign governments. All concerned were aware of 'the terms and conditions' of such aid which, said the American statute,[1] included the rendering to the United States of some 'direct or indirect benefit which the President deems satisfactory'. For almost a year the two governments were to argue about the nature of such 'benefit' or, as it soon became known, 'the Consideration'. There was to be no war debt such as had clouded relations after the 1914–18 war, but if Britain could not repay in cash the American Congress, the American public, and hence the law itself expected something else in return.

Three main sets of influences during 1941 and early 1942 delayed a decision about 'the Consideration'. These were, first, the evolution of American thinking. In particular, the President delayed making up or disclosing his mind on the matter as long as possible. Eventually, early ideas about the replacement of Lend-Lease resources not destroyed in war were to be dropped in favour of a policy that cancelled any physical restitution, and which sought instead a broad commitment to 'liberal' trading practices after the war.[2] Second, the British Government, concerned not to dilute but rather to strengthen the great degree of influence over economic affairs that had been developed during the 1930s, was wary of such an undertaking. Third, there was persisting uncertainty whether there would be extra financial aid to meet continuing expenditures initiated in the USA before the passage of Lend-Lease. These were 'the old Commitments'. To finance them Britain had been disposing of her slender dollar resources, and feared that it would be necessary to make further disposals of the remainder, possibly at a loss. Help to meet 'the old Commitments' would have permitted at least the partial reconstitution of Britain's depleted overseas assets.[3] The fear that the absence of such aid would gravely weaken the basis of a relatively independent economic policy stiffened British unwillingness to accept an obligation virtually to abjure economic controls after the war.[4]

American thoughts about the Consideration had at first flowed principally from the US Treasury, which President Roosevelt had instructed, immediately after the enactment of Lend-Lease, to formulate proposals about an eventual settlement.[5] Repayment in kind was contemplated initially, but within two months this accounting approach was overshadowed increasingly by proposals to reject physical compensation; seeing the issue as political rather than financial, the President shifted responsibility to the State Department (above p 24) where Mr Cordell Hull, Secretary of State, was seeking like a missionary to reduce the intricate and damaging restrictions that had come to hamper world trade during the inter-war years. A particular target was British Imperial Preference which favoured, for instance, British imports of agricultural products from Canada over those from the USA, and which similarly discriminated in favour of British over American exports to imperial territories. Lend-Lease or, more specifically, the terms of its eventual settlement, could be the means of exacting an undertaking from Britain to end such discrimination.

British thinking, not surprisingly in view of the financial impoverishment already suffered, also turned towards a settlement that eliminated, and not just suspended, the dollar sign. Mr Churchill mused widely and profoundly on these issues early in April 1941 in a despatch to Lord Halifax,* British Ambassador in Washington.[6] He noted that both countries had slipped, without thinking about the implications, into an unprecedented relationship which was more complex than a simple division of effort between those doing the fighting (the British Empire and its allies) and their paymaster (the USA). Quoting a letter that Mr J M Keynes had written a month earlier, Mr Churchill noted that American pressure had led Britain to use her own resources even beyond the point of safety in relation to her continuing obligations as an international financial centre; it would be necessary to limit the use of Lend-Lease to 'clearly defensible transactions' and to work for fuller American understanding of British policy. As for the specific question of the compensating benefit to the USA, Mr Churchill feared that this would involve political conditions when it was realised that Britain could not repay Lend-Lease physically. His thoughts therefore turned to the probable involvement of the USA, not yet a belligerent, in the eventual peace settlement; it was time, he felt, to begin thinking about peace aims. This would probably involve differences of view about the future organisation of international trade. At this stage, broad proposals for international co-operation to create a world with more secure trade and payments had not yet been officially formulated, and it was in the more restricted mould of the inter-war

---

* HALIFAX, Edward Frederick Lindley Wood, 1st Earl 1944 (1881–1959); Secretary of State for Foreign Affairs, 1938–40; British Ambassador at Washington, 1941–46.

years that Mr Churchill seemed to envisage the problems. There was a contrast between American abundance of gold and British poverty in gold. Mr Keynes's 'bilateral barter' schemes (see pp 18–19 and p 71) might therefore be necessary; proposals to the United States would endeavour to gain American understanding of British scepticism about arrangements of the gold standard variety and of our need to contemplate policies such as bilateralism. That such thoughts were the antithesis of America's goals, as proclaimed by Mr Cordell Hull, the Secretary of State, was to become particularly clear in the Board of Trade's negotiations (see chapter 2). Around the time of Mr Churchill's despatch there were in fact important stirrings of American intentions on post-war policy, as when Mr Hull told Lord Halifax on 4 April 1941 that he favoured 'early attempts' to discuss 'large issues'. The Ambassador took this to mean informal discussions on trade policy. Two days later the President stressed his own concern to 'try to get clear on some fundamentals of future policy...'. In mid-May he gave public clarification of this concern, declaring that totalitarianism must be banished alike from politics and from international trade; next day (18 May 1941) Mr Hull re-iterated this theme, emphasising American opposition to discriminatory trade practices.[7]

Some two further months were to elapse before the formal embodiment of this American trade policy in a non-monetary 'Consideration'. Mr Keynes's mission to Washington from May to July 1941, principally to deal with the finance of 'the old commitments', not only coincided with that development but also appeared to have accelerated it; it is clear, however, that the State Department had already shaped its broad intentions. A controversial figure in the USA perhaps even more than at home, Mr Keynes had arrived under suspicion of intending to modify the terms recently agreed for the disposal of the American Viscose subsidiary of the British rayon manufacturers, Courtaulds. This disposal of a direct investment in the USA had been required from Britain as a demonstration, ahead of Congressional debate on the Appropriations Bill necessary to provide finance for Lend-Lease, of her readiness to sacrifice overseas assets before resort to Lend-Lease.[8] The suspicion about Keynes's visit was entirely justified. Further, Mr Morgenthau, Secretary of the US Treasury, queried Mr Keynes's status since he bore no letter of accreditation from the Chancellor of the Exchequer (Sir Kingsley Wood*).[9] Worse, Morgenthau suspected, not entirely wrongly, that Keynes had been encouraged by the American Embassy in London to talk in Washington in a manner likely to strengthen at his expense other factions in the US Administration.[10] Not surprisingly Keynes wrote of his first meeting with Morgenthau that he had 'seldom struck any-

* WOOD, Kingsley, Kt 1918; PC 1928 (1881–1943); Secretary of State for Air, 1938–40; Lord Privy Seal, 1940; Chancellor of the Exchequer 1940–43.

thing stickier'.[11] Entangled thus at the outset in rivalries and suspicions, which he laughed off as 'comic',[12] Keynes was soon to compound the clash of so many sentiments. Perhaps deliberately, certainly characteristically, he talked forthrightly to clarify Britain's need to contemplate continued trade and exchange controls after the war; this culminated in late June in his 'Schachtian' intervention (above, pp 22–23).

Before trade policy emerged as its focus, discussion of the Consideration appeared to be largely exploratory during May, June and much of July 1941. Even when American leanings towards a 'trade-policy Consideration' became evident early in Keynes's mission, initially they disturbed neither him nor the British Government. This was in late May when Keynes believed that the State Department would try to frame its proposals to accommodate Britain's probable dependence on trade and exchange controls after the war. In association with the Secretary of State's goal (and that of Britain) of reduced American tariffs, modification or abandonment of the Ottawa agreements of 1932 for Imperial Preference might lie ahead, but London at first seemed likely to agree with Keynes that that prospect was not novel and did not justify bothering the Dominion Governments.[13] Within a month, however, London was less sanguine. Although the Dominions Office seemed unworried, the Colonial Office was sceptical of the Americans' willingness to cut their own preferential arrangements, the India Office was uneasy about any diminution of Imperial Preference, and the Foreign Office advised stalling on any suggestion for commitment about post-war policy. Taking the lead in the inter-departmental discussions, the Chancellor stressed the uncertainty about the nature of the post-war economic position and his apprehension about undertaking obligations which could not be honoured; on Ottawa, this was no time to provoke controversial discussion within the Empire, which should concentrate upon winning the war.[14]

This firm stonewalling reflected British optimism that either there would be no Consideration at all or that it might be largely and acceptably non-economic. An early proposal from Mr Harry Hopkins, the President's principal aide, was that Lend-Lease supplies should be divided into warlike items and non-warlike items, with 'consideration' being applied only or mainly to the latter. This invited the reflection that it was scarcely possible thus to distinguish the civilian from the military effort of war, and that perhaps little or no consideration was therefore appropriate.[15] The Prime Minister and the Chancellor of the Exchequer, seeking in a desperate situation the best of both worlds, disliked the distinction for other reasons. If there were to be a non-economic consideration, it should apply to both kinds of aid. If, however, there were to be *some* economic consideration in the form of reverse Lend-Lease from Britain, they wanted that to apply only to the provision of warlike goods; in return for *non*-warlike goods, Britain wanted to receive dollars to restore her international reserves.[16] In the event the President stopped short of the conclusions to which the awkward distinction had pointed, and political prudence led him also to rule out explicit reference to reverse Lend-Lease, with its suggestion that open American involvement in the war was contemplated.[17] Alternative American proposals, such as the cession of islands, the provision of military bases additional to those provided in 1940 by the destroyers-for-bases deal, and the post-war supply of tin and rubber on favourable terms, had earlier offered the tempting prospect of reducing the balance of obligations to a level which could be met by 'politico-economic' declarations of common purpose.[18] A solution so deceptively simple, potentially so non-committal was, however, to elude the British representatives in Washington. The American President who, Keynes reported in June, regarded the Consideration as 'very much his own' subject,[19] was apparently far from unsympathetic, but during much of 1941 he chose to play for time to devise, and to ensure that Congress was ready to accept, a non-cash arrangement.

The British Government, which had particularly disliked suggestions about the post-war supply to the USA of Empire commodities, pointing out that the Empire and its products were not at the free disposal of Britain, welcomed the American delay in view of the reports from Keynes and Sir Frederick Phillips (principal representative in Washington of the British Treasury). These stressed the hostility of the State Department to Britain's use of bilateralism and of trade discrimination after the war. The two Treasury representatives recommended an attempt to educate Americans about realities, or simply about the policies Britain must follow; the US Administration might be invited to send some expert to verify the facts of British economic problems. London supported the broad assessment (though not the suggestion of an American inspection of the British economy), conscious in mid-1941 of the brittleness of Anglo-American trade discussions. The eventual message to Washington in mid-July was that 'hurried conclusions' on wide issues were inadvisable.[20]

The preliminary phase of exchanges about the Consideration, of sparring about whether there should be one, was by now (July 1941) giving place to a more prolonged phase. This had two aspects: the practical arrangements for Anglo-American discussions on the subject, and the nature of the Consideration itself. In a manner that was to become wearyingly familiar, these two aspects tended to fall out of perspective; there tended to be a blurring of the distinction between the nature of possible discussions about large issues, and preliminary discussions about what those 'large issues', namely the content of the Consideration, should be. This distinction was important because of

American determination from July 1941 to secure first a commitment about trade policy and only then to have discussions, whereas Britain, although enthusiastic about neither, preferred a reverse order of events. Hence an *impasse* threatened to be the road for the Consideration.

(2) EVOLUTION OF THE CONSIDERATION; THE ATLANTIC CHARTER

Soon after reporting in April 1941 Mr Hull's keenness for discussions, Lord Halifax had also reported the President's concern and his characteristic proposal for 'three wise men' from each side to come together 'to sit down and thrash out the main lines of the subject' of Anglo-American policy in the post-war world. The Minister without Portfolio (Mr A Greenwood)* had had oversight of reconstruction problems since August 1940 (see below p 67); in May 1941, when Lord Halifax sent him a copy of his telegram about the President's proposal, he responded enthusiastically to the invitation to consider how best to reply, and for some months was to maintain pressure for discussions to take place.[21] The British Government as a whole was more cautious about the American suggestion. The Chancellor of the Exchequer, notably apprehensive about post-war policy discussions and post-war commitments, pointed out that we had three perfectly good representatives in Washington already.[22] There were other stronger objections to significant Anglo-American discussions at that stage, whether to the proposal to select three wise men, or to the alternative suggestion, inspired by the American-Canadian Commission established in June 1941, for an Anglo-American Commission, which Keynes and others advocated. [23] Undoubtedly senior Ministers were reluctant to consider, let alone to make, commitments about post-war policy. When in June 1941 Mr Greenwood sought the Chancellor's support for discussions, he reported that[24]

'K[ingsley] W[ood] said in a sentence that he had been approached from US about an economic conference and he had said "nothing doing until after the war" '.

The Chancellor was supported in this by the Minister of Production (Mr O Lyttelton),† while the Secretary of State for India (Mr L S

---

* GREENWOOD, Arthur (1880–1954); Member of the War Cabinet, and Minister without Portfolio, 1940–42; Lord Privy Seal, 1945–47; Paymaster-General, 1946–47.
† LYTTELTON, Oliver, 1st Viscount Chandos 1954 (1893–1972); Controller of Non-Ferrous Metals, 1939–40; President of Board of Trade, 1940–41; Minister of State and Member of the War Cabinet, 1941–42; Minister of Production and Member of the War Cabinet, 1942–45; President of Board of Trade and Minister of Production, 1945; Secretary of State for the Colonies, 1951–54.

Amery)* was to prove unremittingly hostile to American ideas on post-war trade.[25] The Prime Minister's view and that of the Chancellor was that an Anglo-American Commission sounded interesting, but that the time (June 1941) was not yet right. To appoint such a Commission 'would mean bringing in the Dominions and the Allies'. They preferred a 'widely drawn' statement in 'the most general terms', and professed satisfaction with Anglo-American co-operation through the informal discussions which Keynes had had in London with American officials, and was then having in Washington; there could be more formal discussions on 'specific practical questions' and they hoped for 'concrete progress from limited discussions on trade matters which are at present taking place or are under contemplation'.[26] Influencing these attitudes was the realisation that time was needed to evolve a British policy, which was to prove no easy task in a coalition Cabinet. Further, the pressures of war in 1941 were such as to discourage Ministers' dreams about peace. Perhaps, too, wider discussions were inappropriate until the nature of the Consideration had been settled. By no means least, the Prime Minister himself was temperamentally lukewarm towards detailed post-war economic plans, partly because he preferred to concentrate on first winning the war,[27] but above all because he looked to the development of broad Anglo-American understanding as the best solution for the economic problems resulting from the war.

The requirement of a 'benefit' to the USA had nevertheless to be translated into an Anglo-American agreement. The President's obligation to make his first regular report on Lend-Lease to Congress in June 1941 imposed upon him the need to display publicly, in contrast to his private inclinations, a sense of urgency. At his request, Keynes accordingly acted out the formality of opening discussions, thereby enabling the President to reassure Congress that work had begun on an agreement.[28] In fact, said Lord Halifax, Mr Roosevelt was as yet uncertain of what he wanted, and, sensing no strong Congressional pressure for early publication of an agreement, felt that matters might be allowed to evolve until he reported to Congress at the beginning of 1942.[29] Mr Roosevelt was striving to devise a politically acceptable form for a sweeping concept of 'many "considerations"', but he found himself disliking 'the kind of "consideration" that could be talked about' and unable 'to talk about the kind he did like'—the former being presumably the simple principle of non-payment in cash or goods for Lend-Lease (and therefore being effectively no 'Consideration' at all), and the latter being international proposals that were 'political dynamite'. The President therefore instructed Mr

---

* AMERY, Leopold Stennett (1873–1955); Secretary of State for India and for Burma, 1940–45.

Acheson,* the Assistant Secretary of State, to formulate a suitable draft.[30]

Thus, in mid-1941 there was only superficially a marking time in Washington on the Consideration; in London, however, some feared, with reason, that the British Government was prevaricating. The immediate difficulty was to devise the Consideration in a form to balance American intentions and British apprehensions about post-war trading arrangements. There lay immediately ahead significant Anglo-American exchanges; an intensive debate in the British Cabinet; and a comprehensive formulation by British officials of proposals for post-war economic arrangements (see chapter 4). Thus, the summer of 1941 saw the real, if confused, beginnings of Anglo-American discussion on the post-war economy. The difficulties in reaching agreement emerged sharply in three Anglo-American encounters: two in July between Mr Keynes and Mr Acheson, and a third in August between the President and Mr Churchill at their Atlantic Conference.

The first encounter was in mid-July. Previously, under strict instructions[31] from London to be 'very discreet' and to 'avoid making far-reaching suggestions, however tentatively', Keynes had joined the Ambassador in meeting the President, who seemed unhurried about the Consideration.[32] He rejected a cash arrangement; did not want for the USA territory, such as islands (this would have clashed with an understanding at the Havana Inter-American Conference of mid-1940); and oracularly rejected reverse Lend-Lease 'for some future occasion'. The President favoured a preliminary unpublished agreement or an *aide-mémoire* about the Consideration. To Keynes's amusement, the President asked him to report his views to Mr Acheson who, whether truly sharing the amusement or not,[33] decided that Keynes 'was a bad emissary' and that he had been 'putting his own conclusions into the mouth of the President'.[34] The Prime Minister and the Chancellor had approved Keynes's report of the discussions with the President, but for his meeting with Mr Acheson they had instructed him to omit from the three pages of draft proposals he had formulated about the Consideration just over two pages, which referred to a wide range of post-war matters: the provision of military bases and of other defence aid to the USA; relief and reconstruction; trade and economic policy; an Anglo-American Commission to prepare plans for economic reconstruction.[35] The surviving items proposed the return, if asked, of Lend-Lease goods not destroyed or consumed during the war and the provision of reverse Lend-Lease by Britain if desired by the USA. Apart from a proposal for a declaration of

* ACHESON, Dean (1893–1971); US Assistant Secretary of State 1941–45; Under-Secretary of State 1945–47; Secretary of State 1949–53.

common purpose, brief references to wider matters were general and restrained. Thus, we should welcome discussions in due course; where Lend-Lease aid did not produce the benefits for the USA intended by the Act, there should be no cash account set up, and any request for goods and services in compensation should not involve interference with 'the normal economic relations' between the USA and the Commonwealth, nor affect the Commonwealth's ability to trade with the USA.

Mr Acheson found Keynes's attenuated draft 'wholly impossible' for it excused Britain 'from any liability to deliver goods or assets whilst we [Britain] on our side entered into no undertaking of any sort or description'. Keynes, who had earlier admitted to London that Britain's proposed 'Consideration' did not look very plausible, could not controvert Acheson, although he asserted that the vagueness and absence of detail reflected the views of the President and the Prime Minister. It would be necessary, Keynes now told London, to 'do at least something to meet them [the Americans] in other directions' if we hoped to exclude the delivery by Britain of goods and assets from the definitive agreement.[36]

What that 'something' would be emerged clearly at the second encounter about a fortnight later, when on 28 July 1941 Mr Acheson presented Keynes with the State Department's draft.[37] This was fortified with the approval of the President, who had reportedly been indignant about the British draft, particularly its reluctant approach to discussions on co-operation.[38] It was much stronger meat than Keynes had thought he had sniffed with the President earlier in the month, and he speculated[39] that the State Department had

'taken the opportunity to introduce their pet idea [Mr Cordell Hull's faith in multilateral free trade] in language which they meant to be technical; whereas the President himself had nothing so definite in view and meant only to require that we should agree to co-operate and to do so in a certain spirit and with a certain good purpose'.

Whether or not this was too sanguine an assessment of the President's views, or of the ability of the State Department to influence them, to Mr Acheson the American draft was 'simple and amazingly liberal'. And so it was in its affirmation that Lend-Lease should not involve war debts, but there was a stout thorn with that rose. This was Article VII of the proposed agreement, which would commit Britain and the USA to co-operate in a post-war commercial policy directed towards the reduction of trade restrictions (see Appendix 1). This would involve ending all forms of trade discrimination which, Mr Acheson admitted in evident understatement, would probably preclude Imperial Preference, import controls, and exchange controls. Keynes thereupon 'burst into a speech such as only he could make' against the outmoded nineteenth century inspiration and gold standard implications of a commitment which Britain could scarcely shoulder 'in good faith'. Acheson explained that the inspiration of the proposed renunciation of discrimination was essentially positive; although Britain would surrender her liberty to discriminate against the USA, the two countries would agree to co-operate to eliminate discriminatory practices throughout world trade. When Keynes had 'cooled off' he recognised agreement on 'broad policies' and wrote to Acheson next day, on his way back to England,[40] that he would endeavour to interpret to the British Government the President's views: and did so, while he himself was rapidly re-assessing his own views on post-war economic policy. Within a further two weeks, the President was able to make his own explanation to Mr Churchill in the third of the three encounters of mid-1941, at the 'Atlantic Conference' on their respective warships in Placentia Bay, Newfoundland: *USS Augusta* and *HMS Prince of Wales*.

This meeting, code-named RIVIERA, implemented Ministers' desire to announce war aims and to extend a series of inter-Allied meetings (although the USA was not yet a belligerent and therefore not yet formally an ally). It produced the joint declaration known as 'The Atlantic Charter'.[41] After President Roosevelt had proposed that such a declaration be made, the efforts to devise it were to reflect both the acute Anglo-American differences that had recently emerged between Keynes and Acheson, and the anxieties within the War Cabinet over post-war trade policy.

An initial draft was presented by Mr Churchill.[42] The economic issues were the subject of its fourth 'Point' which spoke in very general terms of striving to secure 'a fair and equitable distribution' of resources between all nations (see Appendix 3). This Point met neither American concern to outlaw trade discrimination nor that of the British to retain scope to resort to it, especially through Imperial Preference and exchange control. On the American side the President shared Mr Churchill's wish to have statements of broad principle rather than the formal precision of a version, embodying State Department views, being pressed by Mr Sumner T Welles,* Under-Secretary of State (Appendix 4). He nevertheless sought to accomplish Welles's purpose in rewording Mr Churchill's draft, by embodying the essence of the proposed Article VII which had so appalled Keynes: the goal of access for all to the world's economic

* WELLES, Sumner T. (1892–1961); Under-Secretary of State of USA, 1937–43; special representative of President to report on conditions in Europe, 1940; accompanied President Roosevelt at meeting at sea with Mr Churchill, August 1941.

resources should be explicitly qualified as being 'access without discrimination and on equal terms' (Appendix 5).

Mr Churchill's reaction was that this qualification would compromise the post-war operation of Imperial Preference. He stressed that it would be necessary to consult the Dominion and Indian Governments as well as the home Government, and that none of them was likely to approve the Presidential revision. After a vigorous contrast of America's history of protectionist policies with Britain's Free Trade era, Mr Churchill proposed amendments to the US draft[43] (Appendix 6). In particular, these omitted the reference to discrimination, and inserted a qualification that access to markets and raw materials would have 'due respect to their [ie Britain's and the USA's] existing obligations.' Thereby Imperial Preference should be shielded.

The Prime Minister urgently sought the views of the War Cabinet in London. In his absence, this was presided over by the Lord Privy Seal, Mr C R Attlee,* to whom he telegraphed that 'the full War Cabinet, with any others you may think necessary' should meet immediately, and that Mr Attlee should report back at once. The War Cabinet reacted with a mixture of apprehension and acquiescence, and under great pressure of time, to the messages from the Atlantic. Most members of the War Cabinet, and others including Mr Peter Fraser, Prime Minister of New Zealand, met in the small hours. Soon afterwards, two proposals were despatched to the Prime Minister aboard *HMS Prince of Wales*.[44] The first constituted the Cabinet meeting's own version of the troublesome fourth Point. It resembled President Roosevelt's revision, *in*cluding the contested words 'without discrimination', but spoke of extending 'access' only to raw materials, and *not*, unlike that and Mr Churchill's amendment, to 'markets' (or 'trade'). It added, however, the aim of promoting 'the greatest possible expansion' of international trade (Appendix 7(a)). Second, the Cabinet proposed the addition of a paragraph supporting international co-operation to improve living and working conditions (Appendix 7(b)). Scarcely, however, had these suggestions reached *HMS Prince of Wales* than a further, brief, telegram from the Prime Minister was on its way. Mr Churchill's message, which somewhat cut across the results of the Cabinet's deliberations, reported that—much to Mr Welles's regret[45]—the President had accepted his amendments.[46]

Concerned to register its views as fully as possible, the War Cabinet quickly met again within a few hours. There was now an opportunity to have the opinions of the Chancellor of the Exchequer

* ATTLEE, Clement Richard, 1st Earl 1955 (1883–1967); Lord Privy Seal 1940–42; Secretary of State for Dominion Affairs 1942–43; Lord President of the Council, 1943–45; Deputy Prime Minister, 1942–45; Prime Minister and First Lord of the Treasury, 1945–51; Minister of Defence, 1945–46.

and of the President of the Board of Trade, who had not been present at the earlier meeting, and to consider the position in the light of the version of the fourth Point that had been agreed between the President and the Prime Minister. The Chancellor offered his own draft of the disputed Point (Appendix 8). It sought to hedge more fully the declaration of Anglo-American good intentions about future international economic relations, specifically by the qualification that those intentions would be 'within the limits of their governing economic conditions'. After the Chancellor had explained the concern among Ministers that the scope to operate Imperial Preference should not be compromised, the Foreign Secretary, Mr Anthony Eden, expressed a complementary apprehension that 'the greatest danger of all was the American desire to stop this country maintaining exchange control after the end of the war'.[47]

Telegraphing again immediately to the Prime Minister, the Cabinet did *not* send the Chancellor's draft but, pressing its own, explained Ministers' anxieties: to retain Imperial Preference and the ability to resist low-wage competition from, eg, Japan. To secure these, the Cabinet wanted to elaborate its draft with a qualification to the proposed further aim of promoting trade expansion: Britain and the USA would seek this 'with due respect to their existing obligations'.[48] These were in fact precisely the qualifying words included in Mr Churchill's amendments, though with reference to the more vaguely expressed aims of providing general access to markets and raw materials.

Notwithstanding its unease, the Cabinet declared its willingness to accept the Prime Minister's amended version of the fourth Point (Appendix 6) if its own proposals were likely to create 'great difficulty'. In the event, the constraints of pressure of time and the difficulty of conducting simultaneously discussions in the Atlantic and between the Atlantic and London, were again apparent. When informed of the Cabinet's *first* representation, the President preferred to keep to the newly agreed amended version, between which and the Cabinet's draft Mr Churchill professed to see no real difference. The President accepted, with some verbal changes, the Cabinet's proposed additional paragraph on living standards, etc.[49] By the time the Cabinet's *second* representation had arrived, the declaration as a whole had already been agreed and farewells had been made, Mr Churchill was to report; it seemed to him 'impossible to reopen the discussion'. In fact, the War Cabinet appeared satisfied with the outcome. Mr Attlee telegraphed his congratulations to the Prime Minister on the 'final draft which you have much improved. It covers now the points we considered important'.[50]

A comparison with the other drafts of the fourth Point shows that in the final version Mr Churchill had secured a greater degree of generality and a smaller degree of commitment. There was cautious relief in London at what was recognised to be a respite, and a sense of frustration in Washington.[51] The most passionate defender of Imperial Preference, Mr L S Amery, whilst rejoicing at 'the comparatively innocuous character' of the two economic Points (Appendices 9(a) and 9(b)), which he regarded as 'woolly verbiage', warned against signing any Lend-Lease agreement that would exploit a renunciation of discrimination in order to prohibit preferential arrangements.[52] For Washington the setback proved to be but momentary. Aboard ship the President had started with the British draft, lest an American draft be seen as a direct attack on the Empire,[53] but in the final version he had failed to secure the crucial explicit commitment to non-discrimination.

The reaction of the Secretary of State was 'profanely unfavourable',[54] and within days of the President's return from the Atlantic Mr Hull had extracted his authority to try to secure British agreement to publish a clarification of Point Four: that the fluffy Atlantic wording embodied a British undertaking to reduce trade barriers and to eliminate preferences and discrimination after the war.[55] Mr Churchill demurred, and was supported by a warning to Washington at the beginning of September from Mr J G Winant,* the American Ambassador in London, against pressing the point. If it came to a parliamentary debate, said Mr Winant, there could be disagreeable comment upon pressure from the USA, which was not at war, being exercised for concessions from Britain, which was.[56] Mr Hull now dropped this approach, only to shift by the end of September to a more deliberate and determined effort (below p 44) to gain British acceptance of Article VII: 'the only article in the draft... handed to Keynes at the end of July which gave rise to serious difficulty...' the Chancellor wrote to the Prime Minister in September 1941[57]. By this time British officials' discussions on post-war policy, partly in anticipation of the expected requirements for the Consideration, were beginning but were some months away from a full set of recommendations; their aversion, on balance, to more than a very general willingness to consider the eventual abatement of discrimination in trade was, however, already clear. This owed something to the disappointment, in the prolonged Lend-Lease debates between Congress and the Administration, of expectations that several hundred million dollars would be provided to recompense Britain for 'the old commitments'.[58] The resultant probability that, unless some means could be found to fulfil those hopes, there would be a significantly weaker balance of payments after the war, stiffened Whitehall's caution.

---

* WINANT, John Gilbert (1889–1947); Ambassador of the United States to Court of St. James, 1941–46; American Representative on European Advisory Commission, 1943–47.

(3) ANGLO-AMERICAN DEBATE

The eventual British decision about the Consideration emerged from a threefold shading of views that was to persist beyond the war into the negotiations of September-December 1945. First there was the main body of Ministers: largely pre-occupied by the immediate burden of war; oppressed, when they could turn to them, by the prospectively intractable problems of the post-war economy; sensitive not just to their own convictions but also to the genuine divisions, and the difficulties of bridging them, within their own parties, within the Coalition Government, and within the country. Second, there was the Ministry charged with reconstruction problems (under Mr Arthur Greenwood, Minister without Portfolio), anxious to look ahead, to see some action or at least to hear some talking about post-war plans. Third, there were those with recent or continuing contacts with the United States, notably Mr Keynes and Lord Halifax, Ambassador in Washington; measuring more closely the Anglo-American relationship, they recognised the probably irresistible strength of American pressure, and gradually edged themselves and then the British Cabinet away from a wholesale rejection of Article VII, although it was to take determined American pressure to persuade the Cabinet to accept it. Within this group the Foreign Office and Lord Halifax gave the impression of greater readiness to advocate the Americans' proposals; while the Treasury, led by the Chancellor, Keynes, and Sir Richard Hopkins, were reluctant to do so unless they were significantly qualified. Mr Churchill straddled the first and third groups; seeking to head and to lead a perplexed Cabinet, he exploited his personal relationship with the American President in masterly efforts to avoid any commitment and, when commitment seemed unavoidable, to secure reassurance about its implications.

London's resistance, predominantly from the Treasury, reflected pre-occupation with the prospective weakness of the post-war balance of payments. There was fear that an American policy of multilateral free trade not coupled with policies of high employment would expose Britain to a repetition of the 1930s. Such apprehensions largely inspired anxiety to retain scope to exercise discriminatory controls in overseas trade during the post-war years. More narrowly, London sought to protect Imperial Preference. In the extreme form propounded by Mr Amery, the case for that viewed international trade, and the use of the most-favoured-nation clause to encourage trade, as inherently undesirable; intra-imperial trade was an entirely different activity of kith and kin, Imperial Preference being regarded not as discrimination against outsiders but rather as a sensible means of running an essentially private, British, exchange of goods. So hostile was Amery to America's declared trading objectives that he grasped support for Imperial Preference from analogy with a Russian reference to their own 'historical peculiarities'. He asserted, extravagantly but not entirely ludicrously in view of the reports from Switzerland that had induced Keynes's paper on the subject a few months previously, that the peoples of Europe would prefer the Nazi 'New Order' to the American proposals.[59] If other Ministers were less emotional they were generally unwilling to renounce discrimination in trade; refused overtly to appear to barter, by Article VII, Imperial Preference against Lend-Lease; were reluctant to do more than discuss with the US the possibility of shading down discriminatory policies; and felt considerable unease at being pressed for any commitment at all on post-war commercial policy. Moreover, at the same time (August 1941) as discussion on the Consideration was developing America was insisting, in the Washington negotiations for a renewed international wheat agreement, on precisely a type of discrimination that Britain was being pressed to renounce. 'A fantastic piece of chicanery' the outraged Keynes described the wheat scheme.[60]

As delay over Article VII and hence over the formal Lend-Lease agreement persisted during 1941, the Minister without Portfolio periodically recorded concern at the possible impression of prevarication being given to the United States.[61] This was not wholly justified. In addition to the pause associated with the Atlantic Charter there was a major distraction over the alleged misuse, to promote British exports, of Lend-Lease supplies. 'The Export White Paper' of September 1941 sought to deal with this by providing that neither Lend-Lease materials nor their substitutes would normally be thus used; this was at once a reassurance to the USA and an acknowledgement of British dependence on her supplier.[62] A further reason for delay was the need to decide upon and to agree with the Dominion Governments, the India Office, and the Colonial Office a policy on the future of Imperial Preference. This last was by no means the simple issue of imperial unity that its fervent protagonists claimed. London and others certainly recognised its emotional aspects, and London saw it as a straw the more worth clutching as the post-war prospects for the balance of payments worsened. Above all, London viewed Imperial Preference as part of the trade discrimination that it was reluctant to renounce, and it refused to jeopardise either imperial unity or possible domestic trade advantage; nor would it act on preference without assurance that Britain, the Dominions and the rest of the Empire, were all in step. In practice, in late 1941 and early 1942 Britain was more concerned than the Dominions to retain preference, although the India Office and the Colonial Office did enter reservations about American proposals for trade policy.[63] The southern Dominions, however, not only accepted that preferences might be modified, but in their bilateral trade negotiations with the USA appeared ready to gain concessions in a manner that might react adversely on Britain and weaken the whole imperial trading system.[64] There even appeared to be a danger of the Dominions being 'lined up in a common front' against Britain, so that in November 1941 their Governments were cabled to weigh wider considerations in these trade talks.[65]

As these issues were being pondered, Mr Keynes was turning away from his abrasive tussles of June and July with Mr Acheson to urge in August that Britain could strike an understanding with the USA that he hoped might be short of the full Article VII. He argued that the USA was fundamentally reasonable and friendly, though ignorant of British problems. On the other hand, Britain had no excuse for resentment over Article VII, having accepted Lend-Lease in the knowledge that the American legislation had specified that the President was to seek a 'benefit' for the USA. Moreover, there was a tactical case for dealing with the question forthwith while there was a friendly President, rather than with somebody else later, particularly as delay might also waste the chance of waiving the old troublesome war debts from 1914–18.[66] Not least, as will be discussed in chapter 4, Keynes had devised by September 1941 his plan for an International Clearing Union; he hoped that this would ease those post-war problems of international payments, for which policies less multilateral in character, and contrary to the American ideas embodied in Article VII, might otherwise prove unavoidable.

A British decision about Article VII emerged painfully, and, to those on both sides who were anxious for agreement or at least to remove a fount of Anglo-American tension, all too slowly. Yet the issues were such that the few months involved might not seem excessive, least of all during some of the gravest events of the whole war. Initially, the American President, as was his way when uncertain of what he wanted or of his ability to secure it (the latter rather than the former in this instance) did not press hard. In Cabinet [67] at the time of the Atlantic Charter, Mr Greenwood slipped a note to the Chancellor of the Exchequer,who was fiercely opposed to post-war commitments:

> 'How does the new declaration affect clause VII of the Draft Lease Lend agreement[?] We must still [sic] insist on the two being brought into harmony.'

The Chancellor's answer was 'Yes—but I rather gather President is in no hurry about it.'

Hurry or no hurry, Ministers were active during August and September 1941 in re-drafting Article VII: prudently so, for, taking breath only briefly after his failure to 'clarify' the fourth Point of the Atlantic Charter and in contrast with a month earlier, with the support of the American Ambassador in London (above p 40), Mr Cordell Hull was soon pressing for British acceptance of it. The disputed words of the troublesome article declared that 'the terms and conditions' for Britain's receipt of aid and for America's benefits in return should

> 'provide against discrimination in either the United States of America or the United Kingdom against the importation of any product originating in the other country; and they shall provide for the formulation of measures for the achievement of these ends.'

Towards the end of September, an ingenious British re-draft which was subsequently approved by the Dominion and Indian Governments, sought both to respect the principle of non-discrimination, without an explicit disavowal of discrimination, and to protect Imperial Preference.[68] The economic objectives of the Atlantic Charter were re-affirmed; early discussions should be held on the best means to attain them; and the objectionable American section on discrimination just cited should be replaced by provision

> 'for joint and agreed action by the United States and United Kingdom, each working within the limits of their governing economic conditions, directed to securing as part of a general plan the progressive attainment of balanced international economies, the avoidance of harmful discriminations...'

The qualification about 'governing economic conditions' sought to safeguard discrimination and Imperial Preference. Together with the reference to 'balanced international economies' it had already inspired the wording of the text which the Chancellor had unsuccessfully proposed for the fourth Point of the Atlantic Charter (see Appendix 8).[69] The Foreign Office thought the qualification redundant in respect of discrimination, which it regarded as covered by the Charter, though insufficient to protect Imperial Preference; but it successfully objected to the sheltering of Imperial Preference by the addition, suggested by Mr Amery, of a further qualification about 'established obligations' as being far too wide. Instead of the proposed qualifications, it suggested the possibility of an understanding with the USA 'in an agreed minute' or in a concluding sentence of the article itself, that Article VII did not preclude British and American preferential arrangements.[70] Doubtless the addition of an extra paragraph (evidently on Mr Greenwood's prompting)[71] looking forward to early discussions offered a broad umbrella over this and other contentious points; but much more was to be heard of the eventually abortive proposal for an interpretative declaration.

The major issue remained: American insistence on an unqualified renunciation of discrimination. Unable to circumnavigate this obstacle, Ministers sought to scale it down; following discussions with Mr Winant, the American Ambassador, there was added to the British re-draft the patently imprecise phrase about 'the avoidance of harmful discriminations'. From several possible adjectives, one being his own 'Vexatious', Mr Churchill himself chose '*Harmful...* the best word'.[72]

When Lord Halifax presented this draft in mid-October, a cool reception was predictable, not just because of Mr Hull's earlier anger about the Atlantic Charter, but particularly because a recent speech by the Under-Secretary of State, Mr Sumner Welles, had stressed American determination to base post-war economic aims firmly on the elimination of restrictions and of discrimination in trade.[73] Lord Halifax reported Mr Acheson's reaction to the British draft as 'helpful and friendly' though non-committal: Mr Acheson himself noted impatiently[74] that by adding to the original American version 'some slippery words and phrases [it] had robbed of all meaning our prohibition of discrimination'. Several weeks passed before what proved to be the final American revision of Article VII was presented to Lord Halifax early in December 1941, after clearance with the President. This embodied much of the spirit of the British re-draft, and met one especial British anxiety in its reference to the pursuit of appropriate employment policies; it incorporated the re-affirmation of the Atlantic Charter; and it contained the additional paragraph that looked forward to early conversations on implementation, this carrying the qualification about 'governing economic conditions' that the British re-draft had originally attached to the main commitment (see Appendix 2). Once again, however, the critical feature was the reference to discrimination, now terser, now generalised beyond Anglo-American trade, and now blunter and more forthrightly comprehensive. The Consideration would 'include provision for agreed action... directed' amongst other things to

> 'the elimination of all forms of discriminatory treatment in international commerce, and to the reduction of tariffs and other trade barriers...'

Although this re-phrasing clearly covered Imperial Preference (and also American preferences, for example to the Philippines) as well as the Americans' own high tariffs, there were qualifications. Did not the interdependent obligations and the careful approach of the article as a whole allow it to be regarded as a set of noble aspirations rather than as a straitjacket of rigorous commitments? Thus argued reasonable men in the State Department. In Britain, however, reasonable men could not overlook the fierce hostility in high and many other American quarters to Imperial Preference, indeed to the concept of the British Empire. Experience in the various continuing bilateral trade negotiations seemed to have confirmed in practice American bad feeling about Imperial Preference. Moreover, for all the mutuality of British and American commitment that the article envisaged, was there still some asymmetry between the proposal to *abolish* preferences but only to *reduce* tariffs? (Mr Acheson explained that a world agreement to end tariffs appeared an impracticable aim, but not one to end discrimination.) In a remarkable exercise of the ambassadorial function, Lord Halifax strove in early December 1941 to elucidate these matters, and admonished London to accept. If the terms appeared disagreeable, London should nevertheless recognise and trust the Administration's good faith, and realise its political difficulties, notably in the impatient expectation of an awkward Congress that a provisional Lend-Lease agreement would be forthcoming. Stressing that the Americans were unlikely to yield over Imperial Preference, he hoped for British acceptance, and urged the virtue of early rather than damagingly late action.[75]

'Then began two months of blindman's buff', Mr Acheson has written.[76] Superficially apt, for instance in relation to Mr Churchill's agile evasiveness, this description does less than justice to subsequent developments on two counts. First, even without the problem of distilling some sort of decision from a divided Cabinet, the British Government, faced with American intransigence over discrimination and preference, probably required a breathing-space before making a momentous commitment about external economic policy after the war. Second, scarcely had London received Lord Halifax's communications when the attack on Pearl Harbour (7 December) brought America into the war and with that—it appeared to many in Britain—the transformation of Lend-Lease and no less the transformation, indeed the disappearance, of the basis for 'the Consideration'. The instant American action, understandably to ensure supplies for their own forces, was to suspend all Lend-Lease shipments.[77] This encouraged the assumption that aid in the form of Lend-Lease was at an end. Refutation came quickly, two days after Pearl Harbour, that it was not; and also that Article VII was not to be banished. On the contrary, two telegrams from the State Department to the London Embassy, which passed them on to the British Government, recorded the President's determination to continue Lend-Lease as the means of providing aid, and stressed the importance of an Agreement as a basis for Congressional grant of funds for that purpose (see Appendixes 10(a) and 10(b)). These telegrams claimed that Article VII had the virtues already rehearsed to Lord Halifax, and concluded a gloss on it by saying of the contentious matter of discrimination:

˙ ⸱⸱ that we ask is that the British sit down with us to work out the problems which lie ahead so that we may avoid substituting trade warfare in peace time for the present co-operation in wartime'.

London took a profoundly different view, cabling Lord Halifax a few days after the attack on Pearl Harbour that the 'Position is no doubt therefore greatly changed'. It hoped that if the Ambassador shared that view he would suggest to the President the suspension of discussions about Article VII. Time was needed to examine the issues involved, but London doubted that it was opportune now to discuss them, particularly with Australia and Canada. There might, however, be conversations of 'a preliminary and general character' in advance of a settlement of the 'Consideration' question: these could clarify, for instance, British intentions and difficulties, the latter being 'certainly... not understood in America at present'.[78] To this programme the Ambassador sent the sharp reply that he was 'most reluctant' to convey its import to the US Government. Repudiating the initial assumption of a substantial change in the situation because of American entry into the war he averred that, on the contrary, to try to evade agreement would be 'a political blunder at the outset' of developing Anglo-American collaboration. We should invite thereby the suspicion of using the new turn in the war 'as a pretext for evading commitments which we might otherwise have been not unwilling to make'. Moreover, he again argued that the proposed commitment was relatively modest and qualified by obligations equally on the American side. As for London's assertion of the need for consultation with the Dominions, that had already been undertaken when they had not objected to the British redraft; this excuse, he implied, would simply irritate the Americans.[79]

This forceful and informed advice notwithstanding, London maintained its unwillingness to accept Article VII without reservations. There was a contrast, a possible inconsistency, between the clear American affirmation that Imperial Preference was included in the proscription of discrimination, and the Ambassador's assessment:[80] Lord Halifax had argued that, despite pressure on Britain to subscribe to the principle of abolishing discrimination, this would not involve a commitment to abandon preference immediately, nor to abandon it in isolation from wider changes in trading arrangements. In short, a momentous commitment to discuss modification or eventual abolition of Imperial Preference was involved, but it was qualified more extensively than the taut wording of the article made immediately apparent. This was explained, in terms similar to those used earlier in the State Department's telegrams to the American Ambassador in London

(above p 46 and Appendixes 10(a) and 10(b)) by Sir William Malkin,*
legal adviser to the Foreign Office:[81]

'Imperial preference is certainly a "form of discriminatory
treatment" within the meaning of the phrase in the draft;
consequently its ultimate "elimination" forms part of the
programme indicated in the draft article. We should therefore be
committed to negotiating with the United States with the object of
reaching agreement for action by the two countries (and others
"of like mind" who are willing to participate) "directed to" the
realisation of the programme in question, including the elimination of Imperial preference among other forms of discriminatory treatment. This does not of course mean that we should be
committed to abandoning Imperial preference, irrespective of
measure of success reached as to the agreement on the rest of the
programme; the programme must be taken as a whole and we
could not be called upon to abandon Imperial preference except
as part of a scheme which provided for a satisfactory realisation of
other parts of the programme which were of interest to us such as,
eg, "the reduction of tariffs and other trade barriers". In other
words, while the abolition "or possibly modification of" Imperial
preference would be among the objects to be aimed at in
negotiations, the condition in which it could be attained would be
a subject for negotiation and agreement and would naturally
depend upon whether a satisfactory measure of agreement could
be obtained on the programme as a whole. We could not refuse to
discuss the abolition of Imperial preference as a part of the
programme and we should not be entitled to make impossible
conditions as to the price of our acceptance; but apart from this
our hands in negotiations would be tied only by the general effect
of clause 7 and of relevant provision in the Atlantic Charter. As to
preliminary conversations the position would generally be the
same, subject to the proviso that "the best means of attaining the
above stated objectives" is to be considered "in the light of
governing economic conditions". This proviso is important
because any agreement reached with the Americans in the light of
the [sc. above] will govern the subsequent negotiations under the
1st paragraph of the Article.'

All too accurately, and with what must seem justifiable concern
about the political risks of advertising inter-Allied differences during
a dangerous period of the war, London declared that the acceptance
and publication of a document of uncertain meaning would
probably be injurious to Anglo-American co-operation. An agreed

* MALKIN, Herbert William, KCMG 1930 (1883–1945); Legal Adviser to Foreign
Office 1929–45.

interpretation of Article VII, however, could make all the difference and, if appropriate, might be published. Perhaps Lord Halifax could include this matter of an interpretation in discussions with the Prime Minister, newly arrived in Washington?[82] Although the Ambassador had to reply that the Prime Minister had been unable to find time for such discussion, and that the matter was too pressing for prolonged reflection, he nevertheless offered a draft of an 'agreed interpretative document supplementary to Article VII'. This recognised that there would be post-war problems for all, specifically of the balance of payments for Britain and of greater involvement in world trade for the American economy; it emphasised that there must be consultation with the Dominions over any proposed change in Imperial Preference, and that achievement of the aims of Article VII 'must be gradual'.[83] Thus the proposed interpretation sought to weaken the vigour of commitment to the implementation of Article VII without explicitly rejecting its goals.

(4) MR CHURCHILL AND THE CONSIDERATION

At this point there might well have developed the crisis in government over Article VII that was in fact postponed until the first half of February 1942. Neither outright acceptance of the Consideration nor its proposed dilution appeared likely to unify opposing views in Whitehall, which was hopelessly divided.[84] On one side was the Foreign Office which, like Lord Halifax, predicated its case for acceptance of Article VII partly on the alleged need to avoid feeding traditional and especially isolationist suspicions of Britain in the USA: the less account we took or appeared to take of American sensitivities, 'the less likely we are to get our way in the long run'.[85] The Treasury opposed this approach, and Keynes's brutal comment illustrated the critical character of the issue and of the divergence within Whitehall upon it:

'The theory that "to get our own way in the long run" we must always yield in the short run reminds me of the bombshell I threw into economic theory by the reminder that "in the long run we are all dead". If there was *no-one* left to appease, the F.O. would feel out of a job altogether!'

So far, indeed, from assuaging American suspicions we were more likely to stimulate them, Keynes argued,

'by agreeing to unreasonable demands against our better judgement, and then *inevitably* having to find some way of slipping out of our ill-advised words.'

The Prime Minister now arrested temporarily the apparently inevitable twin crises in government and between London and

Washington, although his role is by no means easy to assess since much that passed during his Washington visit from mid-December 1941 to early January 1942 he asserted to be 'private and unofficial' between himself and the President.[86] In a sense it was. Parallel with the continuing Anglo-American exchanges at official level, Mr Churchill now conducted his own negotiations with Mr Roosevelt, evidently hoping that their unique personal relationship would allow the issue of Article VII to be postponed and to wither away, rather than to let it divert energies from winning the war and to cause dissension. Certainly, the record shows the gravity and intensity of concern with military and supply problems during the Prime Minister's visit to Washington.[87] Mr Churchill deflected the endeavours made through the President to discuss Article VII.[88] He subsequently appears to have dissembled, and perhaps to have persuaded Lord Halifax to dissemble, about discussions between the two war leaders, to the despair of official London and official Washington alike. To adopt Mr Acheson's metaphor, this was 'blindman's buff' with the intended 'victim' (Mr Churchill) evading masterfully two sets of 'blindmen' in Washington and London respectively. Having apparently 'mentioned' the proposed Lend-Lease agreement to the President before leaving Washington early in January 1942, the Prime Minister claimed[89] that:

> 'they were both in agreement that time need not be wasted on it at present, the entry of America into the war having ended the "Lease-Lend" period'.

After some talk with Mr Churchill, Lord Halifax, who assessed American official opinion less optimistically, pleaded inability to draft a telegram to London on the Prime Minister's understanding with the President 'for I . . . don't know enough of what passed'. He urged, presciently, that if Mr Churchill himself drafted one, he might 'let the President see it in order to avoid future misunderstandings'.[90] This brought a note to Lord Halifax, in which Mr Churchill displayed so clearly his own feelings that it must be quoted in full:[91]

'LORD HALIFAX

I must regard my conversation with the President as private and unofficial. Therefore I do not feel at liberty to allow it to be quoted. It is, however, a very good guide to my action or inaction, and it squares entirely with my own feelings.

2. All this fussing about what is to happen after the war is premature at the present time, when we are probably a long way from any satisfactory conclusion. It is only the State Department

which is pressing. Mr Morgenthau assured me he was not troubling about it. The views and requests of the State Department were formed in a period separated from us by the gulf which marks the United States involvement in full war through being attacked by the three Axis Powers. Therefore, it is clear the views formed on the earlier basis have no relation to the present situation. I told the President that the Imperial Preference would raise great difficulties in England if raised as a separate issue now but that if raised at the end of the war as part of a large economic settlement, in which the United States would become a low tariff country, it would probably be ~~of no consequence at all~~ [sic] easy to handle. He seemed to think this very sensible, and I am sure he felt, as I did, that we had better address our minds to the struggle on which the lives of our people depend. I should recommend you to stall any demand from the State Department with the usual diplomatic arts. I told the President that I personally was incapable of discussing the subject. For your own information, if the matter became extremely pressing I should have to send over the Chancellor of the Exchequer. But with every month that passes the fighting comradeship of the two countries as allies will grow, and the haggling about the lend-lease story will wane. After all, Lend-lease is practically superseded now.

W.S.C.

10.1.42'

Back in London Mr Churchill capped this apparent prevarication towards the President with his report to the War Cabinet, whose discussions and divisions in his absence had led to the postponement of a decision on Article VII until his return. Mr Churchill stated (17 January 1942) that[92]

'there had been virtually no discussion in regard to the question of consideration under the Lease-Lend Agreement.

'The Prime Minister said that he had taken the line that this question need not be settled as a matter of urgency, and that he had not been pressed on the point'.

This boldness secured the briefest of respites. If in the 'blindman's buff' over Article VII Lord Halifax's endeavours dominated December 1941, and if January 1942 was Mr Churchill's month of sidestepping, the fortnight from the end of January 1942 was to prove inescapably to belong to the Americans. The US Administration had already warned[93] at the end of December that it must make an early statement on Lend-Lease to Congress and that it was therefore anxious to settle the Consideration issue; British officials, concerned that without some agreement it would be

51

difficult to operate satisfactorily the reverse Lend-Lease to the USA that Britain had initiated on America's entry into the war, persuaded a reluctant Mr Churchill to devote much of a special Cabinet meeting in early February to the issue. The Prime Minister grumbled inaccurately that the matter had become 'obsolete rather than urgent',[94] even as the American Administration was moving to secure British acceptance of Article VII with a determination and unity of purpose not frequently seen in the statement or execution of its policy.

Amongst the papers before the Cabinet were four memoranda, which had resulted from its inconclusive discussions during the Prime Minister's American visit. [95] The most important memorandum came from the Minister without Portfolio (Mr A Greenwood). The others were from the Chancellor of the Exchequer (Sir Kingsley Wood), the Secretary of State for India (Mr L S Amery), and the Dominions Secretary (Lord Cranborne). Mr Greenwood's memorandum outlined recent governmental differences on now familiar lines, with some fresh emphases. Those favouring immediate acceptance of Article VII rested their arguments on its alleged necessity for Anglo-American understanding and for the continuance of Lend-Lease appropriations by Congress. Imperial Preference some saw less as a political question than as an anti-depression device to aid primary producers; it would therefore, along with everything else, need to be re-considered in the construction of a new economic system after the war; in any event, the wording of Article VII liberally safeguarded the approach to any modification of Imperial Preference. Against acceptance it was argued that the case was either weak or asymmetrical: weak, inasmuch as Pearl Harbour and the development of reverse Lend-Lease had transformed Anglo-American relations; asymmetrical, indeed unfair, in seeking the *elimination* of Imperial Preference against only a *reduction* of tariffs and other trade barriers. The opponents not only denied the existence of strong American feelings requiring a British gesture for the sake of allied unity, but asserted in strong contrast that Imperial Preference was an indispensable element in fostering 'free co-operation' in the Commonwealth; somewhat melodramatically and scarcely, it must be said, in accurate reflection of views from South Africa, Australia, New Zealand, Canada, and the Colonial Office, they were said to argue that its abandonment would leave a deep wound in the Commonwealth; would also arouse tremendous passions; and would give rise to a clamour for liberation from 'American pluto-democracy'. This lurid phrasing Mr Greenwood took from Mr Amery's memorandum. The Chancellor's memorandum concentrated upon the immediate risks in domestic politics and the post-war risks to economic policy from any commitment, however qualified, to the eventual abolition of Imperial Preference. The Chancellor urged its exclusion from Article VII and urged that the signature of a mutual aid agreement should be conditional upon an 'interpretative document' which should be published. This last point was echoed in the memorandum from the Dominions Secretary who, while expressing his belief that the principal Dominion Governments would support British acceptance of Article VII, felt it 'essential to avoid ambiguity by means of an agreed interpretation with the United States, for use by all concerned when the agreement is published'.

Superficially, two obstacles to the acceptance of Article VII persisted at the beginning of 1942: Imperial Preference and the question of securing an agreed interpretation. Only to a limited extent, however, was Imperial Preference in itself really a major policy issue; rather, it was a special case of a more serious problem. There was indeed reasoned approval by, for instance, the Board of Trade and the Colonial Office as well as by industry, but Preference was above all symbolic for highly emotional imperialists like Mr Amery. It was a symbol, however, to which attachment deepened the greater appeared the probable external weakness of the British economy. More generally, there was distaste for the suggestion of bargaining in exchange for Lend-Lease Britain's freedom to make her own economic policy after the war. The crucial problem was the threat that the elimination of discrimination under Article VII presented to Britain's ability to use 'various forms of safeguarding measures, including import restrictions & bilateral arrangements, wh[ich] may be *vital* to our welfare in the post-war period'—thus did one of his most senior advisers warn the Chancellor.[96] At their harshest, as Mr Churchill's personal adviser (Lord Cherwell)* more than once stressed with distaste, these reservations embodied an attachment to the maintenance of 'the Schachtian system of blocked currencies and barter arrangements with foreign countries, to which we have been reduced in war'.[97] The Treasury, however, stood firm; disclaiming the need for 'Schachtian' justification, it simply emphasised that an international trading system opposite to American hopes might 'be quite inevitable, at any rate for a good time to come'.[98]

(5) ACQUIESCENCE AND MISUNDERSTANDING

On the eve of the Cabinet's attempt to distil from these conflicting views an agreed policy, Washington signalled that the irresistible crunch on Article VII had begun. With imminent questioning by Congress in mind, Mr Acheson, Assistant Secretary of State,

* CHERWELL, Frederick Alexander Lindemann, 1st Baron 1941 (1886–1957); Paymaster-General, 1942–45.

had sought President Roosevelt's guidance at the end of January 1942. Acknowledging Mr Churchill's emphatic preference for deferment, Mr Roosevelt nevertheless declared that the issue of the Consideration must now be settled. In reply to specific queries from Acheson, he wrote on the latter's memorandum that 'I strongly hope the British will accept' the American draft of Article VII. Of the possible alternative, the omission of the article in view of British objections about 'discrimination', the President noted starkly that that would leave the British 'in a much more difficult future economic situation'. [99] (Presumably this meant that a generous settlement of Lend-Lease and the provision of post-war aid would therefore become more problematical). Later that evening, the President having at last clarified policy, Acheson and a colleague (Herbert Feis)* personally reported this to the British Ambassador[100]. Lord Halifax cabled fully to London, and again urged the wisdom of a prompt agreement on American terms. [101] At the same time the Secretary of State instructed the London Ambassador to seek discussions with senior Cabinet Ministers; he stressed that the entry of the USA into the war had not displaced Lend-Lease, the legislation on which remained the American Government's only authority to provide aid and to pool resources. [102]

The Cabinet met on 2 February 1942 and understandably dithered. The Foreign Secretary had ready a draft of an interpretative note on Article VII; this broadly followed the State Department's explanatory telegrams of December and accepted Article VII. The Cabinet rejected this, postponed a decision on Article VII, and asked the Foreign Secretary and the Chancellor, proponents of the opposing views, for alternative draft replies to Lord Halifax. [103] These came within two days.[104] The original Foreign Office draft had aroused Treasury anxieties, with Sir Horace Wilson† unhappy about its unhelpfulness on Imperial Preference,[105] while Keynes reiterated his suspicion of 'appeasement *pur sang*'.[106] The Chancellor's short draft (prepared by Sir Horace Wilson)[107] did not object to the underlying economic aims of the proposed agreement including Article VII, but declared signature of it to be 'inappropriate' until there had been economic discussions, which Britain hoped could soon be commenced. The much longer Foreign Office redraft reproduced the Treasury's acquiescence in the principle of the proposed agreement and reflected Treasury pressure: it suggested an exchange of notes to exclude preferences from the

---

* FEIS, Herbert (1893–1972); Economic Adviser to Department of State 1931–37; Adviser, International Economic Affairs 1937–43; special consultant to Secretary of War 1944–46.
† WILSON, Horace John, KCB 1924 (1882–1972); Permanent Secretary of HM Treasury and official Head of HM Civil Service, 1939–42.

condemnation of discrimination, and to recognise Britain's need, before commitment to their modification, to consult Dominion Governments. Before, however, these drafts could be discussed in Cabinet, indeed within twenty-four hours, the arrival of urgent messages from the President and from Mr Morgenthau, the United States Treasury Secretary, to the Prime Minister and the Chancellor respectively, led the Foreign Office to circulate as a possible alternative its earlier draft, more compliant with American wishes, which at its special meeting on 2 February the Cabinet had rejected. [108]

Urgency, not elucidation, was the content of these messages. Mr Roosevelt sought prompt agreement, 'convinced that... further delay... will be harmful to your interests and ours' and 'that a failure to sign... would do much mischief...'.[109] Mr Morgenthau echoed, emphasising that the absence of agreement was already 'working harm to unity of war effort and purpose'.[110]

Whereas the Chancellor's reply to his American counterpart was of the holding variety,[111] Mr Churchill's forthright reply to the President was to pull punches only by comparison with the language of the preliminary drafts of it. The final version[112] registered British distaste for American pressures and emphasised in particular the unwillingness of the Cabinet to trade Imperial Preference for Lend-Lease. This was not a fiscal question of protection *versus* free trade, declared Mr Churchill, noting that he himself had 'always been opposed or lukewarm to Imperial preference'. Such a bargain would involve American intervention in the domestic affairs of the British Empire. It would lead to dangerous debates in Parliament and to further German propaganda, of the type the President had recently read to the Prime Minister, about American hostility to the Empire. Asserting his desire to work with the President in constructing a free, fertile, economic policy for the post-war world, Mr Churchill hoped that weight would be given to these and to diplomatic representations.

The Churchillian message had distilled a profound sense of grievance from much more outspoken drafts, [113] which prime ministerial red ink had largely softened, though at points it had toughened it. It would be unfair (altered by Mr Churchill to 'it would not be wise') to exact immediate British acquiescence to Article VII, went one draft (see Appendix 11). American entry into war meant that Britain was 'no longer a client' (altered in red ink to 'combatant') 'receiving help from a generous patron' (the red ink said 'sympathiser'). It was now even more true than in the previous 27 months that British survival protected the United States. Thus the 'comparatively small quantities of Lend-Lease' ('check' said the red ink) received under the original arrangements 'ought not to be a cause of the prejudgement of our future co-operation in the economic rebuilding of the world'. Recalling his earlier words to the President on the appropriateness of coupling Imperial Preference and low tariffs in 'a large settlement', Mr Churchill—in this undispatched draft—warned 'of the inappropriateness... of our being forced to part with our freedom of honourable decision with you' on an issue, he added in red ink, 'which in certain aspects touches our freedom [sic], sovereignty and independence. This might be regarded [sic] represented as the acceptance by the British Government and of the British Empire as a condition of tutelage wh[ich] w[oul]d I am sure be a great pity. The keynote of our relations must surely be equality, coupled with rivalry in sacrifice and effort against the common foe, and for the sake of the common cause of liberty freedom [sic] and democracy'.

This draft concluded with a plea that the USA would 'not press upon us unduly a one-sided submission'. A further draft [114] eliminated only the tart allusion to the quantity of Lend-Lease aid, and was therefore presumably a considered statement of Mr Churchill's attitude to American policy. After Cabinet discussion, however, it was decided to revise further the proposed message to the President: the emphasis was to be placed upon the avoidance of any bargaining of Imperial Preference for Lend-Lease.[115] Further, the Cabinet decided that the reply to Lord Halifax's telegram recommending acceptance of Article VII forthwith would be based upon the *less* compliant of the two drafts prepared by the Foreign Office: this embodied a proposed American interpretative note that Britain had stated that 'discrimination' did not cover preferential arrangements, and that undertakings to change Imperial Preference would require prior consultation with the Dominions. An appropriate telegram was thereupon sent to the Ambassador in Washington[116].

Anglo-American tension now intensified. In London Mr Winant, the American Ambassador, received from the Foreign Secretary a copy of the Cabinet's instructions to Lord Halifax. In Mr Winant's view the proposed interpretative document 'defeated the primary objective of Article 7' and he therefore refused the Foreign Secretary's request to explain to Washington the political background to London's opposition to bartering preference for American aid. He thought (setting an example by seeing the Australian High Commissioner in London) that American persuasion of the Dominions could bring indirect pressure on the British Government[117]. Meanwhile he was himself to spend the immediately following week-end with Mr Churchill at Chequers, gaining perspective on British views. [118]

Instant crisis met Lord Halifax in Washington when he gave the Under-Secretary of State (Mr Sumner Welles) 'Very definitely the impression that he was attempting to argue against his own better judgement', explaining that the London draft 'was really all right although on the face of it it seemed to be all wrong'.[119] Mr Welles stressed the intensifying gravity of the matter, a view that two State Department officials, Mr Acheson and Mr Feis, reinforced when later that day they also met the Ambassador.[120] Lord Halifax reported sombrely that they regarded as 'politically impossible' the acceptance of the proposed British reservations about Imperial Preference.[121] Mr Acheson promised, however, to 'discover' whether there were any fresh ideas in the Administration, and within a few days there arrived for Mr Churchill a striking message from the President, which helped the Cabinet at last to accept Article VII (see Appendix 12). In a brilliant weaving of clarification and of persuasion, the President disclaimed any intention to trade Imperial Preference for Lend-Lease; recognised Britain's need to consult and to carry the Dominions with her; and stressed that the central American aim was an understanding 'to have a bold, forthright, and comprehensive discussion' from which 'nothing should be excluded'. He emphasised that the American Administration did not seek, nor did Article VII contain, any commitment by Britain to abolish Imperial Preference; that could no more be expected from Britain than a commitment from the President 'relative to a vital revision of our tariff policy'. In the context of Mr Churchill's own evocation of 'a free, fertile economic policy for the post-war world', which his message twice quoted, Mr Roosevelt deplored as a potential dilution of that spirit the proposed explanatory notes on the agreement.

Mr Churchill read this message to the Cabinet, now recommending the signature of the agreement, without the exchange of interpretative notes.[122] Shortly after the Cabinet meeting, and after consulting the Ministers involved, the Prime Minister cabled the President that his elucidation 'entirely meets my difficulties' and that matters would be concluded forthwith.[123] Within a fortnight they were; after consultations with the Dominion and Indian Governments, the Mutual Aid Agreement was signed on 23 February 1942.[124]

Alas, this did not end the already prolonged Anglo-American tension over Article VII. Granted that the Presidential assurances carried especial weight and that they were made on the basis of the remarkable Roosevelt-Churchill relationship, they scarcely said more than State Department officials and others had already explained about the tentative nature of the undertakings. Did some other influence persuade the British Government to accept? It seems likely. Up to the last, in a draft for Mr Churchill's reply to the President, Sir Richard Hopkins of the Treasury had struggled to protect Imperial Preference and to qualify the apparent commitment of Article VII to 'Victorian ideas of "free trade"'.[125] That his draft was discarded by the Chancellor probably reflected other views in the Treasury, notably the hope of grasping a chance that unqualified acceptance of Article VII would allow Britain 'to preserve some measure of financial independence in the immediate post-war period'. The words were those of Keynes. [126] Mr S D Waley* had prepared a note, evidently blessed by Sir Horace Wilson, who said that it sought 'to indicate the damage we might suffer' from failing to agree. [127] This hoped that eventual settlement with the USA might involve only Lend-Lease aid received before an agreement, and that the USA would at last fulfil British hopes, by providing as much as $800 million for the 'old Commitments' incurred for pre-Lend-Lease supplies. It is a measure of the strength of such hopes that Keynes, hitherto most premonitory about the consequences of the proposed Lend-Lease agreement, now urged acceptance in a paper that elaborated but did not dissent from Mr Waley's advocacy. In the event, the old commitments were *not* taken over; the consequent fulfilment of Mr Keynes's fears 'that we should have so managed our affairs during the war as to have parted with the foundations of independent action immediately afterwards' [128] understandably led to cooler British feelings towards the implementation of Article VII.

Productive of misunderstanding in another way was the decision not to have an agreed interpretation of the controversial article. The President had offered political justification for this refusal, in the potential danger that it might detract publicly from Allied unity; but the lengths to which he and others went to elucidate it undermined that position. As Lord Cranborne†, Dominions Secretary, had noted during the discussions, the issue would be raised in Congress and in Empire Parliaments, in which event 'any ambiguity in the interpretation of the Agreement would be very dangerous', and he had therefore planned 'an agreed interpretation... for use by all concerned...'.[129] Devastatingly, surely, and most unexpectedly, this view was borne out by imprecise reporting of the Cabinet discussions which led to the acceptance of Article VII. Of the two

---

* WALEY, (Sigismund) David, KCMG 1943 (1887–1962); Under-Secretary HM Treasury to 1946; Third Secretary, HM Treasury, 1946–47; European Recovery Dept, Foreign Office, 1948; Alternate UK delegate, Tripartite Commission on German Debts, 1951–52.

† CRANBORNE, Viscount (Robert Arthur James Gascoyne-Cecil), Baron Cecil 1941, 5th Marquess of Salisbury 1947 (1893–1972); Parliamentary Under-Secretary of State for Foreign Affairs, 1935–38; Paymaster-General, 1940; Secretary of State for Dominion Affairs, 1940–42; Secretary of State for the Colonies, 1942; Lord Privy Seal, 1942–43, 1951–52; Secretary of State for Dominion Affairs, 1943–45; Leader of the House of Lords, 1942–45, 1951–57; Secretary of State for Commonwealth Relations, 1952; Lord President of the Council, 1952–57.

main Cabinet documents concerned, the 'Confidential Annex' inadequately reported that the President's message had stated that[130]

'In his view Article 7 contained no commitment in advance to abolish Empire Preference, and it should be excluded from our discussions'.

In the final Minutes,[131] this was altered slightly, but not improved in accuracy:

'In his view, Article 7 contained no commitment in advance to abolish Empire Preference, which should be excluded from our discussions'.

When even Cabinet reporting, by its inaccurate suggestion that the President's exclusion of a specific commitment to abolish Imperial Preference covered also the exclusion of discussion of that issue, could go astray, it is scarcely surprising that misunderstanding of the Consideration persisted.

A notable instance shortly after the end of the war in 1945 concerned Sir John Anderson,* in 1942 a leading member of the War Cabinet, and from September 1943 to July 1945 Chancellor of the Exchequer. In the House of Commons in December 1945 he criticised American proposals on commercial policy, which the new Labour Government guardedly commended to the House (below, p 329), because they appeared to introduce the prospect of eliminating Imperial Preference. [132] He claimed correctly, as if echoing President Roosevelt's emollient words of February 1942, that by Article VII Britain was 'no more under an obligation to get rid of Imperial Preference than the Americans were to get rid of their protective tariffs'. He also claimed correctly that the reference in the Article to the elimination of discriminatory practices 'left rather at large how far Imperial Preference could in this connection be so treated'. Before the acceptance of Article VII, however, Anglo-American exchanges, and the Foreign Office's legal interpretation of it, had reduced very considerably the extent to which discussion of the future of Imperial Preference had remained 'at large'. The argument for having Article VII—'The Consideration' —at all may fall outside the historian's function; this can hardly be said about the powerful arguments emerging from documents and from events, that clearer wording of the Article, or an agreed interpretation, or both, might have spared Britain and the USA much friction during and after the war.

---

* ANDERSON, John, KCB 1919, 1st Viscount Waverley 1952 (1882–1958); Home Secretary and Minister of Home Security, 1939–40; Lord President of the Council, 1940–43; Chancellor of the Exchequer, 1943–45.

CHAPTER 3, SOURCE REFERENCES

1. For 'The Lend-Lease Act' see Hall, *North American Supply,* pp 505–7.

2. The evolution of American policy is discussed in Warren F Kimball, 'Lend-Lease and the Open Door: The Temptation of British Opulence, 1937–42', *Political Science Quarterly, LXXXVI (1971),* 2, pp 232–59.

3. Sayers, *Financial Policy,* pp 383–97.

4. Penrose, *Economic Planning for the Peace,* pp 17, 30. Penrose was economic adviser to the US Ambassador in London from 1941.

5. Kimball, op cit, p 243.

6. W 3379/37/49 of 10 April 1941, CAB 117/52.

7. W 5382/426/49 of 21 April 1941 and reports of the two statements in May in CAB 117/52.

8. The principal reference for the American Viscose deal is D C Coleman, *Courtaulds: An Economic and Social History,* (3 vols, Oxford: Clarendon Press, 1969–80) II, ch XV. See also Hall, op cit, pp 273–6; Sayers, op cit, pp 388–90, 392–3; T 247/43; T 247/103; T 247/113.

9. For Keynes's concern with the American Viscose deal, see: T 247/103 in particular, and T 247/43. For Morgenthau's suspicions about Keynes's lack of credentials: 'The Course of my Negotiations', report with letter from Keynes to Sir Horace Wilson at the Treasury, 19 May 1941; Keynes to Wilson, 21 May 1941; Lord Halifax to Mr Morgenthau, 21 May 1941; 'The Course of my Negotiations, II', report of 26 May 1941 with letter from Keynes to Wilson, 25 May 1941. The foregoing in T 247/113, documents 5, 7, 8, 12; *JMK* XXIII, pp 79–101.

10. The visit had been arranged in conjunction with the American Embassy in London: Penrose, op cit, p 14, and Keynes to Lord Halifax, 24 May 1941, T 247/113, document 10. Keynes clarified matters with Morgenthau, ibid, report to Wilson, 26 May 1941, document 12. Professor Penrose has confirmed orally that in discussions before Keynes left London, Embassy officials hoped that he would ginger up Washington's thinking on post-war policy.

11. Report by Keynes on 'Mr Morgenthau', undated, but evidently May 1941, in T 247/113, document 9; *JMK* XXIII, pp 87–91.

12. Keynes to Lord Halifax, 24 May 1941, and report of 26 May 1941 to Wilson, T 247/113, documents 10 and 12.

13. Telegram 2351 of 25 May 1941 and telegram 2439 of 29 May, both from Keynes to the Treasury, and initial reactions in London: T 160/1105 and CAB 117/52; *JMK* XXIII, pp 101–2. For Keynes's relaxed attitude towards the possible abandonment of Ottawa: letter to Sir Horace Wilson, 25 May 1941, T 247/113, document 11.

14. The relevant documents are in T 160/1105.

15. Telegrams 2273 of 21 May 1941, 2274 of 21 May, 2351 of 25 May, 2439 of 29 May, 2690 of 10 June from Washington to London, and telegram 2959 of 31 May from London to Washington in T 160/1105. The five telegrams from Washington also in CAB 117/52; 2273 & 2351, *JMK* XXIII, pp 92–93, 101–2.

16. Telegram 3317 of 15 June from Prime Minister and Chancellor of the Exchequer to Washington, sources as in n 15.

17. Telegram 3177 of 8 July 1941 from Washington to London, sources as in n 15.

18. Telegram 2351 of 25 May 1941 from Washington to London, CAB 117/52. The Chancellor's red pencil side-lined and starred the critical paragraphs.

19. Keynes to Chancellor, 21 June 1941, T 160/1105; *JMK* XXIII, p 134.

20. Telegrams 3102 of 4 July 1941 from Washington to London and 4074 of 16 July from London to Washington, T 160/1200. The advice against 'hurried conclusions' is in telegram 4022 of 14 July 1941 from the Prime Minister and the Chancellor of the Exchequer, T 160/1105.

21. Viscount Halifax to Mr Eden, W 5382/426/49 of 21 April 1941 (and as a paper dated 6 May); Halifax to Greenwood, 19 May; Greenwood to Eden, 3 June: CAB 117/52.

22. Ibid, Sir Kingsley Wood to Mr Eden, 23 June 1941.

23. American-Canadian Commission: CAB 117/56. Telegram 2690 of 10 June 1941 from Washington to London, and Sir Frederick Leith-Ross to Sir George Chrystal, 1 July 1941: CAB 117/52. J A Stirling of Board of Trade to L P Thompson, 16 June 1941, Keynes to Stirling, 17 June 1941, Keynes to Chancellor, 28 July 1941: T 247/44. Telegram 3317 of 15 June 1941, Prime Minister and Chancellor to Washington, CAB 117/52.

24. Pencil note by Mr Greenwood in CAB 117/52.

25. Mr Oliver Lyttelton to Sir Kingsley Wood, 27 June 1941; Mr L S Amery to Mr Eden, 30 May; to Sir Kingsley Wood 9 August, 18 August, 27 August: CAB 117/52. Amery to Kingsley Wood, 30 May and 10 June, T 160/1105.

26. Telegram 3317 of 15 June 1941, CAB 117/52.

27. Keynes noted of the Prime Minister: 'I know he is reluctant for any post-war conversations to take place'. 17 June 1941, T 247/44.

28. Telegram 2657 of 9 June 1941 and 2690 of 10 June in T 160/1105, and CAB 117/52 refer to Keynes at the State Department.

29. Telegram 3177 of 8 July 1941, CAB 117/52.

30. Memorandum by Mr R Opie of the British Embassy in Washington, 12 August 1941, T 160/1105.

31. Sir Kingsley Wood to Keynes, 5 July 1941, ibid; telegram 3634 of 29 June, ibid, and CAB 117/52.

32. As n 29.

33. Dean Acheson, *Present at the Creation* (London 1970), p 29.

34. As n 30.

35. Telegrams 4022 and 4023 of 14 July 1941, T 160/1105, and CAB 117/52.

36. 'The "consideration" we are in a position to offer does not look very plausible': Keynes to Chancellor, 21 June 1941, T 160/1105 (and *JMK* XXIII, p 135). Report of first Acheson-Keynes discussion: Keynes to Chancellor, 15 July 1941, ibid, and T 247/44; Acheson, op cit, p 29; *FRUS 1941* III (1959), pp 6-7.

37. Acheson's account of meeting in Acheson, op cit, pp 29-30 and *FRUS 1941* III, pp 10-13; Keynes's account and report, with draft agreement in T 160/1105. See also CAB 117/52 and T 247/44; *JMK* XXIII, pp 171-8.

38. Opie's memorandum and further Minute, both of 12 August 1941, in T 160/1105.

39. 28 July 1941, T 247/44.

40. Acheson, op cit, p 30; Keynes's letter, ibid, JMK XXIII, pp 177-8 and *FRUS 1941* III, pp 16-17.

41. See Theoodore A Wilson, *The First Summit. Roosevelt and Churchill at Placentia Bay 1941* (Boston USA 1969). Full text of the Atlantic Charter in Cmd 6321, *Joint Declaration . . . known as The Atlantic Charter, BPP 1940-41*, VIII.

42. Sir Alexander Cadogan of the Foreign Office prepared the draft of a joint declaration, as well as a draft of a 'parallel' declaration to be made by the US,

United Kingdom and Netherlands, on policy towards Japan. He recorded that the Prime Minister approved both rough drafts, 'with alterations': David N Dilks (editor), *The Diaries of Sir Alexander Cadogan 1938–1945* (London 1971), p 398, entry for Sunday 10 August 1941. Mr Churchill recorded that 'the "Atlantic Charter" was in its first draft a British production cast in my own words': Winston S Churchill, *The Second World War. III The Grand Alliance* (London 1950), p 386. Sir Alexander's later recollection was that 'the preamble and first three articles [of the Charter] stand now as I drafted them ... the remaining five ... were considerably modified': draft chapters for an autobiography, ACAD 7/2, Churchill College Archives, Cambridge.

43. Churchill, *The Second World War.* III, p 387, and *Memorandum* on the Atlantic meeting, 20 August 1941, WP(41) 202, p 3, CAB 66/18; Sumner Welles, *Where Are We Heading?* (London 1947), pp 11–12.

44. Telegrams from the Prime Minister to the Lord Privy Seal in the TUDOR series in CAB 120/24, and from the Lord Privy Seal to the Prime Minister in the ABBEY series in CAB 120/25. A selection of the more important telegrams was assembled as a document on 'Conference between the Prime Minister of the United Kingdom and the President of the United States', 18 August 1941, WP(41) 203, CAB 66/18. Draft of proposed Joint Declaration in TUDOR 16, and Prime Minister's comments in TUDOR 15, both of 11 August. First meeting of War Cabinet on 12 August at 1.45 a.m., WM(41) 80th Conclusions, CAB 65/19. Telegram from Lord Privy Seal to Prime Minister, ABBEY 31 of 12 August.

45. Welles, op cit, p 13.

46. TUDOR 20 of 12 August.

47. Second Cabinet meeting on 12 August 1941, WM(41) 81st Conclusions, CAB 65/19. Letters from Sir Edward Bridges, Secretary to the War Cabinet, to the Chancellor of the Exchequer and President of the Board of Trade, 12 August 1941, CAB 120/20. Mr Eden's misgivings seem to have reflected his feelings that, in proposing the Joint Declaration without advance notice, President Roosevelt had 'bowled the P.M. a very quick one': John Harvey (editor), *The War Diaries of Oliver Harvey* (London 1978), p 31, entry for 12 August 1941. Sir Oliver Harvey, Bt., was Principal Private Secretary to Mr Eden.

48. ABBEY 35 of 12 August.

49. TUDOR 23 of 12 August.

50. ABBEY 42 of 13 August. It has been asserted that over the troublesome fourth Point Mr Churchill 'evaded full consultation with his Cabinet and ignored some of their advice' (A P Dobson, 'Economic Diplomacy at the Atlantic Conference', *Review of International Studies, 1984*, 10, pp 143–163, at p 143). The first accusation disregards the Prime Minister's urgent request, noted above, that Mr Attlee should assemble the full Cabinet and report immediately. The other requires conjectures about the approximate times at which telegrams from the Cabinet reached the Prime Minister, and about the interpretation of those and other telegrams passing between them. In contrast, though ignored in that speculative accusation, stands Mr Attlee's warmly appreciative telegram on the final draft.

51. Wilson, op cit, pp 247–8.

52. Mr Amery to Sir Kingsley Wood, 18 August 1941, CAB 117/52.

53. Wilson, op cit, p 187.

54. Ibid, p 247.

55. Ibid, pp 248–9.

56. Wilson, op cit, pp 248–9, and *FRUS* 1941 I, pp 370–2. Penrose, op cit, p 16 notes only Winant's warning but not the reversal of his position at the end of September (*FRUS* 1941 III, pp 37–38)—see text p 43. In implying that the matter was not actively taken up until February (Penrose, p 19), he omits a period of considerable discussion about Article VII.

57. 20 September 1941, PREM 4/17/3, f 473.

58. On 'the old commitments' see Sayers, op cit, pp 383–97.

59. Amery to Sir Kingsley Wood, 25 September 1941, and to Mr Anthony Eden, 30 May 1941, CAB 117/52.

60. R J Hammond, History of the Second World War, *Food* Vol I (1951), p 351; and see note by Keynes on 'Discrimination', 15 August 1941, in T 160/1105, and T 247/43.

61. Sir Frederick Leith-Ross, 23 June 1941, and Mr A Greenwood, 23 June, 4 August, 22 August, 29 September, 28 November in CAB 117/52.

62. Sayers, pp 398–405.

63. See note 13 above; see also USE 41(8) of 18 October 1941; Viscount Cranborne, Secretary of State for Dominion Affairs, to Mr A Greenwood, 13 January 1942; WP(42) 25 of 17 January 1942, memorandum by Chancellor, especially paragraphs 4 and 13; WP (42) 32 of 21 January 1942, memorandum by Viscount Cranborne: CAB 117/53.

64. Inadequate weight is given to Australia's broadly favourable attitude towards Article VII during late 1941 and early 1942 in Roger Bell, 'Australian Economic Relations and Reciprocal Wartime Economic Assistance, 1941–6: An Ambivalent Association', *Australian Ec. Hist. Rev.* XVI–1, March 1976, pp 23–49.

65. Note by Sir Hubert Henderson, 8 October 1941, with supporting note by Keynes, 10 October 1941, T 160/1377; C F Cobbold of Bank of England to S D Waley at Treasury, 1 October 1941, and telegram D No 701 of 22 November 1941 to Canadian, Australian, New Zealand and South African Governments in T 160/1200.

66. Memorandum by Keynes, 27–28 August 1941, T 247/44.

67. 12 August 1941, CAB 117/52.

68. Draft initialled by Mr Churchill, 22 and 23 September 1941 in PREM 4/17/3, f 474. Drafts and extensive comments by Ministers and officials during August, September, and October in T 160/1105.

69. The common source was probably a Treasury 'Note', undated, on the original US draft agreement, accompanying a letter from Sir Kingsley Wood to Mr Arthur Greenwood, 8 August 1941, CAB 117/52.

70. Ibid, N B Ronald to T Daish, 8 September 1941, original in CAB 117/52.

71. Mr A Greenwood to Sir Kingsley Wood, 22 August 1941, CAB 117/52.

72. PREM 4/17/3, f 474. Other adjectives were 'special' and 'arbitrary', ibid, f 473.

73. Ibid, telegram 4649 of 11 October 1941, Washington to London.

74. Ibid, telegram 4755 of 17 October 1941; Acheson, op cit, p 31; *FRUS 1941* III, pp 38–43.

75. Telegrams 5589 and 5590 of 4 December 1941, CAB 117/52.

76. Acheson, op cit, p 32.

77. Hall, op cit, p 340.

78. Telegram 6914 of 13 December 1941, London to Washington, CAB 117/52 (also in WP (42) 21 of 14 January 1942, CAB 117/53).
79. Ibid, telegrams 5953 and 5954 of 20 December 1941.
80. Pencilled comments on telegram 5953 in CAB 117/52.
81. Telegram 7250 of 26 December 1941, 'Private and Personal' from Sir Orme Sargent of the Foreign Office to Viscount Halifax, PREM 4/17/3, ff 393–7. The first sentence of the minute, with 'phrase in Article VII' substituted for 'phrase in the draft', was cited in papers relating to discussions in 1944 about the Anglo-American conversations of September–October 1943 on Article VII: ASD(44)2, in CAB 99/34.
82. Telegram 7724 of 24 December 1941, CAB 117/52.
83. Telegram 6105 and 6106 of 29 December 1941, ibid.
84. Telegrams 20 (DEDIP) of 1 January 1942, and TAUT 357 of 3 January, in CAB 117/52.
85. Mr Nevile Butler of the Foreign Office to Mr S D Waley of the Treasury, 30 December 1941; Keynes's comments of 31 December written on the letter, T 160/1105; *JMK* XXIII, p 224.
86. Mr Churchill to Lord Halifax, 10 January 1942, PREM 4/17/3, f 363.
87. Chiefs of Staff Committee, ARCADIA, Record of Proceedings, Washington War Conference, December 1941–January 1942, CAB 99/17.
88. Telegram 542 of 29 January 1942, Washington to London, CAB 117/53; Acheson, op cit, pp 32–33; *FRUS 1942* (1960) I, p 526.
89. Mr J M Martin, private secretary to Mr Churchill, in a note to Lord Halifax, 6 January 1942, PREM 4/17/3, f 365.
90. Ibid, pencilled comment on above by Lord Halifax, 7 January.
91. 10 January 1942, ibid, ff 363–4 (Copy).
92. WM(42) 8th Conclusions, Minute 1, 17 January 1942: CAB 65/25.
93. Telegram 6105 of 29 December 1941, Washington to London, CAB 117/52; also in WP(42) 21 in CAB 117/53.
94. Mr T L Rowan to Mr Churchill, 1 February 1942, PREM 4/17/3, f 324.
95. In the order listed above: WP(42) 21, 25, 23, 32 in CAB 117/53.
96. Sir Richard Hopkins, 17 January 1942, T 160/1105.
97. Lord Cherwell to Prime Minister, 5 February 1942; see also Cherwell to Prime Minister, 27 September 1941, and 23 January 1942, and to J M Martin, private secretary to Prime Minister, telegram TAUT 142 (undated but evidently January 1942): PREM 4/17/3, ff 310, 470, 329, 372.
98. Sir Richard Hopkins, 22 January 1942, as n 90.
99. Acheson, op cit, p 33, and telegram 542 of 29 January 1942 from Washington to London, CAB 117/53. (See also n 56 above.)
100. Ibid. Acheson's later and possibly inaccurate recollection was that his meeting with Halifax took place the following day: Acheson, op cit, p 33.
101. Telegram 542 as n 99.
102. *FRUS 1942* I (1960), pp 525–7, 30 January 1942.
103. WM 14 (42), CAB 65/25.
104. WP(42) 62 of 4 February 1942 from the Foreign Secretary, and WP(42) 63 from the Chancellor, CAB 117/53.
105. 2 February 1942, T 160/1105.
106. Ibid, 5 February.
107. Draft by Sir Horace Wilson, unsigned, but identified as his in a preceding note by Sir Richard Hopkins of 2 February, ibid.

108. WP(42) 66, CAB 117/53.

109. 4 February 1942, PREM 4/17/3, ff 307–8, and *FRUS* 1942 I, p 529.

110. 6 February 1942, T 160/1105.

111. Ibid, 6 February (despatch 8 February).

112. 7 February 1942, PREM 4/17/3, f 298.

113. Drafts of 5 February, ibid, ff 299–305.

114. Further draft of 5 February, ibid, ff 299–302.

115. WM(42) 17th Conclusions, Minute 4, 6 February 1942, CAB 65/25.

116. Telegrams 845 and 846, London to Washington, 6 February 1942, CAB 117/53.

117. *FRUS* 1942 I, pp 529–32, Mr Winant to Secretary of State, 6 February.

118. Ibid, pp 534–5, 9 February.

119. Ibid, pp 532–3, memorandum of conversation, 7 February.

120. Ibid, pp 533–4, memorandum of conversation, 7 February.

121. Telegram 741, Washington to London, 8 February, CAB 117/53.

122. WM(42) 20th Conclusions, Minute 4, 12 February 1942, CAB 65/25.

123. Telegram 987, London to Washington, T 160/1105.

124. Telegrams to Dominion Governments in CAB 117/53. 'Agreement . . . on the Principles applying to Mutual Aid', published as Cmd 6341 of 1942, *BPP 1941–42*, IX.

125. Undated paper in T 160/1105.

126. Ibid, Memorandum on 'Lend-Lease Consideration' by Keynes, 12 February 1942; *JMK* XXIII, pp 225–8.

127. Ibid, 11 and 12 February.

128. As n 126.

129. Memorandum on 'Lease-Lend Agreement', WP(42) 32 of 21 January 1942, paragraph 8, CAB 117/53.

130. WM(42) 20th Conclusions, Minute 4, Confidential Annex, 12 February 1942, CAB 65/29.

131. WM(42) 20th Conclusions, Minute 4, 12 February 1942, CAB 65/25.

132. 417 HC DEB 5 s, 13 December 1945, cols 452–3. Cited by R N Gardner, *Sterling-Dollar Diplomacy* (Oxford 1956, reprinted with new, extended, Introduction 1969 & 1980), pp 65–66. Gardner perhaps goes too far in the direction of asserting that Article VII provided for the *'elimination'* of Imperial Preference (p 65), much as Sir John did in the opposite direction of thinking that it had only vaguely comprehended Imperial Preference in the proposed agreed action directed *'towards'* 'the elimination . . . of discriminatory treatment in international commerce . . .'. Gardner's exposition thus seems further to illustrate the consequences of the absence, albeit unavoidable, of an agreed and reasonably diffused Anglo-American explanation of Article VII.

CHAPTER 4

Implementing Article VII: The Preparation of Policies

(1) HESITATION ON IMPLEMENTATION

Although the broad guidelines for external economic policy became clear with the signing of the Mutual Aid Agreement in February 1942, serious and continuous thinking about specific post-war plans had already developed within the British Government under the stimulus of the exchanges over the Consideration. Implementation of the crucial Article VII seemed, however, to hang fire after the tension of the weeks preceding its final acceptance. Initially, the early conversations for which it provided were expected to commence in spring 1942[1], but there was instead a prolonged succession of uncertainties. There were, indeed, continuing exchanges in and between the two capitals, and there was to be a major allied Conference, that at Hot Springs in May and June 1943 on post-war food problems. Two and a half years were to elapse, however, from the enactment of Lend-Lease, and one and a half years from acceptance of Article VII, before comprehensive—though informal and non-committal—talks were to be held during September-October 1943 in Washington. But for the good though unfulfilled intentions voiced on both sides of the Atlantic to hold meetings much earlier, this might scarcely be regarded during a grim war as procrastination.

On the American side, several excuses or reasons can be excavated to explain the delay, the most compelling being possibly the Administration's need for time to evolve definite proposals. There was also the risk of diplomatic awkwardness in holding Article VII talks on an overtly Anglo-American basis when other countries had also been, or were being, persuaded to sign that article; and there was also the commitment of the USA, at Pan-American meetings, to inter-American discussions.[2] More domestic political hesitations arose characteristically ahead of forthcoming elections, in this case for Congress in November 1942. Moreover, there was anxiety not to compromise what was hoped to be scope, following those elections, for the wider initiatives in commercial policy that the biennial renewal of the Reciprocal Trade Agreements Act would offer in 1943, and which Mr Cordell Hull, the Secretary of State, hoped to exploit fully.[3] More negatively, the year 1942, with reverses in North Africa and above all with the fall of Singapore and Malaya, was bad both for British prestige and for British standing in the USA. Whilst Americans applauded the Britain of Dunkirk and after, the war in Asia had reminded many of a different, imperial, aspect which they detested; and this anti-imperial sentiment, echoed in American inclinations towards some form of post-war trusteeship for colonial territories, was a brake on Anglo-American collaboration.[4]

On the British side, thinking and plans appear to have been somewhat ahead by March 1942, but the delay, though worrying as it became prolonged, did provide time for clearer formulation of proposals; for attempts to clarify and to resolve domestic differences; to consult the Dominions and representatives of the Indian Government; and to have informal Anglo-American consultations before major plans were to be comprehensively considered.

(2) POST-WAR ECONOMIC PLANNING

Attention to post-war economic planning developed from several directions during 1941. A War Aims Committee of the Cabinet had existed since August 1940, and a Minister without Portfolio (Mr Arthur Greenwood) had been appointed at the end of the year to supervise its work. Concern with post-war problems arose also from the economic blockade.[5] Ministerial and official committees overseeing the resultant export surpluses of internationally traded commodities found themselves concerned with the future use of such surpluses in post-war relief. Further, in considering proposed international agreements during the war about a major commodity such as wheat, they were bound to be concerned with post-war economic policy generally, when such arrangements involved fundamental principles in trade policy.[6] Indeed, with the wheat discussions of 1941 specifically in mind, Mr Greenwood pointed out that post-war questions could not be avoided because in fact they were occurring already.[7] The proposals then floated for a Commission or group of 'Wise Men' to consider post-war policy were rejected.[8] Instead, at the Treasury's suggestion[9], an inter-departmental committee was formed in August 1941 on 'Post-War External Economic Problems and Anglo-American Co-operation'. Under the chairmanship of Sir George Chrystal*, from Mr Greenwood's office, the terms of reference[10] of the Chrystal Committee were 'to formulate the chief problems of post-war external economic policy with special reference to forthcoming discussions with the United States of America'. The Committee was to assemble memoranda and to prepare for Ministers the *desiderata* to be kept in mind during the expected talks.

---

* CHRYSTAL, George William, KCB 1922 (1880–1944); Permanent Secretary, Ministry of Health 1935–40; subsequently Secretary of Committee on Reconstruction Problems, Offices of the War Cabinet.

In practice, with the Committee's encouragement, the Treasury made the running, in organising the preparation of policy, which drew on the work of the Economic Section. In turn, the Economic Section drew on statistical information collated by the Bank of England as administrator of Exchange Control, by the Board of Trade, and by the Treasury itself from other departments and from other governments (see Appendix 27, 'Forecasting the Post-War Balance of Payments'). After its preliminary meeting on 7 August 1941, the Chrystal Committee did not meet formally until the end of the following April[11]. Meanwhile it received memoranda. That the Treasury tended to predominate was partly because the monetary arrangements were recognised to be fundamental, and partly because, under the inspiration of Keynes, the Treasury's contribution was wide in scope and imaginative in presentation. Indeed, discussion on post-war economic policies had been developing actively in the Treasury since spring 1941, when, warning that it was 'very sketchy and half-baked' the author of a brief note on the likely post-war 'exchange situation' had effectively identified the problems.[12] Not for the first time and very far from the last time their elements were recognised to consist of a pressure on living standards in face of the need for substantial domestic investment, under the international constraints of a seriously weakened British balance of payments and a very strong American balance of payments. Discussion intensified during the autumn of 1941 and the winter of 1941–2, in order to present to the Chrystal Committee a paper for the War Cabinet in preparation for the expected conversations on Article VII.

At first, the discussions stayed largely within the Treasury; other departments felt it to be essential to know the Treasury's approach before enlarging the debate.[13] When the debate broadened to include a number of other departments and the Bank of England, it revolved around four sets of documents. From the Treasury came notes on 'Post-War Trade and Financial Policy'.[14]

Keynes produced between September 1941 and January 1942 four drafts of his proposal for an International Clearing Union.[15] Mr (later Sir Hubert) Henderson's* reflections, to which his colleagues attached much weight, were embodied in a note on the balance of payments.[16] By no means least, as will become apparent, the Bank commented forthrightly from its viewpoint as operator of Exchange Control.[17]

Where broad agreement emerged was on the nature of the problem, although Keynes was subsequently, and as it proved prematurely, to evolve more optimistic views both of America's future balance of payments[18] and of the chance of lightening the burden of massive sterling

---

* HENDERSON, Hubert Douglas, Kt 1942 (1890–1952); Economic Adviser, HM Treasury, 1939–44; Professor of Political Economy, University of Oxford, 1945–51.

balances. Agreement emerged on the desirability of a system of international payments that would remedy the defects of pre-war arrangements. On this there was widespread though varying support for Keynes's proposals; these extended to the provision of international liquidity, the promotion of international investment, the moderation of cyclical fluctuations, especially in commodity prices and in producers' incomes, and the reduction of trade barriers.

Where disagreement of a fundamental character developed was over trade policy and, partly by association, over the relationship of policies in the immediate post-war period to possible international arrangements in the longer run. These differences were not resolved by February 1942, nor indeed by the end of the war. The issue was not a question of the timing of the implementation of new international schemes: that is, whether these should be introduced after a transition period, or, with reasonable qualifications, during the transition period itself. The preference of some, particularly of the Bank of England, was for the maintenance of wartime controls during the transition in the belief that these, together with pre-war experience under the Tripartite arrangements of 1936 (see below p 74) would provide a more satisfactory basis than some new scheme for the evolution of long-term arrangements. The differences were thus fundamental; they may be usefully illuminated in the context of discussions stimulated by Keynes's initial proposals of September 1941 for international collaboration, particularly that for an international clearing union.

Between 1941 and 1945 opinion on trade policy fluctuated, favouring initially a substantially controlled system of trade; then swinging with brief euphoria to favouring a more open economy before settling towards a system part-free, part-controlled. With his prestige, and back from over three months in Washington where he had quite thoroughly tested American reactions, Keynes in September 1941 presented in extreme form the two opposing approaches to post-war policy, conscious himself that somehow Britain should—must—avoid a 'non-American' policy. In an unwarrantably neglected excursus, which was a prologue to and more than half as long again as his clearing union plan, he elaborated what might be a 'Schachtian' necessity for detailed controls.[19] Though subsequently modified, its significance remained as an expression of contemporary British apprehensions and as a sombre premonition about Anglo-American relations which post-war events were partially to vindicate. Entitled 'Post-War Currency Policy', this prologue had four sections: 'The secular international problem', 'Our contemporary British problem', 'The analysis of the problem', and 'The alternatives before us'. Keynes dismissed as an historical misinterpretation the belief that 'currency *laissez-faire*' had in the past conduced to economic equilibrium and to the international division of labour. On the contrary, he argued that it had had a deflationary bias against the debtor countries.

In profound contrast to a system of detailed controls Keynes offered a bold scheme for international payments that promptly attracted the label of 'Utopia'. He claimed a three-fold virtue for his 'ideal system' which would solve the problem on multilateral lines by international agreement. It illuminated Britain's post-war difficulties; it showed what was necessary in an alternative to a Schachtian policy; and, if it met American aspirations, it would permit Britain to accept the commitment of Article VII against discrimination. In the shorter-run, however, Britain's acute disequilibrium would delay the introduction of some new system; Schachtian devices were therefore scarcely avoidable. Further, their use or the right to use them should not be renounced until an equally satisfactory alternative was assured for the longer run. Of profound significance for the evaluation of the Anglo-American negotiations at the end of the war were Keynes's expressions of scepticism as early as 1941 about three specific hopes of underpinning from the USA. One, to be revived by Keynes himself at the end of the war, was the hope of 'liberal relief', for 'we should have been helped during the war; it is the others who will be helped afterwards'. Second, significant tariff reductions or restraints on American agricultural exports should not be expected. Third, greatly helpful as a continuously high level of American employment and demand would be, it was too soon to be able to place reliance on that being achieved.

The proximate rationale of this scepticism about future international arrangements was anxiety about the limited awareness in America of Britain's problems, and despair over the restrictionist and discriminatory American proposals during the summer of 1941 for a new International Wheat Agreement. How could Britain in such circumstances abjure discrimination under the proposed Article VII? In default of the bold and more satisfactory alternative he was about to propose, Keynes echoed his earlier paper on 'A New Order' (above, pp 18 – 19). He asserted that a solution lay in Dr Schacht's 'discovery', when in desperation over German balance of payments problems during the inter-war years, of 'something new which had in it the germs of a good technical idea'. Taking up remarks of Mr Henderson, Keynes suggested that Schachtianism could be used for securing butter no less than guns. The prescription was for 'barter-bilateralism'. On a general rather than on a commodity by commodity basis, Britain should seek to refuse imports except where the country concerned would agree to spend the receipts on British exports. There seemed to be scope for such deals with countries for whose products Britain was the principal market, Argentina and her meat being a favourite example. Such arrangements need not be strictly bilateral, but could encompass groups of countries. Bulk purchase would similarly exploit British market strength. The wartime system of payments and clearing agreements could be developed further and, indeed, would be necessary to control the huge overseas sterling balances. More explicit exchange controls on capital movements would be essential to prevent the recurrence of the pre-war disruptive movement of 'hot-money'.

What was the alternative? The plan for an international clearing union proposed the concentration of foreign exchange in the members' central banks, which would clear accounts with other central banks through the Union's 'International Clearing Bank'. A member could meet a shortage of international currency by drawing on the clearing bank within a generous quota system, and if necessary, and possibly compulsorily, by a limited devaluation. In general, alterations in exchange rates were to be kept to a minimum; the aim was to secure exchange rate stability. A persistent debtor might have to withdraw from the Union. To avoid the defect attributed to the old 'currency *laissez faire*' arrangements, that they were biased against debtors, the first draft of the plan proposed that persistent creditors would be compelled to appreciate their currencies, and to transfer excessive balances to the international clearing bank's reserve fund.

Although the clearing union and other international schemes were to capture particular attention, the immediate reality was that extensive controls had been developed for war purposes, and that some controls would be necessary in the transition. Thus, some compromise had to be sought. In a note on the lessons of the 1930s Mr Henderson of the Treasury argued in August 1941 for such a compromise, but of a semi-permanent rather than of a transitional character. This was condemned by another Treasury voice for its Schachtian implications. A further Treasury voice was to stress that the USA might accept exchange control from Britain after the war, but not discrimination against the dollar. From the Board of Trade it was pointed out that the Schachtian solution in Germany had rested on default or repudiation of international debts; the Bank of England was later to note that it had also relied on Germany's relatively compact trading area, whereas Britain's was looser and more scattered geographically.[20] Despite the frankly admitted Utopianism of the Clearing Union, the neatness of an avowedly Schachtian alternative quickly dissolved. Keynes himself was soon to back away from what he came to see as 'the horrid complications and complicated horrors' of bilateralism,[21] in order to concentrate his own advocacy and to mobilise that of the Treasury behind the Clearing Union.

The case for significant economic controls did not, however, disappear if only, as a Treasury paper in late September 1941 said of exchange control, 'for the plain reason that there is nothing else to do' in face of Britain's likely post-war position.[22] There was, indeed, a widespread acceptance in the discussions of a general case for the right to use controls to regulate economic activity, though there was uncertainty about their particular applications. Indeed, an unusual argument came from Mr Henderson, who in general was gravely concerned with the need for exchange and import controls as well as (in the case of colonial territories) for Imperial Preference. At one stage he argued, without convincing his colleagues, that scarcities during the transition period would mean that quantitative restrictions on imports would be redundant and that, equally, Imperial Preference might not matter; controls should be held in reserve for subsequent eventualities.[23] The most powerful advocacy for controls, strongly flavoured with Schachtianism in all but name, came with the forthrightness of confident monetary technicians from the Bank of England. The Bank commented approvingly on Keynes's 'Schachtian' essay. Given that Britain would be an open economy with low reserves, exchange control was essential, particularly to protect London's function as the centre of the international payments mechanism of the sterling area. Whereas, however, exchange controls in Germany could be centralised, the distinctive nature of the sterling system depended upon a variety of local arrangements, including administration of exchange control by commercial banks, and relied ultimately on 'standards of commercial and financial conduct . . . high enough to dispense with regimentation on the German model'. In reassurance, the Bank stressed that such exchange control would not be an innovation, but 'a natural development . . . with which the country had been experimenting since 1931'. It would require support, however, from a policy of trade regulation including discrimination and, if high tariffs were to be avoided, quantitative restriction of imports.[24] These were essentially technical arguments from the managers of the country's foreign exchange reserves. It was to prove difficult to escape such arguments, which were to influence discussions on the Clearing Union proposals during 1941–3, and those on the pattern of post-war external policy during the later stages of the war.

The Board of Trade was rather more eclectic than the Bank, although its conclusions also pointed towards a case for controls when it gave its views to the Treasury in a memorandum by Mr R J Shackle* early in 1942.[25] The Board preferred a post-war world of multilateral trade to one of bilateralism if suitable monetary arrangements (eg, the Clearing Union) made the former possible. It warned, however, of the dangers in the multilateral, free trade, and non-discriminatory policies advocated by Mr Cordell Hull. For instance, there were risks in the uncontrolled use of the most-favoured-nation

* SHACKLE, Robert Jones, (1895–1950); Principal Assistant Secretary Board of Trade, 1942–47; Under-Secretary, Board of Trade, from 1947.

clause in trade treaties, which might operate unfairly as it had done in the past. Imperial Preference was 'primarily political'. Import restrictions would be justified to operate commodity agreements, to deal with competition from low-cost countries, and in connection with the clearing arrangements involved when trading with countries using exchange controls. A special note, apparently prepared by Mr H Clay*, on 'The Commercial Policy of the United Kingdom', paralleled Mr Henderson's arguments in the Treasury.[26] It expressed grave apprehensions that the USA would seek to repeat the policies of the 1920s, which, he averred, would conduce to excessive contraction of income when the trade outlook was poor. Policies such as high tariffs or Schachtian methods to maintain domestic activity appeared impractical, so that the only choice for the United Kingdom appeared to be a degree of barter-bilateralism 'aimed at maintaining the maximum area of freedom of trade consistent with preventing a resumption of the depressed conditions which characterised British export districts between the wars.' A particular justification offered for trade controls was that the sources of trade depression were otherwise beyond British control.

The attempt to reconcile the differing approaches to post-war problems involved two main and obviously associated problems. One was the problem of maintaining adequate employment: how best to blend the determination to exercise domestic control with schemes for international controls and co-operation; and how to be reasonably confident that the management of the United States economy would avoid the export of world-wide depression. Mr Bevin,[†] Minister of Labour and National Service, and a notable trade union leader, was to express particular apprehension of a return to something like the old gold standard, with the danger that some new international organisation would impose deflationary policies and unemployment; he told Keynes that the gold standard 'in the last analysis, was what drove him, against his natural inclinations, to fight [in support of] the General Strike' of 1926. Keynes therefore drafted a safeguarding passage, its inclusion being a condition of the War Cabinet's approval of the Clearing Union proposals.[27] The unease about American economic fluctuations was another, much more worrying matter. Two

---

* CLAY, Henry, Kt, 1946 (1883–1954); Jevons Professor of Political Economy University of Manchester, 1922–27 and of Social Economics, 1927–30; Securities Management Trust, 1930–33; Economic Adviser to the Governors of the Bank of England, 1933–44; seconded to be Economic Adviser to the Board of Trade 1941–44; Warden of Nuffield College Oxford, 1944–49.
† BEVIN, Ernest, (1881–1951); Minister of Labour and National Service, 1940–45; Secretary of State for Foreign Affairs, 1945–51.

American economists, Professor Alvin H Hansen* and Luther Gulick†, had sought to reassure Whitehall in talks in London during August 1941, and in subsequent elaboration of proposals for international co-operation on employment, the use of resources, and on economic development. Not wholly unwelcoming, London felt little confidence that such proposals had sufficient support in the American Administration, and was in any case sceptical of their practicability.[28]

The second problem concerned the relationship between short-term, post-war arrangements and longer-term schemes. On this issue, Keynes soon came to moderate his fascination with wartime controls; they were 'a patched-up contrivance', sustainable in the transition, but were not a satisfactory basis for a permanent system.[29] In contrast, the Bank of England, as has been seen, regarded them as part of an evolutionary process, which could be further developed. Should British policy, then, aim in the transition to work at once towards a new system, or should it recognise with the Bank that to introduce 'an automatic monetary mechanism' might mean an attempt to evade balance of payments problems? On the latter view, would it not be better to build international arrangements on the Tripartite Agreement of 1936 and on the wartime system of monetary and payments agreements? In retrospect the Bank's views can be seen as an accurate forecast of what lay ahead in the post-war years. In 1941–2, however, the pressures of Article VII virtually dictated that an attempt at a more ambitious programme be undertaken. In consequence the Bank's sustained and patiently presented apprehensions about the boldness and enthusiasm attaching to the post-war monetary and trade schemes, though far from being without influence, had a limited impact on the main *direction* of official policy. Thus, Keynes and the Treasury continued to grapple with Britain's post-war problems by taking an active lead in devising schemes to fire American as well as British imaginations—'The more we look at the alternatives, the less we like them'.[30]

(3) THE DRAFTS OF THE CLEARING UNION PLAN

The clarification of ideas and the drawing up of the issues for further debate can be seen conveniently through the successive

---

* HANSEN, Alvin Harvey, (1887–1975); Chairman, US-Canadian Joint Economic Committee, 1941–1943; Special Economic Adviser, Federal Reserve Board, 1940–45.
† GULICK, Luther Halsey, (b. 1892) Government administrator; consultant chief of staff War Dept, 1940–42; staff War Production Board, 1940–44; assistant to director Smaller War Plants Corporation, 1943–44; consultant numerous governmental agencies, administrator various governmental organisations for research and investigation, during and following World War II; member staff US Reparations Mission, 1945 and 1946.

drafts between September 1941 and February 1942 of Keynes's Clearing Union proposal, and in the much longer Treasury memorandum on 'External Monetary and Economic Policy' (the 'Treasury sandwich') in which it was embodied.[31] For convenience, reference will be made to the first four drafts of the Clearing Union plan of September, November, and December 1941, and of January 1942, as I, II, III, IV respectively. It may be as well to stress that concern here is with the evolution of British policy and not with a technical detailed exposition of the Clearing Union proposals as such.

Increasingly concerned that British and American policies for the post-war world should find 'common ground', Keynes looked towards international arrangements within which specific British problems would be less intractable. To stress this he urged, in a declaration that was later to be set aside, that after the war Britain should not become a supplicant for yet more American aid (II, III, IV), although if US intentions were appropriately generous, it might be better for Lend-Lease and relief to continue for perhaps two years until the Clearing Union could operate (IV). 'The assistance for which we can hope must be *indirect* and a consequence of setting the world as a whole on its feet and of laying the foundations of a sounder political economy between all nations' (II, III, IV). The alternatives were unattractive, not least the reliance which some wanted to place on a development of the wartime sterling area. Challenging without naming the Bank of England he asserted that such arrangements would involve bilateral agreements, strict controls, and severe tensions between Britain and some sterling area countries in the effort to control the use of sterling balances. In contrast, a multilateral payments system, such as the Clearing Union, would sustain the liquidity of balances. It would in this respect reproduce the best features of the gold standard, and its atmosphere of freedom would be far more congenial than that of a tightly controlled sterling bloc to the traditional role of the City of London (III, IV). Exchange control on capital movements would be unavoidable, in view of pre-war experience (I, II, III, IV). Broadly, however, the proposed international arrangements would amount to 'financial disarmament' (III, IV), subject to a transition period of three to five years following their adoption (II), and subject also to the right of recourse to trade controls, etc, in cases of prolonged balance of payments difficulties (II). It was over this crucial problem of trade controls, to the retention of which many participants in the Treasury discussions attached so much importance, that the Clearing Union proposals struggled hardest for a compromise. In a first leap towards Mr Hull's desires, the Clearing Union suggested a virtual prohibition of controls, together with a ceiling of 25 per cent *ad valorem* on tariffs and preferences (II). It offered two solvents of fears about domestic employment and over the denial of defensive measures. One involved the association with the Clearing Union of policies to underpin its multilateralism and to impart to the world economy both stability and expansion. These included the maintenance of high levels of employment and income, along lines advocated by the American economists A H Hansen and L H Gulick (II, III, IV); the same authors' proposals for an international (or initially an Anglo-American) investment board to operate anti-cyclically (II, III, IV) in which was the germ, developed by Mr R F Harrod,* of the eventual International Bank for Reconstruction and Development; relief and reconstruction schemes in the immediate post-war years (II, III, IV); and commodity controls to moderate fluctuations in prices and incomes (II, III, IV). Such schemes could be operated in conjunction with and possibly be financed in part by the proposed Clearing Union. The second attempted solvent was the proposal in the later of these drafts largely to abandon the explicit outlawry originally envisaged for trade controls, and to allow them more respectability. Members of the proposed Clearing Union would use their respective debit or credit positions in the Union, ie, the state of their balances of payments, to indicate the appropriateness of a temporary relaxation of the prohibitions in any commercial treaties between them of various expedients (III, IV). Against the possibility of abuse there might be a requirement for approval by the Union's governing body, and also for a general subscription in commercial treaties to the principle that import controls, barter, export controls, and 'excessive tariffs' were undesirable (IV). Finally, the emotive matter of preferences should be treated as beyond the scope of the Clearing Union (IV).

The Treasury paper enfolding the Clearing Union plan assembled for Ministers the questions to be settled if progress were to be made. Early progress was desirable for several reasons: the German propaganda for a New Order, the need to be prepared with policies when the war abated, and above all the expectation of early Anglo-American discussions on Article VII. The paper ranged over the issues in the light of the continuing debate and in terms of the lines along which Anglo-American discussions might develop. After providing a summary for those not concerned with details, the Treasury expounded the country's probable external difficulties after the war on the basis of a report (reproduced as an appendix) by the Economic Section of the War Cabinet Offices. Entitled 'The

---

* HARROD, Roy Forbes, Kt, 1959 (1900–78); Economist, Christ Church Oxford; Mr Churchill's private statistical staff in Admiralty, 1939–40; Prime Minister's Office, 1940–42, and subsequently in advisory capacity; statistical adviser to Admiralty, 1943–45; Economic Adviser, International Monetary Fund, 1952–53.

United Kingdom's Post-War Balance of Payments', this analysis was to underlie much future discussion. It estimated that there would be a total potential external deficit of around £1,000 million during the first five years of peace. On the assumption that Lend-Lease and Canadian Mutual Aid would end with the war, the possibilities of closing the gap satisfactorily depended largely on the hope of substantial increases in exports. There would remain, nevertheless, the risk of continuing difficulties, which might involve both further efforts to increase exports and a restriction of imports. The Treasury echoed the concern of the Clearing Union scheme lest the strong American balance of payments expected after the war should intensify disequilibrium in world trade. It approached this problem by first examining briefly the 'Possible United States contribution to the Solution of the General Problem'. As a preliminary, it wondered, somewhat doubtfully, whether American public opinion after the war would support the Administration's existing 'readiness...to act as fairy godmother to the post-war world'. Gifts or loans of America's excess gold, and lending in general might be available, but carried the danger of encouraging postponement of fundamental domestic adjustment. 'A great programme of foreign long-term lending for sound productive purposes' would certainly be welcome. Too much should not be expected, however, from an admittedly desirable reduction in American tariffs. Under American law, this would require reciprocal concessions; moreover, British exports would not only have to compete with competitors also enjoying tariffs cuts, but as they tended to be luxury goods they were sensitive less to price changes than to 'conditions of prosperity' in the USA. Hence, concluded the Treasury, 'a main way in which the United States could assist the world is by maintaining a high level of internal industrial activity and employment'.

This cautious assessment led the Treasury to warn that the country would probably have 'to rely largely' upon its own efforts. There was consequently a need to retain trade controls. This did not involve an espousal of bilateralism, the hazards of which the paper stressed, but neither could 'unqualified multilateralism' be entertained, for three particular reasons. First, there could be only limited resort to exchange depreciation to correct payments disequilibrium, given the probability of retaliation, the closer linkage of money wages to living costs, and the major constraint upon exchange rates required for the effective working of the sterling monetary system. Hence, quantitative controls might have to be used instead. Second, state trading and anti-cyclical state intervention in Britain and elsewhere were likely to restrict the scope for unregulated trade. Third, American toleration of preferential systems elsewhere (ie, between the USA and the then-American territory of the Philippines), and also of the closer associations of customs or economic unions, would embody a contradiction, indeed a danger, if Britain were nonetheless to be pressed under Article VII to abjure as 'discriminatory' her own system of Imperial Preference.

The obvious message for future policy, that the path forward must be one of delicate compromise, was re-inforced by 'the consideration, to which almost overriding importance must be attached, that it is essential to avoid a head-on collision with the United States'. Wrapped thus in sombre swaddling clothes, the Clearing Union plan was proffered to ministers not as a means of salvation but primarily, as Keynes had originally urged, as an illuminant of major problems and as a basis for discussion. There would be two distinct tasks, each with two aspects. First, it would be essential to persuade the USA of Britain's exceptional post-war problems; then the USA must be persuaded of more general arguments against unqualified multilateralism. Second, in tackling the implementation of Article VII, a distinction should be observed between its two branches. In view of the possibility of differences over trade controls, etc, it would be advisable to mark time on that aspect, and to seek to deal initially with the first branch of Article VII, that concerning broad and improved economic arrangements in the post-war world. The memorandum hoped for ministerial approval for its main themes to be released in the expected Anglo-American discussions, and also sought approval for consultation beforehand with representatives of the Dominion and Indian Governments.

Anti-climax now lay ahead.

(4) SLOW PROGRESS IN 1942

The Treasury memorandum, the arrangement of its arguments being different from that above, with an eye to its official and political readership, duly passed through the Cabinet at the beginning of May 1942, and received ministerial blessing for use on a non-committal basis in Anglo-American talks.[32] But *when* would there be such talks? There were, indeed, regular exchanges between 'resident' American and British officials in London and in Washington. There were to be visits, official or unofficial in varying degrees, between the two capitals. There was the usual flow of reports from the respective embassies. These contacts did not, however, constitute the conversations 'at an early and convenient date' which the second paragraph of Article VII had envisaged, and to which 'the Treasury sandwich' was intended to be the *hors d'oeuvre*. What was so unsettling to British hopes during 1942 and in the first eight months of 1943, what was so unconducive to mutual understanding, to mutual trust, and to eventual agreement between Britain and the USA, was a succession of delays, disappointments, and seeming prevarications over these proposed conversations. In a limited sense, certainly, discussions might have appeared premature inasmuch as they would necessarily have been restricted to generalities until detailed policies had been formulated; indeed, the Clearing Union was the one proposal in the Treasury sandwich with much shape, but even that required much detailed elaboration. Yet it was precisely the discussion of generalities that had seemed desirable to both Britain and the USA during the agonising of 1941–42 over the precise wording and significance of Article VII. Moreover, on specific issues there were arguably the strongest possible reasons for joint, rather than separate evolution of post-war policies, in the common memories of the unsatisfactory peace settlement of 1919, in the determination to avoid repeating the economic miseries of the inter-war years, and in the awareness (stronger perhaps in Britain, with her drastically weakened balance of payments) of the problems created directly by the war. In the event, there was unexpected delay before there were any real discussions; then the discussions were for some time limited to specific issues; when at last, during September and October 1943, there were wider-ranging talks, these were still informal, non-committal and preparatory in nature. There was to be no really comprehensive economic conference, as distinct from conferences on special topics, throughout the period of hostilities.

The first imperative is to describe and to try to explain the delays which coloured the background against which discussion developed. In the autumn of 1941, during the exchanges over the content of Article VII, there had been unease amongst some members of the British Government over the possibility that other members of it were dragging their feet over the holding of genuine discussions with the USA (above pp 33, 40–41). The Treasury, however, had envisaged discussions on the implementation of Article VII for the spring of 1942. As that approached, a date in April 1942 was in mind; Mr Winant, the American Ambassador in London, was expected to return from a visit to Washington with some American experts. Names of such experts were picked over critically in London.[33] Mr Winant stressed the informal character of the expected talks. The Foreign Office echoed this in repeating the Foreign Secretary's earlier wish for wide-ranging non-committal talks by informed but non-specialist people; it was anxious for talks that would remove suspicions that Britain did not look to the same economic goals as the USA; the stress on non-specialists appeared to reflect some concern lest there be a repetition of Keynes's abrasive treatment in June 1941 of post-war questions.[34] London wondered, however, whether the proposed American team would carry much weight; the senior British Treasury official even worried whether it was too soon for such talks; and then Mr Winant returned to London in April without the team.[35] Keynes, with the premonitory qualification of 'not before the end of May' now looked for talks by about mid-summer.[36] Mr Winant was explicitly short on optimism.[37] He continued to press Washington, and the possibility of a rather different and stronger American visiting team was floated, but he was warning the Chancellor in May 1942 that, despite the approval by the President and by Mr Morgenthau, Secretary of the Treasury, of the proposed visit by experts,

> 'conversations would be inconclusive and that we [the British] should have to do a good deal of teaching. He rather ominously suggested that nothing would emerge until we had made a return visit to Washington'.

Amongst the reasons which underlay the American desire to mark time, not least was an *impasse* in the Administration over Lend-Lease matters, which could well have been reproduced in any major Anglo-American discussions. In particular, the President had refused to take over pre-Lend-Lease contracts, thereby destroying a hope which had encouraged Britain's recent acceptance of Article VII (above p 58). Unhelpful also was Britain's poor standing because of her military setbacks in the Far East.[38] The State Department therefore seemed relieved at an opportunity in May 1942, to the evident dismay of Mr Winant, to soft-pedal on the elusive London talks on learning of a prospective visit by Mr Richard Law*, the Foreign Under-Secretary; he was to be accompanied by Mr Nigel Ronald†, the Foreign Office specialist on economic affairs.[39] Moreover, the British Treasury's principal representative, Sir Frederick Phillips, was shortly to return to London; it was suggested that he could inform each side of the other's views.[40] All too clearly the prospects for talks were vanishing. There now was added unexpected delay from the British side. First, the parliamentary timetable held back Mr Law's departure for the USA; and then, following visits to London and Washington by the Russian Foreign Minister, diplomatic prudence indicated a further pause, lest Mr Law seem to be reporting on Russian diplomatic

---

* LAW, Richard Kidston, 1st Baron Coleraine, 1954 (1901–80); Financial Secretary, War Office, 1940–41; Parliamentary Under-Secretary of State, Foreign Office, 1941–43; Minister of State, Foreign Office, 1943–45; Minister of Education, 1945; Leader of United Kingdom Delegation, International Food Conference, Hot Springs and of Mission for Article VII talks in Washington, 1943.

† RONALD, Nigel Bruce KCMG 1946 (1894–1973); Counsellor, Foreign Office, 1939; Assistant Under-Secretary, 1942; Ambassador to Portugal, 1947–54.

activity.[41] By now (June 1942) Sir Frederick Phillips had reported in London his doubts about persuading the United States to hold discussions.[42] He had, however, brought from the State Department a suggested agenda for Article VII talks—'the Pasvolsky agenda' (Mr Leo Pasvolsky,* Special Assistant to the Secretary of State, was chairman of the relevant committee). The British Treasury turned the agenda inside out; the two partners appeared to be far apart in their respective approaches to post-war economic policies.[43] The Chancellor of the Exchequer now doubted whether Mr Law's twice-frustrated visit should ever take place;[44] he did not appear to him to be the appropriate minister to discuss the topics at issue, 'and in any event we should still aim at getting the Americans here'.

That the chance of 'getting the Americans here' was disappearing, Lord Halifax warned from the Washington Embassy at the end of June 1942: Mr Cordell Hull and Mr Sumner Welles, Under-Secretary of State, felt that they were unlikely to be ready for discussions for two or three months.[45]

Mr Redvers Opie,† the Embassy's economist, increased this to three or four months, in view of the differences—and apparent indifference also—within the Administration; he evidently expected an American suggestion to have discussions in Washington.[46] Sir Frederick Phillips, back in the USA in early July, was more emphatic:[47] if there were to be any talks at all, they would have to be in Washington, 'unless there is a complete change here, which I do not expect...'. He sought and received permission, however, as 'our only means of making progress', to disclose the Clearing Union scheme to the State Department, where he had a meeting for this purpose a few days later, although he did not provide a copy of the scheme until Mr Law brought over the latest draft during August.[48]

By mid-1942 then, there seemed to be no early prospect of London talks, nor indeed of wide-ranging talks at all. Instead, the limited exchanges initiated by Sir Frederick Phillips were to be largely typical of Anglo-American formation of post-war economic policies, although this did not become wholly clear at the time. Once the Congressional elections were over, Mr Cordell Hull was in fact to declare, early in November 1942, his continuing interest in 'informal and explanatory conversations, without commitments or publicity' on

* PASVOLSKY, Leo (1893–1953); Economist and US government official; 1936 appointed special assistant to Secretary of State Cordell Hull and forwarded the reciprocal trade agreements programme; 1939 co-ordinator of studies on resources of foreign countries; 1941 chief of the Division of Special Research and director of the Committee on Postwar Problems.
† OPIE, Redvers (1900–1984); Counsellor and Economic Adviser to British Embassy, Washington, DC until 1946; Adviser, UK Delegation, International Food Conference, Hot Springs, 1943; UK Delegate, UN Monetary and Financial Conference Bretton Woods, 1944.

Article VII matters.[49] With some British unease about the low pitch of such exchanges, preparations were made, and January 1943 was the expected time. Again there was postponement. Then, in February, shortly after Lord Keynes had been wondering if substantive talks would ever take place[50], President Roosevelt announced, to widespread surprise and to the profound disappointment of the British Treasury, the calling of a United Nations Conference on the specific and apparently minor topic of nutrition. The immediate rationale of this was to provide a testing ground for allied co-operation without putting at risk some major element in post-war economic planning, by discussion of a subject which nevertheless commanded wide popular interest, and which had been floated for some time on both sides of the Atlantic as deserving close attention.[51] Moreover, the presence of allied representatives in the USA for this conference—on Food and Agriculture at Hot Springs, Virginia, during May and early June 1943—was to provide an opportunity for subsequent discussions, albeit ill-organised, on other matters such as relief, monetary problems, and commercial policy.

Before examining these developments, it is as well to register more firmly the apparent reasons for the postponement of the discussions that had originally been anticipated, and for the adoption of a partial rather than a comprehensive treatment of post-war policies. In July 1942 Lord Halifax had attributed the delays 'wholly to the fact that the United States are not ready'.[52] This appeared to be correct if two senses of the evaluation be distinguished, the second being potentially the more serious from the British viewpoint. First, in addition to the protestations of sensitivity about the feelings of other allies, Mr Cordell Hull in August told the British Minister in Washington, Sir Ronald Campbell*, that at a militarily disastrous period there was 'bitter feeling' about the alleged diversion of effort from waging the war to engage in possibly futile discussions about post-war policies.[53] With the autumn Congressional elections doubtless foremost in his mind (as well, no doubt, as Washington's memory of the mishandling of the Versailles settlement in 1919 – 20) Mr Cordell Hull stressed the great need, 'second only to. . .winning the war', to carry the electorate along with any post-war planning. This led him to a profoundly cautious conclusion: although the US Administration looked to eventual conferences, the time for them had not arrived. It would be ready to have talks with representatives from Great Britain or from

---

* CAMPBELL, Ronald Ian, KCMG 1941 (1890 – 1983); Minister in Washington, 1941 – 45; an Assistant Under-Secretary of State in the Foreign Office, 1945 – 46; Deputy to Secretary of State for Foreign Affairs on Council of Foreign Ministers, 1945 – 46; British Ambassador to Egypt, 1946 – 50.

any other of the United Nations, but these would be informal, unofficial, and would involve no decisions. Mr Hull repeated these views, qualified only in relation to his recognition of urgency over plans for post-war relief in Europe, to Mr Law when the latter, after yet another delay, at last reached Washington about ten days later.[54]

Was prudence in timing really all? There appeared to be a second sense in which the US Administration was far from ready. 'The Pasvolsky agenda' had suggested to the British Treasury that the American approach to post-war problems was much more piecemeal than the British search for fundamentals. Whereas the former began with consideration of the post-war balance of payments problems of the United Kingdom and of other countries, and only circumspectly involved general principles, the latter favoured priority for attention to be concentrated on the causes of the international disequilibrium experienced before the war. A wide-ranging view of world economic problems undoubtedly animated members of the US administration, but the apparent preference for a step-by-step treatment was not shared in Britain. This contrast was partly the result of differences within the State Department, where 'a drawn battle' had produced the *impasse* in discussions during summer 1942.[55] More generally, the contrast reflected the much greater diffusion of power and decision in the American political structure; the hazards which this involved in decision making fostered a preference for the concentration of bargaining power upon two-party ('bilateral') negotiations rather than risk its dissipation upon many-party ('multilateral') negotiations. Not least, as reflected in the choice of food and nutrition as the subject for the first major conference, the President's political judgement, to which in so many other ways Britain was indebted, led him to adopt a gradual, roundabout, and above all cautious approach to discussions on major issues.

How significant was the protracted manoeuvring between London and Washington over the elusive talks? Was the American 'unreadiness' a hard fact which left no choice but to follow a piecemeal approach? This is not self-evident. The urgent concern about talks in 1942 – 3 that was voiced, for example, by Mr Eden, the Foreign Secretary, envisaged a wide non-committal exchange of views, not to secure a precipitate commitment to specific policies but to ensure genuine co-operation in devising them.[56] It is far from clear, however, that such co-operation was feasible. Each country had its distinctive problems and faced its own domestic political complications, while the administration of so imaginative a piece of international co-operation as Lend-Lease repeatedly threw up reminders of the close boundaries of inter-allied harmony. In the event, it was scarcely surprising that consultation and co-operation occurred largely over post-war policies that had been separately devised. Since their preparation, and the securing of a degree of domestic consensus on them, took considerable time, the regret of contemporaries that there was not closer Anglo-American co-operation must be distinguished from impatience at the slowness of decision; the one was understandable, the other perhaps uncomprehending.

(5) RELIEF, COMMODITIES, MONEY AND TRADE

Four main lines of post-war policy were to emerge from the preparations of 1941–2 and in the discussions between the United Kingdom, the USA, and other allies which began in 1943. These concerned relief for the populations of territories affected by the war; proposals to moderate fluctuations in the prices of commodities and in the incomes of their producers; new international monetary arrangements; and commercial policy. So closely interconnected were they all that the order of their presentation is inevitably somewhat arbitrary. Just how interconnected became clear in the evolution of plans for relief. Although not the most important in the long view, they were logically the first to be considered, especially because relief was likely to be required in liberated territories before the formal end of the war, and discussions quickly revealed the need to think about the three other aspects of policy. Following Mr Churchill's pledge of August 1940 to ensure relief for those to be liberated eventually from enemy occupation, a ministerial committee on surpluses was formed, to be concerned with building up relief supplies.[57] About a year later, an inter-allied body was formed to co-ordinate action and to study possible policies.[58]

Relief became one of the many subjects aired in Washington during Keynes's visit in May-July 1941, when the involvement of wider issues became apparent. At first, attention had focused on the surpluses of commodities that had already accumulated and were expected to continue to do so, as a result of economic blockade and of shipping constraints. By 1941, however, there had also accumulated, and were expected to continue to do so, very large sterling balances due to various sterling area countries. American apprehension lest there be some arrangement to trade commodity surpluses against the gradual use of such balances, thus protracting trade and exchange restrictions, led to proposals for some Anglo-American sharing in the purchase of surpluses.[59] This raised the question of financing. Two solutions aired were to be rejected. One would have associated relief finance in some way with the proposed new international monetary arrangements being explored from 1941; thus, the Clearing Union proposal envisaged the provision of finance for relief. American preference for keeping short-run and long-run arrangements separate, and specifically for not entangling 'relief and rehabilitation' with reconstruction, ensured the demise of this approach.[60] A second possibility was to use Lend-Lease procedures;[61] here, even more, was a non-starter since it was impossible to know whether the American Administration could continue Lend-Lease, at least in its original form, after the war.

As the need for a special organisation for relief emerged, however it was to be financed, there was a proposal from Keynes in September 1941 for a 'Relief and Reconstruction Fund', which was embodied the following month in a Treasury memorandum.[62] During the following months, British concern about the financing of relief intensified with the realisation that surpluses were disappearing and that scarcities were more likely. Further, the spread of war to the Far East had added a vast new area to the relief problem. Not least, growing concern with Britain's likely post-war balance of payments difficulties fostered Treasury caution about commitments to finance relief. It was essential, the Chancellor told the President of the Board of Trade (Mr Hugh Dalton*), a proponent along with the Foreign Secretary (Mr Anthony Eden) of major outlays on relief, to discuss such expenditure within the constraints of our balance of payments and in the light of the Article VII discussions then expected about post-war financial and economic policy.[63]

American thinking, which had been moving towards a special organisation for relief and to special arrangements for financing it, led to a memorandum being sent to the British Government in May 1942.[64] By autumn, Anglo-American discussions in Washington had produced a draft agreement for a 'United Nations Relief and Rehabilitation Administration' (UNRRA), the broad lines of which were approved by the War Cabinet.[65] Further drafts and much discussion on organisation and administration were to occupy the next twelve months; but by November 1943, after an Allied conference at Atlantic City, an agreement was signed by representatives of 44 governments to establish UNRRA.[66]

For Britain there were in the UNRRA scheme two elements in particular that combined some reassurance and some hazard for the post-war period. One was the provision, limiting in principle the financial burden, for each member country to contribute one per cent of its national income. Relief was not, however, to be provided to western European countries; it would be directed to those of the south and east. This embodied a treble hazard: the relief funds

---

* DALTON, Edward Hugh John Neale, 1st Baron 1960 (1887–1962); Minister of Economic Warfare, 1940–42; President of Board of Trade, 1942–45; Chancellor of the Exchequer, 1945–47; Chancellor of the Duchy of Lancaster, 1948–50; Minister of Town and Country Planning, 1950–51; Minister of Local Government and Planning, 1951.

might prove inadequate; the western European countries' own needs might be greater than their own resources could readily bear; and, for Britain perhaps most of all, there was no telling yet whether there would be significant American aid for her own recovery needs and, indirectly, to enable her to pay her contribution to UNRRA. A second element in the relief arrangement was the lack of financial provision for relief in enemy territories, during the period of military occupation. There was an evident risk that Britain would be committed to paying for occupied Germany's food when unable to see how to pay for her own.[67] This premonition was to be amply justified in the immediate post-war years.

(6) COMMODITY POLICY

The need for a policy to influence markets for primary products had emerged early in the war as a problem in its own right, distinct, that is, from more dramatic aspirations for a better world. The economic blockade and shipping difficulties had caused the accumulation of surplus commodities. From one angle this raised problems for many colonial producers, while from another it promised welcome resources for relief. Stretching back, however, into the peace years were much longer-term problems of fluctuations in prices and in producers' incomes, and problems also of appropriate policies to influence markets without damage to world trade.[68] All these had become particularly acute in the decade or so before the war. Indeed, in 1938 Keynes, pointing to the severity of fluctuations in commodity prices, and between scarcity and abundance, had proposed the holding of stocks to moderate them.[69] In an atmosphere of approaching war, he linked the proposal to the desirability of accumulating stocks of essential commodities in Britain. A specially appointed committee investigated the scheme, but declared it to be unnecessary.[70] The basic principle, however, of the variation of central holdings of stocks—a buffer-stock system—to moderate price fluctuations, was scarcely assailable. Hence, when commodity problems attracted consideration in post-war planning, Keynes had at hand (as with other matters) virtually a ready-made scheme.

The occasion emerged when in August 1941 the Chrystal Committee on Post-War External Economic Problems included a study of 'international commodity regulation schemes' amongst its tasks.[71] At that stage, this was regarded as falling primarily within the sphere of the Colonial Office and of the Official Committee (of the Ministry of Economic Warfare) on Export Surpluses. Both had for some time been concerned with the issue. In neither case could it be said that a restricted view had been taken, but the necessity for a wider setting was recognised, particularly because of the financing problems, as well as of the lack of sufficient staff in the Colonial

Office.[72] The need was for adequate financial mechanisms as well as for a supply of finance; both needs seemed to be initially met by the wide sweep of the early drafts of autumn 1941 for an International Clearing Union, with their suggestions for using its machinery to finance stabilisation in commodity prices. Keynes, having undertaken that a detailed scheme would be forthcoming, produced a first draft by January 1942.[73] By mid-1942, after much discussion between ministries, this had reached its sixth draft and the status of a printed paper.[74] There was much further discussion and amendment, following 'Tens of thousands of minor or major criticisms from different Departments'.[75] A document on 'The International Regulation of Primary Products', more or less final for the time being, went into print at the end of 1942, as the agreed policy to be recommended to Ministers.[76]

The original stress in the scheme was placed on the management of buffer stocks on lines comparable with that part of the commodity policy advocated by the American Vice-President and former Secretary for Agriculture, Mr Henry Wallace,*[77] although his proposals, unlike this British scheme, were restrictionist. To reduce short-term price fluctuations without going against long-term trends in prices, commodities should be bought or sold, on appropriate conditions, in order to maintain a roughly constant reserve of them (Vice-President Wallace's 'ever-normal granary'). The principal machinery for this would consist of a 'Commodity Control' for each commodity; to standardise the principles to be followed, it was desirable to have a central Commodity Council, which would be prepared to advise on fresh problems so as to avoid *ad hoc* action.

Discussions had quickly revealed two major problems that either linked the scheme with other post-war plans, or, to the severest critics and opponents, separated it from them. The draft Clearing Union proposals had suggested opening an account for a commodity scheme and possibly the provision of short-term finance. The draft plan on Primary Products also suggested the possibilities of finance from central banks and by loans secured on the Controls' stocks, guaranteed by the Clearing Union. The Bank of England, though supporting the aim of reducing price fluctuations, particularly disapproved the association with the Clearing Union, which might well find much of its resources tied up in commodities. Keynes pointed out that the Clearing Union would be better off with commodities than with no specific backing for its members' borrowings.[78] There was also, however, a political case against mingling monetary and commodity plans, in the American

* WALLACE, Henry Agard (1888–1965); Vice-President of the USA, 1941–45; Secretary of Commerce, 1945–46.

preference for a series of separate schemes, rather than to have them all under some single umbrella such as the Clearing Union.

This financial aspect of the commodity proposals was to have further attention, but the second major problem in the proposals proved to be overridingly stubborn, and to foreshadow a future tangle of obstacles to the evolution both of a British policy and of an agreed Anglo-American policy. The issue was that of the regulation of levels of production by such methods as quotas (for exports), restrictions, and subsidies. Buffer stocks, as Mr R F Harrod emphasised in one of his many contributions to a cornucopia of memoranda on post-war policies,[79] sought to deal with the problems of prices and incomes; these had to be distinguished from the characteristic problem of over-production, for which some form of restriction might be necessary. There was in fact widespread doubt whether buffer stocks could help sufficiently without some regulation of production. Three types of criticism emerged in this context. One was friendly. Thus, the Economic Section of the War Cabinet Offices, the Ministry of Economic Warfare, and the Colonial Office, as well as Treasury officials, laboured to devise provisions that would permit regulation of production as an exception, not as a rule.[80] A second type of criticism was sceptical: from its experience with foreign exchange arrangements, the Bank of England feared that the price range of buffer stock operations would give too much scope to speculators, and felt that 'international agreements on prices and quantities' would be necessary.[81] A third and eventually intractable criticism came from the Ministry of Agriculture, which was convinced of the need to regulate output and exports. In the spheres of food and of agricultural policy this was so much a domestic concern, said its principal official, Sir Donald Fergusson,* that he believed that governments would be unwilling to entrust power over them to some international body.[82] The successive redrafts of the Commodity scheme had sought to acknowledge such anxieties by providing for the possibility of resort to export quotas and to output restriction, but hedged this with provisos for the examination of the contribution to producers' difficulties of such devices as tariffs and subsidies.[83] It became clear, however, that the agricultural interests—and certainly the dedicated Sir Donald Fergusson—were resolute against international arrangements which embodied the spirit of Article VII; they favoured arrangements which would permit restrictive policies, stressing the interests of producers rather than those of consumers. This struggle was to intensify, to the eventual detriment of Anglo-American economic

* FERGUSSON, John Donald Balfour, KCB 1937, GCB 1946 (1891–1963); Permanent Secretary, Ministry of Agriculture and Fisheries, 1936–45; Permanent Secretary, Ministry of Fuel and Power, 1945–52.

discussions during the later stages of the war (*see* especially chapters 6 and 8 below).

(7) FOOD POLICY

With the draft commodity plan in virtually final shape, the President's proposal in March 1943 for a United Nations conference on food and nutrition at the end of April threw ministers and officials momentarily off balance. These were not the Anglo-American discussions which had been so long deferred. Such a conference would cut across and might compromise other more fundamental issues. Further, the short notice left inadequate time for preparation and briefing.[84] Transatlantic exchanges brought from the State Department an explanation that although the Conference was seen in the context of Article VII discussions, it was intended to avoid direct intervention by the Conference in wider questions such as economic and financial policy. It was, however, envisaged that it would illuminate, through study of world food problems, those larger issues on which special conferences were expected. Finally, the date of the Conference was postponed to the second half of May.[85] A more positive British attitude to the Conference evolved on contemplation of the risks of a passive approach: food producers were likely to press for restrictionist policies, the recent wheat negotiations providing a warning here; and there was a danger of being caught unprepared with post-war food plans if, as seemed possible in 1943, there was an early end to the war. Britain's object should therefore be to go along with proposals for some new international organisation, but to ensure that it be without executive powers. Attention should be drawn to British achievements and intentions on nutritional matters; the elements of the commodity scheme might be aired, but this particular gathering would be no place for detailed examination of it. Discussion in London developed along these lines in March and April and received Cabinet approval.[86]

At the Conference itself, in the opulence of 'The Homestead' in the resort of Hot Springs, Virginia, all and more of the pressures which London had foreseen for what may be summarised as a protective, restrictionist policy for agriculture, manifested themselves.[87] The British representatives evidently contributed successfully to the avoidance of Conference support for that; not least, the disclosure of British thinking, though not of the detailed proposals, on commodity regulation secured Conference approval for its broad principles. The final Resolutions embodied this, together with an avowal of the undesirability of tariffs, etc, and of the desirability of expanded food production. An interim Commission was to begin work quite soon, and did so in July, six weeks after the end of the Conference, in order to prepare a permanent organisation. This was to emerge about a year later as the Food and Agriculture Organisation (FAO). Britain was to approve it in November 1944; the minimum number of countries required to activate it had assented by mid-April 1945; and the American Congress assented three months later.

(8) INTERNATIONAL MONETARY ARRANGEMENTS: GENERAL

Albeit on a minor theme, the undoubted success of the Hot Springs Conference was related less to food than to the demonstration that there could be international collaboration involving the USA, on post-war plans. The President's intention had thereby been achieved; and for Britain, there had been a valuable opportunity to test ideas on post-war commercial policy, and for a strong team to gain experience in negotiations.

Unquestionably the major issue in post-war international planning was the reconstruction of international monetary arrangements. The agreement of the United States Administration in July 1942 to limited, preliminary discussions on these marked the rough simultaneity of the evolution in 1941–2 of respectively the Keynes plan for an International Clearing Union (ICU) and the White Plan for a Stabilisation Fund (SF). The history of these proposals and of the prolonged discussions which eventually produced the Bretton Woods Agreements of July 1944 has been largely and most authoritatively distilled elsewhere.[88] That process will therefore not be repeated here. Attention in this and in chapters 6 & 7 below will be concentrated upon the relevance of the plans and of the discussions to the aims of British policy; on their achievement or modification or abandonment, and the reasons involved; and on the significance for Britain of the final agreements reached.

Several clearly identifiable *desiderata* had emerged for British policy makers. There should be multilateral clearing of international payments; measures to protect the economy from unduly adverse turns in the current account, as well as to correct them; protection against potentially harmful capital movements; access to an international source of international liquidity other than gold; protection against the potentially depressing effects on world trade and payments from economies persistently in surplus with the rest of the world; and, by no means least, an assurance of an adequate transitional period after the war before the full operation of a new international mechanism.

American policy from 1936 had lain somewhere between the old gold standard, with its fixed exchange rates and implicit requirement of rigorous domestic adjustment, and a managed money policy comparable broadly with that evolved by Britain after departing from the gold standard in 1931, with its operation (from 1932) of a stabilisation fund: the Exchange Equalisation Account. That is, exchange rates should be stable, but not rigid; the monetary authorities responsible for the leading currencies should consult about intended changes, and meanwhile should use the domestic and foreign means of payment in their own stabilisation funds (such as the Exchange Equalisation Account), to diminish fluctuations. Such a policy, embodied in September 1936 in the Tripartite Declaration (above pp 17,74) was of limited scope, but it had ended the comparatively brief, though chaotic, retreat of the late 1920s and first half of the 1930s from international monetary co-operation.[89] It stands with the Reciprocal Trade Agreements Act of 1934 as an American initiative to moderate her own as well as others' policies of economic nationalism. Just as Keynes had drawn for the ICU on his earlier proposals in his *Treatise on Money* (1930), so Dr Harry D White* in the US Treasury drew on the Tripartite Agreement at the end of 1941 when, at the request of Mr Morgenthau, he organised the drafting of the SF. Knowledge of this activity, at least in broad outline, reached London in January 1942 while the ICU was still nominally in the Treasury eggshell.[90]

The SF sought to stabilise exchange rates, and to improve the facilities for international payments with a pool of gold and currencies subscribed by its members.[91] The aims of the SF and of the ICU broadly matched each other in respect of seeking adequate clearing arrangements for trade and therefore currency convertibility. There was a critical difference, however, in their long-run and short-run implications. Whereas both might eventually operate in broadly comparable fashion, the much greater flexibility of the ICU provision for an overdraft system of liquidity, and the more rigid limitation of the SF to a given pool of members' currencies, made the former more and the latter less suitable for the difficult transition from a war economy to more normal conditions; that is, to British eyes, though not to American.

The first phase in Anglo-American monetary discussions was essentially one of elucidation. This 'elucidation phase', which lasted from mid-1942 to mid-1943, sharpened British concern over the inadequacy of the SF to ease the post-war stresses that had dominated domestic British discussion. Each Treasury in summer

---

* WHITE, Harry Dexter (1892–1948); Director of Monetary Research, US Department of the Treasury, in years preceding US entry into World War II; assistant to Henry Morgenthau (Secretary of the Treasury) 1941; at end 1941 also given the authority of Assistant Secretary of the Treasury; in charge of his department's relations with US Army and Navy 1943; formally appointed Assistant Secretary of the Treasury 1945; appointed first American Executive Director of the International Monetary Fund 1946; presided over first meeting of Board of Executive Directors; resigned from Fund 1947.

1942 gave the other copies, as distinct from earlier verbal information, of its proposals. Each put a series of questions about the other's scheme and received answers.[92] The ICU underwent at least two further re-drafts, making six versions in all, by November 1942, and the SF around a dozen re-drafts by April 1943.[93] The many re-drafts of the SF reflected not only a response to the comments it evoked both inside and outside the USA, but also its status as increasingly the reference proposal, rather than the ICU, as the main focus of debate over international monetary plans. By June 1943 Keynes himself, having hitherto discouraged others from doing so, was 'conflating' the two proposals in anticipation of a 'Joint Statement' expected late that year[94] (it eventually emerged in April 1944). The immediate British reaction to SF had been that it was unworkable, but that the American initiative was welcome.[95] At that stage (August 1942) British concern remained primarily with ICU; with one important exception, active concern with SF was scarcely possible for several more months. The exception occurred in late October 1942 when, during a visit to London, White met Keynes informally.[96] This meeting cleared the air for the time being, but not the serious differences between the two schemes. In particular, Keynes regarded the scope of SF as too restrictive and its proposals about exchange rates as too rigid. Emphasising the need to work within American political constraints, White stressed the need to separate from the currency proposals short-term measures (such as post-war relief).

Subsequent Anglo-American exchanges on these and other issues continued in at best a desultory fashion for some months, Mr Hull's avowal in November 1942 of readiness for Article VII discussions notwithstanding. The now familiar impression persisted that such talks would be at a relatively low level. True, in the New Year 1943 the possibility of a consultation among experts was aired on the American side, but if this aroused some British interest it also inspired fears that the American aims might be to secure commitment to a rigid scheme in advance of a major conference on Article VII.[97] Early in 1943 thoughts in Britain were turning to publication of the Clearing Union plan in order to widen discussion,[98] while American thoughts had crystallised into an invitation to widely-based informal discussions in Washington: first a series of two-party talks between the USA and individual countries; then a general, informal conference; and finally brief Anglo-American discussions. These various exchanges, suggested originally for May 1943, were in fact to be held a month later.[99] By that time Keynes's comment of 1945 about the vast gap in mutual understanding between London and Washington would have been extremely appropriate.[100] Not only was the view from the former of the latter extremely bewildering, but London itself appeared confused about events, with the Treasury professing in early June surprise that the exchanges were about to take place.[101]

It is, however, the outcome of the apparently amorphous elucidation phase which is the primary concern here. There had emerged by mid-1943 a clear emphasis on 'currency' proposals; a number of projects originally encompassed by the ICU proposals had been set aside for separate consideration, and the investment proposals (the Reconstruction Bank in the American scheme), slipped temporarily into the background. Four key issues now predominated in the search for Anglo-American accord. Cutting through the technicalities, they concerned the nature and scope of the arrangements to ensure multilateral clearing of international payments; the operation of these arrangements and the access to them by participants; the adjustment mechanisms which the rules would permit for the adjustment of a country's balance of payments; and provisions for policy during the two transitions, which might not be co-terminous: from war to peace, and from the initiation to the full operation of a new international scheme.

Following the elucidation phase there was movement between June and September 1943 towards compromise and towards the identification of gulfs still to be bridged. Broadly, the reduction in the scope and attractiveness of the currency scheme proposed by the United States tended to increase British reluctance to forgo completely the various devices that had earlier been seen as the alternative to the ICU Utopia. In terms of the shaping of policy, Keynes pointed out in July 1943 that there were certain American 'essential conditions', the British acceptance of which seemed possible. There were others which British interests required to be substantially modified.[102] Finally, certain features, unacceptable to Britain were sticking points, in default of concessions on which Keynes recommended that there could well be a temporary break in the Anglo-American debate. There seemed by late summer 1943, first, to be no alternative but to accept the reduction in the overall size of the proposed fund. In some compensation, the SF embodied proposals to help lighten the burden of Britain's huge sterling balances (below, pp 98–99); the SF recognised, with the ICU, the need to control capital movements; and it had embodied since the end of 1942 the 'scarce currency' clause, which provided for easement of the pressure on international liquidity should a shortage of a particular currency persist.[103] This 'scarce currency' clause paralleled the provision in various drafts of the ICU to cancel the excess balances of members persistently in surplus with the Union.

Second, Britain disliked American proposals for the denial of automatic access to the resources of the proposed fund, and for the conduct by its managers of active operations in financial markets, particularly the proviso that they might limit their purchases to those currencies 'in good standing'. Such reservations seemed to undermine the objective of providing resources for multilateral clearing; they might exacerbate the existing weakness of a currency; and the sterling system, certainly in the early post-war years, could prove extremely vulnerable.[104] Around this set of problems revolved discussions on whether the fund should operate with a single, new, international unit such as characterised the ICU and was implicit in its absence of capital, or with a mixed bag of currencies which virtually followed from the American plan to base the fund's resources on members' subscriptions; an associated issue was whether the operation of the fund should be 'active' in the sense outlined above, or 'passive' in the sense that use of its resources depended upon the requests of individual members. Feeling unable to avoid acceptance of the subscription principle, with its implied constraint on the volume of liquidity to be available, Britain pressed hard for 'passivity'.

On the third key issue, that of adjustment, Britain yielded on one major aspect to American insistence that the pound sterling should be valued initially at a fixed rate of $4.03 (or the tidier $4). Acceptance of a fixed rate had been virtually assured once the Bank of England had persuaded the Treasury and Keynes that, at least during the transition, sterling area arrangements and hence a stable exchange rate would have to be maintained. There seems to have been little serious examination of whether $4.03 (or $4) would be an equilibrium exchange rate. Keynes was inclined to think, indeed, that the US dollar might prove to be undervalued by the end of the war, in which case such a rate for sterling would prove a bargain.[105] Further, Keynes's evident distrust of devaluation as a check on excessive imports, and his preference for the greater certainty of controls (see Appendix 27, section 4), qualified the significance that might be attached to the exchange rate. But suppose an alteration of the initial rate were subsequently to appear necessary? Here Britain's concern was emphatically not just to retain but to enlarge the scope for unilateral adjustment, in contrast to the American aim both to limit the extent of changes and to make them dependent on virtually the unanimous agreement of other members.

On the fourth key issue, that of the length of the transition and members' policies during it, there had been a considerable narrowing of the original gap between American and British views. In a sense, nevertheless, those views remained opposed, perhaps doubly so. The American instinct, as was to become starkly evident at the end of the war, was to expect a swift return to 'normal' economic conditions, whereas the British horizon stretched to several years. Insofar, however, as American thinking recognized the possibility of a long transition, it embodied a fear lest that would protract restrictionist policies and allow them to become more firmly embedded. Indeed, precisely such had been Keynes's assessment, and was to continue to inform his advocacy with sceptical colleagues and with the Bank of England of bold measures. As late as April 1943, the published draft of ICU (paragraph 43) still urged against excessive caution in its implementation, and stressed that 'the problem of "proper timing" will be nearly insoluble'. This bold view was based, however, on the hope that the ICU's easement of transitional difficulties would be supplemented, or even superseded, by post-war relief aid and perhaps by the prolongation of Lend-Lease. If such support seemed likely to be absent or inadequate, 'the overdraft quotas [of the ICU might] ... be even more necessary at the outset than later on' (paragraph 42). The less ambitiously equipped SF at first threatened to restore the problems of the transition to their grim pre-ICU appearance. Subsequent changes saw the disappearance of the SF requirement for a member to assume its full obligations a year after joining; but, as noted in connection with exchange rates, it was envisaged that there should be a transition period of no more than three years. British policy was to seek to raise this to at least five years, during which exchange controls could be maintained.[106]

(9) INTERNATIONAL MONETARY ARRANGEMENTS: STERLING BALANCES

With one major qualification, the foregoing encompassed the major issues to be further refined in the Anglo-American discussions of September and October 1943, and subsequently, before their definitive resolution in the Bretton Woods agreements of July 1944. The qualification concerned the relation of 'abnormal war balances' or 'blocked balances' to the proposed currency scheme. This involved for Britain the sterling balances and thereby much more besides: indeed consideration of those balances led to consideration of the future of the sterling area and hence of the broad pattern of Britain's post-war monetary arrangements in general.

Britain had consciously used the accumulation of sterling debt to ease the financing of the war (above pp 1–3). During 1941 and 1942 anxiety began to spread in the Treasury (more slowly than in the Bank of England) over the problems which this accumulation was creating. Of four particular influences giving concern about the growth of balances, the most obvious was the heavy expenditure, contrasting with a shrinkage of British exports, by Britain and her allies within the sterling area; and there was also heavy expenditure by sterling area members in non-sterling, largely non-dollar, countries. A second influence was the constraint of the limited size of Britain's—the sterling area's—reserves. Third, the use of sterling balances to repatriate sterling debts owed to Britain, thus dampening their net increase, appeared in 1942 to be approaching its limits, especially in the case of India. Fourth, in India, as in Egypt, there was a formidable concentration of sterling problems, to which the sensitive political setting compelled attention, though defying solutions to them (it was assumed in London that the treatment of Egyptian balances, second in size only to India's, would follow whatever might be devised for the latter). The intensification of war in the Middle East and its spread to the Far East led to India becoming an arsenal and then a theatre of war, as well as a substantial supplier of troops. Domestic war production and rising earnings brought monetary expansion, inflation, and shortages of civilian goods; these could not, in war conditions, be sufficiently offset by imports, nor by domestic borrowing policies, although in contrast there persisted in some Treasury quarters the apprehension that India might in fact be *short* of sterling after the war.[107] Vigorous discussions in London, and between London and the Viceroy in New Delhi, during 1942 proved unsuccessful in devising mutually acceptable ways to contain the Indian balances, as more systematic attempts in 1943–5 were also to be (below pp 221–3). The difficulties over a policy for Indian balances reflected, however, those in reaching one for the overall problem of Britain's sterling debt.

Serious concern about the balances developed slowly in Whitehall, as already noted. Keynes was an exception. Thus, in November 1940 and again some months later he aired the ingenious attractions of the mutal cancellation of surpluses of sterling and of commodities. The earlier instance envisaged that commodities might be included in India's note issue reserve.[108] In the later, the idea was for sterling balances to be indirectly offset by appropriate financial arrangements for the disposal of surplus commodities under post-war relief plans (above, p 84). With ingenuity unsuccessful, Keynes asserted at this time that the balances 'ought to be funded or blocked at the end of the war', although such an intention should not be disclosed.[109]

The Bank of England had been concerned since the early days of the war lest accumulated sterling balances destabilise Britain's external economic relations. Without action to control or better, to eliminate them, retention well into the peace of controls on foreign exchange and trade and of the sterling system, as these had developed during the war, would be unavoidable: yet the ICU-SF proposals appeared inconsistent with the maintenance of the sterling area conception.[110]

The Bank assembled its views in a notable memorandum of April 1943 on 'Sterling after the War'.[111] The international monetary plans, it noted, would provide for the clearing of *final* balances in international transactions, but a need would remain for appropriate day to day facilities. The keynote was that after the war sterling, with the US dollar, should continue to be used for most international payments, but that sterling's weak reserve position in relation to liabilities required that freedom in its use be developed carefully. There could be no uniform treatment. Exchange control would maintain the distinction between the sterling area and the rest of the world, with more freedom to use sterling in the former than in the latter. With non-sterling countries a variety of payments agreements would probably be needed. The sterling area, in the absence of 'a radical solution' for accumulated balances, would have to operate with an eye to the protection of Britain's balance of payments. In urging that there should be early preparatory action to lay the basis of post-war arrangements, the Bank's recommendations included the intensification of 'efforts to get rid of blocked sterling'.

That the Bank's views of post-war sterling, and its scepticism about the post-war monetary plans, could prove unhelpful to the multilateralism he envisaged, and might involve prolonged austerity for the country, was Keynes's anxiety until the end of the war. Both the earlier and later drafts of the ICU, however, treated these problems of sterling very circumspectly. It would not do, said draft II (November 1941, section I) to risk 'prejudice and suspicion' by hinting that the proposals might particularly benefit the Commonwealth or sterling area. The drafts referred in broad terms to monetary groupings such as the sterling area; they would have a role, so long as they did not create restrictions on the use of the central currency concerned and thereby work against, instead of towards, the goal of multilateralism (II of November 1942, section VIII, and the general sense of IV of January 1942, paragraphs 95–98). The earlier drafts spoke, also in broad terms, of the need to control capital movements, but not until a later draft (August 1942) made shortly after he had seen a draft of the SF with its proposals for dealing with abnormal war balances discussed below did Keynes incorporate specific references to the crucial problem on which, hitherto, prudence had appeared to counsel reticence. In words to be reproduced in the published *Proposals for an International Clearing Union* in April 1943 (Cmd 6437, paragraph 34), a brief reference to the problem of the balances was followed by the suggestion that 'Perhaps there should be some special... provision for... the transitional period only by which, through the aid of the Clearing Union, such balances would remain liquid and convertible...'.

The early draft of SF (April 1942, but not available to the British until July-August that year) offered a drastic solution, to which it gave more attention than to any other topic.[112] During the 1930s German indebtedness and the accompanying blocked mark balances, clearing restrictions (ie, bilateral trade and payments agreements), and exchange controls had clouded international economic relations. To avoid a repetition of this experience after the war in a British, sterling, image, the SF provided that abnormal balances could be sold to the fund. As amended in April 1943, twenty per cent of such balances might be re-sold by the fund. Of the remaining eighty per cent, the original holder and the original debtor would each repurchase half (ie, forty per cent each of the total), together with certain charges, over a period commencing three years after the transfer to the fund of the balances concerned. The fund's acquisition of balances would be limited to a total of ten per cent of all members' quotas in the first two years, after which it would propose means for the disposal of outstanding balances.

These proposals would not have been costless either to creditor or debtor, and it was not difficult to detect drawbacks. Keynes pointed out that formerly-restricted sterling, when eventually repurchased from the fund by an original holder, would then become *free* sterling. This, added to the similar amount of Britain's own eventual repurchase of sterling from the fund, meant that the burden on Britain would ultimately be twice as great as might appear at first sight. The proposals nevertheless offered an opportunity both to ease a potentially appalling strain on post-war Britain and to equip the post-war world with a substantial accession of international liquidity. British reaction was therefore to welcome the proposals, at least in principle.[113] Only gradually did serious misgiving develop. In this there were three main strands. First there was the terminology, which American usage switched from 'blocked balances' to the still objectionable description of 'abnormal war balances' and back again to 'blocked balances'. The last suggestion that the British Treasury and the Bank of England wished to see propagated, however freely they might privately use the description, was that sterling balances were in any way 'blocked'. Their employment might nevertheless be restrained by persuasion, by voluntary restraint, or simply by their functions as currency reserves. This was not all. While the designation 'blocked balances' might be interpreted as including outstanding pre-war German debt, the more restricted 'abnormal war balances' might none the less seem to cover wartime German debts in occupied countries.[114]

The second difficulty followed: would the resources of the fund be adequate to deal with the huge volume of balances? American officials were apprehensive about the chances in Congress and elsewhere for a scheme with resources of the order that could be required. Further, there were doubts about the extent to which resources intended predominantly for clearing *current* payments should be used for *capital* transactions such as the conversion of 'old' balances might seem to involve. There was a danger, too, that the new scheme could be hobbled by identification as a device to bail out Britain; moreover, the stress on the clearing scheme as a post-war arrangement and the eventual exclusion from long term arrangements of such wartime problems as relief, opened up the possibility of also excluding the settlement of wartime balances for the same reason.

The third difficulty, intertwined with the other two, predominated: an international plan for the balances required that there be a *British* policy about them. Such a policy had emerged neither from the ICU-SF discussions during 1942–43, nor from the more or less simultaneous discussions about the fundamental element in any British policy on the balances, namely the treatment of the large and growing Indian balances. Ministers and officials stopped short of proposals, whether from India or from the Treasury, to deal with them. They hoped for better days militarily and politically than those being experienced after the Japanese victories right up to India's borders. They hoped for arrangements that would somehow reconcile the widely differing views of the Treasury, the Bank of England, the India Office, and, by no means least, those of Mr Churchill and his close advisers (below, chapter 9, sections 3 and 4).

These difficulties had the unsurprising result of postponing decisions. For the British travellers to the Washington talks in September 1943, the injunction was that, in respect of 'Abnormal Post-War Balances' they should 'go slow until we knew better what the financial conditions of the post-war period would be': a deferment in which White was shortly to acquiesce.[115]

(10) COMMERCIAL POLICY

The dominant commitment under Article VII was that to future commercial policy, on which intensive British discussions endeavoured to reconcile both internal differences and Anglo-American differences, without losing sight of the aim of encouraging multilateral trade freed largely from restrictions. During late 1942 and early 1943 bold proposals evolved in the plan for a 'Commercial Union' and in the Overton and Hurst Reports (see below). Subsequently these bold ideas were to be dampened, but although no specific Anglo-American agreement on them emerged, the underlying commitment to liberal trading policies was not disa-

vowed; there is therefore continuity between some four years of
wartime discussions on trade policy and the principles to be reflected
in the Anglo-American Financial Agreement of December 1945, and
also in discussions which failed to lead to an International Trade
Organisation, but which did produce the General Agreement on
Tariffs and Trade (GATT) in 1947.

The earlier ICU drafts had recognised the desirability of reducing
trade restrictions, but later drafts had gradually diminished their
emphasis, concentrating more on the monetary issues, and in effect
shunting aside other topics for separate detailed attention. A
substantial part of the main Treasury memorandum of spring 1942,
embodying the ICU, was, however, concerned with the approach to
post-war trading arrangements which would be in harmony with
Article VII. The memorandum favoured making a distinction
between the main American objectives of the expansion of world
trade, and that of eliminating discrimination. Concentrating on
trade expansion, the memorandum urged that although it was
desirable, especially on political grounds, to pursue multilateralism,
it was essential to qualify it with the retention of various physical
controls over trade; this reflected not only Britain's likely post-war
problems of a weak balance of payments, but also more general
considerations, such as the limited efficacy of exchange depreciation. Only a general assurance on commercial policy should be
given to the USA, and commitments should be avoided until the
various proposals for new international arrangements had been
explored.[116] This deliberately left the question of discrimination in
trade for later treatment.

Not least in the Board of Trade itself, whence had come
arguments supporting the retention of a range of trade controls,
there was a growing challenge throughout the later months of 1942 to
this cautious, defensive approach. The fuller exposition and
discussion of a restrictive policy led to a bold initiative, virtually
reversing the earlier attitudes, in an effort to break the apparent
impasse in Anglo-American exchanges. More optimistic than some
others in Government, in the light of Keynesian economics and of
the American 'New Deal', was Mr H T N Gaitskell,* then personal
adviser to Mr H Dalton, President of the Board of Trade. Gaitskell
favoured a bolder view. This evolved as 'A Proposal for an
International Commercial Union' in August 1942 which, he said,

* GAITSKELL, Hugh Todd Naylor (1906–63); Principal Private Secretary to Minister of Economic Warfare, 1940–42; Principal Assistant Secretary, Board of Trade,
1942–45; Parliamentary Secretary, Ministry of Fuel and Power, 1946–47; Minister of
Fuel and Power, 1947–50; Minister of State for Economic Affairs, 1950; Chancellor of
the Exchequer, 1950–51.

'owed a very great deal to Mr James Meade'* of the Economic Section of the War Cabinet Offices. It was indeed a redraft of a paper by Meade with the same title. Mr Dalton was enthusiastic about Gaitskell's version and, after departmental discussions, circulated it at the beginning of November 1942 as a 'Project for a Commercial Union'. Mr Meade was seconded to the Board of Trade to advise on commercial policy.[117]

In the words of the opening sentence of Mr Dalton's formulation, the Commercial Union would seek to meet the Americans on their own proposed ground of multilateral trade by 'a large-scale clearance of pre-war impediments to trade between nations'. There should be drastic all-round tariff cuts; limits to or reductions in discrimination and in import quotas; and comparable treatment for a variety of other trade restrictions. A 'Commercial Union', complementary to the proposed Clearing Union, would operate a code of behaviour and ensure an expansionist commercial policy. With the paper's note of enthusiasm went a note of urgency, underlined by Mr Cordell Hull's willingness to open Anglo-American discussions and by the advice of semi-official American visitors that Britain should take some initiative.[118] With some qualification by the Chancellor, Mr Dalton's proposal for a small committee was accepted, with the appointment of an inter-departmental Committee under Sir Arnold Overton† of the Board of Trade.[119] Quite quickly, by January 1943 this had produced a report, one of the two Treasury representatives dissenting, in support and in elaboration of the paper on the Commercial Union.[120] On the crucial question of quantitative restrictions on trade, this Overton Report proposed that, two years after the end of the war, there should begin a three-year period for their disman-tlement; their subsequent use, special considerations apart, would then depend on the agreement of the body to operate the Commercial Union, to be styled an 'International Commerce Commission'. On preferences, it proposed not only cuts but also a rule of 'no new preferences', save with the approval of the Commission. The report urged that there should be a multilateral negotiation of a multilateral trading convention, rather than

---

* MEADE, James Edward, (1907–   ) Member of Economic Section, League of Nations 1938–40; Economic Assistant (1940–45) and Director (1946–47), Economic Section Cabinet Offices; Professor of Commerce, with special reference to International Trade, University of London (London School of Economics) 1947–57; Professor of Political Economy, University of Cambridge, 1957–68.
† OVERTON, Arnold Edersheim, KCMG 1939, KCB 1943 (1893–1975); Delegate of UK Government to negotiate Anglo-American Trade Agreement, in Washington, 1937–38; Permanent Secretary, Board of Trade, 1941–45; Head of British Middle East Office, Cairo, 1945–47; Permanent Secretary, Ministry of Civil Aviation, 1947–53.

negotiation on the bilateral (ie, two-party) basis favoured by the Americans. It was feared that such bilateral negotiations might require British concessions to the United States to be extended to third countries with no assurance of reciprocity by those countries to Britain; and, equally that other countries might in bilateral negotiations with the USA negotiate concessions that would affect Britain adversely as, indeed, was seriously feared in connection with the apparent willingness of the Dominions to agree to a diminution of preferences in exchange for American tariff concessions.

The rapidly produced Overton Report had the signal effect of stimulating the crystallisation of crucial differences over post-war economic policy. These were differences amongst officials and between Ministers; politically, they cut across both the wartime coalition and across the loose coalitions within each of the two major parties. One official remarked quite fairly that the Overton Report was 'an attempt to strike a balance—in the form of what might be called planned free trade or controlled protectionism—between the extremes of two systems of *laissez faire* and extreme protection which have both been found wanting'. On this, another official elaborated percipiently to his Minister that the choice therefore seemed to be between the Commercial Union, with international planning that would allow scope for some 'internal *"laissez faire"*', and extensive internal controls to deal with 'international *laissez faire*'. He added wryly that nonetheless Labour Ministers were more likely to support, and Conservative Ministers to oppose, the Commercial Union.[121]

The majority support in the Overton Committee had come from the representatives of the Board of Trade, the Department of Overseas Trade, the Dominions Office, the Foreign Office and the Economic Section of the War Cabinet Offices. Only one of the two Treasury representatives approved, the other, Sir Hubert Henderson, registering a weighty 'Note of Dissent'. In the Treasury, which had hitherto dominated the post-war economic discussions, the balance of opinion, including that of the Chancellor himself, was wary or hostile. In other Government quarters there was dissatisfaction at not being consulted, or at the contents of the Report, or over both.[122] These reactions blended in January 1943 with the recession once more of prospects for early Anglo-American discussions, to moderate the hopes of the President of the Board of Trade for speedy action; they persuaded a group of Ministers when they considered the Report in January 1943 to take further soundings. Much as originally envisaged, the Overton Report was therefore referred to the relevant Official Committee (on Post War External Economic Problems and Anglo-American Co-operation)—or, rather, to its Chairman, Sir Alfred Hurst.* His task was 'to collate and present' within a month the views on the Report of all Departments concerned.[123]

A lively debate meanwhile developed around Henderson's views, propounded in his 'Note of Dissent', which he elaborated in subsequent exchanges with other officials and then, in February 1943, in a more 'positive' proposal for 'a sort of British brief' for Anglo-American discussions.[124] His majority colleagues so far respected his advocacy that they presented a collective rejoinder which was subsequently incorporated with the printed Cabinet documents.[125] Henderson echoed the Treasury apprehensions which in 1941 had preceded the optimism accompanying the evolution of the Clearing Union proposals. His views were only partly based on pessimism about the likely post-war weakness of Britain's balance of payments, which led him to caution against the abandonment of tariff protection. He saw a future in which planning rather than market competition would regulate economic life, and in which state trading would govern major areas of overseas expenditure. Quantitative regulation of trade would therefore be a normal requirement; it would also be a means to protect the balance of payments that would be all the more necessary should resort to tariffs be renounced. More generally, reciprocal tariff reductions were unlikely to provide the margin of ease so desirable for the balance of payments, since these were as likely to involve an increase in our imports as in our exports. There would, indeed, be no scope in Britain's likely post-war position for reciprocal tariff cuts. Moreover, the ability to use quantitative restrictions should be virtually untrammelled, dependence upon the permission of an international authority would be derogatory, and it would be potentially destabilising for, and therefore incompatible with, the management of an international currency. In this context, it was undesirable to offer a substantial modification of Imperial Preference. As Britain had emphasised before signing the Mutual Aid Agreement in February 1942, Imperial Preference was not unjustifiably discriminatory; unlike the more formal customs unions which were widely allowed as exceptions to the concept of multilateral free trade, Commonwealth economic links, including the monetary arrangements of the sterling area, were characteristically loose, and this warranted in compensation the use of preferences to sustain members' trade with each other. Moreover, substantial reduction of certain preferences would be both destructive of the living standards of, for instance, West

---

* HURST, Alfred William, KBE 1929 (1884–1975); Under-Secretary HM Treasury, 1932; seconded for service with Import Duties Advisory Committee as Adviser and Personal Assistant to Chairman, 1932; Under-Secretary for Mines, 1940–42; in charge of Reconstruction Secretariat of the War Cabinet, 1942–44.

Indian colonies dependent wholly upon sugar, and unfair if the greater preferences operated by the USA and France in their Caribbean colonies were to persist.

The overall conclusion of Sir Hubert Henderson's 'Dissent' was to dismiss the Overton report as 'backward-looking' towards discredited nineteenth-century arrangements; it was even worse as the basis for an approach to the USA, for its superficially bold proposals might well become minimum terms in American eyes. Henderson was therefore opposed to an approach to the USA, at least on Overton lines. Britain should be content with initiatives on monetary policies and on commodities. We could leave the Americans to make proposals on commercial policy, whilst ourselves defining clearly the position we ought to maintain on major issues; but as for ambitious schemes to govern international trade, scepticism was in order, so long as post-war conditions remained obscure.

Some notable Treasury voices supported Henderson. 'His is a most powerful paper' declared Keynes, who condemned the Overton report for giving insufficient weight to Britain's self-interest; for giving too much away in advance, and for being far too idealistic and lacking in realism.[126] But was not Keynes himself back-tracking or even being hypocritical? Had not the ICU specifically deplored quantitative restrictions?[127] 'Is not Lord Keynes playing fast and loose with the fate of his own child?' inquired a distinguished academic and Treasury colleague.[128] An anti-Overton stance could, however, be rationalised. The doubt by early 1943 about securing American acceptance of the ambitious ICU supported apprehensions about too readily dismantling, let alone renouncing, protective devices for the balance of payments. This was far from all. Would not physical controls be essential for the proper ordering of production (the beguiling description 'programming' for import controls had yet to be appropriated)? Further, state trading, such as bulk purchase of overseas commodities, would remain significant after the war, and would of its nature circumvent normal trading and the normal objections to controls. As for agriculture policy, import quotas would be ideal. Finally, trade controls need not operate against the splendid aspirations for a better international economic order, since they need not be applied on a discriminatory basis, and would therefore not transgress Article VII. Moreover, by balancing trade more accurately, say, than tariffs or alterations in exchange rates might do, they would help rather than hinder the working of a multilateral clearing system.

These tempting arguments of Henderson and others were trebly unacceptable to the signatories of the majority report. On some technical points, particularly on the probable impact of all-round tariff reductions, they disagreed or alleged inconsistency. Second, rejecting the characterisation of the Overton proposals as 'backward looking' they stressed that they should be seen in the context of the various proposed schemes for international payments and commodities; the code envisaged for commercial policy would encompass state trading and national economic planning, for all uses of quantitative restrictions would come under it. Third, the arguments for seeking agreement with the USA could scarcely be defied. In terms of cold international obligation the Anglo-American Trade Agreement of 1938 required Britain to remove wartime trade controls when peace returned.[129] As for the commitment under Article VII, it would not do to wring our hands in regret at having signed it, nor to stall over action on it.[130] A multilateral view was essential, for a reduction in American tariffs, taken by itself, would do comparatively little to help our exports. An offer to consider a reduction in preferences might, however, be a useful counter in a wider attempt to expand international trade. Hence, there was a case for a British initiative, before more limited American ideas had been formulated and hardened to British disadvantage.

All this strong argument notwithstanding, Sir Alfred Hurst's report of early February 1943, somewhat disappointing though it was in its original form, pointed clearly to a tempering of the Overton proposals.[131] Three features command particular attention. First, departments not represented on the Committee, as well as the Treasury, attached 'great importance to the retention, unimpaired, of the power to regulate imports'. Second, the question of subsidies was more complex than appeared in the Majority (Overton) Report, which regarded them as broadly acceptable for home production, though not for exports. They could, however, be a serious financial burden: a point which indirectly supported the proponents of import controls if tariff protection were to be circumscribed. Further, domestic subsidies could be so applied as to become export subsidies, for instance in state-owned or state-subsidised industries which could sell abroad and at home at the same uneconomic price; thus, the coal industry, a major exporter before the war, wished to retain scope for export subsidies. Hurst underlined powerfully the Overton Committee's rather mild recognition that 'a wider prohibition' of state export subsidies than it had suggested might be desirable: he reported the concern of the Ministry of War Transport over the possible threat of foreigners' shipping subsidies (which the Committee had regarded as outside its remit) to Britain's shipping earnings, and also as a concealed export subsidy.

The third feature of Hurst's report followed largely from such points as the foregoing: could Britain really hope for much from some new international trade organisation? This was partly drawing the lesson of past experience, but it also reflected unwillingness to hand over decisions on commercial policy to an international body. Too much, therefore, should not be expected from the proposed Commercial Union. Perhaps the successful pursuit of policies to maintain a high level of employment, about which the Government had recently expressed its determination (and which had been embodied in the Clearing Union proposals) would do more to develop world trade.

A general approach on commercial policy to the USA rather than detailed proposals: this was the upshot of the Hurst Survey. But should there be a British initiative at all? Eschewing a recommendation, Hurst recorded more arguments in favour than against. A 'marking-time' attitude had the support of the Treasury and of recent Washington advices. Against this was the majority view that we should prove our good faith about Article VII. Further, Britain was not a free agent. In separate discussions during autumn 1943 with the British Government, Dominions and Indian representatives, and Allied Governments, had clearly expressed their wishes for a lead in the planning of the reconstruction of world trade. Looming up was another reason for action, in the likely discussion in the United States over the renewal of the Reciprocal Trade Agreements Act in June 1943. A series of bilateral discussions between the United States on the one hand, and Australia, New Zealand, South Africa and Great Britain on the other, had straggled on since 1940–41. The best way to avert the hazards (eg, to Imperial Preference) of such talks might well be to seek multilaterally negotiated arrangements under Article VII.

(11) ACTIVITY OVER COMMERCIAL POLICY, 1943

As the issues in commercial policy became clearer in early 1943, urgency seemed to return—doubly so. Mr Sumner Welles, the US Under Secretary of State, strongly hinted at an American initiative; and the forthcoming Food Conference, remarked the Lord President of the Council (Sir John Anderson) would probably 'lead to a discussion of more fundamental questions such as that of commercial policy'.[133] A clear drive to formulate policy now followed, with successive refinements of the Overton proposals during spring and summer 1943 in an attempt to reconcile the major differences of view. Procrastination could find no shelter behind the recognised need to consult the Dominions before a British approach was made to the USA, for it was flushed out by the Prime Minister himself:[134] 'I think we ought to make up our own minds on the broad principles of our policy before we consult the Dominions'. There followed a memorandum summarising for the War Cabinet under three main heads (A, B, and C) the views amongst which policy must choose; this was presented by the President of the Board of Trade (Mr Dalton) and the Dominions Secretary (Mr Attlee).[135] The two Ministers elaborated these views in a draft telegram for Dominion Governments which, they urged, should forthwith be invited to send experts to London. Early in April 1943 the War Cabinet, having approved the commodity buffer-stock scheme as suitable for mention to the Dominions and if necessary at the Food Conference, though on a non-committal basis, then had a long discussion on the Dalton-Attlee memorandum and on one hostile to the Overton Report, submitted by the Secretary of State for India (Mr L S Amery).[136]

Of the three views on commercial policy, the War Cabinet rejected 'C', which favoured trade controls and bilateral trading arrangements as more or less permanent policy, and which was against a British initiative. It also rejected view 'B', which 'favoured a single multilateral rather than a bunch of bilateral agreements'; looked to an eventual relaxation of quantitative controls on imports, but not to a commitment to their limitation; and which, while accepting the case for an initiative and for support of some new international organisation, was averse to the early surrender to it of the regulation of British commercial policy. This left, but with a significant modification, view 'A', broadly the Overton majority view, that there should be a British initiative to secure 'a multilateral commercial convention' (which the Dalton-Attlee memorandum had outlined) to clear trade barriers as an indispensable element in the quest for 'full employment in our export trades'. The War Cabinet added, however, that to 'meet with general acceptance' view 'A' should be amended[137] 'so as to preserve the freedom of a country to maintain quantitative import restrictions without obtaining the permission of an international monetary authority if it could be shown that the country had an adverse balance of payments'.

The War Cabinet had therefore opted broadly for an Article VII policy subject to a satisfactory role for quantitative restrictions: a position mid-way between view 'A' and view 'B'. (Was this however a disingenuous attempt to have the best of both worlds, by professing to restrict controls in ordinary trade, while developing state trading which would be free of such constraints? The Lord President of the Council was to reassure a puzzled fellow Minister: state trading was intended to observe a code, to be non-discriminatory, and to give no more protection than an agreed tariff ceiling.[138]) It was now the turn of the Chancellor of the Exchequer, with a committee of Ministers, to make the next distillation of possible policy, for which he received the War Cabinet's approval a fortnight later. His approach, already embodied in a memorandum discussed in committee a month previously, was characteristically unhurried, especially in contrast with the hustling of the President of the Board of Trade. The Chancellor's recommendations probably struck a fair balance of prevailing opinion amongst officials and Ministers.[139] There should be an early meeting of Dominion representatives—and of Indian also, added the Secretary of State for India;[140] in case it should meanwhile prove necessary to outline provisional British views to the American authorities, we should provide the Ambassador in Washington with appropriate advice. The proposed instructions to the Ambassador stressed the provisional character of British views which, if occasion demanded, should be expressed orally to the Secretary of State. He was also to be provided with an *aide-mémoire* which should not be presented to the latter unless authorised, when he was to explain our wish for discussions on the same non-committal basis as for those about the ICU proposals.[141] The *aide-mémoire* rehearsed the essence of the Overton scheme with two particular embellishments. One was a stress on British devotion to the principle of free trade: 'any qualifications ...will be due to the special difficulties of the immediate post-war period and the present uncertainty as to what will, in fact, lie within our power and that of other countries'. The other was a determination to resolve the issue of import controls by devising a satisfactory, more or less automatic and objective test to warrant their use in order to keep them within a set of trading rules.

The Dominions, Indian and United Kingdom representatives discussed this *aide-mémoire* in London during June 1943, together with an 'Outline of a Multilateral Convention' which had formed the exposition of view 'A' in the Dalton-Attlee memorandum.[142] The proposals emerged modified but not critically transformed. There was broad support for the general approach to international trade, clearing arrangements, and commercial policy. Australia, New Zealand and South Africa expressed, however, some attachment to bilaterally negotiated trade arrangements, a danger which the British representatives sought to skirt by asking for a pause in existing bilateral negotiations in order to press the wider proposals from which bilateral arrangements might benefit. On protection, general agreement on the desirability of reducing tariffs was qualified by reservations on technical difficulties, as well as about their usefulness for promoting industrialisation and for infant industries. On restrictions and subsidies: broad support for British views. The question of Imperial Preference proved to be a sticking point only for Britain, as the guardian of colonial territories; the Dominion and Indian representatives accepted the likelihood of modifications, but they were emphatic that these should be closely linked with modifications of American and of other countries' trade restrictions. Finally, there was support for a British initiative on the lines of the *aide-mémoire* and in the light of these imperial consultations.

As those consultations were about to begin, the renewal of the Reciprocal Trade Agreements Act led the Ambassador in Washington to report his view that the Secretary of State was likely to urge shortly a resumption of the various bilateral discussions which had dragged since 1940 – 41. The Ambassador appeared to favour such a course, for to exhaust the possibilities of the Act would demonstrate to the United States the need for a more drastic policy.[143] London, hoping shortly to make its approach on commercial policy, rejected that argument.[144] Shortly after the conclusion of the imperial discussions (which Washington had duly noted and perhaps weighed in contemplating resumption of the bilateral talks), the War Cabinet approved the recommendations of a ministerial committee to seek discussions in September 1943 with the USA. These would be on all aspects of Article VII. The Ambassador in Washington was now authorised to approach the Secretary of State, and to hand him the *aide-mémoire*; the 'Outline' was intended as a brief for United Kingdom representatives, but that, too, might be given when appropriate to the United States authorities.[145] Both documents had been amended in the light of the discussions with the Dominions and India. During the first half of August there was a series of formal exchanges between the Ambassador and the State Department.[146] The United States Administration now formally suspended[147] the bilateral Anglo-American trade discussions which had originated in 1940, although with rare exceptions events were to show that this was not a suspension of American preference to negotiate trade agreements bilaterally rather than multilaterally. The way was at last clear, however, for widely-based Anglo-American talks; early in September 1943 a group of British officials, led by Mr Richard Law, Minister of State at the Foreign Office, sailed for the USA.

CHAPTER 4, SOURCE REFERENCES

1. Tel 1091 of 24 February 1942, Washington to London, CAB 117/61.
2. Mr L S Amery to Sir William Jowitt, 16 April 1942, ibid.
3. Note by Mr J A Stirling of the Board of Trade, 2 December 1942, BT 11/1822.
4. Mr Walter Lippmann to Keynes, 2 and 18 April 1942, and Keynes's notes to colleagues 16 April, in T 247/94. See also tel 1505 of 14 March 1942, Lord Halifax from Washington to London, CAB 117/61 on hostility of certain American groups.
5. Memos by Mr E F M Durbin, 17 May and 13 June 1941, CAB 117/51.
6. Mr A Greenwood to Sir Kingsley Wood, 1 January 1942, CAB 117/52.
7. Mr A Greenwood to Mr A Eden, 25 June 1941, ibid.
8. Sir Kingsley Wood to Mr A Eden, 23 June 1941, ibid.
9. A S J Baster, *Reconstruction* Part 1, p 13, CAB 102/619.
10. USE (41) 1 of 6 August 1941, CAB 87/60.
11. Papers in ibid.
12. 26 May 1941, T 247/121.
13. Baster, op cit, I, 12.
14. September 1941, T 247/121.
15. 8 September, 18 November, and 15 December 1941, and end of January 1942, in T 247/116: draft of end of January 1942 also in T 247/122. All four drafts in *JMK* XXV, pp 33–40, 42–66, 68–94, 108–39.
16. 25 September 1941 in T 247/121 and a further note of 24 November 1941 in T 247/116.
17. Memoranda from, correspondence and meetings with, the Bank of England in T 247/122.
18. In his posthumous paper, 'The Balance of Payments of the US', *Economic Journal* LVI, 222, June 1946, pp 172–87; *JMK* XXVII, pp 427–46.
19. T 247/116, *JMK* XXV, pp 21–40.
20. Mr Henderson, 22 August 1941; Professor D H Robertson, 22 August; Mr S D Waley, 21 September; Sir Arnold Overton of the Board of Trade, 16 October; all in T 247/121. Bank of England memorandum of 17 October 1941 in T 247/122.
21. 11 May 1942 in T 160/1376.
22. 'Post-war Trade and Foreign Policy', T 247/121.
23. 24 November 1941, ibid.
24. The Bank on 'J M K Memorandum I', 29 September 1941; further Bank memorandum, 'Post-war Trade and Financial Policy', 17 October; 'Skeleton Draft of Memorandum for Presentation to US Administration', 4 November; meetings between Bank and Treasury, 20 and 25 November, all in T 247/122.
25. 'Post-war Commercial Policy and the Most Favoured Nation Clause', 21 January 1942, BT 11/1872.
26. 14 January 1942, ibid.
27. WM(42) 55, Min. 1, 1 May 1942, CAB 65/26. For correspondence, etc, on this: Keynes to Sir Richard Hopkins, 22 March 1942, T 247/33; Keynes to Hopkins, 22 April 1942; Mr E Bevin to Mr A Eden, and to Sir William Jowitt, 24 April; Jowitt to Bevin, 28 April: T 247/115. The last two items also in CAB 117/61, as are the following: Eden to Bevin 29 April 1942; Bevin's secretary to Sir Edward Bridges, 1 May; Sir George Hurst's note, 8 May. See also *JMK* XXV, pp 142–3. The spirit, though not the precise wording, of the 'Bevin clause' was to be reflected at

several points in the final agreement constituting the International Monetary Fund, and also in an interpretation obtained from the new Fund in September 1946 (below, pp 182–5). At least during 1943–45, Bevin remained apprehensive of the deflationary possibilities of the monetary proposals: Bevin to Sir John Anderson, 15 December 1943, and queries for Mr R Law, 4 January 1944, CAB 123/96; speech in House of Commons (as a member of the Opposition), 4 June 1945, 411 HC DEB 5 s, cols 581–2.

28. Keynes at Bank-Treasury meeting, 25 November 1941, T 247/122. Keynes recalled the matter in ASD (44) (Employment), 1st Meeting, 29 February 1944, T 247/25; Mr Redvers Opie, unsigned note, probably end June 1942, T 160/1377; Penrose, op cit, pp 15–16; Harrod, op cit, pp 527–8.

29. Proposals for an International Clearing Union, 18 November 1941, T 247/116.

30. Drafts II, III, IV of Clearing Union Scheme, T 247/116.

31. Treasury Memorandum: RP(42)2 of 24 March 1942, T 160/1377. It was called 'The Treasury sandwich', according to Harrod, op cit, p 528. References to the drafts are to the versions in T 247/116. These are reproduced, with occasional variations and omissions, in *JMK* XXV, pp 21–40, 42–66, 68–94, 108–39. Horsefield, op cit, III, pp 3–36 reprints two versions: the fourth draft, as submitted to Ministers, but without eight introductory paragraphs, which are reproduced in *JMK* XXVI, pp 108–11; and the version published as a White Paper in April 1943, *Proposals for an International Clearing Union*, Cmd 6437, *BPP 1942–3*, XI.

32. WM(42) 55, Min. 1, 1 May 1942, CAB 65/26.

33. Meeting of officials to discuss the Treasury draft of the Note for the Chrystal Committee, 25 February 1942, T 247/119.

34. US Chargé in United Kingdom to Mr Cordell Hull, Secretary of State, 29 April 1942, *FRUS* 1942 (1960) I, pp 168–9.

35. Mr J G Winant, US Ambassador in the United Kingdom to Mr Hull, 11 May 1942, ibid, p 169.

36. Keynes to Hopkins and Sir Horace Wilson, 18 February 1942, T 247/45, and T 160/1105.

37. Hopkins to Wilson, 6 May 1942, T 160/1377.

38. Above, n 4.

39. Mr Hull to Mr Winant, 14 May 1942, *FRUS* 1942 I, p 170.

40. Memorandum of conversation, by Mr Dean Acheson, US Assistant Secretary of State, 29 May 1942, ibid, p 191.

41. Mr Winant to Mr Hull, 15 May and 5 June 1942, ibid, pp 170, 191–2.

42. Waley to Wilson, 17 August 1942, T 160/1377.

43. T 160/1377, 26 June, 17 July, 10 September 1942, CAB 87/60; CAB 117/61.

44. Note by Sir Kingsley Wood, 25 June 1942, T 160/1377.

45. Tel 304 Saving Washington to London, 30 June 1942, ibid; similar telegram, No.3530 from Washington to London, 2 July 1942, CAB 117/61.

46. Unsigned, undated note by Mr R Opie, T 160/1377.

47. Sir Frederick Phillips to Hopkins, tel 3622, 8 July 1942, CAB 117/61.

48. Ibid; memorandum of conversation, 17 July 1942, *FRUS* 1942 I, pp 192–3; Mr R Opie to Mr A A Berle, Assistant Secretary of State, 28 August 1942 with copy of proposals, *FRUS* 1942 I, pp 203–21.

49. Tel 5573 Washington to London, 12 November 1941, T 160/1377; this cites telegram from Mr Cordell Hull to Mr J G Winant, 10 November 1942, also in *FRUS* 1942 I, p 230.

50. Keynes to Mr A S J Baster, 8 February 1943, CAB 117/37 and also in T 247/10.

51. Eg, Mr S Caine of the Colonial Office, to Keynes, with memo, 5 February 1942, T 247/9. Mr R F Harrod to Hopkins, 9 March 1942, T 247/120; USE(42) 19 of July 1942, CAB 87/60.

52. Tel 3530, Washington to London, 2 July 1942, CAB 117/61.

53. Memorandum by Mr Hull of conversation with Sir Ronald Campbell, British Minister in Washington, 14 August 1942, *FRUS* 1942 I, pp 196–8.

54. Memorandum by Mr Hull of conversation with Mr Law, 24 August 1942, ibid, pp 200–202.

55. Tel 4221, Washington to London, 19 August 1942, T 160/1377.

56. Mr Anthony Eden to Sir William Jowitt, 22 March 1942, CAB 117/61.

57. Note by Mr E W Playfair, 24 October 1940, T 247/41.

58. Penrose, *Economic Planning for the Peace,* p 133 and chapter IX.

59. Keynes's discussion with Acheson, 27 May 1941, Keynes's letter to Acheson 4 June, and Acheson's draft reply to proposal by Sir Frederick Leith-Ross, 1 July, in T 247/104; *JMK* XXVII, pp 20–31. On sterling balances and surpluses: meeting of Surpluses Committee, 6 August 1941, T 247/91.

60. Keynes on Mr Winant's views, T 247/11.

61. Keynes to Mr E W Playfair and Mr G S Dunnett, 5 March 1942, T 247/90.

62. Keynes to colleagues, 18 September 1941, and Treasury memo, 24 October; T 247/90.

63. Sir Kingsley Wood to Mr H Dalton, 1 May 1942, CAB 110/78.

64. 18 May 1942, ibid.

65. WP(42) 478 of 22 October 1942, ibid.

66. Penrose, op cit, chap IX, and *FRUS* 1943 (1963) I, pp 850, 853–7, 878–9, 884, 889, 890–5, 908–9, 926, 978, 997, 1000, 1013–28.

67. Penrose, op cit, pp 156–7; Keynes to Eady, 11 May 1944, T 247/89.

68. See P Lamartine Yates, *Commodity Control* (London 1943).

69. J M Keynes, 'The Policy of Government Storage of Foodstuffs and Raw Materials', a paper read before Section F of the British Association, August 1938, in *Econ. Journ.* XLVIII, 191 (September 1938), pp 449–60; *JMK* XXI, pp 456–70.

70. Report by the inter-departmental committee on exchange difficulties and raw materials, July 1939, BT 11/1037.

71. USE(41) 3 of 8 August 1941, CAB 87/60.

72. USE(41) 5 of 14 August 1941, ibid. See also correspondence between Keynes and Colonial Office officials, T 247/9.

73. Acknowledgement by Sir Frederick Leith-Ross of draft from Keynes, 20 January 1942, ibid.

74. USE(42) 15 of June 1942, CAB 87/60; *JMK* XXVII, pp 135–66.

75. Keynes to Phillips, 6 January 1943, T 247/10, and to Mr R H Brand, 6 January 1943, T 247/90.

76. T 247/10. See also *JMK* XXVII, pp 168–93.

77. US Chargé in United Kingdom to Mr Hull, 12 April 1942, *FRUS* 1942 I, p 164; see Henry A Wallace, 'New Frontiers' in J Samuel Walker, *Henry A Wallace and American Foreign Policy* (Westport, Conn. and London 1976), p 46. See also *JMK* XXVII, pp 22, 112–15, 138–41.

78. Mr B G Catterns, Deputy Governor of the Bank of England, to Hopkins, 2 March 1942, and Keynes's comment, 15 March, T 247/9.

79. USE(42)11 of 10 June 1942, CAB 87/60.
80. T 247/9 and T 247/10.
81. Catterns to Hopkins, 2 March 1942, T 247/9.
82. Correspondence and other papers, February–April 1942, in T 247/119; 30 June 1942, T 247/9; 28 July 1942, 14 January, 12 April, 29 April 1943, T 247/10; Fergusson's views, 29 June and 22 December 1942, CAB 87/60.
83. See, eg, USE(42) 15 'The International Regulation of Primary Products', sections 15 and 16, CAB 87/60. Keynes had recognized the need to introduce into his scheme some provision for restriction of production: meeting of Chrystal Committee, 12 June 1942, ibid.
84. Penrose op cit, pp 119–20; Hammond, *Food,* I, pp 357–8.
85. *FRUS* 1943 I, pp 820–36.
86. Hammond, op cit, I, p 358.
87. Ibid, pp 359–62. For valuable detail, but above all for conveying the atmosphere of the Conference, I am indebted to Lord Robbins, for access to his personal reports in his *Journal*.
88. Horsefield, op cit, and E S Mason & R E Asher, *The World Bank since Bretton Woods* (Washington, DC 1973).
89. For details of the Tripartite Declaration, see R S Sayers. *The Bank of England 1891–1944,* II, pp 475–81, and III, pp 280–1.
90. J M Blum, *From the Morgenthau Diaries: Years of War, 1941–45* (Boston, Mass. 1967), pp 238–9; Horsefield, op cit, I, p 16.
91. Horsefield, op cit, I, pp 21–25 and III, pp 37–82.
92. American questions on the Clearing Union: *FRUS* 1942 I, pp 225–6; British questions on the Stabilisation Fund, tels 907, 908, 909, London to Washington, 24–25 February 1943, CAB 117/71.
93. Redrafts of Clearing Union: Horsefield, op cit, I, pp 27, 50, and *JMK* XXV, pp 159–95, 449–68; of Stabilisation Fund, Horsefield, I, p 31.
94. 31 March and 2 April 1943, T 247/30 and 29 June 1943, T 247/81; *JMK* XXV, pp 308–14.
95. Keynes to Hopkins, 3 August 1942, T 247/33.
96. Horsefield, op cit, I, pp 30, 49; Penrose, op cit, pp 47–49; *JMK* XXV, p 196.
97. Tel 155, Washington to London, 8 January 1943, T 160/1377.
98. Keynes to Eady, 22 March 1943, T 247/30.
99. Professor Robertson to Keynes, ibid, and Horsefield, op cit, I, pp 31–32.
100. House of Lords, 18 December 1945, 138 HL DEB, 2nd Session 1945–6, col 777.
101. Notes on letter of 2 June 1943 from Mr Hume Wrong from Ottawa to Keynes, T 247/30.
102. Keynes's memorandum on the Stabilisation Fund, 19 July 1943, CAB 117/71; *JMK* XXV, pp 316–20.
103. Horsefield, op cit, I, p 45.
104. Ibid, I, p 52.
105. Keynes to Waley and others, 1 July 1943, T 247/30 B.
106. Horsefield, op cit, I, p 21; Eady, reported in ASD (44) 3rd Meeting, 20 March 1944, CAB 99/34.
107. Sayers, *Financial Policy,* p 258.
108. Keynes to Waley, 19 November 1940, discussing meeting on 15 November with India Office officials, T 247/5; *JMK* XXIII, pp 325–8.

109. Keynes to Mr R G Hawtrey, 13 October 1941, T 247/33.

110. Mr C F Cobbold of the Bank, 2 March 1943, cit Waley in memorandum on 'Abnormal War Balances', 19 June 1943, T 247/41.

111. T 160/1270.

112. Horsefield, op cit, III, pp 54–60.

113. Note by Keynes on 'Abnormal War Balances', 22 June 1943, T 247/31 and T 247/81; JMK XXV, pp 305–7.

114. Telegrams 1145 and 1171, Washington to London, 20 February 1943; telegram 907, Washington to London, 25 February 1943; telegram 75 REMAC, Washington to London, 16 June 1943, CAB 117/71. See also Horsefield, op cit, I, pp 48, 52–53.

115. Keynes in meeting at sea, 7 September 1943, CAB 99/33. Keynes reporting talk with White, who agreed with the intention to play down the problem of 'abnormal balances' for the time being: telegram 4125, Washington to London, 15 September 1943, CAB 117/76.

116. Keynes to Eady, 20 November 1942, T 247/2.

117. Professor J E Meade, to whom I am grateful for permission to consult his diary, was later to note that it was 'in May or so of last year [1942] that I first penned the words "Commercial Union"' (entry for 21 September 1943, pp 24–25). Three drafts by Meade of 'A proposal for an International Commercial Union' of 25 July, 1 August, and 17 August 1942 respectively, in T 230/125. Gaitskell's discussions with Dalton, second half of August 1942, BT 11/2000 and Philip M Williams, *Hugh Gaitskell. A Political Biography* (London 1979), p 116. Copies of Dalton's paper, 'The Project of a Commercial Union' in T 230/125, T 247/2, CAB 117/67, CAB 123/221.

118. Eg, Mr I Lubin, Commissioner of Labour Statistics, understood to be a 'Personal Economic Advisor to President Roosevelt', memorandum by Meade, 18 December 1942, T 160/1377 (Lord Halifax, however, was critical of Lubin: telegram 500 of 29 January 1943, Washington to London, CAB 117/68).

119. Sir John Anderson, Lord President of the Council, to Mr H Dalton, President of the Board of Trade, 10 November 1942, CAB 123/221.

120. Report of Committee on Post-War Commercial Policy, 6 January 1943, CAB 123/221, CAB 117/68, BT 11/1824.

121. Mr Gorell Barnes to Lord President, 18 March 1943, CAB 123/221.

122. Colonial Office (26 January 1943) CAB 123/221; Ministry of Food (28 January), Ministry of Agriculture (3 January), Department of Agriculture for Scotland (3 and 4 February), India Office (4 February), N. Ireland Ministry of Agriculture (4 February) CAB 117/67.

123. Meeting of Ministers, 19 January 1943, CAB 117/67.

124. 31 December 1942, T 247/2 and 4 February 1943, CAB 117/67.

125. 29 January 1943, CAB 117/67; 5 March 1943, CAB 117/68; see also Professor L C Robbins's critique, 14 January 1943, CAB 123/221 and CAB 117/67.

126. Note by Keynes, 4 January 1943, CAB 117/67 and T 247/2.

127. Mr Gorell Barnes to Lord President, 18 March 1943, CAB 123/221.

128. Professor D H Robertson, 16 January 1943, T 247/2 and also his comment on the risk of accusations of 'hypocrisy and double dealing' to retain quantitative restrictions when about to publish the Clearing Union plan, 16 February 1943, ibid.

129. Board of Trade memo 20 February 1943, CAB 117/67 and T 230/172.

130. Waley's summary of the views of the majority, 'The Overton Report', 15 January 1943, T 247/2.

131. 7 February 1943, CAB 117/67 and T 230/171.

132. Mr Gorell Barnes to Lord President, 27 February 1943, CAB 123/221.

133. Meeting of Ministers, 23 March 1943, ibid.

134. 27 March 1943, ibid.

135. Ibid, WP (43) 136, dated 5 April 1943, CAB 66/35, and considered by the War Cabinet on 8 April 1943, WM (43) 50th, CAB 66/34.

136. WP (43)97, 5 March 1943, CAB 66/34 and WP (43) 143, 7 April, CAB 66/35 on 8 April 1943, WM (43) 50th, CAB 66/34.

137. Ibid, WM (43) 50th Conclusions, 8 April 1943, CAB 66/34.

138. Sir John Anderson, Lord President of the Council, to Mr R S Hudson, Minister of Agriculture, 29 April 1943, on the basis of a note by Professor L C Robbins, CAB 123/221.

139. Ibid, WM (43) 50th Conclusions, 8 April 1943, CAB 66/34; WM (43) 58th Conclusions, 22 April 1943, CAB 66/34, with Chancellor's memo 22 April 1943, WP (43) 168, CAB 66/36. The Chancellor's earlier memorandum, unnumbered and dated 19 March 1943, concerned 'Post-war Commercial Policy', and had been considered at a meeting of Ministers on 23 March 1943: CAB 123/221.

140. WM (43) 58th Conclusions, CAB 66/34.

141. Ibid.

142. Summary in ibid.

143. Tel 2773, Washington to London, 15 June 1943, CAB 117/61.

144. Tel 4170, London to Washington, 23 June 1943, CAB 117/76.

145. Meeting of Ministerial Committee on Commercial Policy, 23 July 1943, and WM (43) 106th Conclusions, 27 July 1943, CAB 66/35 in CAB 123/221.

146. Telegrams on arrangements in CAB 117/76; see also FRUS 1943 I, pp 1106 and III (1963) pp 108–10.

147. Mr Hull to Mr Winant, 19 August, FRUS 1943 III, pp 107–8.

CHAPTER 5

The Washington Talks September-October 1943

(1)PREPARATIONS FOR TALKS

The informal, non-committal talks of September-October 1943 were the most important Anglo-American exchanges on economic issues not only during the war but also for many years before and since. They were indeed unique; they were conducted at a high intellectual level, ranging frankly over virtually the whole field of economic policy, and they have been appropriately described as having been 'in the spirit of a university seminar rather than of a formal international conference'.[1] Although there was to be eventual disappointment of some of the highest hopes with which the participants emerged, the talks had a lasting and twofold significance. In the general sphere they demonstrated (with some qualifications about Keynes's manner of arguing) how intelligent men properly briefed could seek to resolve international problems. Second and specifically they registered and clarified issues and points of agreement, the understanding of which is fundamental if some later problems of policy are to be seen in perspective.

The apparently modest purpose of the talks was to prepare an agenda for future talks about the implementation of Article VII: to draw up a scheme for discussion, not for immediate agreement. For Britain this encompassed, specifically, commercial policy, commodity policy, monetary arrangements, long-term international investment, and adequate provision for a substantial transition period after the war; all would have to be set in the context of serious balance of payments problems and of determination to avoid heavy unemployment after the war. Other topics were in the event to be discussed, including employment policy itself and cartels, but on these British policy had not yet been sufficiently shaped. On cartels British views were in any event likely to differ in their case by case approach from the American generalised 'trust-busting' hostility. That all these topics were interconnected the British stressed rather more than did the Americans, whose inter-departmental tensions kept the monetary talks formally separate, under the Treasury, while the State Department supervised the other discussions.[2] In contrast departmental differences in both countries over the economic issues themselves underlined the inter-connections whilst illuminating the problems of policy to be resolved. As one British representative pardonably over-simplified the attitudes of the Treasuries and of the trade departments (in Britain, the Board of Trade and in the USA particularly the trade specialists in the State Department), the former seemed broadly to lean to stable exchange rates, thereby throwing into commercial policy the burden of adjustment, whereas the latter's aversion to trade controls implied greater reliance on variable exchange rates.[3] Over-riding such complexities, however, was broad sympathy between American and British principles and aims. Differences arose over the American presumption of a much speedier move to permanent, new, international arrangements than Britain felt to be possible and also over a familiar unsettling paradox deriving from American political considerations: on the one hand there was pressure for Britain to sup-port specific, often rigorous, rules, but on the other the informal, non-committal, and by implication uncertain nature of the Americans' own position was evident throughout. Nowhere was this last element to appear more strikingly, about half-way through the talks, than in a frank off-the-record interchange about the political obstacles to bold international economic policies.

Near farce might have wrecked the long-awaited talks before they began. Britain had sought to respect the Americans' acute anxiety to keep the talks informal and also concealed from public awareness, so that there was consternation aboard ship when some leading financial journalists were discovered on the passenger list. That hazard mastered, members of the mission travelled from New York to Washington in relays to avoid drawing attention to themselves. The instructions 'to slip into Washington unnoticed' were surely forgotten when Lord Keynes in a Pullman car discussed politics and culture in an unquiet distinctively British voice, and when Lady Keynes* sang Tchaikovsky's Casse-Noisette music 'at the top of her voice—dancing it with her hands'.[4] Arrived nevertheless without incident in Washington, members of the mission established personal contacts before the main discussions began. The predominant topics proved to be commercial policy, commodity policy, and monetary policy, the last being the most important, since a substantial abatement of trade restrictions depended largely upon satisfactory arrangements about exchange rate policy and for an adequate supply of international liquidity.

To complete these preliminary comments, it merits emphasis that careful preparation in Britain and aboard ship, followed by efficient organisation and intensive work in Washington, helped to ensure the success of the talks. These administrative aspects, though claiming but brief attention here, underline the major endeavour necessary to

*KEYNES, Lady (Lydia Lopokova) (1892–1981). Ballerina. Married John Maynard Keynes, 1925.

secure agreed post-war policies. At home an official committee and a Cabinet Committee had closely considered the issues. In Washington, the sub-groups of British representatives concerned with the various topics met separately and together to prepare for discussions and to report afterwards; London was fully informed and consulted. The Washington representatives of the Dominion and Indian Governments were kept informed. Plenary meetings brought the British and American representatives together periodically to oversee progress, and there was a good deal of individual and social contact. Back home again, the British mission prepared for Ministers a series of illuminating papers to carry along with the projected policies the varying persuasions represented in the Government; there was, too, the continuing process of consulting the Governments of the Dominions and of India, specifically in fresh discussions in London during February and March 1944.

(2) THE ISSUES IN COMMERCIAL POLICY

The British papers provided the framework of discussion on commercial policy. A major British achievement was to persuade the Americans that a multilateral rather than a bilateral basis for negotiations might be both desirable and possible.[5] Britain feared that in bilateral negotiations, whether between herself or others and the USA, too much might be yielded at her expense and with inadequate reciprocity; whereas only on a multilateral basis could a dramatic all-round reduction of trade barriers be achieved. The American approach retained, however, considerable scepticism about the feasibility of a multilaterally negotiated convention on international trade; notwithstanding, there was an agreement that there should be an international trade organisation with a set of rules to cover a wide range of international economic behaviour.

Three particular issues of commercial policy stood out. The first, not unexpectedly, was agreement that quantitative restrictions (hereafter 'QR') should be eliminated, though the British representatives sought qualifications both for the transition and in case of serious balance of payments difficulties. When it became clear that exchange rate flexibility was likely to be seriously circumscribed, the search for some 'objective test' for the use of QR led to a proposal by Mr Meade to relate it to the level of a country's international reserves. Probably due in part to Keynes's opposition, this was rejected by London, which feared any automatic test, at least of that kind, in favour of a requirement for approval by the proposed Commercial Union.[6] American agreement satisfied British concern to retain access to QR, in principle at least.

Subsidies were a second substantive issue, again reaching beyond general principles of commercial policy. Consideration of the financial power of Congress led the American representatives to regard subsidies as a less dependable device than tariffs; they foresaw difficulty, however, in the abolition of *export* subsidies unless importing countries could be restrained in their use of *domestic* subsidies on the production of commodities in world surplus.[7] The more relaxed British view of domestic subsidies was that they were a safety valve. In contrast, the United States held domestic subsidies to be acceptable for infant industries, whereas British officials objected that poor countries might be unable to raise the finance necessary to operate them. There was consequently no agreed Anglo-American recommendation on subsidies, which, in contrast with 'minor differences' on other matters, remained as one of several 'serious potential difficulties'.

The third main issue of commercial policy, the future of tariffs and preferences, raised critical problems of procedure likely to affect Britain's bargaining position. Conscious of strong American attachment to bilateral trading negotiations under the Reciprocal Trade Agreements Act, Britain was apprehensive of possible arrangements under which a multilateral convention would involve renunciation of preferences and of other 'discriminatory' policies, while the major tariff reduction sought from the USA would depend on bilateral negotiations, which Britain would enter *after* surrendering her bargaining counter of preferences. Britain and the USA did in fact agree in principle on the desirability of multilateral negotiations on tariffs, for the reduction of which they noted a possible formula; should there be bilateral negotiations, these should encompass preferences as well as tariffs. Reassuring as this might appear in procedural terms (though eventually ephemeral), it did not remove the crucial unresolved difference, scarcely narrower than during the protracted exchanges of 1941–42, between American and British attitudes to Imperial Preference. For much less than the substantial tariff cut Britain was seeking the USA expected outright abolition; it contemplated only a limited cut to balance Britain's proposed partial, though drastic, reduction in preferences. The one consolation was that, despite some opposition to any reciprocity for abolition of 'discrimination', there was American willingness to consider some compensating reduction in tariffs. The British mission stressed to London that Imperial Preference remained a serious difficulty; recalling Sir William Malkin's minute of December 1941 that it fell within the discriminatory behaviour to be eliminated under Article VII, they pointed to the risk of antagonising the USA by too rigid a defence of it. To the mission it seemed clear that, while aware of the unwisdom of pressing Britain too far in view of imperial considerations, the US would trade substantial tariff reductions only against the virtual abolition of preferences.[8]

Closely associated with commercial policy was the question of commodity policy; a broad Anglo-American understanding on commodity policy, albeit again on principles rather than on details, was a notable achievement (although its subsequent history disappointed). The British had approached this part of the discussions gingerly, with recent experience at Hot Springs in mind, and wondered whether to reveal their scheme in dribs and drabs, if at all.[9] It became clear, however, that since Hot Springs American experts had been working at their own scheme.[10] Moreover, the atmosphere of debate proved more encouraging than anticipated, helped by a British declaration that the expiring rubber agreement, so disliked by the Americans, would not be renewed.[11] Initially the British scheme drew such strong criticism that momentarily it appeared moribund. In fact, there was a clear split of opinion in the US Administration between free traders and ardent interventionists, the former sceptical of any control and the latter finding the spirit of the British scheme too *laissez-faire*.[12] A degree of reconciliation between them was to bring them closer to British ideas. The agreed final policy document envisaged a smaller surrender of sovereignty than in the British scheme but greater constraint on resort to quantitative control of production. Patient explanation by British representatives, notably by Professor Robbins,* and capped by a last minute intervention by Lord Keynes on the virtues of buffer stocks as an anti-cyclical device, persuaded the Americans.[13] Subsidies, as already noted, remained an unresolved issue, and the American inclination towards the concept of parity for farm incomes with non-farm remained unacceptable to Britain.[14] A further unresolved problem was the need to apply to commodities the anti-cartel policy for manufacturing, on which British representatives had to mark time. Such considerations helped to clinch Anglo-American accord on the desirability of embodying rules and a code in an international commodity organisation, which Britain hoped would be independent of, though associated with, the organisation for food and agriculture proposed at Hot Springs.[15]

(3) MONETARY PLANS

Significant achievement with monetary plans, by no means assured despite their more advanced state, was regarded as indispensable for progress on other proposals. The Commercial Union, for instance, was predicated on adequate post-war clearing and liquidity arrangements.[16] Much remained to be settled, but with typical over-optimism Keynes had asserted in England that most difficulties could be resolved 'in a week-end of conversations'.[17] Certainly, agreements or understandings were reached in Washington on crucial monetary points, but a number remained unresolved or in woolly form, while

*ROBBINS, Lionel Charles, Baron (Life Peer) 1959 (1898–1984); Professor of Economics in the University of London (London School of Economics) 1929–61; Director of the Economic Section of Offices of the War Cabinet, 1941–45.

the time taken proved equivalent to a dozen or so packed week-ends. Moreover, as others have written, Keynes's debating was often tempestuous.[18] On the American side, Dr H D White asked that no official record be kept of one particularly tense meeting. Next day, in the absence of an indisposed Keynes, he pointedly noted of political hurdles for monetary plans that it might be helpful if Congress could go along with experts' views, but that some experts had been showing 'a little less than friendliness at the high levels'.[19] Such frictions, disturbing to some British sensitivities, may or may not have found justification in a belief that distinctively American hindrance to understanding had to be blasted away, but they appear to have been compensated by the undoubted respect which Keynes won for his intellectual dominance and for his overall contribution to the success of the talks.

The pursuit of a joint statement on monetary proposals was concerned predominantly with a stabilisation fund (the American name quickly being adopted). There was to be little examination of plans for an international investment institution, which at this stage provoked controversy, not elucidation. On clearing arrangements and international liquidity initial American and British positions were broadly of rigidity and of suppleness respectively, particularly on exchange rates and on members' ease of access to the proposed Fund's resources. At an early meeting with Keynes, White indicated the potentially critical role of the projected Fund and investment body. With his habitual pessimism about Congress, fortunately to be proved exaggerated in the event, he foresaw not only little likelihood of much extension of Lend-Lease after the Japanese war, but also that 'there would be no third source' of assistance. Reinforcing British caution about the post-war world, this underlined the significance of the sterling area, which White thought Britain should be free to maintain, and it gave point to British anxiety for a relatively prolonged transition.[20] Moreover, if, as Keynes was later to phrase it, the fledgling Fund was not to be 'waterlogged at the outset by tackling the special problems left by the war' there was sufficient excuse to exclude discussion of the delicate question of sterling balances.

In an interview with Keynes, White declared his own willingness to go along with much of the British position if he could be provided with sufficiently strong arguments to deal with the bankers[21] (notably the central bankers of the New York Federal Reserve Bank). Both countries had minutely analysed the other's proposals, and exercises in reconciling them had already been undertaken in Britain. Now asked by White to conflate them, Keynes displayed 'prodigies of ingenuity',[22] despite which the Washington discussions secured but limited agreement on major issues; some six months of transatlantic dialogue proved necessary before the desired joint statement could be published in April 1944. In Washington there was agreement on the broad form of the statement and on the size of quotas; the scarce currency clause introduced in the American draft of December 1942 was elaborated to allow exchange restrictions, but not variations of exchange rates, against a currency declared scarce.[23] Superficially these approached British goals of adequate international liquidity; Keynes had indeed confessed that the quotas envisaged in the Clearing Union had possibly been too high.[24] There remained, however, acute difficulties about access to the Fund, the variation of exchange rates to assist adjustment, and the nature of the transition. All three issues were interconnected, but it is desirable to examine them in turn.

The disturbing proviso about a currency being 'in good standing' before it could be accepted by the Fund was withdrawn under British pressure; but this ensured neither that access would be automatic nor that the Fund would be entirely passive. In contrast to the simple quantitative limit of a member's quota envisaged in the Clearing Union, the Americans insisted on the retention of the Fund's 'policing' authority beyond a country's initial 25 per cent drawing (equal to its gold subscription). Even though the British gained the provision that drawing could take place on a member's 'representation' the American view was that the Fund would not be bound to act on that. If this was essentially a very remote long-stop against banana-republics' misuse of borrowing, it was nevertheless a damper on confidence in the proposed Fund's facilities that invites a parallel with Bagehot's classic discussion on the harm to confidence and to the authority of a domestic central bank, should there be a scintilla of uncertainty about the availability of liquidity in a crisis.[25] Associated with this question of access was Keynes's sustained and unsuccessful attempt, seemingly sterile to many, to have the Fund's holdings of currencies denominated in a single new international unit which would take the name of Unitas from an early American draft (below p 139). He feared that the alternative of a 'mixed bag of currencies' would permit discrimination against a particular currency, specifically against sterling and hence the sterling area, thereby reducing instead of increasing liquidity; whereas the anonymity of Unitas would give simplicity and an air of universality to the use of Fund resources. Against this were American apprehensions that it would merely disguise a channel through which other countries could draw more US dollars than if their currencies were openly identified.[26]

The second acute difficulty, the alteration of exchange rates to assist adjustment, intensified when London, adducing domestic political considerations, cabled its anxieties about the rigidity envisaged after the initial fixing of rates; they ought to be regarded as experimental, while 'precise definition of ranges' of subsequent adjustment seemed 'unwise', and could invite the description of a 'gold standard scheme'.

Coupled with this, London opposed explicit dependence on the Fund's prior discussion and approval of a proposed change in rates; confidentiality might easily be broken, leading to damaging pressure against a currency. To the dismay of the British representatives in Washington, who sought to devise rules, London insisted that there must be discretion for a member to decide whether a fundamental disequilibrium necessitated exchange rate changes; there would then be an obligation to consult the Fund rather than formally to obtain its approval. Parliament would be reluctant to 'surrender the right to protect employment by exchange adjustment ....'[27]. There was limited movement towards the London view during the Washington discussions. Existing exchange rates would be used initially; members could subsequently change the rate unilaterally by up to 10 per cent, and by a further 10 per cent if the Fund quickly agreed.[28] Formally, that was intended to be the foreseeable extent of changes in exchange rates envisaged in Washington once the Fund began operations, so that the position reached was far from British desires.

The third difficulty, that of the transition, lurked everywhere as a potential constraint. It is scarcely a caricature of British views that the grave post-war prospect prescribed a transition of indeterminate length, at the end of which there might be qualified adherence to flexible international commitments. In contrast, the American view comprised a brief transition of no more than one year (a minimum of five years being the eventual *British* requirement) leading to unambiguous implementation of precise and sweeping commitments.[29] The contrast was perhaps of caution *versus* boldness, and between a British fear of a largely uncontrolled economy and an American belief in its superior virtues. There were, however, fears that were by no means wholly American that leisurely transition would dissipate the rare wartime enthusiasm for change and international co-operation. There was, too, apprehension lest wartime controls and accretions of 'transitional' controls might harden into permanence. The commercial policy proposals looked to a two-stage move in the post-war years: a short period in which special restrictions would be allowed, followed by gradual dismantling of major restrictions. Inasmuch as it was desired, indeed was necessary, to keep the commercial and monetary schemes in step, agreement on the transition was essential. This, however, was amongst the business left unsettled which it was hoped to resume in London at the end of the year or early in 1944.[30]

(4) INTERNATIONAL INVESTMENT

An international investment body to aid reconstruction and to reduce economic fluctuations had been a feature of early versions of both the British and American monetary proposals. This slipped temporarily into the background with stress on the currency proposals. Not until the eve of the Washington talks was an up to date American draft of a proposed International Bank ready; it was communicated unofficially to the British authorities and discussed by the Law Mission at sea.[31] Then, as so often, the contrast between the wide-open governmental methods of the USA and the more closed methods of Britain caused difficulties. Halfway through the talks, Presidential authorisation for discussion of the investment scheme was announced. White, wanting to make an early statement to Congress, circulated copies of the draft to Congressmen, although contrary to British understanding there had been no preceding Anglo-American discussion of it.[32] With Congressional leaks in any case likely, Keynes struggled to prevent publication lest, with its representatives in Washington at the time, the British Government be identified with a scheme that it had not been able to examine properly and that he castigated in private as 'loony'.[33] Bathos now took over in a classic illustration of the misuse of press freedom. In London *The Financial News* 'scooped' with publication of a draft of the Bank scheme—but it was an old discarded draft. An infuriated Keynes demanded of London whether there was not some penalty for publishing a secret document obtained illicitly.[34] There was now no serious constraint on publication of the current draft, which shortly after took place. There was, however, virtually no discussion of it during the Washington talks, at the last plenary meeting of which Keynes expressed the hope that White would prepare a new draft.[35]

(5) COMMONWEALTH CONSULTATION

Commonwealth consultation was an essential feature of the Washington talks, commercial policy and the commodity scheme being of especial Commonwealth interest. Australian persistence ensured attention to employment proposals;[36] all were concerned about the monetary plans, particularly as members, Canada excepted, of the sterling area; and the urge of Australia and New Zealand to resume bilateral trade negotiations with the USA had to be deflected if American officials were to be persuaded of the possibilities of a multilateral approach to new trade arrangements.[37] Shortly after the mission's arrival, a Treasury official spoke about its work to Commonwealth representatives, and at three subsequent meetings[38] there were reports by leading British members, followed by discussions. There was no question of Britain acting as spokesman for the Commonwealth, nor any question of seeking to drag its Governments behind British policy. The discussions here and subsequently suggest all the ease, all the delicacy, all the occasional difficulties and tensions in the Commonwealth relationship that involved delay in formulating policy, yet gave the British representatives the reassurance of broad Commonwealth understanding.

The consultations continued when, after Washington, the mission made the almost routine stop of several days in Ottawa to give a full report 'off the record' and to hear Canadian views. The Canadians broadly supported British aims of a multilaterally negotiated commercial convention, while advising of the need to handle carefully Mr Cordell Hull's predilection for bilateral methods. The Canadians would like to have joined directly in future Anglo-American discussions but accepted that this was impracticable; in fact, they were shortly to have their own commercial policy discussions with the USA.[39]

(6) VERDICT ON THE 1943 TALKS

The Law Mission could fairly report that the Washington talks had justified the British initiative. On commercial policy, where the Americans had suspended work on their own document, progress had been 'surprisingly good'.[40] A paper for the War Cabinet in November 1943 embodied agreed papers on what will hereafter be described as 'the Washington Principles'. These related to the understandings about the basis of discussions, both recent and future, of commercial policy, international commodity policy, 'private international business arrangements' (ie, international cartels), and employment policies, though not yet on monetary proposals[41] (see Appendix 13). There was a sense, not of 'unfinished business', but of continuing efforts, with the confident expectation, disappointed in the event, of further talks by the new year.

The hazard in the undoubted success of the talks was that, given their informal, non-committal, preparatory nature, excessive optimism could flourish about a transatlantic debate which, in wartime parlance, was scarcely more than the end of the beginning. In perhaps the most illuminating phase of the talks, the minute-takers were put aside to allow a frank discussion of the political constraints on post-war economic plans.[42] Mr Law, asserting that British public and parliamentary opinion, though likely to provide some difficulties for the Government, had learned a good deal and would broadly support the proposed policies, sought the Americans' view of their own political climate. The American Chairman generalised cautiously that Congress was very active but reasonable; nobody doubted, however, that it would present major hurdles. White, as if forecasting the technique to be employed not only in Congress but also in the British Parliament, placed his hopes on making the policy 'packages as attractive as possible...leaving the contents as potent as possible...'. Others warned of difficulties over agriculture, that the American public might expect reciprocity for any concessions, and that 'for any very drastic innovation the fight would be terrific'. Overall there was agreement that the remarkable inclination of American opinion towards international political co-operation had yet to be matched in the economic sphere; the unanimous conclusion was that 'the only chance was to put across a big scheme in a big way'. The coming months were to reveal the frailty of that chance.

CHAPTER 5, SOURCE REFERENCES

1. Gardner, *Sterling-Dollar Diplomacy*, pp 103–104.

2. Tel 3546 of 19 August 1943, Washington to London, CAB 117/76, and meeting of British representatives, 26 August, CAB 99/33. On the talks as a whole, see *JMK* XXV, pp 338–92.

3. Mr J E Meade's *Diary*, 23 September.

4. Ibid, 11 September.

5. Ibid, 21 September; report of plenary US-UK meeting of 21 September, CAB 99/33; tels 4278 of 25 September and 4439 of 4 October, Washington to London, CAB 117/76; report on commercial policy discussions, 16 October, T 230/172.

6. Tel 6818 from Board of Trade to Washington, 9 October, CAB 117/76 and Meade, *Diary*, 12 October.

7. ASD (44) 2, Report on Commercial Policy dated 21 October 1943, CAB 99/34.

8. US-UK discussions 28 September, T 230/172; plenary meeting 30 September, CAB 78/14; meeting of British officials, 11 October, CAB 99/33.

9. ASD (44) 3, CAB 99/34.

10. ASD (44) 3, International Commodity Discussions—paper for discussions between United Kingdom and representatives of Dominion and Indian Governments, 18 February 1944, CAB 99/34 (copy also in T 247/20).

11. Mr A S J Baster's Report to Sir Alfred Hurst, 22 September 1943, CAB 117/76; Report on Commercial Policy, CAB 99/34.

12. Ibid.

13. Meeting of British officials, 24 September and 14 October, CAB 99/33; Baster's report of 16 October, CAB 117/76.

14. UK-US plenary meeting of 30 September, CAB 78/14; meeting of British officials 5 October, CAB 99/33; ASD (44) 3 of 18 February 1944, CAB 99/34.

15. Meetings of British officials 5 and 6 October 1943, CAB 99/33.

16. Ibid, meeting of 23 September.

17. Mr J G Winant, US Ambassador in London, to Secretary of State, 5 August 1943, *FRUS* 1943 I (1963), pp 1081–2.

18. Gardner, op cit, pp 111–12; Harrod, *Life of . . . Keynes*, pp 557–9. Mr J E Meade vividly recorded Keynes as 'raging' about an American document that 'That is intolerable. It is yet another Talmud', provoking White's rejoinder that 'We will try to produce something which Your Highness *can* understand'—*Diary*, 9 October 1943.

19. Plenary meeting of 30 September, CAB 78/14.

20. Tel 4125 of 15 September, Washington to London, CAB 117/76.

21. Meeting of British officials, 22 September, CAB 99/33.

22. Baster's report of 22 September, CAB 117/76.

23. Meeting of British officials, 23 September, CAB 99/33.

24. Horsefield, *The International Monetary Fund*, I, p 51.

25. Tel 4261 of 22 September, Washington to London, CAB 117/76. Meeting of British officials, 23 September, CAB 99/33. Cf W Bagehot, *Lombard Street* (1873) reprinted in *The Collected Works of Walter Bagehot* (ed N St John-Stevas) IX (1978), pp 147–8.

26. Tels 4241 of 21 September and 4261 of 22 September, Washington to London, CAB 117/76; Meade, *Diary*, 24 September; Horsefield, op cit, I, pp 64–65.

27. Tel 6356 ABIDE from London to Washington of 22 September, CAB 117/76 and

also CAB 99/33; ibid, officials' meeting of 23 September.

28. Horsefield, op cit, I, pp 61–62.

29. ASD (44) 2 of 21 October 1943 and ASD (44) 3rd Meeting, 20 March 1944: CAB 99/34.

30. Ibid, ASD (44) 2.

31. Meeting of 8 September, CAB 99/33.

32. Ibid, meeting of 4 October; Meade, *Diary*, 4 October.

33. Ibid, 11 October.

34. Tels 6777 London to Washington, and 4532 and 4533 Washington to London, all of 8 October, CAB 117/76; Keynes, who more than once found the journalistic ingenuity of Dr Paul Einzig in *The Financial News* a sore trial subsequently complained to Mr Brendan Bracken, Minister of Information and former editor of that newspaper. Bracken replied that the Chancellor of the Exchequer had spoken to him about Einzig, to whom Bracken had in turn spoken, to no effect: correspondence 7–13 January 1944, T 247/34.

35. 16 October, CAB 78/14.

36. 5 September meeting of officials in London, CAB 99/33; tel 230 of 7 September, Australian Commonwealth Government to Dominions Office, CAB 117/76; plenary meeting of 16 October, CAB 78/14; ASD (44) 5 on Employment Policy, CAB 99/34.

37. Talks with Dominion representatives in Washington, AD (BC)(43) 1st Meeting, 22 September, CAB 78/14; tel 4283 Washington to London of 25 September and 4399 of 2 October, CAB 117/76; ibid, tel 281 of 28 October, Australian Commonwealth Government to Dominions Office.

38. Reports by Mr S D Waley of 17 September and Mr Richard Law of 22 September, CAB 99/33, and reports of these meetings, CAB 78/14.

39. United Kingdom-Canada meetings in Ottawa 22, 23, 27 October, ibid; United States-Canada discussions, 3 & 8 January 1944, T 230/172 and CAB 99/34.

40. ASD (44)2, Report of discussions, CAB 99/34.

41. Copy dated 17 September 1943 in ibid, and circulated to War Cabinet as GEN 19/47 of 8 November 1943, CAB 78/14.

42. 1 October, AD (43) 23, CAB 78/14.

CHAPTER 6

1944: Deadlock in Commercial Policy, Progress in Monetary Policy

(1) BRITISH HESITATIONS

Following the broad understandings achieved in Washington, where the British 'Outline' of post-war commercial policy had been used as the basis for the unpublished Joint Anglo-American report, failure to sustain the momentum towards the goals of Article VII would clearly risk the fudging of the whole prospect of joint Anglo-American policies for the post-war world. Fudged it proved to be in respect of commercial policy. The monetary plans, however, which had originally been ahead of commercial policy since 1941 but which had limped a little in Washington, did progress strikingly in 1944. The *Joint Statement by Experts on the Establishment of an International Monetary Fund* in April marked a substantial agreement between British and American views;[1] three months later came the climax of the Bretton Woods Conference to establish the International Monetary Fund and the International Bank. Commercial policy, in contrast, lost its Washington impetus and indeed its Washington birth certificate during 1944. The resumption of the commercial policy talks, originally expected for late 1943 or early 1944, came only in November 1944 after months of tautening political deadlock in Britain, and then in an emasculated form, in a lower key than originally anticipated, with the Washington document diluted by the British Government and virtually discarded by the Americans. Moreover, conscious as it was of domestic political opposition to the trade proposals, the War Cabinet was equally aware, particularly after an aggressive House of Commons debate in May 1944, of comparable hostility to the monetary plans. That hostility appeared to be fundamental (and well-organised). Keynes, who spent 'seven hours in the cursed Gallery [of the House of Commons] lacerated in mind and body' noted that 'the whole thing was smeared by this unreasoning wave of isolationism and anti-Americanism which is... passing over us just now'.[2] If the Bretton Woods agreements nevertheless followed within weeks, disquiet over the monetary plans did not abate; critics were held off only by their persisting hope and the Government's equally persistent avoidance of further parliamentary debate. The agreements escaped full-dress debate until the end of 1945 when, joined with the American Loan, they were to be driven through an uneasy Parliament.

To view first the general attitude in London towards post-war economic policies in autumn 1943 is to discern something like a sideways movement as well as some backward steps in relation to the implementation of Article VII. This shuffling developed with discussion of the masterly reports and series of questions and answers on his mission that Mr Richard Law provided.[3] Critical questions came from several Ministers, notably from Mr E Bevin, Minister of Labour and National Service; Mr R S Hudson*, Minister of Agriculture; and, on a wide range of topics, from Mr L S Amery, Secretary of State for India. There were four major anxieties, which the Washington talks had left unsettled in the hope of subsequent resolution: Britain's defence against external economic fluctuations, particularly against an American slump; the use of import controls and of subsidies to protect agriculture; the possibility of linked reductions of tariffs and preferences; and policy during the post-war transition. Mr Bevin had in 1942 secured from the War Cabinet a stipulation that the monetary proposals must preclude deflation and unemployment as a means to correct external imbalance; the British representatives had striven to infuse this into the spirit of the Washington discussions and of the draft joint statement on monetary policy that had yet to be agreed. Mr Bevin was once again apprehensive, however, fearing that American influence had produced plans resembling gold-standard arrangements. Mr Law pointed to the liquidity to be available in the Fund, the scope to control capital outflows, the provision for adjustment of exchange rates, the action possible against scarce currencies, and the opportunity under the commercial policy proposals to use quantitative restrictions under appropriate circumstances. Further, the gold element in the Fund subscription had been reduced, and the passivity of the Fund in supplying liquidity had been virtually assured. On agriculture Mr Law claimed that in general the Washington understandings had left 'sufficient elbow room for reasonable protective policies, while outlawing the more extreme forms of protectionism', but he faced the evident unwillingness of the Ministry of Agriculture to relinquish freedom to use quantitative restrictions and to accept a limit on subsidies. Tariffs and preferences once again found an implacable defender in Mr Amery. Mr Law explained his view that the reduction or elimination of preferences had to be seen in the context of the reduction of much greater trade barriers, which on balance would aid British exports; but such arguments were to be scarcely effective against entrenched emotionalism about empire and preference.

*HUDSON, Robert Spear, 1st Viscount, 1952 (1886–1957); Secretary, Department of Overseas Trade, 1937–40; Minister of Shipping, 1940; Minister of Agriculture and Fisheries, 1940–45.

There remained the transition problem, which was partly one of re-assurance that there would indeed be a transition period; it involved also concern about the availability of and scope for controls. The Washington conclusions had encompassed a first phase of two to three years, virtually a holding period for existing controls, followed by one of gradual reduction; the Minister of Agriculture, however, wanted freedom for whatever policies might seem necessary for agriculture, industry and the general ensuring of employment.

(2)DISSENT ON TRADE AND AGRICULTURE

On the trade proposals, Mr Law's efforts did not satisfy the Cabinet doubters. Their flow of memoranda, verging on downright obstructionism, increased during the spring of 1944. The critics gained breathing space from Commonwealth considerations, which thrice during the early part of 1944 gave occasion or excuse for hesitation about commercial policy. Time was gained for determined opposition to harden towards the Washington proposals which, as had been feared, lost their impetus. In contrast to the protracted delays before the 1943 talks, it was now London that evaded, and the American Administration which was anxious to resume, Article VII talks. At an early stage, in January 1944, American reports from London were blending explanations of delay in terms of pressure of work on British officials and Ministers with warnings of potential opposition to the Washington proposals. By March the reports were that May was the earliest chance for talks, but a doubtful one. There seemed to be ministerial difficulties in making 'long-range decisions', with the wartime electoral truce apparently weakening. It was a 'dying administration' according to a leading civil servant.[4] Certainly the widely-expected Allied invasion of western Europe foreshadowed the end of the war, and with it the loosening of the political coalition. It was not surprising that there was apprehension within Government over the implications of the trade proposals. The War Cabinet did indeed broadly approve Mr Law's report in February 1944, whilst noting that there were points to watch, especially concerning the transition. Somewhat ominously for the future of the proposals, however, Mr Churchill thought that there should be consideration of alternatives if there should prove to be no Anglo-American agreement. A ministerial committee, on External Economic Policy, was formed to prepare for forthcoming talks with Dominion and Indian representatives and to advise on commercial policy in the transition.[5] This Committee quickly prepared a report that, with qualifications, commended the Washington schemes as a basis for those talks.[6] The qualifications rehearsed the now familiar worries about the monetary proposals (passivity, the sterling area, the transition). On commercial policy it supported the view that to secure a reduction in American tariffs there must be readiness to contemplate though not to advocate changes in Imperial Preference; these should be considered not on a narrowly reciprocal basis, but within a wider context of relevance to efforts to increase British trade. On agriculture the Committee asserted the right for the United Kingdom to control prices, to subsidise production, and to engage in bulk purchase overseas, but it also claimed that the British interpretation of the Washington principles safeguarded these desiderata. On the other hand, the Committee limited its defence of quantitative restrictions on imports to their necessity while the balance of payments was unfavourable.

The War Cabinet broadly approved this report. It could be used for the Commonwealth discussions, though with no cachet of authority from the War Cabinet, which intended to discuss it further.[7] Commitment was indeed scarcely possible, for opposition was mounting. Lord Beaverbrook*, the Lord Privy Seal, had put in a truculent minority report, which deplored the Washington proposals and supported the Bank of England's distaste for the projected International Monetary Fund (below, pp 140–2). Mr Churchill shortly afterwards summarised[8] for the War Cabinet neatly and fairly, though in view of his own free-trading inclinations rather guardedly, four 'fundamental points' relevant to Article VII discussions. On only one, avoidance of dear food, did he more or less lean towards the proposals. On the other three—opposition to any new form of gold standard, the refusal to drop Imperial Preference save in exchange for drastic reductions in trade barriers, and insistence on retaining the wheat subsidies enacted in 1932—he spoke defensively and almost negatively.

Apart from Mr Amery's unremitting attacks on anything favouring free trade or indeed on international trade outside the Empire, the major hostility to the Washington principles came from the Minister of Agriculture, Mr R S Hudson. Behind him massed the political weight of the Tory shires. He opened a no-nonsense memorandum[9] to the War Cabinet forthrightly: 'The Washington proposals as they stand are incompatible with a sound and permanent agricultural policy'. He was now to fight to strangle the Washington child which, some two years before, his officials had in vain struggled less tersely to prevent being born (above, p 88). To assure stable, reasonable prices for consumers and economic stability for farmers, the principle of the levy-subsidy, by which a (possibly limited) levy on imports financed a (possibly limited) subsidy on domestic production, would not be suitable for all products unless imports of them and of their substitutes were controlled. International regulation was

---

*BEAVERBROOK, William Maxwell Aitken, 1st Baron 1917 (1879–1964); Minister for Aircraft Production, 1940–41; Minister of State, 1941; Minister of Supply, 1941–42; Lord Privy Seal, 1943–45.

unacceptable. Sceptical in general of the Buffer Stock scheme for commodities, the Minister noted its authors' recognition of its inapplicability to just those perishable products giving most anxiety to British agriculture. Moreover, resort to closer international supervision of prices and production would be doubly objectionable. First, it would arise only on the proven inadequacy of the buffer stocks mechanism, and therefore might operate too tardily. Second, as Britain was not only the largest but almost the only importer of certain foodstuffs, it would be 'dangerous' both for her producers and her consumers for production and marketing to be dependent upon international regulation. Hence, the 'minimum requirements' were levy-subsidy arrangements, backed by regulation of imports, with seasonal tariffs for certain products: all forbidden under the Washington schemes. In another paper[10] of the same date, disdainful of the commercial policy proposals as a whole, the Minister emphasised the wide political basis of his opposition. The Coalition Government had in November 1940 recognised 'the importance of maintaining after the war a healthy and well-balanced agriculture as an essential and permanent feature of national policy'. He asserted that there were three possibilities. That all-party pledge must be abandoned; there could be no further Anglo-American discussions on the Washington proposals unless they were modified fundamentally; or, in the spirit of the Prime Minister's memorandum of the previous October[11] and the War Cabinet's decision thereon, they should concentrate upon the transition and not bother overmuch with controversial long-term projects.

Before considering these broadsides, the War Cabinet had concluded in April 1944 that the Washington proposals on commercial policy should not yet be published. Work on them was insufficiently advanced and discussions with the Dominion Prime Ministers lay ahead. The Cabinet instructed the President of the Board of Trade, Mr H Dalton, to prepare a memorandum for consideration in those discussions.[12] Mr Dalton's memorandum reiterated the broad Overton-Hurst-Washington case for Anglo-American agreement to move towards more free, multilateral trade, with qualifications for the transition and for special difficulties. On agriculture, however, he pointed out that while non-protectionist levy subsidies (ie, those which did not raise prices to consumers) would not be dependent on international approval, quantitative regulation of imports would be. The War Cabinet considered this memorandum, the two memoranda from the Minister of Agriculture, and memoranda for and against respectively less restrictive trading policy from the Minister of War Transport (Lord Leathers)* and the Secretary of State for

*LEATHERS, Frederick James, 1st Baron 1941, 1st Viscount 1954 (1883–1965); 1940 joined Ministry of Shipping as adviser on matters relating to coal; Minister of War Transport, 1941–45; Secretary of State for the Co-ordination of Transport, Fuel and Power, 1951–53.

India, towards the end of April.[13] It continued to be indecisive. Mr Dalton's conclusions, with a further memorandum summarising the results of the officials' talks, should be laid before the Prime Ministers, with the explanation that HM Government was not committed to the proposals, whereas all favoured the encouragement of Commonwealth and Imperial trade. It should be further explained to them that the Washington proposals, on which their views were to be sought, had raised 'difficulties' not yet resolved and that there were 'doubts' about the position under them of Britain's agriculture.

(3) DEADLOCK IN COMMERCIAL POLICY

The need to take, to assess, and if appropriate to incorporate Commonwealth views in shaping policy had been recognised in Mr Law's preliminary report on his mission. In fact, there were to be three major Commonwealth evaluations during the early months of 1944. The first came unexpectedly when, early in January 1944, delay over the arrival of a Soviet Russian delegation to discuss Article VII prompted the American State Department to invite Canadian and other Commonwealth representatives in Washington to fill the gap.[14] A further meeting between American and Canadian representatives was held in February in New York. The important message from these encounters was that the Canadians found it possible to combine caution about their neighbour's determination to combine drastic tariff cuts and the virtual abolition of preferences with broad support for American intentions. Whilst stressing that for Canada preferences had been of domestic political concern even before the Ottawa agreements of 1932, they emphasised the need for multilateral action and for linking cuts in tariffs with reductions in preferences. In fact, a large all-round cut in most-favoured-nation tariff rates, themselves a form of preference, would largely eliminate, or substantially diminish, preferential margins.

A second and the major Commonwealth pause came in February and March 1944 with discussions in London between HM Government and representatives of the Dominion and Indian Governments.[15] The third in a series of such meetings to consider post-war economic plans (the two earlier had been in October 1942 and June 1943), these discussions brought recognition that modification of Imperial Preference would have to be considered; but perhaps most notably it occasioned elaboration of British reluctance to let slip quantitative restrictions, which were now being disguised as 'the programming of imports'.[16] The duration of the transition, indeed its effective commencement, evoked British unease. The Canadian Government, well aware of the precariousness of the wartime rise in exports to the United Kingdom, hoped to dissuade Britain from a post-war policy of trade restriction. Its representatives advocated a simple one-stage transition; they pointed out that effectively that might begin with re-conversion to a peacetime economy starting before the end of the war; it might advisedly be short should the USA be contemplating an early cut in tariffs. A further consideration was the desirability of initiating the implementation of the two main schemes, monetary and commercial, more or less simultaneously. This brought the more cautious British Ministers and officials against the choice between accepting the unacceptable and excluding the unexcludable in trade arrangements; a third possibility, at which Mr J E Meade in particular worked incessantly and ingeniously, was to devise 'objective tests' that would meet British concern to provide for special problems, yet operate with the automaticity and non-intervention that American policy-makers and British proponents of economic rationality broadly concurred in seeking.

The main impression of British policy during these discussions was clear: cold feet were developing. By the time of the third Commonwealth event, the meeting in May 1944 of Commonwealth Prime Ministers in London, there was no doubt that many Commonwealth feet were also growing colder and were likely to drag over the commercial policy proposals.[17] So ready over two years previously to urge Britain to accept Article VII and initially prepared to accept it themselves when the tense opening months of the Pacific war made them so dependent upon American help, the Australian Government now preferred to dig in behind Imperial Preference. New Zealand echoed, and all bar Canada—Australia, New Zealand, South Africa and India—affirmed that they clung to it. Canada's Mr Mackenzie King* alone echoed the boldness of earlier British proposals in urging his colleagues that to secure serious tariff cuts elsewhere in the world would necessitate comparable reductions in preferences (though not their unilateral modification, as the Canadians had impressed on the Americans already: above, p 134). Moreover, the Prime Ministers were also considering the proposed International Monetary Fund, on which an American proposal for an early conference had been received but not yet formally accepted by the British Government. Mr King reiterated his recent statement to the Canadian House of Commons that his Government's approach to the monetary plans would be 'greatly, perhaps decisively' conditioned by progress on other economic plans, including trade policy.

Mr Churchill went along with the more defensive attitude. He read to the Prime Ministers his summary of some two months earlier of 'certain fundamental points' (above p 132). Further, he read to them the crucial letter from President Roosevelt in February 1942 which had

---

*KING, William Lyon Mackenzie (1874–1950); Prime Minister, President of the Privy Council, Canada, 1935–48; Secretary of State for External Affairs, 1935–46.

finally secured acceptance of Article VII (above, p 57). In doing so, he affirmed his view that the British and Commonwealth Governments had their hands thereby left 'entirely free and safeguarded as regards Imperial Preference, and... [that the letter bound] ... the United States in respect of that issue'. Whether or not this stretched the meaning of the President's letter, which had stressed that no subject should be excluded from post-war economic discussions, it sailed past the difficulty that Article VII required Britain to work towards the elimination of discrimination, which had been recognised at the time of signing to include ultimately the ending of Imperial Preference.

In truth, by this time, there was complete indecisiveness over commercial policy. Very shortly, there was to be talk of 'impasse' and 'deadlock' which seriously delayed resumption of Anglo-American discussions in that sphere. Opposition, based partly on ignorance, gave 'not a dog's chance' to American inspired policy, thought Keynes, who nevertheless struggled to devise ways to break the deadlock:[18] but these involved trying to persuade Americans to accept such policies as import controls and not to regard preferences as 'original sin'. The American Embassy in London reiterated to Washington the essentially political nature of the obstacles. Civil Servants were pessimistic about a resumption of trade talks, but it was not the technical experts who had retreated from the previous year's understandings. Cabinet unity was the problem, particularly over agriculture and Imperial Preference. Perhaps, said Mr Winant, as he had long been urging, some senior American representatives should be sent to London, lest the feeling develop that Washington also cared little about progress on commercial policy.[19]

By now, in mid-1944, a British delegation was in the United States for the monetary conference at Bretton Woods. It had been suggested by US officials to its members, who were inclined to agree, and also to the Treasury in London, that they should afterwards go to Washington to exchange information informally on the position over Article VII.[20] Treasury opinion was unenthusiastic, for the specific reason of the *impasse* over commercial policy and for the wider reason of apprehension over the impact that such exchanges might have upon the Anglo-American discussions on Lend-Lease and the restoration of British exports in Stage II (following the end of the European war) which were expected later in the year. Embarrassed by American persistence, the Treasury, in co-operation with the Foreign Office, suggested an alternative, which the Chancellor broadly approved. Mr Law would shortly be in Washington for conversations about oil and to discuss a range of other Anglo-American problems; could not his discussions extend to cover the position over Article VII with the Secretary of State? Put to the Prime Minister, this brought a cutting rebuke for the Chancellor for appearing 'very light and easy' over the Conservative Party's feelings over Article VII.[21] A few days later, however, Mr Law himself cabled his assessment that Britain's unforthcoming behaviour over Article VII was causing damage in Washington, and he therefore sought and obtained from the War Cabinet authority to explain the reasons.[22] Accordingly, he made excuses to Mr Cordell Hull that the military operations in western Europe were pre-occupying ministers, but that the Chancellor might visit Washington shortly, and that his Government hoped to resume high level commercial policy talks, in which Cabinet Ministers would participate, in the autumn. This removed any need to act on Mr Winant's suggestion to send high officials to London.[23] (In the event, the Chancellor never visited the USA; on the other hand, Mr Morgenthau and Dr H D White of the US Treasury were able to visit London in August 1944, when clarification of Stage II problems eased that particular complication.) For the Bretton Woods mission Article VII was to remain largely a forbidden subject.[24] Two of its members, however, Professor L C (later Lord) Robbins and Professor D H (later Sir Dennis) Robertson*, who had planned to visit Washington to discuss commodity questions with the British supply missions there, were by some tangle of transatlantic communication told that they could discuss such matters also with American officials. They duly had a 'useful but not exciting talk', carefully skirting explicit discussion of Article VII.[25]

If all this relaxed the deadlock on commercial policy a little, it did not end it. At the Cabinet meeting which authorised Mr Law's apologia the Prime Minister did indeed agree to form a Cabinet Committee to re-examine the Washington scheme of October 1943,[26] but that Committee and a group of officials were to struggle for several months before producing a more restricted proposal (see below, pp 194–9). By that time, with the promised resumption of Anglo-American talks overdue, it was to become clear that strong domestic pressures both in the United Kingdom and in the USA upon their respective governments were seriously reducing the chances for a comprehensive agreement on commercial policy.

(4) MONETARY POLICY AND THE BANK OF ENGLAND

On monetary policy, in contrast with commercial policy, Anglo-American agreement was to be achieved between October 1943 and mid-1944. This took longer than expected, to the intense irritation of the US Administration. The delay reflected growing British unease

*ROBERTSON, Dennis Holme, Kt 1953 (1890–1963); Cassel Professor of Economics, University of London, 1939–44; an Economic Adviser, HM Treasury, 1939–44; Professor of Political Economy, University of Cambridge, 1944–57.

and reservations as consideration of the monetary proposals merged with discussions about the immediate post-war problems of the balance of payments (see chapter 9). Those discussions, centring around memoranda by Keynes, suggested that there were two prerequisites for the early implementation of the monetary scheme, particularly of the crucial obligation to maintain free convertibility of currently earned sterling. One was to limit drastically, perhaps by blocking and partial cancellation, the availability of the abnormally high sterling balances accumulating during the war through Britain's overseas expenditure outside North America. The other was to seek financial aid from the USA to meet the dollar deficits of Britain and the rest of the sterling area in the early post-war years. Treasury opinion narrowly favoured the new monetary system. The Bank of England, scorning Keynes's two suggested prerequisites, was against it. As if to reinforce apprehensions about the constraint of sterling balances, a Cabinet Committee, which considered during early 1944 that large portion held by India, was to prove unable to propose any early action.

In this coming together of the monetary scheme and of Britain's specific post-war problems, it was not to prove easy either to secure or to sustain agreed policies. The Law Mission had brought back, not an agreed statement on monetary policy, but only a British draft for one. Moreover there had been scant examination of the ancillary American proposal for a Reconstruction Bank, to which the British authorities were not to give serious attention until April 1944. The draft Joint Statement of October 1943 on the proposed Stabilisation Fund, with its notes of substantial Anglo-American agreement as well as of outstanding differences, had nevertheless represented significant progress; being fundamental to the achievement of other economic plans, the monetary proposals presented a major challenge to agreement.

Following the Law Mission there were roughly five phases. From October 1943 until April 1944 numerous drafts shaped for publication an agreed 'Joint Statement' ('by experts' to avoid immediate commitment by governments). This was the product of discussions in London, between London and Washington, and in Washington, where visiting British Treasury officials compensated for the absence of a senior Treasury official since the death in August 1943 of Sir Frederick Phillips; they supplemented the vigorous efforts of the Ambassador's economic adviser, Mr Redvers Opie. During this first phase, American pressure encountered a Britain apparently dragging its feet. In the next phase, despite the agreement reached on the 'Joint Statement', the Bank of England continued to press its anxiety over the monetary fund; there were also fuller discussions than hitherto on the proposed Reconstruction Bank. During June and July it is convenient to identify three phases. Aboard ship for the international monetary conference at Bretton Woods, the British delegation held productive discussions, especially on the proposed Bank. Next came a preliminary conference at Atlantic City, and then the grand assembly ('the monkey house' as Keynes habitually called such gatherings)[27] at Bretton Woods during the first three weeks of July.

Three major issues had remained unsettled or unclear in October 1943. On exchange rates the Treasury relaxed by the end of the year its attempt to retain scope for more variation than the American preference would allow. Apparently the future outermost limits of departure from declared parities, once the Fund had been established, would be twenty per cent, consisting of ten per cent unilaterally, plus a further ten per cent on consultation with the Fund. This retreat, an acknowledgement of American determination, was less than it seemed. Not only did the Treasury assume that quantitative regulation of imports would be inevitable in the early post-war years, but Keynes added his belief that in any case such controls were preferable to and more precise than exchange depreciation as a remedy for an adverse balance of payments.[28] Moreover, as if to hedge his bets and to read escape possibilities into the existing or future version of the Fund, Keynes was later to declare that 'the 20% was not of course a maximum change'.[29]

A second issue, that of the nuances of uncertainty that the Americans wished to retain over access to the proposed Fund's resources, had not been clarified satisfactorily when, by the end of 1943, the American view was again accepted. There was, however, a British reservation in the hope that there would be breadth and flexibility in the Fund's attitude. Moreover, the issue was partially side-stepped by a formal British statement that, in the most difficult period, that of the post-war transition, it was hoped that special arrangements would avoid the need for recourse to the Fund for the urgent purposes of relief and reconstruction.[30] British concern persisted, however, to ensure that the Fund should avoid discrimination against any particular currency, and that it should provide resources 'passively' on members' representations (above p 122). This had focused on British preference for the Fund's resources and for drawings on them to be denominated in a single new international unit ('Unitas' in the earlier American scheme, 'Bancor' in the British). To the puzzlement of some of his colleagues, Keynes had been an unwavering proponent of the 'Unitas' approach until early 1944, when he recognised the uselessness of trying to overcome American opposition to it; the Treasury hesitated a few weeks longer, yielding finally to the American view in April 1944.[31] There were American assurances that their preferred alternative of a fund ('a mixed bag') of currencies was largely technical and would be less provocative to sceptical New York bankers.[32] In contrast, some new international unit would probably require specific Congressional authorisation with the accompanying troublesome debates.[33] To the sceptics, however, especially to the Bank of England,[34] a 'non-Unitas' fund would embody a potential threat to a monetary sovereignty already prospectively constrained by commitment to convertibility at virtually rigid exchange rates. Such a fund, with holdings of members' currencies, would be a dealer in currencies. The natural tendency to receive the weaker currencies in exchange for stronger would constantly threaten the quality of its portfolio, to offset which it would be bound, whatever its intention of remaining 'passive', to become 'active' in management and hence to operate against weaker currencies. Even a 'Unitas' fund held dangers, for the Americans' name of 'Stabilisation Fund' indicated their leaning to active intervention.

The third and most crucial unsettled issue, that of the arrangements for the transition, brought together all the other apprehensions to put the monetary plans into question. With the difficulties and uncertainties foreseen for Britain's post-war balance of payments, was it wise to let an untried scheme determine policies? Would it not be better first to solve the transition problem and only then construct a more permanent international system? Strong Treasury voices and particularly the Bank of England favoured the seeming prudence of the latter path. A vigorous debate now erupted, in the early weeks of 1944, over whether the Treasury should go ahead with the post-war monetary plans. The debate developed within wider and more prolonged discussions over post-war policy, to which Keynes gave impetus and direction in January 1944 with a memorandum entitled 'Notes on External Finance in the Post-Japanese-Armistice Transitional Period'[35]. The immediate relevance of that memorandum, which is discussed more fully below (pp 225–7), was its argument that Britain's post-war deficits and those of the sterling area would constitute, together with the continuing accumulation of balances, a burden graver than was generally realised. It would be hazardous to depend on sustaining that burden by a modest adaptation of the wartime arrangements of the sterling area and of payments agreements. Drastic measures would be necessary to restrain the expenditure of the balances, and substantial aid from the USA would be indispensable if there were to be early movement towards a less restrictive system of international payments along the lines of the proposed monetary scheme. 'The Austere Alternative' of a much more tightly drawn sterling area than during the war and of dependence on Britain's own resources might be unavoidable and indeed workable, but at the price of worsening the problems that must eventually be solved, and possibly with forbidding implications both at home and internationally.

The Bank was not to be persuaded. In a series of representations in January and February,[36] it made the first of two major attempts in 1944 to deflect the Treasury from the projected commitments and to press its own alternative (the second attempt came in June). The Bank affirmed sympathy with the objectives of exchange rate stability and of greater ease in making international payments, but feared that the proposed fund would make their achievement more rather than less difficult. In the long-term, reasoned the Bank, if the obligation of convertibility at near-fixed exchange rates had the force of an international treaty, Britain would virtually be back on a gold standard.

To orient post-war policy towards what it feared as an unsustainable commitment of convertibility would, the Bank warned, intensify the already worrying problems of the transition. The Bank was profoundly worried about the impact upon the sterling area. As a normal feature the fund was expected to deal directly with members; this would tend to by-pass and to weaken London as a financial centre, and hence to complicate the Bank's already demanding task of the management of sterling. A major blow to the sterling area would result from the attempt to move in the transition towards the goal of convertibility. This would require the blocking of excess sterling balances both inside and outside the sterling area. Exchange controls on current and capital transfers would be necessary within the sterling area to maintain convertibility outside it; this would destroy its rationale, the freedom of transfer, and with that the area itself, which during the war had provided for all its members the especial advantage of the pooling of reserves and for Britain a means of financing its deficits with other members. Effective blocking, if that were possible (and the existence of privately held commercial balances argued against it) would be a curious way to launch a new monetary scheme intended to reduce international restrictions. Above all, by diminishing the attractiveness of sterling as an international currency it would harm invisible earnings, and much else besides: the sterling area comprised business, personal and imperial relationships of proven value, transcending banking matters. In practice, the Bank stressed, it was neither feasible nor desirable to treat the widely differing countries of the sterling area, which was very far from being homogeneous, in a standardised manner. In any case, the Bank emphasised, it was unrealistic to believe that blocking could eliminate the risk of a drain on the reserves of a currency so internationally used as sterling. Balances held for expected payments might well, on political uncertainties, be withdrawn, placing grave strains upon the maintenance of convertibility and of stable exchange rates.

The Bank clearly regarded the proponents of the monetary fund, including Keynes, as failing to understand the sterling area. Moreover, the Bank believed that Keynes had overstated the admittedly serious problem of the sterling area's post-war dollar deficit, partly by miscalculation, partly by overlooking the abnormal, temporary nature of adverse wartime influences on sterling trade. Such considerations led the Bank doubly to reinforce its challenge to the monetary fund. First, there appeared to be less justification for seeking special American financial aid to allow Britain to operate the scheme; in any case, the Bank was extremely doubtful of the chances of a loan, given American political pressures and the strength of many Americans' feelings that they were handing out too much Lend-Lease aid to a Britain that was holding on to excessive gold and dollar reserves. Second, the Bank rejected the equation of potential deficit and unavoidable loan; this offered no guarantee of the elimination of weaknesses in the balance of payments, which would better be tackled by control of domestic demand and of imports, as well as by export policy.

Having argued thus against the proposed monetary fund as such, and against the case for accepting risks in order to operate it, the Bank offered its own prescription. While countries should remain free to alter their exchange rates, to secure the stable rates desired by the Americans Britain could agree with them to maintain an appropriate rate, say £1 = $4.00 (it had been $4.03 since early in the war). This would be backed by the extension of payments agreements, particularly to promote the use of sterling by European and Latin American countries. If there were to be an international institution let it be consultative, with scope to evolve from experience rather than be, as on the existing plans, an ambitious body which, if found inadequate, could seriously damage the cause of international co-operation.

The Bank's was a technician's verdict and was treated with appropriate respect: 'It is difficult for us to advise the Chancellor to endorse a Currency Scheme', wrote one senior Treasury official to another,[37] 'when the Bank of England believes that its present form would be injurious to British interests and have said so expressly, and when we are informed that the American banking system is hostile to the scheme, though perhaps for other reasons'. (It is worth noting that the most interesting alternative to the proposed fund on the American side was similarly oriented to the empirical central banking approach. This was the 'key currency' plan, echoing the Tripartite Agreement of 1936, advocated by Professor John H Williams[*][38] of Harvard University, who was also a vice-president of the New York Federal Reserve Bank.) There was, however, a political aspect to the currency proposals into which the technical experts could scarcely help straying, but which was essentially a matter for governmental decision. As the War Cabinet's Committee on External Economic Policy noted, when formulating instructions for United Kingdom representatives at the

---

* WILLIAMS, John Henry, (1887–1980), Economist; Economic Adviser, Federal Reserve Bank of New York 1933–52, Vice-President 1936–47, Economic Consultant 1956–64.

imperial discussions of February-March 1944, they should not over-stress the difficulties, and should keep in mind the War Cabinet's 'general view in favour of proceeding with a policy . . . on the lines discussed at Washington'.[39]

A powerful rejection of the Bank's case came from Keynes and other economists in government. Keynes reiterated his arguments and defended his statistical calculations.[40] Accepting the Bank's *caveat* that the scale of the balance of payments problem rested on policy, he deplored what he regarded as the War Cabinet's unduly relaxed atti-tude on this, and asked rhetorically of the prevailing outlook whether 'such rashness [was not] likely to end in extreme catastrophe?' The concerted response of the War Cabinet's economists was to stress the grave political and social implications of the Bank's alternative, as well as questioning its technical arguments.[41] In doing so they dealt also with the arguments of the Lord Privy Seal, Lord Beaverbrook, who in the committee, in the Cabinet, and elsewhere, had thrown his support behind what he believed to be the Bank's policy, perhaps not always to its advantage.[42] Although his rejection of the entire Washington proposals had concentrated on the commercial and commodity documents, he had claimed to discover in the monetary scheme the fatal flaw of a new gold standard, Mr Law's refutation notwithstanding (above, p 130). He further asserted that the Bank's critique paralleled his own objection to sterling being made freely con-vertible.

The economists claimed that the traditional banking function of the sterling area could survive within the proposed fund, given a supply of credit from it, suitable arrangements about excess balances, and a degree of inevitable control over capital movements. They ques-tioned, however, the prospect of drawing non-sterling countries closer to a post-war sterling area that, on the Bank's forecast, would involve significant controls; and if such countries did enter it, would the sterling area really gain thereby, with yet more potential deficits to finance? Such an extended role for sterling would gravely harm Britain. It would alienate sterling countries by continuing constraints upon their non-sterling expenditure. It would damage Anglo-American relations, not just by the abandonment of discussions on post-war monetary policy but particularly by giving the impression of being an organised attempt to discriminate against American trade. As for Lord Beaverbrook's striving to link with the Bank's ideas his dream of an empire economy largely independent of the rest of the world, that was unrealistic and even more likely to destroy economic and other co-operation with the United States.[43] His castigation of the monetary scheme as a gold standard overlooked the scheme's flexi-bility; he had also underestimated the extent of convertibility and the strains on the sterling area implicit in the Bank's ideas. The Bank's proposals would lead to a disaster even worse than that of the return to gold at an overvalued parity which it had inspired in 1925, for they would scarcely encourage American provision of financial assistance. They would throw post-war Britain on to her own resources and involve austerity. In an impassioned rejoinder to a personal letter from Lord Beaverbrook, Keynes recalled[44] his own accurate prophecies of earlier disasters from Bank policies, to echo the warning of further disaster from the Bank's alternative, and begged him 'For God's sake have nothing to do with it!'.

Further support for the monetary plans came from the meetings with representatives of the Dominion and Indian Governments in London during February and March 1944. Their monetary committee's report, whilst anxious about those features which continued to trouble British officials and Ministers, and also about the American proposal for an international investment bank, approved the broad principles of the proposed fund. Moreover, though preferring the 'Unitas' type of fund, the representatives felt that it could not be made a condition for accepting the plan.[45]

(5) TREASURY CAUTION

Even now, however, Treasury caution persisted, to the edge of indecisiveness. Although the 'Unitas' question was no longer regarded as a potential breaking point, the Bank of England remained gravely apprehensive about it, and the prevailing Treasury view stressed persisting doubt about the principle of the scheme as a whole. Advice to the Chancellor, who agreed, was of the need to avoid giving the US officials the impression that British acquiescence in the 'non-Unitas' form meant agreement over the proposed fund, which would encourage them to publicise this.[46] There was also the wider problem of whether it would be necessary to keep movement on the monetary plans in line with the slower progress of the other Article VII discussions. In late March and early April three sets of pressures modified these Treasury hesitations. First, the Dominions Office gave a push forward, with a meeting of officials who distinguished the major issues.[47] Following the recent imperial discussions, which a strong Treasury view had seen as a reason for delay in order to ascertain American reaction to them,[48] it was in fact necessary to have an early War Cabinet decision, to give guidance on its views to imperial Governments in advance of the forthcoming meeting in London of their Prime Ministers. On the relation of the monetary plans to Article VII generally, a bargaining procedure was envisaged. Since the United Kingdom's acceptance of the monetary plans depended on the availability to it of trade controls during the transition, endorsement now could be a useful lever to secure American co-operation to reduce trade restrictions. In accordance with the meeting's recommendations, the Dominions Secretary consulted other Ministers closely concerned (the Foreign Secretary, Chancellor, and President of the Board of Trade) and then submitted to the War Cabinet a memorandum stressing the need to form a view.

From Keynes came a second set of pressures, in his concern lest the impression of British diffidence should encourage the Americans to publish the proposals independently, to the detriment of Anglo-American co-operation. This concern did not reflect approval of the Americans' existing procedure, which all in London disliked; it was based not only on anxiety over the risk of longer-term damage to Anglo-American co-operation, but also on a medium-term fear that avoidable disharmony would encourage American insistence on unfavourable terms for post-war aid.[49]

The third set or flow of pressures was American, with in particular 'a very insistent personal message' (the Chancellor's description) from his opposite number, Mr Morgenthau, stressing 'the urgent necessity' for an immediate reply to the President's wish for a Conference on the proposed Monetary Fund and Reconstruction Bank. Further messages of unconcealed impatience and irritation were to follow. The American hope was for a monetary conference in May; this would mean an early publication of a Joint Statement to allow preliminary discussion. The Administration wanted an international agreement before the autumn Presidential election, even if possible before the Democratic Party's nominating convention in July, so that it could be flourished as an example of the President's achievement of a major political objective.[50] All this tensed Anglo-American relations in a characteristic contrast between the relative centralisation of governmental authority in Britain and its relative dispersal in the USA. The Chancellor replied to Mr Morgenthau's message that, with parliamentary debate scarcely avoidable, it would spare embarrassment to know the American position and whether he had correctly surmised that publication would leave the Administration uncommitted. Mr Morgenthau answered testily; it had already been agreed that the monetary proposals concerned the experts, not governments, and he was well aware of the parliamentary constraint.[51] Both Mr Morgenthau and his chief expert, Dr H D White, appeared nervously desperate to push rapidly ahead. White had been fending off informed inquiries about the monetary plans from other countries, and there was a fear that delay would allow the organised opposition to economic internationalism to persuade Congress to adopt some much less satisfactory proposals. Mr Morgenthau complained that embarrassment had already arisen from the delay by British Treasury representatives over publication. About to testify to Congressional committees, he wanted to tell them that publication was imminent (in, say, the third week of April), failing which it might be impossible to hold a conference in 1944.[52]

A lead out of this tangle came from the Chancellor who, with 'one puff of common sense',[53] distilled into policy the recommendations of the Dominions Secretary and of his advisers, whilst firmly controlling American hustling. In a memorandum[54] to the War Cabinet he noted the persisting problems but, stressing the urgency of a decision, recommended acceptance of the principles of the monetary scheme. On procedure, he demurred at American impatience for a wide agreement between a number of countries, to be followed by some sort of conference. It would be better for Britain and the USA to agree and to work together on fundamentals as the basis of an agreement for publication. There could then be wider discussion, above all in parliamentary debate in which the Government would state its own position. On the crucial issue of the transitional arrangements and of the long-term obligations, Ministers should defend the scheme in Parliament by reliance on the transitional exemption from their full operation. We should, however, privately advise the United States of three conditions: the necessity for some international investment body, to provide reconstruction and long-term finance, which lay outside the scope of the monetary fund; the need to delay the fund's operation until the end of the war, and then to introduce its provisions gradually; and the need to qualify British acceptance in the light of experience during the transition (the second and third conditions clearly echoed the Bank of England's representations). On the wider issue of the interconnections with the comprehensive Article VII programme, especially with commercial policy, the Chancellor concluded that monetary discussions could go ahead without waiting for agreement on that.

The War Cabinet, at its meeting in mid-April 1944 which decided to mark time on commercial policy, accepted the Chancellor's advice.[55] Before, however, the Chancellor informed Mr Morgenthau that there could be simultaneous publication within a week, if agreement could be reached, instructions were sent to the Washington Embassy to impress upon the US Treasury the Chancellor's three conditions. This was done verbally and in writing.[56] There followed several frantic days across and on both sides of the Atlantic. A threat of extra complications arose from the US Treasury's desire to tell Congress that there was or quickly would be Anglo-American agreement on a parallel Joint Statement about its plan for a Reconstruction Bank;[57] London, as is explained below (pp 150–52) had been laggard about this, but deflected the problem. Some technical details of the proposed monetary fund had to be omitted to minimise delay. The principal difference in the final form from the draft joint statement of October 1943 was in the threefold amplification of the transitional provisions. A member could delay its implementation of the scheme until it believed itself able to operate it satisfactorily; there was provision to consult the

Fund if transitional measures still operated three years after its establishment; and members would have 'the benefit of any reasonable doubt' over transitional problems.[58]

At Keynes's suggestion the Joint Statement began with some 'Introductory Notes' which he had prepared.[59] These made a favourable comparison with the Clearing Union proposals published a year earlier. A government disavowal of any commitment prefaced the document, which was published more or less in time for Mr Morgenthau. But the Chancellor's steadfast adherence to a timetable that meant waiting for a parliamentary debate fretted the US Administration. Early in May the Secretary of State joined his Treasury colleague to declare that Britain was imperilling the chances of holding a conference, and with it the prospects for economic collaboration generally amongst the United Nations.[60] In fact, on the Americans' second fear, British officials had useful consultations on the Joint Statement during the apparent pause with experts of eight European Governments in London.[61] Besides illuminating technical complexities, these had the broad effect of consolidating support for the Anglo-American proposals. Shortly after, in the second week of May, the House of Commons unenthusiastically approved the 'Principles' in the Joint Statement as 'a suitable foundation for further international consultations' (the later House of Lords debate had fewer and kinder participants).[62] The Chancellor immediately accepted the informal American invitation to a monetary conference, though regretting his own inability to attend.[63] The formal invitation in late May specified a commencement date of 1 July, several weeks later than originally deemed possible; but further hustling over the arrangements lay ahead. The venue, a matter of considerable concern because of Keynes's physical frailty ('For God's sake don't send us to Washington at this time of the year' he scribbled on a cable from the Embassy there)[64] was formally notified as the Mount Washington Hotel at Bretton Woods, New Hampshire. It was out of consideration for Keynes that the smaller preliminary drafting conference in late June was arranged for Atlantic City, New Jersey.[65]

(6) CONVERTIBILITY AND THE EXCHANGE RATE

The holding of the Monetary Conference had at last been settled. The codeword SNAKEBITE was allotted to the administrative arrangements.[66] There was to be a small delegation, headed by Keynes.[67] Two major sets of problems, concerning the Monetary Fund and the Reconstruction Bank respectively, had still to be resolved in London.

The familiar difficulties over the Monetary Fund were sharpened partly by the need to instruct the British delegation, but also by various pressures from the Bank of England. The Bank-Treasury links had been uniquely extended in April 1944 when Lord Catto* had moved from the Treasury to be Governor. At the Treasury he had echoed the Bank's preference for gradualism and eclecticism in adopting any new system of international payments. He had resisted the surrender of the right to vary the exchange rate, and had proposed a clause, 'the Catto clause', to recognise that right, at the less disruptive price of suspension from the Monetary Fund's facilities, rather than withdrawal from it, should the Fund disagree with a member's action. As Governor he now, on the eve of the Bretton Woods Conference, wrote a carefully weighed letter to the Chancellor for consideration in briefing the British delegates.[68] He reiterated the Bank's earlier critique of the monetary plans: not to reject them, but to modify the crucial obligation of convertibility. His case, to be argued in dramatic fashion by Keynes shortly after the Conference, centred on sterling balances (he and Keynes had actively participated in a Cabinet Committee's discussions during 1942–44 on Indian balances). The Bank was apprehensive not solely over 'abnormal war balances' and over those that might accrue during the transition. Even if there were to be arrangements to deal with such balances, overseas holdings of sterling (apart from overseas holdings of other sterling assets, including traders' balances) would normally be substantial for London to function as an international financial centre. For those 'reserves balances', as they may conveniently be distinguished, the Joint Statement, declared Lord Catto, extended the commitment to provide convertibility on demand beyond the needs of current international payment: they could be switched right out of sterling, to be held in other currencies or in gold. The projected transition period of three years appeared too brief for the acquisition of sufficient overseas assets against such liabilities. The proposed commitment to convertibility would therefore facilitate precisely those destabilising movements between currencies that it was intended to prevent. (In the interests of clarity, it should be stressed that the description 'old', occurring in Treasury discussions, was used in a relative sense. It did *not* encompass all long-standing balances, such as wartime accumulations; it referred to those balances that might arise *after* the end of the transition, and which in due course would, if retained by their owners, become 'old' balances. They would be balances that bore a relation to ordinary holdings of sterling comparable with that between an individual's deposit account (or time deposit) and his current account (or demand deposit)).

Yet was there, asked Lord Catto, a need for a broad convertibility provision even for ordinary current international transactions? The aim was not to enshrine convertibility as a pure principle, but the more limited one to ensure 'that earnings in one currency should be freely convertible for current expenditure in another country'. Lord

*CATTO, Thomas Sivewright, 1st Baron 1936 (1879–1959); Financial Adviser to Chancellor of the Exchequer, 1940–44; Governor of Bank of England, 1944–49.

Catto therefore recommended a restricted commitment: countries would provide convertibility 'so far as they are able' and for payments consistent with the Fund's purposes.

At the meeting[69] of Treasury officials with the Chancellor which settled the delegates' briefing, it was agreed to reject the Bank's restricted approach to convertibility, for that 'would cut at the root of one of the major purposes' of the Fund. It was recognised, however, that the Governor had identified, in the Joint Statement's apparent extension of the convertibility obligation to sterling held as countries' overseas reserves, 'an ambiguity and a danger'. These appeared to have arisen from the possible disharmony between three clauses in the Joint Statement. A member of the proposed Fund would be obliged 'Not to impose restrictions on payments for current international transactions with other member countries'; exceptions related to capital transfers and to currencies that the Fund might declare to be scarce, but not to 'discriminatory currency arrangements or multiple currency practices without the approval of the Fund' (IX-3). A member could acquire another's currency from the Fund in exchange for its own under specified conditions; that particularly relevant to the point at issue was that 'the currency demanded is presently needed for making payments in that currency which are consistent with the purposes of the Fund' (III-2a). It was the third clause which had provoked anxiety. A member entitled to draw on the Fund's resources must be prepared 'to buy its own currency from ... [another] member with that member's currency or with gold' (III-5). That obligation, which would *not* apply to balances accumulated before the end of the Transition, would be subject to the exceptions provided in the first clause quoted above (IX-3) relating to capital transfers and to currencies declared scarce. It 'might be held to cover', the Chancellor agreed with the Governor, 'sterling which is held as a reserve in this country; these reserves might at any stage amount to such a large sum that we ought not to be exposed to the claim that they are to be converted at sight into gold or any other currency'.[70] Accordingly the British delegates were instructed to secure the necessary harmonisation of the clauses 'so that the obligation of convertibility is defined as applying to sterling required for current international transactions'.

On another of the anxieties of the Bank (and of the Treasury), the need to be able to vary the exchange rate, the delegates were instructed to press 'the Catto clause' 'but it need not necessarily be made a sine qua non'. Whilst it appeared broadly 'desirable to accept' the constraints of the Joint Statement (IV-4), the delegates should try to secure:

'an overriding proviso reserving to a country, in case of necessity, the exercise of its sovereign rights over the parity of its exchange in consultation with the Fund, subject to the right of the Fund at its discretion to suspend the member from continued use of the Fund's facilities if the Fund disagreed with the exchange policy proposed'.

In explaining to the Bank Governor the Treasury's qualified approach, the Chancellor stressed the need to steer through familiar complexities:

'We think it unwise on the whole to press explicitly for acceptance of the doctrine of the 'floating' exchange rate, partly because the Americans are critical of what we did in 1931, and also because the more we press, particularly in front of other countries, the more likelihood there is of misunderstanding, particularly among holders of sterling, of our actual intentions...'

What of the Bank's advocacy of gradualism in activating the Fund? Keynes had pointed out that acceptance of this would mean re-writing the Joint Statement.[71] Instead of that there should be crucial qualifications. The delegation should press for a transition of five years after the end of the European war or, failing that proviso, at least three years after the Fund's inauguration. Above all, given the American stress on the Conference as a gathering of experts, not of plenipotentiaries, the delegates could not reach final decisions. It should nevertheless be the aim to produce 'a final document' for consideration, on the clear understanding that its acceptability to Government and Parliament would rest on their right to seek appropriate amendments.

That this quest for amendments reflected caution, not lukewarmness, towards the projected Fund the Chancellor emphasised at two points. First, in seeking a lengthier transition, 'The Delegation need not fight this to the last ditch and should avoid creating the impression that we had no hope of making sterling convertible at any early period'. Second, 'he did not attach importance to delaying the setting up of the Monetary Fund and ... thought that if we were to influence the management we should want to adhere from the beginning'.

(7) AN INTERNATIONAL INVESTMENT INSTITUTION

The second outstanding set of problems to be settled before a major conference on post-war financial plans concerned a proposed international investment institution. An ambitious feature of the original American ideas on post-war arrangements and a less prominent one in British thinking, it had subsequently shrunk in scope and importance, particularly in British eyes. The rather disorderly public disclosure of American ideas in October 1943 (above, pp 123–4) had done nothing to arouse British support. Mr Law's main report had, however, detected some possible advantage in it; he suggested, particularly as the Americans were likely to pursue the project, that the Treasury should explore the matter and report to the Cabinet.[72] This was duly done, critical but broadly positive comment coming from the Economic Section of the War Cabinet Offices and from several departments, though the Bank of England was to prove unenthusiastic.[73] Progress depended on that made with the proposed monetary fund, and also in some degree on its prime mover, Lord Keynes, who was slow to act over the Americans' projected Reconstruction Bank.[74] As with other issues, the imperial discussions of February and March 1944 focused minds. A paper by Keynes, who led discussion on it,[75] resulted in the hedged agreement that international arrangements were desirable for reconstruction finance as well as for longer-term development, but that they would need to be on lines drastically different from those envisaged by the Americans. In particular, there should be no tying of loans to expenditure in particular countries, and a member country should be free to decide, in the light of its balance of payments, whether to subscribe to loans. The Bank's broad functions should be to provide expert evaluation and to guarantee the servicing of loans.[76]

Hitherto, American officials had made the running, circulating successive drafts and 'Questions and Answers' on their proposals.[77] A British Treasury sceptic wondered whether an international institution was needed since there would be only two possible lenders after the war.[78] White's view was that an international bank would avoid the taint of 'imperialism' that might attach to unilateral American lending.[79] British views were now, in spring 1944, changing to become more positive, though very concerned to avoid a commitment to lend beyond what the balance of payments would permit.[80] Perhaps above all, the Bank was seen as filling the gap in reconstruction finance left between the respective fields of UNRRA and of the projected monetary fund.[81] As a preliminary constructive move to reassure the American Secretary of the Treasury when the Joint Statement on the monetary fund was at last being agreed, the Chancellor elaborated to him the conclusions of the recent imperial discussions.[82] The encouraging American reply[83] evoked from the hitherto sceptical Keynes the comment that 'it is a very manful effort to meet us'.[84] Shortly, in early June 1944, the Chancellor submitted a paper on the proposed Bank to the War Cabinet. Based on a paper by Keynes and embodying the reservations already noted, it sought and received authorisation for the delegates to Bretton Woods to participate in devising such a project there.[85] By this time they had reached the USA. On board ship a day had been spent in discussing what became known as 'the Boat Draft' for the Bank. This received brief exposure, but virtually no discussion at Atlantic City, the British and American delegates being in broad agreement. This 'Boat Draft' had grafted the principal British concerns on to the American proposals. It became the basis for discussion, and of the articles of agreement, at Bretton Woods, where Keynes was to be the chairman of the Commission concerned with the proposed 'International Bank for Reconstruction and Development'.[86]

CHAPTER 6, SOURCE REFERENCES

1. Horsefield, op cit, I, p 60.
2. Keynes to Mr F W Pethick-Lawrence, 16 May 1944, T 247/35; *JMK* XXVI, p 3.
3. WP (44) 75 of 5 Feb 1944, CAB 66/46 in CAB 123/96 – II.
4. Mr J G Winant to Secretary of State, 24 March 1944, *FRUS* 1944 (1967) II, pp 33 – 34.
5. WM (44) 18th Conclusions, 11 Feb 1944, CAB 65/41 in CAB 123/96 – II
6. WP (44) 121, 18 Feb 1944, CAB 66/47, ibid.
7. WM (44) 24th Conclusions, 23 Feb 1944, CAB 65/41, ibid.
8. WP (44) 145 of 3 March 1944, CAB 66/47, ibid.
9. WP (44) 200, 13 April 1944, CAB 66/48, ibid.
10. WP (44) 203, 13 April 1944, CAB 66/49, ibid.
11. WP (43) 467 of 21 Oct 1943, CAB 66/42, ibid.
12. WM (44) 49th Conclusions, 14 April 1944, CAB 65/42, ibid.
13. Ibid, Pres. B. of T, WP (44) 217 of 21 April 1944, CAB 66/49; Min. of Ag., WP (44) 200, CAB 66/48 and WP (44) 203, CAB 66/49, both of 13 April 1944; Min. War Trans., WP (44) 227 of 25 April 1944, CAB 66/49; Sec. of State for India, WP (44) 224 of 25 April, CAB 66/49.
14. Secretary of State to US Minister in Australia, 17 Jan 1944, and report by Assistant Secretary of State (Mr D Acheson), 2 March 1944; Secretary of State to US Consul General at Cape Town, 24 January 1944; *FRUS* 1944 II, pp 5, 18 – 19, 106.
15. Brief report of 23 February 1944, in CAB 99/34, and fuller summary of US-Canadian talks as Annex I, pp 44 – 49, of report of the London discussions in ASD (44) 16 of 21 March 1944, in WP (44) 192 of 6 April 1944, CAB 66/48 in CAB 123/96 – II.
16. The term 'programming' had been used elsewhere to describe the orderly allocation of scarce resources, for instance of shipping. Its quite different employment as an euphemism for a chosen policy of import restrictions was evidently Sir Wilfrid Eady's idea, Keynes congratulating him for 'a stroke of genius on your part': Keynes to Eady, 20 March 1944, T 247/35.
17. Papers for meetings and memoranda in CAB 99/27; reports of meetings in CAB 99/28.
18. Keynes to Sir Richard Hopkins, 12 June 1944, and Hopkins to Chancellor of the Exchequer, 14 June 1944, T 247/2; *JMK* XXVI, pp 304 – 10.
19. Mr Winant to Secretary of State, 9 July 1944, *FRUS* 1944 II, pp 53 – 54.
20. Keynes to Hopkins from Atlantic City, 25 June 1944, *JMK* XXVI, pp 59 – 64, and Sir David Waley to Hopkins, 4 July, T 231/365; Hopkins to Keynes, 5 July, ibid.
21. Waley to Mr T Padmore, Principal Private Secretary to Chancellor of the Exchequer, 8 July 1944, with Chancellor's comments added 9 & 10 July, T 236/378; Prime Minister to Chancellor, 13 & 16 July, and Chancellor to Prime Minister, 14 July, ibid.
22. WM (44) 92nd Conclusions, 18 July 1944, CAB 65/43 in CAB 123/96 – II.
23. Mr E R Stettinius, Under Secretary of State to Mr Winant, 31 July 1944, *FRUS* 1944 II, pp 63 – 64.
24. Hopkins to Keynes, 70 CAMER of 17 July 1944, T 231/367.
25. Professor L C Robbins from Bretton Woods to Sir Edward Bridges in London, 63 REMAC of 12 July 1944; Bridges to Robbins, 63 CAMER, 14 July; Hopkins to

Keynes, 70 CAMER, 17 July and 76 CAMER, 19 July, ibid. Professor Robbins's *Journal*, 19 and 31 July.

26. CAB 87/97 for papers of the Cabinet Committee on Commercial Policy.

27. Eg, Keynes to Waley, 10 Feb 1943, T 160/1287; to Chancellor, 14 October 1943, T 247/30B; to Hopkins, 25 June 1944, T 231/365.

28. Keynes to Mr J M Fleming, 13 March 1944, T 236/303 and 22 April 1944, T 236/304.

29. 8 May 1944, at third meeting with European financial experts, T 160/1287.

30. Keynes to White, 19 Dec 1943, in WP (44) 192 of 6 April 1944, CAB 66/48, Annex D, pp 27–28, CAB 123/96–II; see also informal letter, Keynes to White, 22 Dec 1943, T 247/30B.

31. Horsefield, op cit, I, pp 64–66; Keynes to Eady and Waley 10 March 1944, T 247/34; numerous memos between Eady, Hopkins, Padmore and Chancellor, 24 March to 3 April, and formal abandonment of Unitas by Treasury in 299 CAMER, London to Washington, 14 April 1944, T 160/1287.

32. Keynes to Eady, 3 October 1943, *JMK* XXV, p 359.

33. Keynes in Article VII discussions with representatives of the Dominions and of India, 2 March 1944, ASD (Money) (44), 4th Meeting, CAB 123/96–II; also in T 160/1287.

34. Note 1 to Bank's memo on 'Currency Plans', 31 Jan 1944, and Eady to Hopkins, 24 March, T 247/27.

35. 11 January 1944. Keynes had undertaken to produce this memorandum following the talks of September–October 1943 which are the subject of chapter 5: Sir Wilfrid Eady to S D Waley, 17 January 1944, T 160/1270. Copy of the memorandum in *JMK* XXIV, pp 1–18.

36. Memo by Mr G F Bolton of Bank of England, 17 January 1944, and a Bank memo of 11 January 1944, T 247/27; comments by Bank on Keynes's paper, 'Notes on External Finance in the Post-Japanese Armistice Transitional Period', T 236/303, with covering letter from B G Catterns, Deputy Governor; to Eady, 9 February 1944; Bank memos to Cabinet Committee on External Economic Policy, 15 February 1944 in WP (44) 121, of 18 February 1944, CAB 66/47 in CAB 123/96–II and of 17 February 1944 in CAB 87/95.

37. Eady to Hopkins, 21 January 1944, T 247/27.

38. Horsefield, op cit, I, pp 17–18 and III, pp 124–7. Copy of Williams's article from *Foreign Affairs*, July 1943, in T 247/30B, with note on cover by Keynes, 'A very intelligent and moderate criticism'. Later, he noted: 'This is an able article, but its criticism is much better than its constructive proposals—which are almost nil. . .' Keynes to Lord Catto and others, 22 February 1944, T 160/1287.

39. WP (44) 121 of 18 February 1944, CAB 66/47 in CAB 123/96–II.

40. 'Notes on the Bank of England's Proposals for the Sterling Area', 15 February 1944, T 236/302; *JMK* XXIV, pp 19–22.

41. Draft reply with covering note of 22 February 1944 from Professor L C Robbins to Lord President of the Council, ibid.

42. WP (44) 95 of 9 February 1944, CAB 66/46; WP (44) 121 of 18 February, CAB 66/47; WP (44) 148 of 6 March, CAB 66/47; all in CAB 123/96–II.

43. Professor J E Meade, memorandum of 22 February 1944, ibid.

44. Lord Beaverbrook to Keynes, 7 March 1944, and Keynes to Beaverbrook, 8 March, T 247/35; *JMK* XXV, pp 415–17.

45. ASD (44) 16, I, para 8, of 21 March 1944, in WP (44) 192 of 6 April 1944, CAB 66/48 in CAB 123/96–II and also in T 160/1287.

46. Note by Eady to Hopkins, 24 March 1944, and note by Sir John Anderson of 27 March on note from Hopkins of 25 March, T 160/1287.

47. Report dated 30 March 1944 of meeting held 29 March; note by Eady to Hopkins, 1 April 1944, T 247/27. Draft memo of 30 March 1944, with covering letter from A W Snelling of Dominions Office to Eady of 31 March, and Eady's note to Hopkins, 1 April 1944, T 160/1287.

48. Eady to Hopkins, 3 April 1944, ibid.

49. Keynes, memo to Chancellor, 16 April 1944, T 247/35; *JMK* XXV, pp 434–6.

50. Mr Morgenthau to Chancellor, 5 April (delivered 7 April) 1944, *via* US Embassy in London, *FRUS* 1944 II, p 107, and Chancellor's comment in WP (44) 198 of 11 April, CAB 66/48 in CAB 123/96 – II. Mr R Opie's report on talk of 11 April with White, with covering letter of 12 April to Waley, T 160/1287. See also Mr A T K Grant from Washington to London, 233 REMAC of 23 March 1944, and Mr Opie in 264 REMAC to London of 4 April 1944, ibid and tel 2335 from Lord Halifax to Chancellor of the Exchequer, 4 May 1944, T 160/1287.

51. Chancellor to Mr Morgenthau, 9 April 1944; Mr Morgenthau to Chancellor, 10 April; Chancellor to Mr Morgenthau in 305 CAMER of 15 April; Mr Morgenthau to Chancellor, 18 April, T 160/1287, and *FRUS* 1944 II, pp 108–9, 112–3, 118–9.

52. Mr R Opie's report of discussions of 22 February 1944 with White and Mr E M Bernstein, T 160/1287; telegrams from Opie to London, 265 REMAC of 4 April and 266 REMAC of 5 April, T 160/1287. Mr Morgenthau's message as in preceding note.

53. Memo by Professor L C Robbins, 13 April 1944, CAB 123/96 – II.

54. WP (44) 198 of 12 April 1944, CAB 66/48, ibid.

55. WM (44) 49th Conclusions, 14 April 1944, CAB 65/42, ibid.

56. 299 CAMER of 14 April (amended by 308 CAMER of 17 April) London to Washington and Opie's reply, 292 REMAC of 15 April; Opie to White, 15 April 1944, T 160/1287.

57. Chancellor's Memorandum 'International Monetary Fund' WP (44) 198 of 11 April 1944, CAB 66/48 in CAB 123/96 – II; Mr Morgenthau to Chancellor, 17–18 April 1944, *FRUS* 1944 II, p 119.

58. Joint Statement by Experts on the Establishment of an International Monetary Fund, Cmd 6519 of April 1944, *BPP* 1943–4, VIII.

59. Draft with covering note from Keynes to Chancellor, 16 April 1944, and draft note by Chancellor for Prime Minister, 17 April, T 160/1287; *JMK* XXV, pp 437–42. Copy of Minute and of Prime Minister's reply in approval, both of 18 April, T 247/35. On publication, the notes were retitled as 'Explanatory Notes'.

60. Mr Morgenthau to Mr Winant, 3 May 1944, *FRUS* 1944 II, p 130.

61. Meetings on 1, 3 and 8 May 1944, T 160/1287.

62. 399 HC DEB 5 s, cols 1935–2046, 10 May 1944 (House of Commons); 5 Series, CXXXI, 1943–4, cols 834–83, 23 May 1944 (House of Lords).

63. Mr Winant to Mr Hull with message from Chancellor to Mr Morgenthau of 11 May 1944, and Mr L W Casaday of US Embassy in London to Keynes, 26 May, with official announcement of 25 May in T 231/359; both items also in *FRUS* 1944 II, pp 131–3.

64. Note on telegram 2279 of 2 May 1944, Washington to London, T 247/29 and similar comment, Keynes to White, 24 May 1944, T 247/35.

65. 435 REMAC of 7 June 1944, Washington to London, T 247/29, and T 231/359.

66. Mr D Capel-Dunn from Offices of the War Cabinet to Mr H E Brooks of HM Treasury, 5 June 1944, T 231/365.

67. After consulting the Chancellor, the Foreign Secretary formally proposed the names of the delegates to the Prime Minister: 6 June 1944, PREM 4/17/8. Lord Keynes was to lead the delegation, the other members being Sir Wilfrid Eady and Professor D H Robertson of the Treasury, Mr N B Ronald of the Foreign Office, Professor L C Robbins of the Economic Section of the War Cabinet Offices, and Mr R Opie, Counsellor at the British Embassy in Washington. Mr R H Brand, the Treasury Representative in Washington, was to be associated with the delegation, and Mr G F L Bolton of the Bank of England was to be available for technical advice. Mr W E Beckett of the Foreign Office was subsequently appointed to act as Legal Adviser to the Delegation.

Immediately after the appointment of the Delegation the Secretary of State for India (Mr L S Amery) and the Lord Privy Seal (Lord Beaverbrook) wrote to the Prime Minister that their dissenting views should be represented on it. With the advice of the Foreign Secretary, who had consulted the Chancellor, Mr Churchill rejected this proposal for what would have been 'a divided delegation'. Papers of 6–22 June 1944, PREM 4/17/8, fols 770–4.

68. Lord Catto to Eady, 24 January 1944, T 247/27, and to Chancellor, 7 June 1944, T 247/35.

69. Note on 'Conference on International Monetary Fund', which raised 'certain questions on which the Delegation wished instructions', T 230/43. Report of meeting, 8 June 1944, ibid, T 247/128, and T 231/359; slightly different Report, T 236/1161.

70. Chancellor to Lord Catto, 14 June 1944, T 236/1161.

71. Note by Keynes, 7 June 1944, T 247/28.

72. WP (44) 81 of 7 February 1944, CAB 66/46, Annex F, CAB 123/96–II.

73. T 231/351, 10 February, Economic Section; 7 February, Colonial Office and Dominions Office; 11 February, Board of Trade; 12 February, Bank of England; 16 February, Ministry of Labour; 18 February, Export Credits Guarantee Department.

74. 'We have, I am afraid, been frightfully dilatory in working out the Reconstruction Bank': Keynes to Mr Harcourt Johnstone, Secretary for Overseas Trade, 22 April 1944, T 247/32, and also in T 247/76.

75. 'Notes by Lord Keynes on the US proposals for a Bank of Reconstruction and Development', ASD(44) 8 and ASD(44) 12 of 7 March 1944, T 247/22, T 231/351; *JMK* XXV, pp 419–27. Draft Minutes of Meeting, ASD (Bank) (44) 1st Meeting, 14 March 1944 in T 247/21. Sir Roy Harrod mistakenly states that Keynes's indisposition prevented his attendance at the discussions; in fact, he attended many of them (Harrod, *Life of … Keynes*, p 573).

76. WP (44) 192 of 6 April 1944, CAB 66/48, Annex E, CAB 123/96–II.

77. For the 'Questions and Answers', see 15 February and 13 April 1944, T 160/351; see also IMC(B)(44) 1 of 12 June 1944, T 247/21. On the American activity, E S Mason and R E Asher, *The World Bank since Bretton Woods* (Washington, DC 1973), pp 12–13, 17–18.

78. Waley to Eady, 28 January 1944, T 231/351.

79. Mr R Opie reporting conversation with White, 247 REMAC, 29 March 1944, T 160/1287.

80. 'Notes by Lord Keynes on the US proposals. . .' ASD(44) 8 and ASD(44) 12 of 7 March 1944, paras 1, 18(ii). See also draft of unsigned, undated letter, evidently of late March 1944 from Keynes to White in T 247/32.

81. Chancellor's memorandum of 13 April 1944, paragraph 12 in IMC(B)(44) 1, T 247/21, and also in *FRUS* 1944 II, pp 120–4. Keynes to Eady, 31 May 1944, T 247/32. Keynes's opening remarks to Commission II at Bretton Woods, ibid, and *JMK* XXVI, pp 72–77.

82. Chancellor's memorandum, as in preceding note.

83. IMC(B)(44) 1 in T 247/21.

84. Keynes to Waley and Eady, 30 May 1944, T 247/32.

85. WP (44) 338, 20 June 1944, CAB 66/51 in CAB 123/96–II. Keynes's paper 10 June 1944, T 247/32, and also in T 231/354; WM (44) 83rd Conclusions, 28 June 1944, CAB 65/42 in CAB 123/96–II; *JMK* XXVI, pp 48–54.

86. Mason and Asher, pp 20–21. Mr A W (later Sir Arthur) Snelling reported that there was no real discussion of the Bank at Atlantic City: 'Notes on the United Nations Monetary and Financial Conference', DO 35/1216.

CHAPTER 7

The Formation of International Monetary Policy 1944 – 45: Bretton Woods and After

(1) ORGANISATION OF THE CONFERENCE

Joint policy-making with the USA during the war was never a greater test of endurance than in the monetary conferences of June-July 1944. An evaluation of what was then achieved must begin with the organisational and personal difficulties encountered. The need to vacate for other users the hotel chosen at Bretton Woods threatened to allow less than three weeks for the main conference. This led to American pressure to begin the preliminary drafting conference at Atlantic City so early that, given the transport constraints associated with the opening of 'the second front' in north-western Europe, it was improbable that the British and some other delegations could arrive in time.[1] Dr White, resigned or insouciant over this, contemplated opening the preliminary discussions without them, suggesting that they might hold parallel proceedings aboard ship; on their arrival discussions could continue or start afresh. Scandalised by what seemed to him a 'frivolous' attitude towards a major conference, the Chancellor inquired incredulously if White expected that Keynes, who had 'contributed more than anyone to the principles of the Monetary Fund . . . would be willing to walk in late with apologies and either ask that the Drafting Committee should begin again or be content to go on from where they have reached. That is no way to plan serious . . . business'.[2] Canadian and Australian resistance was rallied against premature commencement, and the British Ambassador in Washington eventually persuaded the American Treasury to open the Atlantic City meeting on 24 June;[3] this proved to be the day following the British group's arrival in New York.

Transferring a week later to Bretton Woods, the delegation arrived to find that the hotel, closed for two years, had half its rooms unready, despite military help and that the distraught manager was reported to have fled to his room with a case of whisky. The hotel proved too small for all the participants, some having to be housed five miles away, despite the 'doubling up' of all but the senior participants. The British delegation, though comparatively small, suffered 'almost intolerable' conditions, especially the overworked secretarial staff, who referred to their quarters as 'the salt mines'.[4] Unexpected personal strain arose from the almost complete lack of private communications for the several weeks that the British party were away, at a time when relatives were engaged in the fighting in north-western Europe or suffering the attacks of the V-1 flying bombs, which had begun a few hours before they had left London.[5] The pressure of work proved almost overpowering and may not have been eased by the abundance, unusual for many delegates, of good food and of lavish cocktail (and Russian vodka) parties.[6] For much of the Conference half or more of the British delegates usually had committee meetings from morning until well past midnight. All approached physical exhaustion. In an illuminating report, Mr A W (later Sir Arthur) Snelling* of the Dominions Office commented that the delegation had been too small on the technical side and also on the legal side, with a single lawyer, Mr W E (later Sir Eric) Beckett† of the Foreign Office to grapple with the Americans' lawyers. It had been a mistake to combine, especially in so frail though furiously hard-working a person as Lord Keynes, the burdens of being both leader of the delegation, in constant demand from leading representatives of other countries, and also its principal expert. The resultant scarcity of time meant that the delegation itself did not meet daily, sometimes with near disastrous consequences, and did not have regular meetings with Dominions representatives.[7]

(2) THE FINAL SHAPING OF POLICY

The final shaping of British proposals for the International Monetary Fund, on the basis of the Joint Statement, and for the Reconstruction Bank, began on board ship, continued at Atlantic City, and concluded at Bretton Woods. To a much greater extent than the elliptical comment of Keynes's distinguished first biographer conveys[8] ('. . . there was to be hard work . . . It was decided to have meetings on the subject of the International Bank . . .') the British delegates' views on the major issues were clarified and consolidated on the voyage in seven formal meetings amongst themselves and six with Allied delegations aboard.[9] Although the most conclusive work proved to be that on the draft for the Reconstruction Bank, attention concentrated on the re-shaping of the appropriate clauses in the Joint Statement in order to resolve the anxieties of the Treasury and of the Bank of England. By

---

*SNELLING, Arthur Wendell, KCMG 1960, KCVO 1962 (1914-); Private Secretary to Parliamentary Under-Secretary, Dominions Office, 1939; Joint Secretary to UK Delegation to UN Monetary and Financial Conference, Bretton Woods, 1944; accompanied Lord Keynes on missions to USA and Canada 1943 and 1944; Deputy High Commissioner for UK in New Zealand 1947–50, in South Africa 1953–55; Assistant Under-Secretary of State, Commonwealth Relations Office 1956–59; British High Commissioner in Ghana 1959–61; Deputy Under-Secretary of State, FCO, 1961–69; Ambassador to South Africa 1970–72.
†BECKETT, (William) Eric, KCMG 1948 (1896–1966); Second Legal Adviser, Foreign Office, 1929–45; Legal Adviser F.O. 1945–53.

the end of the Bretton Woods Conference this appeared to have been largely accomplished, with the qualification that London was to express grave disquiet about the potential risk in the proposed commitment to convertibility. Moreover, there were to be some disturbing exchanges over the scope for post-war import controls and also over sterling balances. The British delegation was to be successful in shunting aside the rumbling threat to agreement on the Fund from the unsettled problem of wartime, 'abnormal' balances, but it was the effort to accommodate attention to 'normal' balances in the new Fund's articles of agreement that inspired some of the apprehension about convertibility. There were other, though less dominating, anxieties for London during the conference and in the eventual agreements. The concern here, however, is not to provide a full history of these, but to examine the fundamentals in the making of British post-war policy: those features, any one of which could have been 'breaking points' in international discussions.

(3) THE 'CATTO CLAUSE' ON THE EXCHANGE RATE

Despite some British disquiet and a frank warning from the highly respected Canadian representative at Atlantic City that it was likely to be too much for the Americans,[10] the essence of 'the Catto clause' on sovereignty over the exchange rate was secured there. This was to be embodied in the Fund agreement.[11] In drastic dilution, indeed in virtual destruction of the twenty per cent limit on alterations in initial exchange rates envisaged in the Joint Statement, it made explicit a country's right to vary its exchange rate. The Fund must be consulted, but an alteration in the rate despite the Fund's objection would not destroy a member's good standing within the Fund: it would not automatically be expected to withdraw from it, although it might become ineligible to use its resources. The Chancellor cabled the delegation that he could defend the text in Parliament 'as recognising an inherent right on the part of members to modify their exchange rates despite the objection of the Fund'; he wrote on Keynes's report of this achievement that 'This seems very satisfactory'.[12] What had shifted the Americans from their original determination not to 'budge one bit' on increased flexibility, and from their view that the 'difficulties were absolutely basic' and that British insistence would make it 'impossible to reach agreement'?[13] Lord Keynes, whose persistence had triumphed, explained that they had accepted ('in principle', before the full Conference) the British view that it was better to recognise that, ultimately, a member country could always act unilaterally.[14]

In view of the formal stability of the sterling exchange rate after the war until the floating of the pound in 1972, a stability punctuated by agonising over devaluation in 1949 and 1967, two amplifications of this acknowledgement of monetary sovereignty are appropriate. First, the

Bank of England, though broadly satisfied, would have liked to eliminate all reference in Article IV to the scope for two sets of changes of
ten per cent: it feared that, technically, this could put a cloud over a
currency's stability whilst not underpinning the right to alter exchange rates.[15] Second, the choice of an initial par value for sterling in
the Fund raised the embarrassing hazard of giving a view of future
exchange rate policy precisely opposite to that inspiring 'the Catto
clause'. British representatives at Washington in 1943 had accepted a
rate of $4.03. Since then Dr H D White had been pressing for the
arithmetically convenient rate of $4, but he had now (June 1944) aban-
doned this aim. In agreeing with the British delegation that the initial
par value should be that prevailing on 1 July 1944 and that it should
therefore be $4.03, the Treasury feared that by thus emphasising the
rate which had been maintained since early in the war, an impression
could be given of acquiescence in a rigid link to the dollar and thereby
to gold. The Chancellor sought and received from the delegation a
formula designed to avoid that possibility, but the ultimate version of
the Fund agreement was to be quite bare of it.[16]

Why was the chance not taken to tidy up the rate to $4 and to regis-
ter, albeit by so little, the hard fought claim to flexibility? Apart from
the original intention to maintain the rate of $4.03 during the war,
there were two particular justifications, both focusing the constraints
upon sterling if it was to continue as a reserve currency. One was that a
number of European countries had already decided on exchange rates
'in round figures in terms of sterling'.[17] The other was Indian apprehension that a change would foster uncertainty about the future value
of sterling and hence of India's large sterling balances.[18]

(4) ATLANTIC CITY: EXCHANGE AND TRADE RESTRICTIONS

Continuing to overshadow the acceptability of the monetary
scheme as a whole, the importance of the provisions for the transition
to full adoption of its obligations had been demonstrated in a startling,
if brief, flurry at Atlantic City over exchange and trade restrictions.
The British concern was to ensure scope to operate these during the
transition; the Chancellor had stressed his distaste, given the obscurity about post-war arrangements to deal with the balance of payments, for the commitment proposed in the Joint Statement to
eliminate such controls during the transition.[19] A new American proposal at Atlantic City, however, threatened not only to limit controls
during the transition, but also to dilute 'the scarce currency clause'
which had hitherto done much to reconcile British opinion to the monetary scheme. This new proposal was that the agreement would not
override 'existing or future international commitments' on discrimination, restrictions, and trade liberalisation.[20] Strong British reaction

quickly produced reconsideration and re-drafts to be embodied in the final agreement at Bretton Woods in the articles relating respectively to scarce currencies and to the transition.[21] In the former it was to be provided that members would not frustrate the intention of the article by appeal to earlier obligations. In the latter, the British representatives achieved their aim of excluding a specific obligation to remove restrictions during the transition; moreover, the US Administration itself proposed an exchange of notes to deal with the particular problem of the Anglo-American Trade Agreement of 1938.[22]

Anxieties about the transition extended, however, further than this. The Joint Statement has provided for the Monetary Fund to make representations about restrictions, and for members to consult it within three years when continuing them. This implied disagreeable obligations and an unrealistic timetable, particularly if the Fund began operations before the end of the war. With the Americans coming to Atlantic City intent on reducing the period of the transition, and the British set virtually on one of indeterminate length,[23] serious tension threatening the continuance of discussions had to be endured before the issue was settled. The implication in the Joint Statement of a limited period for the transition now disappeared; the Fund was required simply to report on restrictions after three years, and a member was to consult about them after the fifth and each succeeding year.[24]

Perhaps these differences and their resolution were inescapable parts of the step-by-step groping towards an acceptable international monetary code. There was indeed, it was reported, serious American concern lest the new Fund conflict with existing obligations and that some countries might exploit a prolonged transition in order to entrench restrictions.[25] In the context of Britain's future economic policy, however, the initial American proposals may be regarded as warning shots, or at least as smoke signals, indicating a determination—intensified by the feeling that Britain was dragging its feet over the Article VII commitment—to eliminate discrimination and trade restrictions from the post-war world.

(5)THE PLEDGE ON STERLING BALANCES

On a second and associated major problem, the ambiguity in the Joint Statement over the provision for convertibility into other currencies of overseas holdings of sterling, the Treasury and Bank of England were to feel far less reassured by the solution which the delegation proposed, defended, and brought back as part of the agreement for the International Monetary Fund. The problem appeared exceptionally unyielding, being entwined with two other sets of continuing discussions, which will be examined at some length below (chapter 9), about Britain's wartime accumulation of massive debt in sterling bal-

ances. One set concerned those due to India; the other explored the
general problem on the basis of some striking memoranda by Lord
Keynes. By mid-1944 the drift of all these discussions was that ways
must be found, short of unilateral repudiation, to prevent the early use
of these abnormal balances. The prospect of their eventual release
might well, however, persuade their overseas holders to sustain the
prolongation of the sterling area system of pooling and economising
reserves. Whether to Britain's own financial benefit or not, that appeared the least invidious means to meet her obligations.

This tentative projection of post-war policy rested on two potentially conflicting requirements: to make old sterling unusable, yet to
persuade its holders to continue using sterling and to accumulate, in
the ordinary course of international transactions, new balances. Nor
was this all. Further to strain ingenuity, Treasury and Bank agreed
that there must be discretion to limit the withdrawal of normal balances, distinguished above (p 148) as 'reserves balances', should
that threaten the gold and foreign exchange reserves and hence the
maintenance of the expected commitment to convertibility of currently earned sterling. These incompletely formed intentions, largely
unrevealed to those most affected, were manifestly not for scrutiny in
the forthcoming conference. The British view remained as formulated
in 1943, that the future treatment of sterling balances should be settled
outside the proposed new monetary system (above pp 98 – 99 and 148).
There was no agreement, however, between Ministers, officials
and the Bank of England on what that treatment should mean in
terms of policy. Indeed, discussions which were to continue throughout the summer of 1944 had in May and June only just opened on
Keynes's challenging post-war proposals; in those a decisive settlement of sterling balances was fundamental (below pp 216 – 34). On
the specific issue of India's balances a Cabinet Committee on Indian
Financial Questions was about to report (in July 1944) its sense of
helplessness (below pp 221 – 2).

The Chancellor was nevertheless to feel obliged to make virtually
the sole definite, unequivocal statement of wartime policy on sterling
balances. Warnings from India, including press interviews with two
of the Indian delegates as well as newspaper comment, had reached
London early in June, shortly before the British delegation's departure: Britain should not contemplate repudiation or adjustment, nor
an alteration in the financial settlement between the British and
Indian Governments. The Indian delegates affirmed their freedom to
raise the issue of the balances at Bretton Woods.[26]

The British intention had been to seek by private discussions to
calm Indian anxieties. It was also necessary, however, to deal with
pressures of a contrasting kind within the Government itself. Lord
Cherwell, the Paymaster-General and close adviser to the Prime Min-

ister, had reiterated to the Chancellor, both by letter and at a meeting of Ministers, the views he had made familiar at the Indian Finance Committee on the need for drastic treatment of Indian sterling balances: that they should not be funded, but should be drastically scaled down (below, pp 218, 221). He had made it known that he envisaged unilateral action by Britain.[27]

Keynes had promptly advised the Chancellor against Cherwell's views.[28] He doubted whether such British action would be taken; further, whilst *voluntary* reduction would be welcome, it was likely to be too small to do anything to solve the problem. When, in relation to the aim of avoiding the involvement of the proposed monetary fund with the settlement of war indebtedness, Sir Wilfrid Eady* set out these matters for the Chancellor, Sir John Anderson declared of the Indian balances, in a handwritten note:[29]

'There is no question of repudiation. This can be stated.

J.A. 14/6'

Aboard ship, Sir Jeremy Raisman,† the (British) Finance Member of the Viceroy's Council and the principal delegate of the Indian Government was to underline the hazards ahead. To his advice that an alteration of the exchange rate by so little as from $4.03 to a tidier $4 would foster Indian uncertainty about the future of sterling, he added concern that Indian critics would regard as 'highly objectionable' the British delegation's proposal to remove the ambiguity over convertibility by introducing restrictions on the use of balances (Indians hoped to use their balances to finance not only normal trade but also ambitious post-war investment plans). The two principal British delegates, Lord Keynes and Sir Wilfrid Eady, explained that without the proposed safeguards the convertibility of sterling might be delayed; and it was agreed to have further discussions on this Indian anxiety.[30]

British hopes to avoid the airing at Bretton Woods of embarrassing doubts about the creditworthiness of sterling were to be quickly disappointed. The Indian delegation felt that it must satisfy Indian political opinion.[31] In an attempt to do that, it proposed an addition to the purposes and policies of the Fund:

---

*EADY, (Crawfurd) Wilfrid Griffin, KBE 1939 (1890–1962); Deputy Under-Secretary of State, Home Office, 1938–40; Deputy Chairman, 1940–41, and Chairman, 1941–42, of Board of Customs and Excise; Joint Second Secretary, Treasury, 1942–52.

†RAISMAN, Abraham Jeremy, Kt 1939 (1892–1978); Director, Reserve Bank of India, 1938; Secretary, Finance Dept, 1938–39; Finance Member of Government of India, 1939–45; Vice President, Governor-General's Executive Council, 1944; Chairman, British Indian delegation to International Monetary Conference, Bretton Woods, USA, 1944.

'To promote and facilitate the settlement of abnormal indebtedness arising out of the war'.

This was submitted to the relatively small group of delegates comprising the Committee on 'Purposes, Policies, and Quotas of the Fund', one of four Committees of Commission I, on the Fund (the very large Conference of 164 delegates (and advisers) from 44 countries had been divided into three Commissions, the other two being concerned respectively with the Bank (II) and 'Other Means of International Financial Cooperation' (III)).[32]

Sir Jeremy Raisman supported his delegation's proposal with a temperate, sensitive, exposition of the Indian case.[33] He regretted that the plan to deal with abnormal war indebtedness, which had been included in a draft of the Stabilisation Fund (above, pp 98 – 99), had subsequently been dropped. The reason might have been that the balances would be too large for the Fund to manage satisfactorily. The Fund might be affected, however, by arrangements made outside it to deal with the balances, and therefore ought to be concerned with the issue, even though it was beyond the ability of the Conference to settle it.

Support for the Indian case came from the Egyptian delegation which, to some British discomfort, had gone to Bretton Woods fortified by a broadly phrased resolution of the Cairo Monetary Conference earlier in the year that hoped for easy transferability after the war of foreign held balances. The delegation was waiting to circulate its own proposal, similar to that of the Indians, for an addition to the Fund's scope:

'To promote the multilateral settlement of foreign credit balances accumulated during the War'.

With less restraint than Raisman, its spokesman expressed anxiety over Egypt's large sterling balances.[34]

Dr E A Goldenweiser* of the US Federal Reserve System confirmed Raisman's supposition that measures to deal with abnormal indebtedness had been excluded from the Fund's remit because their volume was likely to exceed its capacity. He expected a settlement to be outside the Fund, and favoured setting the matter aside, at least temporarily.[35] Professor Robbins briefly hoped that this would virtually dispose of the hazardous question.[36] M André Istel of the French delegation did indeed support Goldenweiser with a vigorous assertion that settlement of abnormal indebtedness, whether of war or peace, fell outside the Fund's purposes. Other delegates, however, thought differently. The Chairman of the New Zealand delegation wanted the

---

*GOLDENWEISER, Emanuel Alexander (1883 – 1953); Director, Division of Research and Statistics, Federal Reserve Board 1926 – 45.

Fund document to refer to it in some way. Two delegations (Norway and Guatemala) reasoned that the opportunity should be taken to have so important a problem referred to Commission III for more extensive consideration.[37]

These discussions rendered essential a 'clear and uncompromising' declaration of British interests; anything less at that moment, Robbins noted, would have been 'fatal', and accordingly he expressed forcibly H M Government's opposition to consideration of the problem 'by any part of the Conference'.[38] With, however, the Committee Chairman evidently inclined to favour the reference to a larger body (but to Commission I, not III),[39] it proved impossible to prevent it. Indeed, two days later, the Committee experienced a virtual and impressively argued repeat of the discussions, this time around the Egyptian resolution.[40] Although Robbins was obliged 'to stonewall', he was able, in response to an allusion by the Polish delegate to outstanding German *credits*, to point to the contrast with the British wartime debts which, though appallingly large, had been created honourably. At the close, he felt that there was no 'danger of the Conference attempting to force our hand'.[41]

The reality was that by this time private talks were beginning to have their effect. Keynes had communicated to the Indian delegation the Chancellor's assurance, which was to become known as 'the Keynes pledge' after he had elaborated it in his speech a few days later.[42] Robbins and Mr A D Shroff of the Indian delegation, whose views had caused unease, discovered the comforting *rapport* of having been contemporaries at the London School of Economics.[43] In these various ways were matters brought under control before they reached the wider forum of Commission I, where Keynes, Raisman and White 'stage managed' the debate.[44]

Mr Shroff duly made his plea, somewhat restrained and rather despairingly, yet less aggressively than had earlier seemed likely, for assistance from the Fund; he limited his request to help over a period of years to ensure convertibility for 'at least a portion' of Indian balances. Keynes replied that Britain would settle these debts honourably, but would not seek assistance from the Monetary Fund to do so; that was a matter to be settled directly between those concerned. The American technical expert, Mr E M Bernstein*, supported the British stand, adding that the Fund would indirectly facilitate a settlement by its encouragement of orderly financial and trading arrangements. Perhaps by no means least, M Istel undermined the Indian case. The Fund was to be concerned with current payments, not with capital transactions such as the balances would involve. Moreover, much as

---

*BERNSTEIN, Edward Morris (b.1904), Assistant Director of Monetary Research, US Treasury, 1941–46; Assistant to Secretary of the Treasury, 1946; Director of Research, International Monetary Fund, 1946–58.

France sympathised with India, she and other occupied countries did not seek the Fund's aid over their massive balances against Nazi Germany. The Indian proposal thereupon lapsed.[45] The Indians were to carry their resentment back damagingly to India,[46] but for the time being they and the Egyptian delegates were mollified by ill-based prospects of discussions in London;[47] these were never in fact to materialise before Britain committed herself to action over sterling balances in the Anglo-American Financial Agreement of December 1945.

This was clearly a sensitive atmosphere in which to seek a satisfactory compromise, between a commitment to convertibility and a constraint on the use of balances in post-war sterling arrangements, that would assuage Bank and Treasury anxieties. Papers produced on the eve of sailing, agreed aboard, and steered largely unchanged in principle through the Atlantic City and Bretton Woods discussions, embodied two amendments to the Joint Statement[48]. First, from the clause relating to convertibility for current payments there should be excised the apparently ambiguous reference to convertibility of balances. That clause was concerned with the Fund's transactions, ie with its operations when in existence, whereas questions relating to balances and to the code governing restrictions on their use properly belonged to the clause which prescribed members' general obligations, ie, which laid down general principles. Ultimately, with the result of possibly intensifying a conflict over interpretation that was virtually inherent in the problem, the two aspects were to be embodied as distinct sections of a single Article of the Fund agreement. One section (VIII-2) was headed *Avoidance of restrictions on current payments*. The other (VIII-4) was headed *Convertibility of foreign held balances*.

The second amendment to the Joint Statement appeared to undo the effect of the first, to the consternation of the Treasury. There were to be two conditions under which balances (distinguished previously for convenience as 'reserves balances') would be convertible. One was that they had 'been recently acquired as a result of current transactions'. The other was 'that their conversion is needed for making payments for current transactions'. Apart from certain defined circumstances, a country would otherwise surrender to the Fund its discretion in withholding convertibility of balances. To the Treasury, the alarming feature was that the requirements provided not a double safeguard but a choice: that is, the two conditions for convertibility were not to be joint, linked by 'and' but were to be alternatives, separated by 'or'. Thus, not only would 'recently acquired' balances be convertible for both current and capital purposes, but older, accumulated balances (not, to repeat, those amassed in wartime or during the transition) would also be available for current use.

The two conjunctions 'and' and 'or' buzzed for three weeks in the Treasury, in the Bank, and along the transatlantic cables. London saw the re-draft as resolving the ambiguity in precisely the opposite direction to that sought; it would open, not close, the way to the relatively free use of balances and to drains on the reserves. It would be a commitment, the Bank feared, that could not be honoured should the conditions of the 1931 crisis recur. The apparent favouring of 'recently' (or 'currently') acquired balances, if indeed precision could be given to such a distinction, might encourage their premature withdrawal lest they be blocked as they became 'older' balances. Would not the coupling of the two conditions by 'and' be better? Defending its deliberate use of 'or' the delegation stressed that the use of 'old' balances would be limited to current payments. Ordinary balances might be used also for capital payments; to adopt one suggestion, that they should be made explicitly liable to capital controls might well, however, discourage the holding of reserves in sterling after the war by, eg, India. Resort to capital controls might be contemplated where substantial withdrawal could be regarded as a capital transaction. Perhaps convertibility could be limited to current payments in the same currency in order to diminish claims on Britain's reserves, as the Bank Governor had earlier suggested? The delegation replied that that restriction would involve bilateralism, conflicting with the Fund's objective of general convertibility; indeed, to some overseas eyes the constraints already proposed went 'dangerously far' in hazarding the international status of sterling. Reluctant to press London's wishes, the delegation warned that to go farther would feed mistrust of British intentions.[49]

The delegation's attitude appeared to reflect the circumstances at Bretton Woods, and the necessity for sensitive handling of the issue of sterling balances. They had not, however, fulfilled their instructions, London complained. 'The only discretion we gave was . . . to choose the best words', wrote the Chancellor, who found the position 'most tiresome', and agreed that the point should be discussed on the delegation's return.[50] Thus, even before their formal acceptance, the new Fund's potential obligations were causing unease; indeed, soon after the Conference, as will be elaborated below (section 6), this unease was to develop into the contemplation of outright rejection, when it emerged that the delegation's acceptance of the disputed commitment to convertibility of balances rested upon fundamental misapprehensions by Lord Keynes.

(6) CONFUSION OVER CONVERTIBILITY AND STERLING BALANCES

With potentially serious consequences, the Bretton Woods Conference ended in unseemly hustle, much as it had begun. The hustle now was to clear the hotel for fresh and waiting guests. Lord Keynes recalled that '. . . our hosts had made final arrangements to throw us out of the hotel, unhouselled, disappointed, unanealed, within a few hours'. If there was nonetheless a sense of achievement, even of euphoria, over the results of the conference for Britain, this was quickly to fade in London on closer consideration of what had been signed in such a rush: 'We, all of us' said Keynes, 'had to sign before we had had a chance of reading through a clean and consecutive copy of the document. All we had seen of it was the dotted line . . .'.[51] Superficially there was no intergovernmental commitment yet, for all was *ad referendum*. The diplomatic description of a 'Final Act' for the Bretton Woods agreements had been proposed by Mr W E Beckett;[52] it was to be no more than 'technically a formal signed record of what took place . . .'. Lord Keynes specifically emphasised towards the end of the conference that governments were in no sense committed.[53] Alterations to or reservations about the 'Final Act' were to face, however, a stiff three-fold hurdle. They were intended to be submitted to the secretariat, but that had dispersed. The US Government had been authorised to publish the proceedings of the conference and other relevant documents, so that changes would directly involve the United States; but the chief American proponent of the monetary plans, Dr H D White, believed that to secure their approval it was best 'to railroad' them through Congress 'as an indivisible whole incapable of amendment'. Finally, the long-stop in the idea of the 'Final Act', although it was not embodied in the published version, was that the authorised depository of the agreements, ie, the US Government, could consider whether proposed amendments required a further conference: a distant possibility, in a Presidential election year, and with the war in Europe expected to end shortly; and the need for which really depended on the extent to which Congress might seek to change the agreements.[54] Thus the Final Act could prove indeed to be final. Short of outright rejection or possibly hazardous temporising about acceptance, there remained the provisions in the Final Act to seek amendments or interpretations from the executive bodies of the new Fund and Bank when these had been constituted. That meant, however, that governments would be accepting in good faith and hope agreements about which they might have serious reservations.

Four particular issues, of which three were intricately technical, troubled the British authorities over the proposed Fund. They were to take two years to settle. The non-technical difficulty was no less serious, and concerned the location of the headquarters of the Fund and of the Bank. It was fought, notably by Keynes, up to the inaugural meeting of the Fund in March 1946 at Savannah, Georgia. The British Government feared that the probable location of both institutions in the USA would be likely to intensify domestic hostility to the monetary plans. Accordingly, the Chancellor had firmly instructed the delegations at Bretton Woods that it might accept an American location for the Bank, but that it must press for the Fund to be established in Europe—in London or Amsterdam. Failing that, it should seek to delay matters until there had been time for public opinion, and consideration of the location of other international bodies, to influence the eventual decision. Mr Morgenthau told Keynes, however, that Congress would insist on American locations.[55] The British delegation therefore withdrew its proposal to defer the decision, though making a reservation, as instructed by the Chancellor, to cover the possibility of reviving the issue later. All that remained was the precise choice of American location. At Savannah in March 1946 Keynes was to argue for New York, but American insistence on Washington prevailed.[56] As the Fund's first historian suggests, that particular battle, given the inevitability of political control, may have been one 'which had not been worth fighting'.[57]

Of the technical anxieties, the least worrying ultimately, but nonetheless troublesome for some months after the Conference, was the demonstration by an ingenious financial journalist of a paradoxical implication of the Fund's articles: the concern to ensure convertibility and to foster stability in exchange rates appeared to forbid intervention to prevent black markets in currencies, because such prohibition would involve the imposition of restrictions contrary to the Fund's intentions.[58] By November 1944, however, American Treasury officials had agreed that such had not been their intention, and that they would support an appropriate interpretation from the new Fund.[59] Such an interpretation does not, however, appear to have been sought.

The third and far the most grave difficulty over the Bretton Woods agreements also concerned the maintenance, indeed the meaning, of 'convertibility'. This difficulty was inescapably fundamental. For some months after the Conference, Anglo-American discussions on it were to cast shadows over the acceptability of the agreements to the British Government. Then, in somewhat bizarre fashion, the British endeavour to clarify the issues led to fears in the US Treasury that Anglo-American differences, if revealed publicly, could prejudice the chances of Congressional approval of Bretton Woods.

The formula governing the convertibility of balances of a member's currency normally held by others as reserves had appeared to fall short of the Treasury's instruction to keep such balances clear of the convertibility commitment (above pp 167–8). Keynes's defence of that formula was predicated, however, upon his own very special, though disputed, interpretation of it. Serious differences had emerged in its final drafting, half-way through the Conference, amongst the British delegates, and between them and the American and Canadian delegates, over the British proposals on the treatment of balances. As noted above (p 167) the two sets of obligations involved were to be embodied with no fundamental change in the Final Act, under headings respectively of 'Avoidance of restrictions on current payments' and 'Convertibility of foreign held balances' (see Appendix 15). The first set (VIII – 2), in which the word 'convertibility' was *not* used, was concerned with the general principle that members should not unilaterally 'impose restrictions on the making of payments and transfers for current international transactions', save in specified circumstances. Those circumstances were that during the Transition they might 'maintain and adapt' existing restrictions or, in the case of formerly occupied countries, introduce them 'where necessary'; subsequently the imposition of restrictions would require Fund approval, unless the Fund had declared a currency to be 'scarce' (when, however, the restrictions were not to be unnecessarily restrictive).

The second set of obligations (VIII – 4) embodied more elaborate conditions to govern the convertibility of balances, the term 'convertibility' being used to indicate the wider scope of the provision, in contrast to that for 'payments and transfers' in respect of current transactions. Those conditions, which excluded from the convertibility obligation balances accumulated before the end of the Transition, included one of especial concern to Britain. This was a member's unilateral right to suspend the convertibility of balances if it had become ineligible 'for any reason' to obtain resources from the Fund; for example, as was later to be explained, it might have exhausted its drawing rights, or the withdrawal of balances might be deemed a substantial movement of capital that it was not the purpose of the Fund to facilitate, so that a member might be refused resources to finance it (see Appendix 17, Mr H Morgenthau's letter of 8 June 1945 to the Chancellor, sixth paragraph).

Keynes had clearly assumed during the Conference that if a member ceased to be eligible to draw on the Fund, the obligations relating to current payments and transfers would be suspended in the same way as those relating to balances.[60] The Fund in full operation, he was shortly after to note, would be complemented by prohibition of discriminatory import restrictions.[61] It would then be necessary for Britain to have the right to restrict current payments; otherwise it might have to see its international reserves dwindle until the Fund decided whether defensive action could be taken. The American intention and the American view, both shared by the Canadian experts, were the reverse: ineligibility to draw would *not* release a member from the commitment about current transactions (VIII – 2a).[62] Whether or not it was stated clearly at Bretton Woods, the American view, Mr Morgenthau was to explain over ten months later, was that the two sections concerned quite different problems and hence involved different obligations. That concerned with current payments was designed to ensure that traders would be paid in their own currency, so that international trade could take place without fear of exchange control being imposed. The reason for making restrictions dependent on Fund approval, apart from the two specified cases, was that the amounts would be 'moderate', so that it was reasonable to expect a country to avoid such restrictions. In contrast, balances (in the sense of 'reserves balances' as defined above, p 148), might be 'enormous in amount'; a suspension of their convertibility would then be reasonable if a member were ineligible to obtain help from the Fund (see Appendix 17).

Such substantial clarity failed to characterise, or if it were expressed, to influence sufficiently the discussions at Bretton Woods. Subsequently, there was to be prolonged agonising in London as opinion slowly moved towards a horrified understanding of what had been agreed. As Keynes was eventually to express it,[63] 'We have unquestionably given away our right to block current transactions without the approval of the Fund'. The source of the misunderstanding of so significant a matter lay in the pressures of the Conference upon an overworked delegation. The order of exposition in the Joint Statement and in the British draft (reversed in the Final Act) had put the section about *balances* first, and that about current transactions second.[64] This, and the intricate phrasing had conceivably lent colour to the assumption that the former necessarily qualified the latter. Certainly, at Bretton Woods the British on one side and the Americans and Canadians on the other, argued fiercely for and against respectively the specific recognition of such a link. When Keynes appeared to believe that it was implicit in the obligations about current transactions, that they would lapse should a member 'run through . . . rights of recourse to the Fund', he was opposed by Professor D H Robertson, the British expert closely concerned with negotiating the technicalities involved. Such a point had 'never been made explicit in any text', said Robertson, and would be weak ground on which to break; in any case, relief from current obligations could be sought from the Fund before exhaustion of eligibility.[65]

Robertson devised a form of words that he believed might be acceptable to the Americans and Canadians,[66] but they sought a more rigorous formulation, that nothing in the obligations about balances qualified those relating to current transactions; he resisted that. Then the British tried to secure such a linkage, by including conditions governing convertibility of balances amongst those to which obligations relating to current transactions would be 'subject'. The highly regarded Canadian expert, Mr Louis Rasminsky*, now intensified his opposition, seeking even to exclude the 'let-out' for convertibility

*RASMINSKY, Louis (1908–); Chairman, Foreign Exchange Control Board, Canada, 1940–51; member of Canadian Delegation, UN Monetary & Financial Conference, Bretton Woods, 1944; Deputy Governor, Bank of Canada, 1956–61, and Governor, 1961–73.

of balances (Article VIII – 4(b) (v)); so fierce was the resulting disagreement, particularly between him and Keynes, that it threatened to produce a break. Eventually the Americans and Canadians relaxed their stand. The provisions about balances were not of direct concern to them, whereas those barring unilateral restrictions on current transactions, to assure exporters of being paid in their own currencies, were.[67] They did not, however, insist on the explicit *ex*clusion of a link between the two troublesome sections of the Article, nor did the British secure its explicit *in*clusion. The potential ambiguity therefore persisted in a form of words that evidently satisfied fully neither side, proved far from easy to interpret, and had been imperfectly comprehended by some at least of the British delegates.

The vigorous exchanges might well have been thought to have left little doubt of American and Canadian views. Moreover, Robertson had endeavoured to register with Keynes his own clear understanding that the relevant Article of the Fund was to be read in American and Canadian terms; he was indeed to assert later that he had been authorised (by Keynes) 'to delete, in response to the demands in particular of the Canadian delegation' the qualification that the British had tried to introduce.[68] It seems probable, however, that the frantic pressures of the Conference frustrated his attempt to settle the issue. Subsequent recollections indicated that, unable to discuss the point with Keynes, Robertson had had to make it through Sir Wilfrid Eady, from whom he thought he had received verbally Keynes's agreement.[69] Eady, however, had been preoccupied with raising with Keynes an associated problem—the operation of black markets in currencies, noted briefly above (p 170)—as they were both later to recall. There was probably little discussion, perhaps none at all, of Robertson's point.[70] Keynes was even to declare later that his attention had not been drawn to the matter at Bretton Woods, and that it was only sprung on him afterwards by Robertson (whom this assertion greatly wounded).[71] Eady himself confessed to Keynes, a few days after those remarks, in January 1945, that he could not 'remember exactly what happened . . . or whether and when the safeguard . . . appeared and then disappeared from the text'.[72] Robertson, however, thought that his point had been put 'and satisfactorily cleared', and had been 'completely sure of [Keynes's] concurrence'.[73] He was himself to recall that Keynes had reportedly remarked, surely uncharacteristically, to Eady 'Oh all right then'. Keynes's own recollection was that he had said, much more characteristically, 'Dennis and the Americans and Canadians can go to hell!'[74]

On the delegation's return to London there began a search by the Treasury, the Economic Section, and the Bank of England for an agreed understanding of the disputed matter and for the appropriate policy to recommend the Chancellor to adopt towards the Bretton

Woods agreements. Robertson expounded the issues and his own views with compelling lucidity in 'A Note on the International Monetary Fund',[75] to which he added in handwriting the sub-title 'An Essay in Rabbinics' (the sub-title echoed Keynes's quizzical attitude to the able Jewish officials in the United States Treasury, who learned to understand its complete lack of malevolence). Robertson's thesis was essentially that there was an overriding obligation, in the section on current transactions, to maintain freedom of payments. He held this *not* to be indiscriminate convertibility into any currency or into gold, which he described as 'multilaterality'. What it envisaged was virtually a bilateral exchange of currencies; a Canadian exporter to Britain, for instance, could be certain to obtain his own currency in exchange for the sterling proceeds of his exports. The wider provisions for convertibility, with qualifications, of balances accumulated after the Transition, a convertibility which also would not embody 'multilaterality', had been devised with the need to reassure India (and no less Egypt) particularly in mind. The rationale of the conditions under which the convertibility of balances might be suspended reflected a corresponding concern to reassure the member (eg, the UK) from whom such balances were due, and the Fund, of protection against their massive encashment. It also reflected the Fund's concern to discourage damaging movements of capital. Robertson himself believed, however, that Britain did not intend to invoke against holders of sterling the constraints provided. Indeed, he confessed—surely underlining thereby the verbal obscurity of provisions which he had helped to devise—that he had himself, supported by Mr G F Bolton* of the Bank of England, misinterpreted the section on balances. They had mistakenly assured the Indian delegates that it guaranteed that their country's sterling would be convertible, not just into rupees, but 'unconditionally' into United States dollars. It is a further indication of the difficulties experienced in interpretation of Article VIII that Robertson's assurance to the Indians was in fact correct, provided that India remained eligible to have recourse to the Fund. By acquiring rupees from the Fund, Britain would increase correspondingly India's drawing rights in it, allowing her, *ceteris paribus*, to acquire dollars.[76]

Keynes attempted in 'An Essay in Metarabbinics'[77] to refute Robertson's assertion that there was an overriding obligation to maintain freedom of current payments. His view, sustained throughout, was of an obligation between the monetary authorities (central banks) concerned, and therefore within their respective exchange

*BOLTON, George Lewis French, KCMG 1954 (1900–82); Adviser to Bank of England, 1941–48; Director, Bank of England, 1948–68; Director, Bank for International Settlements, 1949–57; UK Alternate Governor of IMF, 1952–57; UK Executive Director, 1946–52.

control arrangements; it was a kind of negative undertaking not to obstruct payments, though *not* a duty to facilitate them at all costs. Were Robertson correct, a central bank would be obliged to sustain convertibility in respect of current transactions, without imposing unilaterally new restrictions, notwithstanding the provisions—which would then look nonsensical—allowing the suspension of the convertibility of balances. This hedging around the nature of the obligations relating to current transactions, whilst it stressed, as Robertson had done that it did not involve wide-ranging convertibility, but rather a form of controlled convertibility between the currencies of trading partners, failed to persuade Robertson; he could not agree that those obligations would be automatically suspended if a member's ineligibility to use the Fund led to suspension of convertibility for *balances*.

When in the USA again, this time for negotiations on Stage II finance during autumn 1944, Keynes first tried, in vain, to discuss the problem with White.[78] Eventually he succeeded in eliciting American views (though not in writing) from Mr E M Bernstein, Assistant Director of Monetary Research in the US Treasury, and Mr Ansel Luxford, White's legal adviser.[79] To his colleagues' astonishment, White, co-architect with Keynes of the Fund, found the point new and of little importance. Bernstein and Luxford entirely supported Robertson. This exchange, felt Keynes, left matters in at least as bad a state as before; but he did not press the issue, following advice from London that the Treasury and Bank had devised a redraft to reflect the British view of the relatively limited scope of the obligations on current transactions. Keynes did not disagree in principle with the redraft, though he suggested abbreviations of it.

By this time, Keynes was recognising the strength of the Robertson-Bernstein view, to the extent of accepting the lack of explicit interdependence between the two sections of Article VIII. He maintained, however, that they were either inconsistent or 'hopelessly obscure', and blamed these alleged defects on oversight by the British delegates at Bretton Woods. The result was an unacceptable risk: that in the event of serious difficulties in the balance of payments, when Britain would be 'much more likely to want to suspend free convertibility than to depreciate', it might be expected to leave that choice of policy to the Fund.[80]

Before there was to be a decision on the policy to pursue, in order to ensure that acceptance of the Fund would retain for Britain discretion to take emergency action to protect the balance of payments, there was to be much more discussion in London. The course of action appeared to lie between seeking a modification of the troublesome clauses, either by redrafting or by public declaration of reservations, and leaving them as they stood while being prepared to offset their effects by appropriate import controls.

It is perhaps a measure of Keynes's intellectual and personal force-fulness that, in a matter where he was demonstrably less than substan-tially in the right, he nevertheless convinced not only the unhappy Robertson (who volunteered to shoulder the supposed blame),[81] but also the legal draftsman, W E Beckett, that the fault lay in the drafting. Indeed, having early in the London arguments supported Keynes's original interpretation, Beckett had by the beginning of 1945 con-cluded that the drafting was bad. Keynes might prevail on a basis of intentions, but in a court of law such as that of the House of Lords, Beckett reckoned that the American interpretation would succeed[82]. Various hands were to discover technical difficulties, however, in devising an amendment to harmonise the apparently conflicting clauses; moreover, such an amendment, as Robertson pointed out, would re-create the original cause of the tense *impasse* at Bretton Woods.[83] Then what of the principal alternative, suggested by White, to by-pass the clauses by trade restrictions? Here again it was difficult to see an escape. In peacetime they seemed unlikely to comprehend all the current transactions invigilated by the Fund.[84] From a different angle, Mr J E Meade's prospect of adequate 'let-outs' from the normal constraint on restrictions expected in post-war trading plans faced the almost certain barrier of non-discrimination,[85] whereas the balance of Treasury opinion favoured retention of the ability to resort to discriminatory restrictions. Mr Meade's bolder suggestion, that the Chancellor could simply refuse to sign an agreement that did not acknowledge the right to restrict imports appropriately, overlooked the prohibition by the existing Anglo-American Trade Agreement (1938) of quantitative import controls in normal peacetime trade. Per-haps above all, the difficulties in future trade policy were being more fully displayed than ever in Anglo-American talks in London during December 1944 and January 1945 (below pp 200–3). Speculation on the possible content of future trade agreements, Keynes stressed, was of dubious help in evaluating the Fund agreement.[86]

Did all this point to the unacceptability of the Fund obligations on convertibility, as they stood? To Keynes himself, conscious of the public and somewhat hostile criticism of the Bretton Woods agree-ments, that appeared as a possibility. The Chancellor could scarcely explain to the House of Commons that the difficulty was the result of our representatives' oversight at Bretton Woods, nor could he readily justify an intention to seek clarification if this involved an admission that he did not understand a crucial Fund article. The Cabinet and Parliament could scarcely be advised to accept the obligations without adequate safeguard; even were the Chancellor to offer such advice, they would probably reject it.[87] Indeed, any step outside the group discussing the problem in the Treasury, the Economic Section, and the Bank of England, which would have publicised the difficulty, might have risked disaster. There seemed to be only one possibility if the convertibility provisions were to be salvaged. That was for the Chancellor to persuade the US Treasury that the drafting was defective, and that it should eventually be corrected to give the British (ie, Keynes's) interpretation; Britain would defer approval of the Fund obligations on convertibility until this was done. Keynes accordingly drafted a letter in such terms at the end of 1944 for the Chancellor to send to Mr Morgenthau. Further discussions and redrafts were to delay its despatch until the beginning of February 1945[88] (see Appendix 16(a)). So far, however, from that leading to a solution it opened fresh difficulties, and the Chancellor's letter was eventually to be resubmitted in a revised, shortened form.

Before those fresh difficulties were provoked, it had seemed, during the first few weeks of 1945, that British agonising over the nature of the prospective commitments to the Fund had subsided. Somewhat less apprehensive views than hitherto were influencing officials and Ministers. Congress was expected to begin shortly its examination of the Bill to accept the Bretton Woods agreements. Professor Robbins and Mr Meade of the Economic Section now argued that the agreements were acceptable in the light not just of the opportunity they allowed for exchange restrictions, but particularly because of Britain's determination not to retain scope for import restrictions. Leaning towards the Economic Section rather than towards Lord Keynes, the Chancellor reiterated to the War Cabinet that there were sufficient safeguards in the scarce currency clause, in the flexible transitional arrangements, and in the recognition of the right to adjust the exchange rate. In reflection of the renewed Anglo-American discussions of recent weeks, he declared that nothing better, possibly something worse, could emerge from a commercial convention. Should not Britain therefore express its opinions on Bretton Woods earlier rather than later, and do so through Parliament, rather than risk having to endure whatever Congress decided? The Chancellor did not, however recommend a parliamentary debate yet on the final acceptability of Bretton Woods, but he suggested a resolution approving the principles. In practice, there might have been little difference between such debates. Noting the uninformed state of public opinion and the activities of some leading opponents of Bretton Woods, Professor Robbins feared a hostile debate, and aired the advantage of Lord Keynes's making a speech in the House of Lords to dispel public ignorance. The War Cabinet embraced such caution; whilst it broadly favoured the scheme, the Minister of Labour and National Service (Mr E Bevin) expressing characteristic unease, it decided to avoid for the present a parliamentary debate that risked open commitment to a position that might be untenable when Congress had concluded its own discussions.[89]

A month later, towards the end of February 1945, unease about the convertibility commitment revived. In Washington, White had given two British officials, Mr R H Brand and Mr R Opie, the US Treasury's response to the Chancellor's letter; he refused, however, to put it in writing.[90] White reiterated the views, supporting Robertson's original exposition, that had been expressed in the discussions Keynes had had with Bernstein and Luxford the previous autumn. He repudiated any suggestion of ambiguity in the troublesome Article VIII. He stressed that, should a member wish to re-impose exchange control on current international transactions on losing eligibility to draw on the Fund, that *would* require Fund approval. Although on its own the US Treasury would take a different view, the weight of opinion in the State Department, in the Federal Reserve Board, and amongst the American public was that Fund members must not be free under such conditions to re-impose exchange restrictions.

The US Treasury's unwillingness to give a written response reflected fear that Congressional questioning might reveal the existence of the correspondence, and that disclosure of Anglo-American disagreement 'might be extremely damaging to the chances of the fund getting through'. The Chancellor's letter had not so far been acknowledged; it had been handed on to White, who wondered if it might be returned to the Chancellor 'so that it should not form part of official record'. If that course, which he preferred, were not accepted, he suggested four other possibilities: that it should be withdrawn, and a revised version, excluding references to the hurried work of the Conference (which might be damaging in the US), substituted, and presumably answered; that such a revised letter should be provided but not answered; that the original letter should be left in, but unanswered; that the original letter should be left in and answered.

At first this new twist in a struggle already running for eight months (since the efforts from mid-June 1944 to reconcile within the Fund reassurances to post-Transition holders of sterling balances with the protection of the UK's gold and dollar reserves) seemed to do little more than underline once more the broad problem with which the Chancellor's letter had been concerned: that there be a satisfactory resolution of the 'possible ambiguity [relating] . . . to the meaning to be attached to the obligation not to impose restrictions on current payments'.[91] That would be a prerequisite to Britain's eventual acceptance of convertibility.

It had become clear, however, that there had entered elements of risk and urgency. Britain had to choose, it appeared to Brand, between three unattractive courses.[92] One would be to gamble on securing a satisfactory interpretation eventually from the Fund's governing body, which White and Bernstein were confident would be 'reasonable'. A second would be to stand by the British interpretation in the hope that the signatories to the Final Act would agree to it, or would accept an appropriate amendment of the agreement. Should the British Government take either of the first two courses, it would have to contemplate informing the US Administration before hearings opened in Congress. In its turn, the Administration, Brand expected, would feel obliged to inform Congress of the Anglo-American dispute; White feared that this would have 'serious' consequences and 'would blow sky high the Treasury's strategy of forcing the plan through without amendment'. The third possibility was that Britain should, in effect, mark time and indeed wipe the slate clean, if only temporarily. Withdrawal of the Chancellor's letter and the absence of an official US record of it would ease the passage of Bretton Woods through Congress. Should Parliament subsequently approve it also, with the British reservation, the position would then have to be considered by all concerned. The major drawback, Brand noted, was its likely result of leaving the US in a 'strong tactical position', though White denied having this aim, claiming that this third course would be in the general interest.

The reaction of officials in London was to advise the Chancellor, who agreed, that the letter could not be withdrawn, although it might be prudent not to press for an answer to it.[93] Discussion of the issues now dragged on, both in London and in Washington. In a series of meetings, held variously with White, Bernstein, and Luxford on the American side, and Brand and Opie on the British, the history and technicalities of the problem were repeatedly dredged without a mutually acceptable clarification emerging.[94] The Americans firmly denied that there was inconsistency between the sections of the disputed Article VIII, and maintained that the obligations relating to current transactions were fundamental, of overriding importance, and more extensive than the British would recognise. On no account would they contemplate unilateral imposition of restrictions on payments; there must for those be Fund approval, for the US could not accept an arrangement under which a member could exhaust its recourse to the Fund and 'thereby secure freedom to impose whatever exchange control it likes'.[95] Such freedom, Bernstein asserted, would 'strike a deadly blow to the Fund'.[96] He nevertheless sought to play down the *practical* importance of the issue, and to indicate that both the US itself and the Fund could be expected to act reasonably. This provoked Keynes, reading the cables and letters from Brand, to remark that Britain could scarcely depend on an *obiter dictum* in such a matter.[97] It might be regarded as a reasonable statement from Bernstein, however, that international organisations like the proposed Fund required each country to take 'some risk over things which it would like to keep within its own control' and that 'we must take the bitter with the sweet'.[98]

By early March 1945 something of a wait-and-see attitude was emerging by default from these frustrating Anglo-American exchanges. Bernstein saw no harm in leaving the disputed Fund article as it was; Keynes saw no point in further argument for the time being, and the Chancellor acquiesced in that view.[99] The dispute did not, however, subside immediately. On the contrary it was to take a fresh and serious turn. When, after some delay, the US Treasury was informed of the British decision to leave the Chancellor's letter with it, White reiterated his earlier anxiety, now evidently much greater: Senate questioning might well compel him to produce it. Not only would disclosure of the Anglo-American difference be 'very damaging' but, 'to use his own words', Brand cabled, 'much the most damaging part of the letter would be statement twice repeated that drafting of plan was deficient through hurry and haste'. Bernstein agreed with White that the 'result might be fatal'.[100] Brand concluded that there was a case for substitution of a revised letter, which would secure the US Treasury's goodwill, whereas rejection of the request would 'be regarded as a churlish refusal to help them in their great fight for Bretton Woods'.[101]

In London the Treasury understood the anxiety of its American counterpart. There was, however, a risk that post-dating the original letter would create a false position. It would imply that Britain had belatedly raised the matter: not only long after Bretton Woods, but also 'at the very last moment, after Congress had been discussing the question for some weeks', objected Keynes. On the contrary it had been pressed from the earliest moment. Given, however, the risk of publication, there might well be a suitably pruned though not re-dated version of the Chancellor's letter, for which he provided a draft, with the addition of a *caveat*: if an interpretation were to be sought from the Board of Governors, that should impose no obligation that the original document had not clearly specified or that the signatories had not recognised. The Chancellor agreed, noting his own concern 'to spare Mr Morgenthau embarrassment'.[102] The revised letter, still dated 1 February 1945, was cabled to Washington at the beginning of May[103] (see Appendix 16 (b)).

Mr Morgenthau replied to the Chancellor early in June (see Appendix 17). By then, both a worsening and an improvement in British hopes for post-war policy had transformed earlier apprehensions. The decline of Lend-Lease aid (above, pp 7–9), growing unease about the post-war balance of payments (Appendix 27), and , by no means least, the uncertain future of the Fund agreement itself, seemed to make more remote the acceptance of uncomfortable commitments about international payments. It was particularly important to await the verdict of Congress on the Fund. By June 1945, Congress had voted to seek (and evidently hoped to

obtain) an interpretation from the Fund, when it had been constituted, on whether the use of Fund resources for short-term purposes
was even more circumscribed than had been originally contemplated.
Together with disappointment over the size of borrowing quotas accepted at Bretton Woods, this raised the prospect that Fund aid would
fall short in availability as well as in volume.[104] (In the event the Fund
was in September 1946 to scotch the issue in economical wording that
permitted flexible interpretation[105]). During 1945 London was coming
to ponder whether the proposed International Bank might prove a
more important source[106]; a transatlantic interchange in March 1945
confirmed that the Bank agreement embodied a let-out specifically to
permit 'in special circumstances' stabilisation loans.[107] Thus, aid outside the Fund's irksome obligations seemed possible.

At the same time a more optimistic outlook on post-war policy was
emerging with the determination to use import controls, transpar-
ently defined as 'import programming'. The application of this was
expected normally to be non-discriminatory. There still remained,
however, the possibility of the discriminatory use of exchange control
on Keynes's interpretation of the Fund requirement about transfers
and payments arising from current international transactions.[108]
When Mr Morgenthau replied to the Chancellor's letter, he affirmed
the Bernstein-Robertson view; he could see no inconsistency, only a
distinction, between the two troublesome sections about balances and
current transactions; that would not become important until after the
Transition, and perhaps not even then. On current payments he
stressed that, specified exceptions apart, restrictions could not be imposed without Fund approval, and he implied that normal arrangements would preclude exchange controls (see Appendix 17). Although
Keynes's reaction was that such doctrine was 'unworkable', he nevertheless declared that the Fund could provide Britain with adequate
protection, given the provision to suspend convertibility of balances,
resort to import licensing, and the application of the principles for
current payments according to the *British* understanding of them.[109] It
was precisely on this last crucial point that American representatives
in Anglo-American trade talks in London were about to recognise the
correctness of the British interpretation. Their proposals for an international commercial convention sought, against British opposition to
mixing monetary and commercial agreements, to close gaps in the
Final Act of Bretton Woods. Those gaps had been left because, in the
absence of an international agreement on a trade convention, restraints on trade were likely to persist and might justify the use of
exchange control. The gaps in the Final Act therefore allowed, they
admitted, discrimination both during the Transition and subsequently, should exchange control be introduced under the Fund articles.[110]
With this recognition, a major anxiety of the previous eight or nine

months had abated; it was to revive, however, later in the year when negotiations for an American loan were to provide a fresh and more advantageous occasion to press successfully the American view. For the present, however, the Chancellor was able virtually to close the issue. He wrote to Mr Morgenthau to stress his understanding that the obligation to provide any foreign currency applied not to the proceeds of current transactions, but only to balances. Noting that if doubts arose in the future, he would request an interpretation from the Fund, he acknowledged that the original problem had by now been reduced sufficiently to avoid practical difficulty[111] (see Appendix 18).

(7) VARIATION OF EXCHANGE RATES, AND FUNDAMENTAL DISEQUILIBRIUM

There remained the fourth and final major issue over the acceptability of the proposed Fund, both before and after its approval by Parliament. This involved the right to alter the exchange rate unilaterally, beyond 20 per cent of its initial parity. Although at Atlantic City this had been secured in principle (above p 160), it was doubly hedged. First, it was contingent upon the Fund's being satisfied that its exercise was 'necessary to correct a fundamental disequilibrium'. Second, should it *not* be so satisfied, it could object, and might do so, the agreement implied, on the grounds of the member country's 'domestic social or political policies'.[112] London's particular concern was to avoid resort to deflation and unemployment as a means to balance of payments equilibrium. It therefore sought to ensure that the concept of 'fundamental disequilibrium', undefined in the agreement, should embrace 'chronic and persistent unemployment', the recurrence of which was most seriously feared. By August 1945, the question had some urgency. With the war ending, post-war economic policy was an immediate problem, and was being viewed by a fresh Government (Labour instead of Coalition) and a fresh Chancellor, Mr Hugh Dalton. A mission was about to seek post-war aid from the United States: Washington was bound to inquire about Britain's attitude to the Bretton Woods agreements, which had recently passed through Congress. Ratification by the end of 1945 by countries with 65 per cent of the total quotas (presumably including Britain as well as the USA) was necessary if the agreements were to come into force. It therefore appeared prudent to secure recognition of the right to devalue to correct the 'fundamental disequilibrium' of persistent unemployment (and possibly to clarify other matters), by following the example of Congress in requesting from the new Fund an appropriate interpretation of the concept. It had to be borne in mind, however, that severe unemployment might arise from causes that did not justify alteration of the exchange rate.[113] The significance of this *caveat* was shortly to become evident.

Early in November 1945, the Chancellor hoped—prematurely—for an early conclusion to the negotiations for US aid. He informed the Cabinet that, should the aid terms prove satisfactory, he would ask the House of Commons to accept the Bretton Woods agreements, but that he would make a declaratory statement of his intention to seek an interpretative declaration from the Fund on the scope for action to avoid deflation and serious unemployment.[114] From the Economic Section, Mr Meade pointed out that the Chancellor's proposed statement to Parliament spoke too imprecisely of a Fund member's right to depreciate its currency for such purposes. Depreciation would be appropriate if the country concerned also had an unfavourable balance of payments (eg, Britain in 1931), but less so in the reverse circumstances (as in the USA in 1933), when it would allow a country to export its unemployment to others. He therefore submitted a reformulation to cover the point.[115] In the Treasury Sir Wilfrid Eady claimed awareness of these basic principles, but appeared untroubled. He regarded the proposed statement as 'purely a political gesture to help the affair through the House of Commons'; the Fund should be able to differentiate between the two cases.[116] Mr Meade, however, viewed the issue as fundamental. If the desired interpretation were secured from the Fund, it should both help Britain directly and protect it against unwarranted depreciation by others.[117] He secured the intervention of the President of the Board of Trade (Sir Stafford Cripps) with Mr Dalton, who, after consulting the Lord Chancellor, approved an amplification of the proposed statement.[118] When the Bretton Woods agreements were presented to Parliament in connection with the Anglo-American Financial Agreement in December 1945, the Chancellor stated[119] that the Fund would be asked to agree that:

'steps necessary to protect a member from unemployment of a chronic or persistent character, arising from pressure on its balance of payments, shall be measures necessary to correct a fundamental disequilibrium'.

Notwithstanding this qualification by reference to the balance of payments, there were to be strong hints of American opposition, lest there result an automatic formula that would bind the Fund.[120] There was, too, caution in London; unless and until the Loan Agreement passed safely through Congress, it was prudent to avoid giving the impression that Britain was in the Fund 'wholeheartedly and forever', and preferable, said the Chancellor, 'to spin out the discussion'.[121] During that discussion the British case was elaborated (notably by Mr Meade in the Economic Section of the Cabinet Office[122]). It now allowed for the possibility that international reserves might fall because of abnormally high outflows or low inflows of capital. The British case concentrated on securing recognition that a country should not be forced either to maintain or to create serious unemployment in order to ensure equilibrium in the balance of payments, but that it should be free to choose instead an alteration in its exchange rate. The Chancellor accordingly approved the despatch to the British Executive Director at the Fund of the following definitive British understanding[123] of the relationship between its domestic and international economic obligations in mid-May 1946:

"In our view the basic criterion of a 'fundamental disequilibrium' under Article IV, Section 5(f), should be whether or not the country in question has a disequilibrium of a chronic or persistent character in its balance of payments. We believe that if a country is continually losing monetary reserves (at any rate, provided that this loss of reserves is not due to an unreasonable failure to control abnormal capital exports or unreasonable interference with normal capital imports) it should at least have the option of putting its balance of payments right by an appropriate depreciation of its exchange rate, although it may not, of course, always choose to deal with the problem in this way.

"This, we take it, must be the basic interpretation of a 'fundamental disequilibrium' in the international sphere, namely whether or not a country has a chronic or persistent adverse balance of payments. Our Interpretative Declaration is a gloss on this basic criterion. It is possible that a country would have a chronic and persistent adverse balance of payments if it had full employment at home, but that it is, at the moment, avoiding such an adverse balance of payments because it has a large volume of general unemployment at home. The accompanying depression in its money income and its purchasing power may serve so long as it lasts, to restrict its demand for imports, and to force out exports. But as and when a country in this position takes effective domestic measures to expand its total national income in order to provide full employment at home, its demand for imports will rise again and it will thus be faced with an adverse balance of payments which will be of a persistent and chronic character, so long as it maintains full employment at home.

"All that we are attempting to claim in this Interpretative Declaration is that we should never, in such circumstances, be forced to acquiesce in persistent unemployment, even though the measures appropriate to remedy it might involve a chronically adverse balance of payments, ie, a fundamental disequilibrium, possibly calling for an alteration in the exchange rate. This is merely the counterpart of the admitted doctrine that we should never be forced to bring our balance of payments into equilibrium by an internal deflation, with the consequent unemployment, but in such circumstances should have open to us the alternative of a suitable adjustment of the exchange rate."

With the Loan Agreement approved by Congress in mid-July, Britain was pledged to implement Fund obligations (and those specific to the Loan) within one year, but uncertainty persisted over when and how the Fund would consider the desired interpretation. Moreover, discouragement came from Dr H D White, now one of the Fund's five Executive Directors, in 'A Note on the Meaning of "Fundamental Disequilibrium" in the Fund Agreement'.[124] He appeared to accept the first paragraph in the British statement on the relationship between unemployment and the balance of payments. He stressed, however, that the concept of 'fundamental disequilibrium' had been deliberately left vague. It had provided the maximum compatible with harmonising different views; it was comprehensive and allowed scope for subsequent interpretation. White believed that the Fund would therefore prefer to avoid hypothesising, and to gain experience and to await a specific case. This was read by the British Executive Director, Mr G F Bolton, and by London as advice not to press the issue, but it was disregarded. Soon, with American expert advice, a formula evidently likely to be acceptable to the Fund, was evolved.[125] This embodied essentially the wording given to the House of Commons in December 1945, with the addition of a requirement for the Fund's acquiescence in an alteration of the exchange rate. Although this promised the Treasury what it had been seeking, the Chancellor, whose determination in the matter had been evident throughout, hesitated over the addition; this was therefore left for consideration on his visit to Washington for a meeting of the Fund Governors at the end of September 1946.[126] The original version, echoing the language of the Fund agreement, had required the Fund 'to determine . . . whether it is satisfied that the proposed change [in the exchange rate] is necessary to correct the fundamental disequilibrium'. The requirement was now modified; the Fund was to decide not that it was 'satisfied', but 'whether in its opinion' the change was necessary, etc. The Executive Directors thereupon issued the desired interpretation; at the same time, they made a much less restrictive interpretation than had been feared earlier of the request by Congress concerning the use of Fund resources.[127] It may be noted, however, that in welcoming the decision on the British request, the Chancellor's statement confined itself to quoting the interpretation shorn of the qualifying addition.[128]

CHAPTER 7, SOURCE REFERENCES

1. 414 REMAC of 1 June 1944 from Mr R Opie in Washington to London; tel 3048 of 6 June from Lord Halifax to London, T 231/359.

2. Ibid, Sir Wilfrid Eady to Mr T Padmore, private secretary to the Chancellor, 3 June; Chancellor to Lord Halifax, 467 CAMER of 4 June; 477 CAMER of 6 June, London to Washington; Lord Halifax to Chancellor, tel 3048 of 6 June.

3. Ibid, tels 84 and 128 of 4 June, Dominions Office to Governments of Canada and Australia; tel 100 of 6 June, Canadian Government to Dominions Office, and tel 131 of 7 June, Australian Government to its Legation in Washington and to Dominions Office; 488 CAMER of 8 June, Chancellor to Lord Halifax.

4. Professor L C Robbins, *Journal*, 1 July 1944; Horsefield, op cit, I, p 89; Mr A S Gambling from Bretton Woods to Mr J Haybittle of HM Treasury in London, 8 July 1944, T 231/367.

5. Several papers in T 231/365.

6. 'The flow of alcohol is appalling... The Americans set a perfect example by giving none [cocktail parties] whatever', Keynes to Sir Richard Hopkins, 22 July, ibid; *JMK* XXVI, p 110. 'This evening...cocktails with the Russians...we vied with each other in demonstrating friendship by excessive consumption of liquor', Robbins, *Journal*, 9 July. Apart from the uncertain relaxation provided by alcohol, there were, however, 'lavish recreational facilities and magnificent scenery', notes an illuminating account of the Conference and of the subsequent history of international monetary experience: Alfred E Eckes, Jr, *A Search for Solvency. Bretton Woods and the International Monetary System, 1941–1971* (Austin, Texas, & London 1975), p 136 and also p 139.

7. Mr A W Snelling's 'Notes on the United Nations Monetary and Financial Conference', DO 35/1216.

8. Harrod, op cit, pp 575 – 6.

9. There were seven meetings of British, Commonwealth and Indian officials, and seven of British and allied representatives aboard ship: T 231/361 and T 231/364.

10. Robbins, *Journal*, 24 June. Keynes to Hopkins, 25 June, p 5, T 231/365; *JMK* XXVI, p 62.

11. Article IV, sections 5 (c)(iii), 5 (f) and 6.

12. 38 REMAC of 7 July 1944, Bretton Woods to London, T 231/366; 43 CAMER of 11 July, London to Bretton Woods, T 231/367; ibid, Chancellor's ms comments of 26 July on Keynes's note of 14 July to Sir David Waley, Sir Richard Hopkins, and Mr T Padmore at HM Treasury. On, and attached to, a copy of this note there was an interchange between Professor D H Robertson and Keynes, dated 18 July, at Bretton Woods. Robertson was decidedly of the view that Keynes had not only secured more flexibility than the Canadians had wished, but also that in his note to the Treasury he had wrongly imputed to the Canadians a willing acquiescence in the change, through a confusion with their approbation of the original provisions in the Joint Statement: T 247/35.

13. Horsefield, op cit, I, p 84: IMC(44)(DEL) 9th Meeting, at Atlantic City, 26 June 1944, T 231/361 and also in T 231/366.

14. 'The essence of our plan is that there is no absolute obligation to obey the Fund in the matter of exchanges', Keynes to Sir Richard Hopkins, 30 June, T 231/365; *JMK* XXVI, p 68.

15. Ibid, Sir David Waley to Hopkins, 30 June and 3 July 1944.

16. Ibid, 4 REMAC of 27 June and 9 REMAC of 30 June 1944, from British delegation via HM Consul-General in New York to London; Chancellor's ms note of 1 July on note of 30 June from Hopkins; 7 CAMER of 2 July and 18 CAMER of 4 July, London to Bretton Woods; 23 REMAC of 5 July, Bretton Woods to London.

17. Ibid, 4 REMAC of 27 June, New York to London.

18. Sir Jeremy Raisman's view as reported in IMC(44)(DEL) 3rd Meeting, 20 June 1944, T 231/361.

19. Joint Statement, X-2.

20. Informal meeting of United Kingdom and US delegates, Atlantic City, 26 June 1944, T 231/361; Professor Robbins, *Journal*, 26 & 27 June 1944.

21. Fund Agreement, *United Nations Monetary and Financial Conference... Final Act,* Cmd 6546, *BPP* 1943–4, VIII, reprinted in Horsefield, op cit, III, pp 185–214: Articles VII–5 and XIV–4.

22. Telegrams 41 and 42 REMAC of 8 July 1944, T 231/367.

23. Discussions on the Transition at Atlantic City, 26 June 1944, T 231/361.

24. Fund Article XIV–4.

25. Telegram 41 REMAC of 8 July 1944, T 231/367.

26. Tels 7678 of 8 June 1944 and 7790 of 10 June from Government of India, Military Finance Department, to Secretary of State for India, mentioned (with tel 7790 attached) in letter from Sir Cecil Kisch of India Office to Sir Wilfrid Eady, 13 June; with Kisch's letter, a document prepared by India Office of interview by Mr A D Shroff, member of Indian delegation to Bretton Woods, and extracts from Indian press: T 231/360.

27. Lord Cherwell to Chancellor, 13 June 1944, T 160/1270; meeting of Ministers, 14 June 1944, ibid; Indian Finance Committee, IF(43)4th Meeting, 29 November 1943; memorandum on Sterling Overseas Liabilities, IF(44)4 of 18 January 1944; IF(44) 1st Meeting, 8 February 1944: CAB 91/5.

28. Memorandum from Keynes to Chancellor, 'External Finance in the Transition', 14 June 1944, T 160/1270.

29. Eady to Sir Richard Hopkins and others, 14 June 1944, with ms note by Chancellor, T 231/360.

30. Discussions with Sir Jeremy Raisman, IMC(44)(DEL) 4th Meeting, 20 June 1944, T 231/361.

31. Snelling's 'Notes on the .. Conference', paragraph 12.

32. Members of Delegations, and Commission and Committee structure: *UN Monetary and Financial Conference . . .*, Cmd 6546, pp 2–11.

33. Snelling's 'Notes', paragraph 28; Robbins, *Journal*, 4 July 1944; US G[overnment] P[rinting] O[ffice], *Proceedings and Documents of the UN Monetary and Financial Conference, Bretton Woods, New Hampshire, July* 1–22 1944 (2 vols, Washington DC, 1948), I, pp 75, 122–4, 127–8; undespatched draft REMAC telegram from Bretton Woods, and 'Summary [by Snelling] of discussion on abnormal war balances in committee 1 of Commission I', both of 4 July 1944, T 230/46.

34. Telegrams 1203 of 14 June 1944, Cairo to London, and 822 of 16 June, London to Cairo, T 231/360; telegrams 28 REMAC of 5 July 1944, Bretton Woods to London, and 25 CAMER of 6 July, London to Bretton Woods, T 231/366; US GPO, *Proceedings . . .*, I, pp 127–8, and 'Summary . . .'.

35. Undespatched telegram and 'Summary'.

36. Robbins, *Journal*, 4 July 1944.

37. Undespatched telegram and 'Summary'.

38. Robbins, *Journal*, 4 July 1944.

39. 'Summary'.

40. US GPO, *Proceedings*, I, pp 335–6; Robbins, *Journal*, 6 July 1944.

41. Robbins, *Journal*, 6 July 1944.

42. Robbins, *Journal*, 5 July 1944; HMSO, *Constitutional Relations Between Britain and India, The Transfer of Power* 1942–7, vol VI (London, 1976), Document 395 of 5 February 1946, pp 880–1, quoting Keynes's statement of 10 July 1944.

43. Robbins, *Journal*, 5 July.

44. The description was Snelling's, loc cit, para 28.

45. Ibid; tels 52 REMAC of 10 July (misdated 7 July) and 53 REMAC of 10 July, Bretton Woods to London, T 231/367. Conference discussions reported in US GPO, *Proceedings*, I, pp 185–7, 331, 335–6, 424–6, 433–4.

46. Ibid, I, pp 424–6; Viscount Wavell, Viceroy of India, to Mr L S Amery, Secretary of State for India, Document no 607 of 27 July 1944, *The Transfer of Power,* vol IV (London, 1973), pp 1127–8.

47. Snelling clearly expected that discussions would take place, and that their prospect would keep the Indians 'quiet for the time being'—'Notes', paragraph 30. In an exchange that was recorded verbatim, Mr G F Bolton of the Bank of England assured the Egyptian delegation that there would be talks 'in good time'—Report submitted by Committee 3 to Commission III at Bretton Woods, 10 July, T 231/370. Professor D H Robertson evidently assumed that there would be talks with the Egyptians and Indians: 'A Note on the International Monetary Fund', 31 July, T 247/38. Two of the Indian delegates expected to have discussions in London, probably informally: tels 82 REMAC of 17 July, Bretton Woods to London, and 94 REMAC of 19 July, London to Bretton Woods, T 231/367. In London, however, a senior Treasury official was puzzled at press reports of discussions on sterling balances planned for autumn; that would be contrary to Ministers' wishes: Waley to Hopkins, 24 July, T 231/368.

48. Draft amendment before sailing, IMC(44)(DEL)(F)1 of 18 June 1944, T 231/362; agreed aboard ship 19 June, IMC(44)(DEL) 2nd Meeting, ibid. Keynes's subsequent proposed revisions of 19 June, IMC(44)(F)3, T 231/363. Further discussions aboard ship 20 June, IMC(44)(DEL) 4th Meeting, T 231/361. Discussions aboard ship with Allied delegations, 20 June, IMC(44)(GEN) 2nd Meeting, T 231/364. Report of discussions on voyage, IMC(44)(F)11, paragraph 15 of 21 June, T 231/366. Final version of proposed clause/article, IMC (44)(DEL)(F)17 of 11 July, T 231/362.

49. Undated note, probably of 3 July 1944, from Mr E R Rowe-Dutton to Waley; 12 CAMER of 3 July, London to Bretton Woods; 25 REMAC of 5 July, Bretton Woods to London; note of 6 July, Rowe-Dutton to Waley; letter of 7 July, Mr C F Cobbold of Bank of England to Waley; 27 CAMER of 7 July, London to Washington: T 231/366. Note of 8 July, Waley to Padmore; 31 CAMER of 9 July and 45 CAMER of 11 July, London to Bretton Woods: T 231/367.

50. Note of 20 July, Waley to Hopkins; note of 20 July, Hopkins to Padmore, with Chancellor's ms comment of 20 July, ibid; tel 79 CAMER of 21 July, London to Bretton Woods, T 231/368.

51. Keynes's memorandum on 'The International Monetary Fund', 29 December 1944, T 247/38 and T 230/168; *JMK* XXVI, pp 146–55. The dramatic description of the exit from the hotel recalls *Hamlet*, I, v, 77.

52. Memorandum by Mr W E Beckett, 20 June, T 231/362. White was reported to have liked the idea; 8th meeting of Delegation, Atlantic City, 25 June, IMC(44) (DEL) 8th, T231/361.

53. 102 and 103 REMAC of 20 July, T 231/367.

54. Keynes to Padmore and Beckett's note, both of 20 September, T 247/38; the comment on railroading in Keynes's memo of 20 December on the IMF, ibid & *JMK* XXVI, pp 146-55; file on 'IMF, Publication of Records of the Conference', T 231/369. At a meeting in the Treasury the Chancellor considered that there 'might have to be a further International Conference to consider amendments by Congress, by ourselves, or by others', 10 January 1945, T 231/372.

55. 9 CAMER of 30 June 1944, T 231/366; 44 CAMER of 11 July, 68 & 69 REMAC of 14 July from Keynes to Chancellor, T 231/367. See also ibid, 32 CAMER London to Bretton Woods, and 50 REMAC of 10 July, Bretton Woods to London.

56. Ibid, 65 CAMER of 15 July, Chancellor to Keynes; 76, 77 and 78 REMAC of 17 July, Keynes to Chancellor; Horsefield, op cit, I, pp 129–30.

57. Horsefield, op cit, I, p 130.

58. Article IV–4(b). P Einzig, 'Is it a Gold Standard?' and the editor's answer, 'Nothing of the kind', *The Banker*, Sept 1944, pp 112–117, 119–20. Keynes to Chancellor, 17 September; G F Bolton to Keynes, 20 September; Professor D H Robertson to Keynes, 20 September; Mr H E Brooks to Keynes, 19 September; Keynes to Dr H D White, 6 October; Mr J E Meade to Professor L C Robbins, 7 November: T 247/38.

59. Ibid, Keynes's memo of 29 December.

60. Note by Professor D H Robertson, 11 July 1944, T 230/168.

61. Keynes's note to Chancellor, 'The IMF-Drafting Queries', 17 September 1944, T 247/38; *JMK* XXVI, pp 134–40. Keynes's note to Mr Meade, 'Bretton Woods—Interpretation of Article VIII', 16 January 1945, T 247/39.

62. Keynes's memorandum 'The International Monetary Fund' of 29 December 1944, section IV, T 247/38; Robertson's note of 11 July 1944, T 230/168.

63. Keynes to Eady, 1 March 1945, T 247/40.

64. See above p 149.

65. Robertson's note of 11 July 1944.

66. Ibid.

67. Robertson to Keynes, 29 August 1944, T 247/38; *JMK* XXVI, p 124. There was 'a rather stormy little meeting... which ended in impasse': copy of draft letter from Robertson to Keynes, January 1945, T 247/39; *JMK* XXVI, p 160.

68. Memorandum on 'International Monetary Fund Article VIII', one of three 'squibs' sent by Robertson to Mr Meade, 27 September 1944. Robertson said that this particular note was 'not being circulated at present even within the Treasury': T 230/43.

69. Professor L C Robbins to Keynes, 17 January 1945, T 247/39. Robertson to Keynes, 29 August 1944, T 247/38; *JMK* XXVI, p 124.

70. All that Keynes could recall was 'Eady coming to me about some drafting point... but no memory or consciousness that it was this one...': letter to Robbins, 19 January 1945, T 247/39 and T 230/168.

71. Keynes's note to Chancellor, 17 September 1944, and memo of 29 December 1944, T 247/38. Robertson carried the wound 'to the grave' (Lord Robbins in discussions with the author).

72. Memorandum from Eady to Keynes, 24 January 1945, T 247/39 and T 236/1161.

73. Robbins to Keynes, 17 January 1945, T 247/39 and T 230/168.

74. Eady to Keynes, 25 January 1945, ibid and ibid.

75. 31 July 1944, T 247/38; *JMK* XXVI, pp 114-7.

76. Joseph Gold, *The Multilateral System of Payments. Keynes, Convertibility, and the International Monetary Fund's Articles of Agreement* (IMF Occasional Paper No.6, Washington DC, 1981), p 3. In his invaluable study, Sir Joseph Gold elucidates with great skill the technical issues surrounding convertibility in the light of later Fund deliberations; his narrative does not, however, encompass the fuller history of Anglo-American exchanges up to May-June 1945 which is discussed in the present account. See also: Gold's review article, 'Keynes and the Articles of the Fund', *Finance and Development*, 18-3, September 1981, pp 38-42. An extensive discussion of the issue, based on British and US records, but which does not indicate the close link with the problems of sterling balances, is provided by A. Van Dormael, *Bretton Woods. Birth of a Monetary System* (London 1978), pp 228-39.

77. 9 August 1944, T 247/38; *JMK* XXVI, pp 117-22.

78. Keynes's letters to White, 6 October 1944 and 12 November 1944, and to Bernstein 19 October 1944, T 247/38; first letter to White and letter to Bernstein in *JMK* XXVI, pp 142-6, 154-5.

79. Keynes's memo of 29 December 1944, ibid and ibid.

80. Telegram 1074 CAMER of 21 November 1944, London to Washington, T 236/1161; memo of 29 December, sections IV and VI.

81. Draft letter from Robertson to Keynes, January 1945, T 247/39; *JMK* XXVI, p 160.

82. Memorandum by Mr W E Beckett, 20 September 1944, T 247/38 and T 230/43; Beckett to Mr H E Brooks of the Treasury, 5 January 1945, FO 371/45662 and extract in T 230/168.

83. Robertson's ms notes on Keynes's memo of 29 December, section VI, T 247/38.

84. Keynes's memo, section V.

85. Meade to Keynes, 10 January 1945 and Keynes to Meade, 16 January, T 247/39.

86. Meade to Keynes, 17 January 1945 and Keynes to Meade, 19 January; Keynes to Eady, 19 January, ibid.

87. Keynes's memo of 29 December, T 247/38, *JMK* XXVI, p 151; Keynes to Robbins, 19 January 1945, T 247/39 and *JMK* XXVI, p 174; draft letter to Morgenthau, January 1945, T 247/38; *JMK* XXVI, p 157.

88. Copy of letter of 1 February 1945 in T 247/39, T 230/168, FO 371/45663, *JMK* XXVI, pp 175-7.

89. Meeting in Treasury 10 January 1945, T 231/372; Cabinet Meeting 25 January, WM (45), 9th Conclusions, Minute 4, Confidential Annex, CAB 65/51.

90. Telegram 177 REMAC of 22 February 1945, Washington to London, personal for Keynes from Brand, FO 371/45663.

91. Telegram 201 CAMER of 8 March 1945, London to Washington, personal for Brand from Keynes, ibid.

92. 177 REMAC, ibid.

93. Memorandum by Mr E R Rowe-Dutton and note by Sir David Waley, 26 February 1945; memo by Mr Rowe-Dutton of 26 March; memo by Sir Wilfrid Eady, 27 March with agreement of Chancellor, 28 March: T 236/1161.

94. Reports of meetings 27 February, 1 March (two reports), and 7 March 1945; letters from Brand to Keynes of 2, 3, & 7 March: ibid and FO 371/45664.
95. Report of meeting of 1 March (by Brand).
96. Ibid.
97. Keynes to Brand, 5 April 1945, T 236/1161 and FO 371/45664.
98. Report of meeting of 1 March (by Brand).
99. Ibid, and Keynes to Waley, 30 March 1945, T 236/1161. Brand had written to Keynes that it was difficult to get things done at the US Treasury, where the staff was overwhelmed with work (letter of 2 March).
100. Telegrams 265 CAMER of 4 April 1945, London to Washington, and 328 REMAC of 20 April, Washington to London, FO 371/45664.
101. Telegram 329 REMAC of 20 April 1945, Washington to London, ibid.
102. Memorandum by Keynes to Eady and to Mr T Padmore, secretary to the Chancellor of the Exchequer, 27 April 1945, with draft of letter, approved by Chancellor 1 May; memo by Eady to Padmore, 30 April, with note by Chancellor of 1 May, T 236/1161.
103. Cable of letter, 343 CAMER of 3 May 1945, London to Washington, ibid and FO 371/45664.
104. Mr F G Lee from Washington to Keynes in London, 16 June 1945, T 231/373; Keynes's memo of 14 June, ibid and T 247/40; Horsefield, op cit, I, p 115.
105. Horsefield, op cit, I, pp 148-9 and III, p 245.
106. Meeting of officials with Chancellor and Financial Secretary to the Treasury, 10 June 1945, T 231/372; Eady to Sir Edward Bridges, 16 August, T 236/378.
107. Telegram SEVER 468 Washington to London, 22 March 1945, and telegram 254 London to Washington, 29 March, T 231/373.
108. Keynes to Mr G F Bolton of the Bank of England, 23 January 1945 in reply to Bolton's letter of 19 January, T 247/39. When Sir Hubert Henderson had raised and rejected the possibility of such an interpretation in September 1944, Keynes had scorned this as 'a mare's nest' (Henderson's note of 19 September, and Keynes's note of 20 September, T 247/38). Four months later Keynes had reversed his view.
109. Mr Morgenthau's reply to Chancellor, 8 June 1945 in T 247/40, and also, with Keynes's comments of 12 June, in T 231/373; *JMK* XXVI, pp 183 – 4.
110. Eady to Keynes, 27 June 1945, T 236/378.
111. Chancellor's reply to Mr Morgenthau, 28 June 1945, T 231/373.
112. Fund Article IV – 5(f).
113. Keynes to Eady, 22 August 1945, and Brand to Keynes, 23 August, T 236/166.
114. Cabinet Meeting, 6 November 1945, CM(45) 50th Conclusions, CAB 128/1.
115. Meade to Eady, 13 November 1945, T 230/83.
116. Eady to Meade, 13 November, ibid.
117. Meade to Eady, 14 November, ibid.
118. Meade to Mr J R C Helmore of the Board of Trade, 12 November 1945; Helmore to President of Board of Trade, 14 November; draft letter by President to Chancellor (14 November ?); Chancellor to President 21 November; ibid.
119. 12 December 1945, 417 HC DEB 5 s, cols 436 – 7.
120. Telegram 131 REMAC of 27 March 1946 from British Embassy in Washington, reporting a critical Press article thought to have reflected US Treasury views, T 230/83.

121. Mr E R Rowe-Dutton to Mr Burke Trend, 21 February 1946 and note by Mr Dalton, 14 May 1946, T 236/166.

122. Papers in ibid and T 230/83.

123. Telegram 7 EAGER, London to Washington, 15/17 May 1946, T 236/166.

124. International Monetary Fund Executive Board Document no 47, August 1946, ibid.

125. Telegram 78 EAGER, Washington to London, 9 September 1946; Mr Rowe-Dutton to Miss P C Shaw, assistant private secretary to the Chancellor, 14 September; 84 EAGER, Washington to London, 13 September: ibid.

126. Note by Mr Dalton, 17 September 1946, on notes between Mr H E Brooks and Mr Rowe-Dutton of 17 September: ibid.

127. Horsefield, op cit, I, p 149 and III, pp 227, 245.

128. Statement of 1 October 1946, T 236/166.

CHAPTER 8

Slow Progress on Trade Policy
1944 – 45

(1) DIFFICULTIES AND HESITATIONS

Some movement on commercial policy, out of deadlock towards the implementation of Article VII, had become unavoidable by the close of the Bretton Woods Conference in July 1944. The prospects of Anglo-American agreement were, however, much less promising than they had appeared at the conclusion of the Washington talks in the previous autumn. Britain was now a reluctant partner. Admittedly, there was in July 1944 an immediate excuse for delay, in preoccupation with the tense military position in Western Europe. There were, however, difficulties over agriculture. There was also anxiety about the scope in a liberal convention on international trade for the special requirements for state trading, especially in the bulk purchase of commodities; moreover, the old fears of too ready a modification of Imperial Preference, and of too hasty a renunciation of quantitative controls over imports had strengthened. Further, Lord Keynes's memoranda of mid-1944 had stressed that Britain might be forced, should adequate American aid not be forthcoming, to rely substantially upon her own resources; it was therefore easy to infer that she would then have to look to certain trade techniques, the use of which should therefore not be lightly renounced. The inclination to avoid elaborate and apparently restrictive commitments increased in summer 1944, with the critical reception in Britain of the Bretton Woods agreements.

During summer and early autumn of 1944 some powerful considerations opposed these hesitations. In particular, apart from substained American concern to resume talks on Article VII, there was the issue of Lend-Lease aid for Britain in Stage II, after the defeat of Germany, which was thought to be likely before the end of 1944. This issue was especially sensitive in the long shadow of difficult Congressional elections and of Mr Roosevelt's unprecedented candidature for a fourth Presidential term in November 1944. To consolidate progress in trade liberalisation in advance of a possible Republican Party victory, the State Department let it be known by early September that it was thinking of sending one of its trade experts to London, perhaps to secure by mid-October a preliminary understanding. This, it was briefly suggested, before that hope was dropped, might be followed by high level discussions should there be in fact a Democratic victory. [1]

British policy had to be formulated under these gathering pressures. Immediately after Mr Morgenthau's visit of August 1944, the process of formulation began with the Cabinet Committee on Commercial Policy (above p 137) receiving its terms of reference[2]:

'to examine the questions raised by the Commercial Policy Scheme, with particular regard to the position of agriculture and the provisions of bulk purchase thereunder'.

There followed three months of exceptionally difficult discussions, largely in an endeavour to accommodate the views of the Ministry of Agriculture and Fisheries; the discussions threatened to become embarrassingly inconclusive while the American trade expert, Mr Harry Hawkins, was from mid-October waiting in the US Embassy to begin talks.

(2) RE-APPRAISAL: AGRICULTURE AND IMPORT CONTROLS

The formulation of policy went through two main stages: first a re-appraisal of the 1943 principles in relation to British desiderata; then an attempt to deal with the problems of agriculture, to retain scope for quantitative restriction of imports, and to employ a degree of discrimination, with particular reference to three techniques to influence production and trade. Those three were levy-subsidies, bulk purchase, and the programming of imports.

At its first meeting (16 August 1944), conscious that Anglo-American discussions on trade were expected to be resumed in October, the Cabinet Committee decided that officials should make an urgent re-appraisal of the 1943 Washington principles, and of the compatibility with them of the three techniques of policy. Under the guidance of the Chancellor of the Exchequer, a committee of officials was therefore assembled from the Treasury, the Board of Trade, the Dominions Office, and the Economic Section. [3]

The officials reported very quickly: by early September. [4] They guardedly advised that the policies thought to be necessary during the transition period did not appear to be at odds with the Washington principles. Those principles would not preclude, they believed, the right which Britain sought to retain to provide unlimited or certainly very substantial subsidies to production in general. Within a multilateral convention, however, 'The most logical solution' appeared to be the application of limits to their use and also to that of tariffs, bulk purchase, and import programming. Those limits might require that the impact on consumer prices should not exceed a given percentage, say twenty-five per cent. Such limits to quantitative restrictions might be waived should there be balance of payments difficulties. That the devices in question would have to operate in a non-discriminatory fashion the officials did not doubt, but they were not apprehensive; hitherto there had been toleration of heavy duties on particular types of production, even though sources of supply were few. It would prove more difficult to stretch the doctrine of non-discrimination so favourably in respect of bulk purchase and the regulation of imports. On the sensitive point of non-discrimination in relation to Imperial Preference, the Cabinet Committee had felt the position to be quite clear when instructing the officials, whose report echoed that view: but with a warning note.

The officials recalled that the exchange of messages between President and Prime Minister in 1942 (above, pp 56–57 and Appendix 12) had stressed that Article VII did not require the elimination of Imperial Preference. There was nevertheless an obstacle in the preferential system itself to the generous protection of agriculture through levy-subsidies. Their use would involve a levy, equivalent to a tariff, on foodstuffs from the Dominions (the Dominions Office noted that this 'would involve a fairly considerable reduction in preferences').[5] The officials concluded that such a prospect, unacceptable to the Dominions, would rule out the use of levy-subsidies desired by the agricultural departments.

Two meetings of the Cabinet Committee, in mid- and late-September, considered the Report. It became evident that the officials had achieved no more than a limited clearing of ground: that Britain remained committed to Article VII and hence to non-discrimination in trade. Defending that ground at the first meeting[6], the Chancellor carried the Committee with him in rejection of quantitative restrictions for *general* use, given the near impossibility of applying them in a non-discriminatory manner. The Committee also accepted the verdict of the Report that the *general* use of levy-subsidies appeared to be impracticable. Not least, it agreed that the US authorities be invited to 'further exploratory discussions' in London in October.

What of agriculture? The officials had reported negatively. Ministers reacted sceptically, without discerning an agreed way to reconcile with the Washington principles arrangements acceptable to the agricultural departments. The Agricultural Ministers had not, however, been represented directly either on the Cabinet Committee or in the group of reporting officials, nor, as will be shown below, had their views been satisfactorily ascertained. It was now agreed that the Ministers concerned should be asked for their views.

The second stage in the formulation of policy was now opening, and it was to be dominated by this attempt to secure compatibility between the aims of the agricultural departments, and their supporters, and the requirements of a multilateral convention. This stage proved to be relatively prolonged and diplomatically embarrassing. Officials and Ministers were still struggling with this problem of agriculture when Mr Hawkins of the State Department arrived in October as Commercial Counsellor to the US Embassy in London, to participate in the expected Anglo-American talks on commercial policy. [7] The effort to grind out appropriate proposals for agriculture threatened indeed to produce a collapse of the attempt to devise a British policy for post-war trade, and thereby to delay yet longer Anglo-American talks and eventual Anglo-American agreement.

The agricultural interests remained as intransigent over international commitments as they had been in 1942–43 (above p 88) and earlier in 1944 (above pp 132–3). This attitude may well have influenced the Chancellor and the group of officials in keeping those interests at arm's length, at least while they consolidated support for Article VII. The Chancellor had decided that the Minister of Agriculture and Fisheries should not receive the minutes of the first meeting of the Cabinet Committee, although he might be informed of the proceedings. [8] In connection with the officials' Report, Sir Wilfrid Eady declared that there had been no opportunity for full consultation with the Ministry of Agriculture, and that in any case its chief official (the dedicated Sir Donald Fergusson) had been away on leave. Other officials of his Ministry had been shown the report, but had declined either to approve or to criticise it. [9] All this Treasury adroitness, if such it was, quickly faded. The Ministry of Agriculture was 'in a high state of indignation' over its treatment; [10] with its sympathisers, it counter-attacked. Mr R A Butler*, President of the Board of Education and MP for an agricultural constituency, quoted to the Committee, at the first of its two meetings on the officials' Report, the Agriculture Minister's forthright Cabinet paper of the preceding April to explain how the proposed multilateral convention and the expansive agricultural aims could be made 'just . . . compatible'. The requirement was for greater flexibility in the limits suggested by the officials; thus the price-raising effects of controls (say twenty-five per cent) could be averaged over a period. [11]

The Chancellor had to recognise that fuller account must be taken of the views of those Ministers interested directly in domestic agriculture and in the regulation of trade in agricultural products. The

---

*BUTLER, Richard Austen, 1st Baron, 1965, (1902–1982); Under-Secretary of State for Foreign Affairs, 1938–41; President of the Board of Education, 1941–44, and then first Minister of Education, 1944–45; Minister of Labour, 1945; Chancellor of the Exchequer, 1951–55; Lord Privy Seal, 1955–59; Leader of the House of Commons, 1955–61; Home Secretary, 1957–62; First Secretary of State and Deputy Prime Minister, 1962–63; Secretary of State for Foreign Affairs, 1963–64.

Minister of Agriculture and Fisheries, the Minister of Food, and the Secretary of State for Scotland (who had oversight of the Scottish Department of Agriculture) joined the Cabinet Committee when it held its second meeting on the officials' Report[12]. Agreement on agricultural policy became no easier. On bulk purchase of imports, Ministers were divided about its compatibility with the Washington proposals. Quantitative restrictions on imports or equivalent controls were indispensable, claimed the Agriculture Minister and the Scottish Secretary; the latter explained that their particular attractiveness arose from the possible difficulties of operating a policy of subsidies. In vain the Chancellor questioned whether quantitative restrictions could be non-discriminatory as required by Article VII; the President of the Board of Trade, originally a Cabinet protagonist of the Washington principles, reserved his views. The alternative of Exchequer subsidy, declared the Agriculture Minister, would be unattractive to landowners; they would be unwilling to undertake the considerable expenditure required for equipment after the war if expected to rely on finance dependent on annual parliamentary vote. Indeed, Sir Wilfrid Eady was shortly to express objection to Exchequer subsidies for agriculture.[13] The technique of the levy-subsidy therefore attracted the support of some Ministers. It might not be appropriate for the whole sweep of the economy, but the Minister of Food claimed that it had worked successfully under the Wheat Act (of 1932); why should it not be used for other commodities?

It had become clear that a more drastic re-evaluation of commercial policy than the Chancellor had anticipated would be necessary. Once again officials were requested to report urgently; this time, to the four non-agricultural departments previously represented were added the Ministry of Agriculture, the Scottish Department of Agriculture, and the Ministry of Food. The remit concerned the need of agriculture for price stability after the war: how would that need, and the use to secure it of the techniques discussed in the earlier Report, accord with or require modification of the Anglo-American principles of 1943? The officials were further instructed to 'consider whether a workable scheme of non-discriminatory regulation' of production and of imports could be devised.

On this occasion officials were neither to report so quickly as before, nor, as they drafted, to find ready agreement. The Economic Section suggested possible routes out of the prolonged *impasse* that would not involve the scrapping of the 1943 principles or their dilution by excessively favourable treatment for agriculture.[14] In particular the price-raising effects of import controls might be constrained flexibly by what became known as the XY formula. This encompassed recognition of the unwillingness of both the US Administration, and of British agricultural officials and some Ministers, to accept the relatively low levels of protection that had been proposed at Washington in 1943. The tariff floor then envisaged of 10 per cent might be raised to, say, 25 per cent, and also regarded as a maximum level of protection, X. The use of protective devices, such as import controls, would be reduced when a country's production exceeded Y; this would be a stated percentage of, say, its pre-war production or of total world production at a given period. As a further device to control imports quantitatively but without discrimination against particular suppliers, Mr J E Meade proposed the auction of import licences. Such ingenuity exasperated the chief Ministry of Agriculture official, Sir Donald Fergusson, who denounced both the Economic Section's theorising and 'political solutions'. He warned that the type of Anglo-American agreement that was envisaged 'would not only cause political uproar but would be followed by widespread resignations among the leaders of the industry from our County and District Committees which would lead to a breakdown of our whole machine. . . '.[15]

(3) AGRICULTURE: THE OFFICIALS' REPORT

The fifth and final draft of the officials' Report on 'Commercial Policy and the Needs of Agriculture' was submitted to the Cabinet Committee early in November 1944.[16] It noted pointedly that 'in the absence of any approved long-term policy or production programme for home agriculture', the agriculture departments found difficulty in formulating their wishes. The Report concluded that it would be impossible to devise acceptable proposals within a convention on commercial policy.

Notwithstanding the earlier report to the contrary, the agriculture departments had, however, asserted that a Convention could be made compatible with a levy-subsidy scheme for agriculture. The necessary modifications to the type of convention envisaged at Washington would involve in particular a much higher degree of basic protection: a tariff floor of twenty-five per cent rather than one of ten per cent. Further, quantitative restrictions of imports in general would have to be permitted. The officials warned that such modifications, which would be 'so substantial as to alter the whole balance' of the Washington proposals, were unlikely to be acceptable to the US or to the majority (at least) of the Dominions which exported food to Britain. Moreover, as the Board of Trade had noted, even if liberal scope to use quantitative restrictions were to be secured, that would be self-defeating; other countries would be entitled to apply them against British exports, and this would eliminate the attractiveness to Britain of the projected convention.

Could the anxieties of the agricultural interests be allayed? Were there alternative policies? A drastic solution would be to seek the exclusion of agriculture entirely from a convention. The Chancellor himself thought that this should be attempted,[17] but the officials' Report advised that complete exclusion was unlikely to be possible in a multilateral convention. Instead, there might be a partial exclusion of foodstuffs or special provisions for them. Such arrangements would be intended to allow greater flexibility than in the case of industrial products in respect of price and income guarantees. There could be more or less automatic checks on the degree of subsidy and of protection, with allowance for such special needs as the stimulation of structural change in a country's economy or the meeting of serious balance of payments problems. Proposals for this special status for foodstuffs would have to be stated with some precision and, thought the officials, could be accommodated within the Washington concepts.

On the sensitive issue in Anglo-American relations of the discriminatory element in trade controls, this Report avowed adherence to non-discrimination, with the usual qualification about Imperial Preference. In their separate Report on 'Non-Discrimination in relation to the Programming of Imports', the officials ingeniously widened the whole issue.[18] They virtually reversed the usual arguments, thereby to meet, indeed to counter, potential American objections. Elaborating a principle they discovered in the Anglo-American Trade Agreement of 1938, they proposed a 'doctrine of commercial considerations'. This would warrant a country adhering to its normal sources of supply, although the availability of apparently cheaper sources might make this appear discriminatory. Such cheapness might, however, be temporary or artificial and could therefore be as open to objection as deliberate discrimination. Here, swinging the accusing finger away from import controls to manipulation of exports, the Report noted the Americans' tendency to protect their own high cost production, at the expense of low cost producers elsewhere. American dumping appeared to be a post-war threat, as the Minister of Agriculture also was shortly to argue to the Cabinet Committee.[19] The Report concluded therefore that there should be scope within a commercial convention for regulation of imports without meeting immovable American insistence on non-discrimination. Agreement should be sought on broad rather than on detailed grounds; although the Economic Section had devised variants of precise rules, the majority favoured accumulating experience on a 'case-law' basis.

The attraction of these proposals was in indicating at last an escape from the *impasse* within the Government and between London and Washington. Even the Minister of Agriculture, though against a multilateral approach and rating low the chances of securing a multilateral convention, regarded the proposals as more practicable than earlier ones, and recognised them as a tolerable basis for Anglo-American talks.[20] The Chancellor now commended them to the War Cabinet.[21] In view of their relevance to the Dominions, some of whose representatives had earlier in the year expressed reservations about the Washington proposals, he followed the officials' recommendation that Dominion Governments should be fully informed. There should not, however, be fresh consultations with them at that stage. There had already been serious delay in resuming talks with the Americans; moreover, it was scarcely appropriate to launch discussions with the Dominions on the proposed special arrangement for foodstuffs, lest that prove to be a non-starter with the Americans. The War Cabinet accepted the Chancellor's view and authorised officials to hold 'exploratory and non-committal talks' with Mr Harry Hawkins along the lines of their reports, with one major exception. To the disappointment, indeed to the despair, of officials, the War Cabinet resolved and the Prime Minister directed that they were on no account to air, 'even by way of illustration', any figures of post-war production or of a possible agreed level of protection such as had been proposed in the reports, by the XY formula, to govern the use of import controls.[22]

If this directive, which recognised strongly divergent views amongst Ministers and officials on the tolerable level of protection, seemed to dilute in advance the substance of Anglo-American discussions, at least those discussions were at last to resume. Moreover, for all their appearance of being a continuation of the 1943 talks, these were to be fresh talks in at least two senses. First, the Americans, never wholly committed to multilateral discussions, had been re-assessing the record of the Washington discussions of 1943. They inclined to favour a new start, to seek initial agreements either in a series of bilateral negotiations or in a 'nuclear' approach within a group of leading countries, before attempting to secure wider adherence to a comprehensive multilateral convention.[23] In a second and ominous sense the talks were freshly inspired. With the end of the German war in sight, and with unintended gaps they were determined to plug in the Bretton Woods agreements, American officials had apparently exchanged the academic seminar of 1943 for hard bargaining to exact fulfilment of Article VII as an accompaniment, or perhaps as a prelude, to Anglo-American arrangements for Stages II and III. This made likely on each side cautious stances that would scarcely facilitate agreement; Britain was anxious that commitments on commercial policy should not out-run reassurance on financial policy, whilst the USA tended to regard policy commitments as a pre-requisite to financial aid. Not surprisingly, against this background the discussions were to stretch indecisively on critical points until Britain's serious post-war position, on the ending of Lend-Lease following Japan's defeat in August 1945, precipitated agreement.

(4) ANGLO-AMERICAN DISCUSSIONS, DECEMBER 1944—JANUARY 1945

The discussions on commercial policy fell into three phases: December 1944 to January 1945; April to June 1945; and August 1945.

Between the first and second phases, a bold Canadian initiative sought to encourage Britain down the Article VII road. Between the second and third phases, Congressional pressures produced an American retreat from multilateralism, which shocked Canadian representatives sought to mitigate.

In thirteen meetings in December 1944 and January 1945, with American officials led by Mr Harry Hawkins, British officials fully discharged their threefold remit over a wide range of topics. They ascertained the views of the State Department, which was anxious to take full advantage of a favourable atmosphere in the USA to go ahead with commercial policy. Mr Hawkins disclosed the contents of a draft Convention on Commercial Policy resulting from extensive discussions in Washington. This would establish an International Trade Organisation (ITO). They reported a satisfactory reception of the suggestion for special provision for foodstuffs, although the bar on quantifying X and Y was a drawback. Finally, British views on the nature of non-discrimination were received sympathetically.[24] Since these discussions were exploratory and for bridge building, these results were perhaps satisfactory at that level; they did, however, reveal very serious divergences, both on the details of trade liberalisation and on the method to secure an agreement. On the details, there were three outstanding differences. Against the American leaning towards generalised percentage cuts in tariffs, British officials noted that such cuts would have a smaller relative effect on high tariff countries than on low tariff ones. They favoured their 1943 principle of a ceiling for tariffs. A second difference, not surprisingly, was over preferences. Here, an American proposal to extend a Canadian suggestion for reciprocal cuts in tariffs and preferences was decidedly unattractive; it would mean a substantial dismantlement by Britain of preferences against 'a mere halving' of American tariffs. When account was also taken of the proposed renunciation of quantitative restrictions on imports after a transition of five years, except in specified conditions which would not necessarily be equitably applied, the balance of American ideas seemed to bear heavily against Britain. Whereas she would be expected to cut tariffs and preferences, and to abandon import controls, only a cut in tariffs would be required of the USA. Against this Mr Hawkins pointed to the Americans' 'negative' undertakings—that they would not adopt certain policies—and to the greater access to escape clauses for Britain than for the USA in the proposed Convention.[25]

The third difference of opinion was potentially the most serious. The Americans' proposals on exchange controls stiffened those of the proposed International Monetary Fund. They reflected their determination that the world 'should not be left to run wild' in trading practices in the transition, and that there should be no revival of the restrictive exchange controls of the inter-war years.[26] In the shorter-term, at the end of a transition period of five years, exchange restrictions should have disappeared, whereas the Fund agreement provided simply for a review of them. Moreover, the draft Convention allowed much less scope for discriminatory policies, even during the transition. Central to British anxiety was the American attitude to 'blocked balances' which the British representatives, though explaining that sterling balances were not really blocked, recognised as directed to the potential obstacle of sterling debts to trade and currency liberalisation.[27] The American proposals undermined the solution for which British discussions had been groping: a combination of the control of excess balances, with revised arrangements for the sterling area, to permit movement towards Article VII goals, supported by American financial assistance. Since an overhang of blocked (or funded) balances would encourage the debtor country to discriminate in favour of trade with its creditors, the Americans preferred all sterling to be freely available. The British response was that that would require Britain to borrow heavily; it would simply transfer the balance of payments burden from the current to the capital account. Further, such borrowing would have to be from the USA and Canada and would be difficult to repay. In the longer-term, London's position as a financial centre would be threatened; there would also be the risk of a slower movement towards multilateral trade, partly because public opinion would be hostile to the implications of such borrowing. The draft Convention, unlike the IMF, left no scope for the further accumulation of blocked balances. The Americans, in a clause that had been withheld from the draft, did indeed acknowledge that the settlement of wartime indebtedness might justify discrimination, but they coupled with this a requirement for consultation with the proposed ITO. As at Bretton Woods, six months earlier, so now British representatives opposed such involvement with sterling balances of an international body.[28]

Perhaps more than any other feature of the proposed Convention, this attempt to toughen the Bretton Woods agreements and to add surveillance by a further institution, obstructed progress on commercial policy, especially as British perplexities about Bretton Woods were still unresolved (above, pp 176–7). In explaining their opposition British officials did not, however, reject Mr Hawkins's broaching of the possibility of quite separate inter-governmental talks on the balances.

On the overall approach to an agreement on commercial policy, strongly contrasting attitudes foreshadowed slow progress at best. For Britain a multilateral convention (such as the Commercial Union proposal of 1942–43) now held diminished attractions, given the complexity of issues and also Britain's need for special post-war arrangements. Of American intentions, there was serious British apprehension; Mr Hawkins was warned against any projected 'railroading through' of a Convention despite other countries' opposition. He therefore undertook to discuss a range of other courses in Washington; these included deferment of discussion of a Convention; a series of steps towards a Convention, beginning with an agreed Statement of Principles; publication of that as either an Anglo-American document or as solely an American one; finally, Congress might be asked to authorise the President to seek international action on the Principles.[29]

Scarcely had Mr Hawkins left for Washington when a curious interchange underlined the indeterminate status of the talks on commercial policy and of Britain's circumspect attitude towards it. On the way to the Yalta Conference in February 1945, President Roosevelt wrote to Mr Churchill to urge that the Article VII talks of 1943 be 're-invigorated' at Ministers' level. The Deputy Prime Minister and the Chancellor, when informed about this, cabled Mr Churchill about the recent talks, of which the President seemed unaware. They opposed early high-level action until matters were clearer, a view which Mr Churchill conveyed in his written reply to the President (they do not appear to have discussed the issue).[30]

(5) THE CANADIAN INITIATIVE, FEBRUARY 1945

The slow pace and uncertainties of the Anglo-American talks now brought a remarkable intervention from the Canadian Government, which had been kept informed of them, and which had become increasingly uneasy about the post-war prospects for Canadian trade. In peacetime Canada's trade surplus with Britain had offset her deficit with the USA. During the war, while American Lend-Lease took care of Britain's enhanced imports from the USA, Canada's Mutual Aid largely financed her greatly increased exports to Britain. Ahead, however, lay the post-war possibility that Britain and the rest of the sterling area would be so short of North American resources that Canada would face an export slump. Canada feared that Britain's sterling indebtedness would induce her to discriminate in favour of imports from other sterling area countries, leaving Canada 'out on a limb'.[31] Canadian officials had already heard Keynes, in the discussions of Britain's future wartime needs from Canada during November 1944, expound post-war problems, and his view that very long-term interest-free loans might be necessary to ease the burden of sterling balances.[32] A few weeks later Mr R S Hudson, Minister of Agriculture and Fisheries, alarmed Ottawa with his blunt advocacy of controlled and preferential trade; it reminded one official of 'a conversation he had had ten years previously 'with Schacht'.[33] With Mutual Aid to Britain for the coming fiscal year yet to be approved by the Canadian Parliament, and with electoral hazards in mind, the Canadian Government shortly decided to act boldly, in order to encourage Britain along the Article VII path and away from discriminatory policies.

In February 1945, three forthright telegrams, two to the Dominions Secretary and one from the Canadian Prime Minister to Mr Churchill, sought to promote liberal international trading policies by, in effect, promising finance for Canadian exports to Britain and the sterling area in exchange for an end to discrimination. Canada feared that the post-war transition might breed affection for trade controls, and was apprehensive that international co-operation on trade was being pushed dangerously into the future; disliking the distinction between Stage II and Stage III, she wanted early movement towards liberalisation. Canada saw no excuse for the wartime exercise of discrimination against her exports, given the generous provision of Mutual Aid; if that fell short, Britain and the sterling area could surely meet at least a small shortfall from their reserves. In Stage III Britain would require increased Canadian imports, whilst Canada would certainly want to maintain exports. Canada therefore offered the possibility of special and substantial long-term credits to Britain; repayment would not commence for some years, and could be deferred in case of difficulties in the British economy. Believing that thereby trade discrimination, and with it a danger of economic isolationism and bitterness in North America, could be avoided, the Canadian Government sought early discussions to secure high level action.[34]

London discussions on this initiative ranged widely before attitudes settled back, perhaps marginally less far back than previously, to caution. In contrast with the enthusiasm of the Paymaster-General (Lord Cherwell) and of Mr Meade of the Economic Section, Professor Robbins (Director of the Economic Section), sympathetic to Canadian motives, offered sober counsel. There was uncertainty over the post-war balance of payments, while the Americans were ready, according to Mr Hawkins, to contemplate in an international agreement 'let-outs' for import restrictions for countries in balance of payments difficulties. It therefore seemed both unwise and unnecessary to accept the Canadian suggestion to jettison import controls immediately. Moreover, the volume of external assistance to underpin that demanded pause. In any case, stressed Professor Robbins, an underlying difficulty over post-war commercial policy was Britain's footdragging since the 'Commercial Union' initiative some eighteen months previously, and this threatened Anglo-Canadian, intra-imperial, and Anglo-American relations. From Washington, Mr R H Brand warned that the Canadian proposals themselves hazarded Anglo-American arrangements. If Britain used reserves or loans for Canadian imports, then the USA might expect similar treatment, and would reduce Lend-Lease. Further, relaxation of sterling area discrimination against Canada and its maintenance against the USA would arouse fears there of an anti-American empire *bloc*.[35]

Evaluation of American views, or, rather, uncertainty about them, inevitably fashioned London's response to Ottawa. The Anglo-American trade talks had broken off only temporarily, and Britain awaited Washington's re-assessments. Congress was considering, in connection with the renewal of the Reciprocal Trade Agreements Act, Presidential authority for tariff cuts which, though substantial, would be less than originally hoped.[36] Further, Congress had yet to re-enact Lend-Lease legislation and to make Appropriations; finance for the rest of the war was uncertain, whilst until that was resolved, President Roosevelt would not consider Anglo-American discussions about Stage III arrangements.[37] In London, by the second half of March 1945, Keynes's challenging memorandum on 'Overseas Financial Arrangements in Stage III' was underlining post-war needs for American assistance.[38] All this made it scarcely possible to grant Canada's wish for firmer shaping of post-war policy. A Committee of 14 (raised by Mr Churchill from 13), an informal meeting of Ministers, and then the War Cabinet assessed these points—and also a characteristic protectionist memorandum from Mr Hudson, rejecting the Canadian viewpoint. Telegrams were then sent to Canada, welcoming her initiative; they avoided both acceptance and rejection, and suggested early discussions in London.[39]

Those discussions took place during the second half of May (almost three months after the original telegrams) in London and in Cambridge; there, combining his Treasury and academic roles, Lord Keynes entertained and presided at his own King's College. By this time, further uncertainties were deferring the major policy decisions sought by Canada. Congress had taken a hard line on the future of Lend-Lease. American reaction to British proposals for agriculture had been unwelcoming. The Anglo-American discussions on commercial policy, resumed in April, were unpromising. Above all, with the end of the European war, the Coalition Government had given place to a largely Conservative Administration; a general election was pending (it was to bring a Labour Government into office at the end of July); officials advised their Canadian counterparts that Ministers were unlikely to be able to meet Mr Hawkins's wish for detailed decisions by early August.[40] Paralleling this, at Cambridge Keynes foresaw no movement on Anglo-American arrangements for Stage III before September. He centred discussions there around his recent memorandum (see below, pp 236-41). Whilst its broad drift appealed to the Canadians, with its vision of a brief transition and of an early adoption of sterling convertibility, Keynes stressed that the original Canadian proposals must be subordinate to the results of a potentially difficult approach to the Americans; he speculated whether the latter could be persuaded to realise that, failing an attitude along Canadian lines towards the association of financial aid with the ending of trade discrimination, wartime controls must continue. This question of discrimination was further examined in London, when Canada sought to end it in exchange for finance of the sterling area's deficit with Canada. Britain compromised, with an undertaking to modify import controls so as to eliminate discrimination where Canada was a normal source of supply. Whilst retaining discretion as to what was essential, Britain would eliminate discrimination against Canada in respect of 'essential' imports, and would endeavour to ensure that the Commonwealth members of the sterling area did likewise. This action was taken in July 1945.[41]

(6) ANGLO-AMERICAN DISCUSSIONS, APRIL–JUNE 1945

The resumed Anglo-American trade talks, the progress of which British officials recounted to the visiting Canadians, lasted from April to June 1945.[42] They remained 'informal and non-committal', and were supplemented by a variety of other discussions before, during, and after a series of seven meetings. On three main counts British and American ideas continued to be sufficiently unharmonised to make early agreement improbable. First, the American representatives' desire to catch what favourable wind there might be in the USA, by looking to an international conference by October, encountered British doubts. Domestic political considerations in Britain, and the need to consult the Dominions and India, made it difficult to contemplate a conference before January 1946. Second, there were unbridged gaps on major topics. On cutting preferences, the Americans regarded the British requirement for large compensating tariff reductions as unacceptable. The proposed regulation of cartels brought the British advocacy of a case-by-case approach into conflict with the American tradition of generalised legal controls. American comment on the special proposals for agriculture seemed misconceived to British officials, who virtually started to argue their case again from the beginning. The Americans' hankering for surveillance of exchange controls beyond that provided by the IMF agreement disturbed British officials. The third and by far the greatest obstacle was the proposed international trade organisation: the procedure to seek international agreement on its principles and on their subsequent implementation.

The American officials proposed a broad agreement between a few key economies (the USA, Britain and the Empire, Russia and France) on detailed proposals. These would then be circulated to other countries as the basis for the international conference, which would distil a statement of principles and conclude a Convention for the proposed

International Trade Organisation. Whilst the British officials accepted the ultimate aim, they saw great dangers in the American approach. They feared that to leave agreement on a statement of principles to the conference itself would risk its breakdown; the American view, however, was clearly that the key group's agreement would persuade or even force the other countries to follow. When in mid-June 1945 the principal American expert, Mr Harry Hawkins, produced his own draft 'Statement of Principles', his British counterparts despairingly remarked that it took little account of their own comments in the earlier talks. Offering their own two-page draft on commercial policy against his thirty-two wide-ranging pages, they advocated brevity. Finally, after discussions on procedure occupying half of this second series of talks, they warned virtually of British non-co-operation; it might be impossible to forecast Ministers' reactions to a document such as Mr Hawkins had outlined, and Britain might feel obliged to keep out of the key group and go to a conference without that committed status. Late in June, in a meeting which underlined all these points, British officials coupled to pessimism about the American approach to international agreement their misgivings about the Americans' proposed method of securing the all-important goal of widespread tariff reductions.

'A new start' in international trade, with all making 'substantial reductions at once' was the professed British aim.[43] The US, however, preferred to seek worldwide changes by a series of bilateral negotiations: 'multilateral bilateralism' had for over a decade been its practice under the Reciprocal Trade Agreements Act. The British officials doggedly pointed out that this could drag on for a long time, and that it could involve many complex negotiations, the outcome of which would be unpredictable. This uncertainty would be a gift not only to critics of a liberal commercial policy but also to those who opposed acceptance of the IMF until trade policy was settled. They begged the American officials to follow a true multilateral policy of general tariff cuts, the abandonment of which 'would be the end of all we hoped to achieve,' and would destroy British enthusiasm for the search for international co-operation in trade policy.

Very soon, indeed within two weeks, this British gloom was to prove well-founded. In early July the US Administration felt constrained to give Congress undertakings, to secure renewal of the Reciprocal Trade Agreements Act, that tariff cuts would be on a selective basis. Thus, general, multilateral ('horizontal') tariff reductions were out. This so shocked the Canadian Government that a meeting was quickly arranged between several of its senior officials and diplomats in Washington, with a group of American trade experts, headed by

Mr Will L Clayton,* Assistant Secretary of State for Economic Affairs. The Americans returned the visit a few days later in Ottawa. Much as the British had done recently the Canadians deplored the implications of abandoning 'horizontal' reductions in tariffs. They commented, for instance, that significant diminution of tariff preferences, including Imperial Preference, would not now be possible. They pleaded, but in vain, that the difficulties in gaining acceptance for the horizontal method could be exaggerated. The Americans, however, stood firm that it was impossible to secure Congressional support; the furthest they could consider going seemed to be the 'multilateral-bilateral' approach. This depressed the Canadians as it had the British. They urged a compromise in a 'nuclear' approach: eight to twelve countries would negotiate tariff reductions and other changes amongst themselves, preparatory to the calling of a more widely based international conference.[44]

Perhaps reflecting these discussions, the recommendations of State Department experts now edged towards the Canadian and British positions, which in fact they favoured. Given Congressional constraints, they proposed the triple blend of a 'selective nuclear-multilateral' approach. This would embody the Canadian compromise suggestion in order to move in a multilateral direction, whilst maintaining selectivity. In case of British rejection, they recommended perseverance with negotiations, and hoped for reconsideration by the Administration and Congress of the broader approach. For the moment, however, Washington had to admit to the disappointed British that there had been a 'very marked change' in American policy since 1943.[45]

(7) ANGLO-AMERICAN ATTITUDES, AUGUST 1945

The third of the three main phases of the 1944–45 discussions on commercial policy was now (August 1945) about to open. In that phase two other issues were also to become involved. These were the terminal arrangements for Lend-Lease and, above all, the form of possible financial aid for Britain after the war. So interwined were these three issues that the following discussion inevitably overlaps with parts of the next two chapters.

Although prospects for these latest commercial policy talks seemed gloomy, they promised to be more significant than ever. They were specifically linked to examination of arrangements for Stage III. Further, they were to be at a high level, for Clayton was to lead the talks whilst visiting London for a meeting of the Council of UNRRA

---

*CLAYTON, William Lockhart (1880–1966); Government service, 1940; became Deputy Federal Loan Administrator; Assistant Secretary of Commerce; Administrator of Surplus War Property Administration; and later Assistant Secretary of State in Charge of Economic Affairs.

(United Nations Relief and Rehabilitation Administration). Dedicated to uncompromising free trade principles, Clayton had recently set out his view on the financial assistance necessary to remove the obstruction that Britain's difficulties held for the movement to freer trade.[46] The terms of such aid, which would be generous, but not a gift, should involve above all a rapid British move to multilateral free trade; as he was to say elsewhere, he believed that only thus in fact could Britain repay credits, which should be 'collectible'.[47] Notwithstanding the crippling in Congress of multilateralism, this was to be the American aim in the talks. Six principal meetings were held in London during the first half of August.[48] They broadly re-registered the existing British position, reinforced by Treasury discussions of tolerable Stage III arrangements (below, pp 242–5), and also by awareness that the new Labour Government would need a little time before wishing to make policy commitments. Lord Keynes's exposition of Britain's external financial problems, and of the need to deal with sterling balances in order to move to early freedom in international payments, appeared to evoke American agreement.[49] There remained, however, acute differences on the practicability of the nuclear approach if matters were to advance quickly. The British officials resisted the suggestion of dealing with preferences separately from tariffs; that would have meant surrendering the possibility of trading one against the other. On quotas and export subsidies, differences persisted, and once again British officials resisted efforts to stiffen the Bretton Woods agreements. Even so, Keynes gave his personal view that much of the basic American document (ie, the proposed Convention on international trade) would be acceptable.[50]

The overriding problem was the relationship of trade liberalisation to the financial assistance which both sides recognised to be essential to achieve it. In mid-August, however, as the talks continued, the sudden end of the war against Japan transformed this into a momentarily desperate issue. Lend-Lease aid was stopped and then prolonged temporarily. As will be discussed more fully below (pp 251–3) a doubly urgent problem now arose. First there was the method of financing supplies and services ordered or arriving after the legal end of Lend-Lease, as well as of payment for stocks of goods and equipment. Second was the possible impact of the terms of such financing upon those of the major financial aid being sought for Stage III. London sought to defer finality on the immediate issue. On Stage III Keynes resisted fiercely ('with typical abruptness' reported the American Ambassador in London) the idea of aid in the form of credits, particularly if they were intended to rank ahead of existing sterling debts.[51] Rather than that, Britain would adopt a bilateral trading policy. This was the threat which Keynes had earlier suggested was Britain's only serious, if disagreeable, weapon; it might be displayed if all else failed to persuade the Americans to accept the British concept of aid.[52] Mr Clayton retorted, however, that to obtain assistance Britain 'must abandon that position'.[53] Escaping from that dead-end by agreeing that drastic measures would be necessary to cut sterling balances, the British participants promptly stumbled on further obstacles: Mr Clayton wanted an early end to preferences, a transitional period much briefer than Britain contemplated preparatory to the full adoption of 'liberalised' trading and exchange arrangements, and a non-discriminatory use of quantitative import controls during the limited period for which they would be tolerated. Underlying all this was a characteristic contrast of emphasis: for Britain financial resources were the substance and trade arrangements more of the shadow, whereas for the USA precisely the reverse was the case.

To avert the *impasse* or clash (perhaps both) which threatened, it now became a mutual aim to seek for September the Washington talks on Stage III which in any case had for some time been in London's mind (below pp 241–2). On the British side this was largely an attempt to delay and to ease the reckoning—the Lend-Lease reckoning of Article VII; but Britain's search for further aid reinforced American determination to secure that. To a leading British expert, the difficulties could be insuperable if the Americans insisted on their existing proposals.[54] In the new Labour Government, which had taken over from the Conservatives in late July, the President of the Board of Trade, Sir Stafford Cripps,* echoed this to the Cabinet in a memorandum that warned that financial aid would be closely linked with a requirement for assurances to the USA on commercial policy.[55] The ebullient new Chancellor of the Exchequer, Mr Hugh Dalton, was more optimistic: aggressively so. In a memorandum initially given very restricted circulation, he asserted that Britain could satisfy American desires whilst retaining a formidable group of 'essential safeguards'. These, on which Keynes and Eady in the Treasury were 'wholly agreed', included in particular 'import programming'; exchange control as discriminatory as might appear necessary in the transition; and the treatment of Imperial Preference 'as an integral part of the tariff system, and not as a special sin which requires separate expiation'.[56]

The Americans were set on a swift settlement on trade and finance, but on terms for the former still unacceptable to the British. Mr Clayton nevertheless wanted to decide essentials before returning to the USA, where the proposed Anglo-American talks could then be concerned with details. The British officials argued, however, that it was

---

*CRIPPS, Richard Stafford, Kt. 1930 (1889–1952); British Ambassador to Russia, 1940–42; Lord Privy Seal and Leader of House of Commons, 1942; Minister of Aircraft Production, 1942–45; President Board of Trade, 1945; Minister for Economic Affairs, 1947; Chancellor of the Exchequer, 1947–50.

desirable to allow the British case to be expounded more fully in Washington. At that distance from the Cabinet, negotiations would be easier, said Keynes, in a plausible assertion that later was to rebound cruelly on him (below pp 319–20). Mr Clayton dismissed such views. Congress had excluded the wide multilateral approach; there was no point therefore, he declared, in spending time on that. He came close to insistence on quick acceptance of the narrow qualified policies that had so disheartened British officials.[57]

With a mutually satisfactory agreement on commercial policy thus continuing to be elusive, the war ended and the peace began with the future shape of Anglo-American trade relations scarcely more resolved than when the war's impact on them had been first considered in 1940–41. Preparations were now begun for fresh endeavours in the negotiations in Washington which were to last from September to December 1945. Before discussing that crucial phase extended attention must, however, be given to the formulation in London, not just under the exceptional pressures of August 1945, but in the previous year and a half, of the overall approach to the USA for financial assistance, in the context of the Article VII commitment to trade liberalisation.

CHAPTER 8, SOURCE REFERENCES

1. Telegram 4783 of 4 September 1944, Washington to London, CAB 123/96 – I.
2. Ibid, WP (44) 442 of 12 August 1944, CAB 66/53.
3. Cabinet Committee meeting, CCP (44) 1st of 16 August 1944, ibid and CAB 87/97. Appointment of committee of officials, notes by Chancellor 24 August, CAB 123/96 – I and by Mr W L Gorell Barnes 24 August, ibid; note by Gorell Barnes to Sir Edward Bridges 25 August, CAB 123/96 – II.
4. By 4 September, about ten days after their appointment, the officials provided a draft report for Sir Wilfrid Eady of the Treasury, who submitted a final version to the Chancellor on 9 September: T 236/172. The report was presented to the Cabinet Committee as CCP (44) 1 of 12 September: CAB 123/96 – II and CAB 87/97.
5. Mr A W Snelling of the Dominions Office to Gorell Barnes of the Treasury, 31 August 1944, T 236/172.
6. Meeting on 18 September 1944, CCP(44) 2nd, and memorandum by Chancellor, signed 18 September, CCP(44) 2 of 19 September: both in CAB 123/96 – II and CAB 87/97.
7. In late October: Gorell Barnes to Bridges, 7 November 1944, CAB 21/1247.
8. Gorell Barnes to Bridges, 24 August 1944, CAB 123/96 – II.
9. Eady, note to Chancellor, 9 September 1944, T 236/172.
10. Mr W Armstrong to Gorell Barnes, and Gorell Barnes to Bridges, 8 September 1944; Bridges to Chancellor, 14 November 1944: CAB 123/96 – I.
11. CCP(44) 2nd meeting, 18 September, CAB 87/97.
12. Ibid, and CCP(44) 3rd Meeting, 27 September.
13. CCP(44) 3rd Meeting of 27 September, CAB 87/97; Eady to Mr T Padmore, 20 October, T 236/172.
14. Note by Economic Section, 14 October, T 236/172.
15. Ibid, Sir Donald Fergusson to Eady, 21 October.
16. CCP(44) 3, 'Commercial Policy and the Needs of Agriculture', 6 November 1944, CAB 87/97.
17. Eady to Mr P A Clutterbuck of the Dominions Office, 24 October 1944, T 236/172.
18. CCP(44) 3, 13 November 1944, CAB 87/97.
19. CCP(44) 5, 13 November, ibid.
20. CCP(44) 4th Meeting, 15 November, ibid.
21. WP(44) 661 of 16 November, CAB 66/58 and Cabinet Meeting of 22 November, WM(44) 153rd Conclusions, CAB 66/44 in CAB 123/96 – I.
22. Ibid; CCP(44) 8 of 28 November, CAB 87/97.
23. Keynes from Washington, 13 November, reporting discussion with Mr Leo Pasvolsky, T 236/378 (and also T 236/172); report of discussion at State Department 12 January 1945 between Mr Joseph C Grew, Mr Clayton, Mr Pasvolsky, and Mr R S Hudson, Minister of Agriculture, T 230/174.
24. Thirteen meetings in December and January 1944 – 45, CAB 123/96 – I; summary in CAB 99/34.
25. ASD(45) 1 of 8 March 1945, 'Article VII Discussions . . .', CAB 99/34.
26. Meeting of 11 January 1945, CAB 123/96 – I.
27. Ibid.

28. Ibid.

29. Ibid, meeting of 16 January 1945.

30. *FRUS, The Conferences of Malta and Yalta 1945* (1955), p 962 and *FRUS* 1945 VI (1969), p 21; CAB 123/96-II; T 236/379.

31. Sayers, *Financial Policy*, pp 359–60.

32. Notes of meeting in Ottawa, 28–29 November 1944, T 160/1377.

33. Letter from Mr Lewis Croome, in charge of British Food Mission in Ottawa to Mr Broadley of Ministry of Food, 8 January 1945; the remark about Schacht was made by Mr Graham Towers: T 236/379.

34. Telegrams 45, 46, 47 of 23–24 February 1945 in several files: CAB 21/1247; AVIA 38/1118; T 236/31; T 230/174.

35. Cherwell, 1 March, CAB 21/1247; Meade, 7 March, T 230/174; Robbins, 5, 19 March, CAB 21/1247; Brand to Keynes, 219 REMAC of 6 March, T 236/379.

36. Acting Secretary of State Joseph C Grew to US Ambassador in UK, 5 March 1945, and Assistant Secretary of State Will L Clayton to Mr H Hawkins at US Embassy, 28 April, *FRUS* 1945 VI, pp 27–28,45–47.

37. Telegram 6276 from Keynes in Washington to London, 22 November 1944, T 160/1244.

38. T 247/49.

39. Notes of 17 and 18 March 1945, CAB 21/1247; meeting of Ministers, Governor of the Bank, Keynes, and others, 20 March 1945, ibid; War Cabinet meeting, 21 March, WM (45) 34th Conclusions, CAB 65/49 with memoranda WP (45) 142, CAB 66/62; WP (45) 167, CAB 66/63; WP (45) 182, CAB 66/63; telegram 515 of 21 March, Dominions Office to Ottawa, AVIA 38/1118.

40. London meetings 25, 29, 31 May 1945, T 230/174; meeting of 28 May, DO 35/1219.

41. Cambridge discussions T 236/31 & 32; T 247/127; DO 35/1219 which also contains report of July action. Douglas Le Pan, who attended the Cambridge discussions as a representative of the Canadian High Commissioner in London, has provided an informal and vivid account in his *Bright Glass of Memory*, A set of four memoirs (Toronto 1979), I 'Introduction to Economics: Lord Keynes and the Audit Room Meetings'. I am indebted to Professor D E Moggridge for this reference. See also *JMK* XXIV, pp 345–53.

A view of the Canadian approach to these discussions has been provided in a wider study by Hector M Mackenzie, 'The Path to Temptation: The Negotiation of Canada's Reconstruction Loan to Britain in 1946', The Canadian Historical Association, *Historical Papers* (Ottawa 1982), pp 196–220.

42. Reports of meetings: CAB 123/96–I.

43. Report of meeting of British and US officials 27 June 1945, *FRUS* 1945 VI, pp 56–60.

44. Memoranda of conversations, ibid, pp 61–74.

45. Ibid, pp 74–76, memorandum by the Executive Committee on Economic Foreign Policy, 21 July 1945.

46. Ibid, pp 54–56, memorandum of 25 June 1945.

47. Meeting with senior United Kingdom Ministers, 21 August 1945, T 247/2.

48. Reports of meetings in *FRUS* 1945 VI, pp 79–88, 90–101, and summary by Mr Clayton, ibid, pp 103–5.

49. Ibid, pp 79–87, meeting of 3 August 1945.

50. Ibid, p 96, meeting of 15 August 1945.

51. Ibid, p 98, meeting of 14 August 1945.
52. Ibid. The earlier suggestion was under the 'Austerity' possibility, in 'Overseas Financial Arrangements in Stage III', paragraphs 23–24, 18 March 1945, T 247/49.
53. Ibid.
54. Note by Sir Percivale Liesching, 14 August 1945, T 230/175.
55. Sir Stafford Cripps to Mr H Dalton, 13 August 1945, T 236/439; 'Article VII and Commercial Policy', CP(45) 116 of 16 August, CAB 129/1 and T 236/380.
56. Chancellor's unnumbered, cyclostyled memorandum of 17 August 1945, 'Economic Relations with the United States', T 236/437, also T 236/380. Eady mentioned his and Keynes's agreement with the memorandum, and its restricted circulation, in a note to Sir Edward Bridges, 28 August 1945, T 236/437.
57. Eady to Bridges, 15 August 1945, T 236/437; Keynes at meetings of UK and US officials with Mr Clayton, 14 August 1945, FRUS 1945 VI, p 99.

CHAPTER 9

The Shaping of Post-War Financial Policy

(1) INTERNATIONAL *v* NATIONAL CONSIDERATIONS

Underlying the contrast between the hard-won agreement on monetary policy and Anglo-American divergences over commercial policy during 1944 and 1945 were daunting perplexities for British Ministers and officials. The longer-term puzzle of the accommodation within international agreements of protectionist agricultural interests and of Imperial Preference, which had fostered Cabinet indecision in spring 1944, was serious enough. That puzzle can, however, be regarded as involving policy clashes rather than economic fundamentals. The fundamentals were the probable weaknesses of Britain's external position not only during Stage III, but even more immediately during Stage II. From early in 1944 some striking memoranda by Lord Keynes illuminated Stage III problems and possible solutions, but firm conclusions were inevitably elusive in view of apprehensions about American policy. Britain's own hopes of equal participation in the concentration of effort against Japan during Stage II were associated with expectations of commencing reconversion to a peacetime economy, and of a relaxation of the 1941 'Export White Paper'. American views, however they envisaged British involvement in the war against Japan, reflected concern that Britain's reconversion should not be faster than that of the USA.[1] With that concern went a determination that the need to maintain controls during reconversion should not be allowed to become an excuse to perpetuate restrictive trading practices. Thus, reports in autumn 1944 of a proposed British meat contract with Argentina doubly enraged Washington: it was support for an illiberal, anti-American régime, and it involved bilateralism and state trading. In order not to imperil the flow of Lend-Lease and hopes of easing restrictions on exports, the War Cabinet therefore decided against a long-term contract and to operate on a month-to-month basis.[2]

The Chancellor had earlier in 1944 warned the War Cabinet that American misunderstanding of British problems 'might reflect disastrously' on the impending discussions about Lend-Lease in Stage II. Hence the reassurance in July through the Minister of State, Mr Richard Law, to the US Secretary of State and the appointment of a

Cabinet Committee on Commercial Policy to re-examine the 1943 Washington proposals (above p 137). In the event, the first major move towards greater understanding, a projected American visit by the Chancellor with other Ministers, was soon to prove less urgent and was dropped. This was largely because in August 1944 Mr Morgenthau, Secretary of the Treasury, visited Britain accompanied by Dr H D White. Mr Morgenthau speculated encouragingly, if vaguely, about the need for some new approach in considering post-war aid for Britain; on trade matters, he echoed Mr Churchill's view that the moment was inappropriate, and that they might better be raised after the November Congressional and Presidential elections.[3] That was scarcely the view of the State Department, which was shortly to urge the President not to bribe Britain with cheap post-war finance into a liberal post-war commercial policy. The Administration should stand upon the existing Article VII commitment; it should delay action on Lend-Lease for Stage II, over and above that needed for strictly military purposes, until Britain's position on post-war commercial policy was clarified. Indicative of an influential American trend against not only easy post-war aid but even against continuance of Lend-Lease during the Japanese phase of the war was the pressure, albeit unsuccessful, for Stage II finance to be partly or wholly in the form of interest-bearing loans.[4] Moreover, it could not be assumed that Congress would accept the Bretton Woods agreements, with their modest financial relief, and in fact a year was to elapse between the 'Final Act' and Congressional approval. Above all, however, preoccupation with securing adequate arrangements for Stage II overshadowed not just those uncertainties, but also the consideration in other than a very provisional and lightly sketched form of post-war policy in general. If an impression of irresolution results, irresolution could be attributed essentially to the unworkability, save under duress of the twelfth hour, of any solution whatever. Unable to finance the second world war entirely from her own resources, Britain had shifted significant burdens either to the USA, or to the Commonwealth and sterling area. A permanent settlement of those burdens appeared to require Britain to make unacceptable trading commitments to the former that evoked formidable objections from the latter. A more drastic type of solution, in which post-war Britain should herself largely bear the financial consequences of the war, implied domestic constraints and economic isolationism on a formidable scale; majority opinion amongst both officials and Ministers was reluctant to contemplate such austerity.

(2) STERLING BALANCES: INDIAN BALANCES

The future treatment of accumulated sterling balances dominated prospective solutions to the post-war external problem. Whether treated as short-term or long-term liabilities, they were potentially the most intractable claimant on exports and on the gold and dollar reserves. For Britain to contemplate the early operation of a multilateral system of trade and payments, as envisaged in the wartime discussions, some means had to be found to eliminate or defer the ability of their holders to spend them.

Net 'quick' liabilities, £476 million at the end of August 1939, immediately before the outbreak of war, had more than tripled, to £1,515 million, by the end of 1942; that amount was to double, to £3,052 million, by mid-1945, shortly before the end of the war (see Appendix 21). Net gold and dollar reserves, however, moved in the opposite direction. They were first run down in the desperate conditions of 1940, and subsequently were checked from rising too far in order to avoid accusations that Lend-Lease aid might be financing their growth. The ratio of net 'quick' liabilities to those reserves, less than one to one at the outbreak of war, approached nine to one by the end of 1942; it had eased to something under seven to one shortly before the war ended, though this reflected a temporary boost to the reserves from expenditure by US and Canadian forces in the sterling area.

The greater proportion of liabilities, reaching eighty to ninety percent of the total between 1942 and the end of the war, consisted of those owing to sterling area countries; they were also potentially the most liquid, given the nominal right of sterling countries to use their balances freely. Within the sterling area, the largest accumulations occurred in the group of countries comprising India (pre-partition), Burma, and the Middle East: more than half the area's total by the end of 1942, and not far short of two-thirds towards the end of the war.

Of the holdings of individual countries, those of India were far the largest and attracted the greatest amount of systematic wartime discussion of sterling balances. India's balances, already £441 million by the end of 1942, were to rise to £1,138 million by mid-1945; over one-third of those of the whole sterling area at the earlier date, they were over two-fifths by the later. In mid-1945 they were about two and three quarters as great as those of the next largest holder, Egypt and the Anglo-Egyptian Sudan, like India a special case, and the only other creditor to evoke comparable anxiety.[5]

Obviously, the achievement of a satisfactory agreement over Indian balances would probably have facilitated a wider solution, but both were to elude Britain.

In large part, the growth of the balances was specifically Britain's responsibility, reflecting the purchase of supplies for her armed forces. Maddeningly for Whitehall, however, they also reflected the unforeseen consequences of political and financial decisions in 1937–40 involving India and Burma.

Following a major review during 1938–39 of Indian defence, the Defence and Financial Settlement of 1940 specified that Britain would meet most of the costs of modernising the Indian Army, and those of Indian forces sent abroad; India's financial responsibility for defence, though extremely heavy for so poor a country, almost entirely stopped at her frontiers.[6] All this meant major burdens for Britain, not only in the Middle East but also in the defence of India during the Far Eastern War; much of the fighting was in Burma, the administration of which had been detached from India in 1937; under the financial settlement, therefore, the cost fell not upon India but upon Britain.

(3) INDIAN BALANCES: PROPOSALS DURING 1942–43

Consideration of Indian balances encountered strong, indeed passionate arguments for each of the two opposing extreme courses of action. One emphasised that Britain had fought the war in defence of India as well as of herself. In financial terms the resultant debt was a deadweight; it was represented by no tangible asset, having been incurred by Britain for war purposes. Moreover, some persistently asserted, contrary to the evidence, that Indian overcharging had inflated the balances. In any case, it would be intolerable for post-war Britain to have to struggle beneath a burden of unrequited exports in order to repay them. Hence, the excessive balances should be partly or wholly cancelled. At the other extreme, Indian opinion naturally resisted such adjustment. The balances represented resources forgone during the war. They would be a post-war compensation to which, as an extremely poor country, India could look, particularly to secure capital goods for economic development.[7]

There was no clear case for either extreme solution. Each, however, had such vigorous support that various compromise proposals were no easier of acceptance, especially in view of the delicate political position in wartime India. It was the strong support for each of these alternatives, rather than some propensity to endless indecisiveness in Whitehall and New Delhi, that appear as the great intractabilities. They ensured the virtual impossibility of agreement amongst the powerful minds involved, which distributed themselves in support of competing proposals for action or inaction. To outline the debates in London and between London and India is to illuminate the ultimate constraints on this critical element in the formation of post-war policies.

In the prolonged discussions from 1942, Mr Churchill and his personal adviser, Lord Cherwell, favoured drastic treatment. They regarded the Settlement as bad, believed that India overcharged for supplies, and argued that Britain had a moral case for diminishing a post-war burden she ought not to carry.[8] In contrast, Vice-regal assessment of India's interests, and of the maintenance of the British presence, warned against this, with the constructive support of the able and much respected Finance Member of the Viceroy's Council,

Sir Jeremy Raisman. Broadly allied to their viewpoint and opposing that of his Prime Minister, whom he regularly reported to the Viceroy as capable only of raging hostility to India, was Mr L S Amery, the Secretary of State for India.[9] Although aware that repayment would have to be gradual, he saw Britain's debts as really an asset, even a blessing, for their expenditure could maintain post-war demand for British exports. If this involved strengthening Imperial Preference and trade discrimination, that accorded exactly with Amery's hostility to Anglo-American endeavours to do the reverse. The Treasury sought solutions between the two extremes. The Chancellor most involved was Sir John Anderson; he was sensitive to Indian representations, having been Governor of Bengal from 1932 to 1937. Action there must be to ease the burden of the balances, but not unilaterally (above p 164). Lord Catto, a merchant banker experienced in Anglo-Indian trade, argued at the Treasury and later at the Bank for careful plans, to be implemented at some future date.[10] Lord Keynes pressed almost until the end of the war for early decisions; then in early 1945 he wavered and reversed, surrendering to the ultimate hope inspiring the prevarications of others on this issue, that the overall post-war settlement would sweep the problem away (below p 221).

London tried unsuccessfully to revise the 1940 Settlement almost immediately, and nagged at it for the rest of the war.[11] Efforts intensified in 1942 with the approaching end of India's debt repatriation and with mounting British outlays. Could there not be reciprocal aid, as between Britain and the USA, and between Britain and Canada? Could not India at least meet more of the costs of her defence? From India the Viceroy, and before the British War Cabinet, Sir Jeremy Raisman both warned of consequences politically and for defence production in seeking such revision. Further, Sir Jeremy explained that any feasible revision would not touch significant expenditure, so that accumulation of balances would persist. He nevertheless aired the possibility both of tempering the rise by Indian acceptance of certain expenditures, and of absorbing some existing balances in a Reconstruction Fund, in funding pensions due to Indian civil servants, and in Indian currency and banking arrangements.[12]

These ideas were unpopular in the Viceroy's Council, which regarded the Settlement as burdensome for India.[13] Neither in 1942 nor later did London enthuse over them, despite qualified support from Keynes and Catto.[14] Advice to Ministers (in 1942) was that the Indian political threat was exaggerated, and that President Roosevelt's declaration, that there should be no war debts to darken the post-war world, should be kept in mind; the existing distribution of war burdens should therefore be regarded as provisional.[15] This uncertainty, indeed the threat of eventual deprivation of the post-war spending power of the balances, was too much for the Indian Government when informed that Mr Churchill had re-drafted an already disagreeable telegram to the Viceroy, to include the possibility of a British counter-claim against India. Eventually (September 1942) the formal message, shorn of the Churchillian addition, affirmed British adherence to the 1940 Settlement, but noted that the question of a financial adjustment, within wider post-war arrangements, would have to be raised when convenient. Mr Churchill left no doubt, however, of his own views in a personal message to the Viceroy. On the prospect that, having successfully defended India against Japan, Britain would then be turned out, yet owing huge war debts to India, he quoted Mr A J Balfour: 'This is a singularly ill-contrived world but not so ill-contrived as that'.[16]

Contrary to Amery's hope, 'this tiresome business of sterling balances'[17] would not stay shelved indefinitely. By the following summer (1943), leaps in Indian balances and in Indian inflation demanded attention. Anxiety increased as the drift of Anglo-American monetary discussions persuaded London to keep direct responsibility for the balances away from the Monetary Fund being evolved (above pp 98–99, 121, 163–7). Doubtless the two-fold rationale of this was powerful: it avoided the exchange of a British controlled debt in sterling for one more or less in American dollars under American influence; and it permitted the survival of hope that a way would be found to avoid their eventual repayment in full. This rejection of internationalisation may have been inevitable. It had, however, the ultimately costly result for Britain of identifying action over the sterling balances as her obligation—and as her burden.

Two limited steps were taken to ease the impact of sterling debt on the Indian economy and Indian opinion. One was to provide extra imports, including gold, to dampen inflation and the growth of balances. A second was to make further accumulations of balances more tolerable: the earmarking in 1944 and 1945 of a limited amount of Indian earnings of US dollars assured India that some at least of her sterling would be convertible after the war.[18] A more comprehensive, longer-term scheme remained desirable, and one came from Lord Keynes in summer 1943. This resembled the previous year's proposals by Sir Jeremy Raisman for the allocation of balances to Reconstruction and Pension Funds, and to currency reserves, but with two major qualifications; these, likely to be attractive to British opinion and the reverse to Indian, both official and unofficial, were that no interest be allowed on funded balances, and that war expenditure involving India should be met by Britain and India by a form of Reciprocal Aid.[19] Lord Catto offered instead a bankers' type of scheme, to segregate usable from non-usable balances. He led that group, a majority, of Treasury opinion which questioned the wisdom of tying balances to Reconstruction and Pension Funds, lest India run short of current sterling; it was inclined to defer action which, it was argued, might wait until Britain was winning the war against Japan and thereby winning respect and acquiescence from India.[20] Keynes himself now retreated, and was inclined to join that group in hesitation over such funding of balances into longer-term debt. He argued that a zero rate of interest on at least a substantial portion was justified by the debt's deadweight character; in any case, a rate lower than that paid to domestic British holders of government debt was appropriate because Indians would not pay British tax on it.[21]

(4) INDIAN BALANCES: INCONCLUSIVE DISCUSSIONS 1943–45

These discussions were associated with the inquiries of a Cabinet Committee during 1943 and 1944 into Indian inflation and the balances. Arguments were similar to, if sharper than, those of 1942. Once again the inescapable accumulation was stressed. Sir Richard Hopkins[22] of the Treasury noted in February 1944 that there was 'no hope of India's giving us' supplies for nothing. Earlier, the Minister of Production (Mr Oliver Lyttelton) had underlined the fundamental dilemma: should cuts be made in India's war production to reduce the accumulation of balances and the pace of inflation there, it was doubtful if Britain could make up the short-fall.[23] Once again, Lord Cherwell[24] claimed that there was 'an excellent moral case for repudiating the bulk of the debt'. Some scaling down was also supported by Mr Hugh Dalton, who, as President of the Board of Trade was to advise on Britain's capacity to supply post-war exports against India's balances; he saw the debt as 'an intolerable burden' and demanded to know the culprits.[25] On this and on the suggestion for counter-claims, a political difficulty was noted by two Ministers with Indian expertise. This was that comparable arguments had been heard from the Indian National Congress about the treatment of *India's* debts to Britain on gaining independence. Britain had rejected the suggestion that they should be cancelled.[26] On the underlying Cherwell (and Churchill) suspicion of Indian overcharging, the Chancellor promised an examination; this was to yield a blistering reply from the Indian authorities,[27] and a broad affirmation of their fair dealing both from a Committee of officials, and from one of Members of Parliament.[28]

No decisive recommendation came from the Cabinet Committee. Its draft report of March 1944, on sterling balances, to be unchanged in the final report of July, cast the old stale crusts on to unknown waters.[29] Reflecting the parallel discussions amongst officials and Ministers of Keynes's memoranda on post-war policy, it stressed that vagueness about the treatment of the general problem of sterling balances was at present unavoidable. Virtually all that could be done about Indian balances was to do nothing, and certainly nothing to prejudice a settlement. The Committee implied that the prospects for an Indian settlement, in default of an overriding general solution, were hopeless. Despite its expectation that India would reject both the Roosevelt principle of avoidance of war debts amongst allies and any dilution of its claims on Britain, it nevertheless hoped for a voluntary contribution; perhaps a rupee devaluation would justify scaling down; or perhaps some form of guarantee could be devised to protect the value of the balances. The Report's frail hopes soon weakened when, even before its formal signature, Keynes at Bretton Woods conveyed the Chancellor's pledge against unilateral repudiation (above pp 164, 166). Thus all depended upon the chances of a satisfactory wider settlement.

On the insistence of the Lord Privy Seal (Lord Beaverbrook) that an Indian solution could be devised separately, the Committee reconvened early in 1945.[30] The Chancellor now confessed himself to be 'frightened of tackling the matter prematurely' lest there result an insupportable obligation that would drive Britain to a form of repudiation. Keynes not only counselled delay over accumulated balances, but also now abandoned his earlier anxiety about further accretions; they now appeared to be of smaller relative importance. The real problem in overseas payments, he declared in this meeting of January 1945, was the flow of finance from North America: to replace at the end of the war America's Lend-Lease and Canada's Mutual Aid, which had come to finance the bulk of Britain's imports. The Committee's discussions echoed the uncertainties and hence the case for delay; it invited the Treasury to provide an assessment of the overall problem of the balances, and to offer 'suggestions as to the objectives. . . and the course which should be pursued.' The Treasury had in fact been attempting to do just that since early in 1944, as will be discussed in Section 6 below, but there were forbidding obstacles. These were indeed being delineated on the same day as the Committee met (above, pp 201–2). In talks on commercial policy between British and American officials, American proposals envisaged stringent action on sterling balances that would involve Britain in heavy, and unacceptable, borrowing from the USA and Canada.

The underlying difficulties were still unresolved in spring 1945, but a policy was shaping, in the doubtless inevitable form of a decision to defer decision. This had a dual aspect, one of desperation the other of hope. The desperation appeared when Sir Wilfrid Eady considered the Treasury's 'fairly urgent obligation' to deliver proposals to the India Finance Committee,[31] only to declare the impossibility of doing so. Indeed, the Treasury advised the Chancellor that it was 'not only premature but very unwise' to contemplate even tentative solutions, given the familiar uncertainties about continuing war expenditure overseas, over the post-war reconversion, and over the availability of

US aid. Eady, pointing to a sombre statistical survey prepared by Mr R W B ('Otto') Clarke*, clearly leaned to advising the Chancellor to mark time.[32] Moreover, hope was present: the hope of some inspired overall settlement of the war's financial legacy in some 'Grand Assize'. This was the vision in a dramatic memorandum more sweeping than Clarke's, which Keynes had just completed.[33] The Chancellor gave its message on 'policy' for sterling balances to the Commonwealth Prime Ministers' meeting in London in mid-April.[34] Though not the time to propound solutions, one could be found; all depended on realism at home, on co-operation from the holders of balances, and above all, on the attitude of the USA. It would be unjust for Britain to be victorious yet burdened with debt comparable in amount with the reparations proposed from Germany. 'He hoped that we would have an agreed policy with the United States and with the holders of Sterling balances so as to ensure that the balances might be used as soon as possible as purchasing power'.

On the specific issue of India's sterling balances matters were in fact worsening. The Viceroy had sought earlier in the year to reassure his Council with the prospect of London discussions about them when the European war was over and when the prospects for the Japanese war were clearer.[35] As that stage approached, a new worry in April 1945 was the Indian talk of post-war restrictions on imports from Britain. This raised the fear that, if exports to India were to be difficult, excess balances, so far from being worked down might have to be frozen indefinitely.[36] A proposal from the Board of Trade to have in India a British High Commissioner to deal with the balances had already aroused doubts. It was still being discussed when the result of the general election involving the defeat of Mr Churchill's 'Caretaker' Administration at the end of July 1945 put Mr Amery, one of its advocates, out of the India Office.[37] By then, however, discussions within the Government were on the wider scale provided in 1944–45 by a series of memoranda from Lord Keynes. These were expanded, continuously revised versions of papers which he had been submitting to officials and Ministers since 1942 to support his pleas for recognition of the gravity of the accumulating problems of the post-war balance of payments, and for early preparations to deal with them.

(5) KEYNES'S PROPOSALS 1942–44

Keynes's powerful memoranda stemmed from the work of the

---

* CLARKE, Richard Williams Barnes ('Otto'), KCB 1964 (1910–75); Ministries of Information, Economic Warfare, Supply and Production, 1939–45; Combined Production and Resources Board (Washington), 1942–43; Assistant Secretary, HM Treasury, 1945; Under Secretary, 1947; Third Secretary, 1955–62; Second Secretary, 1962–66; Permanent Secretary, Ministry of Aviation, 1966, Ministry of Technology, 1966–70.

Economic Section, as instanced in its paper of 1942 on 'The United Kingdom's Post-War Balance of Payments' (see Appendix 27). This concluded that, should the war be over by the end of 1943—an unavoidably arbitrary date as any other would have been in the circumstances—'a serious adverse balance' in the trading account was likely to persist beyond the transition unless exports could be quite substantially increased. In the early post-war years, there would be further weakness from repayment of short-term debt (excess sterling balances), and from reduced capital receipts (ie, 'invisibles') resulting from disposal of overseas assets. Calculations by the League of Nations and by the American National Planning Association were still more unfavourable.[38]

The solutions which Keynes canvassed at this time, in 1942, in his first major essay on wider plans for post-war external policy, foreshadowed the discussions of 1944 – 45. In September 1942, in a memorandum on 'Our Prospective Dollar Balances' Keynes warned of the dangers of Britain's emergence from the war with gold and dollar reserves of apparently respectable size. That would be dangerously deceptive, because the reserves belonged to the whole sterling area. Britain's liabilities to sterling and other countries had meanwhile increased dangerously. Apparently comfortable looking reserves could tempt Britain into excessive contributions to relief. They might mislead the USA into feeling that little aid to Britain was necessary. They would tempt holders of sterling balances to believe that they could withdraw them. Here was the post-war quicksand: these balances were likely by the end of 1942 to be several times the size of the reserves, but the reserves would be fully needed for Britain's own payments deficits immediately after the war. There must therefore be wider understanding, especially in the USA, of this reserves/liabilities contrast.[39]

Even with total balances at the end of 1942 only one-half of what they were to become by mid-1945, towards the end of the war, and with those of the sterling area somewhat less than one-half, the problem was already looking hopeless. Recognising this, Keynes propounded bold solutions. As already noted (above pp 219 – 20) he inclined to favour Sir Jeremy Raisman's ideas for funding Indian balances. At this stage, too, it was possible to hope that the eventual establishment of an International Clearing Union or of an American Stabilisation Fund might ease the burden (pp 98 – 99). Nothing came of any of these ideas, bold solutions, or hopes in 1942 – 3, either for India or for the general issue. Late in 1943, with the underlying problems worse and with the end of the war by no means in sight, a triple stimulus to consideration of the issues came from the Prime Minister's Directive to Departments to produce thoughts on post-war plans;[40] from discussions on Indian war finance; and from preparations for Anglo-

American monetary talks. By early 1944, these elements were falling into rough position; they pointed to the sterling balances as the great potential constraint on Britain's adoption of new international arrangements. The retreat from the internationalisation of sterling balances (above, pp 98 – 99, 121, 163 – 7, 222) certainly avoided the risk of hobbling the projected Monetary Fund; yet the resultant burden upon Britain could keep her at arm's length from it. In the attempt to resolve this problem, the first of two major steps had been the Cabinet decision in early 1944 to favour the bolder international approach, rather than the more cautious approach advocated by the Bank of England (above pp 140 – 4). The second major step proved to be much more difficult, and was not completed when the war ended. This was to devise policies to deal with the sterling balances and to secure overseas finance in order to operate the expected new international arrangements.

In his memorandum of January 1944, which had evoked the Bank's unsuccessful remonstrances, Keynes, backed by the Economic Section, had argued for imaginative measures to contain the sterling threat.[41] This attempt to induce preparation well ahead of the peace contrasted with both the relative optimism of the Treasury and the anxieties and preferences of the Bank of England. The Treasury, which responded to the Prime Minister's Directive that a return to normal conditions could reasonably be expected,[42] was largely unpersuaded so far of any urgency, indeed of any need, to do anything drastic about the sterling balances. The Bank, continuing to press for early decisions about the balances, sought those decisions in the context of a post-war policy of sustained exchange restrictions; this implied a path of austerity which it was Keynes's aim to demonstrate should and could be avoided.

The thrust of Keynes's analysis was that for the first two or three post-war years the combined deficits of Britain (£500 – 700 million) and the rest of the sterling area (£200 – 300 million) with the rest of the world might amount to around £1,000 million; it would be wise to anticipate their *gross* deficit with North and South America at somewhat above that. To rely on the prolongation of wartime sterling area arrangements to contain that deficit would be imprudent; countries would want more freedom; they would need to make up wartime shortfalls of goods; the wartime constraints on imports of shipping shortages would diminish; and a turn-round in the favourable balances of some member countries with the rest of the world could strain the London reserves. To extend the sterling area to include some western European countries, perhaps through bilateral arrangements with Central Banks for mutual credits, was a policy that the Bank of England advocated (above, pp 142, 143; below, p 234). Keynes argued that this could worsen, rather than ease matters, for these countries, too, were likely to be in deficit with the dollar area; they would thus add to the strain on sterling.

The twofold conclusion therefore was, first, that sterling area arrangements should be modified to limit the convertibility of excessive wartime accumulations of balances into non-sterling currencies. In his first attempt (further attempts were to follow) to devise a solution to the problems of the sterling debts, Keynes suggested that there might be an easing of wartime constraints during the transition; sterling countries could then withdraw from the reserves as much in gold and hard currencies as they were contributing. Further drawings would be at the discretion of the Exchange Control. After the transition there might be an agreed settlement for eventual release of excess balances. Such arrangements would offer sterling countries a more attractive choice than leaving the sterling area, when Britain would be unable to allow them to utilise accumulated balances, except for payments within the (now smaller) area.

Second, these proposed arrangements could not in any case be sustained by Britain without American financial aid. Against its possible gross dollar deficit in the transition of over £1,000 million ($4,000m), the area's net gold and dollar earnings from the rest of the world, together with a run-down in London's reserves, could contribute about half that amount. This left some £500 million needed to achieve both financial and diplomatic elbow room for Britain after the war. Credit of this size would need to be inter-governmental, and should be long-term at zero interest; a loan in gold (an idea that attracted others as a form of financial lend-lease) might be considered. It ought to be possible to accept American conditions such as, say, that there should be no restriction on sterling countries' current dollar outlays, and that Britain would not discriminate against American goods. If these proposals looked unattractive, Keynes warned that in fact they might be insufficiently harsh, and could even induce too relaxed an approach to securing equilibrium. On the other hand, not to adopt something like them invited prolonged austerity, further accumulations of sterling balances, and disagreeable corollaries in social, political and international strains.

The broad conclusions of these arguments prevailed: that US aid should be sought, and that there should be drastic action to deal with sterling indebtedness. Nevertheless, the persisting unease of the Bank and of some Treasury voices about them did not reflect acceptance of the bases of the arguments: the gravity of the prospective balance of payments position after the war, and the inability of the wartime sterling area arrangements to survive, without serious modifications including drastic restrictions on the use of accumulated balances, the strains which peacetime would impose. Indeed, the monetary discussions with Commonwealth and Indian representatives in March 1944 assumed a resumption after the war of the more relaxed sterling arrangements of pre-war days, and displayed reluctance to consider the borrowing from America that Keynes had argued was essential to a feasible operation of the sterling area during the transition.[43] Within the Treasury reluctance to do anything for the time being, or to take Keynes's advice to bring matters to a head, persisted. 'After all', noted one senior official, 'we have skated over the thinnest of thin ice for four years... Once the ice gets even moderately thick, I do not believe we need worry at all...'.[44]

This lack of a sense of urgency Keynes strove to remove by even stronger warnings in further memoranda, steadily reinforced with sombre statistics from the Bank and the Economic Section.[45] Such unwillingness to evince anxiety cannot, however, be dismissed as ignorance of the problems: it has to be kept in mind that the increasingly elaborate Keynesian projections of the post-war world were at best a groping into future darkness whilst in the immediate present doubt and perplexity abounded.

(6) PROSPECTS FOR POST-WAR AMERICAN AID, 1944

Outstandingly discouraging was the prospect for the American aid so fundamental to Keynes's bold proposals. For a time in spring 1944, indeed, Mr E R Stettinius,* Under Secretary of State, sought early action whilst the wartime atmosphere of co-operation persisted.[46] This was echoed in some British Treasury musings: might Congress consider favourably joint proposals for post-war aid to Britain and for the monetary agreement expected from the forthcoming Bretton Woods Conference?[47] Alarmingly, however, Mr Stettinius voiced a hardening of American feeling that post-war help to Britain should be on loan terms, bearing interest. To Britain this offered a deplorable contrast to Lend-Lease (and to her own reverse Lend-Lease); as a further prospective burden on a weak balance of payments, it reinforced the Bank of England's sustained opposition to Keynes's design for a wide-sweeping international settlement.

The Chancellor had striven to explain to Mr Stettinius on his visit to London in April 1944 that Britain could not unaided deal with the post-war burdens of sterling, and showed him a memorandum, prepared by Keynes, of her mounting liabilities. Aware, however, of strong American beliefs about the British Empire's wealth, and that its help to Britain had not matched that of the USA, Mr Stettinius preferred to concentrate on Britain's supposed assets, evoking the likely mid-Western reaction: '... when "the farmer from Kansas" learns that the British had 3 billion dollars in 1939, that they have received 10 billion or more of goods under Lend-Lease, and that they

---

* STETTINIUS, Edward R, Jr. (1900–1949); Lend-Lease Administrator, USA, and Special Assistant to President, 1941–43; Under Secretary of State, USA, 1943–44; Secretary of State, 1944–45.

are beginning to accumulate gold and dollars again, he is going to think that the British must now be very rich . . .'.

Somewhat shamefacedly, recorded Keynes, Mr Stettinius had aired to MPs the possibility of a loan of $10 billion.[48] Kites to test British reaction to a possible deal tying American designed strings to badly needed finance this and other American hints may have been, but they surely indicated unfavourable winds in Washington.

Worse was indeed soon to come. On Mr Stettinius's return to Washington, the British Embassy reported that, his own inclinations to the contrary notwithstanding, maintenance of Lend-Lease in Stage II was likely to prove difficult. There was talk of aid being provided, in that final phase of the war, on the basis of long-term credit.[49] The Treasury's very carefully prepared reply emphasised its strong resistance both to that and to any suggestion of interest terms for post-war aid. Though expecting to pay cash for materials required for exports, Britain's need for American aid would in fact increase in Stage II.[50]

Mr R H Brand* was shortly to explain to Mr Stettinius at the end of June that Britain's problems were best understood by looking first, not at Stage II, but at Stage III with its reconversion, massive liabilities, and payments deficits. By now Mr Stettinius was shuffling on early post-war decisions. Only the President and the Secretary of State could seek resolution of the impending Lend-Lease wrangles. Further Anglo-American discussion must wait on the expected (but eventually cancelled) visit of the Chancellor to Washington[51] (above, p 137). Nevertheless, Mr Stettinius made clear shortly afterwards to Mr Richard Law, Minister of State at the Foreign Office, that on post-war aid he was opposed to treating the British 'as pensioners for an indefinite period' by grants or interest-free loans. In what was possibly a sighting shot for American terms, he affirmed, like a Kansas farmer, his belief that 'with the vast resources of the Empire they could . . . find some way to service a debt of somewhere in the neighbourhood of five to ten billion dollars over a thirty-year period at 2 per cent say'.[52]

(7) DISCUSSIONS ON KEYNES'S MEMORANDA, 1944

Following the London visit by Mr Stettinius there was to be further assessment of Stage II and Stage III problems. Taking further the calculations displayed to Mr Stettinius, Keynes produced further memoranda in May and June 1944, which were to be intensively discussed in meetings of officials and of Ministers, and then throughout

* BRAND, Robert Henry, 1st Baron 1946 (1878–1963); Head of British Food Mission, Washington, 1941–44; Representative of HM Treasury in Washington, 1944–46; Chairman, British Supply Council in N America, 1942 and 1945–46; UK Delegate at Bretton Woods Conference 1944 and Savannah Conference 1946.

the summer by a Treasury-Bank committee. The May memorandum, on 'Our Financial Problem in the Transition', underlined the earlier memorandum's arguments about the balance of payments, and sought to concentrate attention upon the crucial elements in policy: the sterling balances and the terms of possible aid from the USA.[53] Reproving the Government for assuming that Britain would be able to import all it needed after the war, he elaborated the potential external weaknesses. Invisible earnings would be poor in the early years. The gold and dollar reserves would lose their brief reinforcement from the spending of American forces in the sterling area. Then there was the problem of Lend-Lease. This was not simply a question of the impact of its expected end when the war as a whole ended; before then, its probable diminution in Stage II, after the defeat of Germany, must be considered.

Keynes now extended the earlier rough estimates of the deficits on the post-war current account to deal more fully with sterling balances. These might reach some £3,000 million by the end of 1944. Roughly half might be neutralised by funding or freezing. Of the remainder, which were 'dangerous' in the sense that they were liable to be used if not controlled, perhaps up to one half, say £500 to £750 million, might be released during the transition.

To deal with the excess balances, Keynes reiterated the view (above, p 140) that post-war conditions would be unfavourable to the maintenance of wartime sterling arrangements. The wartime pooling of foreign exchange earnings, in exchange for sterling balances, did not involve the blocking of such balances, although the Bank of England's management of the subtleties of understanding and of co-operation prevented them from being used freely. He stressed that a switch from dollar surplus to dollar deficit would diminish the forbearance of sterling countries. Since it was scarcely possible or desirable to operate a tightly-run system, nor to allow balances to be freely used, Keynes proposed two main stages towards full convertibility for sterling after the war. In the first, excess balances should be funded, to receive zero interest, or perhaps the very low Treasury bill rate on those balances held as currency reserves. Whilst their reduction by outright cancellation or by gifts would be welcome, this would not materially diminish the burden; their repayment must be contemplated over a period of perhaps forty years. In this first stage, the sterling area should be 'closed', in the sense that access to the reserves would be limited to sterling countries' current earnings of dollars. When it was possible to allow them also to spend freely all their net current non-sterling earnings, the second stage of convertibility would have been reached.

Three types of help from the USA might be contemplated. One was not so much an increase of Lend-Lease aid as a relaxation of American paring-down of it whenever Britain's gold and dollar receipts rose; that would permit a strengthening of reserves. A second was that the USA might be approached to relieve Britain of some of her war expenditure in India's defence. Finally, assistance of between £1,500 and £2,250 million might appear to be necessary during the transitional period, to cover deficits from trade and from the rundown of balances. By drawing on reserves and with help from Canada, this might be reduced to some £750 million, approximately $3 billion; ideally, this might be sought in the form of $2 billion in Lend-Lease and the remainder in cash. The case for thus minimising the aid to be sought from the USA was twofold. First, a relatively easy financial position might diminish the incentive to develop exports vigorously. Second, the terms of any assistance would be more important than the amount to be received, and the more we sought the less acceptable might the American terms be.

Vigorous discussion followed the circulation of this memorandum. On sterling balances the possibility of cancellation (or 'scaling down') was now to be considered more seriously, only to appear difficult, hazardous, and possibly of limited scope in reducing the post-war burden. Amongst officials, Mr R H Brand hoped for scaling down, making a comparison (to be heard in American circles) between Britain's wartime sterling debts and Lend-Lease, which was not expected to be repaid.[54] Sir Hubert Henderson reached a case for scaling down by pointing out that the ultimate real burden was that of the capital, net of the interest; that it would be difficult to refuse post-war convertibility to sterling, and that it would therefore take many years to repay balances from increased export earnings.[55] A less sweeping but still drastic step would be to freeze excess balances. Yet would that be practical, even if applied only to the preponderant Indian and Egyptian balances, asked Mr A T K Grant,* without lowering the prestige of sterling?[56] The stronger meat of cancellation aroused even stronger apprehensions from Sir Wilfrid Eady in facing an immediate and tangible issue: it would hardly be possible, in current negotiations with New Zealand over food supplies, to base the eventual contract on payments that might prove worthless.[57]

These and other aspects of Keynes's memorandum were considered by Treasury, Economic Section, and Bank representatives at meetings in May 1944.[58] Reaching no strong conclusion, they echoed the more or less parallel discussions on Indian balances by underlining the extreme difficulty, perhaps indeed the impossibility, of devising a reasonably satisfactory policy for sterling balances, short of inconceivable generosity by their holders, and in the absence of firm know-

* GRANT, Alexander Thomas Kingdom (1906–). Joined HM Treasury 1939; UK member on Managing Board of European Payments Union, 1952–53; Under-Secretary, Treasury, 1956; Under-Secretary, ECGD, 1958–66.

ledge of likely American assistance. Writing off balances in official hands (ie, of governments and central banks) would help but would not be decisive. The existence of substantial privately held balances raised technical problems, as Henderson had stressed, since they were reflected in the volume of bank deposits in the country concerned; special arrangements might have to be made to control them. If funding into longer-term debt were intended, appropriate timing might prove elusive, given that balances were likely to continue to rise with military expenditure; yet deferment of action until sterling was fully convertible might be inadvisable. Even then there might remain a need to consider a further funding, the prospect of which would diminish the acceptability of current sterling. Only the Bank of England, and those in the Treasury who were sympathetic to its views, could have gained much satisfaction from these discussions, in which recognition of the need for *ad hoc* action and for case by case treatment pointed away from a swift, clear cut solution and towards one more gradual.

It was now the turn of senior Ministers, for whom Keynes prepared a fresh, but broadly similar version of the memorandum that officials had discussed. Two points it particularly stressed were, first the potential strain on the reserves following Germany's defeat, when Lend-Lease aid seemed likely to be reduced, while sterling countries would want to import more dollar goods; second, a much more vigorous approach was necessary to the need to raise exports by some 50 per cent in volume above that of 1938, equivalent to thrice their existing value. At a meeting attended by nine Ministers and four officials, including Keynes, Ministers broadly concurred with the need to control balances, although the Dominions Secretary (Lord Cranborne) doubted if Australia and New Zealand would be agreeable, whilst the Paymaster-General (Lord Cherwell) repeated his preference for radical scaling down; but the Chancellor (Sir John Anderson) that day insisted that there should be no repudiation (above, p 164). The rather weak conclusions were that it was necessary to consider separately the various groups of problems involved, and that 'in due course' it would be necessary to bring the Dominions into discussion on the sterling problem.[59] A further meeting of seven Ministers more specifically concerned with economic affairs met a week later. This yielded the view of the Minister of Agriculture (Mr R S Hudson) that Keynes's memorandum understated the potential contribution of agriculture to import-saving; mixed feelings about the post-war prospects of adequate and sustained growth in exports; and agreement to propose an active 'working party' to stimulate the Departments concerned with exports.[60]

Following these discussions the Chancellor circulated the revised memorandum, preceded by a note on 'Our Overseas Resources and

Liabilities', to the War Cabinet at the beginning of July. When the War Cabinet discussed this later in the month, it was against the triply complex background of the monetary conference taking place at Bretton Woods, the stresses in the USA and at home over Article VII (above, p 136), and the major military preoccupations of a critical phase in the Allied reconquest of western Europe and the German V-1 aerial attack on Britain. The Chancellor made the memorandum's case for preparatory action ahead of the economic problems of Stage II and of the peace. He encountered not only the characteristic reluctance of the Lord Privy Seal (Beaverbrook) and the Secretary of State for India (Amery) to accept Keynes's views, which they regarded as too gloomy, but also the no less characteristic sentiments of the Prime Minister. The sterling debts were not like ordinary commercial debts, Mr Churchill declared, and acceptance of American help, especially in respect of Indian balances, might result in a loss of British political control. He looked to a settlement that would fully reflect Britain's own contribution: 'we should be entitled to present the other side of the account'. Out of this Cabinet discussion emerged agreement to seek early Stage II negotiations with the US, and to encourage agricultural expansion at home, to save foreign exchange. On sterling balances, the Chancellor had argued that funding, though not contemplated for the time being, would need to be in the future; the Cabinet concluded that eventually sterling area arrangements 'would need revision' and that 'early examination with the Departments concerned' was necessary.[61]

That examination had in fact already commenced. A special Treasury-Bank 'Committee on Post-War Exchange Control Problems' had been formed on Treasury suggestion to discuss the Bank's views and Keynes's memorandum; members of the Economic Section attended, as also did a representative of the Colonial Office for discussion of the sterling area's balances.[62]

On much the Committee registered agreement: the need to maintain a system of payments agreements to contain the sterling receipts of certain European countries; to keep the exchange rate at $4.03 to the pound; to adjust the gold price in sterling slightly upwards. Not until the subject of sterling balances was reached did significant differences appear. Even so, there was considerable accord on all but one—a major—set of issues.

The Bank virtually provided the agenda for these discussions. Explaining that, whilst it broadly agreed with Keynes's analysis of the sterling problem, it dissented from his proposed solutions, the Bank outlined its own proposals in a paper on 'Sterling Balances and Transitional Arrangements'.[63] This echoed much of what it had expressed, for instance, in the debate over a year previously on the proposed Clearing Union/Stabilisation Fund (above, pp 96–97). In stressing that the sterling balances were the main problem the Bank noted that, in addition to those balances to be the subject of payments agreements, some others outside the sterling area were already covered, notably, in the case of Portugal, by a commitment to post-war repayment in gold; those of Argentina and Brazil would probably be covered largely by disposal of British investments in those countries. Turning to the sterling area's balances, the Bank reported that these had reached £1,963 million by the end of March 1944, and were expected to be far higher by the end of the war. Only an insignificant proportion was appropriated to special purposes such as the pension funds and sinking funds of Colonial and other Governments. The bulk constituted potential spending power of £1,000 – 1,500 million above the level at which the balances might 'settle down'.

How best to protect against this overhang the gold and dollar reserves and the balance of payments? The former were running in 1944 around £400 million, but would be needed after the war largely for working balances; the value of exports and imports in 1938, adjusted to possible post-war levels of prices, was £810 million and £1,290 million respectively (see Appendix 27).

Although the Bank viewed as unavoidable an attempt to secure from India and Egypt 'a war contribution' by reducing their countries' large holdings, it foresaw strong local hostility to an attempt, along the lines of Keynes's proposals, to block or fund balances, whether held by central authorities or in commercial hands. It would be better, argued the Bank, to secure assurances from the holders of balances not to reduce them below agreed levels within stated periods. It would of course be necessary also to agree upon levels of spending, and here too the Bank differed from Keynes, who had proposed to 'ration' sterling countries' dollar expenditure according to their dollar earnings, unless more dollars could be spared ('dollars' evidently being used as shorthand for non-sterling currencies). The Bank feared that, apart from risking inequity between high and low dollar-earners, such an arrangement held the major disadvantage that it could discourage sterling countries from acquiring further sterling; they might even direct their exports away from Britain, which would then face a need to acquire for dollars goods formerly available for sterling. The Bank therefore preferred to try to operate constraint on the sterling area's overseas expenditure in general.

The Treasury, whilst recognising force in the Bank's case, was reluctant to accept it. In a paper at the end of July on 'The Sterling Area and Its Sterling Balances', it explained its anxiety.[64] With the balances likely to continue rising, the Bank's proposals would not sufficiently restrain sterling area demands for dollars nor for British exports ('unrequited exports' if acquired with accumulated balances), which would need time to recover and to face many other demands on them in the early post-war years. The Treasury preferred a direct limit, the dollar ration dealing with the former, and export licences with the latter. Admittedly sterling might indeed be made to look less attractive than the dollar, but this was inevitable while it remained inconvertible. Against this, the *non*-rationing of sterling would allow sterling countries to use it more freely within the sterling area. To sustain in this manner the usefulness of sterling would facilitate the eventual meeting of Britain's obligations in the only way they could be met, by the use of sterling balances to acquire British exports.

Examining the Bank's memorandum on his return from Bretton Woods, Keynes recognised arguments which the Treasury thought it had adequately refuted earlier in the year.[65] He castigated the Bank's proposals as the pursuit of a technical control of the sterling system, which would strive to sustain the prestige of sterling at the cost of both weakening it in practice and of imposing, in that attempt, unacceptable austerity on post-war Britain. Specifically, by seeking to limit total expenditure rather than its dollar element, the Bank's plan would encourage sterling countries to acquire dollar goods; this would tend to convert all Britain's overseas deficits into dollar liabilities instead of being more widely distributed. Keynes and the Treasury therefore agreed in opposing the Bank. Keynes was, however, to some extent at odds with the Treasury, which was by no means convinced of the case for blocking excess balances. Moreover, although he shared with the Bank anxiety that there should be some action over post-war sterling problems, Keynes was, during 1943–44, inclining to acquiesce in marking time over Indian balances (above, pp 221, 222), while the Treasury continued to think very similarly about the sterling balances as a whole. Matters therefore dragged on inconclusively. The Bank continued to favour a policy of seeking broad understandings with sterling countries to secure informal funding and general constraints on their expenditure, the Treasury the prospect of more formal funding and direct constraints on dollar outlays.[66]

(8) CONSTRAINTS ON POLICY

That there should be difficulties in reaching firm conclusions during 1944 on crucial elements of post-war policy is, however, scarcely surprising. Preoccupations over the Bretton Woods Conference and then with the forthcoming negotiations for Stage II assistance from the US underlined the uncertainty which constrained effective preparation for Stage III.

The Bretton Woods Conference in July 1944 scarcely brightened the financial horizon. The War Cabinet's bar on discussion there of Article VII matters embarrassed British delegates in interchanges with American officials.[67] The proposed IMF was not intended for post-war reconstruction; in any case its resources appeared to be both minimal and to be endowed with about as many dollars as the United States, in its existing mood, might be willing to contemplate providing for post-war stabilisation.[68] Above all, the British delegates' technical success in keeping the treatment of sterling balances in British hands (above, pp 164–7) simply fixed that burden more firmly on British backs. One limited offset was that debate and private discussion made Canadian and American delegates come to appreciate more fully the gravity of Britain's post-war problems;[69] yet this too held danger, lest hints of her true weakness encourage American pressure.

Some precarious steadying of at least the immediate prospects came at last in September 1944 at the second Quebec Conference (code-named 'OCTAGON') between President and Prime Minister. On assistance for Stage II, Mr Churchill secured broad recognition of Britain's needs, but by such strenuous pleading that he remonstrated: 'What do you want me to do... stand up and beg like Fala?'[70] But what of Stage III? A month earlier in London Mr Morgenthau had been reassuring; now at Quebec he dampened any idea of a 'brain wave' for the United Kingdom. The main offering was that his pastor-alisation plan for Germany would allow Britain to develop exports to markets formerly supplied by German industry. This inspired neither the enthusiasm of Mr Churchill nor the support of the Secretary of State and the Foreign Secretary, and it remained on the fringes of policy (above, p II).

To implement the Quebec understandings on Stage II assistance, Keynes was soon in the USA again, with a negotiating team, for a lengthy stay (October–December 1944). He met some leading American bankers, who on balance offered some encouragement on prospects for post-war aid, whilst they went away better instructed on Britain's position.[71] Keynes expounded to them, as in his memoranda, the problems, stressing that economic recovery and the continuing post-war drain of military expenditure would require at least three years for Britain to pay her way. His emphasis on the avoidance of reliance on the proposed new international financial institutions, and that Britain should strive to help itself, earned a central banker's commendation. Given the resolution to avoid aid in the form of loans, it was reassuring that one leading banker reiterated his own publicly stated views, supporting a settlement that would involve Anglo-American trade and monetary co-operation, combined with a grant-in-aid. Another contemplated the loan of gold ('kegs of gold') on a Lend-Lease basis. The central banker warned, however, against hoping for assistance even on the restricted scale suggested by Keynes ($3 to $5 billion) in addition to the $6 billion to be provided for the Bretton Woods institutions.

These informal discussions broadly reflected the continuing unresolved position on aid in Stage III. Official Washington evoked a succession of constraints. There should be no discussion before the Presidential election (of November 1944) to avoid any suggestion of commitments, whilst after it the President was against premature action. A little later Dr H D White favoured awaiting the end of the European war.[72] Then there were the dampeners of fierce Congressional debates: on the renewal of Lend-Lease and its prohibition on post-war use of such aid, and on Bretton Woods (above, pp 8–9 and 177, 178).

In relation to Stage III, these cautionary indications, together with the preparations for Stage II and the subsequent negotiations of October – December 1944, greatly sharpened the awareness of Keynes and the Economic Section and of some in the Treasury of the intensity of the problems to be faced. Projections of the impact on the balance of payments indicated that the first year of Stage II would involve higher disinvestment than in any previous year of the war, with substantial increases in sterling balances (see Appendix 27). The arduous negotiations reinforced the impression that, with Lend-Lease likely to cease with the end of Stage II, further help from the US would be entangled with strings that would be more numerous and tighter the more that Britain failed to limit the many demands on her constricted resources; the result could be an undesirably high degree of British dependence on the US. The implications of those demands—post-war relief, subscription to the new International Bank, occupation costs, reconstruction loans, export credits, repayments of excess sterling balances, and, by no means least, the financial consequences of sustaining Britain's status as a great power—and the need to reduce them, had been themes of Keynes's exhortations to colleagues and Ministers before the negotiations. Afterwards he reiterated them, first in a vivid report on the negotiations, written aboard ship, for the Chancellor.[73] Returned to Britain, he discussed Stage II and Stage III prospects in grave terms at a very full meeting of the Exchange Requirements Committee at the beginning of January 1945. Those present included the Financial Secretary to the Treasury (Mr Osbert Peake); forty-five officials from fourteen departments, including of course the Treasury, and a representative of the Bank of England. A few weeks later, Keynes fulfilled his intention to prepare for the Chancellor a special report on the lessons from the US visit in dealing with the problems of Stage III.[74]

(9) STARVATION CORNER, TEMPTATION, JUSTICE

Even apart from Whitehall's continuing deferment of action and the serious differences between Treasury and Bank ideas to deal with sterling's problems, it is clear that there were transatlantic reasons enough to discourage firm conclusions being made about Stage III prospects. In consequence, the Treasury felt unable to give its own view, let alone that of the Government, on Britain's need for financial help from the USA in Stage III when specifically asked about this by a Presidential emissary so late as March 1945.[75] Keynes had by then, however, launched a fresh and dramatic attempt to avoid the drift towards an unprepared peace, by circulating his promised memorandum. This was entitled 'Overseas Financial Arrangements in Stage III'.[76] In a continuing series, it was his most forceful endeavour, alike in analysis, proposals, and literary accomplishment. Supplemented and amended by further memoranda, it was to be the basis of discussions t, officials and Ministers preparatory to the eventual negotiations of late 1945. It clarified ruthlessly all the arguments that had been heard hitherto. To be more fully described below, its essence was the offer of a bold scheme for an international policy of multilateralism in trade and payments that would simultaneously make sterling's problems more manageable and justify Britain in seeking and America in giving financial assistance; an essential complement to this would be the cancellation or funding of substantial proportions of the sterling area's sterling balances, through agreements with their holders. It would then be possible to undertake, both as a desirable policy in itself and as a means to attract the American aid which would be essential to sustain it, the convertibility of currently earned sterling of sterling area countries within a year of the end of the war. In the rest of the world, currently earned sterling had not ceased to be *de facto* convertible for the USA and Canada. For other non-sterling countries, agreements such as the payments agreements for European countries and those for Latin American countries were expected to regulate and to encourage the use of sterling in broad harmony with sterling area arrangements. This proposed convertibility, though in the spirit of the Bretton Woods agreements, would be informal and need not involve abandonment of the painfully secured transitional arrangements under Article XIV of the Fund. It will be seen that these last two crucial features of Keynes's plan, involving sterling and early convertibility for the sterling area, were to vary one way and another before the final agreement of December 1945.

In the subsequent Treasury discussions there were doubts about particular aspects, but the broad sweep of the proposals was not effectively challenged. Convertibility might be acceptable after two years, at least, but scarcely within one year. Holders of sterling balances were to be expected to contribute to a general settlement, but was it realistic to contemplate some form of sanctions against those unwilling to do so?[77] The appropriate treatment of sterling balances gave great concern; here Mr R W B Clarke's paper for the discussions on Indian sterling balances, that were taking place at the same time, was particularly noteworthy.[78]

Mr Clarke's examination of the balances of thirteen countries or regions in the sterling area illuminated the very great differences between them and the likelihood that there would be markedly differing results if a standard solution were to be applied. The balances reflected various influences: principally that of British war expenditure; US military expenditure (especially in Australia); in a minority of cases a favourable balance of trade, although in only three (India, Australia, Ceylon) was there a favourable balance of any significance with the USA. Much of the problem continued to be concentrated in the balances of India and the Middle East (Egypt and Sudan, Palestine, Iraq), which at the end of September 1944 had accounted for £1,435 million out of the £2,009 million of balances accumulated by the sterling area countries concerned. The balances could be compared with the value of British exports to them in 1937, adjusted for price increases.[79] Overall, they were equivalent to a little over six years' exports. Whereas, however, those of India and of the Middle East ranged from 16.3 to 34 years, averaging 18 years, those of the remainder ranged from 0.3 to 9.0 years, averaging 2.35 years, and therefore constituted comparatively less serious problems.

A critical element in Keynes's proposals was the provision of substantial credit by the USA. There was some Treasury unease on this (and the Bank of England remained steadfastly averse to such borrowing). In discussions with his senior officials, the Chancellor overrode those misgivings, declaring that the alternatives would give scope 'to those who favoured Imperial economic isolationism'.[80]

Revised in the light of Treasury discussions, Keynes's proposals were circulated to the War Cabinet by the Chancellor in May 1945 under the slightly changed title of 'Overseas Financial Policy in Stage III'.[81] There were three main choices for policy, claimed the memorandum, distinguished as Starvation Corner, Temptation, and Justice. The first had been called 'Austerity' in the original version, echoing Keynes's use of that description for the consequences of proposals, similar to those against which he was now warning, from the Bank of England. 'Starvation Corner', a policy of attempting complete financial independence of the USA, would involve essentially the operation of a siege economy in the early post-war years, with rationing and controls more intense than during the war; trade would have to be strictly organised; colonial development and reconstruction in the Far Eastern empire would have to be deferred, and there would be severe constraints on all governmental activities overseas. Keynes denied that economic nationalism and the avoidance of outside aid were desirable means to ensure financial independence. The wartime success of financial policy rested on special factors, whereas Britain's post-war prospects had to reckon with out-dated industries; there was also a burden of excessive overseas commitments, which, he urged, should be drastically cut.

Economic isolation—autarky—though 'not quite unplausible',

would require intensified austerity. It would involve consequences, not just at home but abroad, of the gravest character. Above all, the acceptance and advocacy of 'Starvation Corner' would arouse hostility in Canada and in the USA, and also in some sterling countries to a policy likely to appear as deliberately disruptive of international co-operation.

To all this must be added the realisation that bilateral arrangements were inappropriate for Britain's trade, and that, contrary to some views, they would be unhelpful to the sterling area. Treading with great delicacy amongst the powerful arguments being heard for a 'sterling area' solution to post-war external problems, Keynes stressed that it was its internationalism that underlay sterling's strength and London's financial eminence.[82] Bilateralism would gravely impair both. As a possible policy, should anti-internationalist forces sadly triumph in the USA, it might be invoked as a lesser weapon of last resort, but only and more advantageously if Britain had first striven for the better international solution.

What was the right combination of internationalism and aid? 'Temptation' would arise with the prospect of substantial American credits to permit, along Article VII lines, the early freeing of international payments and the convertibility of sterling. Such a solution, probably easy to negotiate, should be resisted. On financial grounds, it would be objectionable in substituting dollar debt for sterling debt. It might well involve yielding on commercial policy for the sake of financial aid. Worst of all, on political and financial grounds it would be outrageous for post-war Britain to emerge victorious from the war, but carrying a debt similar in amount to the reparations proposed by Russia for a defeated Germany. 'Justice', the third choice, must characterise an acceptable policy, based on reasonable equality of sacrifice through a three-fold re-distribution of war burdens.

'Justice' demanded substantial assistance from the USA, Canada and the sterling countries. In addition to the elimination of any debt from Anglo-American and Anglo-Canadian Mutual Aid, this should consist, in sterling terms, of some £3,200 million. Roughly one-third of this would come from cancellation of British obligations; the remainder would involve fresh finance. (In the event something under one-half of the total proposed aid was to be received. A summary of the various proposals is given in Appendix 19, pp 409 – 10.) The argument for such substantial assistance, which would permit early convertibility, fell into three stages. First, the USA should be asked to make the frequently aired grant to Britain of some $3 billion, in respect of her expenditure in the US on the common effort before the formal American entry into the war. This would strengthen the case for the second part of 'Justice'. This would be a more detailed and more severe policy than Keynes had previously urged towards sterling balances. These fell into two main groups. Those owing to non-sterling countries presented little problem, he declared. Of something under £800 million in all, over £600 million would be covered by various arrangements with the countries concerned. That left £169 million, of which some £100 million owing to Argentina and Brazil could be settled by disposal, on terms assumed to be favourable, of British investments there. For the other and far larger group of balances, those owing to sterling area countries, to which Britain had stronger obligations, there should be a firm control by a mixture of voluntary cancellation and funding; this would leave a manageable proportion to be released, and to be fully convertible for current purposes but not to acquire gold reserves (a proposal to be varied in subsequent discussions). At this stage Keynes envisaged payment of interest on the amounts funded: again, a proposal to be varied later.

On the assumption that the sterling area's relevant balances would reach something over £3,000 million by the end of the war, the respective amounts to be cancelled, funded, and freed might be £880 million, £1,500 million and £750 million. This element in the redistribution of war costs rested on a dual claim: that the common effort demanded that they be shared more equitably, and that the accumulated balances reflected war profits. Between his first main draft and the version of the memorandum circulated to the War Cabinet, Keynes added some harsh assertions, and terse statistical illustrations.[83] The sterling Dominions had been 'slipping out of financial responsibility, and the scale on which they are building up war profits at our expense. . .deserves to be set out nakedly'. Such profits had accrued because, in varying degrees, sterling countries had benefited from British war expenditure without contributing significantly to it (India being a major exception); in some cases, eg, Australia, they had not given to Britain the kind of reciprocal aid that they had themselves received from the USA. Finally there was the special case of South Africa, whose war contribution had been 'notoriously inadequate', to offset which she should pay over £50 million in gold. Those sterling countries which rejected these arguments and refused to operate the scheme would find none of their balances convertible, and would receive less interest on them.

The great virtue of this scheme, asserted Keynes, was that the proposed voluntary cancellation of between one-quarter and one-third of the sterling area's balances would be seen as part of a general redistribution of war costs; it would be broadly comparable with the proposed American contribution by way of retrospective Lend-Lease. Without that American contribution, it would be more difficult to persuade the sterling countries to make theirs.

There remained the third main part of 'Justice'. This would be an American credit of perhaps $5 billion, and one of $500 million (together with adjustment of other financial arrangements) from Canada. These would carry low rates of interest. The overall effect, though leaving Britain still significantly burdened, would be to allow it to contemplate the peace 'without any serious anxiety' economically, save the long-standing worry over domestic industries, about which Keynes wrote brutally.[84]

In sum, this latest proposal in spring 1945 envisaged that substantial American aid and a containment of sterling debt would reduce the attractions of a narrow sterling *bloc* solution, and enhance those of a bolder internationalist approach.

Neither early nor easily would it be possible to negotiate such arrangements for Stage III, nor to ensure meanwhile adequate Lend-Lease aid (which, to reiterate, was expected to end with the war and thus with the commencement of Stage III). On both sides of the Atlantic politicians and officials had many other preoccupations. In Britain, the ending of the wartime Coalition in May, and its replacement by a Conservative ('National') Administration—'The Caretaker Government'— relaxed constraints on political controversy and initiated a relatively protracted period of uncertainty for policy-makers. The general election was not to be held until early July; moreover, the results would not become available until late that month, to allow Service votes from all over the world to be assembled. The American perspective on Stage III discussions was that they must await not only the end of the war in Europe, which proved to be early in May, but also the completion of Congressional hearings on the latest Lend-Lease authorisations, which was not to be achieved until the end of June.[85] Further, a member of the British Treasury's mission in Washington reported, at a London officials' meeting at the end of May, that account must be taken of two further matters commanding American attention: the San Francisco Conference, to establish the United Nations Organisation, which had opened in April and was to continue to late June; and the scrutiny which Congress had commenced at the beginning of the year of the Bretton Woods agreements (and not to be concluded until the end of July 1945). Congress, he thought, inclined to feel that the US might be doing enough for the time being.[86] Reinforcing this American perspective was the unpredictable political transformation resulting from the death of President Roosevelt (12 April 1945); the new President, the former Vice-President Harry S Truman, needed time to establish his eventual authority, and meanwhile faced a Congress unafraid to test its own powers. There was, finally, the delay interposed by the forthcoming conference of the Allies at Potsdam; this was expected to be prolonged, but could scarcely start before the close of the US fiscal year at the end of June.[87] Thus, September appeared to be the first possible time for Stage III discussions. Such delay, Keynes presciently observed, when

urging that preparations should be made accordingly, carried a potentially fatal danger. Britain might 'have no option but to accept the
best we can get' from the Americans. That risk arose from the double
hazard that not enough time would be allowed for protracted negotiations, which might initially (and temporarily) break down so that
Britain might be caught, inadequately safeguarded, by the end of the
Japanese war.[88] It was against this anxious background that, on the
eve of the Allies' Conference at Potsdam (17 July – 2 August 1945), the
Chancellor advised the Prime Minister that he might raise there with
President Truman the issues involved. Consideration should be given
before the end of the Japanese war of procedure to wind up Lend-
Lease, and Stage III discussions might start early in September; for
the latter, there could be formed an American Committee 'to discuss
with a party . . . we would send to Washington'.[89]

(10) DEBATE ON POLICY, JUNE – AUGUST 1945

From June to August 1945 discussions on possible financial proposals to the USA were to concern three major issues: the overall
approach to be adopted towards immediate post-war problems; the
type of American financial aid that might be acceptable; and the scope
for early currency convertibility, especially in relation to the sterling
balances and the sterling area. Consideration of the three issues inevitably overlapped, but they fell into something of a natural and chronological sequence. In particular it was first necessary to consider the
case for an approach to the USA on the lines Keynes suggested. Might
not an easy flow of dollars, asked some senior Treasury voices, encourage too relaxed an attitude to the serious problems of Britain's domestic economy (as indeed Keynes had himself noted)?[90] And might we
not thereby risk selling ourselves into slavery?[91] The Governor of the
Bank of England (Lord Catto) in due course counselled hesitation
over the two dollar props.[92] With respect to the first of these, that there
should be a more itemised claim for retrospective Lend-Lease, he
seemed to doubt the chance of securing all of that. On the second, the
resort to fresh financial aid from the USA, he reiterated his well-
known hostility to any loan, as likely to lead to default and bad relations. Better would be a line of credit against security; that proposition
could attract the American public if the alternative to eventual repayment were to be either the forfeiture of the security, or—invoking
a suggestion heard on both sides during the war—the cession of some
islands, in this case from the Bahamas group.

In the Treasury, Sir Wilfrid Eady's early unease about the implications of Keynes's spring memorandum had by late June 1945 led
him to produce, with the help of Mr R W B ('Otto') Clarke, what was
essentially a counter-proposal.[93] This 'Plan II' was presented
nominally as 'a fall-back' rather than as a rival to Keynes's proposals

('Plan I') but it could in fact be regarded as both. In Keynes's terminology, 'Starvation Corner', which Eady's evident vision of the post-war economy resembled, would be unavoidable if 'Justice' failed and 'Temptation' were resisted. Plan II seemed from the outset to head for 'Starvation Corner'. It presupposed not just that the US Administration would recoil from retrospective Lend-Lease, but that Britain's initial negotiating stance would be determinedly protective, envisaging dependence for some years on substantial and discriminatory trade controls. To reassure American opinion, Eady urged that financial negotiations should nevertheless begin with twin British declarations: of support for a liberal, multilateral, commercial policy; and of intent to secure parliamentary approval for the Bretton Woods agreements. Should negotiations fail, Eady suggested—calling on the Bank of England's unwavering view (above, pp 140 – 4 and 232 – 4)—that strength might be sought in a widening of the sterling area to include France, Belgium, the Netherlands, and their empires.

The weakness of 'Plan II' was the strength of Keynes's 'Plan I', the former's pessimistic outlook on Britain's economic problems being for the latter an argument for bold policies to solve them. That bolder view characterised Keynes's further re-formulation of his proposals. At a meeting of officials in July he proposed to drop the attempt to recover the $3 billion of 'retrospective Lend-Lease', and to seek only a free grant of $4 billion. This, and later changes in August made his scheme even more audacious. The essence of this Keynesian 'Plan I' lay in making the right approach (at the right time). As Mr R H Brand now stressed, with all his authority as Treasury representative in Washington, there was scope to appeal both to Americans' generosity and to their interest in a strong British economy. Further, if a loan were anathema so also could be a free grant: 'The US is the last country the UK should take gifts from if they can be avoided'. Any grant were better disguised. As for the suggested extension of the sterling area into Europe, should negotiations fail, that would be unhelpful; the USA would see it as a 'ganging-up' against them.[94] When the Ministries of Supply and Food, with their concern with imported raw materials and food, stressed the 'enormous difficulties' that 'Plan II' would involve, Sir Wilfrid Eady retreated with it, at least temporarily.[95]

The abandonment of the aim of a combined 'gift' and credit of $8 billion reflected a gloomy assessment of the prevailing American mood. This had indicated that such a large amount could only be obtained on loan terms. Keynes now, in July, suggested limiting to $4 billion the aid to be sought. This figure was offered, rather than the $3 billion estimated in May 1944 (above p 230) in order to take account of the subsequent increased burdens with the lengthening of the war.[96] (In the revision in August, part of which the Chancellor circulated as a printed Cabinet paper, this was to be further raised to $5 billion.[97]) But would such an amount permit Britain to undertake early convertibility under the Bretton Woods proposals? Brand expressed doubts which, he reiterated, the two US experts, White and Bernstein, shared.[98]

Keynes's daring reaction to these and other comments was that Britain must offer even stronger inducements to secure American help. He re-shaped the twin pillars of the scheme, involving convertibility and control of sterling balances respectively, perhaps at the risk of blurring the harsh realities ahead. On the former, he went even farther in July 1945 than previously, having recently strengthened his belief that there would be adequate scope for trade and exchange controls within the rules of the International Monetary Fund (above, p 181). He now proposed acceptance at the end of 1946 of the formal convertibility obligations of the Fund (Article VIII), and the renunciation then of its transitional relaxations (Article XIV).[99] These proposals therefore envisaged a very brief transition period, after which exchange and trade controls such as had been used during the war might require the Fund's explicit sanction. This audacious suggestion was quickly modified following discussions prompted by Mr C F Cobbold* of the Bank of England. It was now proposed to have a qualified interpretation of convertibility during the transition period. Instead of being 'spendable anywhere', released sterling balances would enjoy 'general availability' in the sense of being available for spending but (unlike currently earned sterling) not for automatic transfer into another currency. Further it was not now proposed to renounce the transitional easements of Article XIV, although the operation of 'general availability' would take sterling in that direction.[100]

As further counter-weight to the reduced expectation of American aid, and also as bait to persuade the US that the sterling area would itself contribute to Britain's recovery, the proposed treatment of sterling balances was to be more severe. The sum it was hoped to cancel—amounts being now put in dollars—was increased first from $3 billion (£750 million) to $3.5 billion (£875 million).[101] Then in August, as dreams of dollars swelled to $5 billion, the cancellation envisaged rose to $4 billion (£1 billion) and then to $5 billion (£1.25 billion).[102] The eventual hope, *after* these August projections and at the outset of the negotiations in September, was to be mooted at $4 billion (£1 billion) in the final version of all the preceding memoranda.[103]

At the suggestion of the Board of Trade in May 1945, instead of an initial release of £750 million of balances, equivalent to the discarded hope of $3 billion of 'retrospective Lend-Lease', there could be substituted a more prudent one of £250 million ($1 billion)[104] with grad-

---

* COBBOLD, Cameron Fromanteel, 1st Baron, 1960 (1904–); Deputy Governor, Bank of England, 1945; Governor of Bank of England, 1949–61; Director, BIS, 1949–61.

ual releases of the remainder subsequently. (This proposed release was to be further reduced to £200 million—$800 million—in the Chancellor's second main memorandum of 17 August.)[105] Moreover, dropping a proposal to tie them to purchases in Britain would help to commend the scheme to the Americans.[106] Further easement would come from allowing a lower interest rate on free balances, and none at all on deferred balances. Above all, continuation broadly of the wartime operation of the sterling area in the immediate post-war period would best control the use of sterling. In persuading Lord Keynes of this, Mr Cobbold had also persuaded him that the various sterling countries so differed from each other that a standard solution would be inappropriate.[107]

If realistic, this fall-back to the sterling area nonetheless appeared to deprive the proposed treatment of balances of its original decisiveness. Yet the possibility of such decisiveness may have been illusory. There had been a continuing division about the timing of action. Should it be undertaken at the earliest possible moment, to restrict further accumulations, or should such action be deferred until the probable peak had been reached? In July 1945 Keynes thought that it would be possible to estimate the likely peak and therefore to take early action—but a further dilemma then arose. This was the apparent need to give priority both to existing sterling debt and to future dollar debt. To make a sterling settlement first would be to gamble on the adequacy and terms of American aid. If the USA were to take over the excess balances, Keynes admitted that this substitution of a dollar for a sterling debt would prevent Britain from offering early convertibility. Alternatively, a prior sterling settlement might have the disadvantage that the terms of a subsequent American loan could involve emphasis on Britain's obligation to repay the balances. In fact, as Anglo-American discussions were shortly to make clear, whilst Britain felt obliged to assert the prior ranking of sterling debt, the American view was that any dollar loan must have superior status.[108] The conclusion was that the conflicting claims required harmonisation, whether by starting the American negotiations first, or by seeking sterling and dollar arrangements simultaneously.[109]

All these discussions and memoranda between March and August 1945 clearly formed the basis of policy recommended to and accepted by senior Ministers in their two August papers. A crucial problem remained: when could Anglo-American discussions on post-war financial arrangements begin?

(11) THE CABINET AND POST-WAR POLICY

The final shaping of these proposals into agreed Government policy was to come suddenly. In view of the inadequacy of some literature on the subject, it is of considerable importance to attempt to see this in perspective.[110] In an evaluation of the provenance and content of that policy, it must not be overlooked that for some five months the proposals were digested and modified significantly after discussions involving officials in the Treasury, the Board of Trade, the Economic Section, and the Bank of England, as well as leading Ministers. Then, in mid-August, the initial background of serious but relatively unhurried anxiety gave place to the consternation accompanying the sudden end of the war, and with it the end of Lend-Lease. Ministers' discussions of policy centred around two papers, to which brief allusions have already been made; these were circulated by the Chancellor to the Cabinet in mid-August. They were reproduced substantially from Keynes's memoranda with the omission, however, of the threefold dramatisation of choice ('Starvation Corner', 'Temptation' and 'Justice') of the spring memorandum on 'Overseas Policy in Stage III'.[111] They gave scant attention to the less than multilateral solution of a peacetime elaboration of sterling area arrangements. Further, the 'temptation' that ample American credit might offer was now seen quite differently: too much help (viz, more than $5 billion) 'might make us sufficiently comfortable to relax the full pressure without which we shall not recover equilibrium as soon as we should'.[112]

Keynes's memorandum, 'Our Overseas Financial Prospects', formed, under the same title, the Cabinet paper in August. It asserted that 'a financial Dunkirk' threatened.[113] To help avoid this, American aid limited to some $5 billion (instead of the $8 billion aired earlier) should be sought as a grant-in-aid, or a grant camouflaged as a credit. It assumed that overseas debt could be contained, and recognised that commercial undertakings (such as acceptance of non-discrimination), and possibly territorial concessions might have to be offered to the USA. For the rest, this paper concentrated largely on the implications of Britain's insufficiently realised plight, especially on the economic and political consequences of failure to raise exports and to cut overseas expenditure. All this perturbed the new Prime Minister (Mr C R Attlee), who enjoined particular secrecy over the alarming references to 'a financial Dunkirk', as well as to the prospects of Britain becoming a second class power, and enduring protracted austerity.[114]

The detailed and revised proposals, their justification and their presentation at the Anglo-American discussions, which he considered should be held in early September, were the subject of the Chancellor's second Cabinet paper a few days later, entitled 'Proposals to the United States for financial assistance to follow after Lend-Lease'. The form of the suggested request for an American grant-in-aid was now elaborated: £1,250 million (ie, $5,000 million) over the three post-war years, in one instalment of £500 million and two of £375 million. The policy proposed for sterling was in one respect more considerate than previously of sterling countries' differing problems. So far from supporting or even whispering about the possibility of resort to a restrictive sterling area solution of the external problem, the paper recognised Britain's obligations as holder of their international reserves, and the need for individual consideration of their balances, rather than proposing a single, uniform, prescription. Otherwise the plan, though much as earlier in broad outline, was perceptibly more stringent. The total amount of the sterling area's balances to be contained was now put at £3,000 to £3,500 million. The amounts that it was hoped would be cancelled voluntarily, frozen, and released were now put at, respectively, £1,250 million, £2,000 million, and £200 million (compared with £880 million, £1,500 million, and £750 million). Not only was less sterling to be available, but its burden to Britain would also be lightened: interest would be allowed on amounts released but not on those withheld.[115] Those frozen balances might be released over a fifty-year period, commencing five years after the end of the war, in amounts to be increased wherever possible, and also perhaps 'at a discount' for the purpose of making overseas loans.

What attraction would this scheme hold? For the sterling countries, it had been made more severe and potentially less persuasive than originally envisaged. This reflected the dropping of the proposals, matching the proposed cancellation of balances, to seek from the USA a comparable sum in 'retrospective Lend-Lease'. The supposed bait remained, however. The overall relief to the balance of payments would virtually permit Britain to operate something like the post-transitional payments system envisaged at Bretton Woods. This would be on a *de facto* basis, from, say the end of 1946; the protection offered during the transition by Article XIV of the proposed International Monetary Fund would not be formally abandoned so soon.[116] Freed sterling would be 'available' (a shading down of 'Bretton Woods convertibility') for trade transactions without discrimination; currently earned sterling, though *not* released balances, could also be used to acquire gold and foreign assets.[117] In these ways, the features which the Americans so disliked would be eliminated from the arrangements of the sterling area dollar pool. There could then be scope for the international economic system desired by the Americans and, 'if it can be managed', also by Britain.[118] It must be said that this brief qualification of supposed British desires concealed the Chancellor's strong ambivalence over a commitment to early or even later convertibility. No doubt a memorandum offering a bold initiative was not the place to proclaim serious reservations, such as had characterised earlier discussions, and which were later to threaten the success of the loan negotiations (below pp 316 – 19). In particular, and in the light of known American attitudes, the tone of the Chancellor's bold and liberal 'Proposals' scarcely harmonised with that of a different, third memorandum by him of the same date which, however, was given extremely limited circulation, excluding probably the Prime Minister and the Lord President of the Council, as well as most of the rest of the Cabinet. In that near-secret memorandum, he asserted that very substantial safeguards such as exchange control, quantitative controls on imports, and discrimination were 'essential' (above, p 210).[119]

There remained the question of how best to secure American aid that would not be on commercial terms. For this purpose, the Chancellor's 'Proposals' favoured avoidance of advance proposals, in preference for an attempt to evoke a generous American response. That could emerge after a frank exposition of Britain's problems.[120] This could be threefold. Hard currency resources had been largely expended in the USA before Lend-Lease developed. Heavy war expenditure in the Middle and Far East had been borne with little relief except from India. Finally, in implicit justification of seeking yet more from them, the USA, Canada and the sterling countries, whose help had permitted Britain to concentrate resources on war production and the armed forces, had thereby expanded their overseas trade; in contrast and in consequence of that help, Britain had sacrificed hers.[121]

Was this approach, broadly that with which the British were to enter the Anglo-American financial negotiations in September 1945, formulated hastily and with minimal discussion? Inasmuch as the end of the war found Britain and the USA with no agreed plan for immediate post-war arrangements, and with no time for leisurely rumination, such a question would be understandable. There had been two changes in Government, the first, from Coalition to Conservative ('National') in late May, a week after the circulation to the War Cabinet of Keynes's dramatic analysis and proposals. The second, to a Labour Government in late July, after the general election, came less than three weeks before the end of the war. Discontinuity as well as lack of time for possible reformulation of policies might therefore be allowed some weight. On the other hand, most of the senior Ministers particularly responsible for external economic policy in the new Labour Government had been senior members of the Coalition; in the all-important case of the Treasury, the new Chancellor of the Exchequer, Mr Hugh Dalton, had been President of the Board of Trade for some three years to May 1945, and had been closely concerned with commercial policy discussions. Amongst officials there had been no break in continuity, either of individuals or of discussions on post-war policies. To only a very limited extent, therefore, did difficulties in policy formation appear to spring from governmental changes. They reflected, rather, three more substantial influences. One was the preoccupation, until the Japanese surrender, with the immediate problems of Stage II. After months of anxiety and of strenuous negotiations to secure adequate American assistance (above, pp 8, 236

& 450–2), serious shortfalls in expected supplies (above pp 8–9) were constraints on, not encouragements to, hopes and endeavours in relation to supposedly distant Stage III. Second was the *impasse* in post-war plans for international trade. If there be blame for that, it would require nice judgement to apportion it between the nature of American demands and the dragging of British feet: footdragging in which, moreover, the new Labour Government was quickly to demonstrate continuity with its two immediate predecessors (below pp 266–9 & 274–6). Third and above all, the failure to hold Anglo-American discussions in advance of Stage III was ultimately the consequence of the sudden end of the war, September having been regarded for some months as the earliest feasible time for them.

(12) THE UNPREPARED END OF LEND-LEASE

Apprehension over the absence of arrangements for the winding-up of Lend-Lease was amply evident in London during spring and summer of 1945. There was an unenthusiastic reaction, however, to a relatively low-level approach from the US Administration for discussions that would be based on the assumption that Lend-Lease would end on or soon after the defeat of Japan. British hopes were for its prolongation to, say, at least six months after the war, with then a gradual and orderly ending. Loan terms for such extra aid would be resisted, the aim being to deal with its financing in the broader post-war settlement.[122]

Was there not, however, in view of the increasingly critical American attitude to aid reported from Washington, a case for seeking promptly *some* arrangement, against the early end of the Japanese war that many in Washington were expecting? Keynes persuaded his Treasury colleagues against immediate action. The aim was to seek American generosity for a comprehensive settlement, including Lend-Lease and Britain's Stage III needs, of the financial legacy of the war as a whole. In May 1945, however, Washington did not appear in the right mood for Stage III discussions; it regarded the financial implications of the Bretton Woods agreements, still going through Congress, as being as much as was necessary, or as much for the time being as could be contemplated. London hoped to hold Stage III conversations in September; and recognised the risk that the war would end with no agreement for a tidy end to Lend-Lease.[123]

The two limited steps that were taken simply emphasised the gloomy prospects. Mr Brand was instructed to inquire whether Dr White could accompany Mr Clayton, Assistant Secretary of State, on the latter's expected visit to London in July in connection with post-war relief. This would provide an opportunity for financial talks in advance of the main Stage III discussions.[124] White's instant rejection apparently reflected the unpromising American atmosphere. Any visiting, he said, could be by the British to Washington—'and on their knees' wrote Keynes in the margin of Brand's letter. It was soon to become clear, in fact, that partly because of the prolonged uncertainty in the extended arrangements for the British general election, Mr Clayton's visit could not take place until August.[125] By then, as will be discussed shortly, it was to prove too late to forestall a crisis over Lend-Lease.

The other step was for Ministers, above all the Prime Minister, to urge upon the Americans a more generous attitude over Lend-Lease supplies. This achieved little. It was then arranged that the Prime Minister should approach President Truman personally at the Potsdam Conference during the second half of July. This evoked, in response to Mr Churchill's account of 'the melancholy position' of Great Britain, a 'most warm and comforting' attitude from the President. This was offset, however, by an American note (formally replying to the Prime Minister's earlier urgings) which coupled an assurance of adherence to the 1944 undertakings about Lend-Lease with a complaint that British dollar balances were much higher than contemplated when those undertaking were given. The President therefore hoped that Britain would use its dollars more freely—in a word, that it would require less Lend-Lease. The Chancellor promptly advised the Prime Minister of the true situation: that the balances were no higher than expected several months previously, that liabilities had also increased, and that a 'certain level of reserves was an essential precaution against Britain's being in a weak position at the end of Lend-Lease'.[126] The incident was a warning of difficulties that might lie ahead in Anglo-American discussions, which the President agreed could be held in September.

The hope of easing these difficulties— by 'educating the Americans' about Britain's economic problems, as Whitehall inclined to view matters[127]—was to founder in the middle of the August talks with Mr Clayton, when the war ended suddenly. Those talks had been especially concerned, as discussed above (pp 208–9) with resolving Anglo-American disagreements on commercial policy. Mr Clayton linked this back to the Article VII commitment, and forward to the conditions for financial aid. Early in the talks, Keynes's exposition along the lines of his memoranda had pointed towards acceptance of the kind of international trading arrangements envisaged by the Americans. There would be early convertibility, supported by reduction and funding of excess sterling balances. On the amount and terms of essential aid there was a potential clash. British thinking about the amount reflected estimates that total net deficits in the balance of payments, excluding net releases of sterling balances, could reach £1,500 million ($6 billion) during the first three full post-war years. That was an estimate of the total *deficit*, but Keynes's memoranda had been urging in July and August that the amount of *aid* be kept deliberately below that, in order to sustain pressure for adaptation in the British economy: to, say, $5 billion (above p 246). The reference to the larger potential *deficit* can probably be regarded as a bargaining gambit. Mr Clayton's comment was that American public opinion 'seemed to be settling on the possibility of... $3 billion'. Precision was avoided, however, both sides agreeing that of much more immediate significance was the broad character of an overall settlement which would commend itself to both American and British public opinion.[128]

Alas for these cautious steps towards Anglo-American understanding, the ending of Lend-Lease with the end of the war transformed the discussions into a British struggle to defer agreement on all save the immediate emergency: the continuance of essential supplies and services. Already during early August there had been signs and warnings from the USA of the impending cessation of military aid, even for occupation costs, and of Lend-Lease generally immediately the war ended.[129] Some within the Administration had encouraged British officials in Washington to hope for a breathing space;[130] they had to yield to the convictions of the President, and of his Administrator of Foreign Economic Aid (Mr Leo Crowley), that the law which they had helped to formulate left them no choice but to end Lend-Lease and hostilities simultaneously.[131] Canada followed with the end of her Mutual Aid.[132]

Urgent discussions by British officials in Washington and London concluded that it would be broadly possible to manage with little further military aid,[133] although some temporary easement in fact came.[134] Food supplies for the armed forces and civilians had somehow to be maintained. In unpropitious circumstances, the British aim was to avoid hasty decisions to prolong Lend-Lease supplies on terms that might prejudice those for the major aid to be sought for Stage III. As much as possible should be left for settlement as part of the September negotiations.

The problems to be faced immediately were numerous, complicated, productive of misunderstanding, and tedious for those concerned. Simply to outline them is to indicate the burden which the unfortunate lack of agreed arrangements imposed on Anglo-American negotiations for Stage III; initial muddle added to the sense of grievance which the abrupt termination of Lend-Lease had created. Under previous contracts goods were being produced; some were in transit; others were being loaded when the order came to stop loading; but further contracts would be needed if Britain's people were to be fed and her factories kept working. Supplies were held in stock, and there were installations and equipment, not all of which might be thought worth retaining; to make inventories of all these, as the Americans now required, and to reach agreed valuations, were to be dreary tasks. Under Lend-Lease legislation, moreover, the US auth-

orities were likely to exercise the right of 're-capture' of certain supplies. Then there were shipping services and repair facilities which
had been mutually provided; their continuance for defence purposes,
eg, the repatriation of troops, would clearly be needed.[135]

The proposed switch from the wartime suspension of detailed financial accounting to its peacetime restoration raised irritating difficulties,
for instance over the prices to be charged for commodities hitherto
controlled. To decide on the relative advantages of trading items for
cash, or against credit terms, or as offsets to goods or services supplied
by the other partner, involved somewhat sharp calculation. By no
means least for the potential impact on her external finances, Britain's
arrangements to terminate Reciprocal Aid, and for interim aid until
Stage III had been settled, were doubly enmeshed with those of the
Dominions and India. First, the terms that they might expect would
inevitably reflect those that Britain could secure. Second, should they
opt to pay cash forthwith for American supplies, this would come from
the sterling area's gold and dollar pool.

The draft Presidential directive on the end of Lend-Lease had provided that, forthwith, the only new contracts on Lend-Lease terms
should be those for military purposes approved by the Joint Chiefs of
Staff. Payment for goods arising from existing contracts or already in
transit—the 'pipe-line' supplies—or in stocks held in the countries
concerned could be made in one of two ways (other than by cash).
Some countries had made arrangements under section 3(c) of Lend-
Lease legislation for thirty-year credits at an interest rate of $2\frac{3}{8}$ per
cent per annum. Other countries (such as Britain) could pay 'on such
terms as may be determined by this [the US] Government'.[136]

Under urging from London by Mr Clayton and in Washington by
British representatives there, these proposals were quickly modified.[137] Broadly, Lend-Lease terms would now continue to operate for
shipping services for thirty days (to be extended later, in specified
circumstances, to sixty days) after the formal end of the war on VJ
day, set at 2 September.[138] Fresh contracts for civilian supplies could
be accepted through the Lend-Lease machinery on a cash-
reimbursement basis for sixty days (this was subsequently extended to
approximately six months, to the end of February 1946).[139] Payment
for goods 'in the pipe-line' and held in stocks abroad would now be 'on
terms to be mutually agreed'.[140]

The prospects of mutual agreement quickly appeared as fragile as
the badly shaken feelings on both sides of the Atlantic. American
Lend-Lease officials clearly wanted firm decisions promptly on the
form of payment for pipe-line supplies (the financing of new supplies
and of stocks was a less urgent worry). The British Treasury expected
to defer commitments until the Keynes Mission (below, pp 264–6)
arrived to negotiate them, and meanwhile suffered a tortured ambiv-

alence over the choice between cash payment and credit. Sir Wilfrid Eady feared that to take interim credit facilities might prejudice the terms of longer-term finance; reflecting his dislike for a post-war loan, he declared his unwillingness to encourage the US to believe that they could save the world, especially Britain, by providing credits. Yet cash payment he also saw as a deadly influence on possible loan terms, for 'those on the American side who are more hostile to us may try to bleed us of Dollar reserves in the hope of making us more amenable to negotiations'.[141] These anxieties produced the intention to pay cash for selected items; otherwise, it was reluctantly accepted, even by Keynes with his aversion to borrowing at interest, that it might be necessary to use 3(c) credit arrangements for a limited time or for a limited sum.[142] On further reflection, the Treasury then instructed its Washington representative, Mr R H Brand, to seek credit as far as possible, but to do so on 3(c) terms as a 'last resort' and with the Americans' 'agreement' that this would not affect a later, wider, settlement.[143] All this was within a few days of the Presidential Directive. As Mr Brand had expected, American officials objected. They sought immediate standardised arrangements for the many nations receiving pipe-line supplies. Warning that picking and choosing and delay might risk the availability of 3(c) credit terms, they stopped the loading of supplies for Britain.[144]

A strong remonstrance from the Prime Minister brought a resumption of loading, and re-assurance from the President.[145] Even so supplies occasionally stuttered embarrassingly.[146] On financing, Keynes and Mr Leo T Crowley,* the Foreign Economic Administrator, faced both ways. Formally, after offsets from continued supplies from Britain, 3(c) terms would apply, but informally, it was understood that their precise nature would be decided later. This understanding relaxed without completely removing anxiety. The 'bogey' that the cost of winding-up Lend-Lease (some items of which proved to be more substantial than anticipated) might seriously compromise the terms of post-war aid, haunted the near-three months of negotiations almost to the end. It was then provided, to leap a chapter ahead momentarily, that the financing of the net amounts estimated to be due under various heads should form part of the wider settlement.[147]

---

* CROWLEY, Leo T, (d 1972); first Chairman Federal Deposit Insurance Corporation 1934 – 45; Alien Property Custodian, member of President Roosevelt's Cabinet 1942 – 43; Head, Office of Economic Warfare 1943; Foreign Economic Administrator 1943 – 45.

CHAPTER 9, SOURCE REFERENCES

NB NABOB and BABOON telegrams from Washington and London respectively are cited from files T 236/453–64 (NABOBS) and T 236/465–70 (BABOONS).

1. Mr Cordell Hull, Secretary of State, to President Roosevelt, 8 September 1944, *FRUS* 1944 (1965) III, pp 53–56.

2. Thomas M Campbell and George C Herring, *The Diaries of Edward R Stettinius, Jr,* 1943–6 (New York 1975), pp 171–2,265 and CAB 65/48 (Confidential Annex for 24 November 1944).

3. 18 July 1944, WM (44) 92nd Conclusions, CAB 65/43. Meeting of Mr Morgenthau and Dr White with Chancellor and officials, 11 August 1944, T 247/51. Copy of report also in T 160/1375/3.

4. *FRUS* 1944 III, pp 53–56. In a memorandum to Mr E R Stettinius, Under Secretary of State, Mr John D Hickerson, Chief of Division of British Commonwealth Affairs, recommended that in Stage II civilian supplies should be supplied on the basis of a long-term low interest rate loan: ibid, pp 70–74, 2 November 1944. Mr Stettinius advocated that loan finance should be considered for Stage II: discussion with Mr Richard Law in July 1944, Campbell and Herring, op cit, p 93.

5. Sayers, *Financial Policy*, p 259; GEN 89/3 in CAB 78/37 and PREM 8/35 for approximate balances of certain countries at end-June 1945.

6. Sayers, op cit, pp 252–3. Fuller account in Treasury and India Office memorandum, Financial Relations of United Kingdom and India, IF(43) 4, 27 August 1943, CAB 91/5, also in Fourth Report from the Select Committee on National Expenditure 1944–5, *BPP* 1944–5 (84) III.

7. Sayers, op cit, pp 252–73 *passim.*

8. According to Mr L S Amery, Secretary of State for India, Mr Churchill spoke vigorously in the War Cabinet about 'monstrous injustice' 'the one black spot in our arrangements for the financing of the war' and of 'an unbearable burden on the backs of British work people' — *The Transfer of Power*, III (1971), 26 September 1942, document 40, pp 49–50, and IV (1973), 27 July 1943, document 61, p 125. For Lord Cherwell's views, see memorandum and records of meetings of Committee on Indian Financial Questions, CAB 91/5.

9. Mr Amery to Sir Kingsley Wood, Chancellor of the Exchequer, 23 September 1942, *The Transfer of Power*, III, document 14, pp 24–25, and memorandum of 17 December 1943, IF(43) 17 in CAB 91/5; Amery to the Viceroy, Lord Wavell, 10–11 February 1944, *The Transfer of Power*, IV, document 371, p 718, and 24–25 February 1944, ibid, document 399, p 756.

10. Memos 9 August 1943 in T 247/5 and 30 December 1943, IF(44) 2 in CAB 91/5.

11. Sayers, op cit, pp 252–73 *passim.*

12. The Marquess of Linlithgow, Viceroy of India, to Amery, 31 July 1942, *The Transfer of Power*, II, document 379, p 510, and 20 September 1942, document 773, pp 996–8. Sir Jeremy Raisman, addressing the War Cabinet, 6 August 1942, ibid, document 435, pp 589–90.

13. *The Transfer of Power*, II, 20 September 1942, document 773, pp 996–8; III, 3 October 1942, document 56, pp 73–74; III, 7 December 1942, document 261, pp 349–50.

14. Memoranda by Lord Keynes and Lord Catto, 17 and 30 December 1943, CAB 91/5.

15. Keynes to Waley, Catto and Sir Richard Hopkins (following a note from the Prime Minister) 24 July 1942, T 247/5; draft memorandum by Amery, 16 September 1942, *The Transfer of Power*, II, document 752, pp 973 – 4.

16. WP(42) 422 of 22 September 1942, CAB 66/53; WM(42) 129th Conclusions of 24 September 1942, CAB 65/27; Mr Churchill to the Viceroy 24 September 1942: all in *The Transfer of Power*, III, documents 12, 24, 25, pp 20, 31 – 37.

17. Amery to Viceroy, 30 October 1942, ibid, document 128, p 70.

18. Sayers, op cit, p 264 (in the second full paragraph, a printing error has put £20 million instead of $20 million).

19. Keynes to Sir Theodore Gregory, 11 June 1943, and to Sir Wilfrid Eady, 10 August 1943, T 247/5.

20. Ibid, 9 August 1943.

21. IF(44) 2 of 17 December 1943, CAB 91/5.

22. Hopkins at India Committee, 8 February 1944, IF(44) 1st, ibid.

23. Lyttleton at India Committee, 16 August 1943, IF(43) 1st, ibid.

24. Lord Cherwell, memorandum on 'Sterling Overseas Liabilities', 18 January 1944, IF(44) 4, para 16, ibid.

25. Dalton, memorandum of 5 November 1943, IF(43) 12 and meeting of India Committee, 29 November 1943, IF(43) 4th, ibid.

26. Sir John Anderson, Chancellor of the Exchequer and Mr L S Amery, 29 November 1943, ibid.

27. Ibid; Government of India, Military Finance Department to Secretary of State for India, 1 January 1944, IF(44) 3, following his inquiry of 19 December 1943, ibid.

28. Officials' report: IF(44) 15 of 18 December 1944, ibid. Report by MPs, Fourth Report of Select Committee on National Expenditure, 1944 – 5, *BPP* 1944 – 5 (84) III.

29. IF(44) 5 of 15 March 1944 and IF(44) 12 of 19 July 1944, CAB 91/5.

30. Ibid, IF(44) 4th Meeting, 20 December 1944, and IF(45) 1st Meeting, 16 January 1945.

31. Eady to Keynes, 16 March 1945, T 236/436.

32. Mr Clarke's draft memorandum, 'Settlement of our external financial obligations', 7 March 1945, ibid.

33. Eady to Mr T Padmore, private secretary to the Chancellor, 21 March 1945, ibid. Clarke's memorandum, 15 March, on 'Our External Financial Obligations' and explanatory note, ibid.

34. 13 April, ibid.

35. Viscount Wavell to Mr Amery, Secretary of State for India, 30 January 1945, document 240 in *The Transfer of Power*, V (1974), p 491.

36. Chancellor of the Exchequer at meeting of India Committee of War Cabinet, 14 May 1945, ibid, document 449, p 1033, and Report by Committee on 'India: Industrialisation and Commercial Discrimination', 19 May, ibid, document 456, p 1051.

37. Mr R A Butler in paper for India Committee, 13 April 1945, ibid, document 391, p 882; Amery to Wavell, 28 July 1945, ibid, document 640, p 1298.

38. 31 January 1942 in T 236/302, which also includes post-war forecasts made during 1941. Later drafts of January 1942 memorandum, 7 July 1942, ibid, and March 1943, ibid and T 247/30.

39. Memorandum and Supplementary Note, 'Our Prospective Dollar Balances', 10 September 1942, in T 247/74.

40. 27 October 1943, CAB 56/31.

41. 'Notes on External Finance in the Post-Japanese Armistice Transitional Period', 7–11 January 1944, T 236/303; copy also in T 247/55, *JMK* XXIV, pp 1–18.

42. Treasury memorandum included in paper on 'Problems of the Transitional Period', January 1944, CAB 56/31.

43. Meetings in March 1944, T 236/303.

44. Mr E R Rowe-Dutton to Sir David Waley, 13 April 1944, T 160/1270.

45. 'Our Financial Problem in the Transition', 16 May 1944, T 236/436, T 236/304; revised version for Ministers, entitled 'The Problem of our External Finance in the Transition', 6 June 1944, T 236/304. T 247/55, T 160/1270/Annexe 1, and *JMK* XXIV, pp 34–65 (dated 12 June); 'Statistics bearing on the dimensions of the United Kingdom's problem of external finance in the Transition', 28 July 1944, T160/1375/3 and *JMK* XXIV, pp 76–97 (dated 7 August); 'Decisions of Policy affecting the financial position in Stages II and III', 28 September 1944, T 236/436, T 160/1375/5 and T 247/124 and *JMK* XXIV, pp 114–26.

46. Talks in London, 16 April 1944, Campbell and Herring, *Diaries of Stettinius,* p 55; UK Ambassador in Washington, telegram 2793 to London, 27 May, T 247/124.

47. Sir Wilfrid Eady, 4 May 1944, T 236/439; Mr A T K Grant, 2 June, T 160/1375/1.

48. Note of Chancellor's meeting with Mr Stettinius, 19 April 1944; telegrams 2793 and 2794 of 27 May, Washington to London, T 247/124; Keynes's report to Prime Minister on meeting with MPs 27 April, T 236/439; *FRUS* 1944 III (1965), p 49; Campbell and Herring, *Diaries*, pp 58, 93.

49. Tel 2794 of 27 May 1944, T 247/124 (and also T 160/1375/1).

50. Ibid, papers and telegrams.

51. Tel 3531 of 30 June 1944, Washington to London, T 160/1375/1 (also in T 247/124 and T 231/365); letter from Brand to Sir Richard Hopkins, 29 June, ibid.

52. Ibid, tel 3888 of 19 July 1944, Washington to London; Campbell and Herring, *Diaries*, p 93.

53. T 236/304.

54. Memorandum of 22 May 1944, T 247/55.

55. Memorandum of 22 May 1944, ibid.

56. Memorandum of 22 May 1944, ibid.

57. Memorandum of 25 May 1944, ibid.

58. Meetings of 24 & 25 May 1944, ibid and T 160/1270/Annexe 1.

59. 'The Problem of our External Finance in the Transition', 6 June 1944, T 247/55 and T 236/304; Ministers' meeting, 14 June 1944, T 247/55 and T 160/1270/Annexe 1.

60. Ministers' meeting 21 June 1944, ibid and ibid. Although sterling balances were not noted as having been discussed at this meeting, one of those present, Mr Harcourt Johnstone, Secretary to the Department of Overseas Trade, shortly afterwards wrote to the Chancellor of the Exchequer to support repudiation (unless there were to be pooling of gains and losses). Sir John Anderson's reply once again firmly rejected that course. Exchange of letters, 23 & 28 June 1944, T 160/1270/Annexe 1.

61. WP(44) 360 of 1 July 1944, CAB 66/52, and WM(44) 93, Minute 2 of 18 July 1944, CAB 65/43.

62. Sir David Waley to Mr C F Cobbold of the Bank of England, 31 May 1944, T 231/155. Meetings from 7 June to 27 September, ibid. Correspondence and papers relating to Committee in T 236/61 and T 160/1270/Annexe 1.

63. Lord Catto, Governor of the Bank, to Sir Richard Hopkins, 5 July 1944, & Bank's memorandum of 7 July, in T 160/1270/Annexe 1.

64. Ibid; drafts in T 236/155 and T 236/61.

65. Keynes to Waley & Hopkins, 13 August 1944, T 160/1270/Annexe 1. The version in *JMK* XXIV, pp 66–69, was a draft with acerbic comments in its second paragraph on the Bank of England; these were omitted from the final paper.

66. Bank and Treasury views in T 160/1270/Annexe 1.

67. Robbins, *Journal,* 13, 15, 19, 31 July 1944.

68. Cf Mr A W Snelling's report on the Bretton Woods Conference, paragraph 8(a), DO 35/1216.

69. Eady to Hopkins from Bretton Woods, 22 July 1944, T 231/365.

70. J M Blum, *From the Morgenthau Diaries,* III, *Years of War* 1941–45 (Boston, Mass. 1967), p 371. 'Fala' was President Roosevelt's pet dog.

71. Reports of meetings of 19 & 23 October 1944, T 247/63.

72. Keynes to Mr F G Lee, 23 January 1945, T 160/1375/6; *JMK* XXIV, pp 250–2.

73. 'The Washington Negotiations for Lend-Lease in Stage II', WP(45) 24 of 9 January 1945, CAB 66/60; *JMK* XXIV, pp 192–223 (dated 12 December 1944). See also Hancock & Gowing, *British War Economy,* pp 529–33; Hall, *North American Supply,* pp 443–7; Sayers, *Financial Policy,* pp 470–3. A pungent account of the stress and strains and achievements of the negotiations was given by Mr F G Lee of the Treasury Mission in Washington in a letter to Mr F E Harmer at the Treasury in London, 6 December 1944: T 160/1375; *JMK* XXIV, pp 185–92.

74. Meeting of 9 January 1945, T 231/156; proposal for special report, 'The Washington Negotiations . . .', WP(45) 24, paragraph 43: CAB 66/60.

75. Report of Judge Samuel Rosenman's discussions at the Treasury, 7 March 1945, T 236/449; *JMK* XXIV, pp 253–5; *FRUS* 1945 III, pp 28–29.

76. 'Overseas Financial Arrangements in Stage III', 18 March 1945, T 247/49. 'Overseas Financial Policy in Stage III', 3 April 1945, ibid; 'Overseas Financial Policy in Stage III', 15 May 1945, circulated to the War Cabinet as WP(45) 301, CAB 66/65.

77. Eady to Keynes on convertibility, 27 March 1945, and E R Rowe-Dutton to Keynes on sterling balances, 3 April 1945; Treasury officials' discussion on Stage III, 18 April 1945: T 236/449.

78. 15 March 1945, T 236/436.

79. Ibid, Appendix B on sterling balances.

80. 18 March 1945, T 236/449.

81. WP(45) 301 of 15 May 1945, CAB 66/65.

82. In a note to Eady on 16 January 1945, Keynes had pointed out that 'only 15 per cent, and at the very outside 25 per cent of our imports' came from sources with which satisfactory bilateral arrangements might be possible, although greater availability of shipping in Stage III could raise the proportion: T 247/2.

83. Paras 21–23 of 'Overseas Financial Policy in Stage III', dated 3 April 1945, in T 247/49, were reproduced with the same numbering in the Cabinet paper of the same title, WP(45) 301 of 15 May 1945, CAB 66/65. These paragraphs were severely critical of the financial contributions to the war of Australia, New Zealand and South Africa.

84. 'If by some sad geographical slip the American Air Force (it is too late now to hope for much from the enemy) were to destroy every factory on the North-East Coast and in Lancashire (at an hour when the Directors were sitting there and no one else), we should have nothing to fear...', WP(45) 301, para 8.

85. Brand to Keynes on 'Stage III and the Twilight of Lend-Lease', 5 June 1945, T 236/449.

86. Mr F G Lee at Treasury meeting, 29 May 1945, ibid.

87. Winston S Churchill, *The Second World War*, VI (London, 1954), p 497, in a message to President Harry S Truman, 11 May 1945.

88. Keynes in Treasury discussion 29 May 1945, and in memorandum on Stage III, 21 June 1945, T 236/449.

89. Minute (drafts) from Chancellor to Prime Minister, 28–29 June 1945, ibid. It may be recalled that on 26 July 1945, nine days after the opening of the Potsdam Conference, the Labour victory in the general election resulted in the replacement by Mr C R Attlee of Mr Winston S Churchill as Prime Minister, and by Mr H Dalton of Sir John Anderson as Chancellor of the Exchequer.

90. Sir Wilfrid Eady at Treasury meeting 18 March 1945, and Mr E R Rowe-Dutton's memorandum of 3 April, T 236/449; Keynes's memorandum of 18 March on 'Overseas Financial Arrangements in Stage III', paragraphs 25, ibid and paragraph 33 of the memorandum of 3 April, circulated as a Cabinet paper, 'Overseas Financial Policy in Stage III', WP(45) 301 of 15 May, CAB 66/65.

91. Mr E R Rowe-Dutton's memorandum of 3 April 1945 on Keynes's memorandum of 18 March, T 236/449.

92. 'Stage III', 23 July 1945, T 236/437.

93. 'Financial Policy in Stage III', 25 June 1945, ibid.

94. R H Brand to Eady and Keynes, 20 July 1945, ibid.

95. Ibid, Note of meeting in the Treasury, 20 July 1945, para 4, and also memorandum by Eady to Brand and Keynes of 23 July 1945.

96. Ibid, Note of a meeting in the Treasury, 20 July 1945, and memorandum on 'The Present Overseas Financial Position of UK', 20 July 1945, paragraph 31.

97. Further draft of 'The Present Overseas Financial Position...', 13 August 1945, paragraphs 28 and 35, T 247/50. This was confusingly subtitled '...a first draft', presumably because it was the basis of the (unnumbered) memorandum circulated to the Cabinet on 17 August by the Chancellor, in which the amount of aid to be sought was also put at $5 billion: 'Proposals to the US for financial assistance to follow after Lend-Lease', paragraph 14, CAB 124/913.

98. Brand, Memo to Eady and Keynes, 20 July 1945, paragraph 5, T 236/450.

99. 'The Present Overseas Financial Position', 20 July 1945, paragraphs 26 and 27 (xi), T 236/437.

100. Memo by Mr C F Cobbold of meeting at Treasury, 23 July 1945, draft report of meeting by Mr H K Goschen, and final report of meeting, in T 236/449. Report of meeting also in T 236/437. Proposals about availability of sterling in Keynes's memo, 'The Present Financial Position of UK', 13 August, paragraph 30 (x), reproduced as paragraph 12(x) of the Chancellor's Cabinet Memorandum of 17 August (unnumbered), 'Proposals to the US for financial assistance to follow after Lend-Lease' in CAB 124/913.

101. 'The Present Overseas Financial Position of UK', draft of 20 July 1945, paragraphs 27 and 28 on page 12 (further paragraphs on page 16 are also numbered similarly, in error), in T 236/437.

102. $4 billion in further draft of memorandum, 13 August 1945, paragraphs 28–30, T 247/50; *JMK* XXIV, pp 338–94. $5 billion in the Chancellor's (unnumbered) memorandum to the Cabinet, 17 August, 'Proposals to the US...', paragraphs 10–12, CAB 124/913.

103. 'Proposals for Financial Arrangements in the Sterling Area and between the US and UK to follow after Lend-Lease', 12 September 1945, paragraphs 38–39: PREM 8/35 and GEN 89/1, CAB 78/37; *JMK* XXIV, pp 442–7.

104. Letters from Sir Arnold Overton of the Board of Trade to Keynes, 26 May 1945; Eady to Keynes, 9 June; Eady to Overton, 22 June; Joint memorandum by the Board of Trade and Economic Section. 'Overseas Financial Policy in Stage III', 9 July; meeting in Treasury, 18 July; 'The Present Overseas Financial Position of UK', 20 July, paragraph 28 (vi) on page 14: T 236/436. Draft memo, 13 August, paragraph 30(v) on page 14, T 247/50.

105. Chancellor's memo, 'Proposals...' 12 August 1945, paragraph 12(v).

106. Meeting in the Treasury, 25 July 1945, T 236/437 (copy of report also in T 236/450).

107. Ibid, notes by Mr C F Cobbold of the Bank of England of a meeting in the Treasury, 20 July 1945 to discuss a memorandum from him; meeting at Treasury, 25 July.

108. Meetings of Mr W L Clayton with US and United Kingdom officials, London, 3 and 14 August 1945, *FRUS* 1945 VI, pp 80, 98–100.

109. Discussions at Treasury meetings, 18 and 20 July 1945, T 236/437 (copy of report also in T 236/450).

110. In particular, there is unsatisfactory treatment of the critical issues of the sterling balances, and the proposed convertibility of sterling in the distinguished, widely-used books by Harrod, *The Life of John Maynard Keynes*, chapter XIV, and Gardner, *Sterling-Dollar Diplomacy,* chapter X.

111. 'Our Overseas Financial Prospects', 14 August 1945, CP(45) 112, and unnumbered memorandum 'Proposals to the US...', 17 August 1945. It should be noted that in what he emphasises is 'only the most summary indication' of the case that Keynes was to take to Washington in *September* 1945, the illuminating account by Professor R S Sayers of the Cabinet memorandum of *May* ('Overseas Financial Policy in Stage III', WP(45)301), does not incorporate the substantial alterations made to it during the following three months: Sayers, *Financial Policy*, pp 483–6.

112. 'Proposals to the US...', paragraph 14, CAB 124/913.

113. 'Our Overseas Financial Prospects', 13 August 1945, paragraphs 27 & 28, T 247/50 and also paragraphs 27 & 28 of similarly entitled Cabinet Paper of 14 August, CP(45)112, CAB 129/1.

114. CM(45)23rd Conclusions, 16 August 1945, CAB 128/1.

115. 'Proposals to the US...', paragraphs 12(x), 11, 10, 14, 12(ix).

116. Ibid, paragraphs 10, 17.

117. Ibid, paragraph 12(x).

118. Ibid, paragraph 17.

119. Unnumbered cyclostyled memorandum 'Economic Relations with the United States', 17 August 1945, T 236/437 and T 236/380. Sir Wilfrid Eady, in a note to Sir Edward Bridges on 28 August, said that the memorandum had 'not been circulated to the Cabinet or to the inner group of Ministers'. Copies had gone to the President of the Board of Trade and to the Foreign Office. Eady said that 'I do not think the Prime Minister has seen the paper, nor has the Lord President': T 236/437.

120. 'Proposals', paragraphs 19, 22.

121. Ibid, paragraph 24.

122. Discussion at meeting in Treasury, 29 May 1945, T 236/449.

123. Ibid.

124. Ibid; and 451 REMAC of 11 June, Washington to London, and Brand's letter to Keynes, 12 June 1945.

125. Ibid, Keynes's memorandum on Stage III, 21 June 1945, T 236/449.

126. Extract from summary of conversation at Potsdam, 18 July 1945, T 236/450; telegrams 7650 and 7653 of 19 July, AVIA 38/1120.

127. Keynes to Eady and others, 13 June 1945, T 236/449.

128. 'Memorandum of Conversation' between British and US representatives, London, 3 August 1945, *FRUS* 1945 VI, pp 79–87. This exchange in London may have been a source of the confusion of the $6 billion of the potential *deficit* with the lower amount of *aid* being sought, appearing in Harrod, *Life of . . . Keynes*, p 596, and in Gardner, *Sterling-Dollar Diplomacy,* p 202. Another source may have been Keynes's allusion to the deficit in his exposition at the opening of the Washington negotiations: US-United Kingdom Top Committee, minutes of second meeting, 13 September 1945, GEN 80/20 in CAB 130/6 and *JMK* XXIV, pp 466–72. That an impression existed in Washington of $6 billion of aid being at issue could be inferred from mention of that amount, during a meeting there two days later of Commonwealth and Indian diplomats, in a question from the Australian representative to Keynes, who did not comment upon the reference: AVIA 38/1118, reported also in DO 35/1216.

129. Aid would not be available for occupation troops: Acting Secretary of State, Mr Joseph C Grew to US Ambassador in United Kingdom, 1 August 1945, *FRUS* 1945 VI pp 77–78. Dollar payment was required for certain military equipment from 1 August: Hall, *North American Supply*, p 458. Twelve days later, with the Japanese surrender awaited, Lend-Lease shipments of munitions were halted: ibid, p 460.

130. Telegrams USLON 117 of 13 August 1945 and 120 of 14 August from British Supply Mission in Washington to London, AVIA 38/1120; comment of Chairman (Sir Henry Self) at meeting of British Supply Council in N. America, Washington, 21 August, AVIA 38/1118.

131. Ibid, statement by Mr Leo T Crowley, Foreign Economic Administrator, 24 August 1945; also in GEN 80/7.

132. Hall, *North American Supply*, p 485.

133. Report of Washington meeting, NABOB 65 of 20 September 1945; London meeting, 24 August, CAB 124/913.

134. NABOBS 27 of 5 September 1945 and 67 of 20 September.

135. Meeting of officials in Treasury, 21 August 1945, T 236/1684; meeting of senior Ministers and officials, 23 August, T 236/437, & *JMK* XXIV, pp 420–51.

136. *FRUS* 1945 VI, pp 107–8, 20 August 1945.

137. Ibid, pp 103–6, 18 and 20 August 1945.

138. Ibid, p 124, n39, letter from Mr Clayton to Mr Brand, 13 November 1945.

139. NABOB 109, 2 October 1945.

140. Secretary of State, Mr James F Byrnes to Clayton, *FRUS* 1945 VI, p 106, 20 August 1945.

141. BABOON 1 of 29 August 1945 and 9 of 31 August.

142. BABOON 1 of 29 August 1945, CAMER 593 of 27 August, HM Treasury to Treasury representative in Washington, AVIA 38/1118.

143. BABOON 9 of 31 August 1945.

144. NABOB 11 of 31 August 1945.

145. Prime Minister's telegram for President Truman, no 9086 of 1 September 1945 and President's reply, telegram no 6075 from British Embassy in Washington to Foreign Office, 6 September 1945, PREM 8/35, and also *FRUS* 1945 VI, pp 113–15, 117.

146. American food supplies to an RAF unit in Germany were suspended: BABOON 35 of 15 September 1945.

147. NABOBS 68 and 69 of 21 September 1945, 58 of 14 September, 78 and 79 of 24 September, 191 of 20 October, and 404 of 27 November.

CHAPTER 10

Negotiating the American Loan of 1945

(1) THE BRITISH AND AMERICAN APPROACHES

During the second half of August 1945, whilst undertaking their holding operation over the rundown of Lend-Lease, Ministers and officials were simultaneously and urgently striving to devise a firm policy for the imminent Stage III negotiations. That they succeeded only partially is not surprising. To unavoidable weakness in relation to the US Administration was added hesitation about what to seek or even to discuss. Of the four main issues that the negotiations must embrace, London wished to go slowly on post-war monetary plans and commercial policy, and to concentrate first on immediate financial issues together with the Lend-Lease settlement. To the Americans, however, all four issues were intertwined within the Article VII framework, in which commercial policy was their dominant concern. Moreover, they appeared to consider that the essential issues could be quickly settled in principle. London, however, had always expected more protracted, more difficult negotiations. In this conflict of approaches, the negotiations were to develop unfavourably, and were to stumble repeatedly before their unwelcome outcome for Britain.

(2) APPREHENSIONS, AND THE INEVITABILITY OF BORROWING

British apprehensions and intentions took shape during the last ten days of August. There was an intense round of discussions amongst British officials in Washington, and amongst officials and Ministers in London. By this time, the principal papers had circulated, apart from the Chancellor's memorandum on prerequisites in commercial policy (above pp 210 and 247–8). Mr Dalton was likely, however, to have let his views be widely known, and in any case their essence was to be aired by Keynes at a crucial meeting on 23 August, which was to settle the lines on which negotiations with the US for financial assistance should be conducted.

The pessimism of three senior Ministers was made explicit in a memorandum from them to the Prime Minister immediately before that meeting.[1] The Ministers were the Foreign Secretary, Mr Ernest Bevin; the Chancellor of the Exchequer, Mr Hugh Dalton; and the

President of the Board of Trade, Sir Stafford Cripps. They feared that American help would be in the form of a credit, which would involve 'a fairly high rate of interest and also acquiescence in Bretton Woods and their commercial policy'. The alternative to acceptance of such terms would be to rely on Britain's own resources and on those of the Empire and 'our immediate friends'. Whilst they affirmed that 'we should hate being driven to adopt an exclusive policy' (in effect, Keynes's 'Starvation Corner'), they believed that knowledge of its implications, and presumably exposition of them to the Americans, would provide negotiators with a bargaining counter so far lacking; the Ministers recognised that 'in the end we may have to come to some arrangement with the United States'. Such knowledge would also be a guide to necessary action should negotiations nevertheless fail. Accordingly they urged that a secret inquiry be instituted forthwith to assess what such a policy would involve.

Treasury advice on the Ministers' memorandum was that there was no immediate alternative to borrowing from the US.[2] This would be the case even if reliance on non-American sources were to be attempted. Indeed, the inescapable need to borrow during 1946 might preclude, or at least render more difficult, early resort to a 'non-American' policy. Such a policy would depend on securing 'somehow' the export of scarce goods to the supplying countries if they were not to demand dollars no less scarce in order to purchase goods from the USA instead. Further, it would be necessary to cut military expenditure abroad 'very drastically' and to finance what remained by persuading overseas countries to hold yet more sterling. On the most favourable assumptions, however, there would still be a deficit with the US in 1946, which the Treasury put at around $1,000 million (£250 million). The alternative of going without certain supplies altogether in order to avoid that deficit would involve not just sustained but increased deprivation: in personal consumption and in the cessation of imports of manufacturing requirements from the USA. It would certainly be reasonable to seek to restore production to pre-war levels during 1947 and to raise the proportion available for export, which had been much lower in 1938 (fifteen per cent) than in 1913 (forty per cent); but increased production would not of itself guarantee external equilibrium. It would not even be enough to re-direct engineering output towards exports on a scale not so far considered. It would also be necessary to secure export markets by bilateral, discriminatory measures that the Americans might regard 'as something like economic warfare calling for retaliation'; yet no commitment on such matters could be made to the USA. Much, however, would depend on the outcome of negotiations with the USA and with other countries. Reiterating that borrowing was unavoidable for 1946, the Treasury concluded that, should this have to be undertaken on commercial terms, everything must be done to reduce the need to do so again for 1947.

(3) THE BRITISH TACTIC

Before these comments had been formally presented, immediate policy had been decided at a major meeting on 23 August. The Prime Minister was in the chair. Five other Ministers, including the three responsible for the memorandum, were present as well as five senior officials, the Ambassador to Washington, and Keynes, whose proposals for the conduct of negotiations were the meeting's main concern. Those proposals followed the lines of recent discussions, with an important clarification of the preferred form for American aid: a free grant of $4 or $5 billion, which would neither be repayable nor bear interest.[3]

It was evidently realised that to expect an outright grant was over-sanguine. If there was optimism about aid, it attached to broad prospects rather than to precise details. A week before the meeting, in a memorandum to Treasury colleagues, Keynes had underlined this.[4] In particular, he stressed the demanding character of negotiations ahead. Acknowledging as justified the apprehensions of the Foreign Secretary, Mr E Bevin, lest Britain be driven to accept unwise international obligations, he dismissed as quite out of sympathy with the publicly entrenched attitudes of the US Administration the bolder hopes which had momentarily tempted Mr Bevin towards optimism; those hopes, strengthened by discussions with a leading American financier, Mr Winthrop W Aldrich*, had been that it might be possible to avoid, at least temporarily, all commitments on the Bretton Woods monetary plans and on commercial policy. Keynes declared, not just that such commitments would be required, but that Britain could meet them. The Bretton Woods plans incorporated sufficient safeguards to be workable even in the event of an American slump; the associated and necessary reservations on commercial policy, particularly control of imports, would involve 'a stiff tussle', but that could end largely in Britain's favour. Keynes argued that Anglo-American negotiations over the details of possible commitments should take second place, in point of timing, to those over Britain's financial problems; these were particularly acute with the impending demise, after a brief prolongation into the peace, of Lend-Lease. He stressed, however, that the form of financial assistance remained 'one matter of extreme difficulty', and emphasised that initially the Americans would 'certainly' offer some kind of interest-bearing, repayable credit.

---

* ALDRICH, Winthrop Williams (1885–1974); Chairman, Chase National Bank, 1934–53; US Ambassador to the Court of St. James, 1953–57.

Talk of an outright free grant, without interest and non-repayable, can be seen to resemble not so much serious beliefs as an attractive marker, to compare the most favourable possible outcome with the least favourable. Thus, at the meeting of Ministers and officials, Keynes advised that American terms 'might vary from an out and out grant in aid to a commercial credit'. More precisely, even though it was realised that a grant might have to be 'dressed up' as a credit, he stressed that Mr Clayton was thinking on different (ie, more rigorous) lines. Thus, whilst he recommended that anything other than a free grant should be taken only after prolonged consideration by Ministers, he hesitated to support the preference of the President of the Board of Trade for a grant and nothing else. Mr R H Brand was sceptical not only of the chance of securing a free grant but even of the wisdom of seeking one; he gained 'general approval' for an approach that would rely on 'the strength of our case' to inspire an American offer of aid in the form Britain desired. This unfortunately left open the question of what to do should American reactions be different.

The briefing, as the meeting of 23 August may be regarded, encompassed policy on the likely accompaniments of financial arrangements that would include generous aid and a satisfactory settlement of Lend-Lease. Thus, it was at first contemplated, in order to liberalise sterling area payments, that an offer should be made to settle sterling balances along lines previously considered (above, pp 239 – 40, 244 – 5). An early move to more general convertibility was also envisaged. Even the cautious and respected Mr Brand had recently modified his previous scepticism about the wisdom of early convertibility[5] (above p 243). He hazarded that, dependent on the trend of the negotiations, the amount of American help, and the likelihood of sterling area support should a subsequent reversal of such policy prove necessary, then 'the balance of advantage would seem in favour of convertibility'. Britain's adoption of the Bretton Woods plans, Keynes asserted, with the meeting apparently acquiescing, would be feasible if 'not coupled with dangerous concessions under. . .commercial policy' and provided, of course, that Parliament approved. On commercial policy the meeting also appeared to accept Keynes's confident twin expectations: that no 'detailed commercial treaty' would be at issue, only the association with an American invitation to other countries to an international conference in 1946; and that 'reasonable satisfaction' could be secured over the substantial British reservations which had hitherto obstructed Anglo-American agreement on trade policy. Finally, there might be a *douceur*, something to touch American imagination, by the gift of an island, perhaps one symbolic of US heroism.[6]

Next day, in a statement to the House of Commons deploring the abrupt manner in which Lend-Lease had been ended, the Prime Minister announced that conversations were to be held immediately in

Washington to deal with the resulting problems. They were to be led on the British side by the Ambassador, the Earl of Halifax, and by Lord Keynes. Three days later, apparently with no further formal briefing – the broad objectives were presumably familiar from Keynes's memoranda – a small party left by ship.[7] After a brief visit to Ottawa, they reached Washington on 7 September, and negotiations opened formally four days later.[8]

The proposed tactic was twofold and was clear enough. First the British case should be so presented that its strength would lead the Americans to suggest what was needed, sparing the Mission from making specific and possibly embarrassing proposals. This involved the hope not only of a free grant but also of American assistance in the settlement of sterling balances. Only later, towards the end of September, was London to modify the decision of the 'briefing', and to instruct the Mission to try to defer offering written proposals, and so to conduct discussions that suggestions for drastic treatment of sterling balances should appear to come from the American side (below pp 279 – 81). The aim was to seek at the outset, not unnaturally, preferred British goals. That did not involve blind faith that relatively easy terms for aid, such as a free grant or an interest-free loan, were in prospect. Rather, it reflected a judgement that the chances of obtaining such terms, given the sympathy expressed by some Americans, should be explored at the commencement of negotiations.[9] Subsequently, it would be unsurprising for the British so to manoeuvre that disagreeable terms, even if regarded as broadly reasonable in London, should nevertheless appear to be of American inspiration.

This part of the tactic succeeded so well in one respect that some subsequent and apparently authoritative comment has inferred, not only that Keynes believed a grant to be possible, but also that he persuaded Ministers and officials to share his supposed enthusiasm.[10] Given, however, his evident hesitations at the 'briefing', some further explanation is necessary, and it appears to lie in Keynes's discussions, *en route* for Washington, in Ottawa.[11] There, Mr Graham Towers*, Governor of the Bank of Canada, urged the desirability of the policy that Keynes himself had explicitly rejected a few weeks earlier, namely to seek assistance of $8 billion: $3 billion as a grant, and $5 billion as a line of credit if needed. Although Keynes's own most recent memorandum a few days earlier had spoken of seeking aid of $5 billion, he felt that 'basically Towers' advice is very good indeed': a feeling that he himself, unlike some in London, was not long to sustain.

It was none the less in London itself that responsibility for what was to prove an unsatisfactory approach to the negotiations lay. There was

---

* TOWERS, Graham Ford (1897–1975); Governor, Bank of Canada 1934–54.

at the time, and remains still, occasion for surprise at the restricted composition of the 'briefing' meeting. In contrast with some earlier discussions on Stage III, there was no representative of the Bank of England, which opposed resort to American aid and acceptance of Bretton Woods. There was no Board of Trade official present, nor were there representatives of the Economic Section, from both of which groups would have come more informed and more pessimistic views on the prospects of agreement on commercial policy than the meeting heard.[12]

It was indeed this second part of the British tactic which proved to be, very soon, especially questionable and frail. It was an attempt to defy the long-familiar American view of commercial policy as the hinge of any financial settlement. On the day after the 'briefing' meeting, Mr Clayton lunched with Keynes, Brand, and Eady, and handed them a paper with the proposed agenda for the forthcoming discussions; the heading noted that they would 'take place within the framework of Article VII of the Master Lend-Lease Agreement' (ie, for Britain, the Mutual Aid Agreement of February 1942). This clearly indicated that commercial policy was to be a central issue. The British representatives agreed that there could be concurrent discussions of the other two groups of topics: Lend-Lease and associated matters, and financial problems (transitional finance, sterling area arrangements, and 'convertibility – anticipating the Bretton Woods formula'). They sought to avoid, however, agreeing that a separate group of negotiators should be provided to deal with commercial policy; Keynes held to the line he had expounded to Ministers and colleagues the previous day, that only general,not detailed issues were involved. The aim, Eady subsequently reported to the Board of Trade, was to avoid the risk that 'a head-on collision' over commercial policy might hamper financial negotiations, by the simple device of not including in the Washington delegation those competent to undertake commercial policy discussions. If that ploy succeeded, commercial policy would not arise until later, when there would be time enough to despatch experts.[13]

Eady's views were not wholly acceptable to the Board of Trade, which arranged that one of its senior officials, Mr J R C Helmore* should join the Mission as an observer.[14] This arrangement fell far short of satisfying American insistence on the priority of commercial policy. The day before the 'briefing' meeting, that is, two days before the small Anglo-American group discussed the proposed

---

* HELMORE, James Reginald Carroll, KCMG 1948, KCB 1954 (1906–72); Private Secretary to the President of the Board of Trade, 1934–37; Under Secretary Board of Trade, 1946; Second Secretary Board of Trade, 1946–52.

agenda for the Washington negotiations, Mr James F Byrnes*, the Secretary of State, had emphasised the US position to the Ambassador in London: that the grant of a credit to Britain would require a reduction not only of wartime restrictions on trade, but also of those existing before the war.[15] Responding approvingly a few days later to a report by Clayton and a colleague, on discussions with the British, including those on the proposed agenda, he declared that[16]

'The British should understand that not only are the arrangements [over financial aid and commercial policy] tied together but financial conversations would be fruitless unless conducted simultaneously with and as a part of larger discussions. . . '

In London, Mr Harry Hawkins immediately called at the Foreign Office 'in considerable distress' to urge that the Mission include forthwith leading experts on commercial policy.[17] The Treasury and the Board of Trade, in a joint memorandum of 31 August, concluded that given the newness of the Government, the demands on Ministers' time, and the need to ponder Clayton's proposals, delay could scarcely be avoided; the problem was how best to argue with the US Administration for delay. A meeting of much the same group of Ministers as previously (but with the Financial Secretary to the Treasury, Mr W Glenvil Hall[†] representing the Chancellor) considered this memorandum, under the Prime Minister's chairmanship. The President of the Board of Trade, Sir Stafford Cripps, whilst acknowledging American determination, set against that Keynes's belief that initial concentration on financial issues, in order to explain Britain's position more fully, would modify American attitudes on trade questions. When the Foreign Secretary, Mr Ernest Bevin, and the Lord President of the Council, Mr Herbert Morrison[‡], expressed doubts about Keynes's chances of success, the President of the Board of Trade stressed the practical impossibility of sending to Washington the trade experts needed to undertake preparations in London; the Prime Minister secured the other Ministers' agreement to this stand. It was therefore resolved to advise the Americans that full discussion of commercial policy must

---

* BYRNES, James F (d 1972); US Senator 1941–43; Justice of the Supreme Court 1941–42; Director of Economic Stabilisation 1942–43; Director of War Mobilisation 1943–45; Secretary of State 1945–47.
† HALL, William Glenvil (1887–1962); Financial Secretary, HM Treasury, 1945–50.
‡ MORRISON, Herbert Stanley, 1st Baron 1959 (1888–1965); Minister of Supply, 1940; Home Secretary and Minister of Home Security, 1940–45; Deputy Prime Minister, 1945–51; Lord President of the Council and Leader of the House of Commons, 1945–51; Secretary of State for Foreign Affairs, 1951.

be deferred; trade specialists would go to Washington 'as soon as practicable'; and contact on commercial policy issues would be maintained through the Board of Trade's observer.[18]

(4) LONDON VIEWS AND WASHINGTON VIEWS

What were the prospects for achieving British aims? Arrived in Washington, Keynes reported that '...the atmosphere is perhaps rather too good.. One's experience in Washington has always been that when things look beastliest all will be glowing three months hence, and vice versa...'.[19] The Washington atmosphere soon proved discouraging. The official primarily blamed for the Lend-Lease tangles (above, pp 251–3) remained for a little time yet as a standing obstacle to sympathetic American treatment of British needs. This was Mr Leo T Crowley, known amongst the British as 'the Baboon' and as the inspirer of the code name for the major cable series during the negotiations ('Baboon' from London to Washington, and then, by the usual approximate reversal, 'Nabob' from Washington to London). Of the two principal negotiators on the American side, Judge Fred M Vinson*, the recently appointed Secretary of the Treasury, did not evoke much *rapport* with the British. With the Assistant Secretary of State, Mr Clayton, British relations were easier, but he was a formidable negotiator with his near-religious belief in free trade, and with his determination to couple any financial aid to clear requirements for the reduction of trade and exchange restrictions that had grown up during and before the war. Behind Vinson and Clayton were the numerous officials of State Department and Treasury, with specialist groups assessing the likely trends in Britain's balance of payments and her financial needs. Then there was Congress, anxious to return to 'normal', highly suspicious of Imperial Preference and of the sterling area, set on reducing taxation, and determined to scrutinise closely the numerous claims from wartime allies – not from Britain alone – for financial assistance. By no means least there was the Press and American public opinion. Some influential members of the Administration were thought to be inspiring Press comment favourable to Britain, but there remained much hostility in newspaper articles. Moreover a Gallup Poll in late September was to show 60 per cent disapproval of a loan (not a grant) of $5 billion to Britain.[20]

In some respects London provided scarcely less of a problem for the British Mission than did Washington. Hitherto Keynes had prodded and pushed and pulled officials and Ministers to face disagreeable realities and to contemplate bold policies. With his

* VINSON, Frederick Moore (1890–1953); Secretary of the US Treasury, 1945–46; Chief Justice of the US from 1946.

leadership now thousands of miles away, the different groups tugged amongst themselves and at the Mission.

A small group of senior Ministers formed a Committee on Financial and Commercial Policy. In addition to holding several formal meetings, for three months they met most evenings, together with two senior Treasury officials (Sir Edward Bridges*, who was also Secretary to the Cabinet, and Sir Wilfrid Eady) and Mr Douglas Jay†, Personal Assistant to the Prime Minister.[21] The Chancellor of the Exchequer drew support from the President of the Board of Trade for prolonged resistance to credit terms. The Foreign Secretary was uneasy about any assistance with strings, and preferred either no loan, or a relatively small one on strictly commercial terms. Sir Wilfrid Eady reflected Bank of England views in his distaste for finance on credit terms, and in an increasingly determined conviction, shared by the Secretary of State for India (Lord Pethick-Lawrence‡) that an imposed settlement of sterling indebtedness was impracticable. The Lord President of the Council, advised by the Economic Section, and supported by the Secretary of State for the Dominions (Lord Addison§), was less apprehensive about Britain's ability to service a loan at interest. He favoured an agreement that would keep broadly in view the Article VII commitment to a liberal trading policy.[22]

Finally the Mission had its own problems. It was quite small, but faced a formidable range of tasks involving many technical minutiae about military and civilian supplies. There were discussions with the British and Commonwealth Military and Supply Missions, and with the Dominions and Indian diplomatic representatives in Washington.[23] The termination of Canadian Mutual Aid, and some looking ahead to the negotiations expected in Ottawa on the conclusion of those in Washington, required sometimes intricate exchanges with Canadian officials. There were press conferences and, by no means least for Keynes, a flow of Congressional and other visitors. Keynes suffered both physically, with at least one heart attack, and nervously, with phases of acute irritability which London's misunderstandings or stubbornness did not soothe. He had never been so

---

* BRIDGES, Edward, KCB 1939, 1st Baron 1957 (1892–1969); Secretary to the Cabinet, 1938–46; Permanent Secretary, HM Treasury, 1945–56.

† JAY, Douglas Patrick Thomas (1907–   ); Assistant Secretary, Ministry of Supply, 1941–43; Principal Assistant Secretary, Board of Trade, 1943–45; Personal Assistant to Prime Minister, 1945–46; Economic Secretary to Treasury, 1947–50; Financial Secretary to Treasury, 1950–51; President of Board of Trade, 1964–67.

‡ PETHICK-LAWRENCE, Frederick William, 1st Baron, 1945 (1871–1961); Secretary of State for India and Burma, 1945–47.

§ ADDISON, Christopher, 1st Baron 1937, 1st Viscount 1945 (1869–1951); Secretary of State for Commonwealth Relations, 1945–47; Leader of House of Lords, 1945–51; Paymaster-General, 1948–49; Lord Privy Seal, 1947–51.

busy, and as the negotiations threatened to collapse was to complain that he was near the end of his reserves.[24] If the balance of evidence is that no other man could have done better or as well, the effort undoubtedly exacted a heavy personal price from Keynes.

(5) ORGANISATION

The conduct of the negotiations rested on an elaborate structure. The Mission itself had a steering committee which met formally four times during the twelve weeks or so in Washington. Jointly with the American representatives the principal arrangements involved a Combined Steering ('Top') Committee, below which were finance, lend-lease, commercial, surplus disposal and military committees. On each side the respective Administrations monitored progress and influenced negotiations. Apart from formal meetings of committees (and of sub-committees) there were numerous Anglo-American discussions at the US Treasury and at the British Embassy, as well as at the personal level. Of particular significance in determining policy, there were the many cables, letters and telephone calls between the Mission and London, besides the advice and impressions of the London atmosphere offered to the US Administration by its London Embassy.

(6) THE BRITISH CASE

During the transatlantic voyage, Keynes's further re-working[25] of his estimates yielded the figure of $5 billion as the amount of American aid required to carry Britain into 1949, when the economy might 'break even'. This averaged the rough estimates of 'a (most unlikely) minimum deficit of $4 billion' and a 'maximum which we ought not to allow ourselves to exceed', of $6 billion. Though slightly firmer than previous estimates, because the end of the war had removed the running uncertainties over Mutual Aid flows, these were necessarily speculative. The firmest seemed to be of a net overseas deficit for 1946 of $3,200 million, within a range of $2,500 – $3,500 million. Earlier estimates for 1947 and 1948 of $2,200 million and $800 million respectively brought the total to around $6 billion. This figure, and the estimate of $5 billion that it was hoped would be financed by US aid, rested on three sets of assumptions. First, there might be drawings of some $1,000 million from the gold and dollar reserves, and of some $600 million of further credit from other sterling countries. Second, imports would be kept some 23 per cent *below* the pre-war volume, and their sterling prices would be no more than doubled. Exports should rise by at least 80 per cent over their low level of 1945 during 1946; by 1949, the aim (calculated by the Economic Section to be necessary) was that this assumed level for 1946 would be rather more than doubled again to give exports some

271

50 per cent above the pre-war volume. (The estimated overall deficits also sought to take account of delayed war outgoings or receipts, as well as of continuing Government expenditures on defence and on military occupation of former enemy territory.) Third, and above all, it was assumed that indebtedness to the sterling area and to other countries could be satisfactorily controlled, and that aid would come from Canada. Since an initial release of $800 million of sterling balances was contemplated in the Keynes proposals, juggling with estimated deficits and such further drains or possible offsets produced the rounded figure of $5 billion. This was clearly the barest minimum. That sum would require strict controls on imports, and hence on domestic consumption and investment. It would have to support the gamble of an early operation of convertibility, with only a restricted access to the transitional relief originally envisaged in the Bretton Woods agreement for the International Monetary Fund; in particular it was contemplated that the United Kingdom would offer to abjure the use of discrimination in sterling area imports during the transition.

The presentation of the British case in Washington began formally with a Press Conference (12 September) and then three sessions (13, 14 & 17 September) of the Anglo-American 'Top' Committee.[26] At the Press Conference the Ambassador and Lord Keynes held broadly to the intention to state the facts of Britain's position, but not to make proposals; hints of the approach to the negotiations nevertheless emerged in the questions and answers. Keynes particularly stressed that the British preference was to work closely with the United States, and that the alternative of a more isolated, restrictive policy would be regarded, in the absence of adequate aid, as a regrettable necessity but not as in any way desirable. At the three Committee sessions, Keynes's exposition followed and elaborated that with which his colleagues and some of the Americans present were familiar. At the first, the stress was on the bleak prospects for the balance of payments. At the second it was on the unfavourable relationship between diminished overseas assets and greatly increased liabilities, and expressly on the sterling balances problem. In the final session, Keynes underlined the severe consequences of Britain's intense concentration of resources for war, concluding with an evidently impressive reference to the views of the former German production minister, Albert Speer: that that effort, probably decisive, had been markedly greater than Germany's.

Although these expositions appeared to give a promising start to negotiations, they evoked no proposal of assistance from the broadly sympathetic Americans. Indeed, their immediate reactions boxed in the hope that it would initially be enough to rely on the strength of the British case. An intervention by Mr Clayton during the second session underlined the American concern for decisive treatment of sterling balances, and that proposals should come from the British side. Mr Vinson reacted sourly to Keynes's reflections on Britain's comparatively large national debt, and to his implication that aid to Britain would impose a relatively small burden on the USA. Mr Clayton voiced a common apprehension that, notwithstanding wartime deprivation, the British standard of living, thanks to American assistance, might have improved during the war.[27] All in all, it quickly became clear, both in the negotiations and outside, that Americans were not disposed to ponder degrees of relative sacrifice, which at its most sensitive involved comparing casualties.[28] They wanted to clean up the past quickly, and to deal with the present and future.

By now seriously weakened, the British strategy soon collapsed. Not only had the hope of an American initiative on aid disappeared, but so also had that of avoiding major discussion of commercial policy. At two meetings (19 & 20 September) of the Combined Finance Committee shortly after the initial exposition of Britain's case, there was sustained pressure for Britain's representatives to quantify their problems, and to give more precise indications of treatment of the sterling balances. Keynes now aired cautiously the possibility of cancellation of around one-third of the $12 billion of such balances that were expected to have accumulated by the end of 1945. Similar pressure over the amount of aid sought by Britain brought his statement that, whilst $6 billion over the next three to five years might appear necessary, just $5 billion exclusive of the amount needed to settle Lend-Lease might suffice, even allowing for the associated risks to be taken: the risks of the minimisation of import controls, the ending of restrictions upon the convertibility of sterling countries' overseas earnings involved in the operation of the sterling area dollar pool, and of Britain's undertaking by the end of 1946 the formal obligations of the International Monetary Fund. To all this, the disappointing, unhurried, American response was a promise to gather information on the sterling balances and on Britain's prospective balance of payments in 1946.[29]

What was going wrong? In some senses, very little beyond explicable delays. Keynes himself had forecast a 'running-in' period. There was inevitably some sparring for positions. Special delaying influences were of reshuffling and resignations amongst American officials as President Truman continued to reshape the Administration inherited from the late President Roosevelt. Reporting one particular tense Anglo-American meeting, Keynes remarked of the persisting confusion about the financing of terminal Lend-Lease that '. . . our party faces a new audience every week.'[30] Yet there was something more disturbing in the evident marking time on financial discussions. This was the Administration's continuing determination that negotiations on commercial policy, and allied topics, should accompany those on finance. The intention was not that agreement on the latter should explicitly be made dependent on the former, but that there should be parallel, simultaneous negotiations. There was, however, a particular aspect of commercial policy on which Clayton was explicit and determined: that without the abolition of Imperial Preference there would be no financial assistance.[31] Preference, in American eyes, formed with the sterling area dollar pool and sterling balances a trinity of British drags on international trade.

(7) 'THE COMMERCIAL POLICY FIRST ELEVEN' GOES TO WASHINGTON

British hopes of avoiding substantial discussions on trade policy were indeed, in the second week of September and with the negotiations barely opened, about to collapse. In London the officials who had hitherto been closely involved in the earlier Anglo-American trade discussions, but who had been left behind, had been greatly disturbed by the manner in which the Mission had been arranged. They were appalled by its expectation of securing a financial settlement without a complementary commercial policy agreement. They were dismayed by Keynes's belief that he could negotiate without their expertise, he himself not having been particularly closely involved in the technical minutiae of the earlier discussions.[32] Meanwhile, American pressure was being sustained on both sides of the Atlantic. In London Mr Hawkins, disclaiming any intention to link financial and commercial matters as a means of exploiting Britain's financial weakness, continued to represent to British officials Mr Clayton's view, cabled from the USA, of the American case. That view, which Sir Percivale Liesching of the Board of Trade shared, was that a commercial policy agreement could be negotiated on its own merits. Reiterating that such negotiations must be conducted in parallel with those on finance, Clayton stressed the need for 'a United Kingdom team of equal standing to that engaged on financial policy' to be in Washington. There was a brief period, of no more than six months, providing an opportunity, which should be grasped, for securing cuts in US tariffs.[33]

In Washington there were similar pressures on the Mission. Agreeing to the establishment of an Anglo-American Committee on commercial policy, and proposing that the Board of Trade representative be elevated from the status of observer to membership of that committee, Keynes assured Clayton that a further group of trade specialists would come out when ready. He hoped thereby to have removed American apprehensions. In London, however, especially at the Board of Trade, opinion was now turning to acceptance of American representations and to reversal of the end-August views on the conduct of the Washington negotiations. Keynes was instructed to seek postponement of the meeting of the new commercial policy committee until the fresh representatives arrived. Keynes resisted this, and was backed by a personal telegram from the Ambassador, the Earl of Halifax, suggesting that the trade team be kept 'on short call to come to join in when the right moment arrives'.[34] At this point Keynes did not help his case for leaving matters where they were, when he appeared to demonstrate precisely that lack of expertise on certain technical matters that had aroused concern in London. He had been attracted, when in Ottawa, by a suggestion of Mr Norman Robertson*, the Canadian Under-Secretary of State for External Affairs, on a point that Keynes admitted was new to him. This concerned the difference between trade preferences bound by treaty and other preferences which, not being so strictly governed, could be altered with less difficulty. A mutual offer by Commonwealth countries to lift commitments to 'bound preferences', Robertson had suggested, would ease Anglo-American trade negotiations.[35] From Washington Keynes asked whether Ministers were willing to take such a step. On a second unresolved issue in the earlier Anglo-American discussions, he asked how far they were ready to meet US ideas on the regulation of cartels. London's response to the first inquiry was that such an initial concession would be unwise, and to the second that Liesching would bring instructions, when he arrived with the rest of the trade experts. Keynes was meanwhile to stick to financial issues.[36]

London was standing firm after worried officials from the Board of Trade, Ministry of Agriculture and the Treasury had concluded that the 'Commercial Policy first eleven' should go to Washington, having first discussed matters with Ministers. A meeting of a small group of Ministers was quickly arranged, with the Prime Minister in the Chair; officials from the three Departments, and Professor Robbins from the Economic Section were present. The President of the Board of Trade, leaving no doubt of his disquiet, dominated proceedings, completely overshadowing the Chancellor of the Exchequer.[37] Recalling the earlier decisions to delay discussions on commercial policy in Washington, and that the Board of Trade representative should simply be an observer, Sir Stafford Cripps expressed no confidence in the competence of the existing Mission to

* ROBERTSON, Norman Alexander (1904–1968); Under-Secretary of State for External Affairs (Canada), 1941–46 and 1958–64.

negotiate on commercial policy, and he deplored, as throwing away 'our chief bargaining weapon' the proposal to unbind bound preferences. He would accept no responsibility for negotiations opened before arrival of the qualified London team. His colleagues acquiesced, and went on to discuss and to approve a memorandum from him, which set out the major considerations to guide the negotiators.[38] Noting the commitment under Article VII of the Mutual Aid Agreement of 1942, this favoured seeking a multilateral commercial convention, subject to safeguards previously discussed, which Ministers now re-emphasised. There was agreement particularly on the need to retain adequate scope for discrimination in controlling imports. That meant avoidance of too rigidly defined a transition period, and securing the availability of discrimination subsequently, in the event of balance of payments difficulties. Finally, Ministers agreed that the additional British representatives would have the status of 'principal advisers to HM Ambassador on commercial policy', thereby constraining more narrowly Keynes's role in the negotiations.

Notwithstanding a further desperate protest in another personal Ambassadorial cable, Ministers adhered to their revised tactic,[39] and in some embarrassment locally in Washington, the Mission reluctantly arranged to postpone the proposed meeting on commercial policy.[40] These interchanges and the resultant delay in financial negotiations appeared to Keynes, at the time and subsequently, to have materially prejudiced their outcome, by robbing them of their initial momentum.[41] That may indeed have appeared to be so, yet it was scarcely unforeseeable or unavoidable. In trying virtually to evade, at least temporarily, major issues in commercial policy, the original 'briefing' meeting had defied the long-familiar reality of American views. The subsequent back-tracking in sending out the experts, after all, simply recognised American *force majeure* in this matter.

(8) COMMERCIAL POLICY DISCUSSIONS

The trade team was led formally by Sir Percivale Liesching* of the Board of Trade. He worked in close co-operation with Professor L C Robbins, Director of the Economic Section. There were three more experts from the Board of Trade, and one each from the Colonial Office, the Ministry of Agriculture, and the Ministry of

---

* LIESCHING, Percivale, KCMG 1944; KCB 1947; GCMG 1951; KCVO 1953 (1895–1973); Assistant Under-Secretary of State, Dominions Office, 1939–42; Second Secretary, Board of Trade, 1942–46; Permanent Secretary, Ministry of Food, 1946–48; Permanent Under Secretary of State, Commonwealth Relations Office, 1949–55.

Food. Mr Helmore was to return to London as the resident expert there on the trade talks.

Once in Washington, the trade experts quickly reached understanding with their American counterparts on most issues: within eleven days. It would be easy to contrast this with the slow progress of the financial talks hitherto and subsequently. To do so, however, would be to overlook two major differences. First, the task of the new team was to clear the way as swiftly as possible for the financial negotiations; and, second, whereas the commercial policy talks involved understandings, with reservations on both sides, about broad principles for further debate at a future international conference, the financial discussions envisaged early commitments to specific major actions by both sides. It must nevertheless be recognised that Sir Percivale Liesching's conduct of the negotiations, for which his Minister was to praise him by name in the House of Commons,[42] was masterly: in his preparation, in his presentation of the British case, in his handling of American arguments and, by no means least, in his exposition of events to the representatives of the Dominion and Indian Governments.

American documents formed the principal agenda for the commercial policy negotiations. They proposed the establishment of an International Trade Organisation, and procedure for calling an international conference of leading nations (a 'nuclear group') to achieve this.[43] The British hoped that American tenacity had relaxed sufficiently to make it possible to negotiate over Imperial Preference on a straightforward bargaining basis. Eventual British adherence to the trade proposals would in any case be conditional upon that of a majority of the nuclear group. At the subsequent Anglo-American meetings on commercial policy, the British tactic was twofold: to seek to bargain towards understandings on major objectives, but to leave differences and details to be worked out by technical sub-committees for later consideration. The prudence, indeed the necessity, of this approach quickly emerged. In the powerful interchanges over Imperial Preference at the first two meetings, the American determination remained unchanged, to the great disappointment of the British representatives. Whatever American tariff reductions might be bargained in the first stages against cuts in preferences, those remaining (the 'residual preferences') would have to go without further compensating tariff reductions. Thus, the elimination of preferences would not necessarily bring the drastic cuts in tariffs desired to facilitate British trade expansion.[44]

Political factors were paramount here. The two chief American representatives, Mr Clayton and Mr Vinson, judged that Congress and public opinion would not be satisfied with much less than complete abolition of preferences as the price of aid. The British declared that such a price would be unacceptable in Britain. On both sides, it may be remarked, economic arguments for and against were inferential; nobody provided demonstrations of the economic costs and benefits of preferences which, in retrospect, seem to have been less significant than the struggles over them might suggest.[45] With alert Dominion and Indian Governments watching the negotiations for any slippage – from their capitals, from London, and in Washington itself – this matter demanded careful handling.

Liesching met American views head-on. He recalled the US interpretation of Article VII in 1942 (above, p 57) and the agreed Anglo-American statement of 1943 amplifying that. Those documents had recognised the difficulties, whilst acknowledging the goal, of reducing tariffs sufficiently to warrant the virtual elimination of preferences. A more recent complication was the American abandonment of the across-the-board cuts originally envisaged in favour of selective reductions in tariffs (above, pp 207 – 8); the resultant and great uncertainty about the overall international significance of tariff cuts evoked similar uncertainty about their adequacy as a justification for the abolition of preferences. To surrender Britain's one substantial bargaining weapon for such uncertain results could not be contemplated. Indeed, serious bargaining would be scarcely possible at all if, along American lines, preferences were to be condemned in any case. You can't make a horse-trade, remarked Keynes, who participated in these Anglo-American meetings, if the other side knows that your horse will fall dead in three months.[46]

Agreeing to leave preferences for further British proposals to be evolved, the Anglo-American discussions then swiftly accomplished understandings on most other trade and related issues. Liesching had originally proposed a relentless timetable to cover them in four meetings by the end of the first week in October. In fact, five meetings were to prove necessary, stretching to the end of the following week, but that remained a remarkable achievement. Broad agreement on objectives was reached on the approach to calling a trade conference, on export taxes, state trading, and on subsidies of exports and of home production. Even the objectionable (to Britain) attempt to introduce more stringent rules on exchange controls than under the Bretton Woods agreements (above, pp 201 – 2) was satisfactorily overcome, and there was Anglo-American convergence on the proposed treatment of cartels.[47] Drafts for final agreement were either ready or being prepared; of the major issues, only that of preferences remained to be taken up later. Much detailed work, much anxious discussion both in London and between London and the Washington team, were yet to come before the final agreement at the beginning of December (see below, pp 326–9). The path had, however, been cleared to the financial negotiations.

(9) CONTRASTING US AND BRITISH VIEWS ON FINANCE

Financial discussions had slowed down, but had not ceased, during the month between the despatch in September of trade experts and the conclusion of their preliminary work. There soon appeared, however, a fundamental contrast between the attitudes of the two sides towards financial questions. Especially during the early exchanges, the form of finance, by way of an interest-bearing credit or loan, and the wider accompanying conditions weighed more with the Americans than its amount. On the British side, the amount and the potential annual cost of servicing it, if it were not to be a free grant, governed the acceptability of American conditions. These differing approaches, bringing prolonged debate over the character of the finance to be provided, hindered agreement over conditions, which appeared less tolerable to the British the further that their early hopes of relatively easy finance receded. From the negotiations there resulted repeated tension, with breakdown a recurrent possibility. As regards the pattern of events, the result was a far from orderly chronology. There can nevertheless be discerned three broad phases of unequal length as financial negotiations quickened from late September. In the first and prolonged phase London struggled, with some encouragement from the Washington Mission, to secure at least a proportion of aid as a grant, or as a credit or loan at a zero or low rate of interest. With London's quick disillusion but slower retreat over that, the real struggle emerged in mid-November, when the American draft agreement assembled a series of proposals individually distasteful to Britain into an initially unacceptable package. In the concluding phase, in late November and early December, London sought strenuously, and with some notable successes, to modify the broadly similar final document.

(10) PROPOSALS FOR A STERLING SETTLEMENT: PRELIMINARIES

Following the five preliminary meetings of exposition and discussion (13–20 September), Keynes sought authority to put in writing to the Americans ideas already expressed to them verbally and informally.[48] Essentially those were the ideas outlined in his memorandum circulated by the Chancellor to the Cabinet in mid-August (above, pp 246–8), and little changed in the revised final version completed *en route* for Washington.[49] The request evoked considerable anxiety in the Treasury about the hazards of putting on to paper that part concerning the proposed reduction of sterling balances, before their holders had been consulted. Sir Edward Bridges advised the Prime Minister that:

'Lord Keynes should not go on written record, in a document submitted on behalf of the British Government, as taking the initiative in proposing a scaling down of our obligations to other countries...who have not been consulted beforehand by us...[The way] to get over this difficulty [is] by postponing putting in any written document until a state has been reached at which we could say that the initiative for this proposal has come from the Americans...'.

The Prime Minister agreed.[50] The reply to Keynes not only stressed this reluctance to present the sterling area proposals in writing, but also suggested changes in them and in the manner in which they might emerge.[51] The changes included an emphasis on the voluntary nature of any settlement. On advice from the Bank of England, balances arising from the post-war 'winding-up' period should be excluded from early convertibility ('availability'); moreover, that period and hence the date at which current earnings became available might vary between countries.[52] Above all, London asked Keynes to try to put on to the Americans the onus for proposing that substantial assistance from them would depend on Britain's reaching agreement with her principal creditors to reduce their claims:

'Tactically...we should very much like you to try to get some indication from American administration in a form which could be used if necessary, that they would expect an adjustment of our sterling indebtedness and the release of some part of the sterling balances after the adjustment to be ingredients in any scheme to which they would be expected to make a very large financial contribution. In speaking of use...we have in mind that...we should be able to say that the suggestion had come to us from the American administration. We should not excuse ourselves for we would maintain that it was a suggestion which in our opinion also was in accordance with realities of position. But important political point would have been gained that initiative appeared to be that of American Government...We are not sure that you need press for a written statement...It would be enough if you obtained it in sufficiently clear terms at a sufficiently high level for us to be able to say that during the discussions the American administration at a high level had raised the matter with us...'.

To this Keynes responded that Vinson and Clayton were quite clear that a reduction in sterling indebtedness must form part of any settlement; that Clayton had left the Washington representative of Egypt, one of the largest sterling creditors, in no doubt of American views; and that the Americans had invited the British 'to communicate at once the lines that a possible solution might take'.[53] Vinson and Clayton, he was later to recall, had agreed with the lines of the two key paragraphs in London's instructions to him: on, respectively, the link between aid and a sterling settlement, and the desirability of an American initiative on the issue.[54]

At this stage, at the end of September, there was no suggestion of a British retreat from the general character of the sterling settlement that had been discussed previously in London and now in Washington. The *tactical* problem of its presentation in the negotiations having been solved, the attention of Keynes and London did not concentrate on the draft, which Vinson and Clayton had invited, for almost four weeks. During that period, anxiety over the possible sterling settlement was overshadowed by that over the broader issues of the amount and form of American aid.

(11) NO GRANT-IN-AID

Before the negotiations had opened, indeed while in Ottawa *en route* for the USA, Keynes had written to colleagues in London of his growing doubts about the chances of securing an undisguised grant-in-aid.[55] Those doubts were soon to be reinforced in Washington, where the US Treasury was evolving a scheme, associated particularly with Dr H D White, to provide Britain with around the desired $5 billion. This, however, would be not a grant but a loan, and there was serious opposition to its proposed interest-free basis. Moreover, the proposals contemplated an arrangement, which revived apprehensions evoked by earlier ideas of White's (above, pp 98 – 99), for American involvement in a sterling settlement by taking over liability for part of the balances.[56] Not until early October, however – and then only briefly – did the White scheme seem likely to become a serious element in the negotiations (below, pp 288 – 92). Meanwhile hopes for a grant-in-aid had virtually disappeared by late September, but optimism about the chances of securing some form of interest-free finance persisted a little longer. In a memorandum for the Chancellor on 'The Terms of Assistance' (completed 26 September), which he began drafting before two discouraging meetings between himself, Lord Halifax, and Vinson and Clayton, Keynes affirmed that 'substantial assistance' was in prospect, on the basis of the familiar proposals for commercial policy, the sterling area, and for the operation of the Bretton Woods agreements. On the form of aid, the prospects for a grant-in-aid were 'poor'; he sought guidance should the US Treasury offer, as he hoped, a loan that would be repayable but without interest. Keynes remarked that the annual costs of $100 million for such a loan, repayable over 50 years, would not easily be regarded as an impossible burden. There might be a period of grace before repayment commenced, and also devices to ease repayment, such as lower initial and higher later instalments, and an escape clause. An escape clause to allow deferment of payments might be activated by a low and falling level of Britain's international reserves under the Bretton Woods definitions; this was the suggestion of Mr Graham Towers, Governor of the Bank of Canada. An alternative which Keynes proposed with characteristic ingenuity, recalling a feature of the Clearing Union plan, would emphasise the economic strength of the creditor; whether a sterling country or the USA or Canada, it would not be entitled to receive repayment of debt from Britain so long as its reserves, on Bretton Woods definitions, were high and rising.[57]

Before this memorandum had been completed, Vinson and Clayton, at an informal – 'surreptitious'[58] – meeting with Keynes and Halifax (25 September) had changed the issue on which guidance was sought from London. Not only would there be no grant-in-aid, but to ensure Congressional approval, a credit would have to bear interest, although it 'would be kept as low as possible', and an escape clause would further ease the potential burden. The British representatives, holding to their brief of a grant-in-aid, declared such terms to be unacceptable; both sides agreed to reflect on what had been said, and to meet again very shortly. At this second meeting (27 September), reiteration of British views brought from Vinson and Clayton recognition that there might be 'special financial terms' for aid; perhaps, the British suggested, and the Americans agreed, there could be some *douceur* for the USA, such as the prolongation from 99 to 999 years of their lease of West Indian naval bases?[59] On the terms of a credit, the Americans remained initially very firm, however, and 'repeated in unison that neither a grant-in-aid nor an interest-free loan was practical politics'. Clayton, stressing that he held a more optimistic view than the British of their future, raised the possibility of an escape clause as a safeguard. But why not, asked the British, some combination of a grant-in-aid and a line of credit at a low rate of interest? After first rejecting that too as politically impractical, though attractive, Vinson eventually agreed not to exclude it as a possibility.

These discussions and 'all other currents of opinion reaching us from various quarters' sustained the Mission's hopes that an interest-free loan of $5 billion, repayment of which would cost $100 million annually for fifty years, was possible, within 'a general

Anglo-American economic concordat'. Keynes therefore sought authority to discuss such arrangements non-committally.[60] Assuming, however, that the Americans might insist on an interest charge, mitigated by an escape clause, Keynes completed his memorandum by propounding to London half a dozen manipulations of grant, interest-free loan, and credit at interest. All would provide $5 billion and have an escape clause. His own preferences were for either a grant-in-aid of $2 billion plus a credit of $3 billion at two per cent, or an interest-free loan, the latter possibly in the form of earmarked gold in an effort to sidetrack the question of an interest rate. Failing those two methods, a perpetual loan at two per cent, or a repayable one at two per cent, with low instalments in early years, might be considered. The two remaining ideas were for a long-term loan repayable over seventy years at one per cent, and – 'Probably not a starter' – a combination of grant-in-aid of $2 billion and interest-free credit of $3 billion. Except in the last case, a period of grace of ten years would apply before the commencement of interest payments or capital repayments or both. Annual costs would be below $100 million for the grant and interest-free loan, and above that, on average, for a straight two per cent loan; otherwise, juggling with maturities, interest rates, and periods of grace would keep the annual costs to $100 million.[61]

London's initial reactions were of hesitation to accept the full implications of Keynes's assessment. For some days there was intense exploration of it by transatlantic telephone, cables, and air mail, as well as by discussions amongst Ministers and officials. A combination of grant and loan could be contemplated and so could an interest-free loan. London preferred the latter, which indeed 'knowledgeable people' there, according to Eady, regarded as the only type of loan that would be acceptable.[62] Eady nevertheless wondered, along with the Chancellor, whether its annual burden of $100 million in repayment might be too great. Both of them hankered after a grant-in-aid in the form of retrospective Lend-Lease (above, pp 239, 242, 243, 247), but Keynes had already advised that that was 'most certainly not a good starter'.[63] From the Economic Section, Mr Meade persuaded Eady and the Chancellor that $100 million would be bearable; he pointed out the danger (in Eady's draft telegram for the Chancellor's reply to the Mission), when looking ahead to Britain's ability to find dollars to repay a loan, of confusing a dollar shortage with the state of the balance of payments with the rest of the world; the 'scarce currency' clause of the new International Monetary Fund might take care of the former. Moreover, $100 million was a very small percentage of Britain's overseas earnings, and would be even smaller if the intended expansion of exports by fifty per cent were to be achieved.[64]

Alternatives to substantial American aid would be difficult; the extreme domestic austerity that they would require might not frighten the Government, thought Eady, but Meade pointed out not only that it would involve a drastic cut in imports, but also that a switch from American to non-American supplies could raise costs.

The Chancellor was sufficiently influenced to drop his initial reluctance to consider an interest-free loan. Whilst he viewed a loan entirely on an interest basis, 'even without conditions', as unacceptable, he offered for the consideration of senior Ministers (meeting of 5 October) Keynes's two preferred possibilities: a combination of grant and loan, and an interest-free loan, each costing annually up to $100 million. There could be no serious doubt about the need for some $5 billion of help from the USA. A sum less than that would not permit the desired easing of trade controls, and inability to acquire American supplies would result in drastic cuts in food rations, food production and imports of raw materials.

But what of the conditions likely to be attached to aid? The Foreign Secretary aired the possibility of avoiding them by a smaller and straight commercial loan. It was pointed out that this would be as costly as the larger interest-free loan, which would also bring wider benefits. Three particular conditions had to be considered: the Americans' aim to eliminate Imperial Preference, their hostility to State Trading (eg, British bulk purchase of commodities), and their expectation of British acceptance of the Bretton Woods scheme. The President of the Board of Trade warned that these issues should be regarded less as strings to financial aid than as prerequisites; moreover, an agreement might be secured on commercial policy during the negotiations recently commenced in Washington (above, pp 276–9), only to encounter Congressional difficulties: views elaborated to Ministers by one of his senior officials. He therefore concluded that 'we should go more slowly on the finance side and leave developments to the Commercial Policy side'. The Chancellor, however, expressed confidence in Britain's ability to satisfy the Americans on all three points, given appropriate assumptions: that changes in Imperial Preference would be limited, that broad economic considerations would govern the choice of suppliers under State Trading, and that an interpretative declaration in relation to Bretton Woods would be secured (above, pp 182–5). Ministers accepted the Chancellor's lead. They agreed that, whilst leaving the initiative over terms to the Americans, the Mission could negotiate for $5 billion in whatever form seemed appropriate, though a straight grant plus a line of credit, to be used as necessary, would be preferred. Repayment should not exceed $100 million annually over fifty years. The *caveats* were that the accompanying conditions must be satisfactory, that Britain retained import controls to protect the balance of payments, and – whilst there was no mention of an escape clause – would suspend debt service if a world dollar shortage or world deflation were to make it burdensome.[65]

On receiving London's instructions,[66] Keynes and Halifax had a long meeting (9 October) with Vinson and Clayton, who firmly ruled out a grant as part of aid, and emphasised that Congressional considerations dictated that interest be charged. Clayton, perhaps over-optimistically in the light of discussions only three days previously in the Americans' own 'Top Committee', nevertheless sustained British hopes (as he did also in a press conference the same day).[67] There could possibly be a loan of $5 billion, with interest at two per cent; it would be repayable over fifty years, commencing after a five years' grace period, and sweetened by a waiver so devised as to dress up the credit to look both like an interest-free loan and one bearing interest. Initially, repayments would be at an annual rate of $100 million, equivalent to capital repayment only, if maintained for fifty years. When, however, British exports reached $6 billion annually, a further $50 million would be payable each year. The average level of British exports in 1936–38 on which the British Mission based its calculations, was £866 million, or $3,464 million approximately (below, p 303). Achievement of the cautious aim to increase exports by fifty per cent (in volume) above the pre-war level (above, pp 271–2 and Appendix 27) would not activate the interest payment; the achievement of the bolder goal of an increase of seventy-five per cent in volume would be necessary for that. Hence, the extra $50 million for interest would not be expected to fall for payment in the early years.[68]

Senior Ministers reacted unenthusiastically, feeling 'reluctant to admit that we are in any sense dependent upon the U.S. to get ourselves out of our present difficulties' and having gained confidence in their ability to protect the balance of payments.[69] At a further meeting (12 October) the Chancellor argued that the proposed conditions should not be accepted prematurely; he urged that they should continue to seek a complete or partial interest-free grant, and to resist annual payments exceeding $100 million, although at least one Minister regarded a higher figure to cover two per cent interest as tolerable. In the discussions, a waiver was held to be objectionable, as it offered scope for future Anglo-American misunderstandings as well as for unwanted American scrutiny of British statistics. All present preferred aid to be in the form of an overdraft (line of credit) rather than a loan, in order to restrict costs according to the amount used. Agreeing that Keynes be informed of these views, Ministers recognised that on receiving his reply they must be prepared to consider further concessions.[70]

While London was pondering Washington had been deciding. Their experts viewing Britain's prospective balance of payments more favourably than did the British themselves, the American Financial Committee had moved towards, though it did not settle upon, a significantly lower figure for aid than $5 billion (11 October). Aid would be by line of credit, although White saw an advantage to Britain of a loan which, by its magnitude, would reinforce her reserves and thereby also confidence in sterling. The terms would be those which Britain had been resisting: a group led by Mr Vinson secured agreement to an interest charge, which they favoured on political grounds; for simplicity it would be a fixed rate, eased however by provisions for a waiver of interest and deferment of capital repayments.[71]

(12) THE TERMS TAKE SHAPE

This firming of American policy proved a bitter blow to the British Mission. A long and somewhat unsatisfactory meeting (15 October) between the two principals of each side to discuss London's rejection of Clayton's suggested terms for a credit of $5 billion was followed next day (16 October) by a much larger Anglo-American meeting. This, though inconclusive, was sufficiently disappointing to dissipate much of the optimism with which Keynes had sought to infuse his colleagues. Hitherto the figure of $5 billion had scarcely been in dispute as the amount of aid needed; now, however, there was 'a long and rather irritating discussion about our figures', designed, it seemed, 'to prove that we need only 3 or 4, when we maintain it must be 5: and there is so much room for doubt on the figures that discussion is pretty fruitless'.[72]

Following these meetings, the Mission decided, not without one or two members of it wondering whether the negotiations might be better suspended, to cable to London in the hope of bringing matters to a head. In what a colleague justifiably described as one 'of the best pieces of writing he has ever done'[73], Keynes declared that the prose of the harsh reality of what the Americans felt able to offer must be substituted for the poetry of the larger scale, untrammelled generosity, for which at the outset the Mission had hoped. A break in negotiations, with the risk of 'perhaps irreparable injury to our own body politic and economic or...[of] shattering the basis of day-to-day Anglo-American co-operation' was not to be contemplated.

Aid of $5 billion was now clearly unlikely, but even if provided its servicing costs would greatly exceed the annual limit of $100 million hitherto stipulated, and would therefore be unacceptable. Yet the obstacle of that annual burden would make no argument with the Americans, since they countered with the offer of a waiver. To avoid such terms and their associated obligations by seeking a smaller sum was impractical for several explicit reasons, of which the most compelling were Britain's virtually inescapable needs and American insistence on the familiar commitments. In any case, such a loan with limited commitments, even if possible, would carry, given commercial instead of specially low borrowing rates, much the same servicing costs.

Were there other possibilities? Keynes broached two, each comprising two elements. One proposal was the earlier combination of a grant, of $2 billion, with a credit of $3 billion; this would nominally cost two per cent, but effectively less as the servicing would be delayed two years. The other suggestion was for a loan of $4 billion, costing about one per cent in interest when allowing for delayed servicing; coupled to this would be access for ten years to a credit of $1 or $2 billion at two per cent.

The not very strong hopes for these two ideas vanished quickly: within twenty-four hours, at a further meeting between the four principals (19 October). The Americans had wanted a speedy settlement, and when serious financial negotiations had begun in late September, they had envisaged completion within a month.[74] By mid-October, however, continuing delays in the negotiations were such as to put at hazard the Administration's intention to secure by the end of the year the implementation of the Bretton Woods agreements, the passage through Congress of legislation for a loan to Britain, and the issue of a call for an international conference on commercial policy.[75] The American negotiators now endeavoured to move forward. They made definite proposals: $3½ billion at two per cent, plus settlement of Lend-Lease on the disagreeable 3(c) terms, this latter reflecting Vinson's unawareness of what had been previously understood (above, pp 252–3). As a condition of such aid, smaller and more costly than had been hoped, the same commitments would be expected concerning the sterling area that London and the Mission had regarded as just compatible with much more ample finance.[76]

The impact of the slow start to the financial negotiations and of London's reluctance to accept the American realities was now being felt. The desired $5 billion seemed to have slipped from reach. As Keynes groped for it, an initial American inflexibility raised British apprehensions of an unavoidable breakdown in negotiations. But what, he asked, had become of Clayton's recent suggestion of $5 billion at two per cent? The answer came in two parts. First, it became clear that British rejection so far of an escape clause had been partly responsible for the smaller offer. By boldly disregarding London's aversion, and by raising the possibility of a waiver of interest, Keynes found the Americans more willing to explore arrangements other than those they had just presented. Second, political constraints had been felt. These now included controversy in the the USA over tax cuts which Vinson, as Secretary of the Treasury, was himself advocating to Congress. As these would come to $5 billion, political prudence indicated a skirting of that precise figure in discussing aid to Britain.[77] Keynes therefore talked in terms of $4½ billion for a credit. To wind up Lend-Lease there should be an extra sum, which the Mission hoped would be no more than $500 million (which would thus bring the total back to $5 billion), and this should be on the same terms, Vinson having quickly retreated from the misunderstanding about 3(c) terms. $4½ billion was still too much for the Americans' comfort; they preferred a limit of $4 billion, exclusive of Lend-Lease financing. It had become clear, however, that an improvement on their opening offer of $3¼ billion was possible, so that scope remained for negotiations to continue. The Mission therefore recommended London to consider seriously the possible terms for gross borrowing of $5 billion, of which $4½ billion would be 'new money'. If a five years' grace period were incorporated, the nominal rate of two per cent would fall to 1.6 per cent during the subsequent fifty years of repayment. The annual cost, corrected by the Americans from their earlier estimates of $150 million, would be $159 million, but the waiver would make that more tolerable.

Finance on the terms now contemplated might appear disappointing and burdensome, but the case for it was 'that we are now more convinced than before that nothing better than this is on the map'. Mr Graham Towers, Governor of the Bank of Canada, who had flown to Washington at the suggestion of the Mission to assess the position on both sides and to offer advice, reluctantly took the same view. A loan at interest, much as he regretted it, could not easily be dismissed if accompanied by a waiver, so long as the 'target' figure for Britain's overseas income, the shortfall of which would activate the waiver,was sufficiently high for that as well as to finance adequate imports.[78] Thus fortified, Keynes completed his report on the credit terms by outlining the possible forms and operation of a waiver of interest and deferment of capital repayments.[79]

(13) PROBLEMS OF A STERLING SETTLEMENT: WHITE'S PLAN

There followed a relative lull of over two weeks in the formal negotiations, the four principals agreeing not to meet again until London had replied. In London, however, preoccupation with the new Government's legislative programme and above all with the Budget (23 October) delayed the response to Washington. During this relative lull, major difficulties emerged over the proposed settlement for the sterling area, to produce, in combination with those that had developed over the amount and terms of credit, a crisis in the negotiations by the end of October.

Largely on the sidelines in the recent discussions, the sterling area aspect of the projected financial assistance commanded greater attention from mid-October in connection with White's ingenious plan to finance a reduction of sterling balances. At the outset of negotiations, the Mission had become broadly aware of its nature and of its potential advantages for Britain, though wary of its contrary implications for the status of sterling. Not until the second week of October, however, did it seem to have attracted sufficient *American* support for Keynes to take it really seriously and, adducing colleagues' support, to urge London to do likewise.[80]

White's plan contemplated aid of $5.5 billion interest-free, or possibly of $5 billion to which would be added a nominal sum for interest of $0.5 billion; in either case, therefore, $5.5 billion would be repayable by Britain. The aid would be in two parts, of which the relatively unproblematical part would be a credit of perhaps $3 billion for Britain's own needs. A further $2 billion or $2.5 billion would be provided directly for the sterling area countries, whose balances would be divided along lines broadly comparable with those of the original British conception: some to be cancelled, some blocked (or 'funded'), and a small proportion released. The amount of these balances was taken as approximately $11 billion (£2.75 billion) at the end of June 1945; a further amount of $2 billion (£0.5 billion) was expected to accrue by the end of 1946, when the British proposals envisaged that the sterling area would be 'liberalised' by the ending of restrictions on the expenditure of its currently earned sterling. Account had therefore to be taken of $13 billion (£3.25 billion).[81] The White Plan proposed cancellation of $4 billion (£1 billion). A further $2 billion (£0.5 billion) would be nominally freed but effectively funded by an undertaking on the part of the sterling countries to maintain that amount as minimum working balances in London. That left $5 billion (£1.25 billion) of the $11 billion (£2.75 billion) of balances at end-June 1945; here ingenuity took over. These $5 billion would be funded as a long-term debt by Britain to the sterling countries from whom, however, the United States would offer to buy them at a price of, say, half their face value; that would be the present discounted value of the funded balances on the basis of their maturity date and the rate of interest, three per cent, thought to be appropriate for the discounting. Applied to the whole $5 billion, $5 billion of funded balances would be taken over in exchange for the immediate provision to their holders of $2.5 billion (£625 million). The other $2.5 billion could be regarded as the interest on the advance by the United States to the sterling countries of the present discounted value of the debt taken over; but if the advance of $2.5 billion, which as the original debtor Britain would have to repay, bore no interest, as White hoped, then the discounting would have been costless. Should the offer of credit interest-free raise problems, they might be evaded by making gold loans; or, as in one version, $2 billion might be advanced to the sterling countries, but $2.5 billion would be repayable to cover an interest charge.[82]

These proposals covered $11 billion (£2.75 billion). To cover the expected increase in balances to $13 billion (£3.25 billion), the sterling countries would be expected to make an interest-free long-term loan of $2 billion (£0.5 billion) to Britain.

The outcome of the White Plan's elaborate proposals would have been to transform Britain's projected debt of $13 billion (£3.25 billion) to the sterling area at end-1946 into one of $9.5 billion (£2.375 billion), of which only $4 billion (£1 billion) would be owed to the sterling countries, and the remaining $5.5 billion (£1.375 billion) to the USA. This would compare favourably with the most recent version of Keynes's proposals, which would have resulted in a debt of $14 billion (£3.5 billion): $5 billion (£1.25 billion) of a new American credit; and, after outright cancellation of $4 billion (£1 billion), the same amount as under the White Plan, a remaining debt to the sterling countries of $9 billion (£2.25 billion), of which $800 million (£200 million) would be released immediately, and the remainder funded. Thus, under the White Plan, for an extra $0.5 billion (£125 million) of debt to the USA, Britain's sterling debt would be $5 billion (£1.25 billion) lighter than under Keynes's scheme, making in all a reduction of practically seventy per cent in the debt to the sterling countries; Britain's net indebtedness would be $4.5 billion (£1.125 billion) lighter.[83]

The great though not the sole imponderable in this financial sleight-of-hand would be the sterling area. It would indeed benefit by gaining access to $2 billion or $2.5 billion (£500 or £625 million) in scarce dollars instead of $800 million (£200 million) in sterling. It would, however, be expected to face the disappearance of half of its balances ($4 billion by direct cancellation, $2.5 billion conjured away by 'discounting'), and in addition a fresh loan to Britain.

THE KEYNES AND WHITE SCHEMES FOR THE SETTLEMENT OF THE STERLING BALANCES OF THE STERLING AREA

Billion

	Keynes Scheme	White Scheme
I Disposition of balances:		
1. To be written off	$4 (£1)	$4 (£1)
2. To be funded: (a) to be released immediately in dollars if 'discounted' by USA		$2.5 (£0.625)
(b) 'discounting' cost		$2.5 (£0.625)
(c) total to be funded	$8 (£2)	$5 (£1.25)
3. To be released immediately in sterling	$0.8 (£0.2)	
4. Minimum balances to be maintained in London (in sterling)		$2 (£0.5)
5. Loan in sterling to UK to cover increases in balances June 1945 – Dec 1946		$2 (£0.5)
6. TOTALS (approx.)	$13 (£3.25)	$13 (£3.25)
II Resultant debt of UK:		
7. (a) to sterling area (approx.)	$9 (£2.25)	$4 (£1)
(b) to USA	$5 (£1.25)	$5.5 (£1.375)
(c) Total (approx.)	$14 (£3.5)	$9.5 (£2.375)

Sources: see text.

'Too fancy' to win Vinson's support,[84] the White scheme was unacceptable to London, where concern deepened with a confusing 'leak' in the American press.[85] In the British Treasury, a characteristically meticulous critique by a senior official was directed particularly against both a comprehensive settlement involving sterling and the suggestion of uniform treatment of sterling debt. These would be impossible, for they required what could not be contemplated: a conference of the major sterling creditors, including above all India, the 'stumbling block to this (and perhaps to any) scheme'.[86] The Bank of England tersely commented that if the scheme left sterling countries with overseas funds solely in dollars, this 'would presumably force them to remove all their current banking business from London to New York'. In a further note the Bank reiterated its own earlier assertion that a uniform settlement was not possible and that, even so, arrangements for individual countries would involve many difficulties. The Bank favoured a policy of asking the Americans to entrust to Britain the devising of the best means to use dollar aid to liberalise the sterling area; to reassure the US Administration, it proposed a form of words that was broadly to inform the relevant section of the eventual final agreement[87] (section 10, in Appendix 24). The Chancellor's cabled response to the Mission was to express the hope that the White scheme would not reappear on its existing lines; he would prefer the sterling area to be kept out of the discussions, whilst acknowledging the desirability of some American aid being directed towards easing its problems. Recalling earlier exchanges about the sterling proposals (above, pp 279–82) as well as some of London's more recent instructions, he emphasised that in any sterling settlement the involvement of sterling area countries must be on a voluntary basis; overall writing down of balances, he noted, would be difficult, and he cited 'the calculated awkwardness of the Indians'.[88]

(14) THE CABINET'S PROPOSALS

On the White scheme at least speedy comfort could be offered to London. It was already being pushed aside, both by Vinson's dislike for its convoluted approach to minimising interest charges and by influential American opposition to direct involvement with Britain's sterling debts.[89] At the same time, however, the latest American terms had precipitated British doubts not just about the form, but over the whole concept, of a sterling settlement, and thus over the original vision of an interlocking Anglo-American agreement. Would those terms permit Britain to undertake broad commitments on trade, Bretton Woods, and the liberalisation of the sterling area? Following new rumours in the American and British press of difficulties in the negotiations, with a suggestion of a breakdown,

Eady cabled Keynes urgently to ascertain Vinson's and Clayton's views. The reply drew attention to the most recent discussions, in which they had affirmed that they expected implementation of the original proposals; Keynes too recalled the earlier exchanges about these. In the absence of subsequent pressure from the Americans, he had not so far presented the written version of the proposals which they had invited; a draft of that was to be sent to London the following day, as a possible annex to a final agreement, and was to provoke intense, acrimonious debate between London and the Mission.[90] Immediately, on the crucial role of a sterling settlement in an Anglo-American agreement, Keynes was quite explicit:[91]

> '...as you already know large concessions by the sterling area are of course an absolutely essential and, we think, not unreasonable condition for American assistance. They started this way and are most unlikely to change their position'.

That acceptance of the commitments would require assistance of – 'elbow room up to' – $5 billion (effectively $4.5 billion net of the Lend-Lease settlement) Keynes himself stressed to the Chancellor.[92] Similarly, in advice to Mr Herbert Morrison, Lord President of the Council, Mr Meade emphasised the need for $5 billion, pointing to the grave implications as well as the costs of the alternatives; he urged acceptance of annual costs of $159 million, tempered by a suitable escape clause.[93] The Treasury, however, had strong reservations, assuming that the Americans would not go beyond $4 billion of new money: would it not be prudent to match fewer dollars with fewer obligations?[94] The Chancellor, with advice from Eady that reflected the latter's consultations with Mr C F Cobbold, Deputy Governor of the Bank of England, circulated his views to the Committee of Ministers in a strongly worded draft telegram in response to the American terms. Of the projected commitments, he declared that:

> 'All these might have been safely undertaken with $5 billion grant in cash or possibly on an interest free basis, but they are neither safe nor a good bargain for $4 billion at 2 per cent interest'.

Regretting that there should be any interest charge at all, the Chancellor was unwilling to recommend one of two per cent, which he regarded as 'a commercial rate...for what was not...a commercial transaction'. Moreover, he was against any interest being paid on that part of a credit intended for the sterling area, where its purpose would be to finance American exports. The Chancellor also advised against a waiver of interest that would be related to Britain's external earnings; he reiterated that the difficulties of operating one could harm Anglo-American relations.[95]

Given these considerations, the Chancellor presented two proposals, to be known as Alternative 'A' and Alternative 'B'. The former was to be offered to the Americans in an attempt to secure 'a quick and firm deal'. A fifty-year loan of $2.5 billion at one per cent, with a grace period of five years, would be sought to cover Britain's essential imports in 1946 and 1947, and a Lend-Lease settlement. An option would be requested on a further $2 billion, interest-free, also for fifty years; this would underpin an offer to the sterling countries 'to make their sterling as freely available for current expenditure outside the area as inside', in return for 'an appropriate contribution' to a settlement of sterling balances. With such American assistance, Britain could contemplate qualified commitments on trade policies and on Bretton Woods: with credit terms less favourable than desired, a more prolonged transition period would be necessary before operating them fully.

If 'A' proved unacceptable to the US, then Alternative 'B' envisaged borrowing kept down to $2 billion, adequate only to settle Lend-Lease and to finance dollar imports for 1946. An appropriate interest rate would be two per cent on finance that would be more commercially orientated, for there would be much narrower commitments: Parliament could be expected not to approve adherence to Bretton Woods before the end of 1946 at earliest, and movement on commercial policy would encounter increasing difficulties both from Parliament and the Empire.

In the Ministers' meeting (26 October) three – the Prime Minister, the Lord President, and the Dominions Secretary (Lord Addison) — were willing to consider a waiver, but they encountered the successful opposition of the Chancellor and the President of the Board of Trade as well as official advice from Eady against one. The Chancellor urged the negotiating advantage of first trying the two proposals, in the hope of avoiding a waiver. On Alternative 'A' there was little dissent, although there were doubts about the American reception of it. Alternative 'B' was approved less readily, and with the amount to be sought raised to $3 billion. On one side were apprehensions lest the eventual annual costs might prove higher, on the originally suggested sum of $2 billion, than for the larger amount under 'A'. In contrast, the Foreign Secretary repeated his preference for a commercial loan free of commitments, and he proposed $3 billion as closer to requirements. The chances for that figure, thought the President of the Board of Trade, were questionable, but presented as $2.5 billion plus an amount for Lend-Lease, it might evoke a more favourable American view of 'A'. Instructions were therefore to be sent to the Mission, Ministers agreed, to submit to the Americans these two proposals:

Alternative 'A' for $4.5 billion and Alternative 'B' for $3 billion. The telegrams to Washington largely repeated the Chancellor's arguments in his draft telegram and in the meeting.[96]

The Washington Mission had suffered suspense awaiting London's seemingly leisurely response; its members were conscious of American pressures, as well as their own hopes, for an early settlement, against which they had booked a provisional sailing for home that assumed a mid-November conclusion. The new London instructions appalled the Mission, and opened a fresh period of suspense, Keynes being driven 'white with rage and [to] talking about resigning'; his colleagues initially feared that London's views made a breakdown in negotiations simply a matter of time.[97] In London's telegrams the notes of a double retreat sounded quite clearly and gloomily: retreat from initial hopes of easy conditions, and retreat from British intentions to undertake early liberalisation of trade and payments. The first was almost certainly inevitable. The second was perhaps predictable in the light of earlier and continuing discussions, especially those involving the Bank of England; it was, however, scarcely possible to accomplish this second retreat, despite tense exchanges between the two negotiating teams, and between London and the Mission. It seemed to one member of the Mission that London might be clinging 'to the lunatic idea that we could break with the Americans on everything they really care about and still get enough finance on some terms or other to get us through'.[98] Not surprisingly, perhaps, the British representatives' reactions to Ministers' proposals, and also to Treasury suggestions that they had exaggerated the amount of finance needed for the sterling area, were as acerbic as they were swift; they sought, however, to prevent a collapse of the negotiations, and therefore to persuade London to reconsider its views. Warning of a risk that American opinion might be hardening, and questioning Ministers' assessment of Congress, they declared that, if the larger sum, partially at interest, under Alternative 'A' were not forthcoming, there would be little chance for 'B', with its rejection of Anglo-American co-operation. Whilst very doubtful over the chances for 'A' they nevertheless recommended that, if it were to be proposed, there should be coupled with it a waiver, which the US wanted as a means of avoiding overt default on repayments.

Over finance for the sterling area there was a transatlantic battle of statistical projections. From the Treasury, Mr R W B ('Otto') Clarke claimed that the area's needs had been over-estimated, and that its dollar earning power had been under-estimated. Keynes checked his own calculations. For the three years 1946–48 a total deficit of some $2,000–2,500 million faced Britain. The sterling area might have a total credit with Britain of some $3,500 – 4,000 million (including gold sales of $1,500 million). If there were some further accumulation of balances, say $1 billion, that gave net British requirements ranging between $4,500 and $5,500 million – say $5 billion. $750 million might be withdrawn from the reserves, when $4.25 billion would be required. If London seemed to believe that Britain might manage with borrowing somewhat less even than $2 billion from the USA for its own needs, that might imply borrowing over $2.25 billion extra from the sterling area (by increasing yet further their balances in London). Which sterling area countries, Keynes asked tartly, would be the lenders, and how would they oblige unless previously there had been repayment of existing balances?[99]

This unsettling debate over the need for the finance which was being negotiated dragged on through the cables for some time longer.[100] Meanwhile, decisions had to be taken on the character and conditions of whatever aid might be offered and accepted, in the knowledge that the Americans were trying to operate to a very tight timetable, which had already been set back; they hoped to complete by the second week of November, barely two weeks after London had despatched its two alternative proposals to the British Mission.[101]

The Chancellor's immediate response to the Mission's very sceptical reception of the 'A' and 'B' alternatives was to relax, to the extent of urging that effort be concentrated on securing 'A', with authority secured from the Prime Minister to offer two per cent instead of one per cent on the $2.5 billion being sought for Britain's own needs.[102] This was still too far, however, from an adequate negotiating position. The Ambassador and Keynes hesitated to present the revised terms. In particular, and backed by a separate personal telegram from Brand, they urged acceptance of a waiver.[103] These points apart, some further delay in negotiations was desirable as well as probably unavoidable, for two members of the Mission, Professor L C Robbins and Mr E Hall-Patch, were returning temporarily to London: ostensibly to discuss Anglo-American differences over Imperial Preference, but above all to remove misunderstandings about the sterling area proposals.[104] London's anxiety, aroused by the White scheme, had not abated when the fading of that was followed by Keynes's draft of the sterling area proposals (24 October).[105] London's accompaniment of the 'A' and 'B' proposals with diluted intentions about sterling had brought Keynes's sharp reminder that 'on this we are certainly committed up to the hilt'.[106]

Continuing debate by cable, and discussions in London in which Professor Robbins participated, helped to remove misunderstandings over the sterling area proposals at the beginning of November, albeit only temporarily, as became evident shortly (below, pp 313 – 18). Ministers now moved much closer to accepting the inevitability of terms at which they had hitherto jibbed; terms which, however, had become effectively much worse, for the US was clearly likely to offer credit substantially less than the original $5 billion which it had earlier seemed prepared to consider.

Revised proposals from the Chancellor were to be approved by senior Ministers after a strenuous late night meeting(5/6 November), attended by Robbins and Hall-Patch as well as by six other senior officials. So significant were the changes that approval was sought of the full Cabinet, a lengthy two-session meeting of which was held within hours (6 November) in order to secure a decision before the Prime Minister's departure for atomic energy talks in Washington. The Chancellor found the vigorous Cabinet debate 'heavy work',[107] much unhappiness being voiced over the American attitude and over its implications for the sterling area. Strong support for the Chancellor and the President of the Board of Trade now came from the Foreign Secretary, whose unwillingness to see further sacrifices imposed on the population had overcome his repugnance to the American conditions. The Committee's recommendations prevailed. This was a victory particularly for the three senior Ministers, the Chancellor noting negatively in his diary, on the rejection of opposing views, that 'nothing much can be done in this Cabinet when Bevin, Cripps and I are in firm coalition as today'.[108]

In detail, the Chancellor's proposals were that Alternative 'B' should be dropped, and that Alternative 'A' should be pressed, with two per cent being offered if necessary for the interest-bearing $2.5 billion. In default of that being acceptable to the US, the Mission could go to as much as $4 billion at two per cent, with an option on a further $1 billion at the same rate; repayment would be over fifty years, after a five years' grace period. Given the costs of the latter case, a waiver would be essential; helping to tip the balance in the Ministers' Committee, against Eady's resistance, were the opinions of Robbins and Bridges, Robbins asserting that the waiver could be so devised as to preclude 'any inquisition'.

In respect of the crucial commitments to be undertaken, the keynote was the caution already evinced in face of less attractive terms than had been hoped. On the sterling area, proposals fell into two parts. First, the voluntary character of any settlement was again emphasised in relation to sterling balances. Ministers had before them the advice of the Secretary of State for India (Lord Pethick-Lawrence) that Indian opinion would not tolerate any reduction or blocking; the Secretary of State for the Colonies (Mr G

H Hall) protested that 'any significant scaling down' of the Colonial Empire's balances would be inconsistent with government policy towards the Colonies.[109] These two groups accounted for some two-thirds of the net balances of the sterling area at the end of June 1945;[110] the Prime Minister aptly commented that 'there was little chance of substantial writing down of sterling debts'. But it was the second part of the proposals, said Professor Robbins, which would most interest the Americans in considering aid, and that was the liberalisation of the sterling area; it was agreed to offer the gradual reduction of discrimination by the sterling area against dollar expenditure.[111]

On wider aspects of Anglo-American co-operation, Ministers would agree, first, to support the American proposals for the establishment of an International Trade Organisation, given the aid sought; the President of the Board of Trade was optimistic of overcoming the remaining major difficulty over Imperial Preference (below, pp 326–9).[112] Second, Ministers would recommend the Bretton Woods 'Final Act' for parliamentary approval, subject to a lengthy transition period and to securing from the new Monetary Fund an interpretative declaration safeguarding policies to protect employment and the balance of payments (above, pp 182–5).

(15) THE WAIVER: LONDON'S ATTITUDE

Agreement to consider a waiver in the terms for a credit ended prolonged resistance by London, notably by the Chancellor. Distasteful to London, to the Americans it was attractive as a means of going to the limit or beyond, in giving aid, of what might otherwise have aroused strong Congressional apprehensions. That is, it would avoid repetition of the overt defaults, which continued to rankle, on loans associated with the war of 1914–18. A waiver would also avert two particularly distasteful contingencies. One would be the British use, in facing balance of payments difficulties, of quantitative trade restrictions possibly discriminating against the USA. The other would be an appeal to the International Monetary Fund to activate the 'scarce currency' clause in respect of the US dollar, an action which would be like 'a red rag' to Congress.[113] A further attraction to the Americans of a waiver would be that it would permit a shorter period than otherwise of 'grace' before repayment of a credit began.

London's attitude to repayments, to which it adhered steadfastly, was defined early in October. This followed intense discussions by Ministers and officials of major telegrams from the Mission and of a memorandum in which Keynes stressed the poor prospects for earlier British hopes of easy financial aid. London declared that[114]

'fundamental conditions for regular service [of a loan] are (i) that there is no general and obstinate deflationary policy possibly originating from American policy which might make weight of annual payments intolerable, (ii) that United States is in general balance either by imports or by suitable lending policy so that there is no world shortage of dollars. . . .'.

In the absence of such conditions there would be suspension of debt service, provision for which should be included in the terms of any loan. Initially, such liabilities must be of 'manageable proportions', insisted the Chancellor, but he declared that no informed person was likely to regard that as true of the terms envisaged in early October by Mr Clayton;[115] on a loan of $5 billion at two per cent interest, repayable over fifty years, these required annual payments of $159 million, compared with London's limit of $100 million (being the capital repayment of the same sum on interest-free terms). There would be scant attraction in acceptance of a larger burden with an escape clause related to Britain's capacity to pay; even if such a clause did not cause initial trouble with Congress, for fifty years it would risk, when invoked, creating Anglo-American friction.[116] London had therefore pushed aside Keynes's kite of late September, which Canadian support had encouraged him to fly, of an escape clause related to international reserves (above, p 282). The Chancellor preferred to persist with hopes of easier finance.

In Washington, where by mid-October the Mission assessed the position to be grimmer than London seemed willing to admit, the American response to London's unease about servicing a new loan was to invite Keynes to formulate a waiver of interest, related to Britain's capacity to pay.[117] Two types of escape clause emerged: a 'London waiver' providing for deferment, to be based on the Chancellor's 'fundamental' and general international conditions; and a 'Washington waiver', providing for cancellation of interest on the narrower basis of British capacity to pay.[118] Keynes first devised a 'London waiver' for deferment of capital repayment, to operate if international convertibility seriously deteriorated, or a prolonged depression occurred in world trade, if the International Monetary Fund declared the dollar to be scarce. London's opposition to an escape clause failed to produce better terms from the Americans. Only when it was quite clear that the Americans were determined about the requirement of an interest rate charge, and that Britain was trapped in a weak position when a waiver was offered to ease the potential burden, did the British Mission venture to air informally to Vinson and Clayton the possibility of a 'Washington waiver'. London remained cautious, fearing a repetition of the circumstances of the 1931 financial crisis,[119] believing that the terms for further American financial assistance would, in such conditions, compromise unacceptably the independence of British economic policy.

It was to take the Chancellor from early October to early November to move towards acceptance of a 'Washington waiver', which he insisted must work automatically;[120] but there was to be a struggle before that requirement was more or less satisfied (below, pp 321–2).

As soon as the Cabinet had approved (6 November) the proposals under Alternatives 'A' and 'B', details of which had already been despatched to the British representatives, the Chancellor cabled that they could 'go ahead with our blessing'.[121] It quickly became clear, however, that it would be difficult to move ahead as hoped. Not only were London's proposals unacceptable to the Americans, but their own views were hardening. Within days, the most serious tensions so far in the negotiations were to develop, and were to lead to continuing crisis from the middle of November until an agreement was eventually signed early in December.

Initially, conscious that in trying for interest as low as one per cent they might lose that and more, the three senior British negotiators (Halifax, Keynes and Brand) proposed to Vinson and Clayton (6 November) that a credit of $4 billion should be granted along the lines of Alternative 'A', with two per cent on the interest-bearing tranche, and that there should also be finance for the Lend-Lease settlement (the Cabinet had authorised acceptance of up to $½billion). A waiver would operate if export earnings fell below the cost of pre-war imports. The Americans' reception of this was discouraging. They had $3½ rather than $4 billion in mind, and on Lend-Lease they were still, after all, unwilling to confirm that terms would be the same as for a credit. Not least, there was 'the heaviest going' over the suggestion that $2 billion of the credit should be provided, interest-free, specifically for the liberalisation of the sterling area. Vinson and Clayton stressed that, whilst a credit would be conditional upon liberalisation, the two were not to be associated; indeed, they were now 'violently' opposed to White's scheme. Accordingly the British team hurriedly revised the paper embodying the proposals so that it would be available for the Americans' own 'Top Committee' the following day; it then excluded discussion of accumulated balances, and spoke in general terms of making sterling available without discrimination[122] (see Appendix 20 for extracts from this memorandum).

(16) THE EMERGENCE OF THE AMERICAN TERMS

The American Committee considered the British proposals in the light of their technical experts' assessment of British needs in relation to prospective deficits in the balance of payments, to gold and dollar reserves, and to help that might come from other countries, particularly from Canada; somewhat to the embarrassment of the British negotiators, Mr Graham Towers had hinted to the Americans that $1 billion might be forthcoming.[123] Two main questions concerned the Committee. First was the amount of the credit. It became clear that, notwithstanding earlier discussions, which had produced as a compromise figure that of $3½ billion already presented to the British, Clayton continued to press for $4 billion. It was agreed, however, to leave the amount on one side until clarification with the British of convertibility matters. The second main question concerned an interest charge; it was agreed that this should apply to the whole credit, at two per cent. There was broad agreement on other matters already familiar in the negotiations, such as the provision of a grace period before repayment, and of deferment of payments in case of balance of payments difficulties. There was, however, a new element in the proposed commitment on convertibility: that it should extend beyond the sterling area countries, by the elimination of the discriminatory arrangements which restricted the use of sterling by most *non*-sterling countries.[124]

Hitherto discussion of convertibility had concentrated on that proposed for the current earnings of sterling area countries, and for balances released to them. During the war, Monetary and Payments Agreements (subsumed for most purposes under the head of 'Payments Agreements')[125] with allies and neutrals had provided, broadly, that currently earned sterling could be used freely within the sterling area, although not (other than in the distinctive cases of the USA and Switzerland, which enjoyed full convertibility of current sterling) outside it. The continuance of such arrangements into the difficult early post-war years, allowing the projected Anglo-American financial settlement to be confined to the sterling of the sterling area, had been taken for granted: for example, in the memorandum that Keynes prepared for the War Cabinet in spring 1945 (above, pp 239 – 40). Indeed, well before then, as the end of the war was thought to be approaching, negotiations were being undertaken with a number of countries. It was apparently only at a late stage in the Anglo-American negotiations, when White was shown the draft British proposals about sterling (5 November), that the Americans realised that they did not encompass payments agreements. Reporting this to London, Keynes noted that such agreements would need re-shaping; he declared, however, that he had never suggested the possibility of commitments involving non-sterling countries, and said that White was 'now under no illusion' that on this Britain clung to its transitional rights.[126] London was apprehensive of American intentions, rumours of which had recently weakened sterling, and warned against ('. . . as you would shun the devil') discussion of payments agreements.[127] Keynes responded that the American attitude was partly the result of lack of understanding of payments agreements, etc, but was largely 'doctrinal'. It would be necessary at least to harmonise the existing treatment of American sterling receipts with whatever form of convertibility lay ahead (that would be a largely technical matter). On the wider issue, he suggested that it might be helpful to include in the final document a clause looking to agreement on non-sterling convertibility after completion of a sterling area settlement. In broadly assenting, the Treasury stressed that such a clause must not diminish the transitional rights.[128]

There was to be no easy or quick solution to these new convertibility problems, nor to those concerning the amount and terms of a credit. When White had informed the American committee of the British intention to maintain the payments agreements, Clayton's reaction was that their discriminatory features must go.[129] At the outset of a series of meetings that followed (9, 10, 12 & 13 November) between the Anglo-American principals, he and Vinson made clear not only their rejection of Alternative 'A' but also their concern that the convertibility to follow financial assistance should cover the currently earned sterling of the payments agreements countries. Halifax and Keynes struggled to bridge the differences, with little success. Tense exchanges between a sick Clayton and a tetchy Keynes were reported; 'we seemed to touch bottom in the negotiations'.[130] Keynes was briefly tempted to settle forthwith, but was dissuaded from that course; and, shortly afterwards, encouragement for Halifax and Keynes in their stand against the American terms evidently came from the Prime Minister, by then in Washington (12 November).[131]

As these exchanges between principals continued, uncovering further differences and difficulties, the American technical experts were 'in purdah', preparing a draft of their proposals.[132] The British Mission, anxious about the terms and about Keynes's apparent physical and nervous exhaustion, looked forward to receiving the proposals, less in the expectation that they would be agreeable than in the hope that they would provide clarification. In the event the British representatives were to be horrified on receiving the American draft (15 November). Not only were the terms as bad as Vinson and Clayton had outlined, but they were phrased, in an attempt to cover technical details, in a manner that appeared niggling and even offensive.[133]

The US proposals had two features in particular which evoked fears of a collapse of the negotiations. One was the provision for deferment (*not* a waiver) of annual repayments of a credit. This would operate under three main conditions. The first was that, as certified by the new International Monetary Fund, the annual average of Britain's overseas earnings from exports, together with net invisible income, had fallen in the five years preceding its invocation below a level sufficient to purchase the pre-war volume of imports. Annual pre-war imports were taken as the average of the three years 1936 – 8. Their value, to be adjusted for subsequent price changes, was £866 million. This was calculated on a basis which gave a high valuation and therefore made the deferment relatively more accessible. A second condition, however, referred to the state of Britain's gold and foreign exchange reserves: that they had fallen, in the calendar year preceding resort to deferment, to less than twenty per cent of the value of imports over the preceding five years. Thirdly, the deferment must also apply to Britain's non-dollar obligations: the repayment of sterling balances and the servicing of new loans made to the United Kingdom from 1 January 1945. This was not all, however, for the deferment device could also operate in reverse. That is, the US could call the latest deferred instalment for repayment, in addition to the annual repayment currently due, if Britain's overseas earnings and reserves rose above the defined levels. Further, should releases of sterling balances, or repayment of loans received since 1 January 1945, be accelerated a comparable acceleration should be made in repayment of the American credit.[134]

The other major difficulty in the US draft concerned the proposed approach to the treatment of sterling balances. The United Kingdom would be expected to undertake to make an early settlement; to limit the release of balances to an amount that, by the end of 1951, would not exceed British gold and foreign exchange reserves at the time at which the US credit became effective; and to restrict annual releases, from the end of June 1951, to no more than $150 million during the life of the credit.[135]

That these two features, both unacceptable, the second probably unenforceable as well, could compromise the negotiations followed from discussions in London and from what had passed between London and the British Mission. The deferment device, although – superficially – automatic, as the Chancellor had insisted, would in fact require just the sort of close surveillance of the British economy of which he was so apprehensive. The second feature, indeed those aspects also of the first which sought to link repayments of dollar and sterling obligations, encountered London's continuing retreat from the original hopes of securing a clear-cut settlement of sterling balances. This problem had been somewhat overshadowed hitherto by the struggle over the basic terms for a credit. Having emphasised the voluntary character of any settlement, London had come to recognise by early November the scant chances of securing substantial cancellation (above, pp 297 – 8). Keynes's draft for the Americans on 'Sterling Area Arrangements' (above, p 293), essentially a repetition of proposals broadly agreed in London before the Washington negotiations had opened, had referred to the British aim of reducing balances by about one-third as well as to the amount of possible releases. This was amended so as to exclude mention of particular amounts after Sir Wilfrid Eady had cabled London's strong objection, adding 'My personal judgement is that American obduracy for a quantified commitment on cancellation might bring the talks to a real deadlock'.[136]

(17) TENSION OVER THE AMERICAN TERMS

A full meeting of the Anglo-American Finance Committee had been arranged to discuss the proposals immediately (15 November). So convinced were the British representatives that the draft would be as unacceptable to London as to themselves that they planned to refuse discussion of it and to seek instructions from London, warning of the grave position.[137] On this occasion, the Ambassador was clearly in charge, and presented the British assessment.[138] A preliminary handicap to discussion was the omission of the precise amount of the proposed credit. Acknowledging that some relatively new details on generalised convertibility and on the ending of discrimination in trade controls presented difficulties, which it might nevertheless be possible to resolve, Lord Halifax stressed the sombre implications of the lack of common ground over the two major problems. After the pressure on the United Kingdom to accept a waiver in order to make the servicing costs of a credit less unmanageable, the proposed deferment provisions, he told the Americans, were far different from what the British had contemplated, and they could not consider them. As for the proposals to deal with sterling balances, they went far beyond what was tolerable: negotiations with sterling countries must be the responsibility of the United Kingdom, and could not be the subject of direction by the USA. He warned that if the draft embodied 'the final and considered view of the US Administration the United Kingdom Government would be forced to the conclusion that the present negotiations had failed'. Negotiations might be resumed subsequently, perhaps after a year, but meanwhile British approval of Bretton Woods and of the proposals for commercial policy would be suspended.

The Ambassador's dignified exposition[139] did not, after all, end the proceedings, for Vinson and Clayton, perturbed by the British reaction, stressed that the proposals should be regarded as a draft, not as an ultimatum, and that they were an attempt to match oral understandings with Congressional necessities. Thereupon substantial discussion ensued, in which an evidently tense Keynes[140] examined each paragraph in turn. He thought that the proposals on general convertibility, soon and ever since to be productive of controversy, 'did not involve substantial points of principle', although he noted that a more gradual move towards it had been in mind and would be both desirable and more practicable. Elaborating the Ambassador's criticisms he underlined three issues. First, the reserves criterion for deferment implied a level of reserves that, taking account of liabilities, would be unrealistically and unacceptably far too low. Further, while the US draft provided for governmental consultation should international monetary conditions seem to warrant that, Keynes, with the 'London waiver' in mind (above, p 299), sought 'special provision' to protect the United Kingdom position as regards payments to the US in the event of a substantial breakdown of multilateral clearing. A second major criticism was of the nature of the proposed relief. Whereas there had been envisaged a generous minded, straightforward, waiver of interest, there was now instead a proposal for deferment which could be recouped as Britain recovered from the difficulties causing the original deferment. To Lord Halifax's description of this as involving 'something like economic servitude', Keynes added that it might be seen 'as an attempt to keep the United Kingdom on the bread line'. Any proposal in that spirit, and in terms requiring continuous surveillance of British economic policy, would realise the worst fears of the British Government, and would stand no chance of acceptance. The third criticism was that, in dealing with sterling balances, the requirement of precise arrangements would necessitate prior agreements with the major countries concerned, so that American reliance on British intentions was to be preferred. Further, the proposed restriction of releases and repayments would hamper Britain both in bargaining with sterling countries and in relations with non-sterling countries that held balances; the most that could be accepted would be some arrangement to define the degree to which such payments would rank in priority with those for servicing an American credit.

The American explanations of the principal terms in dispute were clear enough. The intention of the reserves criterion was that borrowers, of which the United Kingdom would not be the only one, would repay when able to do so; and comparable considerations had inspired the 'reverse deferment'. As for the restrictions on sterling repayments, the concern was that new credit should not be used to repay old debts.

Thus the differences were clarified, though not settled. Breakdown had, however, been averted. It was agreed that, while technical experts were to continue consultation, the senior US representatives would reconsider the waiver/deferment provisions.

Four days later (19 November) a further meeting of the Anglo-American Finance Committee considered revised US proposals.[141] These emerged as more tentative and less like a definite memorandum than the British representatives had anticipated: somewhat to their consternation. They had hoped that a more precise document, suitable for transmission to London, would permit a brief meeting in which Halifax could make the running in order to limit the strain on Keynes – and to limit *his* strain on the discussions.[142] But, Vinson having explained the American hope to reduce differences before a more definitive document went to London, there was once again an unexpectedly detailed discussion, with Keynes in the event 'very good — much more himself',[143] and largely presenting the British arguments.

Although the revised draft and discussion of it made some movement towards British views, that did not apply to two major British concerns. The amount of the credit remained unsettled. Thinking partly of the overall amount to be serviced, and starting from the reiterated British need for a minimum of $4 billion of 'new' money, the British had in mind no more than $½ billion for the Lend-Lease settlement. The Americans, however, had in mind a lower amount of 'new' money – $3½ billion – but a larger sum for Lend-Lease, Vinson indicating that the British limit was new to him. After inconclusive discussions, the amounts of the gross credit and of 'new' money were left for further consideration. No movement was made, either, on the unchanged American proposal for convertibility of all currently earned sterling (excluding that arising from military expenditure to the end of 1948) by the end of 1946. Keynes stressed that convertibility should not be one-sided, on the part of the United Kingdom, but must be mutual; he argued unsuccessfully for the substitution of a British proposal to provide for negotiations to ensure that payments agreements would not operate to prevent 'free availability' of currently earned receipts on either side.

The movement towards British views concerned the proposed sterling settlement and, to a limited extent, the deferment/waiver problem. In respect of the former, the revised US draft had substituted for the objectionable clause, requiring a British commitment to secure agreement and to limit releases, a more general statement of British intent to secure settlement of sterling balances. This did not differ significantly from the undertaking subsequently incorporated in the final agreement: 'varying according to the circumstances of each case', balances would be divided into three categories (not necessarily equal in size). One would be of balances to be released immediately and to be freely convertible. Another group would be released gradually, from 1951. Finally some balances would be written off ('adjusted' in the final agreement) 'as a contribution to the settlement of war and post-war indebtedness and in recognition of the benefits which the countries concerned might be expected to gain from such a settlement' (for the similar wording of the final agreement, section 10, see Appendix 24).

Following British disappointment over the deferment proposals, the Americans now offered a waiver of the interest element of repayment of a credit. This was tied, however, to conditions such as the British had previously rejected or sought to modify. On two relatively minor aspects Keynes tried, unsuccessfully, to make the waiver operate more favourably for Britain. Could not the critical level for overseas earnings be rounded up to the nearest £25 million, from £866 to £875 million, providing a modest cushion against the maintenance of import restrictions? Vinson, however, if sympathetic saw political risks in using an imprecise figure. Then, with the 'London waiver' still in mind, Keynes pointed out that payments difficulties might arise for Britain from restrictions by third countries on the convertibility of their currencies. He therefore proposed that in the calculation of Britain's reserves a deduction should be made for accruals of such currencies from current transactions (or an addition in case of their net decrease). The US reaction was that, in effect, their proposals on reserves were sufficiently non-specific. In any case, the reserves criterion for operation of the waiver, changed slightly in detail but not in surveillant character from that attaching to the previous deferment proposal, was one of the two major aspects to which the British Mission expected London would object most strongly. The other was the tying of the waiver's operation to comparable action on Britain's non-dollar obligations: three issues arose, which remained unresolved after prolonged discussion. One, unrevised from the previous draft, related to the servicing of non-dollar loans to Britain from the beginning of 1945, until the US credit was repaid. That meant, with the initial five years' grace period, over fifty-five years. Keynes protested against both the retrospective requirement and future commitment, and proposed that the obligation might apply only to loans made during 1946. From the American side, which stressed the domestic political need for such a provision, White proposed that it should cover only the next five years. Keynes rejected that as impractical, given the economic uncertainties facing Britain, but it was effectively incorporated into the final agreement (section 5(iii) in Appendix 24).

The second issue in the operation of the waiver arose from the British request that the sterling balances of Colonial dependencies be excluded from calculations relating to the possible acceleration of repayments of British obligations. The spirit of this was later to be embodied in the American terms and in the final agreement, in the exclusion of such balances from reductions as a consequence of the invocation of the waiver (below, p 322, and Appendix 24, section 6(iii)). Immediately, however, the problem was effectively subsumed in the general intensive discussion on the third issue concerning the waiver: the now implicit limits on repayment of sterling debt. The revised draft had indeed dropped the previously proposed limits on this, only to embed them indirectly, in the British view. Any increase of sterling repayments above a stated level, now $175 million annually at British suggestion instead of the previous $150 million, was to be accompanied by an equal increase in repayment of the US credit. Such a provision, Keynes declared, would effectively mean that, given Britain's likely dollar shortage, no increase would be made in repayments of sterling (such a linkage, he was later to add, could also be harmful, for extra re-payment to the US of scarce dollars would tend to deflate world trade).[144] The strong American concern for broadly equal treatment of dollar and non-dollar debt remained unshaken, however, and the British representatives agreed to inform London accordingly when reporting this and other Anglo-American differences.

At this stage, the British Mission despatched the American draft, with a request for specific instructions on major difficulties.[145] First was the amount of the credit. With $4 billion of 'new money' thought to be in American minds, the Mission asked for instructions to seek that sum, on the terms already discussed, but to resist the less favourable terms and the sum of over $750 million being sought by the Americans for the Lend-Lease settlement. Should a gross sum of $4½ billion be available, the British representatives thought that up to $600 million for Lend-Lease might be accommodated (leaving therefore rather less than $4 billion of 'new money'). Authority was sought to discuss a formula linking a waiver to the reserves, but to oppose the disagreeable feature of accelerated repayments. On convertibility, authority was requested to accept it for the sterling area at the end of 1946 on the conditions already discussed at length and agreed with London. The question of wider convertibility, and, associated with this, that of discrimination in import restrictions led the Mission to plead for flexibility. Such flexibility might involve acquiescence in American demands for early abrogation of Britain's rights under the nascent International Monetary Fund, which would have allowed controls on trade and payments to be used more freely in the Transition than subsequently. Pointing out that non-discrimination and convertibility were 'central' to the Americans' offer of credit, the Mission stressed that 'If we cannot give them sufficient satisfaction here, any negotiation on the present lines will fall to the ground'. The early surrender of discrimination, Keynes had recently noted,[146] would entail a major consequence only in the cost of dollar oil, which, however, it was hoped might be manageable.[147] On convertibility for the payments agreements countries, which the US wanted to operate simultaneously with that for the sterling area, the *minimum* that the Mission now hoped from London was agreement to undertake negotiations for 'free availability' for such countries' sterling receipts; before according this, it was necessary, the Mission and London had just agreed, to ensure that there would be reciprocity.[148] Momentarily, however, the Mission now urged London to consider going the whole way much earlier than anticipated, that is to provide general convertibility from the end of 1946. It would be difficult, they argued, once convertibility had been granted to sterling countries, to limit that allowed to other countries. They therefore sought authority 'to be in a position at the last lap to go to Clayton with this ultimate concession if he will meet us on any other outstanding matters'. This request, after yet further and even more rapid reflection, and while Bank and Treasury memoranda were already condemning it (below), they withdrew next day. The realisation that the American draft would deprive Britain not just of rights against members of the International Monetary Fund, but also of those against *non*-members made it unacceptable 'even in the last resort'.[149] But alarm had been caused in London and also, probably, damage to confidence in the Mission by this collectively performed double turnabout.

To all these requests the Ambassador and Keynes urged London to reply speedily: the position in Washington was deteriorating as the negotiations dragged on, with their 'subject . . . gone stale', whilst Keynes himself felt that he was 'now rather near the end of my physical reserves'.[150] They advised against attempting wholesale re-shaping of the American proposals. That might provoke suspicion that Britain contemplated withdrawing from understandings already reached, and could cause delay which would endanger the now very compressed timetable for ratification of the Bretton Woods agreements. It seemed to them more prudent to give 'a stiff reply with counter proposals on the same pattern as their draft'.[151]

(18) A BRITISH DISPUTE OVER CONVERTIBILITY

London's reactions to the initial convertibility proposals from the Mission were of scarcely qualified and contemptuous rejection. 'Political dynamite' was an immediate Treasury verdict on the proposal to abandon discriminatory controls; every currency in which the United Kingdom incurred a deficit would become a 'hard' currency. It would apparently require renunciation of the 'scarce currency' clause of the Monetary Fund: a right to discriminate which, said the Bank, we could not surrender. On sterling area convertibility, the Treasury held to its insistence on adequate aid and on a previous settlement of balances. It was, however, on general convertibility that London concentrated its opposition. Treasury and Bank alike stressed that it could not be contemplated on a non-reciprocal basis, and that the abandonment of the transition period so early as proposed was unthinkable.[152] The Chancellor pointed out to colleagues that 1946 would be a 'completely artificial year, both from the point of view of exports and the choice of sources of supply'. A senior Treasury official reflected London's thinking in advising that it was necessary to distinguish between 'the merely distasteful' and the 'vitally dangerous'. Early general convertibility was of the latter type, and would endanger the country's financial and economic future; American insistence on it would have to be regarded as a breaking point in the negotiations.[153]

(19) THE PRIME MINISTER'S INITIATIVE

Summarising reactions to the American draft as a whole, there was much that 'we could not stomach', the Chancellor cabled to the Mission.[154] He had reported gloomily and pugnaciously to colleagues on the Ministers' Committee that it read 'like a moneylenders' agreement and a bad one'.[155] Detailing his objections to the proposals over the waiver, the liberalisation of the sterling area, and the shortened transition period, he concluded that the Americans should be told 'quite plainly' that an agreement on such lines would be unacceptable. In a draft telegram to the Mission, submitted for colleagues' approval – which was not entirely forthcoming – he favoured 'clearing...the brushwood' and seeking a simple agreement; that would be limited to specifying the amount and purpose of a credit, and to providing for subsequent Anglo-American consultation on issues that might arise. He proposed that the total amount to be sought should be reduced to $4 billion, to include up to $600 million for the Lend-Lease settlement. He rejected a number of proposals: the link between a waiver and the level of Britain's reserves; that for an early end to discrimination in import restrictions; the early adoption of convertibility for the current earnings of the sterling area and of the rest of the world; and hence also the early end of the transition.

In ensuing discussions with senior Ministers, the Chancellor did not shrink from the possibility that his proposals might risk a break in negotiations, but his colleagues, notably the Foreign Secretary (Mr E Bevin), warned against action likely to precipitate that. Instead of his bluntly phrased draft telegram they agreed that the Prime Minister should make a formal approach to President Truman, to explain what appeared to be feasible, and what was not, in the US proposals.[156] Initially, however, these explanations would be cabled to the Ambassador for comment and, in effect, as new instructions in the negotiations.

The Prime Minister informed the Ambassador[157] that agreement should be possible on the following:

(1) *'Amount of Credit* not less than 4 billion including Lend/Lease at 2 per cent, to be repaid over 50 years beginning after 5 years'.

(2) 'Liberalisation of the sterling area on the lines in' Keynes's memorandum on the sterling area.[158]

(3) 'Recommendation to Parliament of Bretton Woods as soon as we reach a financial agreement'.

(4) 'Commercial policy as in the documents recently agreed'.

London was *not* prepared to agree on:

(5) 'Completion of the negotiations with creditor countries by the end of 1946'.

(6) 'Abrogation at the end of 1946 of our transitional rights under Bretton Woods'.

(7) 'Formally ranking the American debt ahead of all other external obligations'.

In addition, the Prime Minister expressed a preference for the waiver in *both* forms originally proposed: the London 'deferment' under adverse international trading conditions, and the Washington waiver of interest on a simple basis of reduced capacity to pay. Failing such provisions, Ministers would be prepared to rely on a clause providing for Anglo-American consultation in circumstances that would otherwise have activated one or both of such waivers.

The grave implications for the eventual convertibility of sterling, and immediately for relations between the Mission and London of parts of the Prime Minister's message (items 2 and 5) were at first not perceived either in London or in Washington. That message, re-phrased, was given to Vinson and Clayton (25 November). They were shocked but, with Clayton too unwell to discuss properly, agreed to reconsider matters.[159] At technicians' level came reassurance of American determination to continue negotiations.[160] In advance of fuller discussions the following day, the Ambassador advised delay in approaching the President.[161] For their part, the British representatives lacked enthusiasm about some of the new instructions. On the lower limit for a credit, whilst appreciating the scope to reduce their bid, they were apprehensive. It would 'cut things dangerously fine' to have only $3.4 billion of 'new money'; indeed, there might be even less as the Americans were seeking, indeed appeared to be insisting upon, at least $750 million for the Lend-Lease settlement.[162] Apprehension was also the reaction over London's lukewarm words on the waiver. All in the Mission were 'greatly disturbed'. Stressing its 'inestimable value both practically and politically' as a possible precedent for other settlements and in the light of the prospective burden on the balance of payments, they warned of their wish to be dissociated from rejection of an appropriate waiver.[163]

At the Anglo-American Finance Committee (26 November),[164] significant progress was to be made. On the closely connected issues of the waiver and of priority for dollar repayments, the Americans withdrew the reserves criterion for activating the waiver. Vinson, who was reported as never having been wholly convinced of the case for that requirement, yielded to appeals from the British representatives to trust the *bona fides* of the British Government; the final terms were to include an undertaking to take account of reserves before invoking the waiver.[165] As for the priority of dollar repayments, although that had nominally disappeared on the abandonment of the proposal for increased repayments when British reserves rose, a flavour of it persisted. This was in the two features embodying the *pari passu* principle, which were intended to demonstrate to Congress that the United Kingdom would not be able, by making undue repayment of non-dollar debt, to weaken its capacity to repay the US. On one feature, the acceleration proposal, a vigorous British attack shook even the obduracy of the most stubborn American representative.[166] The other feature was the proposal that repayment of non-dollar debt outstanding at the time of a credit should be financed, until the end of 1951, from sources other than that credit. London had protested that such a requirement would be extremely difficult to operate,[167] and Vinson agreed to its provisional deletion. When, however, the Americans' own Financial Committee reconsidered the two matters (28 November) it decided that, although the acceleration proposal could be scrapped, the constraint on the use of the credit should, after all, be retained.[168] This was to be embodied in the final agreement (section 6(i)); it was regarded on the British side as meaning that drawings on the credit were not to exceed the total of the United Kingdom's own balance of payments deficits to the end of 1951.[169]

Much less headway was made on the Prime Minister's injunction to resist an early date for surrender of transitional rights under Bretton Woods. The British unsuccessfully proffered simple undertakings. Between the United Kingdom and the US, there would certainly be no exchange restrictions, other than those that might be allowed under the articles of the International Monetary Fund; in respect of the US, Britain would not use the transitional rights.

Beyond that the British sought to limit commitments on exchange control and trade discrimination to their reduction 'as rapidly... as world economic conditions permit... and... to the greatest extent compatible with the restoration of the United Kingdom's external position... '.[170] The Americans stood out, however, for a fixed and early date, adducing the familiar need to satisfy Congress; one of their negotiators stressed that it 'would be a serious matter if... despite... very substantial financial assistance... there was to be nothing to show... in the shape of a specific undertaking that the United Kingdom would abandon protective discriminatory measures by a given date'.[171]

These crucial issues went back for further American consideration, but before they were to be settled, a bitter controversy erupted, not directly with the Americans, but between London and the British Mission, over the early provision of convertibility for the sterling area.

(20) THE CRISIS OVER STERLING CONVERTIBILITY

The possibility of an early move to convertibility for sterling area countries, it may be recalled and emphasised, had been accepted on all sides in the negotiations: by London, and by the American and British negotiators in Washington. Such convertibility, for current earnings, would be subject to the amount and terms of aid being satisfactory. The Prime Minister's rejection of a fixed date to complete negotiations over the accumulated sterling balances had not appeared to qualify his re-affirmation of the conditional British offer to liberalise the sterling area by the end of 1946 (with balances arising from military expenditure in the early post-war period excluded from current convertibility).[172] That there might be difficulty in reconciling the rejection and the re-affirmation was not immediately apparent. The British Mission accordingly included the commitment on convertibility, with the now routine qualifications, in their presentation of the Prime Minister's message to Vinson and Clayton. When, however, they reported this to London, the Chancellor swiftly replied that 'We do not wish this formal and public promise to be made' – a promise to 'release all current earnings throughout the whole of the sterling area as from the end of 1946'.[173] This horrified the Washington Mission. Words like 'sabotage' and 'betrayal' now passed in telephone, cable, and written communications.[174] Professor Robbins personally cabled Sir Edward Bridges his distress at what he saw as a withdrawal of assurances he had received on his recent London visit; he feared that this 'must wreck the negotiations' and declared that if it led to Keynes's resignation he 'should feel in honour bound to go with him'.[175] The whole Mission cabled a detailed review of the issue, concluding that adherence to the Chancellor's instructions, rather than to their own understanding of what had gone before and which they had believed the Prime Minister's message had supported, would seem to challenge their *bona fides*. They had assumed that objections to a time limit applied to negotiations on accumulated balances; they had, however, regarded the prospect that balances might otherwise be blocked as an incentive to sterling countries to reach a settlement. Reiterating that the commitment to early convertibility for the sterling area must be accepted, the Mission insisted that non-acceptance, withdrawing all that had long been promised to the Americans, would end hopes for an agreement.[176]

In London also there was rapid re-appraisal of the recent past, with opposite conclusions. It is difficult to disagree with the emollient conclusion of Sir Edward Bridges in replying to Professor Robbins, 'that there . . . [had] been a genuine misunderstanding', nor is it surprising that he had been 'tempted to quote a number of passages in support of the position held' in London.[177]

How had so grave a misunderstanding arisen? Two particular sources can be identified. The first reflected the contrasting emphases of Washington and London in the negotiations. The Mission faced the consistent American determination to secure an early end to discrimination and inconvertibility, the uncertain aspects being the Americans' estimates of the finance that Britain needed and that Congress would authorise. In contrast, London's stress was on Britain's financial needs; the uncertainties concerned the extent of the commitments that Bank, Treasury, and Parliament would regard as sustainable in relation to the amount of aid forthcoming. London had never, indeed, been enthusiastic about early convertibility; only Keynes's persuasiveness while still there, on the spot, had secured acquiescence in the double gamble of seeking substantial U.S aid and of contemplating early liberalisation.

The second source of misunderstanding was more complex. It involved differences over the interdependence of convertibility and settlement of sterling balances, and also over the wartime operation of the sterling area. The Bank made a careful analysis, which it passed to the Treasury, of numerous telegrams between London and the Mission in Washington; these undoubtedly tended to support the Bank-Treasury conclusion on the conditional nature of the proposed commitment on sterling area convertibility. Moreover, quoting the same document as that cited in the Prime Minister's message (see Appendix 20, paragraph II), the Bank noted that it carried 'the strong implication . . . that the current earnings [of the sterling area] will be dealt with in the same way and in the same negotiation as . . . the accumulated balances'.[178] But were matters sufficiently clear, when that same document had undermined the 'strong implication' that the Bank detected, by insisting, as had previous telegrams from London, that there be no commitment over quantification, or to a time limit for a settlement of sterling balances? A prospective settlement so uncertain in character sat ill with the Americans' known views. They sought early, decisive moves to sterling convertibility, thereby to end the discrimination they associated with the sterling area. On this rationale of convertibility, Keynes agreed, and London disagreed, with the Americans. In his draft of the sterling area memorandum towards the end of October, Keynes had both recognised and played down this discriminatory association, in terms which he quickly admitted were exaggerated. Under the controls evolved during the war, constraints on the use of sterling were so much greater outside the sterling area than within it that, he asserted, 'the whole purpose of...exchange control...has been to increase the availability of sterling and to enhance the attractiveness of...London balances...'.[179] A senior Treasury official rejected this abruptly as 'economical of truth' and insisted that the true source of discrimination was in exchange control, based on the unavoidable facts of the abundance of sterling and the scarcity of dollars.[180] Keynes would have none of this. He dismissed as not worth his attention Treasury amendments to his draft, designed to obscure what he held to have been the discriminatory character of the operation of the sterling area. In a famous and sometimes mis-quoted telegram[181] he scathingly rejected, as likely to 'cause surprise to the Americans in relation to Egypt and the Middle East', a crucial assertion: that, with individual sterling countries operating their own exchange controls, London had 'without exception provided foreign exchange for any expenditure authorised' by them.[182] His riposte to the Treasury, which had been echoing this view of the Bank of England ('The Old Lady of Threadneedle Street'), was that 'Some fig leaves which may pass muster with old ladies in London wilt in a harsher climate'. With this rough 'exchange of compliments', which Sir Wilfrid Eady of the Treasury feared would touch Bank susceptibilities, the struggle had far from ended. In what proved to be as much a forecast of imminent trouble as a verdict on that of the immediate past, he reflected that 'The simple truth is that Maynard [Keynes] has gone badly wrong on the whole of the handling of this draft of the Sterling Area'.[183]

The divergence between Keynes, who broadly held the assent of his colleagues in Washington, and the sceptics of Bank and Treasury, over the sterling area became particularly evident in the dispute over convertibility for the area. London argued that to give convertibility before securing a settlement with individual sterling countries of their balances would deprive it of the essential sanction that the former offered to procure the latter. Further, just as a time limit to settle balances would be an unacceptable handicap (above, pp 311, 314), so would a time limit for the grant of convertibility; leading sterling countries would interpret that as tantamount to being also a settlement of the balances.[184] In sharing objections to a time limit to settle balances, Keynes favoured, however, early convertibility. He did not believe that wartime restrictions on it were long sustainable. In contrast, as has been seen, he viewed the sterling balances as having been and as capable of continuing to be controlled, as a potential means of limiting sterling area expenditure under convertibility. Such an approach virtually reversed the Treasury's order of emphasis, that balances were largely *not* controlled, and that *in*convertibility was a necessary and sustainable protection; and, equally contrary to the Treasury, that approach led to the assertion that the two issues of settlement of balances and adoption of convertibility could be separated.

(21) LONDON'S DRAFT TERMS

The Chancellor defended London's position by reminding the Mission (28 November) that Keynes's memorandum, completed on the eve of the negotiations, had envisaged the release of current earnings *after* the overall scheme for an Anglo-American agreement had come into operation.[185] To concede convertibility in advance of that would be to surrender Britain's only bargaining point, as the threat of unilateral blocking of balances was not to be contemplated. The US should realise that to insist on early convertibility would jeopardise settlement of balances, especially as some were in commercial, not governmental, hands (and therefore less easily controlled). To a Cabinet meeting (29 November) the Chancellor submitted a draft of an Anglo-American financial agreement.[186] After opposition from some Ministers and a warning from the Chancellor that no better terms were likely to be secured, it was approved. Though going farther than originally contemplated to meet American views, the draft reiterated London's major objections and reservations, which a clutch of telegrams elaborated for the Washington Mission.[187] The amount of credit to be sought was yet again revised, upwards: to $4½ billion, to allow for both a higher Lend-Lease settlement and an earlier end of discriminatory import controls than had been contemplated. Dissatisfaction persisted about the terms of the waiver. Above all, London underlined its apprehensions over the twofold loss of flexibility as a member of the new International Monetary Fund, as the price for a financial agreement. One was that instead of a transition period of five years, implicit in the relevant Article (XIV) before Britain assumed the full obligations of the Fund, the American terms prescribed an extremely brief transition: around fifteen months if convertibility for all currently earned sterling, and non-discrimination in trade, were to operate within a year of the coming into force of a loan agreement. The other was that the American terms would deny Britain the benefit of the 'scarce currency' clause (Article VII) of the Fund, and hence the use after the transition of discrimination in trade controls, save in respect of abnormal conditions: to permit the use of inconvertible currencies accumulated before the end of 1946, in order to secure necessary imports; and in favour of countries whose economies had been 'disrupted by war'.[188]

On the critical issue of the transition and of full current convertibility, the Government guardedly offered to 'proceed not later than the end of 1946 to make arrangements' for the current earnings of sterling area countries to be freely convertible, without discrimination; at the same time, it would seek a settlement on a voluntary basis of sterling balances. Thereby, claimed the Chancellor, 'we were merely undertaking to carry out, without committing ourselves to an absolutely rigid time limit for completion, the negotiations which it had always been our intention to undertake with the sterling countries'. For the current earnings of the US and of other non-sterling countries, the proposals were as before: convertibility for the former would be immediate, thus reaffirming the existing position under exchange control, and for the latter it would be a British aim to achieve it as early as world economic conditions permitted.

Discriminatory import controls, London advised, could be lifted by the end of 1946, but a double check to finality on this should be sought: by *ex*clusion of explicit reference in the proposed terms to Britain's abandonment of the transition provisions of the IMF, by which discrimination was allowed (Article XIV); and by *in*clusion of an affirmation of the availability of the 'scarce currency' clause (Article VII). That provision would permit discrimination to be applied against a particular currency if the Fund formally declared it to be 'scarce'. Its absence would arouse criticism in Parliament[189] to which some eighteen months previously Keynes had commended it as a reassuring feature of the proposed new international monetary system.[190] Further, as the President of the Board of Trade had stressed to the Cabinet,[191] the proposed constraints on discrimination should be made consistent with the Americans' own proposals on commercial policy, still being discussed with them. Those proposals allowed discrimination in, for instance, the correction of balance of payments difficulties and in Britain's 'long-standing trade arrangements' for certain imports (ie, bulk-purchase contracts) from the Dominions and Colonies. London accordingly instructed the British representatives to seek retention of the clause, either explicitly or, given the known American sensitivity to suggestions that the dollar would be scarce (above, p 298), implicitly; they should in the latter case seek affirmation of the right to discriminate 'with the authority of the IMF' and should ensure that it was 'clearly understood' that the Fund's declaration of a currency's scarcity would allow invocation of the projected agreement's review clause in order to allow discrimination.

In a further batch of telegrams[192], the Washington Mission's sharpest reaction to the London draft was against the closely hedged approach to convertibility for the sterling area, which prompted reiteration of the 'unanimous conviction that the course we are told to take must be disastrous'. In order to secure settlement of balances, why contemplate reliance on an 'empty threat' of a non-enforceable withholding of convertibility? Even if enforceable, it was scarcely practicable to relax it piecemeal, country by country.[193] The Mission once again put its suggestion of a sanction which, it must be said, echoed proposals in both the eve-of-negotiations memorandum in September and in that on the sterling area of early November: that convertibility might be granted, but that countries failing to make a satisfactory settlement of their sterling balances should be warned not to expect early release of a portion of such balances, nor the subsequent release at stated dates of the remainder.[194] 'The pace of that release', stressed the Mission, 'has always been our real bargaining weapon'.[195] London, however, had again rejected that view, declaring that an agreement such as that being sought was no place for that kind of 'undefined half threat'.[196] The Bank, which had no taste for blocking, argued that it was difficult to distinguish between current and past earnings. Keynes's main supporter in the London discussions had remonstrated fiercely, but in vain, that that argument was inconsistent with the advocacy, by the Bank and its Treasury supporters, of the controlled release of balances as an alternative to formal sterling convertibility.[197]

Unyielding so far on convertibility, London insisted that its reservations be presented to the Americans. With only a month to the end of the year, American anxiety to secure by then ratification of the Bretton Woods agreements was the major pressing reason to settle early.[198] The Ambassador warned, however, that to regard that as an opportunity to bargain for the British proposals would risk accusations of blackmail. With that advice, following a tense week of transatlantic recriminations, the Ambassador undertook to obey renewed instructions from the Prime Minister and the Chancellor to submit the London text to the Americans – but, even so, he preferred to delay, and to await the imminent arrival from London of Sir Edward Bridges.[199]

(22) CRISIS OVER TERMS AND OVER KEYNES: SIR EDWARD BRIDGES TAKES CHARGE

Throughout the negotiations there had been in London a current of mistrust of Keynes, mingled with the downright opposition to his ideas at the Bank and amongst senior Treasury officials. The temptation to blame him, surely inaccurately in view of the preliminary discussions (above, pp 264 – 5), for raising false hopes of generous American finance, tended to foster London's lack of confidence. Thus, to range from the general to the particular, there was Sir Wilfrid Eady's comment that 'I am always a bit anxious about K. when he is being idle and ingenious',[200] and his judgement that over the sterling area problem Keynes had gone 'badly wrong' (above, p 315). The Chancellor himself, when formulating to senior Cabinet colleagues the near-final instructions to be despatched by the Prime Minister, had evidently come to feel that, where given something of a free hand, Keynes had played it too freely for London's comfort.[201]

Certainly Keynes himself constituted a problem in the negotiations. His colleagues became uneasy about his conduct towards the Americans and all too evident lack of *rapport* with Mr Vinson; yet, as one particular incident clearly illustrated, he was indispensable (above, p 306). But there was justifiable apprehension about the general health of a man known to be frail physically, although this must be seen in the context of pressures which, especially towards the end of negotiations, had driven all his colleagues close to exhaustion.[202]

The negotiations were complex and inevitably lengthy; they encompassed numerous relatively subsidiary negotiations, although the issues of financial and commercial policy produced most tension. Given the triple handicaps of prolonged absence from London, of distance, and of communications it was to be expected that misunderstandings and even mistrust would develop between the Mission and the Treasury. Keynes had indeed foreseen all this and the eventual dispatch of a senior person from London to report and perhaps to take over negotiations. His own return for consultation had been considered, but rejected partly on health grounds and partly for fear of creating with the Americans a wrong impression that might jeopardise the negotiations.[203] Even so, would Keynes's return for consultation have had much better success than that of Professor Robbins proved to have had in dissipating the confusion over sterling area policy?

A visit by Sir Edward Bridges had originally been suggested by Keynes himself,[204] but he could scarcely have contemplated the circumstances in which, at the beginning of December, it now occurred. For the second time (the first being over commercial policy at the outset of the negotiations) London was by-passing Keynes. Telegrams arrived for Bridges 'personally'; that and their contents, together with the views of Sir Edward's fellow visitor from the Treasury, Mr A T K Grant, indicated London's apprehension that Keynes was unlikely to conclude an agreement acceptable to the Cabinet. That his resignation, which he had frequently contemplated, had not been forthcoming 'had certainly not been for want of trying on their part'; Keynes's vindication came swiftly, however, as Bridges appraised the Washington setting with its problems for the Mission. He soon appeared to be at one with them when, two days after arrival, he reacted to a 'Baboon' telegram from London with a dismissive 'Let them Baboon away'.[205]

If Parliament were to ratify Bretton Woods by the end of the year, a possibility contingent upon acceptable conditions for an American loan, it would be necessary to commence the parliamentary debates by 12 December in view of the Christmas recess. To ensure production of papers in time, it would be necessary to complete negotiations by 5 or 6 December. Leaving London at only three hours' notice,[206] Sir Edward Bridges reached Washington on 1 December. In prolonged and exhausting meetings next day (a Sunday) the two delegations sieved the revised US draft and the British counter-proposals to distinguish those issues on which agreement was more or less possible from those intractabilities which had precipitated the despatch of Bridges. 'We all felt by the time we had finished that we knew pretty well what they would give and what they wouldn't ', noted Lord Halifax, adding that 'Bridges says they [ie, London] will grumble but accept'.[207]

On several points there was verbal tidying-up and some more flexible phrasing. The major problems to be settled concerned the amount of the credit; the waiver; and, embracing the crucial questions of convertibility and discrimination in trade, the length of the transition before Britain would be expected to assume the full obligations of the International Monetary Fund and her position in relation to the provisions of its 'scarce currency' clause.

(23) RESOLUTION OF MAJOR DIFFICULTIES:

(a) The Amount of the Loan

Both sides had been circling around a gross figure for aid of close to $4.5 billion. Prolonged lack of agreement about the amount to be provided for the Lend-Lease settlement sustained uncertainty about the amount of 'new money'; revised British hopes had been that it would at least approach $4 billion, whereas the Americans saw only $3.5 billion. At last the amount of the loan was resolved, by President Truman's compromise of £3.75 billion;[208] in addition, a sum of $650 million was to settle outstanding Lend-Lease payments due from Britain (see below, pp 325 – 6). With the total thus only $100 million short of the minimum of $4.5 billion that the Mission had thought to be necessary, Bridges recommended acceptance; the balance might be obtainable, but it was inadvisable to try.[209] As for the terms for repayment and interest, they were as already discussed. Repayment would begin after five years, when also interest at two per cent per annum would commence to be paid; over the fifty-year period this would involve annual costs of approximately $140 million (£35 million), with the effective interest rate being 1.6 per cent.

(b) The Form of the Waiver

Although London had eventually accepted the principle of a waiver, and had resisted its dependence on rigid constraints upon both the level of reserves and repayment of non-dollar debt, the terms and conditions remained to be agreed. London raised two particular objections to those proposed. The use of a five-year moving average of overseas earnings as a reference level it deplored as 'nonsensical', for it meant that it might become possible to invoke the waiver only after a succession of bad years, by which time overseas earnings might be improving.[210] The Washington Mission disagreed, and claimed that the moving average principle had made less necessary, to American eyes, a specific link with Britain's reserves.[211] When pressed on the point early in December, the Americans insisted on retaining it, as more defensible to the US public than possible alternatives.[212] In the event, that is when Treasury officials examined the waiver mechanism shortly after US ratification of the financial agreement, and when Britain first contemplated resort to the waiver, at the earliest opportunity in 1951, it certainly proved to be more cumbersome than may have been anticipated. Together with the form of the waiver itself, which was never operated as originally devised, it was eventually to be replaced by simpler arrangements.[213]

A further objection was to the proposed coupling of the waiver on the US credit to repayments of non-dollar debt. Treasury and Bank of England officials feared that this would prove unworkable or harmful in the light of the technicalities of sterling area payments mechanisms.[214] For instance, fluctuations in sterling balances would reflect the unpredictable balances of payments of sterling countries; British development aid to the Colonies might affect both their sterling balances, and their dollar earnings or dollar expenditure, in a manner defying the proposed commitments to the USA.[215] The Chancellor therefore pressed for the Americans to accept, as they had done on the issues of the relevance of Britain's reserves and of world economic conditions, a broad assurance that the waiver would be invoked only 'after taking due account' of repayments to other creditors.[216] To secure such a change, replied the Mission, would be 'One of the hardest tasks you have set us', although they shared London's dislike of these American proposals. To underline the problem, they pointed out that the suggested change confronted a major American sticking point, since it could be interpreted as making the activation of the waiver result from priority being given to non-dollar repayments, thus implying subordinate status for the new dollar debt. Further to stress the gravity of the matter, the Mission declared that it was one 'which we have debated for endless hours and days'.[217] They nevertheless struggled for some easement, their task being further complicated by London's renewed attempt at the end of November to secure the addition of the 'London waiver', ie, a deferment of capital repayment; but that would have revived previously unacceptable American requirements, and proved unobtainable.[218]

The Americans' wish for a successful conclusion to the negotiations helped to secure a compromise on non-dollar debt. They would not accept the Chancellor's suggestion that, in invoking the waiver, it would be sufficient for Britain to affirm that it would take account of non-dollar creditors; nor would they accept the modified reference to 'equitable treatment as between all...external creditors' which Sir Edward Bridges proposed soon after his arrival.[219] There was American sympathy, however, for the problems of the Colonies, and they quickly yielded exemption of their sterling balances from the proportionate reductions of repayments of non-dollar debt otherwise required on operation of the waiver.[220] Arrangements more favourable to Britain were not to be obtained, said Sir Edward, who viewed as 'not unreasonable' the constraint on non-dollar payments in computing the case for the dollar waiver.[221] Thus were finally shaped the intricate commitments of sections 5 and 6 of the agreement.

(c) Discrimination, Convertibility, and the Transition:
   The Final Crises Over the Terms

The agreement to end discrimination, by the end of 1946 in the British draft terms, within a year of the agreement becoming effective in the American, did not yet reflect the British concern to qualify it by the 'scarce currency' clause of the IMF. The commitment to end exchange control, ie, to operate general convertibility, likewise omitted any reference so far to that clause, whilst including two references to the relinquishment by Britain of the Fund's transition easements. Those references were respectively to the convertibility of US current earnings when the agreement became effective (no more than a formalisation of the existing position under wartime exchange control); and of those of other non-sterling countries a year subsequently. As for convertibility of the sterling area's current earnings, the American terms continued to incorporate a provision for that to operate not later than the end of 1946. There was, however, a proposed easement of both the general and the sterling area convertibility commitment, to allow for 'exceptional cases...after consultation'.[222]

On the contentious question of current account convertibility for the sterling area, Bridges confirmed, as Keynes had already reported, that the Americans regarded that as already agreed. The most that 'by hard fighting' he could secure, in addition to the let-out for 'exceptional cases', was the change of date from the end of 1946 to one year after the agreement became effective: the same as for convertibility of sterling receipts outside the US and the sterling area. That concession, however, was traded against the bringing forward by an equivalent period of the ending of discrimination: the end of 1946 instead of within one year of the agreement as the British and most recent American drafts had contemplated.[223] By this time (3 December), Bridges felt that there was 'not much left to argue about', with one qualification: on wider convertibility the Americans had held firm, but had betrayed sufficient uncertainty on detail to encourage Bridges to invite London to press its case very explicitly.[224] That case was threefold. With the sterling area's early convertibility now unavoidable, there were first the two remaining intractabilities: the scope for discrimination through specific retention of access to the 'scarce currency' clause, and the availability of the transitional rights before the operation of general convertibility. To apprehensions over these, the three-man group of Prime Minister, Chancellor, and President of the Board of Trade, whom the Cabinet now agreed should settle the negotiations, added a third concern.[225] This was the denial by the proposed agreement, during the 55 years that it would run, of Britain's right to leave the International Monetary Fund if, for instance, it wished to undertake a substantial devaluation.

So apprehensive were the Ministers that they came very close to suspending negotiations. The Chancellor believed that to do so over Bretton Woods should provide 'a clear and limited issue', to Britain's rather than the USA's advantage; and he began to consider how he would announce the crisis to the House of Commons.[226]

The three Ministers accordingly told the US Ambassador in London and cabled the Washington Embassy that the three objectionable features ran counter to the Bretton Woods agreements, singling out Britain for exclusion from its safeguards. They could scarcely commend that agreement, thus restricted, to Parliament, which would vote them down if they did.[227]

The final crisis now erupted. Although willing to yield on the 'scarce currency' provision and over British freedom to withdraw from the Monetary Fund, Mr Vinson and Mr Clayton emphasised that for them a breaking point would be British rejection of early general convertibility, and hence of a brief transition. Those requirements had been essential reasons for the Administration to consider a loan; deviation from them would alienate significant political and business groups.[228]

Now London had to consider whether to break. Treasury officials, stressing the need for the loan, and believing that they could provide the Chancellor with an adequate justification in Parliament for surrendering transitional rights, advised him against a break. The Treasury offered three suggestions: to restrict the application of convertibility, to postpone it to a later date, or to elaborate the provision for 'exceptional' conditions in order to make the end of the transition depend on Anglo-American consultation.[229] The Prime Minister instructed Bridges, after transatlantic telephone discussions and cabling, which had left no doubt of the critical position, to try the second and third.[230] The time difference momentarily caused this high drama to approach knockabout farce when a late night search through Washington for Mr Vinson eventually located him in the same hotel as the British delegation, actively participating in a lively party. In the subsequent impromptu discussions, he firmly rejected both the proposal to delay convertibility to the end of 1948 (instead of one year after the agreement became effective), and, even more strongly, what he regarded as the pretence of a consultation provision.[231]

Although the senior State Department official, whose approval of his decision Vinson had been able to obtain, now concluded that the negotiations had at last collapsed,[232] the senior British delegates determined that this was not to be, and accordingly cabled to London their recommendation to accept the American requirement for early general convertibility. The Ambassador personally cabled the Prime Minister and Foreign Secretary his regret at the failure to move the Americans, but urged acceptance in the light of the damage that a rejection and break would do to Anglo-American relations. Collectively, the delegates elaborated the rationale of the American position, in particular the American view that the lengthy transitional period envisaged at Bretton Woods had been predicated on the prospective deficiency of members' post-war resources, which, however, the US line of credit would remedy for Britain. The delegates doubted whether 'a significant amount' was involved in providing convertibility over and above that of the separate commitment for the sterling area. Account should be taken of provision in the draft agreement for the lapse of the relevant clause, as also of that eliminating Anglo-American discrimination in import restrictions, by the end of 1951 in favour of more comprehensive arrangements by multilateral agreement. In relation to those major trading partners which were likely to remain for a time outside the Monetary Fund, Britain would retain considerable freedom of action. That left a few countries in South America and Europe, in respect of which, however, the provision for Anglo-American consultation might limit convertibility.[233]

The Chancellor noted privately that, in relating the attenuated transition period to their provision of a large credit, the Americans had 'a serious argument'. Seen thus, the dispute 'seemed rather trivial against the great background of 4.4 billion dollars and Anglo-American Agreement'.[234] The Cabinet made one last, restrained attempt to modify the commitment. With only two Ministers recorded as arguing against, it decided to accept the agreement, but at the suggestion of the Foreign Secretary, the Prime Minister sought to defer the operation of full convertibility from one year after the agreement became effective, (then assumed to mean one year from about March 1946), to the end of 1947; this would ease the parliamentary problem, but should not be regarded as a sticking point. Not surprisingly, the Americans felt obliged to decline, and the two delegations now prepared for the formal signing of an agreement which, it is time to recall, was part of a more comprehensive 'Article VII' settlement.[235]

(24) THE SETTLEMENT OF LEND-LEASE

In addition to the provision of financial aid, two essential elements of that settlement were an agreement on the winding-up of Lend-Lease and Mutual Aid, and an understanding on commercial policy. Complementing all three was a statistical paper derived from the British delegation's exposition of 'The Quintessence of our Case' as well as from the statistical material more generally employed in the Washington talks.[236]

But for the greater significance politically and for subsequent events of the financial negotiations, those over Lend-Lease, which skilfully tied up in a 'complete and final' settlement[237] the many complex issues of the immediate past, might have earned the admiration which they merit. Those issues, outlined previously (above, pp 251–2), required detailed examination in relation to US financing of a vast range of civilian and military supplies during 1941–45, not only for Britain, but also for her transactions with the Commonwealth, India, Middle Eastern countries, and her allies. Moreover, although the extensive assistance of military and civilian supply missions in Washington was indispensable, the burden and responsibility lay heavily also on the Keynes Mission along with its preoccupations over finance and commercial policy.

The dragging of the loan talks ensured enough time for the hard-pressed negotiators to present their results for incorporation in the financial agreement.[238] Broad categorisation, drastic writing down of original values, forthright bargaining on both sides, and finally a 'mug for mug clause' (Keynes's description[239]) to cover for both sides any oversight, secured, with less than two pages of the White Paper on the agreement to summarise it, the settlement of many billion dollars of Mutual Aid. An authoritative extended account having already been published,[240] only its major features need be outlined here. The sum of $650 million added to the new loan, on the same terms as for that and thus more favourably than had been originally feared (above, pp 252–3), provided $118 million for the balance due by Britain for supplies after VJ Day (2 September 1945), and $532 million to cover all other items. The two countries, agreeing to meet any resultant adjustment by cash payments, had yet to complete the detailed valuations; they accomplished this by March 1946.[241]

(25) COMMERCIAL POLICY

Most of the outstanding issues in commercial policy, following the preliminary agreement of early October, were settled quickly, although the exclusion of some controversial protectionist practices, such as shipping subsidies, from the proposed arrangements caused British unease. The final understanding depended largely upon the resolution of Anglo-American differences over Imperial Preference and on the concurrence of the Dominion and Indian Governments in British policy. In this London took a more direct role than in other aspects of the negotiations. The Mission in Washington, although consulting the representatives of those Governments, did not regard them as the most appropriate through whom to settle.[242] In discussions with those in London and through cables to their home Governments, Ministers strove to secure agreement with British policy, hoping also that the Washington Mission could persuade the local representatives to cable home favourably.

American and British officials rapidly evolved a formula which sought to satisfy American demands for assurances about the elimination of Imperial Preference as 'a selling point' for the provision of financial aid.[243] To this was attached a proposal, in effect for a gesture, to abandon apparently minor preferences which nevertheless covered about one-quarter of the trade affected by preferences. The formula reflected what had been discussed in London before the trade experts went to the USA, and was threefold: there should be an undertaking not to raise the existing level of preference, by adopting the principle that there should be no new preferences and that existing margins of preference should not be increased; existing commitments were not to prevent cuts in harmony with reductions in tariffs and other trade barriers; finally, embodying after all the Canadian suggestion to unbind 'bound preferences' (above, p 275), tariff cuts involving most-favoured-nation arrangements (by which concessions to one trading partner might be extended to third parties) would automatically reduce or eliminate preference margins.[244]

London and the Dominions had misgivings, particularly about suggestions of precise commitments and of bargaining preferences against aid.[245] After hard debate, the Washington Mission reported hopefully on an American draft embodying the formula, but omitting the proposal to abandon 'minor' preferences. London was not yet satisfied. To the Treasury and the Economic Section the formula appeared promising, but not to others. The Dominions Office feared that official American interpretation of it would tend to give Congress and the public an impression contrary to that which the British negotiators intended the formula to convey, and that this would present difficulties for the Dominions.[246] The President of the Board of Trade was similarly disturbed. After initial cuts in tariffs and preferences, the Americans' legal limit of a fifty per cent cut would prevent the subsequent elimination of residual preferences, but they themselves appeared not to realise this. He therefore felt unable to commend the formula to fellow Ministers or to Parliament unless it were supported by an agreed Anglo-American explanation.[247]

With the help of Professor Robbins's personal elucidation of the Washington atmosphere, the President of the Board of Trade gained Cabinet approval for an 'Explanation of Preferences Formula'. This stressed that there would be no advance commitment to reduce any preference, and that reduction or elimination must be reciprocated elsewhere.[248] The Americans responded with a demand for amendments committing the Dominions; this was despite warnings by Professor Robbins, newly returned from London, of its unacceptability, and from Sir Percivale Liesching that it could provoke suspension of negotiations. This brief crisis ended with the Americans, concerned to clinch agreement in order to move ahead promptly, yielding.[249] The British stand was quickly vindicated, only

Canada broadly approving the proposals. New Zealand, South Africa, and India acquiesced in Britain's support of them, but reserved their own positions, while Australia, apprehensive over the effects on employment and on a forthcoming general election, was vehemently opposed. Indeed, the Australian Prime Minister cabled to the British Prime Minister his pessimism over the chances of securing adequate US concessions, and hence of acceptable terms for aid to Britain; he offered Australian support for an alternative post-war policy based on the sterling area.[250]

Appraising these reactions, London felt that it had adequately safeguarded the position, and in Washington the Commercial Policy Committee regarded its work as completed, save for procedural details over publication. Proving to be far from routine, this last stage illuminated underlying American and British apprehensions over the reception in the respective countries of the pending settlement. Well aware of the interdependence of the commercial and financial agreements, both sides agitated over the choice and implications of the timing of publication. London in addition sought to minimise any published hint of British commitment to the trade proposals. The American timetable had envisaged that, with a financial agreement assumed to be imminent also, proposals for and invitations to the projected conference on the establishment of an International Trade Organisation could be published during the second week of November, and would shortly after be sent to Congress.

At first, apparently acquiescing in this, the Cabinet expected that the President of the Board of Trade would follow the American publication with his own public welcome, preparatory to further government statements.[251] The timetable quickly disintegrated, however, against the background of delays over preference and of financial tension. In contrast with the by no means unanimous American concern that simultaneous publication of the trade proposals with a financial agreement would detract from the former's political impact, London and the Washington Mission urgently pondered the risks from damaging criticism at home of publication in advance of a financial agreement, particularly if that had not then been secured.[252] Above all, on the edge at last of apparent decision, London was as hesitant as ever it had been during the preceding five years over explicit commitment to American-style trade liberalisation. Although broadly approving the proposals, London shrank from outright agreement, in favour of being 'associated' with them; noting the difficulties with New Zealand and Australia, it insisted that they be clearly seen as American proposals.[253]

In Washington the US trade experts riposted that London's

difficulty in commending the trade proposals to Parliament paralleled that of their own Administration in offering the British a loan before Congress had approved. The clear implication, that close association of the trade and financial proposals made sense, shortly brought agreement on simultaneous publication.[254] This arrangement, probably more in British than in American political interests, may have eased somewhat the Cabinet's twin problems, to the extent that its qualified commendation of the trade proposals helped to distinguish their tentative nature from the firm commitments of the financial agreement, and hence to weaken suspicions that one had been bargained for the other. The White Paper on the trade proposals[255] embodied a brief joint statement by Britain and the USA, guardedly recording agreement 'on all important points', their acceptance of them 'as a basis for international discussion', and their intention to use their 'best endeavours... in the light of the views expressed by other countries'. Caution was re-inforced in the statement, originally to have been made in advance by the President of the Board of Trade, with which the Prime Minister was to follow his announcement to the House of Commons of the financial and Lend-Lease agreements. In the subsequent debate, the President's own contribution to non-commitment was the heroic assertion that 'These are not bilateral proposals... They are proposals by the two of us ...'.[256]

(26) SIGNATURE AND RECEPTION OF THE AGREEMENT

With all major difficulties resolved, and with the completion of the supporting statistical White Paper, the Financial Agreement was now signed in Washington at the start of a busy day which also included a press conference, a cocktail party, and a happy dinner party at which the newly relaxed British delegates felicitated each other and their staff.[257] There was relief, too, in London, where Sir Wilfrid Eady had anticipated in fine Treasury style the approaching end of three months of very late nights and very early mornings, reflecting the time difference, which were required to deal with ceaseless transatlantic cabling: '... soon, *nox una dormienda*' ('soon, a night's sleep', in effect).[258]

Major anxieties lay ahead of the expected financial easement. In Britain the Agreement was received very unfavourably. The Chancellor himself privately regarded as 'tepid' his own support of it, and presciently noted his 'cynical and secret reflection' that eventual revision was certain: perhaps, and possibly unilaterally by Britain, within a year or two.[259] On both sides in both Houses of Parliament there was hostility. In the House of Commons the opposition Conservative Party, rather than approve it, abstained, in order to discourage Conservative peers from voting against it.[260] In the House of Lords, so strong indeed was opposition that rejection of the Agreement seemed a likely outcome at the opening of the two days' debate. Keynes, however, made an outstanding speech on the second day. He presented dramatically the difficulties of negotiation, the benefits and opportunities offered by the Agreement, and the case for accepting it. This transformed the debate. When the question was put, the numerous peers who were unhappy about it limited their discontent to abstention, thereby allowing formal approval to be secured.[261]

Enthusiasm was also lacking in the USA where there was, indeed, a good deal of sustained hostility to it among the vocal sections of influential opinion. Above all, Congress was expected to scrutinise the painfully negotiated Agreement very critically; its prolonged and often hostile examination was to foster doubts about eventual approval of the Loan.[262]

There was a further anxiety, and of immediate concern. An essential element in a financial settlement, which could by no means be taken for granted, was a loan from Canada. To secure this, together with agreement on Britain's substantial wartime debts to Canada and on winding up Mutual Aid, was the next task of the Treasury.

CHAPTER 10, SOURCE REFERENCES

NB As in chapter 9, NABOB and BABOON telegrams from Washington and London respectively are cited from files T 236/453–64 (NABOBS) and T 236/465–70 (BABOONS).

1. Copy dated 22 August 1945, T 236/142.

2. Ibid, 'End of Lend/Lease—Balance of Payments, Memorandum prepared in the Treasury', 31 August 1945.

3. Meeting of Ministers, 23 August 1945, T 230/175; also T 236/437; *JMK* XXIV, pp 420–5.

4. Keynes's memorandum of 15–16 August 1945, T 247/2.

5. Mr R H Brand, note on 'Stage III', 14 August 1945, T 236/437.

6. Inconclusive discussions on the cession of Tarawa in the Gilbert Islands, scene of bitter fighting by US Marines, in FO 371/44623 and DO 35/2124–5.

7. 413 HC DEB 5 s cols 995–8, 24 August 1945.
   The ship party comprised Lord Keynes (with Lady Keynes); Mr F E Harmer of the Treasury; and Mr E L Hall-Patch, recently of the Treasury, now of the Foreign Office. In Washington they were joined by Lord Halifax and Mr Brand; Mr F G Lee of the Treasury and Mr R B Stevens of the British Civil Secretariat were Secretaries for Committee discussions. Initially a small group, it could and did draw on the advice of the substantial British civil and military Missions in Washington, as well as on that of the diplomatic representatives of the Empire and Commonwealth.

8. The first meeting of the US–UK Combined Top Committee was held on 11 September 1945: GEN 80/9 in CAB 130/6; also *FRUS* 1945 VI (1969), pp 122–6.

9. 'So pretty well all were agreed that we should start along those lines', Sir Frederic Harmer has recalled in a private communication. 'To fail after trying very hard was disappointing, but nobody's convictions were shattered'.

10. Harrod, *Life of ... Keynes,* pp 596–7; Gardner, *Sterling-Dollar Diplomacy,* pp 189–90; Hugh (Lord) Dalton, *High Tide and After: Memoirs,* III (London 1962), pp 73–74.

11. Keynes, 'Some highly preliminary Notes on the forthcoming conversations', 9 September 1945, T 236/438, with letter of 10 September to Sir Wilfrid Eady; *JMK* XXIV, pp 457–8.

12. See Lord Robbins, *Autobiography of an Economist* (London 1971), pp 204–5.

13. Eady to Sir John Woods, 25 August 1945, T 236/437.

14. Ibid, 595 CAMER of 28 August from Eady to Brand in Washington. See also DOTEL 55 of 7 September, Cabinet Offices to Washington: 'We are going ahead with our gambit of attempting discussion of finance first and commercial policy second', AVIA 38/1118.

15. Byrnes to US Ambassador in London, 22 August 1945, *FRUS* 1945 VI, p 109.

16. Ibid, p 110, 27 August.

17. Mr N B Ronald to Eady, 30 August 1945, T 236/437.

18. 'Financial Negotiations and Commercial Policy', memorandum prepared in the Treasury and Board of Trade, and discussed at meeting of Ministers, 31 August 1945, T 236/437; meeting also reported in T 236/380 and T 247/2.

19. Keynes to Eady from Washington, 10 September 1945, T 236/438; *JMK* XXIV, p 453. A similar comment in a letter to Mr R Gordon Munro in Ottawa, 10 September, T 247/127.

20. Memorandum by Mr F G Lee to Keynes and note by Keynes to Mr H Dalton, Chancellor of the Exchequer, 11 September 1945, T 236/438.

21. Douglas Jay, *Change and Fortune: A Political Record* (London 1981), p 136.

22. Reports of Committee meetings, with memoranda, under GEN 89 in CAB 78/37.

23. Reports of meetings in AVIA 38/1119 and DO 35/1216.

24. Evidence from a wide range of files reflecting Keynes's extensive activity, and 835 REMAC of 20 November 1945, Keynes to Sir Edward Bridges and Eady, T 236/439.

25. 'Proposals for Financial Arrangements in the Sterling Area and between the United States and United Kingdom to follow after Lend-Lease', 12 September 1945, GEN 89/1 in CAB 78/37; also in PREM 8/35; *JMX* XXIV, pp 427–51. Considered by committee of Ministers 14 September, GEN 89/1st Meeting, CAB 78/37.

26. Text of Keynes's remarks at Press Conference, 12 September 1945, GEN 80/11 in CAB 78/37. Verbatim report consulted by courtesy of Mr Paul Bareau. Meetings of US-UK Top Committee, 13, 14, 17 September, GEN 80/20–22 in CAB 78/37; *JMK* XXIV, pp 466–84.

27. Reports of meetings, ibid, and information from Mr P Bareau.

28. Comparisons of relative sacrifice evoked 'almost unanimously adverse reaction' in Washington, according to Mr P Bareau. Keynes was advised that a friendly US expert feared that such comparisons would harm the British case with Americans, and he himself wrote to Eady that 'I hear from every quarter great American resentment': F G Lee to Keynes, 24 September and Keynes to Eady, 27 September 1945, T 236/438. Keynes also cabled London that 'We are told five times a day by everyone we meet that any suggestion that Great Britain has borne an excessive financial burden or has made any efforts or sacrifices which compare favourably with the United States seriously prejudices our case, and if the comparisons are valid that makes it all the worse', 738 REMAC of 28 September, T 236/439.

29. First and second meetings of the Finance Committee, 19 and 20 September, GEN 80/28 and 29.

30. NABOB 191 of 20 October.

31. Eg, Mr W L Clayton to Secretary of State, 18 August 1945, *FRUS* 1945 VI, p 104; NABOB 132 of 9 October.

32. Robbins, *Autobiography* . . . , pp 204–5: 'It would be difficult to overstate the consternation . . . Indignation meetings were held. The relevant ministers were moved to protest . . . arrangements were hastily made to get together a properly constituted delegation to join the lone party in Washington and assume its due share in the conversations'.

33. BABOON 21 of 8 September 1945.

34. BABOON 29 of 11 September; NABOBS 49 and 50 of 13 September.

35. NABOB 49, and Keynes from Ottawa to Sir Percivale Liesching, 4 September 1945, AVIA 38/1118 and T 247/2.

36. BABOON 33 of 14 September.

37. Sir Edward Bridges to Prime Minister, 12 September 1945, PREM 8/35, ff 397–8; meeting of Ministers 14 September, GEN 89/1st Meeting, CAB 78/37.

38. GEN 89/2 of 13 September 1945, CAB 78/37.

39. NABOB 57 and BABOON 34 of 15 September.

40. NABOB 59 of 15 September 1945. In Washington the Ambassador stressed that everybody should offer the same explanations for the change of tack on commercial policy: Keynes to Brand, 14 September, AVIA 38/1118.

41. NABOB 70 of 21 September 1945; *JMK* XXIV, p 49; telegram 7816 of 22 November, T 236/441.

42. Sir Stafford Cripps, President of the Board of Trade, 10 December 1945, 417 HC DEB 5 s, col 488.

43. Reports of preliminary and main meetings on Commercial Policy during late September and early October in GEN 80/39, 41, 44, 45 in CAB 130/6 and GEN 80/47–49 in CAB 130/7.

44. First and second meetings of Commercial Policy Committee, 1 & 2 October 1945, GEN 80/41 & 44.

45. I Drummond *Imperial Economic Policy* 1917–1939 (London 1974), chapters 6 & 7.

46. NABOB 114 of 3 October 1945; also quoted by Liesching at meeting of Dominion and Indian representatives in Washington 4 October, DO 35/1216.

47. NABOB 160 of 12 October 1945.

48. NABOB 70 of 21 September 1945; *JMK* XXIV, pp 500–1.

49. GEN 89/1 of 12 September 1945, CAB 78/37.

50. Bridges to Prime Minister, 25 September 1945, PREM 8/35, f 363.

51. CAMER 673 and 674 of 25 September 1945, T 236/439.

52. 'Documentary Record . . .' by Mr L P Thompson-McCausland of the Bank of England, 28 November 1945, section 6, noted that the Bank's comments had referred particularly to fresh accruals: T 236/438.

53. REMAC 738 of 28 September 1945, T 236/439.

54. NABOB 209 of 23 October 1945.

55. Keynes to Eady and others, 4 September 1945, T 247/2; *JMK* XXIV, pp 475–6.

56. 'Some highly preliminary Notes . . .', 9 September 1945, T 236/438 and *JMK* XXIV, pp 456–7.

57. 'The Terms of Assistance', GEN 89/4, CAB 78/37; also with letter of 26 September 1945 to Chancellor of the Exchequer, T 247/47 and *JMK* XXIV, pp 503–8.

58. Diary of Lord Halifax, II, A–78–17, 25 September 1945, consulted by courtesy of the Earl of Halifax.

59. Telegrams 6444 of 26 September 1945, and telegrams 6490 & 6491 of 27 September reported the meetings of 25 and 27 September: GEN 89/4 in CAB 78/37, and also T 236/439.

60. Telegram 6490.

61. 'The Terms of Assistance'.

62. Eady to Keynes, 28 September 1945, *JMK* XXIV, p 520.

63. 'The Terms of Assistance', paragraph 6.

64. Mr J E Meade to Lord President of the Council, 4 October 1945, CAB 124/913.

65. GEN 89/2nd Meeting, 5 October 1945, CAB 78/37.

66. Telegram 10094, London to Washington, 8 October 1945, T 236/439.

67. Keynes in postscript to letter of 12 October 1945 to Eady, T 236/438; *JMK* XXIV, p 543. The date of the press conference, unclear in Keynes's letter, was 9 October (information from Mr P Bareau).

68. Telegram 6733 of 9 October 1945, T 236/439.

69. Eady to Keynes, 12 October 1945, *JMK* XXIV, p 544.

70. Meeting of Ministers 12 October 1945, GEN 89/3rd Meeting, CAB 78/37.

71. US Financial Committee, 11 October 1945, *FRUS* 1945 VI, pp 145–8.

72. Information from Sir Frederic Harmer.

73. Ibid.

74. Tel 6444 of 26 September, Lord Halifax to Foreign Secretary and to Chancellor, T 236/439; also in GEN 89/4 of 2 October, CAB 78/37.

75. NABOB 177, paragraph 8, of 18 October; *JMK* XXIV, p 549.

76. NABOB 191 of 20 October, paragraph 4; *JMK* XXIV, p 557.

77. Ibid; Senate Committee on Finance, 79th Congress, 1st Session, Misc. Vol 3, Senate Reports, pp 565–888; 79–1, Report no. 656 (US Government Printing Office, Washington DC, 1945).

78. NABOB 191 of 20 October and NABOB 192 of 19 October; *JMK* XXIV, pp 557–64 (NB, with so many telegrams being sent, some would occasionally fall out of strict chronological order, as with these two NABOBS).

79. NABOB 191.

80. Keynes to Eady, 12 October, T 236/438; *JMK* XXIV, p 540. Broadly favourable 'Comments on Harry White's Scheme' by Mr R H Brand, 8 October, T 247/47. Details of White's scheme in memorandum by Keynes, 'Dr Harry White's Plan' with letter to Eady, 5 October, T 236/438; *JMK* XXIV, pp 532–5.

81. These estimates of sterling balances, to which revisions of no significance for the broad magnitudes discussed here were made subsequently, were laid before the US – UK 'Top Committee' at the opening of Keynes's presentation of the British position: GEN 89/3 of 25 September, Appendix B, Statement II, in CAB 78/37 and also in PREM 8/35, fol 358.

82. Gold loan: memorandum, paragraph 5. Nominal interest charge: NABOB 159 of 12 October.

83. 'Proposals for Financial Arrangements. . .', 12 September 1945, paragraph 39, GEN 89/1 in CAB 78/37; *JMK* XXIV, pp 442–7. In his memorandum on White's plan (paragraph 7) Keynes made a slip in writing $8 billion instead of $9 billion as the residual sterling debt.

84. 'Dr Harry White's Plan'.

85. Leak in *The Sun* of Baltimore: letter from Keynes to Eady, 12 October, T 236/438 & *JMK* XXIV, p 543; NABOB 159 of 12 October.

86. Mr E R Rowe-Dutton on 'The White Scheme', 15 October, T 236/438.

87. Note by C F C (ie, Mr C F Cobbold) 16 October, and letter from Cobbold to Eady with draft memorandum on 'what could now usefully be said to the delegation in Washington', 23 October, T 236/438.

88. BABOON 140 of 20 October.

89. NABOB 211 of 23 October.

90. NABOB 215 of 24 October.

91. NABOB 209 of 23 October.

92. NABOB 178 of 18 October; *JMK* XXIV, p 556.

93. Mr J E Meade to Lord President of the Council, 24 October, CAB 124/913.

94. Mr R W B ('Otto') Clarke, playing 'devil's advocate', memorandum to Eady, 23 October, T 236/438.

95. Eady to Cobbold 20 October, and Cobbold to Eady with draft memorandum 23 October: T 236/438; draft telegram in GEN 89/7 of 25 October, CAB 78/37.

96. Chancellor's Memorandum of 25 October for Ministers' Committee, GEN 89/7 and meeting of Ministers, 26 October, GEN 89/4th, CAB 89/37; BABOONS 155 and 156 of 27 October.

97. Information from Sir Frederic Harmer.

98. Ibid.

99. BABOON 162 of 31 October and NABOB 247 of 1 November.

100. Further telegrams in T 236/471.

101. NABOB 232 of 29 October 1945, and NABOB 258 of 2 November.

102. BABOON 158 of 29 October 1945 and 'Explanatory Note' in memorandum by Chancellor of the Exchequer, 29 October, GEN 89/10, CAB 78/37.

103. NABOB 233 of 29 October 1945, and NABOB 235 of 30 October.

104. Tel ASKEW X 249 of 26 October 1945 from Board of Trade to Washington, AVIA 38/958 and NABOB 400 of 27 November.

105. NABOB 215 of 24 October 1945.

106. NABOB 233 of 29 October; similar comments in NABOB 259 of 2 November. London's hesitation: BABOON 156 of 27 October, and tel 11034 of 2 November, T 236/440.

107. Chancellor's memorandum of 4 November 1945, GEN 89/10, in CAB 78/37. Ministers' meeting of 5 November, GEN 89/5th, ibid. Cabinet meetings of 6 November, CM(45)49th in CAB 128/2 and CM(45)50th, Confidential Annex, in CAB 128/4. Dalton Diary No 33, British Library of Political and Economic Science, entry for 6 November.

108. Dalton Diary, loc cit.

109. Memorandum of 30 October 1945 by Secretary of State for India, GEN 89/8, and memorandum of 4 November by Secretary of State for the Colonies, GEN 89/9: CAB 78/37.

110. GEN 89/3 and PREM 8/35.

111. GEN 89/5th.

112. Ibid.

113. NABOB 355 of 18 November 1945, BABOON 315 of 29 November, NABOB 420 of 29 November, all use this phrase, which also appears in the Chancellor's memorandum of 22 November, GEN 89/13 paragraph 8, CAB 78/37.

114. Tel 10094 of 8 October 1945, London to Washington, T 236/439.

115. Ibid, tel 10274 of 12 October, London to Washington, paragraph 10.

116. Idem, paragraph 13.

117. Ibid, tel 6733 of 9 October 1945, Washington to London.

118. NABOBS 295 and 296 of 7 November 1945.

119. BABOON 156 of 27 October 1945 and BABOON 206 of 6 November.

120. BABOON 206.

121. BABOON 218 of 6 November 1945.

122. NABOBS 295, 296, & 297 of 7 November 1945; information from Sir Frederic Harmer; sterling area memorandum in NABOB SAVING 32 of 7 November.

123. Information from Sir Frederic Harmer.

124. US 'Top Committee', 7 November 1945, *FRUS* 1945 VI, pp 157–62.

125. Sayers, *Financial Policy*, pp 247 – 50 and 444 – 60. Both types of agreement provided for the balancing of payments, as far as possible, between Britain and the country concerned, and for the treatment of any surplus in a manner least likely to impose demands upon sterling. Payments agreements were the more favourable form for Britain: settlements were made only in sterling, so that in case of a surplus on one or other side, Britain did not give, but would receive, credit. It may be added that the Treasury saw such agreements as 'the first step towards a multilateral clearing system . . . [and] informed the American Treasury about them as they were made': Chancellor's memorandum of 22 November 1945, GEN 89/13 in CAB 78/37.

126. Tel 7406 of 5 November 1945, Washington to London in T 236/440; *JMK* XXIV, p 581.

127. Tel 11187 of 6 November 1945, London to Washington, T 236/440 and *JMK* XXIV, p 583.

128. Tel 7491 of 8 November 1945, Keynes to Eady, T 236/440 and *JMK* XXIV, pp 587 – 8; tel 11322 of 9 November, Eady to Keynes, T 236/440.

129. *FRUS* 1945 VI, (7 November), p 161.

130. Information from Mr P Bareau.

131. Information from Sir Frederic Harmer.

132. NABOB 339 of 14 November 1945.

133. Information from Sir Frederic Harmer.

134. 'US Draft Memorandum of Understanding on Financial Matters' dated 14 November 1945, Annex to Minutes of third meeting of US-UK Finance Committee of 15 November, GEN 80/69, paragraphs 3 & 4, CAB 130/7.

135. Ibid, paragraph 8.

136. BABOON 198 of 5 November.

137. Information from Sir Frederic Harmer and Mr P Bareau.

138. GEN 80/69, CAB 130/7.

139. Information from Sir Frederic Harmer.

140. Ibid.

141. GEN 80/70, CAB 130/7. Report of meeting also in *FRUS* 1945 VI, pp 162 – 7.

142. 'Something in the nature of "a Mutiny on the Bounty" had occurred with a view to keeping as much of the talking as possible to the Ambassador and away from the Lord' (ie, Keynes), according to Mr P Bareau.

143. Information from Sir Frederic Harmer.

144. NABOB 401 of 27 November 1945.

145. NABOBS 370, 371 & 372 of 21 November reported and discussed the US draft of 18 November, which is reproduced as an Annex to minutes of 4th meeting of the US – UK Finance Committee of 19 November, GEN 80/70, CAB 130/7.

146. NABOB 353 of 17 November.

147. A British oil expert in Washington, Mr Maurice (later Lord) Bridgeman feared that the cost of dollar oil would be heavy: tel 1154 ELFUNOCOP of 19 November, Washington to London, T 236/441. Sir Percivale Liesching of the Board of Trade thought that there would be little to lose from forgoing discrimination, provided that the amount and terms of a loan were satisfactory: NABOB 406 of 27 November.

148. NABOB 358 of 17 November.

149. NABOB 370 of 21 November, NABOB 383 of 22 November.

150. 835 REMAC of 20 November, T 236/441. Cf also Keynes to his mother, 21 November, *JMK* XXIV, p 593.

151. Tel 835 REMAC of 20 November and tel 7825 of 22 November, T 236/441 and *JMK* XXIV, pp 590 and 595.

152. Note by Mr E R Rowe-Dutton, 21 November, and notes by Mr L P Thompson-McCausland of the Bank of England, 21–22 November, T 236/441. Rowe-Dutton's memorandum also in T 236/438.

153. Memorandum of 22 November, GEN 89/13, paragraph 12, CAB 78/37; Rowe-Dutton's memorandum, T 236/441.

154. Tel 11789 of 23 November, T236/441.

155. Memorandum for Committee of Ministers, 22 November, GEN 89/13, CAB 78/37.

156. Ibid, meeting of 23 November, GEN 89/6th.

157. Tel 11790 of 24 November, T 236/441. The order in which the points were made in the telegram has been retained, but they have been given a more convenient numbering.

158. Here the telegram specifically mentioned paragraphs 11, 12, 14 and 15, of NABOB SAVING 32 of 7 November, reproduced in Appendix 20.

159. Tel 7893 of 25 November, T 236/441; *JMK* XXIV, pp 596–7.

160. Information from Mr Bareau.

161. Tel 7894 of 25 November from Ambassador to Prime Minister, T 236/441.

162. Ibid, tel 7893 of 25 November; *JMK* XXIV, pp 596–7. American insistence on at least $750 million: minutes of a special meeting of 24 November between US and United Kingdom representatives, GEN 80/82 in CAB 130/7 and *FRUS* 1945 VI, pp 168–73.

163. Tel 7893 of 25 November; *JMK* XXIV, p 597.

164. GEN 80/76 in CAB 130/7.

165. Section 5(a): see Appendix 24.

166. Mr Marriner S Eccles, Chairman of the Board of Governors of the Federal Reserve System (his name, however, was omitted from the list of those present).

167. BABOON 299 of 24 November.

168. *FRUS* 1945 VI, p 167, n 21.

169. NABOB 395 of 25 November.

170. 'Draft C' appended to minutes of meeting, GEN 80/76.

171. Loc cit, Mr E G Collado.

172. In the earlier discussions, towards the end of September, about sterling convertibility, no date had been given for a 'winding-up' period, during which further balances were likely to be accumulated, but would be excluded from early convertibility: above, p 280. BABOON 189 of 3 November feared that the end of 1946, when the original plan for sterling convertibility might operate, would provide too early an end for 'winding-up', and preferred that flexible phrasing should avoid that difficulty. NABOB SAVING 32 of 7 November, with the revision of the plan agreed between the Mission and London, stipulated the exclusion but not a date: paragraph 11, Appendix 20, pp 411–12. By mid-November, presumably after Anglo-American discussions, the exclusion was incorporated in the draft US terms, and referred to military expenditure to the end of 1948: drafts of 14 & 19 November, GEN 80/69 and GEN 80/70, CAB 130/7. The exclusion was to appear in the final agreement, section 7: see Appendix 24.

173. NABOB 396 of 25 November, and BABOON 303 of 26 November.

174. Tel 11897 of 27 November, Eady to Keynes, and Keynes's reply, tel 7933 of 27 November, T 236/441.

175. Tel LETOD 388 of 26 November, AVIA 38/1118.

176. NABOB 400 of 27 November.

177. DOTEL 212 of 27 November, AVIA 38/1118 and T 236/441.

178. 'Documentary Record relating to our commitment on release of current balances' by LPT-McC[ausland] of the Bank of England, 28 November, T 236/438.

179. NABOB 215 of 24 October, paragraph 8; qualified by tel 7406 of 5 November paragraph 5, T 236/440 and *JMK* XXIV, p 580.

180. Mr E R Rowe-Dutton in BABOON 202 of 5 November, paragraph 6; *JMK* XXIV, p 578.

181. Tel 7446 of 7 November in T 236/440; *JMK* XXIV, pp 583–4.

182. BABOON 203 of 5 November, paragraph 3.

183. Eady to Cobbold at the Bank of England, 9 November, T 236/440.

184. BABOON 299 of 24 November.

185. BABOON 312 of 28 November; Memorandum of 12 September, paragraph 39, in GEN 89/1, CAB 78/37.

186. CP (45) 312 of 28 November 1945, 'Draft of a Financial Agreement', CAB 129/5; CM(45) 57th Conclusions, Minute 3 (Confidential Annex), 29 November 1945, CAB 128/4.

187. BABOONS 314 to 317 of 29 November 1945.

188. US draft of 14 November 1945, paragraph 7, and draft of 18 November, paragraph 8, in GEN 80/69 and GEN 80/70 respectively, CAB 130/7.

189. BABOON 317 of 29 November 1945.

190. House of Lords Official Report, 23 May 1944, Parl Debs 5th Series, vol cxxxi, 2nd vol, Session 1943–44, col. 838–49; reprinted in *JMK* XXVI, pp 9–21.

191. CM(45) 57th Conclusions, Minute 3, 29 November 1945, CAB 128/4.

192. NABOBS 417 to 420 of 29 November.

193. NABOB 419; *JMK* XXIV, p 600.

194. Memorandum, paragraph 39(xiv), GEN 89/1 in CAB 78/37; NABOB SAVING 32, paragraph 15, of 7 November: see Appendix 20.

195. NABOB 419, which also recalled earlier references in NABOBS 372 of 21 November and 402 of 27 November.

196. BABOON 317 of 29 November, and also BABOON 312 of 28 November.

197. Mr J E Meade, Diary, 2 December 1945.

198. BABOON 321 of 29 November and BABOON 323 of 30 November.

199. NABOB 423 of 30 November, and information from Sir Frederic Harmer.

200. Eady to Mr B Trend, private secretary to Chancellor, 2 October 1945, T 236/439.

201. Chancellor at Ministers' meeting 23 November 1945, GEN 89/6th Meeting, CAB 78/37.

202. Information from Sir Frederic Harmer and Mr P Bareau.

203. Keynes, note to Eady, Bridges & Padmore 15/16 August 1945, T 247/2; telephone conversation with Eady, 1 October, T 247/47; information from Mr P Bareau..

204. Letter from Bridges to Keynes, 5 November 1945; information from Professor D E Moggridge.

205. Information from Mr P Bareau.

206. Dalton Diary, 7 December 1945.

207. GEN 80/86 & 87, CAB 130/7 and *FRUS* 1945 VI, pp 185-8; Halifax, Diary, 2 December 1945, cit Birkenhead, *Halifax,* p 555.

208. *FRUS* 1945 VI, p 187, n 48.

209. NABOB 446 of 3 December 1945.

210. BABOON 299 of 24 November 1945, and BABOON 316 of 29 November.

211. NABOB 420 of 29 November 1945.

212. NABOB 445 of 3 December 1945.

213. The principal Treasury files concerned with the waiver are OF 229/02/A to D; OF 110/208/03/A to P; OF 110/208/08/A & B; OF 361/252/025/A to D; OF 361/252/026/A & B. Also relevant are OF 275/252/02; OF 270/145/03. Papers concerning the possible invocation of the waiver in file on 'US and Canadian Loan Agreements. Use of the interest Waiver Clause 1951-55' (Permanent Secretary's Office, file no. 22 and C.3/57). In 1957 agreement was reached with the USA to replace the Waiver provisions of the 1945 agreement, by a greatly simplified arrangement: Britain could request deferment of annual repayments including interest on up to seven occasions, the deferred instalments being repayable, with interest on them, at the end of the originally scheduled period for repayment of the Loan: Cmnd 120 of March 1957, 'Agreement to Amend the Financial Agreement of 6th December 1945 between the Governments of the United States and the United Kingdom', *BPP* 1956-7 xxxiii. By Cmnd 121 of March 1957, *BPP* 1956-7 xxxii, a similar arrangement was made in respect of the Loan from Canada, the subject of chapter II.

214. Mr E R Rowe-Dutton of the Treasury, 'The Washington Talks', 21 November 1945; notes by Mr L P Thompson-McCausland of the Bank of England, 21-22 November; Treasury memoranda, unsigned and undated, on the same subjects, all in T 236/441.

215. BABOON 299 of 24 November 1945, paragraph 5.

216. BABOON 315 of 29 November 1945, paragraph 4.

217. NABOB 418 of 30 November 1945.

218. NABOB 445 of 3 December 1945; 7th meeting of US-United Kingdom Finance Committee, 2 December GEN 80/87, CAB 130/7 and *FRUS* 1945 VI, p 187.

219. NABOB 433 of 2 December 1945, paragraph 4, and NABOB 445 of 3 December, paragraph 3(c).

220. 7th meeting of US-United Kingdom Finance Committee, 2 December 1945, GEN 80/87 and *FRUS* 1945 VI, p 185, NABOB 436 of 2 December and NABOB 442 of 3 December; Financial Agreement, section 6(iii).

221. NABOB 446 paragraph 5 and NABOB 448 paragraph 2, both of 3 December 1945.

222. NABOB 445 of 3 December 1945 and *FRUS* 1945 VI, p 186; references at this stage to sections 6 and 7 related to what became sections 7 and 8 respectively in the final text.

223. NABOB 445; 7th meeting of US-United Kingdom Financial Committee, 2 December (second meeting that day), GEN 80/87, CAB 130/7; *FRUS* 1945 VI, p 186, n 44.

224. NABOB 446 of 3 December 1945.

225. CM(45)58th Conclusions, Minute 2,3 December 1945, CAB 128/4; BABOONS 338 and 339 of 3 December 1945.

226. Dalton Diary, 7 December 1945.

227. BABOON 338 of 3 December 1945; *FRUS* 1945 VI, pp 188–9.

228. US-United Kingdom Finance Committee, 4 December 1945, GEN 80/88, CAB 130/7 and *FRUS* 1945 VI, pp 190–3; NABOB 458 of 4 December 1945.

229. Eady to Chancellor, 5 December 1945, T 236/438.

230. BABOON 349 of 5 December 1945.

231. Information from Sir Frederic Harmer and Mr P Bareau; NABOB 463 of 5 December 1945.

232. Ibid.

233. NABOBS 463–5 of 5 December 1945.

234. Dalton Diary, 7 December 1945.

235. CM(45)59th Conclusions, Confidential Annex, 5 December, CAB 128/4; BABOON 350 of 5 December 1945; US-United Kingdom Combined Finance Committee 5 December, GEN 80/89, CAB 130/7 and *FRUS* 1945 VI, pp 193–4.

236. GEN 80/19; NABOBS 183–5 of 18 October 1945, 309 of 8 November; BABOONS 225 of 7 November, 336 & 337 of 3 December, 347 of 4 December; files T 236/2403 & 2404, *Statistical Material presented during the Washington Negotiations*, Cmd 6707 of December 1945, *BPP* 1945–6, XXI.

237. Paragraph 2 of Joint Statement, following the text of Financial Agreement, Cmd 6708, *BPP* 1945–6, XXV.

238. Keynes to meeting of representatives of Dominion and Indian Governments, 5 December 1945, AVIA 38/1121.

239. Ibid.

240. By R G D (Sir Roy) Allen in *Journal of the Royal Statistical Society*, CIX ,III, 1946; published also as Appendix III to Sayers, *Financial Policy*.

241. Cmd 6778 of March 1946, *BPP* 1945–6, XXV.

242. They were 'of varying calibre': NABOB 132 of 9 October 1945.

243. BABOON 115 of 15 October 1945.

244. NABOBS 132–4 of 9 October 1945.

245. BABOONS 99 of 11 October, 102 and 103 of 12 October 1945; report of London discussions between Chancellor of the Exchequer, President of the Board of Trade, and representatives of Commonwealth Governments, BABOON 115 of 15 October 1945.

246. NABOB 186 of 19 October 1945; tels ASKEW X 242 of 22 October London (Mr J R Helmore) to Washington (Sir Percivale Liesching), AVIA 38/958.

247. Ibid, tels ASKEW X 243 of 22 October and X 249 of 26 October 1945, London (Helmore) to Washington (Liesching); memorandum by Board of Trade, 25 October, GEN 89/6, and meeting of Ministers, 26 October, GEN 89/4th Meeting, CAB 78/37.

248. Ibid, memoranda by Board of Trade 5 November 1945, GEN 89/11 and 89/12; meeting of Ministers, 5 November, GEN 89/5th Meeting, CAB 78/37.

249. NABOBS 308, 310, 311 of 8 November and 312 of 9 November 1945.

250. BABOONS 242–50, 256–8 and 261–2 of 9–12 November 1945; NABOBS 320 of 10 November and 321 of 11 November.

251. NABOBS 258 of 2 November 1945, BABOONS 238 and 239 of 8 November, and meeting of Ministers, 5 November, GEN 89/5th Meeting, CAB 78/37.

252. BABOONS 210 of 5 November and 251 of 10 November 1945; NABOBS 326 of 11 November and 334 of 14 November.

253. BABOONS 289 of 19 November and 293 of 21 November 1945.

254. NABOB 390 of 26 November 1945.

255. Cmd 6709, *Proposals for Consideration by an International Conference on Trade and Employment, BPP* 1945 – 6, XXVI.

256. Draft statement proposed by President of the Board of Trade in his memorandum of 22 November, GEN 89/14, circulated at meeting of Ministers, 23 November, GEN 89/6th Meeting, CAB 78/37; Prime Minister's Statement of 6 December 1945, 416 HC DEB 5 s cols 2662 – 70; speech by President of the Board of Trade, 12 December, 417 HC DEB 5 s, col 484.

257. Information from Sir Frederic Harmer and Mr P Bareau.

258. BABOON 339 of 3 December 1945. The Latin tag was presumably from Catullus: '*nox est perpetua una dormienda*', *Catulli Carmina,* ed Robinson Ellis (Clarendon Press 1937), V, line 6.

259. Dalton Diary, 14 December 1945.

260. Birkenhead, *Halifax,* p 557; House of Commons debate, 12, 13, 14 December 1945, 147 HC DEB 5 s, cols 421 – 558, 641 – 746, 804 – 14.

261. House of Lords debate 17 & 18 December 1945, 138 HL DEB, 2nd Session 1945 – 6, cols 677 – 775, 777 – 898. Keynes's speech, 18 December, cols 777 – 794; *JMK* XXIV, pp 605 – 24. Noting that 'before Keynes spoke there were strong rumours of some sort of adverse resolution', Lord Robbins recalled that 'After Keynes's speech, which I heard, the atmosphere had completely altered . . . and he came into the lobby to talk to my wife and myself more elated and flushed with triumph than I had ever seen him before, even at the last meeting at Bretton Woods' (letter to author, 19 November 1981).

262. The British and American debates are discussed in Gardner, *Sterling-Dollar Diplomacy,* chapter XII. The passage of the agreement through Congress is the subject of a doctoral dissertation of the University of Kentucky: Richard Paul Hedlund, *Congress and the British Loan* 1945 – 1946: *A Congressional Study* (1976).

CHAPTER 11

The Negotiations for the Canadian Loan 1946

(1) CANADIAN AND BRITISH ATTITUDES

The termination and settlement of Canada's substantial wartime financial support for Britain, and then the negotiation of peacetime aid, presented problems superficially akin to those which had arisen in relation to the USA. There were, however, special considerations; some were to prove sufficiently sensitive to produce serious Anglo-Canadian tension. The easy, or at least the obvious, path of simply reproducing the American terms did not initially attract all responsible Canadians. They wished to avoid strengthening existing resentment that wartime Canada had seemed subservient to the USA and to Britain. Yet to provide easier terms would invite domestic political accusations that Britain, still relatively a rich country, was unfairly stretching Canadian generosity.[1] Nor could the Commonwealth relationship be exploited: better, came informed advice,[2] 'to eschew [that] above all else' and to recognise that 'Any Agreement for a long-term Credit . . . . . will require to be fundamentally a business operation in order to satisfy the Canadian Parliament and public opinion in the light of the terms of the US Credit'.

Comparable political considerations operated in Britain. The hostile reception of the United States loan left no doubt of the significance for Anglo-Canadian relationships of the forthcoming negotiations.[3] Further to complicate these anxieties was mutual concern that nothing should be done to endanger the passage through Congress of the Anglo-American Financial Agreement.

(2) THE POSITION AT THE END OF THE WAR

As with American Lend-Lease, the war's sudden end had found Canada and Britain unprepared for an orderly termination of the Mutual Aid which had governed their financial arrangements since 1943. In a sense, however, the Canadian position was slightly clearer, although less favourable in relation to Britain, than that of the Americans. The Canadian Acts and agreements were more precise than the American counterparts in their stipulation that, on the end of hostilities in any theatre of war, relevant war supplies would revert to Canadian ownership. Further, domestic politics created the possibility of the cessation of Mutual Aid even before the end of the war; that was reflected in the superficially reassuring provision of the Anglo-Canadian agreement, that it was to continue until mutual agreement on its termination.[4]

(3) EARLY DISCUSSIONS

Anglo-Canadian discussions had aired the question of post-war aid in principle, although not in detail, well before the formal discussions of early 1946. Thus, at a meeting of November 1944 Keynes had talked of an interest-free loan repayable over perhaps fifty years.[5] A few months later, the trade policy initiative and then the Cambridge discussions made plain Britain's needs and Canada's sympathetic approach to them (above, pp 203–6). Financial aid from Canada was to be assumed in Keynes's proposals that preceded the Washington Mission. Much then depended on the course of the American negotiations upon which the Canadian authorities were kept informed by the British in Washington; by visits there of their own officials; and then by members of the Mission who, on the conclusion of the agreement, briefly visited Ottawa.

Canada's first reaction in mid-August 1945 was to follow the USA and to end aid. This immediately faced Britain with anxieties about the possible recapture of Canadian supplies, the payment of cancellation charges for contracts, and the financing of future supplies, especially of food. The Canadian decision had, however, reflected domestic political preoccupations, and broad rather than specific policy towards recipients (especially Russia) of wartime aid.[6] That Britain was to be regarded as a special case quickly became clear in Ottawa-London exchanges. These included a remonstrance, particularly over the possible prejudice to British discussions with the USA, from the British Prime Minister to his Canadian counterpart, Mr Mackenzie King, who replied reassuringly.[7] Interim arrangements were shortly to be clinched by Lord Keynes when briefly visiting Ottawa *en route* for Washington. As with Lend-Lease, Mutual Aid was to provide finance until the formal end of the war on 2 September 1945; cancellation charges would be borne by Canada; and Canada would renounce rights of recapture, thus sparing Britain the wearisome Lend-Lease burden of making inventories of stocks and surpluses. Pending a full post-war settlement, the Canadian Government would continue to procure supplies for Britain. Finance for these and for the sterling area generally would come from receipts from various British claims, including those in respect of supplies and services to Canadian forces overseas; if necessary, the Bank of Canada would accumulate sterling. The one qualification to these generous arrangements, which evidently greatly relieved the Chancellor, was Keynes's reminder that the Canadians' aid was linked with their well-known concern for liberal trading policies, and that Britain should not 'disappoint them if we can help it'.[8]

There were two particular pressures towards early Anglo-Canadian agreement. First, the Canadians did not want post-war economic difficulties to reduce Britain's normal import surplus in the two-way trade. A second pressure arose from British anxiety to secure appropriate financial arrangements, encompassing those of the sterling area as a whole. Not only would those arrangements determine the limited volume of trade that could be contemplated during the transition, but they had to be seen in context, as the second stage in a wider three-stage agreement. The first was the American agreement; the third would be (rather, was *intended* to be) that with sterling area countries.[9]

The financial issues were fourfold. First was the settlement of $2,043 million of Mutual Aid received from Canada from January 1943 to 2 September 1945. (It should be noted, however, that total Canadian aid during the war was almost twice as great as this.[10]) Second, there was the balancing of numerous claims and counter-claims. A major item involved over $400 million due from Britain for the costs of the wartime Air Training Scheme in Canada. A similar amount was likely to be due for interim supplies since the formal end of the war (2 September 1945). Broad estimates of amounts due *to* Britain indicated that the overall balance in Canada's favour would be between $400 and $650 million.[11] A third issue was the 1942 loan of $700 million. Hitherto this had been interest-free. It had been reduced by applying the proceeds of the sale of Canadian securities held outside Canada; by the end of 1945 it had fallen to about $540 million. It had originally been agreed, however, to conclude more regular arrangements, which would settle the question of interest, at the end of the war.[12] The fourth and final issue, and very far from least, was the provision of fresh finance, over and above the settlement of the wartime accounts, to narrow the expected sterling deficits with Canada in the early post-war years; to deal with those needs a billion dollars and more of new money was the British aim.

At first, British thoughts had been of a loan of $500 million.[13] To the embarrassment of the British team facing difficult American terms, the Governor of the Bank of Canada dropped a hint to the Americans during October 1945 that Canada might help with as much as $1 billion (above, p 300). As American terms began to shape, so did Keynes's views of what the terms for Canadian aid might be:[14] perhaps that $1 billion, at a low rate of interest, with provision for a waiver of payments. There would have to be a settlement of Britain's wartime debts to Canada. These should be on an interest-free basis, and their amount should be held down to the level of Britain's investments in Canada: a sensitive item in Canadian minds.

The dragging of the Washington negotiations kept deferring the visit of the British representatives to Ottawa. Eventually, without Keynes, they had time, early in December 1945, only for exploratory discussions and for an explanation of the Anglo-American Financial Agreement, which had placed the Canadians in a delicate position. They regarded the terms as harsh, but recognised the difficulty of deviation from them in their own projected lending to Britain.[15] Early discussions on this appeared somewhat urgent to the British, who proposed them for mid-January. The Canadians had domestic preoccupations leading them to prefer early February, but the visit of Canadian Ministers to London in January 1946 (suggested by British officials in Ottawa) was to provide an opportunity for them to convey Ottawa's views on an Anglo-Canadian settlement.[16]

Within a few days of the return to London of the Washington Mission, British tactics began to emerge from two meetings of officials in the week before Christmas 1945.[17] The first, attended by the British High Commissioner in Ottawa, Mr Malcolm MacDonald* and his financial adviser, dealt principally with trade policy. Some Canadian anxieties had been covered by the Anglo-American agreement. Beyond that, there was a risk, warned Keynes, that Britain might borrow more than was prudent from Canada simply to satisfy the latter's concern to expand her trade. Further, Canada seemed unlikely to be able to supply much of the essential equipment needed for Britain's re-conversion. It was therefore agreed to avoid major concessions on imports of manufactures until the financial negotiations. The case for caution over imports was underpinned by signs of increased sterling area expenditure on Canadian imports (which would effect London's Canadian dollar resources). Political considerations in Canada, however, made it desirable for Britain to clarify and relax somewhat existing import controls. At the January discussions, increases during 1946 of some twenty per cent by value and 13.3 per cent by volume over pre-war levels of imports were to be as far as the Board of Trade felt able to go; Canadian Ministers had hoped to secure increases of fifty per cent and 33.3 per cent respectively.[18]

The financial approach, a main concern of a second officials' meeting, was essentially to seek the best possible terms, ie, a loan at zero interest, and to entertain worse terms only to the extent that the Canadians extinguished or eased existing British obligations. Subsequent discussions fixed on the amount of 'new money' to be sought at $Can 1.25 billion. This was a somewhat arbitrary figure. It owed more to the earlier hints of Canadian thinking, and to a notional figure of $Can 40 million as the amount which Britain could repay annually, than to precise calculation. Thus, to incorporate the old loan at a reduced

---

* MacDONALD, Malcolm John (1901–83); Secretary of State for Colonies, 1938–40; Minister of Health, 1940–41; UK High Commissioner in Canada 1941–46.

amount of about $500 million, and to allow some $250 million for the balance of outstanding accounts, should this go against Britain, would bring the total gross borrowing to $2 billion. This would allow annual repayments over fifty years, on an interest-free basis, of $40 million. That figure in turn floated around the Treasury less in its own right than on the back of other calculations. A senior Treasury official, evidently with Keynes's approval of his draft telegram in this connection, regarded five per cent of the desired level, by 1949, of export earnings of $5,800 million, ie, $290 million annually, as the maximum tolerable burden for servicing the American loan, repayment of some sterling balances, and servicing a Canadian loan. The American loan would cost $140 million instead of the $100 million originally contemplated; it was necessary to have something in hand for sterling area negotiations, for which annual repayments of $150 million had been 'in mind'; constraint upon the cost of a Canadian loan was therefore essential.[19] By the time that these guidelines were re-stated, negotiations in Ottawa were revolving around a possible loan of $1.75 billion. Compared with annual costs of the American loan of $4.4 billion, $40 million looked modest (a proportionate, comparable cost would have been over $55 million). Initially, however, the British negotiators were seeking to avoid an interest element; repayment over fifty years would then involve $35 million annually, so that something below $40 million appeared a reasonable bargaining basis.[20]

In relation to sterling's balance of payments with Canada, there was comparable statistical roughness. Bank of England estimates indicated a deficit for 1946 of some $650 million, of which $500 million would be Britain's and the remainder from the rest of the sterling area.[21] Sir Wilfrid Eady of the Treasury was to refer in the negotiations to estimated deficits of $750 – 800 million and $500 – 550 million for 1946 and 1947, although finance was being sought to support the balance of payments until something like equilibrium was achieved in 1949.[22] It was not, indeed, intended to eliminate the whole of the expected deficits with Canada, for the previously normal pattern of sterling deficits was likely to persist.[23] It was nevertheless foreseen that there could be a significant shortfall, but proposals to meet this by gold payments (Keynes's idea), or by Canadian accumulation of sterling (Mr A T K Grant's suggestion) were rejected in the preliminary Treasury discussions. It can be concluded that, as with the American loan, the amount to be sought (and to be obtained) from Canada was a reflection less of British economic desiderata than of what appeared politically possible.

(4) BRITISH AND CANADIAN APPROACHES TO THE NEGOTIATIONS

The British delegation was to be led by Sir Wilfrid Eady, with Mr C F Cobbold, Deputy Governor of the Bank of England. Lord Keynes felt unable to go, remaining in Britain to oversee with Sir Edward

Bridges and Mr R W B Clarke the London handling of the negotiations. The Chancellor savoured the reversal of roles: Keynes would be able 'to send Baboons [the telegram series from London during the Washington negotiations] to Eady, and get a bit of his own back . . .'. But 'Baboon Can' seemed inappropriate and, more suitably, the Treasury went 'to Kew Gardens rather than the Zoo' and labelled telegrams from London and Ottawa 'Maple' and 'Beech' respectively.[24]

Canadian Ministers and officials formulated their approach to the financial negotiations, loosely and tentatively, only after the arrival of the British party.[25] There were two strong political influences, in addition to the constraint upon the Canadian Government of a small parliamentary majority. One was the French-Canadian Minister of Justice, Mr Louis St Laurent.* Reflecting long-standing dislike in Canada, especially in his political base in Quebec, of overseas involvement in its economy, he jibbed at a loan when Britain still owned substantial investments on which Canada paid her many million dollars annually.[26] Second, the Prime Minister, Mr Mackenzie King, himself inclined to be suspicious of international financial arrangements, was particularly cautious, as Mr Vinson and Mr Clayton had been about the United States Congress, over what it would be possible to persuade the Canadian House of Commons to accept.[27] The policy to emerge, with far from unanimous backing, was that, in addition to terms similar to those of the American loan, ie, repayment over fifty years at two per cent interest, Canada would bargain her special claims on Britain against concessions on trade where these were not already covered by the more general terms of the Anglo-American Financial Agreement. Mutual Aid itself required no settlement, but payment, deferred or in loan form, was envisaged for the various amounts due from Britain.

(5) NEGOTIATIONS IN OTTAWA

Although negotiations were to stretch through most of February into early March, the main issues were isolated by mid-February in three days of formal meetings.[28] Less formal contacts helped to clarify attitudes, whilst technical experts from both sides worked through detailed accounting problems. Sir Wilfrid Eady's exposition at the formal meetings echoed that of Keynes in Washington five months earlier. It concentrated on the overall weakness, on both capital and current account, of Britain's balance of payments during the early post-war years. Easement of that position would facilitate currency convertibility and trade liberalisation. Britain wished to borrow no more than necessary, and that meant seeking $1.25 billion from Canada. Without such aid, Britain would be deprived of the substan-

---

* ST. LAURENT, Louis Stephen (1882–1973); Canadian Minister of External Affairs, 1946–48; Prime Minister of Canada, 1948–57.

tial flow of Canadian food. More generally, he was to stress the overriding importance of Congressional approval of the much larger American loan; failure to secure that would prevent Britain from operating the Bretton Woods arrangements and those of the proposed International Trade Organisation, and would drive her to extreme economic nationalism and austerity.

Despite the favourable impact of Eady's exposition, supported by Mr Cobbold's explanation of sterling area problems, tension developed as Mr St Laurent voiced unwillingness to contemplate fresh loans without some compensating arrangement over British investments in Canada. British estimates put these at $770 million in Canadian dollar securities, $480 million in Canadian sterling securities, and $200 – 300 million in direct investments: some $1,500 million in all. Mr St Laurent urged that these be treated as cover for the proposed new loan, which their gradual run-down would repay. The loan would embody existing British obligations under the old loan, the Air Training Scheme, and the balance due to Canada on miscellaneous war and post-war transactions. There would thus be a relatively small residual of 'new money'. Moreover, Canada's payment of interest on British investments would provide Britain's interest on the new loan. The British delegation objected strongly.[29] The loss of investment income would further complicate the difficulties of sterling trade with Canada. Worse, the proposals would prejudice Britain's chances of obtaining with other countries the settlements necessary to allow her to undertake early convertibility and trade liberalisation. In relation to the as yet unapproved American loan, the greater severity of Mr St Laurent's proposals would be contrary to its terms, and would invite unfavourable revision of them. As for the contemplated sterling settlement, the chances of that would vanish if Canada required full repayment, with interest, of wartime indebtedness.

Whilst recognising the British case for assistance, the Canadian Prime Minister privately warned leading British representatives to take account of the severe political constraints which made it impossible to meet their two main requests.[30] The search for compromise on these, and interest-free credit and cancellation of the amounts due to Canada (excluding the old loan) now dominated negotiations. Various schemes were to be aired, first on the somewhat rigorous lines demanded by Mr St Laurent. He pondered a three per cent loan, eased by payment of interest in sterling instead of dollars. The old loan might be continued interest-free for five years, but he favoured an interest charge on the Air Training Scheme liability. The Canadian Cabinet decided, however, to offer cancellation of the latter, provided that Britain's sterling creditors made a similar gesture. The British rejection was to stress the unacceptability of the likely burden;[31] the

War Office was to add to that case, by reminding the Treasury that Canada's decision to withdraw by the end of summer 1946 the Army Division that it had provided for the occupation of Germany threatened to impose a further burden, which the Ottawa discussions should seek to avoid.[32] As for a three per cent loan, that was unacceptable; such terms, onerous to Britain, would appear so favourable to Canada that, as the Foreign Office agreed, they would be regarded in the USA as being contrary to the Anglo-American Agreement.[33]

The vigorous British rejection of Canadian proposals outraged the Canadian Prime Minister, who was already angered by British pressure for interest-free aid; when this had been supported by the Governor of the Bank of Canada, he suspected a conspiracy.[34] A break in negotiations might easily have developed at that point, but both sides sought to avoid that; from British representatives in Washington came advice that a breach would prejudice the passage of the American loan.[35] The British High Commissioner in Ottawa (Mr Malcolm MacDonald) and Mr C F Cobbold, Deputy Governor of the Bank of England, were to return to London to advise the Cabinet on the position. In Ottawa, Ministers and officials hastily considered ways of resolving both their own internal differences and those with Britain.[36]

To meet British insistence on avoiding heavy annual service, the Canadian Deputy Minister of Finance (Mr W C Clark*)canvassed briefly a proposal for an interest-free loan, to be amortised over thirty-two years. The annual servicing cost of some $40 million, and the size of the new loan, would bear equal proportions to those in the American agreement. This was unacceptable to the British in its exclusion of a waiver, thereby risking heavy burdens in future difficult years, and risking more immediately a temptation to the United States Congress to remove the waiver provision from the American loan.[37] The proposal in fact proved to be a non-starter in the Canadian Cabinet; the Prime Minister regarded it, or variants of it, as 'too involved', and the majority of the Cabinet viewed an interest charge as politically unavoidable.[38]

Hesitating over terms which might appear worse than the Americans', or which might be insufficiently simple for domestic presentation, the Canadian Cabinet narrowed its choice to two possibilities: a low rate of interest (one per cent) with postponement for five years of the settlement of various claims on Britain; or the same rate of interest as on the US loan (two per cent), with significant cancellation of debt. The decision went to the second; the Canadian Cabinet's offer proved to be, with one exception, the final agreed terms, after further bargaining by London. There would be a new credit of $1,250 million at two per cent, payment of this and capital repayment to begin after five

---

* CLARK, William Clifford (1889–1952); Deputy Minister of Finance, Canada, from 1932.

years; the old loan would be continued interest-free until then, when it would be reviewed, the proceeds of disinvestment by overseas owners of Canadian securities meanwhile reducing the outstanding amount; the Air Training Scheme liability of $425 million was to be cancelled; finally—the item to be modified in favour of a fixed payment by Britain—settlement of the balance of miscellaneous mutual claims would have to be agreed.[39]

(6) CONCLUSION OF THE AGREEMENT

Noting that Canadian considerations favoured quick action, the British delegates indicated that limited scope remained to bargain on fundamentals. In particular, to press for interest-free credit, which would cause a split amongst Canadian Government MPs, would be unwise, unless coupled with trade concessions; they did not, however, rule out entirely the chance of a rate of one per cent instead of two per cent.[40]

The Chancellor, believing that a quick, 'clean', settlement should aid the passage of the American loan, took up these points in the Ministers' Committee.[41] He made two main proposals. First, he supported Mr Cobbold's proposal to try for a lower rate of interest, but on a larger amount of $1.75 billion, which would incorporate the old loan. The appeal of this, besides the lower annual cost, and avoiding continuance of the unsatisfactory arrangements over the old loan, was that it would be differentiated from the American loan and thus from the latter's terms. Ministers did not, however, consider any *douceur* in trade concessions. Second, the settlement of certain outstanding mutual claims threatened to be delayed and to involve an unknown amount. On one more clearly defined part the British delegates had stood firm on a limit of $50 million to be paid to Canada; believing that it might be possible to overcome Canadian reluctance to settle forthwith, they suggested a British offer to pay Canada up to $150 million to cover all claims. Incorporation of the extra $100 million in the loan was another possibility, preferred by Mr Cobbold. Separate treatment, however, had its attractions especially if coupled with cancellation of the Air Training Scheme liability. Such elimination of debt might aid negotiations over sterling balances.

On the two major proposals, Ministers followed the Chancellor. They gave delegates discretion, in the interests of an early settlement, to accept the Canadian offer of $1.25 billion at two per cent, provided that mutual claims could be settled at no more than $150 million, whether by a cash payment or partially by addition to the new loan. To underline the burdens on Britain, however, the delegates should endeavour to remind the Canadian Government that Britain might seek a contribution towards the heavy occupation costs in Germany.[42]

Informal soundings of the Minister of Finance and his Deputy, Mr

J L Ilsley* and Mr W C Clark, quickly persuaded the British delegates to seek London's consent, which came immediately, to abandon attempts to modify the Canadian terms, other than for the residual claims.[43] That British sticking point, after some hesitation lest they appear alone as making sacrifices to help Britain, the Canadians soon conceded.[44] It later emerged that 'by implication' Sir Wilfrid Eady had agreed that the payment of $150 million would be in 'gold' or 'gold equivalent'—and it should be gold, he noted.[45] That arrangement evoked some subtle contrasts in Canadian and British policy making. In June 1940, on the fall of France, Britain had paid to the USA $158 million in respect of costs already paid by France on contracts that she now took over. A subsequent attempt, shortly before Lend-Lease eased financing problems, to gain access to French gold held in Ottawa failed.[46] The Canadian Government refused from considerations of honour and of French-Canadian sensitivity. Recollection of that episode appears to have re-inforced Mr Mackenzie King's prickly attitude in the 1946 negotiations.[47] On the British side, the liberation of France in 1944 – 45 had permitted settlement of Anglo-French claims; this included an arrangement by which, against military equipment, France was to repay the $158 million.[48] Mr A T K Grant of the Treasury noted that the roughly simultaneous receipt of this would offset the drain on the reserves from the payment of $150 million to Canada. Lord Keynes, who had expected a two per cent Canadian credit to be accompanied by complete cancellation of residual claims, and who had helped to devise the Anglo-French scheme, sourly commented 'Not much consolation'.[49]

Formalisation of Anglo-Canadian understanding was in two main parts: a financial agreement, and a supplementary agreement on the settlement of mutual claims.[50] This separation originally had the attraction that the US Congress was thought to be less likely to give troublesome attention to the linking of Britain's Canadian securities with the old loan if there were no reference to that in the financial agreement.[51] In the event, it was to be included in the latter, but only in general terms. That apart, the supplementary agreement concerned matters settled once and for all. In contrast, implementation of part of the financial agreement was to be contingent upon that of the US loan, which otherwise its terms broadly followed.

The belated realisation that Britain might have secured too good a bargain had caused Canadian Ministers to be 'suddenly haunted', Sir Wilfrid Eady cabled to London, 'by political bogeys.... which we must accept as facts'. Britain was to have the new Canadian loan immediately it was approved, but Congressional rejection of the US

* ILSLEY, James Lorimer (1894 – 1967); Minister of National Revenue, Canada, 1935 – 40; Minister of Finance, 1940 – 46; Minister of Justice and Attorney-General, Canada, 1946 – 48.

loan would deprive Canada of the much desired abolition in Anglo-Canadian trade of exchange controls and of discriminatory trade restrictions; by largely British drafting, a clause in the financial agreement had made that dependent upon the operation of the comparable clause in the American agreement. A further clause modelled on one in the latter had been elaborated, albeit in general terms, to provide for consultation should Congress reject the loan. The Canadian Administration now insisted that operation of the clauses to continue the old loan and to cancel the Air Training liability should await Congressional approval of the US agreement. Together with similar postponement of the exchange control and trade commitments, which in any case were dependent on the US action, these requirements were embodied in an exchange of letters between the Canadian Minister of Finance and the Chancellor of the Exchequer. The letters were to be included in the parliamentary records (though not in the more formal published documentation) of the agreements. Sir Wilfrid Eady regarded all this as 'slightly fantastic' but as acceptable. It did not harm Britain; with an American loan, the arrangements for the old Canadian loan and for the Air Training liability would go through, but without it Britain could scarcely be expected to pay interest on the one and to repay the other. As for the impact of the Canadian requirement upon Congress, there would be none.[52] Very shortly, after some technical revisions, the agreements were approved in early March 1946 by both Governments, and by the British Parliament. The Canadian Parliament approved them two months later.[53]

During the waiting period one or two worries were eased. Might Canada resume her pre-war practice of settling her trading surplus with Britain by sales of sterling in New York, thereby drawing on Britain's US dollars? In that case, ought not Britain to be able if necessary to draw the Canadian loan in US dollars, as presumably the Anglo-Canadian Financial Agreement intended? To this inquiry from a Bank of England official, a somewhat nettled Treasury reply viewed 'these contingencies [as] ..... somewhat remote', and Mr Cobbold, in support of this, subsequently clarified the matter. The Canadian loan was not tied, but it would scarcely be proper to use it all up on payments outside Canada, whilst on Canada's part, he doubted if free sales of sterling in New York were an early probability.[54] Another problem was the financing of British purchases in Canada until ratification of the loan. Canadian thinking seemed to prefer accumulation of sterling, rather than British sales of gold or special legislative provision by Canada; London agreed.[55]

Two months or so after the passage of the Canadian loan, Congress approved in mid-July the Anglo-American Financial Agreement. The remaining sections of the Canadian agreement were now promptly activated.[56] The greater part of the post-war financial settlement—for hopes of substantial cancellation of sterling balances were clearly unreal—had been completed.

CHAPTER 11, SOURCE REFERENCES

1. Tel 2288 of 11 November 1945 from United Kingdom High Commissioner in Ottawa to Dominions Office (for HM Treasury), T 236/629, tel BEECH 15 from British Delegation in Ottawa to DO (for HMT), 16 February 1946, T 236/630.

2. Mr R Gordon Munro, Financial Adviser to United Kingdom High Commissioner in Ottawa, 'Notes on forthcoming United Kingdom-Canadian financial negotiations', 15 December 1945, T 236/629.

3. Note by Sir Wilfrid Eady, 21 January 1946, T 236/630.

4. Article XI of Canada-United Kingdom Agreement of 11 February 1944, Hall, *North American Supply*, p 518; tel 1715 of 18 August 1945, United Kingdom High Commissioner in Ottawa to Dominions Office, T 236/628.

5. T 160/1377.

6. Report by Mr Munro, tel 1726 of 21 August 1945, Ottawa to Dominions Office, T 236/629.

7. Telegrams relating to this are in T 236/629, especially the following: telegram 1486, Dominions Office to High Commissioner of the United Kingdom in Ottawa, 17 August 1945; tel 1715 United Kingdom High Commissioner to DO, 18 August, T 236/629; tel 203, Canadian Prime Minister to British Prime Minister, of 31 August. Mr Mackenzie King realised that he had been 'rather peppery'; the United Kingdom High Commissioner toned down the reply from Mr Attlee: tel 1742 of 23 August, Ottawa to London, and tel 1510 of 23 August, London to Ottawa.

8. Report of Ottawa meeting, 3 September 1945, T 247/127. Telegrams from Keynes and related papers sent from United Kingdom High Commission in Ottawa to London, 2–7 September, are in T 236/629.

9. Sir Wilfrid Eady's opening exposition in the Anglo-Canadian negotiations, 11 February 1946. Eady's remarks were repeated in the Memorandum on the discussions, 13 February 1946, T 236/630. These and some other documents in the negotiations are reproduced, not always in full, in Donald M Page (ed), Department of External Affairs, *Documents on Canadian External Relations*, vol 12, 1946 (Ottawa, 1977).

10. The value of goods and services received by Britain from Canada during the war came to $7,441 million. There were offsets from supplies and services provided to Canadian forces abroad, and substantial receipts from the three major items of trade in goods and services, and from sales of securities. Most of the remaining deficit was met formally by Mutual Aid of $2,043 million during 1943 to 1945, following less formal but similar assistance in 1942, in all $2,276 million; by the interest-free loan of $700 million, reduced to some $540 million by the end of 1945; and, also in 1942, by 'The Billion Dollar Gift' of military and civilian supplies. Total Canadian aid therefore came to approximately $4 billion. See Hall, op cit, pp 239–42 and 483–88; Sayers, *Financial Policy*, chapter XI.

11. Note by Mr A T K Grant for Sir Wilfrid Eady, 18 January 1946, T 236/630.

12. For the background to this loan, see Sayers, op cit, chapter XI, esp pp 341–6.

13. $500 million mentioned in NABOB 178 of 18 October 1945, T 236/629.

14. NABOB 306 of 7 November 1945, ibid.

15. Mr Munro's 'Note...' of 15 December 1945, ibid.

16. Keynes from Washington to Sir Edward Bridges and Sir Wilfrid Eady in London, 14 November 1945, tel REMAC 826 (repeated as PILIF 826 to HC in Ottawa); Mr R H Brand and Mr R G Munro, tel 2503 of 10 December from

Ottawa to London; United Kingdom High Commissioner in Ottawa to DO, tel 31 of 5 January 1946, ibid.

17. 19 & 20 December 1945, T 236/630.

18. Meeting at Board of Trade 21 January 1946, ibid.

19. Draft telegram with Keynes's pencilled corrections, and tel 253/MAPLE 11 of 15 February, London to Ottawa, ibid.

20. Ibid.

21. Dec 1945, ibid.

22. Report of Anglo-Canadian meeting in Ottawa of 11 February 1946, page 7, ibid.

23. Mr R W B Clarke's draft ('RWBC 27'), the basis of tel 197, DO to Keynes in Washington (and as tel 1980 to United Kingdom HC in Ottawa) 10 November 1945, T 236/629.

24. In addition to Sir Wilfrid Eady and Mr Cobbold, the British group included Mr A T K Grant and Mr E Jones of HM Treasury, Mr R H Brand from HM Treasury Delegation in Washington, Mr R Bridge of the Bank of England, and Mr S Holmes and Mr G R Bell from the United Kingdom High Commission in Ottawa. Mr P S White of the office of the Exchequer & Audit Dept in New York also joined the delegates: notes by Sir Edward Bridges 2 January 1946 and by Chancellor 3 January; Mr Grant to Sir Alexander Clutterbuck of DO 23 Jan; T 236/630.

25. *Documents on Canadian External Relations,* vol 12, pp 1388–96, and J W Pickersgill and D F Forster, *The Mackenzie King Record,* III, 1945–46 (Toronto 1970), p 160.

26. Ibid, p 161; report of meeting of 12 February 1946, T 236/630.

27. Pickersgill & Forster, op cit, pp 160–75 *passim.*

28. Reports of meetings on 11, 12, 13 February 1946 are cited here from T 236/630. Copies are also in Bridges Papers (Canadian Financial Negotiations 1946), and in AVIA 38/312.

29. Memorandum by United Kingdom Delegation, 13 February 1946, T 236/630.

30. Pickersgill & Forster, op cit, p 166.

31. Ibid, pp 166–7 and *Documents,* vol 12, p 1411 and BEECH 26, United Kingdom HC in Ottawa to London, 22 February, T 236/630.

32. War Office to Treasury, 25 February, ibid.

33. FO to Treasury, 23 February, ibid.

34. Pickersgill & Forster, op cit, pp 165, 168.

35. Ibid, 168–72; Mr Cobbold at Ministers' meeting on 'Financial and Commercial Policy' 26 February 1946, GEN 89/8th Meeting, CAB 78/37.

36. Ibid, 172–4, and BEECH 26 of 22 February, United Kingdom HC Ottawa to London, T 236/630.

37. BEECH 30 of 26 February, Ottawa to London, ibid.

38. Ibid, and Pickersgill & Forster, op cit, pp 172–4.

39. BEECH 30.

40. Ibid.

41. Chancellor's note to Lord President of the Council, 27 February 1946, Bridges Papers, and Ministers' Committee of 26 February 1946, GEN 89/8th Meeting, CAB 78/37.

42. Tels MAPLE 25, 26, 27 of 27 February, London to Ottawa, T 236/630.

43. BEECH 33 of 27 February, Ottawa to London, and MAPLE 30 of 28 February, London to Ottawa, T 236/631.

44. BEECH 37 of 1 March and BEECH 38 of 2 March, ibid.
45. Notes by Mr R G Munro and Sir Wilfrid Eady, 25 March; tel 584 of 23 March, Ottawa to London; Mr Grant to Mr L P Thompson-McCausland of the Bank of England, 28 March: ibid.
46. Sayers, *Financial Policy*, pp 335–6.
47. Pickersgill & Forster, op cit, p 171.
48. T 247/57, 99 and 100.
49. Note by Mr Grant and comment by Keynes, 2 April 1946, T 236/631.
50. Not published as a White Paper until September 1946, as Cmd 6904, *BPP* 1945–6, XXV.
51. Para 5 of BEECH 37 of 1 March, Ottawa to London, T 236/631.
52. BEECH telegrams 38 of 2 March, 39 of 3 March, 44 of 4 March, 48, 49, 50 of 5 March, ibid.
53. United Kingdom House of Commons 7 March 1946, 420 HC DEB 5 s, cols 510–20; Canadian approval 7 May, reported *The Times* 8 May 1946.
54. H Siepmann of the Bank of England to Sir David Waley, 12 March; Mr Grant to Waley, 14 March; draft reply, Waley to Siepmann, no date; Mr Cobbold to Waley 15 March: T 236/631.
55. Tel 511 of 13 March, Ottawa to London, ibid.
56. J C Ilsley, Minister of Finance, to United Kingdom High Commissioner in Ottawa, 16 July 1946, T 236/632. A valuable account of the Canadian approach to the negotiation of the loan to Britain has appeared since this chapter was first drafted: Hector M Mackenzie, 'The Path to Temptation: The Negotiation of Canada's Reconstruction Loan to Britain in 1946', The Canadian Historical Association, *Historical Papers* (Ottawa 1982), pp 196–220.

CHAPTER 12

Conclusion: An Incomplete Financial Settlement

(1) WAITING, HESITATION AND DOUBTS

The completion of the post-war financial settlement as originally envisaged, by decisive containment of sterling indebtedness, was not to be achieved. Instead of providing a *coda* to the American and Canadian agreements, the treatment of sterling balances became a major theme of post-war economic policy. The broad principles of wartime management were adapted to peacetime. At first this arrangement was tentative; but after the brief attempt in mid-1947 to implement the general convertibility required by the Anglo-American Financial Agreement, it was to persist, albeit with eventually diminishing significance, for a quarter of a century.[1] This chapter briefly outlines these developments, which will be examined more fully in a subsequent volume.

The unenthusiastic reception in Britain, not least in Parliament, of the Anglo-American Financial Agreement reflected a predisposition to be free of the constraints that it would impose.[2] Less wide-ranging and weaker financial commitments would therefore have been tolerable, indeed welcome, to many and became more likely possibilities with the anxious waiting for the verdict of Congress on the US loan. The Chancellor was reluctant meanwhile to contemplate more than limited negotiations on sterling balances, preferring to delay most until after ratification by the US of the financial agreement. Should ratification not come, however, to the necessity of managing without the loan would be added the impossibility of renouncing monetary and trade controls as required respectively by the International Monetary Fund and the proposed International Trade Organisation. Britain would be unable to adhere to those institutions. During the first half of 1946, thoughts in London were of possible alternative policies: increasingly so as the short-term prospects of the balance of payments were re-assessed.

(2) THE BALANCE OF PAYMENTS: IMPORTS AND GOVERNMENT EXPENDITURE OVERSEAS

Policy about imports and about the balance of payments in general was shaped in provisional fashion. It evolved more or less simultaneously and in association with the beginnings of systematic analysis of the balance of payments (see Appendix 27, section 2), and with the formation for the first time of a group of officials specifically instructed to give continuing attention to it.

During the closing stages of the war, Treasury thinking about the daunting questions of the means of providing for and financing post-war imports tended to assume the continuation, where appropriate, of wartime methods; whilst some of these were to retain a place in peacetime, wider views were, however, to be necessary. With the shift from American Lend-Lease and Canadian Mutual Aid, and from the accumulation of sterling debt, preoccupation with dollar saving would have to merge into a wider concern with the balance of payments as a whole. Keynes's dominating memorandum of spring 1945 sharpened the discussions and the apprehension of the prospective gravity of the external position. Whichever path were to be taken of the three he outlined ('Austerity', 'Temptation', 'Justice'), '. . . in the short-run we cannot depart far from Austerity', he had warned.[3]

Senior Treasury officials agreed in June 1945 on the desirability of establishing a committee to take an overall view of external economic policy.[4] From Mr R W B Clarke came a programme, a potential inspiration for such a body, in a wide-ranging and imaginative paper entitled 'Towards a Balance of Payments'.[5] This built on work already done in the Economic Section and which underlay Keynes's various memoranda on post-war policy. The paper examined British problems in the light of broad international considerations: economic conditions in the USA, European recovery, and developments in smaller and poorer countries. Clarke re-affirmed the improbability of securing external equilibrium before 1950 (at this stage, the Japanese war was widely expected to continue for another eighteen months). This prospect offered an opportunity to avoid piecemeal, discriminatory, narrowly based policies in foreign exchange and trade, for they could not bring equilibrium any nearer; in the relatively long haul ahead, policies could and should be undertaken in the light of their impact on the longer-run improvement of the balance of payments as a whole. Although early convertibility of sterling was to be avoided (the Washington financial negotiations being still in the future), the aim should be multilateralism; during the transition, however, scope should be retained for bilateral policies, lest events dictate recourse to them.

Shortly after the formation of the new Labour Government (in late July 1945), Sir Edward Bridges was instructed by Ministers to formulate proposals for the organisation of a national economic plan, in the sense of the management of the nation's economic resources (such organisation would carry further the developments that had already been set afoot by the previous Government to implement employment policy, as outlined in the White Paper on that in 1944).[6] His recommendations led to the establishment of an official Steering Committee on Economic Development, with five Working Parties of officials. One, to be responsible for Economic Surveys, was based on the Economic Section, which had already been at work on such Surveys, and the Central Statistical Office; it was effectively under Mr James Meade, Director of the Economic Section. Another was the Balance of Payments Working Party; this proved to be predominantly a Treasury responsibility, with Sir Wilfrid Eady as Chairman and Mr Clarke as its most vigorous member.[7] All these bodies were under the Lord President of the Council (Mr Herbert Morrison), whose responsibilities included co-ordination of economic policy.[8]

The longer-term aim was to look ahead for five years. Although that aim was not to be neglected,[9] it was quickly to be overshadowed by shorter-term considerations. An early Treasury goal was to secure equilibrium in the balance of payments, excluding terminal wartime expenditure, by the end of 1947. Officials soon set a slightly more ambitious date of mid-1947, and the Cabinet formally adopted that in April 1946.[10]

Under great pressure and with a sense of its highly provisional character, a draft of the Economic Survey for 1946 was produced towards the end of 1945. It estimated a balance of payments deficit for 1946 of £750 million, corresponding with that eventually used in the Washington negotiations. That was bad enough, but Clarke, whose approach and conclusions were not entirely acceptable to Meade, reached a little later a grimmer estimate of £821 million.[11] This was even worse than an extra nine per cent or so, for with the Washington negotiations now concluded it was clear that the amount of the US credit was to be smaller than hoped, and the obligations more onerous than feared (in the event both sets of views on the deficit for 1946 proved to be over-pessimistic). The higher figure was that which went to the Cabinet early in February 1946, accompanied by a dramatic appeal from Keynes to restrict government expenditure overseas, which was seen as the greatest obstacle to the achievement of equilibrium.

The need to reduce government expenditure overseas had been stressed from three sources. The Economic Survey envisaged very substantial cuts in manpower in the Services and in the industries supplying them.[12] From papers prepared by Clarke for the Balance of Payments Working Party, and discussed by it, came an estimate of military and other government expenditure overseas of £400 million, which one member described as 'staggering'.[13] By no means least, the Bank of England, which as administrator of Exchange Control had the most comprehensive oversight of international payments, warned the Chancellor—who in turn evoked the concern of the Prime Minister—of the continuing rise in sterling balances because of the Government's overseas expenditure.[14]

A quick preliminary survey was made of the problem by Clarke. In the first of two papers at the end of January 1946, he suggested that, on existing commitments, there might be little scope to reduce overseas military expenditure below some £300 million in 1946.[15] In a second paper[16] he turned to other government commitments abroad, of less certain amount: occupation costs in Germany (less receipts from German exports); assistance to liberated countries in Europe (less amounts that France and the Netherlands, for instance, might be able to find for goods from Germany and the sterling area); expenditure in the liberated colonies in south-east Asia (where Britain would need to control imports and the rundown of sterling balances). Scrutinising these potential drains country by country, he noted that they could amount to £300 million net, in addition to the cost of military commitments, in 1946 'if we were open-handed' and to a net total of around £400 million for 1946 – 48. The combined burden of military and government expenditure overseas in 1946 could therefore reach some £600 million, fifty per cent more than the estimate that had been described as 'staggering'. (Clarke had, however, settled on £300 million, rather than a higher figure, for *military* expenditure, in anticipation of Ministers' approval of cuts. One may surmise that the disparity between the *overall* figure of £400 million in the Balance of Payments Working Party report, and that of £600 million aired in the later papers, reflected a similar anticipation of decisions on cuts in respect of other government expenditure overseas. In citing nevertheless a possibly higher figure of £600 million in all, Clarke may therefore have been stressing conceivable dangers, in order to encourage the taking of firm action to control such large potential outlays).

In a paper closely reflecting Clarke's work, Keynes catalogued these prospective expenditures, and thundered that existing commitments must be drastically reduced.[17] Unchanged, they might involve during the three years 1946 – 48 as much as £1,500 million gross, or £1,000 million net. In contrast, allowance had been made for £600 million (net) in the Washington negotiations. There was no margin in the country's resources for such outlays, to which had to be added those for subscriptions to the new International Monetary Fund and World Bank, and for the release of a substantial amount of sterling balances. He therefore urged immediate reconsideration of three particular threatened drains on resources: 'political loans' to overseas countries; the weakening of the economy of occupied Germany in such fashion that Britain incurred heavy costs in supporting it; and military expenditures outside Europe.

Following intensive discussions involving the principal departments with import programmes, the Chancellor submitted Keynes's 'flaming warning', as Sir Edward Bridges had called it,[18] to the Cabinet, together with the memorandum from the Balance of Payments

Working Party on the import programme for 1946. His introductory note stressed the 'bad picture' they portrayed, and that even with the US and Canadian loans a deficit of over £800 million could not be contemplated. He therefore proposed a cut in imports of some £50 million (approximately 4.5 per cent).[19] This was duly considered by the Cabinet,[20] which already faced something of a crisis over food supplies, a major item in imports, centring around dried eggs;[21] there was also pressure to improve the nation's diet as a means of encouraging production for export. Its decision was to allow some increase in food imports for the first half of the year, to be offset by subsequent reduction, but to seek further decreases in proposed expenditure by the Services. Estimates for the latter had just been cut by about £200 million (almost fourteen per cent); the Chancellor was shortly to ask, through the Cabinet's Defence Committee, for a further cut of £120 million (roughly ten per cent).[22]

By this time (February 1946) Ministers and officials had gone a useful distance in adjusting policies and organisation to deal with the problems of the post-war balance of payments. What, however, if Congress were to reject the US Loan?

(3) 'WHAT HAPPENS IF WE DO NOT GET THE US LOAN'

Discouraging cables about the difficulties being encountered in Congress over the Anglo-American Financial Agreement were being received from the Washington Embassy as the import programme was being reconsidered.[23] Hitherto, attempts to consider what might be done, were no Loan to be forthcoming, had not gone very far,[24] but now, in February 1946, the Chancellor invited Treasury thoughts on what to do in such an eventuality.[25] Mr Clarke, who had earlier queried the assumptions on which US aid had been sought and negotiated (above, pp 242 and 295 – 6) quickly submitted proposals on 'What Happens If We Do Not Get The US Loan'.[26] By their nature, such exercises resembled statistical conjuring (especially coming from Clarke), but they clearly appeared to be a necessary precaution.

The import programme and projected government expenditures overseas that had just been considered would have increased the estimated overall deficit, in the three years 1946 – 48, from the Washington figure of £1,250 million to £1,650 million. To provide a solution to the problem of dealing with this, should Congress reject the Loan or attach fresh (and presumably unacceptable) strings, Clarke made four major assumptions. The USA would not withdraw the credit of $650 million for settlement of Lend-Lease, nor would it prevent Britain from borrowing dollars on commercial terms. There would be moral support from the Dominions and from European countries, with economic aid more likely to come from the former than from the latter. Britain would keep out of the Bretton Woods institutions and the projected International Trade Organisation, and would perhaps evolve substitute arrangements. Finally, and not least, sterling balances negotiations should be dropped, and leading European countries should be associated with sterling countries in order to pool and to economise dollar resources; thereby, it could be inferred, would emerge the substitute international arrangements. Thus fortified, Britain could concentrate on securing a greater proportion of necessarily reduced imports from non-dollar sources, and also on both expanding exports and diverting them to where (eg, North and South America) they would most ease the strain on the balance of payments. Even so, substantial borrowing from the sterling area and other non-dollar countries, in addition to trading surpluses with them, would be necessary to finance the Government's overseas expenditure: an effort which might prove inadequate, with 'the most furious political implications'. With that necessarily speculative qualification Clarke believed it to be possible to 'develop a perfectly workable multilateral system based on sterling, excluding USA'.[27] A memorandum on these lines was to go to Ministers in March 1946,[28] after revisions of detail and of exposition in the light of discussions with Keynes.

Keynes was relatively optimistic about securing the Loan, but had agreed that alternative policies should be explored in case the worst happened. Although not wholly persuaded by Clarke's figuring, he broadly agreed with his conclusions. Loan or no Loan, government expenditure overseas stood out as the great difficulty. The scale of reductions necessary in the absence of the Loan had yet to be recognised, declared Keynes, and 'even on the assumption of an American Loan, the position is all but intractable.' It was a melancholy fact that 'it comes out in the wash that the American Loan [of £937 million] is primarily required to meet the political and military expenditure overseas' [of £1,000 million].[29]

Clarke believed that the country 'could wriggle through' if necessary.[30] Such an uninviting exercise, the Treasury broadly agreed, could be deferred whilst waiting for a decision on the Loan; meanwhile, there were discussions with other departments, to devise possible economies, and with the Bank of England. A draft was prepared of a communication to sterling area countries should the Loan fall through. In mid-May a 'War Book' was to be hurriedly prepared, and a memorandum on 'Rejection of US Loan. Suggestions for immediate action', was produced, embracing cuts in major groups of imports.[31] Notwithstanding these prudential steps, the broad policy remained one of hopefulness and of 'wait and see'. This was encouraged by Keynes's patient optimism following a visit during March to the USA; his view, and that of all those in the American Administration whom he met, was that 'the American Loan [was] . . . quite safe unless some quite unexpected factor develops'.[32]

Uncertainty was nevertheless to persist longer than expected when Keynes had reported Administration views 'that the thing would be through by the end of May and perhaps sooner'.[33] Early in May, the Prime Minister agreed that, with rejection or at least a postponement of Congressional approval possible, there might have to be a further review of policy.[34] The Senate's approval came very shortly after, but before that of the House of Representatives was to be given, there were to be some two further months of doubt; in early July Clarke was touching up the draft memorandum for the Cabinet on possible action should rejection be the outcome. The Treasury, however, remained sufficiently optimistic to have opened in mid-June a fresh file on 'Action to be taken on the approval of the Loan Agreement', and Clarke switched gears to consider 'What happens if the Loan goes through'.[35] Full Congressional approval and then President Truman's signature on the legislation came at last in mid-July. Clarke closed the original file, on possible rejection, 'with mixed feelings', musing that pro- and anti-Loan parties would find in it support for their respective views.[36]

(4) THE TREATMENT OF STERLING BALANCES

The absence of American aid might have permitted a retreat—a release—from attempts to negotiate satisfactory settlements of sterling balances. Its availability required the implementation of the undertakings about them in the Financial Agreement. The difficulties of accomplishing that quickly became apparent.

By the end of 1945, after increasing at a faster pace than had been anticipated in the Washington negotiations, net sterling liabilities amounted to £3,567 million (gross, £3,602 million). Balances due to overseas sterling countries were £2,327 million net (£2,348 million gross), and to non-sterling countries £1,240 million (£1,254 million gross).[37] Against the prospect of drastic treatment of these the monitory voices from the Colonial and India Offices had continued to sound, as had the disapproving views of the Bank of England.[38] Indeed, from a senior official of the latter came stress on the moral distastefulness of cutting balances of colonial territories that went beyond the technical considerations that were the Bank's usual functions.[39] When in February 1946 a Ministers' Committee considered 'Negotiations on Sterling Area Balances', there could be detected not far below the expressions of intention and hope the sense of ultimate bafflement characterising earlier, wartime, discussions.[40] The Chancellor expected there to be talks with Ministers visiting Britain from Australia, New Zealand and South Africa; but the Dominions Secretary expressed unease lest 'our best friends received the worst treatment'. On the Colonies the Chancellor anticipated discussions with the Colonial Secretary who, however, warned that those countries, with over thirty per cent of sterling countries' balances, were too poor to give much scope for cancellation.

In respect of other large creditors, the Chancellor favoured awaiting passage of the US Loan, but offered moderate encouragement only about Argentina, with some eleven per cent of *non*-sterling area holdings of balances. He received discouragement about the largest single sterling area creditor, India (as yet undivided) which, together with Ceylon, held little short of sixty per cent of sterling countries' balances. Indian Congress MPs, supported by the British Finance Member of the Viceroy's Council (now Sir Archibald Rowlands*), wanted early negotiations. They also sought confirmation of 'the Keynes pledge' at Bretton Woods, that Britain would not unilaterally cancel Indian sterling balances (above, p 166). Keynes acknowledged, the Chancellor concurring regretfully, that such confirmation might be given, but that this need not prevent Britain from proposing some cancellation. The Secretary of State for India (Lord Pethick-Lawrence) was pessimistic about the chances of this, and feared deterioration without an assurance to India about early negotiations. Ministers decided against negotiations, however, until the resolution of the Indian political crisis had produced an all-Indian Government, and until the US Congress made a decision on the proposed loan to Britain.

This caution, this hesitation flavoured with hints of procrastination, was to shape overseas financial negotiations into three overlapping phases. The first, with European countries, had already begun. The second, beginning in 1946, largely concerned the two substantial non-sterling area holders of sterling, Argentina and Brazil. Finally, early in 1947 negotiations began with major sterling area creditors.[41]

During the war and immediately after, in some cases growing from the financial agreements necessitated by the operations of the economic blockade and of exchange control, agreements had been negotiated with many European countries. Where these were 'monetary agreements' they provided for the relatively free use of the respective currencies, at agreed rates of exchange, in transactions between the countries concerned and their associated currency areas; in most cases (except Scandinavian countries) there was a limit, after which settlement was in gold. The more restricted 'payments agreements' required overseas countries to settle in, and therefore to be prepared to hold, sterling. By early 1946 agreements of one or other kind had been concluded or were being negotiated with most countries in Western Europe.

---

* ROWLANDS, Archibald, KCB 1941, GCB 1947 (1892–1953); Adviser to the Viceroy on War Administration (India), November 1943; Chairman of Enquiry into Bengal Administration, October 1945; Finance Member of Governor-General's Executive Council, India. 1945–46; Permanent Secretary, Ministry of Supply, 1946–53.

These arrangements depended upon sterling being used more widely; in that respect, they made cancellation and blocking of balances more difficult. On the other hand, some in the Treasury feared, the prospect of such cancellation and blocking, should the US Congress ratify the Loan agreement, might undermine those arrangements. Such apprehensions forced a ragged retreat during 1946 from the bold general approach of the Keynes memoranda of 1944–45, towards a piecemeal policy that was to prove unable to contain the threat of excess balances.

Treasury views moved towards recognition that, neither repudiation nor blocking being possible unilaterally, the holding of minimum balances for a limited period (to 1951) should be sought country by country. Determination persisted, however, especially with the Chancellor, to secure cancellations, sometimes modified to hopes of obtaining 'contributions' from the largest holders of balances; indeed, in March 1947 when, eight months after it had become available, the US loan was rapidly disappearing, he instructed that every agreement involving balances must provide for some cancellation. Although subsequently persuaded that this should not apply to *non*-sterling area holders, he nevertheless publicly deplored shortly after, in May 1947, the untoward burden of the balances. Made publicly at an Anglo-Brazilian function, that protest ruffled current negotiations with Brazil, holder of hitherto small, but now rapidly growing balances. It reflected concern lest the absence of cancellation in an ensuing agreement should sustain the Indian and Egyptian refusals in recent preliminary discussions to consider reduction of their balances.

In truth, hope of significant cancellation was fast receding. The Bank of England, necessarily and closely involved in the technical problems, had always disapproved that policy. The views of the senior Treasury official concerned, Sir Wilfrid Eady, who was collaborating with the Deputy Governor, Mr C F Cobbold, in numerous financial negotiations, harmonised with those of the Bank. This accord strengthened feelings that Britain had no alternative but to persuade overseas holders of sterling that it remained useful; they should therefore continue to hold it as a reserve, and to use it in international payments. The Bank noted the concern of Egypt and India, as well as that of other poor countries owning large balances, that those balances should remain, in principle, available to be drawn down; a senior Bank official suggested that 'a heavy initial release may, in many cases, save a deal of friction, and be the best use we could make of the dollar credit'.[42] Should not those needs prevail over Keynes's early and sustained insistence to the contrary (but from April 1946, when he died suddenly, without Keynes himself to defend the case)? He had insisted that, even with the US Loan, Britain could not make substantial releases of balances for many years; without the Loan, the external position would be so bad that drastic contraction of overseas commitments would be required if serious burdens on the domestic economy were to be avoided.

(5) AGREEMENTS WITH HOLDERS OF STERLING

Shortly after Congress had in July 1946 ratified the United States loan, a second phase in negotiations demonstrated the broad pattern which the Bank-style approach was to give to many agreements (the first phase had covered wartime and early post-war agreements with European countries). There were, with often important variations of detail, three main features. First, substantial balances were segregated into a special account, usually called an 'A' account or 'Number Two Account'.[43] Second, releases from such accounts might be made for special purposes, and also in agreed annual amounts for a stated period. Third, annual releases and currently earned sterling, which would comprise a 'Number One Account' or a 'B' account would be freely convertible for use anywhere, in accordance with the Anglo-American Financial Agreement. The agreement negotiated with Argentina between July and September 1946 thus provided for the hiving-off of £130 million of balances. Long-term funding of these would have required a higher interest rate than Britain would contemplate. These balances, earning one-half per cent interest per annum, could be used to repay Argentine debt held abroad, and above all to purchase British-owned assets, particularly the railways, in Argentina. A special feature, occurring only exceptionally in the various financial agreements, but in this case an adaptation of a wartime arrangement, gave a gold guarantee on the remaining 'blocked' balances. From these were to be released £5 million annually for four years, as well as the interest, this sterling to be spendable anywhere; currently earned sterling could similarly and immediately be used. Comparable arrangements, including the gold guarantee, were reached informally with Brazil in May 1947.

By now, and with the third phase of financial negotiations, those with sterling area countries, already begun, the Treasury was recognising the near-inevitability of such provisional agreements, sometimes of understandings, not formalised on paper, to cover at most five years. Indeed, agreements with Egypt and India, by the former's choice and because of the latter's impending partition, initially covered only the second half of 1947. On preliminary visits to these countries (as well as to Iraq and Iran) early in 1947, Sir Wilfrid Eady and Mr Cobbold met emphatic refusals to cancel any balances. Full negotiations with Egypt in June brought agreed blocking in a Number 2 account, with specified releases to cover the rest of the year. A special feature was that Egypt's use of exchange control required her to leave the sterling area, in which there was formally freedom of current and capital transfers. For India, which however remained in the sterling area, arrangements were in other respects broadly similar.

These negotiations were completed just in time to corral the largest holdings of balances before mid-July 1947. Then, in accordance with the Financial Agreement, Britain was obliged, a year after its ratification, to provide full convertibility for any sterling not cancelled or blocked. Doubtless, as the Treasury had feared during the negotiation of that agreement, such a time constraint would put Britain at a disadvantage in seeking settlement of sterling liabilities. By the due date, about one-third of the balances, a much greater burden than had ever appeared manageable, remained free. Of the remaining two-thirds (over £2,000 million) covered by various arrangements, only £38 million were to be cancelled. The Chancellor attempted in February 1946 to secure cancellation of one-half of the net balances of £42 million owing to New Zealand, with the remainder to be released gradually. This attempt encountered New Zealand's distaste for such action to be used as a precedent with poorer countries, such as India, which it felt should not be asked to make significant cancellations. Eventually, in March 1947 New Zealand made a gift of £10 million in recognition of the British war effort. The Chancellor similarly approached Australia, in May 1946, suggesting cancellation of one-half of its estimated net balances of £85 million; rejecting this, the Australian Prime Minister (Mr J 'Ben' Chifley), whom his New Zealand counterpart, Mr Peter Fraser claimed to have influenced, objected that Australian balances were close to and in the following year likely to fall below their safety level. In the event, the balances increased, and in March 1947 Australia gave £20 million towards the costs of the Pacific war; a further gift of £8 million was made in August 1948 to ease British economic difficulties. These, the only cancellations to be made, were welcome, but were of token magnitude, and were far below the proportions and amounts originally hoped.

(6) CONVERTIBILITY AND ITS SUSPENSION, JULY – AUGUST 1947

Did Britain's failure to immobilise and reduce a sufficient volume of sterling by mid-July 1947 constitute a breach of the Anglo-American Financial Agreement? Formally, the requirement had been to seek to make agreements, and that had been done. But had 'every endeavour to secure the early completion of these arrangements'[44] been made? It could be said and was said that the all-important obligation, and the Americans' overriding concern, was that balances not blocked or cancelled should become freely convertible;

and that, with minimal qualifications, Britain undertook to do in mid-July 1947.[45] Months before, however, there had already developed serious doubt about the possibility of achieving or of maintaining convertibility. As early as November 1946 two senior British officials had indicated as much to the State Department.[46] American officials received these and similar communications in subsequent months with evident sympathy. They felt unable, however, to contemplate a serious relaxation of the commitment to convertibility. They saw a danger that the existence of large free balances might provide an excuse for prolongation of a practice that it had been a sustained American purpose to eliminate: discrimination in trade against the US in favour of sterling area countries.[47]

The exceptionally hard winter of 1946–47, and the accompanying fuel crisis, intensified Britain's domestic economic difficulties. Overseas, not only a weakening balance of payments, but also substantial conversion of sterling balances into gold and dollars were depleting the American Loan; intended to last at least three years, over half of it had gone in a year by mid-1947. (An even higher proportion of the Canadian credit had gone). The rest of the Loan was expected to go by early 1948, in default of further aid. The Marshall Plan for massive American aid to assist European recovery could not yet, however, ease British external burdens. Although publicly aired a month before convertibility was due, it was at that point only an invitation for European countries to devise proposals. Britain was therefore left to seek American approval to postpone convertibility for certain countries with which agreements had not yet been made. This was given, but for a very limited period only;[48] before its expiry the essay in convertibility had collapsed, after some five weeks, following increasingly heavy drains, which could not be sustained, on the gold and dollar reserves.

The brief implementation by Britain of the convertibility obligations of the new International Monetary Fund (Article VIII) was now suspended. Discussions with the US Administration, initiated shortly before the crisis, produced understanding that Britain would now revert for a time to exchange control and trade discrimination.[49] The post-war financial settlement had not exactly been toppled because, not having been fully constructed, it had never really stood up.

If a successful elimination of excess sterling balances could have been achieved, that would largely have closed the books on war finance. The failure to secure that, indeed the impossibility of securing such a settlement, meant that an overhang of wartime financial problems was to provide, far into the peace, justification or excuse for a pattern of external economic policy markedly different from that anticipated in the more optimistic moments of the financial negotiations of 1945.

CHAPTER 12, SOURCE REFERENCES

1. The formal extension in 1972 of exchange control to almost all overseas countries effectively eliminated the distinguishing features of the sterling area, namely the freedom of members to make within it transfers of current receipts and of capital. See Bank of England, *Report and Accounts for the Year ended 28th February 1973* (1973), p 22.

2. 6 December 1945, 416 HC DEB 5 s, cols 2662–84; 12, 13, 14 Dec 1945, 417 HC DEB 5 s cols 421–558, 641–746, 804–14; HL DEB 17–18 Dec 1945, cols 677–898.

3. Keynes to Sir David Waley, 21 March 1945, T 236/1076.

4. Papers in T 236/1079.

5. Circulated May-June 1945, ibid; commenting on Clarke's paper, Mr P D Proctor of the Treasury remarked that hiterto he had thought simply in terms of one body for imports and another for exports, 11 June, ibid. Clarke's paper reprinted in Sir Richard Clarke, *Anglo-American Economic Collaboration in War and Peace*, edited by Sir Alec Cairncross (Clarendon Press, Oxford, 1982), pp 96–122.

6. *Long Term Economic Planning*, Treasury Historical Memorandum No 7, (1964), paragraphs 43–49.

7. See especially T 236/308, T 236/1078, T 236/1088 and T 230/11.

8. Draft memorandum by Lord President of the Council, 22 January 1946, T 230/55.

9. An early paper by Mr Clarke, 'Agenda for Balance of Payments Working Party', 27 September 1945, set the task as planning for at least five years ahead: T 236/1078. At its third meeting on 28 January 1946, the Working Party agreed that a sub-committee should be formed to report on prospects of the balance of payments to 1950, a proposal which was expected to fit in with the plans of the Economic Survey Working Party to prepare an economic survey for 1950: T 236/1088. See also file on 'Import Policy...Estimates for 1950', T 236/1103 and *Long Term Economic Planning, passim*.

10. 'Agenda...', 27 September 1945, T 236/1078; first meeting of Balance of Payments Working Party, 20 November, T 236/1088; *Long Term Economic Planning*, paragraphs 80, 86.

11. Economic Survey for 1946, EO(45) 5 of 14 December 1945, Table B, CAB 134/186; note by Treasury on 1946 import programme, 24 January 1946, BPWP/2/46, T 230/11 and further version, 7 February, T 236/1078; discussions of Balance of Payments Working Party, 3rd meeting, 28 January, T 236/1088; Cabinet Paper of 8 February, CP(46)53, CAB 129/7.

12. CAB 134/186.

13. Mr H Broadley of the Ministry of Food at Balance of Payments Working Party meeting, 28 January 1946, T 236/1088.

14. Chancellor to Prime Minister, 9 January 1946, PREM 8/195.

15. 29 January 1946, T 236/1640.

16. 31 January 1946, T 236/406.

17. 'Political and Military Expenditure Overseas', 7 February 1946: T 236/406 and T 236/1079. These files have copies of the first draft, orginally thought not to have survived by the editor of *JMK* XXVII, where the second draft of 11 February is reprinted on pp 465–81.

18. Bridges to Chancellor, 7 February 1946, T 236/1078.

19. Chancellor's note on 'The Overseas Deficit', CP(46)53 and Keynes's memorandum, CP(46) 58, 8 February 1946, CAB 129/7.

20. CM(46) 14th Conclusions, Minute 4, 11 February 1946, CAB 128/5.

21. Meeting of Ministers and officials, 8 February 1946, T 236/1079, and papers, 9 February, ibid.

22. Memorandum by Chancellor of the Exchequer, 'Service and Supply Estimates for 1946 A', 13 February 1946, CAB 131/2, and meeting of 15 February, DO(46) 5th Meeting, CAB 131/1.

23. Cables in T 236/2410.

24. See chapter 10, p 263, and Mr Douglas Jay to the Prime Minister, 19 October 1945, PREM 8/35.

25. Waley to Clarke, 6 February 1946, T 236/1079.

26. 12 February 1946, T 236/2410 and T 247/47; reprinted in Clarke, op cit, pp 139–45.

27. Clarke's memorandum.

28. 'Preparatory Action in Case Congress rejects the Loan', 11 March 1946, CAB 124/913.

29. Keynes to Waley on 'Mr Clarke's Note...', 13 February 1946, and 'If Congress Rejects the Loan', 22 February, T 247/47, reprinted in Clarke, op cit, pp 145–6 and 151–2. Clarke's revision of his estimates: papers in T 236/2410.

30. 'If Congress rejects the Loan', 20 February 1946, T 247/47.

31. Papers in T 236/2410.

32. 'Random Reflections from a visit to the USA', 4 April 1946, a paper written by Keynes after visiting the USA for the inaugural meetings of the IMF and World Bank: T 247/47, CAB 124/913, *JMK* XXVII, pp 482–7.

33. Ibid.

34. Mr Douglas Jay to Prime Minister and Prime Minister's agreement, 7 May 1946, CAB 8/195.

35. T 236/2412, with Clarke's memorandum of 24 June 1946, and revision of 10 July.

36. Note of 15 July 1946, T 236/2410.

37. End-1945 statistics from *Sterling Balances Since the War,* Treasury Historical Memorandum No 16 (1972), and Bank of England, *UK External Liabilities and Claims in Sterling: 1945–62 (old series)* (1968). The different bases on which statistics from other sources were compiled prevent exact comparison between the position in June 1945 and that at the end of 1945. The White Paper on *Statistical Material presented during the Washington Negotiations,* Cmd 6707 table 7, gives for end-June 1945 total external liabilities of £3,355 million and net quick external liabilities of £3,052 million. Later estimates were that net sterling liabilities increased between end-June and end-December 1945 by £334 million: Sayers, *Financial Policy,* p 497, Table 8–11. During the Washington negotiations, Keynes had made a working assumption that sterling liabilities might rise by some $2 billion (about £500 million) between the end of June 1945 and end of 1946: US–UK 'Top Committee', 14 September 1945, GEN 80/21, CAB 130/6; Finance Committee, 20 September, GEN 80/29 ibid; 'Dr Harry White's Plan', T 236/438; *JMK* XXIV, pp 476,493, 534.

38. Above, pp 297–8 for memoranda by the Secretaries of State for India and the Colonies respectively. Bank of England views in T 236/2682.

39. H. Siepmann of the Bank to Mr E R Rowe-Dutton, 24 January 1946, ibid.

40. Meeting of Ministers on Financial and Commercial Policy, 7 February 1946, GEN 89/7th Meeting, CAB 78/37.

41. The remainder of this chapter draws upon two Treasury Historical Memoranda, although not upon their authors' views, which are not necessarily acceptable: Sir Hugh Ellis-Rees, *The Convertibility Crisis of* 1947, THM 4(1962), T 267/3, and Mr R S Symons on *Sterling Balances*.

42. Mr L P Thompson-McCausland of the Bank to Mr H Siepmann, 17 January 1946, T 236/2682.

43. It might seem logical to relate '1' to 'A' and '2' to 'B', but readers must be assured that such logic did not prevail.

44. Section 10(1) of the Anglo-American Financial Agreement: see Appendix 24.

45. Symons, paragraph 88.

46. Sir David Waley of HM Treasury and Mr R G Munro, of the UK Treasury Delegation in Washington, 21 November 1946, noted in a messsage from the Secretary of State to the US Embassy in London, 18 January 1947, *FRUS* 1947 III (1972), p 2.

47. Eg, Minutes of Sixtieth Meeting of the National Advisory Council on International Monetary and Financial Questions, 17 April 1947; Minutes of Sixty-eighth Meeting, 10 July; Aide-Mémoire from Department of State to British Embassy in Washington, 24 July 1947, ibid pp 7, 8, 34–35, 41–43.

48. Minutes 68th Meeting of NAC, 10 July 1947, ibid, pp 36–41.

49. Sir John Balfour, Chargé d'Affaires in Washington, to Secretary of State, 2 August 1947, and Secretary's reply, 4 August, ibid, pp 49–50.

APPENDIX 1

The Mutual Aid Agreement of 1942: US Draft of Article VII, July 1941

ARTICLE VII

The terms and conditions upon which the United Kingdom receives defense aid from the United States of America and the benefits to be received by the United States of America in return therefor, as finally determined, shall be such as not to burden commerce between the two countries but to promote mutually advantageous economic relations between them and the betterment of world-wide economic relations; they shall provide against discrimination in either the United States of America or the United Kingdom against the importation of any produce originating in the other country; and they shall provide for the formulation of measures for the achievement of these ends.

Source
Draft handed by Mr Dean Acheson to Mr J M Keynes, 28 July 1941, CAB 117/52.

APPENDIX 2

The Mutual Aid Agreement of 1942: Final Version of Article VII

ARTICLE VII

In the final determination of the benefits to be provided to the United States of America by the Government of the United Kingdom in return for aid furnished under the Act of Congress of the 11th March, 1941, the terms and conditions thereof shall be such as not to burden commerce between the two countries, but to promote mutually advantageous economic relations between them and the betterment of world-wide economic relations. To that end, they shall include provision for agreed action by the United States of America and the United Kingdom, open to participation by all other countries of like mind, directed to the expansion, by appropriate international and domestic measures, of production, employment, and the exchange and consumption of goods, which are the material foundations of the liberty and welfare of all peoples; to the elimination of all forms of discriminatory treatment in international commerce, and to the reduction of tariffs and other trade barriers; and, in general, to the attainment of all the economic objectives set forth in the Joint Declaration(*) made on the 12th August, 1941, by the President of the United States of America and the Prime Minister of the United Kingdom.

At an early convenient date conversations shall be begun between the two Governments with a view to determining, in the light of governing economic conditions, the best means of attaining the above-stated objectives by their own agreed action and of seeking the agreed action of other like-minded Governments.

* Cmd. 6321.

Source
Agreement...on the Principles applying to Mutual Aid, Cmd 6341 of 1942, *BPP* 1941–2, IX.

APPENDIX 3

The Atlantic Charter, Fourth Point,
Mr Churchill's Draft

'Fourth, they will strive to bring about a fair and equitable distribution of essential produce, not only within their territorial boundaries, but between the nations of the world'.

Source
WP(41)202 of 20 August 1941, p 2, CAB 66/18; also Churchill, *The Second World War, III, The Grand Alliance,* p 386.

APPENDIX 4

The Atlantic Charter, Fourth Point, Draft by Mr Sumner Welles, US Under Secretary of State

'Fourth, they will strive to promote mutually advantageous economic relations between them through the elimination of any discrimination in either the United States or in the United Kingdom against the importation of any product originating in the other country; and they will endeavour to further the enjoyment by all peoples of access on equal terms to the markets and to the raw materials which are needed for their economic prosperity'.

Source
Welles, *Where Are We Heading?*, p 8; also Wilson, *The First Summit*, pp 190–1.

APPENDIX 5

The Atlantic Charter, Fourth Point, Amendment of Mr Sumner Welles's Draft by President Roosevelt

'Fourth, they will endeavour to further enjoyment by all peoples of access without discrimination and on equal terms to markets and raw materials of world which are needed for their economic prosperity'.

Source
Telegram TUDOR 16, Prime Minister to the Lord Privy Seal (Mr C R Attlee), 11 August 1941, WP(41)203, CAB 66/18; also WP(41)202, p 8, ibid. See also Sir Llewellyn Woodward, History of the Second World War, *British Foreign Policy in the Second World War*, II (London 1971), p 200.

APPENDIX 6

The Atlantic Charter, Fourth Point, Mr Churchill's Amendments to President Roosevelt's Version*

'Fourth, they will endeavour *with due respect to their existing obligations* to further the enjoyment by all peoples of access, [without discrimination and] on equal terms, to the [markets] *trade* and to the raw materials of the world which are needed for their economic prosperity.'

Source
Telegrams TUDOR 15 & 16 of 11 August 1941, Prime Minister to Lord Privy Seal, WP(41)203, and report in WP(41)202, p 3, CAB 66/18.

---

* The President's version, with Mr Churchill's omissions in square brackets, and additions italicised.

APPENDIX 7(a)

The Atlantic Charter, Fourth Point:
The War Cabinet's Proposed Version

'Fourth. They will endeavour to further enjoyment by all peoples of access, without discrimination and on equal terms, to raw materials of the world which are needed for their economic prosperity, and *with due respect to their existing obligations* to promote greatest possible expansion of markets for the interchange of goods and services throughout the world'.

Source
Telegram ABBEY 31, Lord Privy Seal to Prime Minister, 12 August 1941, WP(41)203, except for italicised words, which were proposed as an amendment in telegram ABBEY 35 of 12 August, ibid.

APPENDIX 7(b)

The Atlantic Charter:
The War Cabinet's Proposed Additional Point,
the Basis for the Eventual Fifth Point*

'Fifth. They support the fullest collaboration between nations in the economic field, with the object of securing for all peoples freedom from want, improved labour standards, economic advancement and social security'.

Source
Telegram ABBEY 31 of 12 August 1941.

---

* See Appendix 9(b)

APPENDIX 8

The Atlantic Charter, Fourth Point, Proposed Version by the Chancellor of the Exchequer (Sir Kingsley Wood)

'Fourth.—They will endeavour, with due respect to their existing obligations (or engagements), to further, within the limits of their governing economic conditions, the progressive attainment of a well-balanced international economy, which would render unnecessary policies of discrimination, and other impediments to the freedom of trade'.

Source
WM(41)81st Conclusions, 12 August 1941, CAB 65/19.

APPENDIX 9(a) & (b)

The Atlantic Charter:
Final Agreed Texts
of Fourth and Fifth Points

(a) 'Fourth, they will endeavour, with due respect for their existing obligations, to further the* enjoyment by all States, great or small, victor or vanquished, of access, on equal terms to the* trade and to the raw materials of the world which are needed for their prosperity'.

(b) 'Fifth, they desire to bring about the* fullest collaboration between all nations in the* economic field, with the* object of securing for all improved labour standards, economic advancement and social security'.

Source
Telegram TUDOR 22 of 12 August 1941, the Prime Minister to the Lord Privy Seal, WP(41)203 (asterisked words omitted); WP(41)203, p 9; Cmd 6321, *Joint Declaration . . .*; Churchill, op cit, p 393; Woodward, op cit, p 202.

APPENDIX 10(a) & (b)

The Mutual Aid Agreement of 1942, Article VII: Two Messages from US Department of State to HM Government, December 1941

(A) MESSAGE FROM THE DEPARTMENT OF STATE DATED 9th DECEMBER 1941

The President since the outbreak of war with Japan has emphasized his determination to continue in full vigor the lend-lease program. It is of the highest importance that no factor such as the absence of a Lend-Lease Agreement between the two Governments should operate to cause in Congress any reluctance to furnish the necessary funds or cause differentiation between appropriations necessitated by the outbreak of hostilities with Japan and those needed in the broad view of the war. It is highly important also that the terms of the agreement should be kept on the broad plane of our draft, and encouragement should not be given to narrower conceptions which will not redound to both countries' long basic interest.

The draft of Article 7 handed to Lord Halifax is general in nature and is obviously of mutual benefit. It defines basically the economic objectives of the two Governments and provides for the opening of conversations in detail to reach agreement concerning ways and means of arriving at these objectives. In essence Article 7 charts a broad course and commits the two Governments to co-operate in making headway along that course. The new pursuance of the agreement proposed will be based of course upon governing economic conditions. It is difficult to see what more could be done to meet the difficulties which from the British standpoint have been presented.

The provision envisaging the participation of other nations and the reiteration of the objectives of the Atlantic Charter render the article a declaration of purpose around which all peoples of similar mind may rally.

The interests of both countries would be served by a speedy agreement.

(B) MESSAGE FROM THE DEPARTMENT OF STATE
DATED 9th DECEMBER 1941

The first sentence of Article 7 is self-explanatory in its statement of purpose, namely, to find terms that will not burden commerce between the two nations but will rather promote mutually advantageous economic relations between them and between other nations. The balance of the Article gives assurance (1) that the final settlement will be arrived at by negotiation, and (2) that it will be of such a character that as a forward step toward world-wide reconstruction other nations can join in it.

The Article on the negative side provides that the final settlement shall not be an incubus upon relations between ourselves and the British but will be an instrument for improving relations mutually and our relations with other countries. On the positive side it commences by recognizing the primary importance of increased economic activity, both national and international, in employment, production and the consumption and exchange of goods. It is against this background and in conjunction with it that there are added the objectives of eliminating discriminatory treatment, reducing tariffs and achieving the other objectives of the Atlantic Charter. Recognition explicitly is given in the Article that the liberalization of commercial policy is a question which requires action by all participants and that high standards of productivity and consumption are required to succeed in it. The Article does not lay down self-executing substantive provisions but points a broad course and commits the two nations to co-operate in making headway along that course. The Governments will, in collaboration, recognize the governing economic conditions in seeking the best means of making the goals attainable. No attempt whatever is made to impose a formula which itself will be the touchstone to solve all problems, but rather to provide that they shall be solved by agreement and consultation. It is obvious that there will be a difference in the problems confronting the two nations as well as those confronting other nations. No uniform solution is imposed by the Article which does provide for common counsel and agreed action rather than the principle that at the end of the war each nation for itself will attempt to carry out a position.

As imparted to us on numerous occasions, British pre-occupations with their current and post-war problems, have been prominently in mind in preparing this draft. They have been met by providing (1) that whatever is determined under Article 7 shall be determined by agreement attained after the conversations provided for; (2) that the determinations shall be arrived at in the light of governing economic conditions so that, for instance, if the removal of discriminations and reduction of trade barriers should be found in fact impractical save by gradual stages, there is nothing in this agreement to prevent adjusting action to such findings; and (3) that the field of questions to be considered and included in the final settlement shall not be limited to questions of commercial policy only, but shall embrace all measures for promoting increased employment, production, consumption and exchange of goods. Thus there is no ground for the argument that the conversations proposed and the scope of the final agreement would ignore or prejudice the problems of the British position after the war. The agreement, on the contrary, furnishes the best method possible of solving them.

The draft is not only moderate in that it confines itself to a statement of objectives but from the British standpoint the objectives themselves are reasonable. We request from Britain no unilateral commitment but impose on ourselves identical obligations. Nor do we ask Britain to join with us in seeking the attainment of objectives which would be beneficial to us but injurious to Britain. What is sought on the contrary is the creation of conditions in the period after the war which would operate not merely to our advantage but to their advantage and that of all peoples. It might indeed be argued that inasmuch as the prosperity of Britain depends to an even larger degree on the condition of international trade than does that of the United States, they are even more vitally concerned in the conditions we are seeking. The objectives which are laid down are those which are set forth in Point 4 of the Atlantic Declaration, to which the Prime Minister undoubtedly subscribed because he considered them in the best interests of the British as well as of others.

As regards the provision concerning discrimination, all that we ask is that the British sit down with us to work out the problems which lie ahead so that we may avoid substituting trade warfare in peace time for the present co-operation in war time.

Article 7 lays down a broad programme about which all liberal forces in both countries can rally and which can inspire hope for the future of the British, American and other peoples if developed with sufficient vigor.

Source
WP(42)58 of 2 February 1942, CAB 117/53.

APPENDIX 11

The 'Consideration' for Lend-Lease:
Mr Churchill's Undespatched Draft Telegram
to President Roosevelt

10, Downing Street,
Whitehall.

FORMER NAVAL PERSON TO PRESIDENT.

Yours of the 5th.

Cabinet considered this matter on Monday when a very
general opinion was expressed that it would be unfair
for us to be forced to agree to Clause 7 with its
reference to "no discrimination" before the discussions
which we are willing to begin at once have taken place.
However a reply has been prepared which will be considered
in a few days. As I told you I consider situation is
completely altered by entry of the United States into the
war.   This makes us no longer a client receiving help
from a generous patron, but two comrades fighting for life
side by side.   In this connection it must be remembered
that for a large part of 27 months we carried on the
struggle single-handed, and that had we failed the full
malice of the Axis Powers, whose real intentions can now
be seen, would have fallen upon the United States.   This
would be all the more true if we were to fail now.   In
these circumstances the comparatively small quantities of

-2-

304

Lend-Lease goods which have reached this country before the

pooling arrangements were made ought not to be a cause

of the pre-judgment of our future co-operation in the

economic rebuilding of the world. ³) Again as I told you

the question of Imperial Preference might easily fall into

its place in a large settlement in which the United States

became a low tariff country and it might well be that you

would find us more forward even than Congress in pressing

for the sweeping away of all obstructions on International

trade.   Here it must be remembered that for more than

half a century we practised a most extreme system of free

imports both into the United Kingdom and into all

Colonies under our control.   We were forced to abandon

this policy only by the continued rise of Protective

Tariffs in other countries.

4.   It is not a question of division in this country

upon the lines of Protection versus Free Trade, though

there is danger of that, but of the inappropriateness in

time and circumstance of our being forced to part with our

-5-

305

freedom of honourable discussion with you upon the issue,

§Personally as you know I have been all my life an opponent

of Imperial Preference, and I care little for it as such,

but I feel very strongly that the natural manner in which

to settle this matter is for the full discussion to take

place without our hands being tied beforehand by a

declaration which might be read that we regard any

inter-Empire trade arrangements as "discrimination". § I

earnestly hope that you will consider this point of view

and will not press upon us unduly a one-sided submission

when all depends upon the most whole-hearted common

action.   However I will put the matter before the Cabinet

again.

5.2.42.

Source
PREM 4/17/3 ff 303–5. A re-typed version of this undespatched message, amended in
the light of Mr Churchill's manuscript changes, is in ibid, ff 299–302 and has been
reprinted in Warren F Kimball (ed.), *Churchill & Roosevelt. The Complete Correspondence*
(3 vols, Princeton, NJ, 1984), I, pp 345–6.

APPENDIX 12

The 'Consideration': President Roosevelt's Message for Mr Churchill

COPY

PRIME MINISTER'S
PERSONAL TELEGRAM 21

SERIAL No. T 219/2

EMBASSY OF THE UNITED STATES
OF AMERICA.

12 February 1942.

Secret.

My dear Mr. Churchill:

      I have the honor to transmit to you the following dispatch received from the President this date:

      No. 105. "For the Former Naval Person and Winant from the President in regard to the proposed exchange of notes relating to article seven of the Interim Lend-Lease Agreement, referred to in your message No. 25, I want to make it perfectly clear to you that it is the furthest thing from my mind that we are attempting in any way to ask you to trade the principle of imperial preference as a consideration for lend-lease. Furthermore, I understand something of the nice relationships your Constitution requires of your Home Government in dealing with the Dominions. Obviously the Dominions must not only be consulted but I assume you must have their approval on any affirmative changes in existing arrangements which might be developed in the broad discussions which you and I both contemplate. It seems to me the proposed note leaves a clear implication that Empire Preference and, say, agreements between ourselves and the Philippines are excluded before we sit down at the table. All I am urging is an understanding with you that we are going to have a bold, forthright, and comprehensive discussion looking forward to the construction of what you so aptly call 'a free, fertile economic policy for the post-war world'. It seems perfectly clear to me that nothing should now be excluded from those discussions.

None of us know how those discussions will turn out,
although, as I told you when you were here last, I
have great confidence that we can organize a different
kind of world where men shall really be free economically
as well as politically. The idea of attaching notes
to this interim agreement would seem to me to give an
impression to our enemies that we were overly cautious.
I believe the peoples not only of our two countries but
the peoples of all the world will be heartened to know
that we are going to try together and with them for the
organization of a democratic post-war world and gladly accept your intimation that we might get going at once with
our economic discussion. What seems to be bothering the
Cabinet is the thought that we want a commitment in
advance that Empire Preference will be abolished. We are
asking for no such commitment, and I can say that
article seven does not contain any such commitment. I
realize that that would be a commitment which your
Government could not give now if it wanted to. And I am
very sure that I could not, on my part, make any commitment relative to a vital revision of our tariff policy.
I am equally sure that both of us are going to face in
this realistic world adjustments looking forward to your
'free and fertile economic policy for the post-war world',
and that things which neither of us now dreams of will
be subjects of the most serious consideration in the not
too distant future. So nothing should be excluded from
the discussions. Can we not, therefore, avoid the
exchange of notes which, as I have said, seems to dilute
our statement of purpose with cautious reservations, and
sign the agreement on the assurances which I here give
in reference to the matter that seems to be the stumbling
block. I feel very strongly that this would demonstrate
to the world the unity of the American and British people.
In regard to coming to a meeting of minds with you at an
early date, I only need to say to you that there are very
important considerations here which make an early

understanding desirable. In saying this, I want again to
tell you that I am not unmindful of your problem. We
have tried to approach the whole matter of Lend-Lease in a
manner that will not lead us into the terrible pitfalls of
the last war."

Very respectfully yours,

(sd) H. FREEMAN MATTHEWS.

Source
CAB 117/53.

APPENDIX 13

'The Washington Principles'

This Appendix summarises the agreed Anglo-American documents on Commercial Policy, Commodity Policy, Cartel Policy, and Employment Policy which resulted from the Washington talks of 1943. They were circulated early in November 1943 in one of the official papers reporting the talks: GEN 19/47 of 8 November 1943, CAB 78/14. Subsequently the agreed documents were incorporated in an extensive memorandum on 'Anglo-American Discussions under Article VII', which Mr Richard Law, the Minister of State, submitted to the War Cabinet: WP (43) 559 (Revise) of 17 December 1943, CAB 123/96 – II and CAB 66/44. This memorandum included covering reports on the topics (except Employment Policy), and documents on monetary policy, including an Anglo-American *draft* Statement of Principles.

The wording used below, apart from that in square brackets, is that of the original paper, GEN 19/47.

Informal Exploratory Conversations Between Officials of the United States and the United Kingdom Regarding the Formulation of an Agenda for Discussions Looking Toward the Implementation of Article VII of the Mutual-Aid Agreement Between the United States and the United Kingdom.

SECTION ON COMMERCIAL POLICY

I TARIFFS

1. *Multilateral tariff action*

There are set forth below for further study tariff-reduction provisions for possible inclusion in a general multilateral convention on commercial policy. All... are multilateral tariff-reduction formulas except the last (see E, below), which is a proposal for multilateral provisions... to negotiate bilateral tariff agreements.

It is the view of both the United States and United Kingdom groups that if a workable multilateral tariff-reduction formula acceptable to a large number of nations providing for a drastic reduction of tariffs without nullify-ing exceptions can be found, it would be superior.

In the view of the United Kingdom group, . . . a precise obligation to limit the use of other protective devices would be impossible without an equally comprehensive and closely defined obligation covering tariffs. . . [;] this could be achieved only if the convention provides for simultaneous multi-lateral action to reduce tariffs.

The United States group does not associate itself with the views set forth. . . above.

2. *Alternative provisions for the implementation of tariff reduction.*
  A. The reduction of all duties by X per cent of their height at a given time, or to Y per cent ad valorem (or its equivalent in the case of specific duties), whichever may result in the lower duty, but no duty need be reduced below Z per cent ad valorem (or its equivalent in the case of specific duties).
  B. The uniform reduction of all duties in all countries by a given percen-tage of their height on a given date.
  C. The reduction of all duties by a given percentage, except that no duty need be reduced below a specified ad valorem rate.
  D. The uniform reduction by a given percentage of the overall ad valorem equivalent of each country's entire tariff calculated in comparison with its total imports. It is assumed that there would be provision preventing any increase in duties.
  E. The inclusion in the proposed commercial policy convention of a provi-sion whereby each country would agree to negotiate with its principal suppliers bilateral agreements providing for tariff reductions on its major dutiable imports. This would of course involve dealing by the same method with preferences heretofore regarded as exceptions from the most-favoured-nation clause.

3. *Revenue duties*
It is assumed that any provisions for the simultaneous reduction of tariffs in all countries would not apply to revenue duties, which could be increased.

4. *Infant industries and security industries*
There are strong arguments against. . . exceptions for the protection of national defence or 'infant' industries. . . But in order to obtain the adher-ence of countries which are industrially undeveloped. . . it may be necessary to contemplate some modification of this rule.

5. *Other tariff measures*
It is believed that. . . other. . . tariff measures. . . should be explored later. . .

6. *Comments*

It is believed that a major obstacle to the application of an equitable multi-lateral tariff-reduction formula is the technical problem of uniform tariff valuation... and that further investigation of methods to overcome this obstacle might be useful...

7. *Conclusions*

Further study would appear to be required.

II PREFERENCES

1. ... No convention of the kind proposed would give final effect to... [the] obligations of [Article VII of the Mutual Aid Agreement] unless it makes definite provision both for an adequate reduction of tariffs and for the ultimate substantial abolition of preferences.

3. The provisions of the proposed commercial policy convention looking toward the abolition of tariff preferences would not apply to customs unions which already exist. However, future customs unions... should be reviewed by the proposed commercial policy organisation.

III PROHIBITIONS AND QUANTITATIVE RESTRICTIONS ON IMPORTS

1. Existing import prohibitions and restrictions would be abolished subject to specified exceptions...

2. *Exceptions*

(a) *Balance-of-payments difficulties.* The use of quantitative restrictions to safeguard a country's balance of payments would be permissible.

(b) *Commodity agreements.* The use of quantitative restrictions when necessary to implement a recognized international commodity agreement would be allowed.

(c) *Other exceptions.* The convention would provide for necessary and legitimate exceptions...

3. *Temporary emergency exceptions*

In the emergency period during and immediately following the war import prohibitions and quantitative limitations would be permitted... to meet emergencies...

4. *Rules of fair conduct*

The provisions... with respect to import prohibitions and restrictions would include provisions... to minimise discriminatory and other objectionable practices in... [their] administration...

5. *Exchange restrictions*

Exchange restrictions should not be applied in a manner inconsistent with... provisions for the use of quantitative import restrictions.

IV EXPORT TAXES AND RESTRICTIONS

1. There should be agreed action looking toward the abolition of export taxes and restrictions.

V SUBSIDIES

1. Subsidies are preferable to tariffs and other import restrictions as a means of protecting domestic industries...

2. However, export subsidies and other government action which results in... prices lower than those... charged... in the home market... are objectionable...

3. [P]rovision should be made looking to the elimination of export subsidies...

6. Provision would be made for review... where a country believed that domestic subsidies were in effect concealed or indirect export subsidies...

VI STATE TRADING

1. .... It is not unlikely that conditions created by the war will tend to result in state trading on a more extensive scale than heretofore.

2. [M]ethods and arrangements for trading between private-enterprise countries and state-trading countries... [should] take account of this...

VII INTERNATIONAL COMMERCIAL POLICY ORGANISATION

1. The creation of an appropriate international commercial policy organisation seems essential to the successful operation of any general multilateral commercial policy convention...

6. Parties to the convention should be required to give each other most-favoured-nation treatment...

SECTION ON COMMODITY POLICY

I GENERAL PRINCIPLES

1. International commodity arrangements should be so framed as to be in harmony with the general expansionist policy which, it is hoped, will be the guiding economic principle... in the post-war period...

2. [T]he primary objectives... should be:—

(a) The mitigation of violent short-term price fluctuations.

(b) A system which would... help to counteract business cycles.

(c) ... [A] state of affairs under which price adjustments would follow changes in the basic conditions of supply and demand...

(d) Provision for special action on an international basis.

II INTERNATIONAL COMMODITY ORGANISATION

1. An international commodity organisation should be established.

III METHODS OF INTERNATIONAL COMMODITY POLICY

1. *Buffer stock arrangement*

2. *Quantitative regulation arrangements*

IV SUBSIDIES

1. The United States group have drawn attention to the importance of insuring that... one of the basic objectives— ... increasing opportunities for supplying world requirements... from countries in a position to supply such requirements most effectively—should not be jeopardised by any widespread use of subsidies.

The United Kingdom group recognise the force of the considerations put forward by the United States group... But they are not able to accept... that subsidies should in all cases be accompanied by a quantitative limitation on the amount of subsidized production.

3. It is agreed... that further consideration should be given to... insuring that subsidization is kept within moderate limits...

V FURTHER ACTION

It is recommended that arrangements should be made for further informal discussions... within three or four months...

SECTION ON PRIVATE INTERNATIONAL BUSINESS AGREEMENTS

I GENERAL CONSIDERATIONS

1. Consideration has been given... to the question of whether... action... should be undertaken to deal with... the activities of international cartels.

II OUTLINE FOR FURTHER STUDY

1. [T]he United States group propose that further consideration should be given to...
   a) Registration of all private international agreements...
   b) Prohibition by international agreement of objectionable international cartel activities...

III NEED FOR INTERNATIONAL APPROACH

1. Both groups... are agreed... on the desirability of further detailed studies... on a joint basis...

SECTION ON INTERNATIONAL CO-ORDINATION OF MEASURES FOR THE MAINTENANCE OF HIGH LEVELS OF EMPLOYMENT

I SPECIALIZED INTERNATIONAL ECONOMIC ORGANISATIONS

It is hoped that four new international institutions may ultimately emerge as a result of informal economic discussions:—
   (a) An international stabilization fund for currencies
   (b) An international investment bank
   (c) An international commodity organisation
   (d) An international commercial policy organisation

4. To the four bodies mentioned above there should be added the International Labour Organisation and the Projected Permanent Organization on Food and Agriculture... also perhaps temporary agencies such as United Nations Relief and Rehabilitation Administration.

II COORDINATION OF SPECIALIZED INTERNATIONAL ECONOMIC ORGANIZATIONS

1. Clearly the policies pursued by these different bodies should be . . . co-ordinated . . . and . . . it is desirable that there should exist some organisation with wider terms of reference . . .

2. It is suggested that an Advisory Economic Staff should be established as the nucleus and operative section of such an organization, headed by a Director of influence . . .

APPENDIX 14

The Avoidance of Restrictions on Payments in Respect of Current International Transactions and of Accumulated Balances: the Joint Statement, April 1944

III

5. So long as a member country is entitled to buy another member's currency from the Fund in exchange for its own currency, it shall be prepared to buy its own currency from that member with that member's currency or with gold. This requirement does not apply to currency subject to restrictions in conformity with IX (3) below or to holdings of currency which have accumulated as a result of transactions of a current account nature effected before the removal by the member country of restrictions on multilateral clearing maintained or imposed under X (2) below.

IX

3. Not to impose restrictions on payments for current international transactions with other member countries (other than those involving capital transfers or in accordance with VI, above) or to engage in any discriminatory currency arrangements or multiple currency practices without the approval of the Fund.

X

Transitional Arrangements

1. Since the Fund is not intended to provide facilities for relief or reconstruction or to deal with international indebtedness arising out of the war, the agreement of a member country to III (5) and IX (3), above, shall not become operative until it is satisfied as to the arrangements at its disposal to facilitate the settlement of the balance of payments differences during the early postwar transition period by means which will not unduly encumber its facilities with the Fund.

2. During this transition period member countries may maintain and adapt to changing circumstances exchange regulations of the character which have been in operation during the war, but they shall undertake to withdraw as soon as possible by progressive stages any restrictions which impede multilateral clearing on current account. In their exchange policy they shall pay continuous regard to the principles and objectives of the Fund; and they shall take all possible measures to develop commercial and financial relations with other member countries which will facilitate international payments and the maintenance of exchange stability.

3. The Fund may make representations to any member that conditions are favourable to the withdrawal of particular restrictions or for the general abandonment of restrictions inconsistent with IX (3), above. Not later than three years from the coming into force of the Fund any member still retaining any restrictions inconsistent with IX (3) shall consult the Fund as to their further retention.

4. In its relations with member countries the Fund shall recognize that the transition period is one of change and adjustment and in deciding on its attitude to proposals presented by members it shall give the member country the benefit of any reasonable doubt.

Source
Joint Statement by Experts on the Establishment of an International Monetary Fund, Cmd 6519, 1944, *BPP* 1943–4, VII.

APPENDIX 15

The Avoidance of Restrictions on Payments in Respect of Current International Transactions and of Accumulated Balances: The International Monetary Fund, July 1944

ARTICLE VIII. GENERAL OBLIGATIONS OF MEMBERS

SECTION 1 *Introduction* In addition to the obligations assumed under other articles of this Agreement, each member undertakes the obligations set out in this Article.

SEC. 2. *Avoidance of restrictions on current payments.* (*a*) Subject to the provisions of Article VII, Section 3(*b*), and Article XIV, Section 2, no member shall, without the approval of the Fund, impose restrictions on the making of payments and transfers for current international transactions.

SEC. 4. *Convertibility of foreign held balances.* (*a*) Each member shall buy balances of its currency held by another member if the latter, in requesting the purchase, represents

(i)   that the balances to be bought have been recently acquired as a result of current transactions; or

(ii) that their conversion is needed for making payments for current transactions.

The buying member shall have the option to pay either in the currency of the member making the request or in gold.

(*b*) The obligation in (*a*) above shall not apply

(i)   When the convertibility of the balances has been restricted consistently with Section 2 of this Article, or Article VI, Section 3; or

(ii) when the balances have accumulated as a result of transactions effected before the removal by a member of restrictions maintained or imposed under Article XIV, Section 2; or

399

(iii) When the balances have been acquired contrary to the exchange regulations of the member which is asked to buy them; or

(iv) When the currency of the member requesting the purchase has been declared scarce under Article VII, Section 3 (*a*); or

(v) When the member requested to make the purchase is for any reason not entitled to buy currencies of other members from the Fund for its own currency.

Source
United Nations Monetary and Financial Conference, Final Act, Cmd 6546, *BPP* 1943–4, VIII.

APPENDIX 16(a)

The Interpretation of Article VIII of the International Monetary Fund: Original Letter from Sir John Anderson, Chancellor of the Exchequer to Mr Henry Morgenthau, Jnr, US Secretary of the Treasury, 1 February 1945

A question has arisen of the interpretation of a certain clause in the Final Act of Bretton Woods which is causing me some difficulty and perplexity. It arises out of a possible conflict or inconsistency between Section 2(a) and Section 4(b) of Article VIII of the Fund. This has been already the subject of some discussion between Lord Keynes and Mr White.

The truth seems to me to be that we have here a piece of ambiguous, and probably inconsistent, drafting, which is not surprising in view of the inevitably hurried work of the last days of the Conference. The result is that no clear meaning emerges; and at some stage this will have to be tidied up. I only wish that the fundamental point at issue was sufficiently trivial for us to overlook it at the present stage. But that unfortunately is not the case. Critics of the Plan have already fastened on the point, and I shall probably be expected on a matter so important as the obligation of convertibility to give Parliament some clear guidance as to what obligation in this respect we are being asked to assume.

The essential point is this. The obligation under VIII 4(a) lapses under VIII 4(b)(v) if the member has exhausted his facilities with the Fund. In such circumstances, therefore, he resumes his discretion how far and for how long he shall continue to exhaust his ultimate gold reserves by maintaining *de facto* convertibility. I shall be expected to explain whether this is in any way undone by VIII 2(a), with the result that, in the above circumstances, the discretion is given to the Fund, instead of to the member, to decide up to what point the member shall be required to deplete his gold reserves (which represent a country's iron ration for many purposes, including war) before resuming liberty of action. I do not see how I could advise either the Cabinet or Parliament to be content with a lesser safeguard in this respect than that which appears to be given by VIII 4(b). Nor is it likely, if I gave such advice, that it would be accepted. Furthermore, the critics of the Fund, who I am sorry to say are none too friendly, would be given an opportunity to claim that it was a regrettable deception of public opinion to allow what appears to be a clear safeguard in one sub-section to be taken away by what is a far from clear, and indeed dubious, interpretation of another sub-section of the same clause.

I expect you will share my feeling that, in the case of a text prepared so hastily as the Final Act yet so difficult to amend, it would be a bad and dangerous precedent to seek by subtle interpretation to impose any obligation which did not appear, clearly and unambiguously, on the face of the document, or which had not been understood and accepted by all those who signed it.

Nevertheless an attempt to secure an amendment here and now is, I agree, inadvisable, as well as difficult, since it would open the door to other changes. I propose, therefore, to assure Parliament, when the time comes to seek its judgment, that they are not being asked to accept any obligation beyond what clearly appears on the face of the document, and that we shall have to regard a satisfactory clearing up meanwhile of any possible ambiguity in the drafting as one of the essential conditions prerequisite to our being in a position to accept eventual convertibility under Article XIV.

You may be interested to know that my colleagues have recently been discussing whether or not it would be advisable for the Government to initiate an early discussion in Parliament on the general principles of the Final Act, before Congress has pronounced. We have decided that it will be better that Congress should have spoken before we bring matters to a head here. In any case, the Parliamentary timetable does not leave room for a debate here before the congressional discussions begin, if our latest news about the date of these is correct. Since a debate here, in which some critical and hostile remarks may be made, simultaneously with the discussions in Congress might be inconvenient or embarrassing, this is an additional reason why it may be better to postpone, though I shall probably be seeing privately some groups of members of Parliament for the purpose of elucidation of the proposals.

Source
T 247/39; also T 230/168, FO 371/45663; *JMK* XXVI, pp 175–7.

APPENDIX 16(b)

The Interpretation of Article VIII of the International Monetary Fund: Amended Letter of 1 February 1945, despatched 3 May 1945, from Chancellor of the Exchequer to US Secretary of the Treasury

A question has arisen of the interpretation of a certain clause in the Final Act of Bretton Woods which is causing me some difficulty and perplexity. It arises out of a possible conflict or inconsistency between Section 2(a) and Section 4(b) of Article VIII of the Fund. This has been already the subject of some discussion between Lord Keynes and Mr White.

The essential point is this. The obligation under VIII 4(a) lapses under VIII 4(b)(v) if the member has exhausted his facilities with the Fund. In such circumstances, therefore, he resumes his discretion how far and for how long he shall continue to exhaust his ultimate gold reserves by maintaining *de facto* convertibility. I shall be expected to explain whether this is in any way undone by VIII 2(a), with the result that, in the above circumstances, the discretion is given to the Fund, instead of to the member, to decide up to what point the member shall be required to deplete his gold reserves (which represent a country's iron ration for many purposes, including war) before resuming liberty of action.

I shall probably be expected on a matter so important as the obligation of convertibility to give Parliament some clear guidance as to what obligation in this respect we are being asked to assume.

It would, it seems to me, be proper for me to assume that, in the event of the Board of Governors' being asked to give a decision under Article XVIII of the draft constitution of the Fund, there will be no question of imposing by subtle interpretation any obligation which has not appeared clearly and unambiguously on the face of the document or which had not been understood and accepted by all those who had signed it.

I propose, therefore, to assure Parliament, when the time comes to seek its judgment, that they are not being asked to accept any obligation beyond what clearly appears on the face of the document, and that we shall have to regard a satisfactory clearing up meanwhile of any possible ambiguity in the drafting as one of the essential conditions prerequisite to our being in a position to accept eventual convertibility under Article XIV.

Source
Telegram 343 CAMER of 3 May 1945, T 236/1161 and FO 371/45664.

APPENDIX 17

The Interpretation of Article VIII of the International Monetary Fund: Letter from US Secretary of the Treasury to Chancellor of the Exchequer, 8 June 1945

This is in reply to your letter of February 1, 1945 inquiring about a possible inconsistency between Section 2(a) and Section 4(b) of Article VIII of the Fund.

I can see no inconsistency whatever in these sections. Article VIII Section 2 is designed to assure people engaged in international business that no member of the Fund will prevent their being paid for the goods they export and for other current obligations. The section states, subject to specified qualifications, that ''no member shall, without the approval of the Fund, impose restrictions on the making of payments and transfers for current international transactions.'' With this provision international business can proceed without the restrictions that would result from the imposition of exchange controls on current transactions.

The exceptions to the general principle of Section 2 are enumerated very clearly and in unmistakable terms. If a currency should be declared scarce, a member may impose restrictions in accordance with Article VII, Section 3(b); and any country covered by the transitional arrangements may during the transitional period maintain and adapt to changing circumstances wartime restrictions on payments and transfers for current international transactions. No other exceptions to the general principle of Section 2 are specified because, I believe, no other exceptions were intended.

Section 4 of Article VIII deals with a different problem. Under this section each member (or its central bank) is obligated to buy balances of its currency held by another member (or its central bank) if the balances have been recently acquired as a result of current transactions or the conversion of these balances is needed for making payments for current transactions. There then follow the conditions under which the obligation does not apply, all of the exceptions being specifically listed.

In our view Section 2 and Section 4 have different obligations to meet different problems. Section 2 is concerned to see that an exporter is asssured of payment for his exports in his own currency. Under Section 4, the exporter no longer owns the foreign currency, for it has been acquired by his central bank. Under Section 2, the currency represents the accruing proceeds of current trade and is being presently acquired or will be acquired in the near future by a private trader. Under Section 4, the currency balances have already been acquired by a central bank, and they may represent balances resulting from recently completed transactions or even balances long accumulated from past transactions.

The financial obligations contemplated by the two sections are of a different order. By their nature, the sums involved in Section 2 are moderate in amount; the sums involved in Section 4 may be enormous in amount, for they can include the accumulated balances of years. As a practical matter, a country can be asked not to restrict payments and transfers to traders for current transactions. On the other hand, the burden of converting large accumulated balances held by foreign central banks may be too great for a country when it cannot secure the help of the Fund.

These are the reasons why restrictions on current payments may not be imposed without the consent of the Fund except in the two cases specified in Section 2, although the convertibility of balances held by foreign central banks can be restricted when a country no longer has access to the Fund and under the other conditions specified in Section 4.

As you are aware the distinction between these sections of Article VIII do not become significant until the end of the transitional period and may not be of consequence then.

We have explained these points in greater detail some time ago in conversations with Mr Brand and Mr Opie.

Source
T 247/40 and T 236/1161.

APPENDIX 18

The Interpretation of Article VIII of the International Monetary Fund: Letter from Chancellor of the Exchequer to US Secretary of the Treasury, 28 June 1945

I am much obliged to you for your letter of the 8th June about Article VIII of the final Act of the Fund.

I agree that the question of inconsistency between Section 2(a) and Section 4(b) of Article VIII will not arise immediately, and may, indeed, in practice have little effect.

But I must confess that I do not see the meaning quite so clearly as your letter suggests. It rather depends on the interpretation given to the words in Section 2: "no member shall, without the approval of the Fund, impose restrictions on the making of payments and transfers for current international transactions".

We have assumed that these words forbid a member to impose legal restrictions which would prevent a holder of its currency from spending it to pay for goods or to buy any foreign currency, provided that the price of the foreign currency is within the permitted range, and that the currency offered in exchange represents the proceeds of current trade. Section 2(a) does not, in our view, put the central monetary authority under an obligation to buy for its own currency any foreign currency arising out of a current transaction which may be offered to it, or to provide in return for its own currency any foreign currency which a trader may desire to cover a current transaction. It is, in our view, the obligation of the United States Monetary Authority, for example, to provide foreign currency arising solely out of Section 4.

You may rely on me not to raise the matter unnecessarily, but if it is necessary to allay doubts, I may have to tell Parliament that if at some future time the question were to arise on an actual issue, we should ask the governing body for an interpretation to the effect that the only obligation of a member's monetary Authority to provide foreign currency is that which arises out of Article VIII, Section 4, convertibility of foreign-held balances. I am glad that as a result of our correspondence we have this point narrowed down to dimensions which need not in practice give us difficulty.

Appendix 18 (continued)

Source
Final draft, initialled by Chancellor, T 236/1161, and copy of despatched letter, T 231/373.

APPENDIX 19

Principal Proposals for US Aid, and Accompanying Conditions, Compared with the Main Features of the Anglo-American Financial Agreement of 1945

$ Million

	(i)	(ii)	(iii)	(iv)	(v)	(vi)	(vii)	(viii)
Amount of aid:								
3750								X
4000			X					
5000	X	X		X	X	X	X	
'Retrospective Lend-Lease'								
3000	X	X						
Grant-in-aid			X	X		X	X	
Credit terms	X	X			X			X
Sterling balances								
Cancel 3000	X							
3500			X					
3520		X						
4000				X				
5000						X		
Fund 6000	X	X						
8000						X	X	
12000				X				
12500			X					
Release 800						X	X	
1000			X	X				
3000	X	X						
Statement of Intent on sterling balances								X

$ Million

	(i)	(ii)	(iii)	(iv)	(v)	(vi)	(vii)	(viii)
Interest on funded balances	X	X						
Convertibility: Early	X	X	X					X
'Availability'				X		X	X	
End Sterling Area dollar pool				X		X	X	X
Renounce IMF article XIV transition		X						X
Non-discrimination in trade (implicit or explicit in proposals)	X			X	X	X	X	X

Sources

(i) Overseas Financial Arrangements in Stage III (T 247/49), 18 March 1945.

(ii) Overseas Financial Policy in Stage III (ibid), 3 April 1945, and as Cabinet Paper WP (45) 301 of 15 May 1945.

(iii) The Present Overseas Financial Position of UK (T 236/436), 20 July 1945.

(iv) The Present Overseas Financial Position of UK (T 247/50), 13 August 1945.

(v) Our Overseas Financial Prospects (T 247/50), 13 August 1945, and as Cabinet Paper CP (45) 112 of 14 August 1945.

(vi) Proposals to the United States for Financial Assistance to follow after Lend-Lease (CAB 124/913), 17 August 1945.

(vii) Proposals for Financial Arrangements in the Sterling Area and between the US and the UK to follow after Lend-Lease (T 247/50), 12 September 1945.

(viii) Financial Agreement between the Governments of the United States and the United Kingdom dated 6th December 1945, Cmd 6708.

APPENDIX 20

British Proposals for a Settlement of Accumulated Sterling Balances

Extracts from telegram NABOB SAVING 32 of 7 November 1945 on 'Sterling Area Arrangements'. Quoted by the Chancellor of the Exchequer in memorandum on 'Washington Financial Talks', GEN 89/13 of 22 November, for the Committee of Ministers on 'Financial and Commercial Policy', 23 November, GEN 89/6th Meeting: CAB 78/37. Cited by the Prime Minister (Mr C R Attlee) as a possible element in an Anglo-American agreement in telegram 11790 to Washington, 24 November: T 236/441.

11. The Government of the UK would be prepared on the basis of aid on a scale appropriate to the size of the problem, to proceed not later than the end of 1946 to make arrangements under which the current earnings of all sterling area countries would be freely available to make purchases in any currency area without discrimination, apart from any receipts arising out of military expenditure by the UK which it may be agreed to treat on the same basis as the balances accumulated during the war; and in addition to treat similarly a portion of the accumulated balances forthwith, and further portions by instalments in future years for the purpose of meeting current needs. This would require that a part of the accumulated balances should be retained until they become similarly available: thus unless the amounts released were reasonable in relation to the requirements of the holders, the position of the holders might be changed for the worse.

12. The result would be that any discrimination arising from the so-called 'dollar pool' would be entirely removed, in the sense that each member of the sterling area would have both its current earnings and its available sterling balances at its free disposition for current transactions anywhere.

14. The representatives of the UK agreed that they would naturally welcome common action along such lines. At the same time they affirmed that they could not properly press a unilateral settlement on the countries which had shown such great trust in them during the war and had in this way given the UK essential support in contributing to the common victory. Any such settlement must be by mutual agreement. Nor would any settlement be a fair one which worked on a rigid formula or on cut-and-dried lines, since other factors ought to be taken into account besides the present size of the accumulated balances. They agreed, however, that the principles underlying the thesis of the US representatives were fair and constructive and in the inter-

ests of all parties. They would, therefore, be ready at an early date to discuss a re-settlement with those concerned on the basis of dividing the accumulated sterling balances of each country into three categories, one category being freed at once and becoming convertible into any currency for current transactions, one category being similarly released by instalments over a long period of years, and one category being written off as a contribution to the success of the scheme as a whole and in recognition of the benefits which the countries concerned might be expected to gain from it. For the countries in question would have to recognise that, failing such a settlement as that under discussion and without aid from the US, it would be physically impracticable for the UK to repay the balances except over a long period of years and at a rate about which it would be impossible to enter into any definite commitment in advance. Thus it might be hoped that the sterling area countries would agree that it was in their own interest, as well as fair and reasonable, to come into such a general settlement, rather than to stay out of it.

15. The UK representatives would seek to arrive at voluntary agreements with the sterling area creditors varying according to the circumstances of each case by which each would make an appropriate contribution to the common plan by arrangements which would include a scaling down of the sterling claims. Of the sterling balances scaled down as above a limited part would be released immediately and the remainder by instalments over a period of years. As regards the subsequent releases it would be necessary to protect the position of the UK by a clause permitting postponement of releases in certain contingencies. Conversely there might be a provision to the effect that releases could be anticipated in cases where a particular country holding sterling balances was in a position such as might have called for assistance by way of a loan from the UK in normal times. More precise arrangements than the above could not be specified in advance of discussion with the countries concerned. The UK representatives however, agreed with the view that countries unwilling to enter into an agreement on these lines, which the UK would consider satisfactory and fair in relation to the contributions of others, could not expect to participate in the special releases which would become available to participants in the scheme and would have, out of the sheer inescapable necessities of the case, to accept a lower priority of release of balances than those countries entering into the common scheme and to depend on the UK's future capacity to repay after the UK's obligations under the common scheme had been fully met. Nevertheless all future sterling earned by members of the sterling area, whether participants in the scheme or not, would be freely available for the purpose of current transactions, subject to the qualification relating to military expenditure in paragraph 9 above.

APPENDIX 21

The UK's External Liabilities, by Area, and Net Gold & US Dollar Reserves 1938 – 45

£ million

	End Aug 1938	End Aug 1939	End Dec 1939	End Dec 1940	End Dec 1941	End Dec 1942	End Dec 1943	End Dec 1944	End June 1945
Sterling Area									
Dominions					139	189	236	342	384
India, Burma, Middle East					399	695	1,141	1,537	1,732
Other Sterling Area Countries					318	388	473	555	607
Total Sterling Area					856	1,272	1,850	2,434	2,723
North & South America					240	256	278	280	303
Europe (including dependencies of European countries)					180	242	281	299	267
Rest of World					23	48	56	60	62
TOTAL LIABILITIES	760	476	556	735	1,299	1,818	2,465	3,073	3,355
of which Overseas Loans				2	107	303	307	300	303
Net quick external liabilities	760	476	556	733	1,192	1,515	2,158	2,773	3,052
NET GOLD & US DOLLAR RESERVES	864*	605*	548*	74	97	172	322	421	453

(* Including an estimate of private holdings subsequently requisitioned)

Source
Cmd 6707, December 1945, *Statistical Material presented during the Washington Negotiations, BPP* 1945–6, XXI

APPENDIX 22

Estimated External Disinvestment by the UK
September 1939 – June 1945

	£ million
Realisation of external capital assets	1,118
Increase in external liabilities	2,879
Decrease in gold & US dollar reserves	152
Unallocated	49
TOTAL	4,198

Source
Cmd 6707, Table 9, which has the qualification 'as far as recorded: probably an under-estimate'.

APPENDIX 23

Estimated Average Balance of Payments 1936 – 1938 and Estimates of UK Overseas Expenditure and Income for 1946

£ million

	1936 – 38 Average	1946 (a)	1946 (b)
Imports	– 884*	– 1,290	– 1,150
Exports	+ 496*	+ 645	+ 650
Balance	– 388	– 645	– 500
Net Government expenditure overseas	– 7	– 298	– 300
Net invisible income	+ 352	+ 149	+ 50
Estimated deficit	– 43	– 794	– 750

* including silver bullion & specie (imports £18m, exports £19m).

Sources
1936 – 38 Average, Cmd 6707, Table 10.
1946 (a), from statistics submitted at the opening of the Anglo-American negotiations in Washington, September 1945, GEN 89/3 in CAB 78/37 and PREM 8/35.
1946 (b), estimate as revised during the Washington negotiations and reconstructed by Mr R W B Clarke, in memorandum of 23 February 1946, T 247/47 (see also below, Appendix 27 on 'Forecasting the Post-war Balance of Payments', Table 3 (b), p 458).

APPENDIX 24

Financial Agreement between the Governments of the United States and the United Kingdom (Cmd 6708 of 1945)

It is hereby agreed between the Government of the United States of America and the Government of the United Kingdom of Great Britain and Northern Ireland as follows: —

1. *Effective date of the Agreement.*

The effective date of this Agreement shall be the date on which the Government of the United States notifies the Government of the United Kingdom that the Congress of the United States has made available the funds necessary to extend to the Government of the United Kingdom the line of credit in accordance with the provisions of this Agreement.

2. *Line of Credit.*

The Government of the United States will extend to the Government of the United Kingdom a line of credit of $3,750,000,000 which may be drawn upon at any time between the effective date of this Agreement and 31st December, 1951, inclusive.

3. *Purpose of the Line of Credit.*

The purpose of the line of credit is to facilitate purchases by the United Kingdom of goods and services in the United States, to assist the United Kingdom to meet transitional post-war deficits in its current balance of payments, to help the United Kingdom to maintain adequate reserves of gold and dollars and to assist the Government of the United Kingdom to assume the obligations of multilateral trade, as defined in this and other agreements.

4. *Amortisation and Interest.*

(i) The amount of the line of credit drawn by 31st December, 1951, shall be repaid in 50 annual instalments beginning on 31st December, 1951, with interest at the rate of 2 per cent. per annum.

Interest for the year 1951 shall be computed on the amount outstanding on 31st December, 1951, and for each year thereafter interest shall be computed on the amount outstanding on 1st January of each such year.

Forty nine annual instalments of principal repayments and interest shall be equal, calculated at the rate of $31,823,000 for each $1,000,000,000 of the line of credit drawn by 31st December, 1951, and the fiftieth annual instalment shall be at the rate of $31,840,736.65 for each such $1,000,000,000.

Each instalment shall consist of the full amount of the interest due and the remainder of the instalment shall be the principal to be repaid in that year. Payments required by this section are subject to the provisions of Section 5.

(ii) The Government of the United Kingdom may accelerate repayment of the amount drawn under this line of credit.

5. *Waiver of Interest Payments.*
    In any year in which the Government of the United Kingdom requests the Government of the United States to waive the amount of the interest due in the instalment of that year, the Government of the United States will grant the waiver if:—

(*a*) the Government of the United Kingdom finds that a waiver is necessary in view of the present and prospective conditions of international exchange and the level of its gold and foreign exchange reserves,

and

(*b*) the International Monetary Fund certifies that the income of the United Kingdom from home-produced exports plus its net income from invisible current transactions in its balance of payments was on the average over the five preceding calendar years less than the average annual amount of United Kingdom imports during 1936 – 8 fixed at £866,000,000, as such figure may be adjusted for changes in the price level of these imports. Any amount in excess of £43,750,000 released or paid in any year on account of sterling balances accumulated to the credit of overseas governments, monetary authorities and banks before the effective date of this Agreement shall be regarded as a capital transaction and therefore shall not be included in the above calculation of the net income from invisible current transactions for that year. If waiver is requested for an interest payment prior to that due in 1955, the average income shall be computed for the calendar years from 1950 through the year preceding that in which the request is made.

6. *Relation of this line of credit to other obligations.*
    (i) It is understood that any amounts required to discharge obligations of the United Kingdom to third countries outstanding on the effective date of this agreement will be found from resources other than this line of credit.

(ii) The Government of the United Kingdom will not arrange any long term loans from Governments within the British Commonwealth after 6th December, 1945 and before the end of 1951 on terms more favourable to the lender than the terms of this line of credit.

(iii) Waiver of interest will not be requested or allowed under Section 5 in any year unless the aggregate of the releases or payments in that year of sterling balances accumulated to the credit of overseas governments, monetary authorities and banks (except in the case of colonial dependencies) before the effective date of this agreement, is reduced proportionately, and unless interest payments due in that year on loans referred to in (ii) above are waived. The proportionate reduction of the releases or payments of sterling balances shall be calculated in relation to the aggregate released and paid in the most recent year in which waiver of interest was not requested.

(iv) The application of the principles set forth in this section shall be the subject of full consultation between the two Governments as occasion may arise.

7. *Sterling Area Exchange Arrangements.*

The Government of the United Kingdom will complete arrangements as early as practicable and in any case not later than one year after the effective date of this agreement, unless in exceptional cases a later date is agreed upon after consultation, under which immediately after the completion of such arrangements the sterling receipts from current transactions of all sterling area countries (apart from any receipts arising out of military expenditure by the Government of the United Kingdom prior to 31st December, 1948, to the extent to which they are treated by agreement with the countries concerned on the same basis as the balances accumulated during the war) will be freely available for current transactions in any currency area without discrimination with the result that any discrimination arising from the so-called sterling area dollar pool will be entirely removed and that each member of the sterling area will have its current sterling and dollar receipts at its free disposition for current transactions anywhere.

8. *Other Exchange Arrangements.*

(i) The Government of the United Kingdom agrees that after the effective date of this agreement it will not apply exchange controls in such a manner as to restrict

(*a*) payments or transfers in respect of products of the United States permitted to be imported into the United Kingdom or other current transactions between the two countries or

(*b*) the use of sterling balances to the credit of residents of the United States arising out of current transactions.

Nothing in this paragraph (i) shall affect the provisions of Article VII of the Articles of Agreement of the International Monetary Fund when those Articles have come into force.

(ii) The Governments of the United States and the United Kingdom agree that not later than one year after the effective date of this agreement, unless in exceptional cases a later date is agreed upon after consultation, they will impose no restrictions on payments and transfers for current transactions. The obligations of this paragraph (ii) shall not apply

(*a*) to balances of third countries and their nationals accumulated before this paragraph (ii) becomes effective; or

(*b*) to restrictions imposed in conformity with the Articles of Agreement of the International Monetary Fund, provided that the Governments of the United Kingdom and the United States will not continue to invoke the provisions of Article XIV Section 2 of those Articles after this paragraph (ii) becomes effective unless in exceptional cases after consultation they agree otherwise; or

(*c*) to restrictions imposed in connection with measures designed to uncover and dispose of assets of Germany and Japan.

(iii) This Section and Section 9 which are in anticipation of more comprehensive arrangements by multilateral agreement shall operate until 31st December, 1951.

9. *Import Arrangements.*

If either the Government of the United States or the Government of the United Kingdom imposes or maintains quantitative import restrictions, such restrictions shall be administered on a basis which does not discriminate

against imports from the other country in respect of any product; provided
that this undertaking shall not apply in cases in which

(a) its application would have the effect of preventing the country imposing such restrictions from utilizing, for the purchase of needed imports, inconvertible currencies accumulated up to 31st December,
1946; or

(b) there may be special necessity for the country imposing such restrictions to assist, by measures not involving a substantial departure from
the general rule of non-discrimination, a country whose economy has
been disrupted by war; or

(c) either Government imposes quantitative restrictions having equivalent effect to any exchange restrictions which that Government is authorised to impose in conformity with Article VII of the Articles of
Agreement of the International Monetary Fund.

The provisions of this Section shall become effective as soon as practicable,
but not later than 31st December, 1946.

10. *Accumulated Sterling Balances.*
(i) The Government of the United Kingdom intends to make agreements
with the countries concerned, varying according to the circumstances of each
case, for an early settlement covering the sterling balances accumulated by
sterling area and other countries prior to such settlement (together with any
future receipts arising out of military expenditure by the Government of the
United Kingdom to the extent to which they are treated on the same basis by
agreement with the countries concerned). The settlements with the sterling
area countries will be on the basis of dividing these accumulated balances into
three categories:

(a) balances to be released at once and convertible into any currency for
current transactions;

(b) balances to be similarly released by instalments over a period of years
beginning in 1951; and

(c) balances to be adjusted as a contribution to the settlement of war and
post-war indebtedness and in recognition of the benefits which the
countries concerned might be expected to gain from such a settlement.

The Government of the United Kingdom will make every endeavour to
secure the early completion of these arrangements.

(ii) In consideration of the fact that an important purpose of the present
line of credit is to promote the development of multilateral trade and facilitate
its early resumption on a non-discriminatory basis, the Government of the
United Kingdom agrees that any sterling balances released or otherwise
available for current payments will, not later than one year after the effective
date of this agreement, unless in special cases a later date is agreed upon after
consultation, be freely available for current transactions in any currency area
without discrimination.

11. *Definitions*
For the purposes of this agreement:

(i) The term "current transactions" shall have the meaning prescribed in
article XIX (*i*) of the Articles of Agreement of the International Monetary
Fund.

(ii) The term "sterling area" means the United Kingdom and the other territories declared by the Defence (Finance) (Definition of Sterling Area) (No. 2) Order, 1944, to be included in the sterling area, namely "the following Territories excluding Canada and Newfoundland, that is to say;

(*a*) any Dominion,

(*b*) any other part of His Majesty's dominions,

(*c*) any territory in respect of which a mandate on behalf of the League of Nations has been accepted by His Majesty and is being exercised by his Majesty's Government in the United Kingdom, or in any Dominion,

(*d*) any British Protectorate or Protected State,

(*e*) Egypt, the Anglo-Egyptian Sudan and Iraq,

(*f*) Iceland and the Faroe Islands".

12. *Consultation on Agreement.*
Either Government shall be entitled to approach the other for a re-consideration of any of the provisions of this agreement, if in its opinion the prevailing conditions of international exchange justify such reconsideration with a view to agreeing upon modifications for presentation to their respective Legislatures.

Signed in duplicate at Washington, District of Columbia, this 6th day of December, 1945.

For the Government of the United States of America:
FRED M. VINSON,
Secretary of the Treasury of the United States of America.

For the Government of the United Kingdom of Great Britain and Northern Ireland:
HALIFAX,
His Majesty's Ambassador Extraordinary and
Plenipotentiary at Washington.

JOINT STATEMENT REGARDING SETTLEMENT FOR LEND-LEASE, RECIPROCAL AID, SURPLUS WAR PROPERTY AND CLAIMS.

1. The Governments of the United States and the United Kingdom have reached an understanding for the settlement of Lend-Lease and Reciprocal Aid, for the acquisition of United States Army and Navy surplus property, and the United States interest in installations, located in the United Kingdom, and for the final settlement of the financial claims of each government against the other arising out of the conduct of the war. Specific agreements necessary to implement these understandings setting forth the terms in detail, and consistent herewith, are in the course of preparation and will shortly be completed.

2. This settlement for Lend-Lease and Reciprocal Aid will be complete and final. In arriving at this settlement both governments have taken full cogni-

zance of the benefits already received by them in the defeat of their common enemies. They have also taken full cognizance of the general obligations assumed by them in Article VII of the Mutual Aid Agreement of 23rd February, 1942, and the understandings agreed upon this day with regard to commercial policy. Pursuant to this settlement, both governments will continue to discuss arrangements for agreed action for the attainment of the economic objectives referred to in Article VII of the Mutual Aid Agreement. The Governments expect in these discussions to reach specific conclusions at an early date with respect to urgent problems such as those in the field of telecommunications and civil aviation. In the light of all the foregoing, both governments agree that no further benefits will be sought as consideration for Lend-Lease and Reciprocal Aid.

3. The net sum due from the United Kingdom to the United States for the settlement of Lend-Lease and Reciprocal Aid, for the acquisition of surplus property, and the United States interest in installations, located in the United Kingdom, and for the settlement of claims shall be $650,000,000 subject to the accounting adjustment referred to below. This amount consists of

(a) a net sum of $118,000,000 representing the difference between the amount of the services and supplies furnished or to be furnished by each government to the other government after V-J day through Lend-Lease and Reciprocal Aid channels, less the net sum due to the United Kingdom under the claims settlement, and

(b) a net sum of $532,000,000 for all other Lend-Lease and Reciprocal Aid items, and for surplus property, and the United States interest in installations, located in the United Kingdom and owned by the United States Government.

The actual amounts due to the respective governments for items included in (a) above other than claims will, however, be ascertained by accounting in due course, and the total sum of $650,000,000 will be adjusted for any difference between the sum of $118,000,000 mentioned above and the actual sum found to be due. All new transactions between the two governments after 31st December, 1945, will be settled by cash payment.

4. The total liability found to be due to the Government of the United States will be discharged on the same terms as those specified in the Financial Agreement concluded this day for the discharge of the credit provided therein.

5. In addition to the financial payments referred to above, the two governments have agreed upon the following:—

(a) appropriate non-discriminatory treatment will be extended to United States nationals in the use and disposition of installations in which there is a United States interest;

(b) appropriate settlements for the Lend-Lease interest in installations other than in the United Kingdom and the colonial dependencies will be made on disposal of the installations;

(c) the United States reserves its right of recapture of any Lend-Lease articles held by United Kingdom armed forces, but the United States has indicated that it does not intend to exercise generally this right of recapture;

(d) disposals for military use to forces other than the United Kingdom armed forces of Lend-Lease articles held by the United Kingdom armed forces at V-J day, and disposals for civilian use other than in the United Kingdom and the colonial dependencies of such Lend-Lease articles, will be made only with the consent of the United States Government, and any net proceeds will be paid to the United States Government. The United Kingdom Government agrees that except to a very limited extent it will not release for civilian use in, or export from, the United Kingdom and colonial dependencies, Lend-Lease articles held by the United Kingdom armed forces;

(e) the Government of the United Kingdom will use its best endeavours to prevent the export to the United States of any surplus property transferred in accordance with this understanding.

6. The Government of the United Kingdom agrees that, when requested by the Government of the United States from time to time prior to 31st December, 1951, it will transfer, in cash, pounds sterling to an aggregate dollar value not in excess of $50,000,000 at the exchange rates prevailing at the times of transfer, to be credited against the dollar payments due to the Government of the United States as principal under this settlement. The Government of the United States will use these pounds sterling exclusively to acquire land or to acquire or construct buildings in the United Kingdom and the colonial dependencies for the use of the Government of the United States, and for carrying out educational programmes in accordance with agreements to be concluded between the two governments.

7. The arrangements set out in this statement are without prejudice to any settlements concerning Lend-Lease and Reciprocal Aid which may be negotiated between the Government of the United States and the Governments of Australia, New Zealand, the Union of South Africa, and India.

APPENDIX 25

Principal British Commitments on Convertibility, Discrimination, and Sterling Balances Under the Anglo-American Financial Agreement of December 1945

	On Agreement becoming effective	'Early'	Not later than 31 December 1946	Not later than one year after effective date of Agreement
Convertibility for current transactions of current receipts of sterling:				
USA	×			
Sterling area				×
Rest of World				×
Convertibility for current transactions of released sterling balances				×
Non-discrimination in quantitative import restrictions			×	
Endeavour to secure a settlement of sterling balances		×		

APPENDIX 26

Financial Agreement Between the Government of Canada and the Government of the United Kingdom
Cmd 6904 of 1946 (BPP 1945 – 6, XXV)

NOTE

The Financial Agreement between the Government of Canada and the Government of the United Kingdom dated 6th March, 1946, is scheduled to "The United Kingdom Financial Agreement Act, 1946," of the Canadian Parliament which received the Royal Assent in Canada on 28th May, 1946, and entered into force by Royal Proclamation on 30th May, 1946. In accordance with Article 9 the two Governments determined that the Agreement should enter into force on that date.

In accordance with an exchange of notes dated 6th March, 1946, Articles 5, 6 and 7 of the Financial Agreement remained in abeyance until it should be known whether the United States Congress approved the Financial Agreement between the United States and the United Kingdom dated 6th December, 1945. Articles 6 and 7 were later brought into force by a further Royal Proclamation dated 16th July, 1946, while Article 5 took effect automatically as from that date.

Financial Agreement between the Government of Canada and the Government of the United Kingdom

The Government of Canada and the Government of the United Kingdom of Great Britain and Northern Ireland agree as follows:

ARTICLE 1

Credit

The Government of Canada will extend to the Government of the United Kingdom a credit of $1,250,000,000 which may be drawn upon at any time prior to December 31, 1951.

ARTICLE 2

Purpose of the Credit

The purpose of the credit is to facilitate purchases by the United Kingdom of goods and services in Canada and to assist in making it possible for the United Kingdom to meet transitional post-war deficits in its current balance of payments, to maintain adequate reserves of gold and dollars and to assume the obligations of multilateral trade.

ARTICLE 3

Amortisation and Interest

(i) The amount of the credit drawn by December 31, 1951, shall be repaid in 50 annual instalments beginning on December 31, 1951, with interest at the rate of 2 per cent per annum. Interest for the year 1951 shall be computed on the amount outstanding on December 31, 1951, and for each year thereafter interest shall be computed on the amount outstanding on January 1 of each such year.

Forty-nine annual instalments of principal repayments and interest shall be equal, calculated at the rate of $3,182,300 for each $100,000,000 of the credit drawn by December 31, 1951, and the fiftieth annual instalment shall be at the rate of $3,184,073.665 for each such $100,000,000. Each instalment shall consist of the full amount of the interest due and the remainder of the instalment shall be the principal to be repaid in that year. Payments required by this Article are subject to the provisions of Article 4.

(ii) The Government of the United Kingdom may accelerate repayment of the amount drawn under this credit.

ARTICLE 4

Waiver of Interest Payments

In any year in which the Government of the United Kingdom requests the Government of Canada to waive the amount of the interest due in the instalment of that year, the Government of Canada will grant the waiver if:—

(a)   The Government of the United Kingdom finds that a waiver is necessary in view of the present and prospective conditions of international exchange and the level of its gold and foreign exchange reserves; and

(b)   The International Monetary Fund certifies that the income of the United Kingdom from home-produced exports plus its net income from invisible current transactions in its balance of payments was on the average over the five preceding calendar years less than the average annual amount of United Kingdom imports during 1936–1938, fixed at 866 million pounds as such figure may be adjusted for changes in the price level of these imports. If waiver is requested for an interest payment prior to that due in 1955, the average income shall be computed for the calendar years from 1950 through the year preceding that in which the request is made; and

(c)   Interest payments due in that year on any credit made available to the Government of the United Kingdom to which a similar provision for waiver of interest applies are also waived.

ARTICLE 5

Exchange and Import Arrangements

The Government of the United Kingdom and the Government of Canada agree that in respect of (a) the operation of exchange controls and arrangements, and (b) quantitative import restrictions, each will grant to the residents and products of the other, treatment not less favourable than that provided for in any instrument of agreement with the government of any other country signed prior to the date of this Agreement.

ARTICLE 6

Outstanding Interest-Free Loan

The two Governments agree that the interest-free provision of the loan made to the Government of the United Kingdom under the War Appropriation (United Kingdom Financing) Act, 1942, will continue until January 1, 1951, and that the other arrangements with regard to the loan will continue as at present until that date. The two Governments agree to enter into discussions before January 1, 1951, with regard to the question of interest on, and the terms of repayment of, any balance of the loan then outstanding.

ARTICLE 7

British Commonwealth Air Training Plan

The Government of Canada agrees to cancel the amount owing by the Government of the United Kingdom to the Government of Canada with respect to the British Commonwealth Air Training Plan, which amount the two Governments agree is $425,000,000.

ARTICLE 8

Consultation on Agreement

The two Governments agree that they will consult with each other as they may deem necessary on the working of any provision of this Agreement, and that if in the opinion of either Government reconsideration of this Agreement is justified by the prevailing conditions of international exchange or by any major change in the international financial situation which materially alters the prospective benefits and obligations flowing from this Agreement they will forthwith consider what changes in its provisions they should agree to make. Any changes agreed upon by the two Governments will be subject to such legislative approval as may be necessary.

ARTICLE 9

Entry into Force

This Agreement is made subject to such legislative approval as may be necessary and shall enter into force in whole or in part at such time or times as shall be agreed upon by the two Governments.

In witness whereof the undersigned being duly authorized thereto by their respective Governments have signed this Agreement.

Signed in duplicate at Ottawa, this sixth day of March, 1946.

For the Government of Canada:

J.L. ILSLEY,
Minister of Finance.

For the Government of the United Kingdom:

MALCOLM MACDONALD,

High Commissioner for the United Kingdom.

Agreement on the Settlement
of War Claims between the Government of
the United Kingdom and
the Government of Canada

The Government of the United Kingdom and the Government of Canada, in order to arrive at a prompt and final settlement of all outstanding accounts between them arising out of the war, agree as follows:

ARTICLE 1

The Government of the United Kingdom will pay to the Government of Canada the sum of $150,000,000 and thereupon each of the two Governments will, with the exceptions noted below, cancel all claims against the other which arose on or after September 3, 1939, and prior to March 1, 1946, in respect of supplies, services, facilities and accommodation delivered or furnished during that period, whether such claims are known or unknown.

ARTICLE 2

The two Governments agree that such payment and cancellation shall be in full settlement of all such claims and neither Government will raise or pursue any such claims against the other.

ARTICLE 3

The settlement covered by this Agreement includes without limitation thereto—

(*a*)   All claims of the Government of Canada in respect of the construction for the Admiralty of ships which were in the course of construction on September 1, 1945, and which were to be completed by agreement between the two Governments;

(*b*)   All claims arising out of the operations of the Inspection Board of the United Kingdom and Canada and in this case the period covered by the settlement shall extend to March 31, 1946, the Government of Canada taking over all the assets and liabilities of that Board as of that date;

(*c*)   All claims of the Government of the United Kingdom arising out of the operation by the Department of Munitions and Supply of Canada of joint production projects and all claims relating to the period before March 1, 1946, arising from past or future renegotiation of contracts or the retroactive adjustment of prices paid by or charged to the Government of the United Kingdom in Canada;

(*d*)   All claims between the two Governments arising from the sharing of profits or losses before March 1, 1946, under contracts or arrangements made before that date and where projects covered by profit or loss sharing agreements continue in operation beyond that date, shares of profits or losses accruing on and after that date shall not be affected by this Agreement except in the case of the Inspection Board covered in paragraph (b) above;

(*e*)   All claims between the two Governments arising from the disposal in the United Kingdom of surplus war assets of the Government of Canada, or from the disposal in Canada of surplus war assets of the Government of the United Kingdom, provided that this Agreement shall not prejudice the right of either Government to remove any of its surplus war assets from the country of the other, either for its own use or for transfer to others; and

(f) All claims of the Government of Canada in respect of the costs incurred by it under contracts entered into before March 1, 1946, for the manufacture of locomotives and rolling stock in Canada for the Government of India; without prejudice to the right of the Government of the United Kingdom to recover the amount of such claims from the Government of India.

ARTICLE 4

(i) The balance in the United Kingdom Suspense Account held by the Bank of Canada on February 28, 1946, shall be paid to the Government of the United Kingdom.

(ii) The balance in the United Kingdom Cash Receipts Account held by the Receiver General of Canada on February 28, 1946, shall be paid to the Government of Canada without prejudice to the right of the Government of the United Kingdom to claim reimbursement from third countries in respect of payments made on their behalf out of the United Kingdom Cash Receipts Account.

ARTICLE 5

The settlement covered by this Agreement shall not include the following—

(a) The loan to the Government of the United Kingdom under the War Appropriation (United Kingdom Financing) Act, 1942, which is covered by another agreement;

(b) The amount of $425,000,000 owing by the Government of the United Kingdom to the Government of Canada with respect to the British Commonwealth Air Training Plan, which is covered by another agreement;

(c) Claims of the two Governments arising out of the sharing of military relief expenditures which are to be dealt with in accordance with the procedures already established or to be established;

(d) Claims arising out of established procedures under which periodical settlements are made in regard to payment of pensions and war service gratuities, reimbursement of expenditures for salaries, pay and allowances, travelling and living expenses of personnel on an individual basis, the transfer of personal funds of prisoners of war and other similar payments of a routine nature;

(e) Claims arising out of the settlement of accounts between postal administrations;

(f) Balances held by departments of either Government on behalf of and to the order of departments of the other Government.

ARTICLE 6

Each Government agrees to repay to the other amounts paid since February 28, 1946, in respect of claims cancelled under this Agreement.

ARTICLE 7

The two Governments will consult together, through their appropriate departments and representatives, concerning the interpretation and implementation of this Agreement.

In witness whereof the undersigned, being duly authorized thereto by their respective Governments, have signed this Agreement.

Signed in duplicate at Ottawa this 6th day of March, 1946.

For the Government of Canada:

J L ILSLEY,
Minister of Finance

For the Government of the United Kingdom:

MALCOLM MACDONALD,

High Commissioner for the United Kingdom.

APPENDIX 27

FORECASTING THE POST-WAR BALANCE OF PAYMENTS

APPENDIX 27

Forecasting the Post-War Balance of Payments

(1) THE BACKGROUND TO THE FORECASTS

Forecasts or, rather, bold and virtually speculative estimates of the United Kingdom's prospective balance of payments at various uncertain future dates were an essential feature of thinking about post-war economic policy. In a report of 1942 for the War Cabinet's Committee on Reconstruction Problems, 'The restoration of the balance of payments' was noted as one of 'three outstanding tasks' in the post-war transition; the others were the restraint of inflation and the transfer of resources from war to peace uses.[1] More immediately, shorter-run forecasts were essential for the wartime economy, in order particularly to ascertain the amount of help to be sought from the US and Canada, and the amount of overseas disinvestment to be faced. These two forecasting aspects tended to merge closely on several occasions, notably during 1941 – 42, in early response to closer Anglo-American ties under Lend-Lease; in 1943, in connection with the Washington talks that summer; during the second half of 1944 in calculating the amount of aid to be sought for war finance and export revival in Stage II (the concentration of the war against Japan); and during 1944 – 45 as Lord Keynes dramatised the case for seeking post-war aid from the US and Canada, and for the adoption of bold policies by the Government.

The post-war purpose was to eliminate the prospectively large deficit on current account, and to restore convertibility. The questions to be faced were starkly simple. What might be the likely shortfall of current receipts compared with current payments in a 'normal' post-war year? What domestic measures and assistance from overseas— widely understood as ranging from financial assistance to a liberalised world trading system—might diminish and ultimately eliminate that gap? What short-term policies might prove to be necessary during the transition?

The very lengthy period involved in this forecasting necessarily made the answers to these questions very tentative. Initially, the necessarily arbitrary assumption in 1941 was that the European war would be won by the end of 1943. Two years of transition from a war to a peace economy would follow. A further three years would be necessary to restore fully a peacetime economy. That meant seven years in all. The entry of Japan into the war in December 1941 interposed between the end of the European war (end of Stage I) and the full transition (Stage III) a further period. This Stage II, the concentration of the war against Japan, was officially estimated at various times to last three years, then two years, and finally eighteen months; for *economic* planning, in late 1944 on what was thought to be the eve of Stage II, Keynes treated it as effectively likely to last twelve months (below p 452). Thus, assuming that the transition could begin in Stage II, the total forecasting period could have been eight years (two before the end of Stage I, three for Stage II, and a further three for Stage III). Even in Keynes's view of late 1944 it could be five years (one of Stage II, one further 'transition year', and three years of Stage III).[2]

Given the formidable uncertainties of wartime losses still to be endured, even the shortest period contemplated may seem to have been impossibly long for useful forecasting. The need to forecast could not, however, be ignored. After the challenge of Hitler's 'New Order' for Europe (above, pp 18–19), there came in 1941–42 the quite different impulse of prospective Anglo-American discussions about post-war economic policies (chapter 3). That those discussions would put in question the unilateral regulation of trade, such as Britain had employed since the early 1930s, but that they might also widen export opportunities through a liberalisation of international trading and monetary arrangements, became abundantly clear during 1941–42 with the shaping of the Atlantic Charter and of Article VII of the Mutual Aid Agreement of February 1942. Hence there were reasons enough for a reconnaissance in force of the future balance of payments.

(2) THE NATURE AND QUALITY OF THE STATISTICS

The statistical material on the balance of payments was collated by the Bank of England; it came from information provided by Exchange Control, which it administered, and, through the Treasury, from government departments and overseas governments.[3] The most important analysis to result was the Bank's quarterly 'Statement of the Exchange Position and Balance of Payments Estimates', known as 'The Bank Dossier'. The Economic Section of the War Cabinet Secretariat, which had emerged in January 1941 from a more limited economic advisory service,[4] quickly assumed a central role in preparing estimates of future trends in the balance of payments. The Treasury took the lead in formulating policy, the evolution of which drew on many departmental sources and on the Bank, in both day to day exchanges and more formal Committee work.

The uneven quality of the statistical material was to become an increasingly serious problem. Even using 'reliability grades' with some quite broad ranges of margins of error, Professor C H Feinstein

433

has concluded that the quality of statistics of international transactions declined during the war.[5] His gradings, with spans of margins of error in parentheses are: Firm ($\pm$ less than 5%); Good ($\pm$ 5% to 15%); Rough $\pm$ 15% to 25%); Conjectures ($\pm$ more than 25%). Compared with the inter-war years, the deterioration was as follows:

Exports and imports of goods, and total goods
and services.........................from 'Good' to 'Rough'
Exports and imports of
services.......................from 'Rough' to 'Conjectures'
Net property income from
abroad........................from 'Good' to 'Conjectures'

Before the war concern over the balance of payments had not acquired the intensity which was later to evoke fuller, less inexact, knowledge of the many elements involved. In 1939, notes the Bank's most recent history,[6] 'coverage was still very inadequate'. For the current account, statistics of trade and of the main earnings from shipping were regarded as reasonably satisfactory; less so were those of receipts of interest, dividends, and profits, and from miscellaneous financial services and remittances. On short-term capital account the 1931 financial crisis had underpinned the advocacy of the Macmillan Report of that year[7] for fuller knowledge of short-term assets and liabilities; in responding to this, the Bank was steadily to increase the scope and usefulness of information provided to the Government on these. On longer-term capital the statistical position was weak. Reasonably useful estimates of (largely portfolio) investment abroad could be derived from statistics of income received abroad, but those statistics were not comprehensive; information was wholly inadequate on dealings in existing securities, on inward and outward direct investment, and on the influx of refugee capital which was thought to have been significant in the immediate pre-war years.

During the war, notwithstanding the operation of exchange and other controls, the decline in the overall quality and usefulness of balance of payment statistics was to be particularly reflected in the 'Balancing Item'. Ideally, the deficit on current account should have been statistically equivalent to recorded disinvestment. In practice there was very considerable difference between them, the recorded deficit exceeding recorded disinvestment. The Balancing Item, in concept an accounting necessity, arose from errors and omissions relating to receipts and payments put under particular heads, and from the evidence of other transactions which could not be so assigned because of imprecision about their amount, or source, or both; of an even lower order were 'unidentified receipts'. The essence of the large Balancing Item in wartime was that the reliability of much information did not reach the Bank's exacting standards. As it explained,[8] 'The expression "unidentified receipts"'...does not imply total ignorance of their nature but is a short title for receipts that cannot be evaluated within the limits of acceptable approximation'. The drift of official opinion and of the Bank's detailed work on the composition of the Balancing Item was that the greater part may have arisen from current account transactions. This meant that throughout the war the deficit was over-stated.

Sustained efforts to improve statistics developed during 1944–45; the Treasury had called for fuller information from Departments to assist the Bank of England's formulation of balance of payments estimates.[9] A relatively large and growing Balancing Item gave concern. An illustration of the complexities it represented came in the Bank's response to Keynes's invitation to comment on his memorandum of May 1944, 'Our Financial Problem in the Transition'. This had included an estimate of the balance of payments for 1943, with a figure of £650 million for disinvestment, which in effect was the (adverse) balance of overseas transactions in cash, together with valuations of Lend-Lease and Reciprocal Aid between Britain and the USA, and of Mutual Aid between Britain and Canada.[10] The Bank, excluding non-cash items in its analysis, pointed out that the stated amount of disinvestment was less than the difference between *known* expenditure and *known* receipts. Applying its 'usual method of concentrating first on expenditures, for which our information is relatively good, and then of inferring the total of our revenues from the net disinvestment figure', the Bank concluded that 'our revenues must have included some £130 million beyond anything which we can account for in our estimates'. At this stage, recalling experience with receipts from Canada and the USA, the Bank was prepared to attribute most or all of the £130 million to the non-sterling area (NSA): or even more than that, with therefore a negative balancing item for Britain's transactions with the rest of the sterling area (RSA). But this was not all. Britain's deficit with the NSA was £240 million, so that adjustment for the £130 million would leave £110 million. Since only £40 million of the total disinvestment of £650 million related to the NSA, it had to be assumed that the remaining £70 million out of the £110 million came from the surplus with the latter of the RSA; that brought an equivalent increase of British liabilities to the RSA.[11]

An outline of the statistical deficiencies accompanied the Bank's most detailed analysis and forecasting of the balance of payments so far, in October 1944.[12] The Bank first explained that its tables 'summarised the separate balances of payments between the UK and more than thirty other countries or groups of countries'. To compile these it depended on sources of uneven quality. Exchange Control gave 'accurate data' for expenditure in NSA countries, but little, apart from export proceeds, on receipts from them. For statistics of transactions with the RSA it was dependent on government departments, the Ministry of War Transport facing particular difficulties in providing satisfactory information; on the India Office, and on certain Dominions High Commissioners. Export figures had to be compiled from a range of United Kingdom and other trade accounts, 'adjusted so far as possible to allow for freight and insurance earnings and for the lag between shipment and payment'. This last qualification underlined the artificiality of the wartime balance of payments, as well as its limited usefulness as a basis for predicting post-war trade flows in relation to the national income; for the estimates were on a cash basis, and therefore transactions had not necessarily occurred in the periods for which they were entered. A further, wartime, complication was that, in reaching its estimates, on the one hand the Bank *ex*cluded goods and services supplied under American Lend-Lease, Canadian Mutual Aid, and British Reciprocal Aid; on the other hand, it *in*cluded cash transactions associated with these arrangements. As the Bank fairly noted, its estimates were 'nothing more than a statement of Receipts and Payments on Current Account. . . .'.

Taking first the current account, some of the resulting statistical weaknesses were a wartime intensification of those existing before 1939, including various 'City' financial services, trade financing, and remittances. The quality of statistics of shipping earnings had deteriorated, however; they had become 'very incomplete', largely in respect of trade between non-United Kingdom ports, sterling payments for chartering of Allied ships, and foreign expenditure in British ports. Far the largest group of receipts, regarded with great uncertainty, comprised the essentially wartime item of those from overseas governments. They arose from: expenditures by their armed forces and civilian employees (especially from the USA and Canada) in Britain and the RSA; British expenditure for Allied armed forces; the supply by the United Kingdom of munitions; and expenditure by Allied Governments based, or formerly based, in London. Estimates of this last item, the Bank noted, were 'very conjectural and certainly incomplete'.

For the capital account, controls and reporting provided information on many items, such as realisation of British-owned assets overseas, sales of British Government obligations, and changes in net banking liabilities. Inadequacies persisted, however, the Bank declaring of foreign investment in the United Kingdom or by the United Kingdom in the sterling area that 'we are almost totally in the dark'.

The Balancing Item to emerge for 1943 was very substantial compared with that for 1942, and was expected to be somewhat larger in 1944. The Bank cautiously suggested in October 1944 that the 'true' current deficit lay somewhere between that estimated and estimated disinvestment. The Bank's successive adjustments, which by August 1945 had reduced the Balancing Item for 1944 from a forecast £165 million to £60 million, appeared to support that imprecise division, the reductions being based on improved information, 'relaxing the standard of identification' and 'further research'.[13]

Those improvements came too late to be of much help to post-war forecasting. There were, however, other and far-reaching developments in reaction to dissatisfaction with balance of payments statistics. During autumn 1944 the Economic Section was preparing an Economic Survey for 1945. In anguished tones, a Treasury statistician protested[14] that 'The section on "export trade and the balance of payments" handles guesses provided by the Bank and myself with a horrifying confidence... None of the items are accurate; many of them... are just guesses. When... a figure is taken out from its context, it should be qualified as being a rough estimate'. Shortly, from three directions there were to be essays in the improvement of balance of payments statistics, at meetings called by the Economic Section in December 1944; by the Central Statistical Office in January 1945; and also in January, by Keynes in the Treasury. These drew from a common representation, including besides themselves the Bank of England, Board of Trade, and, from the Ministry of Production, Mr E A G Robinson, who had been closely concerned, when in the Economic Section, with the initial forecasts of 1941 – 42.[15]

The first of these meetings ranged widely over statistical problems arising from the Economic Survey, a revision of assumptions being necessitated by the prolongation of the expected end of the European War, and by the Stage II discussions in Washington on future Lend-Lease aid. This meeting arranged for fuller information to be gathered; it agreed that an existing committee of the Bank, Central Statistical Office, and Treasury examining balance of payments problems should be widened. That widening done, a newly constituted 'Interdepartmental Committee on Estimates of Balance of Payments' duly met, and gave particular attention to eliminating as far as possible the uncertainties comprising the Balancing Item; in that connection, the Bank had submitted two papers outlining its methods, and the problems to be faced, along the lines already described.[16] Keynes's call a few days later for a similarly based meeting was provoked by the large Balancing Item estimated for 1944 in the Bank's latest Dossier. From the Bank, at that meeting, came rough guesses about the amounts of disinvestment and insurance earnings that might be involved; there was pressure from all concerned to investigate the *lacunae* in war expenditure overseas by Departments, and in receipts from expenditure by Allied Governments. Perhaps above all Keynes pressed the Bank for greater boldness in interpreting the Balancing Item, urging that 'It was preferable to have a series of guesses which could be changed later, than to have a complete blank'. The pressure was repeated as the war was ending; a meeting with the usual representation was assembled by Keynes at the end of July 1945. Its remit included, besides forecasting for Stage III, 'a further investigation. . .into. . .the large balancing item. . .in present figures'.

There was demonstrably a need for a more systematic approach to the balance of payments, both administratively and analytically, than hitherto. This was recognised during 1945, in the closing months of the war and during the early months of peace. The constraint of foreign exchange was to replace that of shipping. Forecasting of exports and imports was to be part of overall post-war economic planning. A powerful intellectual stimulus came in June 1945 from a far-seeing paper, 'Towards a Balance of Payments', by Mr R W B Clarke of the Treasury.[17] Though starting from the Economic Section's earlier forecasts, it went well beyond these to consider a variety of policy issues. During summer 1945 this positive approach was reflected in discussions on the formation of a committee for external economic policy. With the new Labour Government (from late July), economic planning was a major consideration, and in September an official Steering Committee on Economic Development was formed. Soon that Committee, persuaded that balance of payments questions were 'to some extent separate' agreed to the formation of a Balance of Payments Working Party as a major official committee, able to report directly to Ministers; it began regular meetings in November 1945.[18]

Analytical considerations reflected, even more than the defects of particular statistics, the inadequacy of existing information on the balance of payments. During 1945 and 1946, the need to consider the most appropriate presentation of international transactions drew increasing official attention. Early in 1945, following Keynes's meeting at the end of January, Treasury statisticians in London and Washington were seeking United States estimates of dollar expenditure in the sterling area to help identify the inflow embodied in the Balancing Item.[19] Even as this was revealing the complications of different countries' accounting, there came from the United States Department of Commerce a 'Proposal for New Standard Forms for Presentation of Balance of Payments Data'. This was studied carefully in London; a considered interdepartmental reply, critical but not dismissive, was despatched in June.[20] At about this time, a League of Nations Committee of Statistical Experts was being re-convened to discuss broadly the same issue. Its report, received early in 1946, likewise received interdepartmental examination, a considered reply expressing reservations about the large scale of the suggested demand for statistics.[21]

British thoughts had also been turning towards a more useful presentation of international transactions. The tasks of officials convened under Keynes's chairmanship shortly before the end of the war, to consider balance of payments matters, included the compilation of 'a balance sheet of outstanding items affecting our external financial position but not entering into the balance of payments tables so that *all* factors affecting the deficit be known and measured'.[22] Some six months later, in February 1946, the Bank of England was to write to Keynes at the Treasury to propose such an improvement. In addition to the usual current and capital accounts, there should be a 'Supplementary Account' to 'house those items which are both abnormal and frequently uncertain or only known with considerable delay'. Keynes not surprisingly welcomed the proposal. In the Treasury Mr R W B Clarke who, with his colleague, Mr E Jones, had already discussed matters with the Bank, had prepared a paper setting out the three accounts envisaged, and their details.[23] The case for the 'supplementary account' was that the items in it involved a drain on the reserves 'rather than upon the dynamics of our balance of payments position', in which the current account was the crucial element. The structure of the accounts needed periodical reconsideration to keep in step with policy needs; thus, in 1949 or 1950 a revision would be necessary to bring out the crucial facts from the point of view of the waiver on the United States Loan of 1945, repayment of which was to commence at the end of 1951. The overall necessity Mr Clarke summed up succinctly:

'If one is going to make policy apply to the balance of payments one must get the statistics in a form which permits it'.

In the event practice was to lag behind precept, when, for instance the revelation of various items (eg, oil receipts, investments, and profits) in other than disguised amounts might have risked embarrassment, or, at least, misunderstanding.[24] Indeed, within weeks of Mr Clarke's paper, Lord Keynes was protesting to colleagues, in one of his last memoranda a few days before his death, that balance of payments figures were being used in an unsatisfactory fashion in official papers.[25] Within a few days, however, the Balance of Payments Working Party had agreed to an inquiry into the issue.[26] This was not the end of difficulties in presentation of the balance of payments, and certainly not over a presentation appropriate for the invocation of the Loan Waiver, which had been a major concern of Keynes's paper. There was now emerging, however, a clear contrast between the increasingly full and illuminating balance of payments accounts in the post-war period, and the very raw, unfashioned material with which wartime forecasters had to struggle.

(3) THE FORECASTS OF 1941–42

Forecasting initially concerned three sets of magnitudes which would indicate the notional shortfall of overseas receipts. First, based on pre-war trade, came a projection of the volume and cost of imports in a 'normal' post-war year, with adjustments for possible levels of post-war international trade and of prices, as well as for higher levels of domestic employment. Next, meeting only a small part of the cost of imports, came estimates of net 'invisible' earnings; compared with pre-war years, these would be reduced by disinvestment during and immediately after the war, and by shipping losses. That left the greater part of import costs to be covered, and led to the third set of magnitudes. If the current account were to be balanced from current earnings, what level of exports would be necessary? If exports failed to increase sufficiently, major policy issues would arise: should imports be restricted? Ought domestic import substitution to be fostered? Might Anglo-American collaboration to foster a more liberal, more multilateral system of trade and payments enhance export prospects?

This summary description inevitably oversimplifies the forecasting problem. There could not be much more than intelligent guesses about underlying trends in British and overseas prices, and hence in the terms of trade (the ratio of export prices to import prices), and therefore in the purchasing power after the war of a given volume of British exports. Particularly for the post-war transition period, the range of possible shipping earnings had to be assessed very flexibly, in reflection of unknown shipping losses yet to come, the possible acquisition of enemy shipping at the end of the war and the loss of Lend-Lease ships to be returned to the USA, not to say the unknown level of post-war international trade. The chances of substantial reconstruction aid from the USA and Canada permitted endless speculation about the shorter-term, as did the hopes of dealing satisfactorily—or the fears of failing to do so—with the mounting balances due to sterling-using countries, and of obtaining from them further credit in peacetime.

During 1941, several papers from members of the Economic Section[27] provided the groundwork for the first draft (November 1941) of the first comprehensive survey of 'The United Kingdom's Post-War Balance of Payments'. This was followed by discussions with other economists in government and with the Bank of England. The 'final version'—'final' only for the time being—followed consideration by a committee drawn from these groups, and had specific emendations from Keynes.[28] This paper provided the grim basis of facts and fears for the Treasury Memorandum of May 1942 on 'External Monetary and Economic Policy', which was prepared in connection with expected Anglo-American discussion on Article VII (see chapter 4, pp 76 – 78). During the next three years or so there were to be several revised versions, involving elaboration and a search for greater precision, but the broad thrust of the arguments of the 1941 – 42 draft, and of the Treasury Memorandum of May 1942, remained intact, to shape post-war export policy and specifically, during the second half of 1945, to influence the approach to the Anglo-American financial negotiations. Those arguments were twofold: that a resumption of a peacetime economy would face Britain, in a 'normal' peacetime year, with the need to raise the volume of exports by about fifty per cent, *ceteris paribus*, to secure balance of payments equilibrium; and that, before achieving such formidable expansion, it would be necessary to deal with a deficit of the order of £1,000 million in the transition to, and in the early years of, a peacetime economy.

The balance of payments deficit in a 'normal' peacetime year was put in the Treasury Memorandum at £150 million, with a wide margin each side of £100 million.[29] This assumed that prices of imports and of exports would have risen by fifty per cent and forty per cent respectively, compared with 1938 (ie, the terms of trade would have worsened by seven per cent). Costs for the same volume of imports as in 1938 would have risen from £858 million to £1,290 million; invisible earnings might yield roughly the same in money terms (£330 million against £322 million), and therefore effectively be over thirty per cent lower. That would leave £960 million to be found from exports or from reduced imports, or by procuring a significant improvement in the terms of trade. As the last seemed doubtful, the burden would fall on the other two. A comparison of the levels of British exports and of international trade in 1937 with those in the following, less prosperous, year suggested that a post-war rise in world economic activity over that of 1938 of some ten per cent could yield a fifteen per cent rise in British exports, equivalent to a volume two per cent above that of 1937. If the deterioration in the terms of trade could be assumed to produce a proportionate increase in the relative incomes of primary producers, and thence similarly in British exports to them, a further increase of some eight per cent would result. These two influences would raise exports in 1938 prices by £71 million and £39 million respectively, from a total of £471 million to £581 million, an increase in volume of some twenty-three per cent. Adjustment to assumed post-war prices indicated exports of around £810 million, leaving a gap of some £150 million, within appropriately wide margins.

Consideration of the routes by which these estimates were reached underlines the uncertainties involved.[30] Initially, the likely volume of post-war imports was largely based on the effect of an assumed reduction of unemployment from the 1938 level of almost thirteen per cent to five per cent. This suggested an increase in output of around nine per cent, but a slightly lower increase of eight per cent in imports, to take account of abnormal stocking of imported food in 1938, and assuming a marginal propensity to import raw materials of 18.5 per cent (slightly higher than the *average* of 1938). So far, this would have indicated increased imports at 1938 prices of approximately £69 million. Further calculations reduced this gradually: agricultural production had expanded during the war; the population might well show the decline already being expected before the war; and the demand for imported raw materials would not rise commensurately with the decline in unemployment, since a higher proportion of the population than in 1938 would be embodied in the defence forces. These allowances lowered the possible increase in imports to £40 million at 1938 prices. Yet further scrutiny in the light of the overall deficit being forecast indicated that these increased imports might be eliminated through import substitution by domestic manufactures, offset a little by the cost of the necessary raw materials.

Estimation of prospective receipts from invisibles was somewhat easier because they were less dependent upon guesses about British domestic developments. The disposal of overseas assets since the end of 1938 was likely to have reduced overseas interest income, estimated as a yield of four per cent on investment, by £29 million at 1938 prices by 1941. Interest on overseas short-term liabilities, assumed to be three per cent, would have increased outgoings by £9 million; that might rise, however, to roughly double when account was taken of, first, the income forgone (£4 to £8 million) in rebuilding by £100 – 200 million the country's international reserves; and, second, a corresponding rise of interest costs on many existing short-term liabilities, perhaps £10 million annually. The effective loss of investment income could therefore be put at around £55 million by the end of 1941. Lend-Lease would diminish but not avoid the continued run-down of assets and growth of liabilities; by the end of 1943 those influences could add £36 million to the loss, and disinvestment to meet deficits during the first two peacetime years a further £18 million. Thus far, the gross drop, from a 1938 figure of some £200 million, would be £109 million, possibly offset by roughly half of that amount coming from increased earnings due to higher import prices, and a further £20 million from better trading conditions abroad; the net loss would then be perhaps £35 million in post-war prices if the war ended at the end of 1943; if it ended a year earlier, the fall would be £15 million. Splitting the difference, and allowing for the war to end possibly before 1943 gave a fall in investment income from £200 million in 1938 to £175 million (at post-war prices).

Net shipping earnings seemed likely to fall by the end of 1943 to less than two-thirds of their 1938 level, but to be capable, on a variety of assumptions about losses, acquisition, loading levels in peacetime, and the distribution amongst different trades, of reaching some ninety per cent of 1938 levels by the end of 1947; rather more optimistic assumptions about the acquisition of enemy vessels led to an estimate of 100 per cent. Adjustment for an increase of fifty per cent in prices yielded earnings of £125 million in a 'normal' peacetime year, a fall in real terms of almost twenty per cent from the £100 million of 1938.

Estimates of total invisible earnings embraced investment income, shipping earnings, and receipts from commissions and miscellaneous remittances; net, these came to the region of £330 million in post-war prices, effectively a fall of about one-third from the £322 million of 1938.

Assembling these more detailed estimates produced the possible deficit of £150 ± 105 million in a 'normal' post-war year, as set out in Table I below.

The two transition years (assumed to be 1944 and 1945) offered special short-run problems of supply, pricing, shipping availability and costs, and of world conditions generally. In this context, the forecasters looked to the experiences of 1919–20, the comparable period following the previous world war, for lessons on what to expect and to avoid.[31]

There was a twofold task. The first part was to calculate the physical possibilities of importing. This depended largely on the availability of shipping. The starting point was the level of imports in 1941: £1,072 million. It seemed possible to foresee import capacity very close to that, at £1,050 million, in 1944, and in 1945 £1,290 million, virtually the level of 1938 imports of £1,287 million (these and other amounts in this and the following two paragraphs are on the basis of assumed post-war prices). But now came the second part of the task, to estimate minimum imports needed *and* affordable. Again, the starting point was 1941: from total imports of £1,072 million could be excluded military stores and finished goods (in 1941, largely machine tools), leaving £879 million, further reduced by stock changes, to £821 million, covering predominantly imports of food and tobacco, raw materials, and petroleum products. To accommodate a larger employed population would require more imports: perhaps, allowing for a greater labour intensity in production and the use of more home-produced materials, some £50 million extra in the first transition year and £80 million extra in the second. This meant that imports of around £900 million would be the minimum needed, although this amount might scarcely support the desired post-war level of employment.

In invisible earnings, shipping might provide exceptional short-run benefit, as scarcities might raise freight rates to double pre-war levels (compared with the fifty per cent increase assumed for post-war prices generally): earnings of £110 million and £120 million were estimated for 1944 and 1945 respectively. In contrast, investment income could be expected to be well *below* the reduced amount expected for that later 'normal' peacetime year. It had fallen two years after the previous war to one-half of the pre-war level; now, to general post-war recovery problems must be added the impact of fighting in areas from which investment income might have been expected to come. It was therefore assumed that £80–100 million annually, compared with a

TABLE 1

ESTIMATE OF THE BALANCE OF PAYMENTS IN A 'NORMAL POST-WAR YEAR'

£ million

Retained Imports 1938	858	
Less Government and ⎫ Private Stocking ⎰	25	
	833	

Adjust for increased employment, *less* ⎫
    increases in domestic production ⎬
    of food and raw materials ⎭
	27	

Estimated Imports at 1938 prices	860	
Adjust for 50% higher prices	430	
Estimated Imports at post-war prices		1,290 ± 40
Estimated post-war ⎫ Invisible Exports ⎰		330 ± 40

Gap to be filled by ⎫
    Exports *or* Reduction ⎬
    in Imports ⎭
		960 ± 80

Exports in 1938	471	
Add for increased activity	71	
for changes in terms of trade	39	
Total at 1938 prices	581	
Add for 40% higher prices	232	
Total at post-war prices	813	
Total rounded		810 ± 25
Remaining gap		150 ± 105

Source: Adapted from RP(42) 2 of 24 March 1942 'External Monetary and Economic Policy', Appendix I, 'The United Kingdom's Post-War Balance of Payments', T160/1377.

pre-war £200 million, was the most to be expected in the first two post-war years. Amongst other invisible earnings, those from commissions were most uncertain, but again the earlier experience suggested a fall; moreover, a greater proportion of trade would not go through 'normal' commercial channels, thereby reducing prospective earnings. Against all these earnings had to be set government overseas expenditure. This was impossible to estimate, and a purely token figure of £50 million was given for each of the two years.

Within the sweeping guesses indicated above, net invisible earnings were put at £200 million and £235 million for the first two post-war years, reduced to £150 million and £185 million by the token figure for government expenditure. Taking these latter figures against import costs left a financing need of either £900 million and £1,065 million for the *physical maximum* of imports, or £615 million and £715 million for the *'Bed-rock minimum'*. What were the prospects for exports and for the peacetime deficit? An inquiry by the Post-War Export Trade Committee into 'Post-War Planning for Exports' was begun as the Treasury Memorandum was being prepared. This gathered valuable information on many exporting industries and on the problems of expanding exports. Inevitably however, given all the uncertainties, its Report was more speculative in its recommendations than in its industrial surveys, perhaps less clear, and certainly more productive than those in arousing controversy (eg, over the implied resort to bilateralism with sterling area countries in order to work off their excess balances).[32]

Exports were slipping in 1942, with the easement on import costs from Lend-Lease and the pressures of the 'Export White Paper'. Export recovery, in the light of the experience of 1919–20, was adjudged to be possible in the first and second transition years to volumes of around seventy per cent and ninety-two per cent respectively of the 1938 level. Higher volumes, at ninety-two and 120 per cent respectively, might be achieved through maintenance of strict controls on supplies and on the home market, and by an export drive. The more optimistic figures would bring export volumes after two years to roughly the level calculated for a 'normal' post-war year. They would bring receipts of £650 million and £800 million respectively (compared with the more cautious £500 million and £650 million); this assumed prices for exports of fifty per cent above those of 1938, rather than the forty per cent assumed for a 'normal' year, reflecting the likely existence of sellers' markets in the early post-war years. Significantly higher prices might, indeed, be possible, but a warning came from 1919–20: high export prices then (three and a half times those of 1913, compared with three times in the case of imports) had brought retribution in the damaging competition they had stimulated for staple British exports.

The prospective deficit in the two transition years could now be deduced: on the more favourable view of exports, which was adopted for the War Cabinet memorandum, £250 million and £215 million respectively; on the less favourable view, £400 million and £415 million. Further variants could be deduced by assuming, as with a 'normal' post-war year that imports were reduced to the barest minimum. These possibilities are set out in Table 2.

TABLE 2

ESTIMATES OF THE BALANCE OF PAYMENTS IN THE TWO TRANSITION YEARS 1944 AND 1945 (ASSUMING THE WAR TO END AT THE END OF 1943)

	(i) Assuming such Imports as can be shipped		(ii) Assuming Bed-rock Minimum Imports	
				£ million
	1944	1945	1944	1945
1. Imports	1,050	1,250	900	900
2. Invisible earnings, net	200	235	200	235
3. Government expenditure overseas	50	50	50	50
4. (2 *minus* 3)	150	185	150	185
5. Net payments overseas (1 *minus* 4)	900	1,065	750	715
6. Exports: possible	500	650	500	650
7. Exports: optimistic	650	850	650	850
8. Deficit: possible (5 *minus* 6)	400	415	250	65
9. Deficit: optimistic (5 *minus* 7)	250	215	100	(135)ϕ

ϕ Surplus

Source: Adapted from RP(42) 2 of 24 March 1942 'External Monetary and Economic Policy', Appendix I, 'The United Kingdom's Post-War Balance of Payments', T160/1377.

For the five years of the post-war period as a whole, the prospective deficit could be put in the region of £1,000 million; this was very rough and rounded-up, as so many estimates unavoidably were in guessing about the post-war balance of payments. It is reached by adding to the £465 million, for the two transition years, deficits of £150 million, within wide margins of error, for the succeeding three years.

The frailty of these estimates was recognised in discussions both before and after the Treasury Memorandum went to the War Cabinet in May 1942. On three aspects in particular uncertainty persisted: the burden of short-term liabilities, ie, sterling balances; the level of government expenditure overseas during the transition; and the possible understatement of pre-war investment income and of inward investment. Increased burdens from the first might be deferred, it was hoped, until well into the transition. Keynes had originally suggested[33] allowing an annual cost of £50 million, but the Memorandum allowed half that. Subsequent calculations depended on guesses about interest rates, the accumulation of balances, and the broad policy to be

446

adopted towards them. The most pessimistic estimate of interest rates (assuming a level of balances at the end of the war over one-quarter greater than proved to be the case) would have required an increase in the volume of exports of eleven per cent above that of 1938 to meet them, and a similar increase for the early repayment of one-third of the balances.[34]

Next, Government expenditure overseas. Declaring the impossibility of stating this, the forecasters in early 1942 had inserted a token amount of £50 million for each of the two transition years. Later in 1942, in preparation of a version of the forecasts for Anglo-American talks (which did not come until 1943), Keynes argued for higher figures. The Economic Section, pondering whether the increase would be gross or net, eventually increased the amount for the first transition year by £100 million, to £150 million, raising the projected deficit for that year to £350 million.[35] By 1944, however, Government expenditure overseas was recognised as likely to be several times higher if the Transition were to commence during the war years of Stage II. When attention turned to Stage III, as in Keynes's memoranda, this item grew into a major threat to the balance of payments and, indeed, clearly appeared to be just that in the early months of the peace (above, pp 358 – 9).

Finally, were statistics of the pre-war balance of payments misleading? If the current account deficit had been exaggerated, eg, by omission or poor recording of various invisible earnings, then the exaggeration would have been carried into the post-war forecasts.[36] Much more serious would have been the omission or under-recording of capital inflows. Such underestimation, given the known loss of investment income in wartime and continuing disinvestment, would have meant that the deterioration of the balance of payments had been even worse than considered. The discussions of 1944 – 45 on the Balancing Item had sought to explore these issues. It must be said at once that a thoroughgoing reappraisal of the pre-war position some thirty years later did not significantly change the picture: a current account deficit of £55 million compared with the £65 million of the Treasury Memorandum of May 1942. Within that deficit, net receipts from invisibles, etc, appear to have been over £100 million lower than thought. Net income from overseas investment is little changed. The biggest amendment is in the much lower figure for shipping earnings, to allow for the high proportion of British imports carried in British ships; the rough counterpart was a lower figure for import costs, and hence a less unfavourable balance of merchandise trade than recorded before the war.[37]

The capital account was another matter. 'Is the United Kingdom Balancing Item a wartime phenomenon?' pondered the Bank in August 1945,[38] adding that 'A recent attempt of ours to make an estimate of capital movements in 1938 achieved no more than to show that the information on securities was too uncertain to provide evidence of value...'. A quarter of a century or so later, the Bank did produce a Balancing Item for the 1930s. Excluding the exceptional year 1931, this came to a net amount during 1932–38 equivalent to thirty-eight per cent of the volume of sales and repatriations of overseas investments during the war. Evidently Keynes's anxiety had been justified.[39]

(4) DEBATE OVER THE USE OF DEVALUATION TO IMPROVE THE BALANCE OF PAYMENTS

During 1943 some optimism emerged amongst Government economists about the post-war balance of payments, and led to an important debate about the role of exchange rate changes in improving it.[40] That optimism and that debate followed the British initiative for a 'Commercial Union' (pp 100–1) and the Anglo-American discussions of September-October. The resulting 'Washington Principles' (see Appendix 13) appeared to offer scope to achieve a controlled conversion to a peacetime economy as part of an agreed, orderly, international approach to the maintenance of long-term equilibrium in the balance of payments. A comprehensive case for this view was provided by Mr J E Meade in December 1943, in a lengthy memorandum on 'The Post-war International Settlement and the United Kingdom Balance of Payments'.[41]

Mr Meade argued that there need be no serious obstacle during the immediate post-war transition to working for the eventual adoption of the Washington Principles. The major differences between American and British views concerned the length of the transition and the scope of quantitative controls in imports; British instincts were for the former to be longer and the later to be more flexible than American spokesmen wished. Provided that those differences could be overcome, the memorandum envisaged two complementary approaches to a satisfactory balance of payments. The UK's own measures would in particular involve import controls and, especially in the transition, flexibility in the exchange rate, i.e. devaluation; internationally, there should be credits and loans, the development of institutions to sustain the world economy, and Anglo-American planning of exports, as in the war, during the immediate transition.

Mr Meade's colleague, Mr J Marcus Fleming,* supported the devaluation argument.[42] First pointing out that Meade's was a special case (where supply elasticities of exports were infinite) he generalised the argument, using like him the economist's formal apparatus of elasticities; he did not dissent from the main conclusion that a relatively small change in the exchange rate, say of ten per cent, would be

* FLEMING, John Marcus (1911–1976); Ministry of Economic Warfare, 1939–42; Cabinet Offices, Economic Section, 1942, Deputy Director, 1947–51.

worthwhile. There was, however, swift obstruction of the exchange path to equilibrium. From two other economists in government came scepticism about these and other papers that favoured the Washington proposals on trade policy. Mr R F Kahn* from the Ministry of Supply and Lord Keynes from the Treasury both expressed doubts on technical points in the devaluation argument; they chaffed their colleagues for deriving their confidence in it from a lingering faith, which they had seemed elsewhere to have abandoned, in how a *laissez-faire* world was supposed to work. Above all Kahn and Keynes expressed their preference, to ensure the exclusion of imports that could not be afforded, for the certainty of controls over the uncertainty and slow reactions likely with devaluation.

Although this debate among the economists, drawing in other economists and officials, was to continue for some months,[43] the Treasury and the Bank of England shunted it aside. Sir Wilfrid Eady informed the Director of the Economic Section, Professor L C Robbins, of the Treasury's belief that, notwithstanding British proposals in the Clearing Union scheme, early depreciation would be unhelpful. He pointed to Britain's foreign liabilities as requiring the maintenance of confidence in sterling; he noted that discussion of devaluation in the Washington talks had impelled 'two leading New York bankers' to seek reassurance, which the Bank with his approval had offered, about sterling's exchange rate.[44]

In discussions with the Treasury shortly after, in January and February 1944, the Bank was to stress the desirability of exchange rate stability (above, pp 141–2). Mr Meade continued to argue for an exchange rate policy, and gained support when Mr R W B ('Otto') Clarke joined the Treasury. In an imaginative and wide ranging memorandum[45] that elaborated further the various memoranda that had come from Mr Meade and the Economic Section, Mr Clarke in May 1945 urged that the existing exchange rate of $4 (more correctly, $4.03) to the pound should not be treated as 'fixed and immutable'. The 'inconclusive' evidence about the correct level for exchange rates might lead sterling into Stage III at $4. Subsequently, a greater rise in domestic prices than in the USA, and greater pressures from 'full employment' policy, might leave sterling looking overvalued. There would then be less danger to the balance of payments, and less hazard in accepting the constraints of the commercial policy proposals on the use of import restrictions, if the exchange rate could be moved: perhaps to $3.50.

Keynes, broadly approving the rest of the memorandum, differed strongly over the exchange rate of $4, which he considered to be more

---

* KAHN, Richard Ferdinand, Baron (Life Peer) 1965 (1905–   ); Temporary Civil Servant in various Government Departments, 1939–46; Professor of Economics, Cambridge University, 1951–72.

competitive than Clarke allowed. In line with the optimism he was to develop in his later, and posthumously published, article Keynes doubted whether American economic trends need threaten Britain's balance of payments. Clarke admitted that his draft had been too pessimistic, but noted the difficulty of assessing the future position when sterling would be made convertible. His concern had been that there should then be 'something in hand in the exchange rate'; present evidence, he conceded, favoured Keynes's view that there would be.[46] There the internal debate in the Treasury rested. That outcome is not particularly surprising. The whole drift of discussions about post-war monetary arrangements had been towards acquiescence in stable exchange rates, for instance in connection with the proposed International Monetary Fund. This trend was underpinned by the expected constraints upon variations in exchange rates from the post-war maintenance of wartime features of the sterling area, and by the sensitivity to any change in sterling's value of holders of large balances, such as India. The exchange rate debate revived in the aftermath of the convertibility crisis of 1947, for a few weeks during 1948, with Clarke arguing for devaluation, and again in the following year in the months preceding the devaluation of 1949.[47]

(5) FORECASTING AND THE FINANCE OF STAGE II

During 1944 there was a reassessment of the basic forecasts of 1941–42. This was in connection with the financing of Stage II, for which it became clear during 1944 that American aid might be more difficult to obtain. Hitherto, those imports not provided under American Lend-Lease or Canadian aid had been financed to a decreasing extent by exports and to an increasing extent by disinvestment (largely in the form of increased sterling balances). Even were aid to be continued on the existing basis yet more heavy disinvestment would, without easement, so worsen the already weak balance of payments as to hamper British ability to co-operate with the USA in implementing post-war commitments (eg, the liberalisation of trade and payments).[48] The British response to these problems was to prepare a case, for the Anglo-American negotiations during autumn 1944 on Stage II, that a beginning should be made forthwith on the revival of Britain's export trade, helped by Lend-Lease and the ending of the restrictions of 'The Export White Paper' of 1941 (above, pp 10–12). The argument was threefold. First, Britain wished to take a full part in the war against Japan, maintaining the same war effort proportionately to that of the US as during the war against Germany. Without increased export earnings, however, that would mean either further disinvestment or a reduction in civilian consumption. Yet both Allies expected some demobilisation in Stage II, so that there would be spare manpower, available for export industries. Second, increased export earnings would ease the burden of sterling balances, the holders of which could then be allowed to use them more freely. Third, relief in Stage II was essential if Britain were to prepare for the massive export expansion necessary in Stage III for economic recovery, and therefore to be as ready as other countries, including the USA, to resume post-war trade.[49]

The forecasts for the post-war balance of payments were revised for use in Stage II planning. Broadly, the size of expected deficits increased, firmly underpinning the need for the volume of exports to rise by at least fifty per cent (although Keynes was gloomily inclined by early 1945, after the Stage II talks, to regard 100 per cent as 'more realistic' if even less attainable).[50] Account had to be taken of higher prices; of a possibly greater worsening of the terms of trade than originally anticipated; and of much higher government expenditure overseas, since the transition must now be treated as beginning, not in 'post-war years', but in the war period of Stage II.

A very wide range of estimates, such as characterised Keynes's memoranda of 1944–45 on the post-war balance of payments, resulted: between £1,300 million and £2,000 million for the cumulative deficit before equilibrium could be achieved. The explanation of this wide range lay, in addition to the statistical patchiness, in the two differing sets of assumptions that were legitimately made, that the transition might last two years or only one year respectively. The Economic Section had continued to work on the basis of two transition years. It now argued that substantial American aid during the first year could taper off in the second as exports recovered. For inter-departmental preparation of the case for North American aid in Stage II, the Economic Section drew on two particular sets of estimates. The Treasury put the deficits for the two years at £650 million and £250 million respectively. In Stage III, the deficit might run at £300 million in the first year, with a further net deficit of £100 million before balance was reached at the end of the third year.[51] This implied a cumulative deficit of £1,300 million. From the Board of Trade came export forecasts, following consultations with departments and other bodies ('in particular the Whisky Association'). Given some optimism that all the necessary manpower would be made available at the beginning of Stage II, the value of exports could rise by over 80 per cent in each year, ie, by almost 250 per cent in all; the volume achieved could be fractionally above that of 1938.[52]

The estimate for the cumulative deficit had very soon to be revised. Fuller information led the Bank of England, on whose statistics the forecasting so largely depended, to see 'an even darker picture' (though stressing that 'the whole computation is necessarily based on sweeping assumptions').[53] The Economic Section revised its forecast for the first year's deficit to £836 million.[54] If the estimates for the succeeding years remained unchanged, (attention being concentrated, however, on this first year), that implied a total deficit, before equilibrium was reached, approaching £1,500 million.

The final document for the Anglo-American negotiations on Stage II revised—that is, Keynes in particular revised, up to the last minute—those assumptions and details.[55] It assumed that Stage II would last, not two years, but one year. This was in line with the US Army's working plans for demobilisation, as recorded in September 1944 at the Quebec Conference, although Anglo-American military plans supposed a period of eighteen months.[56] It forecast a very heavy deficit in that year, with falling dollar receipts from US and Canadian troops as they went to the Continent or returned home. The estimated deficit (now being calculated in dollars), was put at $3 billion (£750 million), even after some $900 million of expenditure in the USA had been met in cash. Before US and Canadian aid, the notional disinvestment could exceed $6 billion (£1,500 million); that would be the level at which the prospective deficit would be running at the beginning of Stage III, in the absence of significant reconversion and of US aid. Cuts in imports, in government expenditure overseas, and in the use of foreign shipping could reduce Stage II deficits, but the total might well reach $4–5 billion (£1,000–1,250 million). Thus, for the two Stages combined, deficits could total some £2,000 million.

(6) THE END OF THE WAR, AND THE BALANCE OF PAYMENTS IN STAGE III

The early end of the war was to destroy the underlying chronology of these estimates. The immediate problem was the balance of payments in the first year of peace, and beyond that of securing external equilibrium within a tolerable period. The Stage II that was barely three months old, with recovery barely started, had now merged abruptly into the first year of Stage III. Uncertainty characterised the future external position as surely as when the wartime forecasters strove to outline it. This uncertainty became very clear in the continuous adjustment of estimates of the balance of payments for 1946, both of particular items and of the overall deficit; of the cumulative deficit before reaching equilibrium; and of the time needed for that.

For the deficit in the first year of Stage II the Economic Section had in May 1945 revised its estimate down to £744 million. This was somewhat lower than the Bank's estimates of just over £800 million (£813 million in March, £810 million May and June 1945).[57] At this period Keynes was already regarding such figures as too low for the first year of *Stage III*. He was asserting that, even with drastic measures to cut Government expenditure and to raise exports, the deficit might approach £1,000 million.[58] By July and August 1945, notwithstanding some scepticism from Mr Clarke, who thought that £800 million might be more appropriate, Keynes was forecasting for the War Cabinet that in 1946, being treated as the first year of Stage II, it would be around £950 million.[59] That deficit was predicated on the adoption of a bold drive for reconversion, without waiting for the war to end. Behind the worsening of £200 million compared with the Economic Section's forecast was a projection of a steep rise of £550 million in imports, a smaller but substantial rise in exports, and a drop in Government expenditure overseas of £150 million. This was the raw material for the Government's decision in late August to send a Mission to the USA to negotiate financial assistance.

By that point, Keynes had begun to reduce his estimates of the cumulative deficit. He had warned in October 1944 that it might reach £2,000 million, and had repeated this for the War Cabinet in May 1945. In mid-August his estimates came to £1,700 million, with the qualification that 'we are in the realm of pure guesswork'.[60] Yet further reconsiderations and revisions were to follow in the next few months. They reflected both the continuous efforts at improvement, and the urgent pressures of the Anglo-American financial negotiations in Washington, particularly in the light of reduced hopes by mid-October of obtaining more than $4 – 5 billion in aid. The Bank now forecast a deficit in 1946 of £664 million; it assumed a lower level of imports and a higher level of exports than in Keynes's mid-August 'guesswork', but was less hopeful about invisible earnings.[61] Aboard ship in early September, Keynes revised his estimate: first down to £750 million, then to a range of £625 – 875 million and then to £800 million, the figure that he presented shortly after to the American negotiators.[62] Moderate optimism (as in the Treasury about exports) was offset by caution about invisibles. Other forecasts during the next few weeks were close to these. Early in the negotiations, the Mission's principal statistical expert, Mr F E Harmer* reached a figure of £780 million. A little later, on assumptions that he described as 'all optimistic', Mr Clarke in London offered an estimate of £725 million, and a range of £700 – 800 million.[63] These estimates, together with those for the cumulative deficit and for the achievement of equilibrium were all shaken up in mid-October 1945, when it became clear that aid would fall short of $5,000 million (£1,250 million). That became the ceiling, *ceteris paribus*, beneath which the cumulative deficit would have to be contained. Keynes now re-estimated the deficit for 1946, on an improved view of prospective invisible earnings, at £750 million.[64] Estimates for succeeding years were also adjusted from those which he had essayed on the eve of the negotiations; the overall revisions were to be assembled and reconstructed some months later by Mr R W B

---

* HARMER, Frederic Evelyn, Kt 1968 (1905–   ); HM Treasury, 1939–45; Temporary Assistant Secretary, HM Treasury, 1943–45; served in Washington 1944 and 1945 in connection with Anglo-American economic and financial negotiations.

Clarke (Tables 3(a) and 3(b) following this Appendix).

The Economic Section agreed about the scale of the expected deficit for 1946, but differed on its composition.[65] It was less optimistic about invisibles and lowered its export forecast, following a pessimistic revision by the Board of Trade; but its lower figure for imports was a technical matter of using a valuation basis of fob (free on board), rather than of cif (cost, insurance, freight) as in Keynes's calculations (the figure of £750 million was to be the figure eventually used, though 'with a fairly large measure of uncertainty' in the statistical material published at the time of the Financial Agreement in December 1945).[66]

The cumulative deficit which Keynes put to the Americans in mid-October, £1,250 million compared with the £1,700 million of two months earlier, raised the question of how long the Transition might endure. Keynes's estimate in May had been three to five years after the end of the Japanese war; that can be interpreted, with 1946 being regarded as the first transition year, as between the end of 1948 and the end of 1950. His mid-August estimate was 'by 1949', and in September it was by 1949 or later. In mid-October, in mid-negotiation, it was by 1949 or 1950. At that time London was assuming a period of three years,[67] although there was already pressure for a shorter period. The problem of stretching out the Transition, something Keynes had mooted, threatened to involve constraints on food consumption and on raw material imports, which would hamper recovery. Thus a case could be seen, as in the Stage II discussions a year earlier, for pushing on with recovery rapidly, if possible. Indeed, the Central Planning Committee requested in September 1945 that there should be a target of June 1947 for achieving equilibrium, although the chairman of the Balance of Payments Working Party noted that it must be assumed that five years at least would be necessary to complete the process.[68]

(7) THE VALIDITY OF THE WARTIME AND EARLY POST-WAR FORECASTS

How correct in the event did the forecasts prove to be, particularly in relation to the overall balance of payments and to the gold and dollar deficit (and hence to the need for US and Canadian credits)? If to the first part of the question the brief answer is that they appear to have been reasonably correct, and to the second that they were well short of the mark, some *caveats* are appropriate.

The forecasts were not prophecies but, rather, warnings of the outer limits of constraints and dangers in the external prospects for the economy. The amount of external aid represented a broad, ultimate check to the size of the overall deficit, and influenced policies intended to restrict the latter. In various ways, Government, business, and the population as a whole responded with reduced overseas expenditure, export promotion, and the acceptance of prolonged austerity within the limits and easement of the US and Canadian credits. The quality of balance of payments statistics constitutes a special difficulty, however, in evaluating the outcome. During the post-war years the statistics were steadily improved, significant changes being made in their calculation and presentation as well as in their accuracy.[69] Wartime and early post-war forecasts are therefore to be compared less with the much revised statistics published in the 'pink books' from 1959,[70] than with the earliest contemporary publications in the series of balance of payments White Papers. Equilibrium of a sort was approached in the current account during the second half of 1948 (see Table 3(c)), and therefore at the earliest edge of Keynes's zone of estimates, but there was uncertainty whether it could be sustained.[71] The overall statistical balance was indeed unsatisfactory; it embodied surpluses with some 'soft currency' economies, but substantial deficits with 'hard currency' economies, particularly those of the dollar area. This was a weakness which the devaluation of sterling (and the currencies of most of the rest of the sterling area) against the US dollar in 1949 sought to remedy. There had been an underestimate, not least by Keynes,[72] of the intensity of the post-war world's dollar shortage.

For the current account for the three years 1946 – 48, the eventual Washington forecast had been of a cumulative deficit of £1,250 million (see Table 3 (b)). The earliest contemporary figures to be published for the period, without being qualified as 'provisional', gave a cumulative deficit of £1,120 million. In terms of reliability grades noted earlier, this ranks the forecasts as 'good'.

Of the three major components of the current account, the trade deficit of £862 million compared with an estimated £950 million. In relation to imports and exports, assessment of forecasts is complicated both by sharper rises in their prices and by more adverse terms of trade than had been anticipated. Imports were well within the 'good' range in respect of forecast costs, but scarcely reached eighty per cent of the 1938 volume, even in 1948; controls were effective. Exports, higher in both value and volume, brought receipts more than one quarter higher than expected, putting the Washington forecast apparently into the 'conjecture' grade. If, however, export prices had continued at the lower level forecast and attained for 1946 (detailed forecasts had not been attempted beyond that year),[73] receipts would have placed the forecasts comfortably within the 'good' grade. A second main element, the net surplus on invisible transactions of £340 million compared with an estimated £300 million, may also rank as a 'good' out-turn. Finally, net expenditure overseas by the Government, relatively modest before the war, greatly worsened the deficit. Driven down by sheer necessity (above, pp 358–60) to £598 million, almost exactly the £600 million envisaged as a maximum tolerable level, this reflected expenditure on the armed forces in particular, on relief and rehabilitation, and on supporting the devastated economy in the British occupation zone in Germany.

Emphasis on the current account in forecasts of the post-war balance of payments had reflected certain assumptions or hopes. These were, in particular, that the exchange rate was unlikely to be altered, that overseas confidence in sterling would be sustained, that overseas investment would be negligible and that repayment of sterling liabilities would be strictly limited. In practice, only the first of these proved justified during 1946–48. A loss of confidence in sterling was a serious element in the crisis of summer 1947. Although in 1946 overseas assets were reduced and sterling balances were slightly increased (ie, borrowing in sterling rose), whilst in contrast there was a small net addition to gold and dollar reserves, these changes were short-lived. During 1947 and 1948, net capital movements were outwards, there was substantial net repayment of sterling liabilities, and the gold and dollar reserves fell. These items brought the cumulative deficit for 1946–48 to £1,673 million.

This financing requirement of £1,673 million was on a firm statistical base, and was not subject to the drastic revision necessary for the early estimates of the current account. It exceeded the combined US and Canadian credits by £423 million. On the one hand it had not been expected, either before or during the two sets of negotiations in Washington and Ottawa respectively, that those credits would or should cover the entire deficit.[74] On the other hand, the sources of the deficit extended well beyond the United Kingdom's own current account; they included not only the acquisition of overseas assets and the repayment of sterling liabilities already noted, but also operations of the sterling area as a whole.[75]

The United Kingdom's own cumulative deficit with the dollar area on current account came to £1,185 million for 1946–48. Subscriptions to the new IMF and World Bank required £64 million. The deficits of the rest of the sterling area with the dollar area came to £423 million, with a further £10 million for its IMF and World Bank subscriptions: £433 million falling on Britain's gold and dollar resources. British gold purchases from the sterling area reduced the shortfall by £221 million. Thus far the deficit comes to £1,461 million. Other items, attributed to the sterling area as a whole, in particular net gold and dollar payments to non-sterling countries outside the dollar area, amounted to £212 million, bringing the final total to £1,673 million.

This overall gold and dollar deficit of Britain and the rest of the sterling area was largely financed by using almost all of the US and Canadian credits, mainly in 1946–47, and by drawing on the United Kingdom's exiguous gold and dollar reserves. The new IMF provided modest aid in 1947–48 to the United Kingdom, and to other sterling countries in 1948; a gold loan of £80 million from South Africa reinforced the reserves in 1948; and the first receipts under the European Recovery Programme ('The Marshall Plan', launched in 1947), also came during 1948. Thus, notwithstanding the broadly relevant forecasts of the United Kingdom's own current account deficits for 1946–48, more extensive pressures for gold and dollars had ensured the virtual exhaustion, and confirmed the inadequacy, of the US and Canadian credits less than half way through the five years they were intended to cover.

TABLES 3(a) to 3(e)

ESTIMATES AND OUT-TURN OF THE BALANCE OF
PAYMENTS OF THE UNITED KINGDOM 1946–49

TABLE 3(a)
Estimates for 1946–49 prepared by Lord Keynes

£ million

	1946	1947	1948	1949
1. Imports	1,300	1,400	1,400	1,450
2. Government expenditure overseas	450	250	200	150
3. Total	1,750	1,650	1,600	1,600
4. Exports	600	1,000	1,300	1,450
5. Net invisible income	50	100	100	150
6. Government receipts from Allies & Dominions	150			
7. Total	800	1,100	1,400	1,600
8. Deficit: (3 *minus* 7)	– 950	– 550	– 200	NIL
	1,750	1,650	1,600	1,600

Source: 'Our Overseas Financial Prospects', Cabinet Memorandum of 13 August 1945, CP (45) 112, CAB 129/1; reprinted in *The Collected Writings of John Maynard Keynes*, XXIV, ed. Donald Moggridge, (Cambridge 1979), p 404.

TABLE 3(b)

Estimates for 1946–48 used in the Anglo-American Negotiations in Washington September–December 1945*

£ million

	1946	1947	1948	Total 1946–48
Imports f.o.b. ϕ (excluding oil)	1,150	1,250	1,350	3,750
Overseas war expenditure	300	175	125	600
	1,450	1,425	1,475	4,350
Exports	650	975	1,175	2,800
Net Invisibles	50	100	150	300
	700	1,075	1,325	3,100
Deficit	750	350	150	1,250

ϕ The import figures used in Table 3(a) and in the Washington negotiations were on a c.i.f. (cost, insurance, freight) basis, instead of the more usual f.o.b. (free on board) basis used here. Net oil expenditure and receipts were included in net invisibles.

* As rearranged by Mr R W B Clarke of HM Treasury from discussions during the Washington negotiations. He commented that 'there was never a detailed statement for 1946–8...However, I think...the figures are compatible with the figures...[used] in Washington'.

Source
Memorandum by Mr Clarke, 'What happens if [we do not get the US Loan]', 23 February 1946, T 247/47. Reprinted in Sir Richard Clarke, *Anglo-American Economic Collaboration in War and Peace*, 1942–1949, ed Sir Alec Cairncross (Clarendon Press, Oxford, 1982), pp 153–4.

TABLE 3(c)

Early Post-War Statistics of the Balance of Payments 1946 – 48

£ million

	1946	1947	1948			1946 – 48
			Jan-June	Jul-Dec	Year	Total
1. Imports	1,097	1,541	(899)	(869)	1,768	4,406
2. Government overseas expenditure(net)	295	207	(78)	(18)	96	598
3. (1) + (2)	1,392	1,748	(977)	(887)	1,864	5,004
4. Exports	889	1,100	(730)	(825)	1,555	3,544
5. Invisibles(net)	123	18	(92)	(107)	199	340
6. (4) + (5)	1,012	1,118	(822)	(932)	1,754	3,884
7. Surplus(+) or Deficit(–) on current account = (6) minus (3)	– 380	– 630	(– 155)	(+45)	– 110	– 1,120
8. Net gold and dollar deficit	226	1,024	(254)	(169)	423	1,673
9. Net change in UK external assets (decrease + increase –)	+ 117	– 264	(– 79)	(– 21)	– 100	– 247
10. Net change in sterling liabilities (decrease – increase +)	+ 38	– 130	(– 20)	(– 193)	– 213	– 305
11. Total overseas disinvestment	380	630	(155)	(– 45)	110	1,120

Source
Adapted from Tables I and IV of *United Kingdom Balance of Payments* 1946 to 1949, Cmd 7793, November 1949, *BPP* 1948 – 9, XXII.
Note: because of rounding, component items may not sum exactly to totals.

TABLE 3(d)

Composition of the Net Gold and Dollar Deficit 1946–48

£ million

	1946	1947	1948	Total 1946–48
A. *On United Kingdom account*	– 310	– 657	– 311	– 1,278
1. Deficit on current account with Dollar Area	– 325	– 580	– 280	– 1,185
2. Other transactions	+ 22	– 26	– 25	– 29
3. Gold and dollar subscriptions to IMF & World Bank	– 7	– 51	– 6	– 64
B. *On Rest of Sterling Area account*	+ 17	– 203	– 26	– 212
4. Deficit with Dollar Area	– 62	– 280	– 81	– 423
5. Gold and dollar subscriptions to IMF & World Bank	– 3	– 7	—	– 10
6. Purchases of new gold by United Kingdom	+ 82	+ 84	+ 55	+ 221
C. *On Whole Sterling Area account*				
7. Net gold and dollar receipts from, and payments to, other countries	+ 67	– 164	– 86	– 183
D. *Total net gold and dollar deficit (A + B + C)*	– 226	– 1,024	– 423	– 1,673

Source Table IV of Cmd 7793. In subsequent White Papers on the balance of payments the net gold and dollar deficit was given in dollars as well as in sterling.

Note: because of rounding, component items may not sum exactly to totals.

TABLE 3(e)

The Financing of the Gold and Dollar Deficit 1946 – 48

	1946	1947	1948	Total 1946-48 £m	Total 1946-48 US$m	1946	1947	1948
				£ million			US $ million	
Change in gold and dollar holdings (decrease + increase −)	− 52	152	54	154	626	− 215	618	223
Drawings on US Credit	149	707	74	930	3,750	600	2,850	300
Drawings on Canadian Credit	130	105	13	248	998	523	423	52
Drawings on IMF: by United Kingdom	–	60	15	75	300	–	240	60
: by other sterling area countries	–	–	17	17	68	–	–	68
South African Gold Loan	–	–	80	80	325	–	–	325
Receipts under European Recovery Programme ('The Marshall Plan')	–	–	169	169	682	–	–	682
TOTALS	226	1,024	423	1,673	6,749	908	4,131	1,710

Note: because of rounding, component items may not sum exactly to totals.

Source
Adapted from Table V of Cmd 7793 (sterling valuations), and from Table VII of
United Kingdom Balance of Payments 1946 to 1949 (No 2), Cmd 7928, April 1950, *BPP*
1950 XV (dollar valuations).

APPENDIX 27, SOURCE REFERENCES

1. WP(42) 347 of 1 August 1942, p 6, paragraph 6; with this, RP (42) 21 of 1 July, p 1, paragraph 3: CAB 66/27.

2. For the variations in the estimated duration of the three stages, see W K Hancock and M M Gowing, *The British War Economy,* p 517.

3. Notes by Mr E Jones of the Treasury, 11 December 1943, T 236/306.

4. D N Chester, 'The Central Machinery for Economic Policy', in D N Chester (ed), *Lessons of the British War Economy,* (Cambridge, 1951), pp 8–9.

5. C H Feinstein, *National Income, Expenditure and Output of the United Kingdom, 1855–1965,* (Cambridge, 1972), pp 20–22, 114–5.

6. R S Sayers, *The Bank of England 1891–1944,* III, p 315.

7. *Report of the Committee on Finance and Industry,* Cmd 3897 of 1931, *BPP* 1930–31, XIII.

8. Bank of England, 'The Balancing Item of the United Kingdom', 17 August 1945, T 236/306.

9. Paper dated 6 January 1945, ibid.

10. T 236/304. The version prepared for the War Cabinet, 12 June 1944, ibid and T 247/55, and *JMK* XXIV, pp 34–65.

11. Letter from Mr C F Cobbold, Bank of England, to Keynes, 13 June 1944, with accompanying papers, T 236/306.

12. Ibid, Exchange Position and Balance of Payments Estimates, end of June 1944, dated 9 October 1944.

13. Ibid, Exchange Position . . .; meeting 30 January 1945 in the Treasury on 'United Kingdom Balance of Payments'; paper of 17 August 1945 on 'The Balancing Item . . .'.

14. Ibid, E Jones to Sir Wilfrid Eady, 7 November 1944.

15. Ibid, Economic Section, 19 & 20 December 1944; Central Statistical Office, 4 & 10 January 1945; Keynes, 22 & 30 January 1945. The second date in each case is the date of the meeting.

16. Ibid, CS (BP)(45) 1, 'Methods used in preparing present estimates of United Kingdom balance of payments', and CS (BP)(45) 2, 'Further information required for preparation of estimates of the United Kingdom balance of payments', both dated 12 January 1945.

17. 11 May 1945, circulated 11 June 1945, T 236/1079. Reprinted in Sir Richard Clarke, *Anglo-American Economic Collaboration in War and Peace, 1942–1949,* ed Sir Alec Cairncross, pp 96–122.

18. 5 June 1945, Clarke to Sir David Waley, and 6 June Waley to P D Proctor and Sir Wilfrid Eady, T 236/1079; Steering Committee, 12 September 1945, CAB 21/2215; first meeting 20 November 1945, T 236/1088.

19. Papers from February to August 1945 in T 236/306.

20. T 236/306, E Jones reporting to 2nd meeting of I-D Committee on Estimates of Balance of Payments, 21 February 1945. Other papers in T 236/307.

21. T 236/307, Mr H Leak of Board of Trade to Mr J Stafford, Central Statistical Office, 1 June 1945; Report in ibid (dated 31 December 1945).

22. T 236/437: meeting of 31 July 1945, with a further meeting under Mr R W B Clarke, 1 August 1945.

23. T 236/307: Mr H C B Mynors of Bank of England to Lord Keynes, 8 February 1946; Keynes's reply, 11 February; Clarke to Keynes, 4 February, and Keynes's reply, 11 February; Clarke to Mr D Jones at Bank of England, 22 February.

24. References in T 236/308 and T 236/2296-8.

25. 'Notes on the form of Balance of Trade and Balance of Payments Statistics', in April 1946. Copies in T 230/7, T 236/307 and T 236/308.

26. 4th meeting of Balance of Payments Working Party, 18 April 1946, T 236/1088.

27. T 230/4, Economic Section papers. T 230/5, draft of 31 January 1942 and Keynes to Professor L C Robbins, 3 & 6 February 1942.

28. T 160/1377.

29. Drafts in T 230/4 and T 230/5, and the Treasury Memorandum.

30. A smaller loss on overseas income would arise if, as in fact proved to be the case after the war, interest were received on international reserves: eg, short-term dollar assets.

31. T 230/4, 'The Balance of Payments after the last War', Appendix D to drafts 6-10 November 1941 and 28 November 1941.

32. Papers in T 230/130-3 and 135. Summarising the Report in 1943 Miss Nita Watts of the Economic Section inclined to feel that it was confused: T 230/131.

33. Ibid, Conversation between Keynes, Mr E A G Robinson and Mr J E Meade, 3 December 1941.

34. T 230/6: 'The Balance of Payments of the United Kingdom in the Post-Transitional Period', paragraphs 7, 43.

35. T 230/5: Keynes to Robbins, 16 July 1942; Economic Section to Keynes, 20 July; Miss N Watts to Robbins, 5 October; Keynes to Robbins, 6 October; Comments (undated) by Miss Watts.

36. Ibid, Comments by Mr J E Meade on re-draft of Economic Section's balance of payments memorandum, 25 November 1943.

37. Sayers, *Bank of England*, III, Appendix 32, 'The Balance of Payments in the Inter-War Period', and Feinstein, *National Income*, pp 115-27.

38. T 236/306: 'The Balancing Item . . . ', 17 August 1945.

39. Sayers, III, p 313; *Statistical Material presented during the Washington Negotiations*, December 1945, Cmd 6707, *BPP* 1945-6, XXI, Appendix III.

40. The *pessimists* included Professor H Clay, who had been Vice-Chairman of the Board of Trade Committee on post-war export trade: H Clay, 'The Place of Exports in British Industry After the War', address at Chatham House, 25 June 1942, *Economic Journal*, LII (1942), pp 148-53. Memorandum, 'United Kingdom Post-War Balance of Payments', T 230/6, the conclusion of which Mr J E Meade rejected as being 'exactly the reverse of the truth' in a long letter to Sir David Waley, 14 July 1944, T 230/6.

41. 13 December 1943, T 230/5.

42. Ibid, 6 December (evidently in reply to an earlier draft of Meade's than that on file), 'Exchange Depreciation and the Balance of Trade'.

43. Ibid, R F Kahn to Meade, 7 January 1944 and Meade's reply, 12 January; *JMK* XXVI, pp 283-304.

44. Ibid, Sir Wilfrid Eady to Professor Robbins, 23 December 1943.

45. 'Towards a Balance of Payments', 11 May 1945, Clarke, *Anglo-American Economic Collaboration in War and Peace, 1942-1949*, pp 94-122.

46. Ibid, pp 122–4. Keynes's posthumous article: 'The Balance of Payments of the US', *Economic Journal*, LVI, 222, June 1946, pp 172–87; *JMK* XXVII, pp 427–46.

47. Above pp 94, 141–2, 164; OF 145/146/09.

48. Mr J E Meade to Mr J H E Woods, Ministry of Production, 21 July 1944, T 230/41; Lord Cherwell to the Prime Minister, 7 September 1944, PREM 4/18/6.

49. Ibid, 'British Requirements for the First Year of Stage II'.

50. Meeting of officials of Exchange Requirements Committee on 9 January 1945, with Sir Wilfrid Eady of the Treasury in the Chair, to discuss 'Great Britain's external financial position in the Transition period', following the Stage II discussions with the US and Canada: T 231/156.

51. Memorandum by Mr E Jones of the Treasury, 'The United Kingdom Balance of Payments, Stage II and Stage III', circulated 14 July 1944, T 230/6.

52. Papers by Mr H Leak, Board of Trade, 26 July 1944, ibid. Interdepartmental meetings 9 & 19 July 1944, T 230/41.

53. Mr L P Thompson-McCausland, Bank of England, to Mr J E Meade, 10 August 1944, T230/6.

54. Ibid, meeting of 14 August 1944, and draft papers for the Economic Survey, 19 October 1944.

55. Keynes from Washington to Chancellor of the Exchequer, 16 October 1944; T 160/1375, and *JMK* XXIV, pp 136–8.

56. CCS (174th Meeting), 14 September 1944, Château Frontenac, Quebec. General Marshall said that 'for demobilisation purposes the United States Army were using a time factor of one year': CAB 99/29.

57. 'Economic Survey. Overseas Liabilities and the Balance of Payments', 16 May 1945. The Bank: 'Tentative Estimates' for Stage II, Year 1, 14 March 1945, and table accompanying letter of 21 June 1945 from Mr D Jones, Bank of England, to Miss N Watts, Economic Section: T 230/6.

58. 'Overseas Financial Prospects in Stage III', May 1945, paragraph 24.

59. Keynes to Clarke, 6 June 1945, and Clarke to Keynes, 11 June 1945, T 247/74; 'Our Overseas Financial Prospects', 14 August 1945, paragraphs 16–17 and *JMK* XXIV, pp 403–4.

60. 'Our Overseas Financial Prospects', paragraph 16.

61. 'Estimates of United Kingdom Balance of Payments', revised, 27 September 1945, T 236/306.

62. 'Proposals for financial arrangements in the Sterling Area, and between the US and the United Kingdom to follow after Lend-Lease': £750 million in draft of 4 September; £625–875 million in draft of 12 September; papers as presented to the Americans. All in PREM 8/35.

63. Mr F E Harmer, 21 September 1945, T 247/46; Mr Clarke, memorandum on 'The Amount and Terms of Aid from USA', 10 October 1945, T 230/142.

64. NABOB 178, for Chancellor of the Exchequer from Keynes, 18 October 1945.

65. Memorandum by Miss N Watts of the Economic Section, 'United Kingdom Dollar Requirements 1946/48', 2 November 1945, T 230/142.

66. *Statistical Material presented during the Washington Negotiations*, December 1945, Cmd 6707, paragraph 15.

67. Economic Section, 'United Kingdom Dollar Requirements', paragraph 8(iii), T 230/142.

68. 27 September 1945, T 236/1078.

69. See in particular *United Kingdom Balance of Payments* 1946–57 (HMSO, London, 1959) and 'Statistics of the United Kingdom Balance of Payments', *Economic Trends*, No 89 March 1961 (HMSO, London). See also an illuminating paper by Mr O Nankivell of the Central Statistical Office, 'Measuring the United Kingdom Balance of Payments', read to the Economic Statistics Study Group of the Manchester Statistical Society, 16 November 1962.

70. *United Kingdom Balance of Payments* 1946–57.

71. *United Kingdom Balance of Payments* 1946 to 1949, Cmd 7793, November 1949, *BPP* 1948–9 XXII, Table 1, and *Economic Survey for* 1949, Cmd 7647, March 1949, *BPP* 1948–9 XXIX, paragraphs 59 & 60.

72. In his last article, 'The Balance of Payments of the US', loc cit.

73. Meeting of US-UK Combined Top Committee, 13 September 1945, GEN 80/20, CAB 130/6; *JMK* XXIV, p 472. '*Statistical Material presented during the Washington Negotiations*', Cmd 6707, paragraph 15.

74. Above, pp 240, 246, 272, 346. US-UK Finance Committee, 20 September 1945, GEN 80/29, CAB 130/6; *JMK* XXIV, pp 495–6.

75. The first post-war White Paper on the Balance of Payments illustrated the difficulty which could be encountered in trying to distinguish between the United Kingdom and the rest of the sterling area as sources of the gold and dollar deficit. The 'whole of British oil companies' dollar expenditure is allocated to the United Kingdom though much of the output is sent to the Rest of the Sterling Area. Any logical allocation becomes impossible in dealing with the loss of reserves to countries which convert only part of their sterling receipts into gold or dollars. This loss is therefore shown as attributable to the whole sterling area . . .': *United Kingdom Balance of Payments* 1946 and 1947, Cmd 7324, February 1948, *BPP* 1947–8 XVII, pp 5–6.

INDEX

An asterisk * indicates a brief biography.

467

Anglo-American Commission:—*continued*
W. Churchill), 34, 35; Keynes, 33.
consultation, 311.
co-operation, 286, 298.
differences, 308.
discussions on post-war economy, 35–40
passim, 432, 433, 440.
on Commercial Policy:
Dec.1944 – Jan.1945: 200–203: Art VII
of MAA, 203; balance of payments
burden, 202; 'blocked balances', 202;
BW Agreements, 202; British borrowing, 202; Canada, 201; Convention on
Commercial Policy, 201, 202, 203; discrimination, 202; exchange controls,
201–2; financial aid for Britain, 202;
foodstuffs, 201; Mr. H. Hawkins, 201,
202, 203; import controls, 201; IMF,
201, 202; International Trade Organisation, 201, 202; non-discrimination,
201; preferences, 201; President
Roosevelt and, 203; quantitative restrictions, 201; sterling, 202; sterling balances, 202; tariff cuts, 201; trade liberalisation, 201; trade and currency
liberalisation, 202; the transition, 201,
202; XY formula, 201.
April-June 1945: British agricultural proposals, 206; British warn of non-co-
operation, 207; Canada deplores US
approach, 208; cartels, 206; change in
American policy, 208; Convention for
International Trade Organisation,
206–7; dangers of American approach,
207; early agreement improbable, 206;
exchange controls, 206; Mr. Harry
Hawkins, 207; multilateral bilateralism,
207; nuclear approach to tariff reductions, 208, 209; preferences, 206; proposed international trade organisation,
206; tariff reductions, 206, 207.
August 1945: arrangements for Stage III, 208,
209, 210; BW Agreements, 209; bilateral trading threat, 209–10; Mr. W. L.
Clayton, 208–9, 210; Convention on
international trade, 209; differences of
emphasis, 210; export subsidies, 209;
financial aid for Britain, 208, 209;
Keynes, 209; LL, terminal arrangements, 208; multilateral free trade, 209;
'nuclear' approach, 209; preferences,
209, 210; quotas, 209; sterling balances,
209, 210; tariffs, 209; trade liberalisation and financial assistance, 209; the
Transition, 210.
*See also Commercial Policy, Trade Policy, Washington
Principles.*
Anglo-American Financial Agreement (1945),
1, 100, 183, 300, 307, 329, 409–10;
breach, possible, 366–7; British draft,
316–9; British counter-proposals, 320;
Canadian Loan and, 342, 345–9 *passim*;
Ch. Ex. (Mr. H. Dalton) and BW, 183;
commitments, principal British, 423; Conservative Party, 329; Conservative Peers,
330; consultation on convertibility, 324,
325, 356, 366; draft, 279, 325; Sir Wilfrid

AA Financial Agreement—*continued*
Eady and US Loan, 348; hostility in USA,
325, 329–30; and IMF, 183, 185; interdependence with commercial policy agreement, 284, 328, 329; non-ratification, consequences of, 356, 360–2; President
Truman, 362; reception in Britain,
329–30, 356; review clause, 318; signature, 329, 362; statistical White Paper,
329; and sterling, 293, 306, 366; sterling
balance agreements, 366–7; sterling balances, 167, 365, 366, 367; text, 416–20;
Treasury (HM) and, 366; US Congress
and, 183, 185, 330, 356, 360, 362, 363,
364; US draft, 320.
Negotiations (Sept.-Dec. 1945), 2, chap 10
passim; accelerated repayment proposal,
303, 312; agreement on commercial
policy, 278–9, 326–9; Agriculture,
Ministry of, 275, 276; Mr. W. W.
W., 264*; alternatives to, 356; Alternative 'A', 294–5, 296, 297, 300, 302;
Alternative 'B', 294–5, 296, 297, 300;
Ambassador to USA (Lord Halifax),
266, 272, 275, 276, 281, 282, 285, 286,
287, 296, 300, 302, 304, 305, 306, 309,
311, 318, 320, 324; American conditions, 284; American determination to
continue, 311; American opinion, 295;
American policy, 286; Anglo-American
economic concordat, 283; Anglo-
American monetary plans, 130, 182,
348; Anglo-American statement of
1943, 278; approach to, 248; Art VII of
MAA, 5, 267, 270, 276, 278, 325; Australia, 328; BABOON telegrams, 320;
balance of payments, sterling countries,
295–6, 321; balance of payments, UK,
271–2, 273, 276, 286, 298; BE, 267,
270, 280, 291, 292, 293, 295, 309,
314–5, 318, 319, 321; Bank and Treasury memorandum, 309; Board of
Trade, 267, 268, 274, 275, 276; Mr. R.
H. Brand, 265, 267, 296, 300; BW and
US credit, 264, 267, 281, 282, 284, 287,
290, 292, 298, 304, 309, 311, 318, 320,
324–5; breakdown possible, 287, 292;
Bridges, Sir Edward, 270*, 280, 297,
313, 314, 320, 321, 322, 323, 324; 'briefing' for, 262, 264–5, 266, 267, 276;
British Delegation (or Mission), 266,
267, 286, 288, 293, 295, 311, 313, 316,
318, 319, 322, 325, 326, 327, 328;
British tactic, 266–7, 276, 277; BW,
263, 264, 265, 267, 272, 273, 278, 284,
294, 323; Byrnes, Mr. J. F., 268*;
Cabinet, 297, 300, 316, 317, 320, 325,
327, 329; Canada, Canadians, 266, 275,
282, 288, 300, 328, 338; Canadian Aid,
270, 272; cartels, 275, 278; Mr. R. W.
B. Clarke, 295–6, 360–2; Mr. W. L.
Clayton, 265, 267, 268, 269, 272–3,
274, 277, 281, 282, 285, 286, 287, 293,
299, 300, 302, 304, 311, 313, 324; Colonial balances, 298, 307, 321–2, 417;
Colonial Office, 276; Colonial Secretary
(Mr. G. H. Hall), 297–8; Colonies, aid

Economic Section—*continued*
policy, 449; exports, 224; Sir Donald
Fergusson, 198; government expenditure overseas, estimates of, 444, 447;
import controls, 197, 198; import
licences, auction of, 198; import programming, 194; Indian balances, 230;
an international investment institution,
151; 'invisibles', 224; Keynes, 227,
230–1; Keynes's memoranda, 223,
230; Mr. J. E. Meade and, 198, 283,
358; Report on Non-Discrimination in
Relation to Programming of Imports,
199; Overton Report, 102; the post-war
external problem, 6, 23, 224, 227; post-
war financial policy, 246; protection,
197–8; quantitative restrictions, 195;
short-term debt, 224; sterling balances,
225, 230–1; subsidies, 194; tariffs, 194;
the Transition, 194, 224, 451; Treasury-
Bank Committee, 232; 'The United
Kingdom's Post-War Balance of Payments', 77, 223–4; Washington Principles, 194–8; XY formula, 197–8.
Survey for 1945, 437.
  for 1946, 358.
Surveys: balance of payments, 358; Central
Statistical Office, 358; Ec. Sec., 358,
436; Mr. J. E. Meade and, 358.
Warfare, Ministry of: commodity regulation, 88. official committee on export
surpluses, 86.
Eden, Mr. R. A., 19*; *see Foreign Secretary.*
Egypt: BW, 165; Cairo Monetary Conference,
165; Mr. C. F. Cobbold, 365; Sir Wilfrid
Eady, 365; exchange control, 366; foreign
credit balances, 165, 166; and Indian balances, 165; IMF, 165, 166, 167; leaves
sterling area, 366; sterling balance agreement, 365; sterling balances, 96, 165, 167,
238, 281, 364, 365; and sterling problems,
96, 315.
Empire, The British: commodities and the US,
32; finance of war, 19; imports from, 21; as
sterling creditor, 2.
Employment, and post-war policy, 73.
  policies: and Australia, 124; Washington
Principles, 125.
  policy: Labour Government and, 357; White
Paper on, 357.
European countries: monetary agreements,
363–4; payments agreements, 325,
363–4; sterling balances, 363–4, 365.
Exchange control, 315, 316, 317, 322, 323; and
balance of payments statistics, 433, 434,
435; BE and, 68, 72, 96, 97, 226; Ch. Ex.
(Mr. H. Dalton) and, 210, 248, 317; and
collapse of convertibility, 367; Sir Wilfrid
Eady and, 210; US Administration and,
367.
  controls, 5, 21, 278, 315; Americans and surveillance of, 206; Atlantic Charter, 37,
39; BE, 72; Board of Trade, 22, 73;
commercial policy discussions, 201–2,
206; current payments, 181; and dollar
pool, 2; Foreign Secretary (Mr. A.
Eden), 39; Mr. Hubert Henderson, 72;

Exchange controls—*continued*
and hot money, 71; ICU, 75; IMF, 178,
179, 181, 201, 202, 244; inter-war years,
202; Keynes, 31, 71, 75, 181, 210, 244;
post-war, 31, 71; sterling countries, 2;
and trade policy, 37; the Transition, 95,
181, 202, 210; HM Treasury, 71–72,
210; Dr. H. D. White, 178, 179.
depreciation: Ch. Ex. (Mr. H. Dalton),
182–5; debate, 448–50; and 'fundamental disequilibrium', 182–5; ICU,
100; IMF, 182–5; Keynes, 139,
448–50; Mr. J. E. Meade, 183; HM
Treasury, 100.
Equalisation Account, 16, 91.
rate: confidence in sterling, 449; dollar at
$4.03, 161, 232; flexibility in, 448;
Treasury-Bank Committee, 232.
  US, inter-war, 17.
policy: BE, 149–50, 160–1; BW Conference, 160–1; Lord Catto, 148, 160–1;
Catto clause, 148, 149–50, 160–1; Ch.
Ex. (Sir John Anderson), 150; and convertibility, 147–50; IMF, 149–50;
Joint Statement, 149–50, 160; and
trade restrictions, 117, 118, 161–2; the
Transition and exchange and trade
restrictions, 161–2; HM Treasury and,
149–50.
Rates: American pre-war policy, 90–91; BE
and, 94, 142; BW, 160–1, 177; Catto
clause, 160–1; Ch. Ex. (Sir John
Anderson), 177, (Mr. H. Dalton) 185;
ICU, 71; IMF, 139, 185; inter-war, 16,
17; Keynes, 94, 139; stability, 160; stability, BE and, 141, 142; SF, 92, 94,
121, 122–3; sterling monetary system
and, 77; in the Transition, 94; HM
Treasury, 139; and unemployment,
182-5; variation, and fundamental disequilibrium, 182–5.
Requirements Committee: Keynes and, 236;
members, 236; and Stages II and III,
236.
Restrictions, 312, 313; BW Agreements,
177; Mr. J. E. Meade, 177; Professor L.
C. Robbins, 177.
Export Council (1940), 20, 21.
  drive, 445.
  earnings, 450, 451–2.
  expansion, 451.
  industries, 445, 450.
  planning, 448.
  production, 455.
  recovery, 445.
  subsidies, 209, 278.
  taxes, 278.
  trade, 450.
  Trade Committee, Postwar: enquiry and
report, 445.
  White Paper (1941), 6, 10, 11, 21, 25, 42,
215, 445, 450.
Exports, 361; American, to sterling area, 293;
and balance of payments deficit, 77; Canadian, 203, 204; dangers of high prices, 445;
export drive and US trade policy, 20–22;
Export White Paper (1941), 6, 10, 11, 21,